I0884561

HEGEL
AND
CONTEMPORARY
CONTINENTAL
PHILOSOPHY

SUNY series in Contemporary Continental Philosophy
Dennis J. Schmidt, editor

and

SUNY series in Hegelian Studies
William Desmond, editor

HEGEL AND CONTEMPORARY CONTINENTAL PHILOSOPHY

EDITED BY

Dennis King Keenan

STATE UNIVERSITY OF NEW YORK PRESS

Published by
State University of New York Press, Albany

Printed in the United States of America

For information, address State University of New York Press,
90 State Street, Suite 700, Albany, NY 12207

Production by Kelli Williams
Marketing by Michael Campochiaro

Library of Congress Cataloging-in-Publication Data

Hegel and contemporary Continental philosophy / [compiled by] Dennis King Keenan.
p. cm. — (SUNY series in contemporary Continental philosophy)
Includes bibliographical references and index.
ISBN 0-7914-6091-6 (hardcover) — ISBN 0-7914-6092-4 (pbk.)
1. Hegel, Georg Wilhelm Friedrich, 1770–1831. I. Keenan, Dennis King, 1960– II. Series.

B2948.H3174 2004
193—dc22

2004006978

10 9 8 7 6 5 4 3 2 1

for Rene McGraw, O.S.B.

Contents

Preface xi

Acknowledgments xxiii

1. **Jean Wahl**, "Mediation, Negativity, and Separation"
—from *Le malheur de la conscience dans la philosophie de Hegel* (1929) 1

2. **Alexandre Kojève**, "The Idea of Death in the Philosophy of Hegel"
—from *Introduction to the Reading of Hegel* (1947; lectures delivered: 1933–34) 27

3. **Jean-Paul Sartre**, "Husserl, Hegel, Heidegger"
—from *Being and Nothingness: A Phenomenological Essay on Ontology* (1943) 75

4. **Georg Lukács**, "'*Entäusserung*' ('Externalization') as the Central Philosophical Concept of *The Phenomenology of Mind*,"
—from *The Young Hegel: Studies in the Relations between Dialectics and Economics* (1948) 95

5. **Maurice Merleau-Ponty**, "Hegel's Existentialism"
—from *Sense and Non-Sense* (1948) 127

6. **Maurice Blanchot**, "Literature and the Right to Death"
—from *The Work of Fire* (1949) 135

7. **Frantz Fanon**, "The Negro and Hegel"
—from *Black Skin, White Masks* (1952) 169

8. **Jean Hyppolite**, "Logic and Existence"
—from *Logic and Existence* (1953) 175

9. **Georges Bataille**, "Hegel, Death and Sacrifice" (1955) 187

10. **Jacques Lacan**, "The Subversion of the Subject and the Dialectic of Desire in the Freudian Unconscious,"
—from *Écrits* (1966; lecture delivered: 1960) 205

11. **Theodor W. Adorno**, "World Spirit and Natural History: An Excursion to Hegel"
—from *Negative Dialectics* (1966) 237

12. **Gilles Deleuze**, "Conclusion"
—from *Difference and Repetition* (1968) 251

13. **Louis Althusser**, "Marx's Relation to Hegel"
—from *Hegel et la Pensée Moderne* (1970; lecture delivered: 1968) 255

14. **Hans-Georg Gadamer**, "Hegel's 'Inverted World'"
—from *Hegel's Dialectic: Five Hermeneutical Studies* (1971) 273

15. **Jacques Derrida**, *Glas* (1974) 291

16. **Luce Irigaray**, "The Eternal Irony of the Community"
—from *Speculum of the Other Woman* (1974) 315

17. **Julia Kristeva**, "Negativity: Rejection"
—from *Revolution in Poetic Language* (1974) 327

18. **Emmanuel Levinas**, "Death and Time"
—from *God, Death, and Time* (1993; lectures delivered: 1976) 337

19. **John Sallis**, "Hegel's Concept of Presentation: Its Determination in the Preface to the *Phenomenology of Spirit*"
—from *Delimitations: Phenomenology and the End of Metaphysics* (1986; first published: 1977) 353

20. **Giorgio Agamben**, "Excursus 7 (after the final day)"
—from *Language and Death: The Place of Negativity* (1982) 379

21. **Slavoj Žižek**, "'Not Only as *Substance*, but Also as *Subject*'"
—from *The Sublime Object of Ideology* (1989) 389

22. **Judith Butler**, "Stubborn Attachment, Bodily Subjection: Rereading Hegel on the Unhappy Consciousness"
—from *The Psychic Life of Power: Theories in Subjection* (1997; first published: 1995) 417

23. **Jean-Luc Nancy**, "Freedom," and "We"
—from *Hegel: The Restlessness of the Negative* (1997) 437

Bibliography 449

Index 453

Preface

Contemporary continental philosophy stands in the wake of the work of G. W. F. Hegel (1770–1831).[1]

The significance of the work of Hegel was hardly recognized by French contemporary continental philosophers before the work of Wahl and Koyré. Jean Wahl (1888–1974) published *Le malheur de la conscience dans la philosophie de Hegel* in 1929. Though it was later considered an important study (which exercised a significant influence on Sartre), at the time it was a relatively isolated work unrelated to the philosophical concerns of French thinkers of the time. "Mediation, Negativity, and Separation," a chapter of *Le malheur de la conscience dans la philosophie de Hegel*, appears here for the first time in English translation. The other significant thinker working on Hegel in France at the time was Alexandre Koyré (1892–1964). Though he did not write an extended study of Hegel, he wrote important articles on Hegel: "Rapport sur l'état des etudes hégéliennes en France" (1930); "Note sur la langue et la terminologie hégéliennes" (1931); and "Hegel à Iéna" (1934 and 1935), which contains generous excerpts of the pre-*Phenomenology* period 1803–06 of the work of Hegel that were previously untranslated into French.[2]

At the invitation of Koyré, the Russian émigré Alexandre Kojève (1902–1968) delivered lectures on Hegel from 1933 to 1939 at the École Pratique des Hautes Études. These highly idiosyncratic lectures on the *Phenomenology* (which made the master-slave dialectic famous) insisted on an anthropological foundation to Hegel's thought. Though inspired by the early Marx's recapitulation of the Hegelian view of action and work (in the newly discovered manuscripts of 1844), Kojève sought in Hegel a more fundamental theory of action, work, and historical progress than he found in Marx. The lectures attracted a remarkable audience that included Bataille, Lacan, Levinas, and Merleau-Ponty. The notes from these lectures were assembled and published by Raymond Queneau in 1947 as *Introduction à la lecture de Hegel: Leçons sur la*

Phenomenologie de l'esprit. The English edition of the text—*Introduction to the Reading of Hegel* (edited by Allan Bloom)—did not include the important essay "The Idea of Death in the Philosophy of Hegel." This essay was the focus of Bataille's essay "Hegel, Death and Sacrifice," which in turn played a major role in Derrida's reading of Bataille's reading of Hegel in "From Restricted to General Economy: A Hegelianism Without Reserve" from *Writing and Difference* (1967).

While Kojève treated the human and the natural world as ontologically distinct domains, Jean Hyppolite (1907–1968) treated time as a monistic absolute that governs both domains. Paying homage to Wahl and Koyré, Hyppolite wrote: "I should say that the first real shock came from Jean Wahl, and that reading the *Conscience malheureuse dans la philosophie de Hegel* was a sort of revelation. [. . .] Reading 'Hegel à Iéna' was for me (with the translation of texts on time) as basic as the *Conscience malheureuse*."[3] Though the work of Wahl and Koyré were indications of the first stirrings of a reassessment of Hegel in France, it was Kojève and Hyppolite who were responsible for the renaissance in Hegel studies in France. Hyppolite's French translation of Hegel's *Phenomenology of Spirit*—the first French translation of the *Phenomenology*—appeared in 1939 and 1941. In 1946–47, he published *Genesis and Structure of Hegel's* Phenomenology of Spirit. In *Logic and Existence* (1953), Hyppolite considered what he called Hegelianism's "most obscure dialectical synthesis": the relation between the phenomenology and the logic. According to Hyppolite, the phenomenology and the logic mutually presuppose one another. Hyppolite's non-reductionistic interpretation of the relation between the phenomenology and the logic significantly challenged the anthropological interpretation of Hegel made famous by Kojève. *Logic and Existence* fanned the flames of French anti-humanism already ignited by Heidegger's "Letter on 'Humanism'" (1947), and influenced the work of Althusser, Deleuze, Foucault, and Derrida, all of whom studied the works of Hegel under Hyppolite.

Both Heidegger's "Letter on 'Humanism,'" as well as Jean Beaufret's letter (to which Heidegger was responding), mentioned Sartre's essay *Existentialism is a Humanism* (1946). In *Being and Nothingness: A Phenomenological Essay on Ontology* (1943), Jean-Paul Sartre (1905–1980) offered a humanistic reading of Hegel. Though he drew upon Hegel's master-slave dialectic to describe the conflictual relation of the existential self and the other, his reading of the relationship was ultimately a defense of the Cartesian *cogito* in the face of its sublation into historical and social being. Sartre wrote:

> But if Hegel has forgotten himself, we can not forget Hegel. This means that we are referred back to the *cogito*. In fact, if, as we have established, the being of my consciousness is strictly irreducible to knowledge, then I can not transcend my being toward a reciprocal and

> universal relation in which I could see my being and that of others as equivalent. On the contrary, I must establish myself *in my being* and posit the problem of the Other in terms of my being. In a word the sole point of departure is the interiority of the *cogito*.[4]

Like Kojève's anthropological reading of Hegel, Sartre placed the human subject in the position of being the absolute.

Like Sartre, many contemporary continental philosophers were fascinated by the work of Marx, and this fascination often provoked a re-reading of Hegel. In *The Young Hegel: Studies in the Relations between Dialectics and Economics* (1948), Georg Lukács (1885–1971) suggested that *Entäusserung* (externalization) was the central philosophical concept of the *Phenomenology*. This concept, along with *Entfremdung* (alienation), played a major role in the 1844 manuscripts of Marx, alongside of which Lukács read the work of Hegel. In his review of Lukács' *The Young Hegel*, Hyppolite wrote: "[T]he understanding of Hegel, and the variety of interpretations of his philosophy, force upon us a confrontation with Marxism. It has to be recognized that Marx is one of the best commentators upon Hegel."[5] Another thinker concerned with the relationship of Hegel to Marx was Louis Althusser (1918–1990), who was invited by Hyppolite to speak on the subject at his seminar in 1968.

In "Hegel's Existentialism"—inspired by a lecture of the same title by Hyppolite—in *Sense and Non-Sense* (1948), Maurice Merleau-Ponty (1908–1961) wrote: "All the great philosophical ideas of the past century—the philosophies of Marx and Nietzsche, phenomenology, German existentialism, and psychoanalysis—had their beginnings in Hegel."[6]

The works of Kojève and Hyppolite were drawn upon by Maurice Blanchot (1907–2003) in his essay "Literature and the Right to Death" from *The Work of Fire* (1949). Literature begins, Blanchot wrote, "at the moment when literature becomes a question."[7] This question—"the 'question' that seeks to pose itself in literature, the 'question' that is its essence"[8]—is posed *to* language *by* language that has become literature. This question *is* "an irreducible *double meaning*"[9]: death as possibility and as impossibility. "[L]iterature," Blanchot wrote in the concluding sentence of the essay, "is the form in which this double meaning has chosen to show itself behind the meaning and value of words, and the question it asks is the question asked by literature."[10] This question is what Blanchot, in *The Space of Literature* (1955), called "double death." The reading of "Revolution" in "Literature and the Right to Death" marked the first instance of Blanchot's irreducibly ambiguous reading of the following passage from the preface to Hegel's *Phenomenology of Spirit*: "[T]he life of Spirit is [. . .] the life that endures it [i.e., death] and maintains itself in it."[11] Literature begins at the moment when it becomes a question, that is, at the moment when an initial reading of this passage, which reads death as possibility, turns into a reading of this passage that reads death as impossibility. Death, as this turning *itself*, leaves a trace of itself in the production of an interminable step/not beyond (what Blanchot, in another work, called "*le pas au-delà*"). Revolution is what Blanchot called one of a writer's temptations. He read the experience of the writer alongside the experience of natural consciousness in Hegel's *Phenomenology*. A writer's temptations are those decisive moments *in* the work or production of the *Phenomenology*, those "decisive moments *in* history,"[12] which *seem* (at least on a first reading) to describe the very process of literary creation, the destructive act of transformation that is a step into the next shape of the dialectical progression. But these decisive moments are fraught with ambiguity. They are decisive moments *in* the work of the *Phenomenology* when work is discovered to be at a certain distance *from* that work.

Like Blanchot, Georges Bataille (1897–1962) considered the ambiguity of the following famous passage from the preface of Hegel's *Phenomenology*:

> [T]he life of Spirit is not the life that shrinks from death and keeps itself untouched by devastation, but rather the life that endures it and maintains itself in it. It wins its truth only when, in utter dismemberment, it finds itself. It is this power, not as something positive, which closes its eyes to the negative, as when we say of something that it is nothing or is false, and then, having done with it, turn away and pass on to something else; on the contrary, Spirit is this power only by looking the negative in the face, and tarrying with it.[13]

In "Hegel, Death and Sacrifice" (1955), which focused on Kojève's "The Idea of Death in the Philosophy of Hegel," Bataille called this passage "a fundamental text." He wrote: "There is no doubt from the start of the 'capital importance' of this admirable text, not only for an understanding of Hegel, but in all regards."[14] In the second part of Bataille's essay, Bataille suggested that sacrifice bears witness to the *entire* movement of death, that is, it bears witness to death not only as the most proper possibility (insofar as it is appropriated), but also as expenditure without reserve. Sacrifice bears witness to death as possibility turning into death as impossibility.

Like Bataille, Jacques Lacan (1901–1981) was present at Kojève's lectures on Hegel's *Phenomenology*. Lacan often situated his work within the context of a "return to Freud." His description of the dialectic of desire in the Freudian unconscious was influenced by his reading of the master-slave dialectic, which in turn was influenced by Kojève's reading of Hegel. One of Lacan's most oft-repeated formulas was: "Man's desire is the desire of the Other."

Other contemporary continental philosophers who approach the work of Hegel through the lens of Freud and Lacan include Irigaray, Kristeva, and Žižek. Luce Irigaray (1930–) called into question the Hegelian master-slave dialectic that underlies the hierarchical relation between the sexes as an adequate or appropriate way of considering sexual difference.[15] She was fascinated with the figure of Antigone, because "she is neither master nor slave," and "this upsets the order of the dialectic."[16] In the "Eternal Irony of the Community" (1974), Irigaray considered Hegel's dictum that womankind is the everlasting irony of the community. The irony of woman's position is that she makes possible the step into the universality characteristic of the community, while at the same time, threatening this step. On the one hand:

> Powerless on earth, she remains the very ground in which manifest mind secretly sets its roots and draws its strength. And self-certainty—in masculinity, in community, in government—owes the truth of its word and of the oath that binds men together to that substance common to all, repressed, unconscious and dumb, washed in the waters of oblivion.[17]

On the other hand:

> But at times the forces of the world below become hostile because they have been denied the right to live in daylight. These forces rise up and threaten to lay waste the community.[18]

In *Revolution in Poetic Language* (1974), Julia Kristeva (1941–) was concerned with (among other things) the thetic moment (rupture and/or boundary) instituting symbolism. The thetic moment is situated at the margin of the unconscious or semiotic *chora* and the signification of the symbolic order. For Kristeva, negativity (or what she called "rejection") is not static like negation. It is a process that she called the fourth "term" of the (Hegelian) dialectic. Though negativity appears in the work of Hegel, Kristeva maintained that it is repressed. The work of Hegel represses rupture. The Freudian notion of rejection, or expenditure, constitutes the key moment interrupting the unity that Kristeva thought forms the end of Hegelian negativity.

The theoretical space of the work of Slavoj Žižek (1949–) was molded by three centers of gravity: Hegelian dialectics, Lacanian psychoanalytic theory, and contemporary criticism of ideology. It is the work of Lacan, however, that is (according to Žižek, quoting Marx) "the general illumination which bathes all the other colours and modifies their particularity," "the particular ether which determines the specific gravity of every being which has materialized within it."[19] In the introduction to *The Sublime Object of Ideology* (1989), Žižek wrote: "[F]ar from being a story of its progressive overcoming, dialectics is for Hegel a systematic notation of the failure of all such attempts—'absolute knowledge' denotes a subjective position which finally accepts 'contradiction' as an internal condition of every identity. In other words, Hegelian 'reconciliation' is not a 'panlogicist' sublation of all reality in the Concept but a final consent to the fact that the Concept itself is 'not-all' (to use this Lacanian term)."[20] One of the aims of this work was "to accomplish a kind of 'return to Hegel'—to reactualize Hegelian dialectics by giving it a new reading on the basis of Lacanian psychoanalysis."[21]

Like many others, Frantz Fanon (1925–1961)—a citizen of Martinique and educated in France in psychiatry—was inspired by the master-slave dialectic in Hegel's *Phenomenology*. In "The Negro and Hegel"—the second section of a chapter of *Black Skin, White Masks* (1952) titled "The Negro and Recognition"—Fanon read the struggle for recognition in the master-slave dialectic alongside the relationship of the "White Master" and the "Negro slave."

In an interview, Emmanuel Levinas (1906–1995) said that Hegel's *Phenomenology* was "one of the finest books in the history of philosophy."[22] Levinas's most striking acknowledgement of Hegel is to be found in "The Thinking of Being and the Question of the Other" from *Of God Who Comes to Mind* (1986). In a list of "expressions of transcendence" in the history of philosophy that included Descartes' idea of the infinite, Plato's "good beyond being," Aristotle's agent intellect, and Bergson's renewal of duration, Levinas included "the search for recognition by the *other man* in Hegel."[23] But this reference to the master-slave dialectic in the *Phenomenology* did not mean that Levinas was reconciled to the work of Hegel. In another interview, Levinas described Hegelian dialectics as "a radical denial of the rupture between the ontological and the ethical."[24] Levinas undertook a sustained reading of Hegel in a lecture course titled "Death and Time." Delivered in the academic year 1975–76, the lectures were the last of his regular teaching duties at the Sorbonne. They were edited and annotated by Jacques Rolland, and published with another lecture course ("God and Onto-theology") in *God, Death, and Time* (1993). The reading of Hegel focused on the beginning of the *Science of Logic* (the dialectic of being and nothing), and that part of the *Phenomenology* titled "The ethical world. Human and Divine Law: Man and Woman" (as well as a brief consideration of the chapter on religion).

In an interview published in *Positions* (1972), Jacques Derrida (1930–) mentioned that *différance* is "at a point of almost absolute proximity to Hegel."[25] He said:

> We will never be finished with the reading or rereading of Hegel, and, in a certain way, I do nothing other than attempt to explain myself on this point. In effect I believe that Hegel's text is necessarily fissured; that it is something more and other than the circular closure of its representation. It is not reduced to a content of philosophemes, it also necessarily produces a powerful writing operation, a remainder of writing,

> whose strange relationship to the philosophical content of Hegel's text must be reexamined, that is, the movement by means of which his text exceeds its meaning, permits itself to be turned away from, to return to, and to repeat itself outside its self-identity.[26]

Glas (1974) was one instance of such a reexamination. Toward the end of *Glas*, the Hegel column (i.e., the left-hand column of each page) considered the first shape of natural religion in Hegel's *Phenomenology*. Hegel characterized the first shape of natural religion—essential light or luminous-essence (*Lichtwesen*)—as a shape of shapelessness. What fascinated Derrida was that, according to Hegel, this all-burning essenceless play of light that never determines itself as for-(it)self, and as such puts the history of Spirit out of order, *can be what it is* (namely, an "all-burning essenceless play of light that never determines itself as for-(it)self, and as such puts the history of Spirit out of order") *only if it turns into its contrary*.

Jean-Luc Nancy (1940–), whose work is often associated with the work of Derrida, considered in *Hegel: The Restlessness of the Negative* (1997) themes that marked his thought at least since the publication of *The Inoperative Community* (1986). In Nancy's work, one detects the insistent desire to describe an originary sociality that cannot be characterized in terms of sovereignty and the law.

In *Language and Death: The Place of Negativity* (1982), Giorgio Agamben (1942–) considered "both the proximity of and the diversity between Hegel's Absolute and Heidegger's *Ereignis*." This consideration was situated within the context of a response to the question: "*If the Voice indicates the taking place of language as time* [. . .], *how is it possible to think the Voice in itself, to think absolute time*?"[27]

Martin Heidegger (1889–1976), one of the first contemporary continental philosophers to recognize the significance of the work of Hegel, delivered a lecture course on the opening chapters of Hegel's *Phenomenology* in 1930–31. These lectures contained statements about temporality, ontological difference and dialectic, and being and time in Hegel. They followed an important consideration of Hegel in section 82 of *Being and Time* (1927) and preceded important considerations of Hegel in "Hegel's Concept of Experience" from *Holzwege* (1972) and "Hegel and the Greeks" from *Wegmarken* (1967). Unfortunately, it was not possible to secure permission to reprint any of these works.

One of Heidegger's most famous students, Hans-Georg Gadamer (1900–2002), applied his own hermeneutical theory to that part of Hegel's *Phenomenology* titled "Force and Understanding" in a hermeneutical study titled "Hegel's 'Inverted World'" (1971). In the foreword to a collection of hermeneutical studies on Hegel, Gadamer wrote that he was confronted with Hegelian dialectic at an early age by Nicolai Hartmann and thereafter by Martin Heidegger.

Another important German thinker who considered the work of Hegel is Theodor W. Adorno (1903–1969). In *Negative Dialectics* (1966), he emphasized that philosophy (and in particular, Hegelian philosophy) can no longer hope to grasp the totality. The concept of the "model," presented in the third part of the book, represented an effort to grasp the system of the false totality in an anti-systematic way. The second of the three models presented by Adorno consisted of "an excursion to Hegel," which consisted of speculations on the role of the universal in the Hegelian world spirit.

Subjects of Desire: Hegelian Reflections in Twentieth-Century France (1987) was originally the doctoral dissertation of Judith Butler (1956–). It traced the trajectory of desire from Hegel's formulation of it in the *Phenomenology* through its appropriation by Kojève, Hyppolite, Sartre, Lacan, Deleuze, and Foucault. Butler returned to the proximity of Foucault and Hegel in *The Psychic Life of Power: Theories in Subjection* (1997), where she suggested that Foucault's concern with "the double-edged implications of subjection (*assujetissement*: the simultaneous *forming* and *regulating* of the subject) is in some ways prefigured in Hegel's account of the bondsman's liberation into various forms of ethical self-beratement."[28]

According to Hegel, philosophy must offer an initial "presentation" of itself to allow the uninitiated to step beyond the prejudices of common sense into philosophy. "The radically disorienting, inverting movement into philosophy must be *presented*. An initiatory presentation (*Darstellung*) is demanded." In "Hegel's Concept of Presentation" (1977), John Sallis (1938–) read the *Phenomenology* as the production of this presentation, and its preface as "the introduction to the introduction to philosophy."[29]

Not all contemporary continental philosophers are as sympathetic to the influence of the work of Hegel. Gilles Deleuze (1925–1995) said: "What I detested more than anything else was Hegelianism and the Dialectic."[30] In the Preface to *Difference and Repetition* (1968), he wrote that the signs of the fact that the subject dealt with in the book are manifestly in the air "may be attributed to a generalized anti-Hegelianism."[31]

But some of those "anti-Hegelian" continental philosophers who attempt to "flee Hegel," acknowledge the problematic nature of such an attempt. In a lecture titled "The Discourse on Language" (1971), Michel Foucault (1926–1984) said: "[T]ruly to escape Hegel involves an exact appreciation of the price we have to pay to detach ourselves from him. It assumes that we are aware of the extent to which Hegel, insidiously perhaps, is close to us; it implies a knowledge, in that which permits us to think against Hegel, of that which remains Hegelian. We have to determine the extent to which our anti-Hegelianiam is possibly one of his tricks directed against us, at the end of which he stands, motionless, waiting for us."[32]

This book is a collection of works that attest to the overwhelmingly disturbing wake of the work of Hegel on contemporary continental philosophy.

The selections in this book are arranged in the order in which they were published (the only exceptions are those selections that were initially delivered as lectures, and published many years later; in those cases the date of the lecture takes precedence over the date of publication).

Notes

1. One could argue that analytic philosophy likewise stands in the wake of the work of Hegel insofar as analytic philosophy finds its very origin in its struggle to distinguish itself from idealism; see Peter Hylton, "Hegel and Analytic Philosophy," in *The Cambridge Companion to Hegel*, ed. Frederick Beiser, 445–486, (Cambridge: Cambridge University Press, 1993), and Peter Hylton, *Russell, Idealism and the Emergence of Analytic Philosophy* (Oxford: Oxford University Press, 1990).
2. Jean Wahl, "Le rôle de A. Koyré dans le développement des études hégéliennes en France," in *Hegel-Studien* Beiheft 3 (1966): 15–26; Alexandre Koyré, "Rapport sur l'état des études hégéliennes en France," in *Verhandlungen des ersten Hegel Kongresses vom 22. bis. 25. April 1930 im Haag* (Tübingen: J.C.B. Mohr [Paul Siebeck], 1931): 80–105, "Note sur la langue et la terminologie hégéliennes," in *Revue Philosophique de la France et de l'Étranger* 111–112 (1931): 409–439, "Hegel à Iéna," in *Revue philosophique de la France et de l'étranger* 118 (1934): 274–283, and *Revue d'Histiore et de Philosophie religieuses* 5 (1935): 420–484.
3. Jean Hyppolite, 'Discours d'Introduction," in *Hegel-Studien* Beiheft 3 (1966): 11.
4. Jean-Paul Sartre, *L'être et le néant: Essai d'ontologie phénoménologique* (Paris: Librairie Gallimard, 1943), 300 / *Being and Nothingness: A Phenomenological Essay on Ontology*, trans. Hazel E. Barnes (New York: Washington Square Press, 1956), 329.
5. Jean Hyppolite, *Études sur Marx et Hegel* (Paris: Librairie Marcel Rivière, 1955), 82 / *Studies in Marx and Hegel*, trans. John O'Neill (New York: Basic Books, 1969), 70.
6. Maurice Merleau-Ponty, "L'existentialisme chez Hegel," in *Sens et non-sens*, 125–139 (Paris: Les Éditions Nagel, 1948), 125 / "Hegel's Existentialism," in *Sense and Non-Sense*, trans. Hubert L. Dreyfus and Patricia Allen Dreyfus, 63–70 (Evanston: Northwestern University Press, 1964), 63.
7. Maurice Blanchot, "La littérature et le droit à la mort," in *La part du feu*, 291–331 (Paris: Éditions Gallimard, 1949), 293 / "Literature and the Right to Death," in *The Work of Fire*, trans. Lydia Davis, 300–344 (Stanford: Stanford University Press, 1995), 300.

8. Ibid., 311 / 322.
9. Ibid., 330 / 344.
10. Ibid., 331 / 344.
11. G. W. F. Hegel, *Phänomenologie des Geistes*, ed. Wolfgang Bonsiepen and Reinhard Heede, in *Gesammelte Werke*, vol. 9 (Hamburg: Felix Meiner Verlag, 1980), 27 / *Phenomenology of Spirit*, trans. A. V. Miller (Oxford: Oxford University Press, 1977), 19.
12. Blanchot, "La littérature et le droit à la mort," 309 / "Literature and the Right to Death," 318, emphasis added.
13. Hegel, *Phänomenologie des Geistes,* 27 / *Phenomenology of Spirit,* 19.
14. Georges Bataille, "Hegel, la mort et le sacrifice," in *Œuvres complètes*, vol. XII, 326–345 (Paris: Éditions Gallimard, 1988), 330–331 / "Hegel, Death and Sacrifice," trans. Jonathan Strauss, in *Yale French Studies* 78 (1990): 14.
15. Luce Irigaray, *Éthique de la différence sexuelle* (Paris: Les Éditions de Minuit, 1984), 17–18 / *An Ethics of Sexual Difference*, trans. Carolyn Burke and Gillian C. Gill (Ithaca, New York: Cornell University Press, 1993), 10.
16. Ibid., 115 / 119
17. Luce Irigaray, ". . . l'éternelle ironie de la communauté . . . ," in *Speculum de l'autre femme*, 266–281 (Paris: Les Éditions de Minuit, 1974), 280 / "The Eternal Irony of the Community," in *Speculum of the Other Woman,* trans. Gillian C. Gill, 214–226 (Ithaca, New York: Cornell University Press, 1985), 225.
18. Ibid.
19. Slavoj Žižek, *For They Know Not What They Do: Enjoyment as a Political Factor* (London: Verso, 1991), 2.
20. Slavoj Žižek, *The Sublime Object of Ideology* (London: Verso, 1989), 6.
21. Ibid., 7.
22. Emmanuel Levinas, *Ethique et infini* (Paris: Librairie Arthème Fayard et Radio-France, 1982), 33–34 / *Ethics and Infinity*, trans. Richard A. Cohen (Pittsburgh: Duquesne University Press, 1985), 37–38. Levinas says this in the context of remarks regarding Heidegger's *Being and Time*: "It [i.e., *Being and Time*] is one of the finest books in the history of philosophy—I say this after years of reflection. One of the finest among four or five others . . ." In response to the interviewer's question "Which ones?," Levinas responds: "For example, Plato's *Phædrus*, Kant's *Critique of Pure Reason*, Hegel's *Phenomenology of Mind*; also Bergson's *Time and Free Will*."
23. Emmanuel Levinas, *De Dieu qui vient à l'idée*, 2nd ed. (Paris: Librarie Philosophique J. Vrin, 1992), 185 / *Of God Who Comes to Mind*, trans. Bettina Bergo (Stanford: Stanford University Press, 1998), 119.

24. Richard Kearney, *Dialogues with Contemporary Continental Thinkers: The Phenomenological Heritage* (Manchester: Manchester University Press, 1984), 66.
25. Jacques Derrida, *Positions* (Paris: Les Éditions de Minuit, 1972), 60 / *Positions*, trans. Alan Bass (Chicago: University of Chicago Press, 1981), 44.
26. Ibid., 103–104 / 77–78.
27. Giorgio Agamben, *Il linguaggio e la morte: Un seminario sul luogo della negatività,* 3rd ed. (Torino: Giulio Einaudi, 1982), 124 / *Language and Death: The Place of Negativity*, trans. Karen E. Pinkus and Michael Hardt (Minneapolis: University of Minnesota Press, 1991), 99.
28. Judith Butler, "Stubborn Attachment, Bodily Subjection: Rereading Hegel on the Unhappy Consciousness," in *The Psychic Life of Power: Theories in Subjection*, 31–62 (Stanford: Stanford University Press, 1997), 32.
29. John Sallis, "Hegel's Concept of Presentation: Its Determination in the Preface to the *Phenomenology of Spirit,*" in *Delimitations: Phenomenology and the End of Metaphysics,* 40–62 (Bloomington: Indiana University Press, 1986), 41.
30. Gilles Deleuze, "Lettre à Michel Cressole." An appendix to Michel Cressole, *Deleuze* (Paris: Éditions Universitaires, 1973): 110 / "I Have Nothing to Admit," trans. Janis Forman, in *Semiotext(e), Anti-Oedipus* 2, no. 3 (1977): 112.
31. Gilles Deleuze, *Différence et répétition* (Paris: Presses Universitaires de France, 1968), 1 / *Difference and Repetition*, trans. Paul Patton (New York: Columbia University Press, 1994), xix.
32. Michel Foucault, *L'ordre du discours* (Paris: Éditions Gallimard, 1971), 74–75 / "The Discourse on Language," in *The Archeology of Knowledge and The Discourse on Language*, trans. Rupert Swyer, 215–237 (New York: Pantheon Books, 1972), 235.

Acknowledgments

The following works have been reprinted with the kind permission of the people and institutions indicated.

Jean Wahl, "Mediation, Negativity, and Separation," in *Le Malheur de la conscience dans la philosophie de Hegel*, trans. Christopher Fox and Leonard Lawlor, 81–118 (Presses Universitaires de France, 1951, deuxieme edition). Used by permission of Madame Béatrice Wahl.

Alexandre Kojève, "The Idea of Death in the Philosophy of Hegel," trans. Joseph J. Carpino, in *Interpretation: A Journal of Political Philosophy* 3, no. 2, 3 (1973): 114–156. Used by permission of Marc Carpino.

Jean-Paul Sartre, "Husserl, Hegel, Heidegger," in *Being and Nothingness: A Phenomenological Essay on Ontology*, trans. Hazel E. Barnes, 315–339 (New York: Washington Square Press, 1956). Used by permission of Philosophical Library, New York.

Georg Lukács, "'*Entäusserung*' ('Externalization') as the Central Philosophical Concept of *The Phenomenology of Mind*," in *The Young Hegel: Studies in the Relations between Dialectics and Economics*, trans. Rodney Livingstone, 537–568 (Cambridge, Massachusetts: MIT Press, 1976). Also used by permission of Merlin Press, P.O. Box 30705, London, WC2E 8QD, UK.

Maurice Merleau-Ponty, "Hegel's Existentialism," in *Sense and Non-Sense*, trans. Hubert L. Dreyfus and Patricia Allen Dreyfus, 63–70 (Evanston: Northwestern University Press, 1964). © Éditions Gallimard, Paris, 1996.

Maurice Blanchot, "Literature and the Right to Death," in *The Gaze of Orpheus, and Other Literary Essays*, trans. Lydia Davis, ed. P. Adams Sitney, 21–62 (Barrytown, New York: Station Hill Press, 1981).

Frantz Fanon, "The Negro and Hegel," in *Black Skin, White Masks*, trans. Charles Lam Markmann, 216–222 (New York: Grove Press, 1967). From BLACK SKIN, WHITE MASKS by Frantz Fanon, translated by Charles Lam Markmann. Copyright © 1967 by Grove Press, Inc. Used by permission of Grove/Atlantic, Inc.

Jean Hyppolite, "Logic and Existence," in *Logic and Existence*, trans. Leonard Lawlor and Amit Sen, 177–189 (Albany: State University of New York Press, 1997).

Georges Bataille, "Hegel, Death and Sacrifice," trans. Jonathan Strauss, in *Yale French Studies* 78 (1990): 9–28.

Jacques Lacan, "The Subversion of the Subject and the Dialectic of Desire in the Freudian Unconscious," in *Écrits: A Selection*, trans. Alan Sheridan, 292–325 (New York: W. W. Norton & Company, 1977). "Subversion of the Subject and the Dialectic of Desire", from ECRITS: A Selection by Jacques Lacan, translated by Alan Sheridan. Copyright © 1966 by Editions du Seuil. English translation copyright © 1977 by Tavistock Publications. Used by permission of W. W. Norton & Company, Inc.

Theodor W. Adorno, "World Spirit and Natural History: An Excursion to Hegel," in *Negative Dialectics*, trans. E. B. Ashton, 323–338 (New York: Continuum, 1973). Excerpts from NEGATIVE DIALECTICS by Theodor W. Adorno. English translation Copyright © 1973 by The Continuum Publishing Company Reprinted by permission of the Continuum International Publishing Group, Inc.

Gilles Deleuze, "Conclusion," in *Difference and Repetition*, trans. Paul Patton, 262–264 (New York: Columbia University Press, 1994). From *Difference and Repetition* by Gilles Deleuze © 1994 Columbia University Press. Reprinted with the permission of the publisher.

Louis Althusser, "Marx's Relation to Hegel," in *Politics and History: Montesquieu, Rousseau, Hegel and Marx*, trans. Ben Brewster, 161–186 (London: Verso, 1972).

Hans-Georg Gadamer, "Hegel's 'Inverted World,'" in *Hegel's Dialectic: Five Hermeneutical Studies*, trans. P. Christopher Smith, 35–53 (New Haven: Yale University Press, 1976).

Jacques Derrida, *Glas*, trans. John P. Leavey, Jr. and Richard Rand (Lincoln: University of Nebraska Press, 1986), 236–262. Reprinted from GLAS by Jacques Derrida, English translation by John P. Leavey, Jr., and Richard Rand, by permission of the University of Nebraska Press. Copyright 1986 by the University of Nebraska Press.

Luce Irigaray, "The Eternal Irony of the Community," in *Speculum of the Other Woman*, trans. Gillian C. Gill, 214–226 (Ithaca, New York: Cornell University Press, 1985). Reprinted from Luce Irigaray: *Speculum of the Other Woman*, translated by Gillian C. Gill. Translation copyright © 1985 by Cornell University Press. Used by permission of the publisher, Cornell University Press.

Julia Kristeva, "Negativity: Rejection," in *Revolution in Poetic Language*, trans. Margaret Waller, 109–116, 147–148, 157–159 (New York: Columbia University Press, 1984). From *Revolution in Poetic Language* by Julia Kristeva © 1984 Columbia University Press. Reprinted with the permission of the publisher.

Emmanuel Levinas, "Death and Time," in *God, Death, and Time*, trans. Bettina Bergo, 71–87 (Stanford: Stanford University Press, 2000). © Editions Grasset & Fasquelle, 1993.

John Sallis, "Hegel's Concept of Presentation: Its Determination in the Preface to the *Phenomenology of Spirit*," in *Delimitations: Phenomenology and the End of Metaphysics*, 40–62 (Bloomington: Indiana University Press, 1986).

Giorgio Agamben, "Excursus 7 (after the final day)," in *Language and Death: The Place of Negativity*, trans. Karen E. Pinkus and Michael Hardt, 99–106 (Minneapolis: University of Minnesota Press, 1991). Used by permission of Giorgio Agamben.

Slavoj Žižek, "'Not Only as *Substance*, but Also as *Subject*,'" in *The Sublime Object of Ideology*, 201–231 (London: Verso, 1989).

Judith Butler, "Stubborn Attachment, Bodily Subjection: Hegel on the Unhappy Consciousness," in *Intersections: Nineteenth-Century Philosophy and Contemporary Theory*, eds. Tilottama Rajan and David L. Clarke, 173–196 (Albany: State University of New York Press, 1995).

Jean-Luc Nancy, "Freedom" and "We," in *Hegel: The Restlessness of the Negative*, trans. Jason Smith and Steven Miller, 66–79 (Minneapolis: University of Minnesota Press, 2002). Copyright 2002 by the Regents of the University of Minnesota.

Thank you . . .

to the staff in the Academic Vice President's office, for the use of their scanner,
to John Cayer of the DiMenna-Nyselius Library at Fairfield University, for locating a number of references through interlibrary loan,
to Christopher Fox and Leonard Lawlor, for translating the Wahl selection,
to Kathryn Cole, Courtney Darts, James DiGuglielmo, Tim Eberle, and Kristy Farrell for proofreading the galleys, and
to John Sallis, for his encouragement and support.

Special thanks to my beautiful wife Liz.

Finally, this book is dedicated to Rene McGraw, O.S.B., of St. John's Abbey and St. John's University in Collegeville, Minnesota, who sparked the flame of philosophical wonder in my life.

CHAPTER 1

"Mediation, Negativity, and Separation"

—from *Le malheur de la conscience dans la philosophie de Hegel* (1929)

Jean Wahl

The unhappiness of consciousness is appeased in the idea of the death of a God. The texts that we have cited commit us to considering two different ideas, which have necessarily appeared from time to time: the idea of mediation and the idea of negativity. Through either idea we will find ourselves at the center of our concerns, but we will find ourselves at this center by considering things from a viewpoint that will make us pass from history to logic or to a metalogic, as well as to a kind of mysterious history of divinity. And we will be able to go towards the idea of sacrifice, towards the still more mysterious idea of separation in the divine.

However great the proper importance of history is for Hegel, at any given moment, history has been transcended. And what has appeared on the scene all of a sudden is the mystery of theological mediation, of divine negativity and of the infinite.[1] The philosophy of history stops being philosophy and history at the moment of Christ's appearance and disappearance. It becomes religious speculation. History is opened up. And the divine appears not only in the unfolding of history, but also, in a sense, in history's being torn apart.

By unifying elements from the systems of Fichte and Schelling, Hegel has discovered an interpretation of the Christian mysteries (cf. Kroner, II, p. 231), toward which these two philosophers were already tending—at first a more or less obscure way, but in a way that they were going to make explicit in their turn.

In Christianity, Spirit gives to itself the form of consciousness, thinks itself as a real man who can see the divinity immediately and thinks itself as the divinity seen by men in an immediate way. Only by starting from the immediate can one reach real mediation. And it is not by chance if Christianity presents to us an immediate mediator. The Christ, God, is put into the dialectic of the immediate in order to mediate man better and make the concrete universal appear in him (*Phänomenologie*, p. 568) [PS 460/GW IX 406].[2] One must no longer think therefore that the sensible exists on one side and the concept on the other. The concept encloses the sensible within: "the moment of immediate being" (ibid) (PS 460/GW IX 406). The dinner at Emmaus is eternally true, if the presence at the tomb is eternally false, and the absolute essence reaches its highest point when, seeming to descend into the sensible world, it presents itself as a "here" and a "now" (p. 571) [PS 477/GW IX 419–420]. "Spirit forgives the evil and gives up its own simplicity and its hard immutability" (p. 591) [PS 492/GW IX 433]. At the same time as the immutable is formed in Christianity, it also stops being immutable in the strict sense. This is the outcome of the whole *Phenomenology*.

We have somehow an *energeia kinesis*, a *noesis* which is no longer content with attracting things, but which, descending toward things, condescends toward them, is the things themselves. There is a movement of the immutable, and this movement is gift and forgiveness.

The dualities, which more or less all philosophies maintain, disappear. One sole thought divides itself, in order to return to itself in a richer way (cf. Kroner, II, 214). The absolute religion is the revealed religion or God appearing in what is other than Himself (*Phänomenologie*, p. 569) [PS 475/GW IX 418]. One then attains the unity of being for itself—concept, thought—and being for the other (ibid, p. 570) [PS 476/GW IX 419]. God loves his opposite as himself because in this opposite He recognizes himself. Through the same process by which God becomes man, man becomes God.

Through the idea of mediation, logic and theology met up. "The *syllogismus* is the *principium idealismi*" Hegel said in his 1801 dissertation. He opposed the philosophies of reasoning to the philosophies of judgment. Kant would have triumphed over dualism had he focused his attention on the specific characteristics of reasoning, and not on those of judgment. In his *First System,* Hegel was studying the subject of the proposition, the pure *Dieses*, so that one can say that the subject's starting point is simultaneously psychological and logical. "The subject is the pure individuality of substance," the empty quality of the "this" which is a pure nothingness. What will therefore be at issue will be to relate—thanks to the reasoning that concludes while the discernment separates—individuality to generality just as the theological mediation gathers together men and God. Hegel thinks he can logically found the idea of mediation upon which Novalis was insisting so forcefully. The real will be the mediated immediate. And just as there are three stages of reasoning, likewise there will be three stages which philosophy will have to traverse in order to grasp reason in its development. As Hegel said in his *First System,* "The two extremes are subsumed under the middle; they are each one for itself; and they are each for the other" (*First System*, Ehrenberg, p. 85). In the middle, we grasp the notion as the unity of the general and the individual. In reasoning, we see Spirit's movement uniting and separating the ideas. Through reasoning, the wound is closed (*Schluss*). Mediation is the remedy to the contradiction from the idea suffers.

Now, unhappy consciousness is essentially mediation. Through it one will go from the inferior immediate to the superior immediate. Through it the propositions "I am finite" / "God is infinite"will be reconciled—but in a mysterious way and in a way that exceeds the classical laws of reasoning. All the psychology of humanity, and even all humanity itself, will appear as a great process of reasoning. Logical mediation and theological mediation will be united. The priest will serve as the mediator between us, as immediate individuals, and the mediator. And theology will be the logic of God.

The *Dieses* is, in effect, not only the disappearing "this" which is described in the *Phenomenology*. While he may have written a phenomenology, Hegel has thought a noumenology. The *Dieses* of perception encloses within itself "a living relation and an absolute presence" (*Naturrecht*, p. 359) [NL 90/GW IV 447].

Because it is mediation, consciousness, and particularly unhappy consciousness, is negation. It is the act of passing from one idea to another. Is it not thereby the same to say that consciousness is the essential negativity of ideas, the two ideas of negativity and of mediation being all the more tightly connected, since the unique thing that they refer to is the very connection of notions? Unhappy consciousness therefore is an aspect of the dialectic that is immanent to Spirit. We can say that it is the dialectical element separated, as much as it can be, from the speculative element, or if one prefers, the negative dialectic insofar as it is separate from the positive dialectic. It is this perpetual agility of chaos of which Friedrich Schlegel will speak; it is this infinite elasticity of the ether of which Hegel speaks in his *First System*.

The very idea of movement, in effect, is only understood through the idea of negativity (about which Bosanquet gave a profound interpretation), or rather the two ideas imply one another and finally form only one. Negativity is incompleteness; it is the note of the melody that inclines towards the next; it is the movement of a statue, such as that of Rodin, which seems to lose its balance at that very moment that it acquires it; it is the movement of life, or as Hegel says, the immanent pulsation of the spontaneous movement of vitality. Unhappy consciousness is "the simple negativity insofar as it becomes conscious of itself" (*Phänomenologie*, p. 569) [PS 475/GW IX 419].

We can approach this idea from certain pages of the treatise on *Natural Law* from the beginning of the *Phenomenology*: the infinity of consciousness is nothing other than that absolute "restlessness" that characterizes movement. Just as consciousness is differentiation from that which is not different, just as it is the notion of infinity, it is self-consciousness, but, we can add, consciousness of itself as another.

The *Phenomenology* will be the study of the different aspects which consciousness takes. And since in every one of these aspects there is a conflict, we can say that in each of them we will find this unhappy consciousness. Unhappy consciousness undoubtedly is manifested more clearly in a particular epoch, but it renews itself under one form or another in all the epochs of the life of humanity.

One must understand that rational consciousness can only be expressed through a series of incomplete manifestations, by a string of conflicts and errors that are constantly rectified. The true is the negation of its negation, Hegel said in his 1801 dissertation, and he develops this idea in the system of 1802. It is in this manner that unhappy consciousness, insofar as it is this multiplicity of successive consciousnesses, is a necessary element of the happiness of consciousness, being identical in its essence to the very movement of the dialectic.

Moreover, Hegel was able to find in Fichte on the one hand, and in Schelling on the other, some elements which directed his thoughts in this regard.[3] In *Faith and Knowledge*, he establishes an identity between negation and indifference: "There is for us, says Schelling, no subjective and objective; and the absolute is considered by us only as the negation of these oppositions, and their absolute identity." But it was necessary to transform this identity into an identification, in order to turn indifference into negativity, in order to turn Schelling's absolute into that of Hegel. The idea of sacrifice was the center of Schelling's philosophy. But because he lacked the idea of pain, at least in the first version of his philosophy, because he lacked the serious, the pain, the patience, and the labor of the negative (*Phänomenologie*, p. 15) [PS 10/GW IX 18], the divine sacrifice does not yet in Schelling have a truly tragic character.

As early as the Jena period, Hegel had seen that it was necessary to oppose the idea of immanence to the "transcendence" of the Schellingian principle. He had seen that it was necessary to substitute the activity of the *Aufheben*[4]—destructive restlessness of the realities that it let, in a sense, subsist—for the passivity of the *Aufgehobensein*. The idea of negativity was no longer then that of a pure and simple negative, empty and abstract, like indifference. The idea of negativity was now that of a plentitude of movement, that of a relation and at the same time a unity, and thereby something positive, something which is the absolute itself. And yet it had to harmonize with the idea of the subject. In other words, we have to return from Schelling to Fichte. Already at this moment Hegel was uniting, following Ehrenberg's remark, Fichte's dialectical movement and the Schellingian idea of totality. Hegel thus arrived at the idea of the "true infinite."[5]

No surprise that Hegel had to see his former thoughts on the paradoxes of consciousness and his new thoughts on theology, morality, and the state, adjusting themselves to one another. He had to see himself realizing from that moment on that negativity, which is the force of passion, also looked to be the force of logic.

In the very examination of the systems of Kant, Jacobi, and of Fichte, thought is known as "infinity and the negative side (meaning) of the absolute, which is the pure destruction of the opposition and of the finite but likewise the source of eternal movement, that is, of the finite, of the finite which is infinite since it destroys itself—nothingness and pure night of the infinity where truth takes its flight, as from a deep secret" (*Glauben*, p. 156) [FK 190/GW IV 413]. By studying the three philosophies of Kant, Jacobi, and Fichte, and by studying the negation which is the judgment that concerns them, thought recognizes itself as united with being. Its negation was therefore another aspect of this affirmation which is the common foundation of the philosophies of Schelling and of Hegel. Hegel explains this affirmation, moreover, in Schellingian terms when he writes: "the pure concept or the infinity as foundation of Nothingness, where all beings disappear" (*Glauben*, p. 157) [FK 190/GW IV 413]. But the Schellingian indifference, the absolute considered as the negation of the subjective and the objective, is replaced by the movment of negativity, the negativity that goes, by uniting them, from the finite to the infinite, from the subjective to the objective. Thereby one reaches the aspect of infinity, the negative meaning of the absolute itself.

The concrete ideal of the *Aufheben* is going to be substituted for idea of the *Sollen*. There are two infinites. The *Aufheben* allows us to catch a glimpse of the concrete infinite, in opposition to the abstract infinite of the Fichteans.[6]

There is an active negativity, a creative negativity. The idea of negativity is an aspect of the very idea of freedom. Thanks to the negative what Hegel calls the "deliverance from the finite" is accomplished. Thanks to negativity, the world moves; thanks to it, the world is purified; thanks to it, the world is just. And this is through the return of negativity to itself, by its reflection on itself that the idea of Spirit becomes complete. It is its negativity that turns Spirit into the true absolute.

In effect, there must be an absolute reality, Hegel wrote in *Glauben und Wissen*, a non-dualistic reality. But there also must be a non-dualistic negativity, an infinite, a nothingness (p. 135) [FK 173/ GW IV 402]. This is the destructive aspect of reason.

This negativity will be the ideality of nature just like the ideality of God; both become at the same time what they are. The disappearance of the "this" and the "now" occurs in nature as well as in us. The dialectic is objective as well as subjective. Movement is dialectic. Because ideality is dialectical, it is movement. This means that nature is Spirit. As Goethe said in his *Faust*, nature constantly tries; and it is for that reason that it will be, like Faust, delivered.[7]

There is therefore an ideality immanent to nature as there is a reality immanent to Spirit (*Differenz*, p. 264) [D 172/GW IV 76]. And Schelling had seen that.

The sharp point of spirit, the progress of matter to the infinite are only the two opposite limits of the same process of contraction and expansion, conceived in the same way as Bruno had conceived it.

And time is precisely this essential ideality, which is in nature itself. This is the negation of every definite idea insofar as every definite idea is an isolated affirmation. Thereby we can say that time is a universal affirmation. As Schiller writes, "what must live immortally in the song—must perish in life," and Goethe: "because everything must be destroyed in nothingness—it must maintain itself in being."

Through time one heads towards true memory which is the interiorization of the movements of time, and in this sense it is a double ideality.

But negation has still another role in Hegel's thought. If it is true to say that an idea denies itself, it is also true to add that it is through its negation that one becomes conscious of the idea. Thus, the feeling of the loss of life is knowledge, is the joy of life. We are led back to the idea that by the negation of the negation, one arrives at the true; by losing life, one conquers it. The genuine concept is the negation of negation; and Spirit, going out from itself, returns to itself.

After having studied the ideas of mediation and negativity, we must now say a few words about the ideas of separation, of diremption. By examining separation, we easily see how Hegel has somehow beaten out the final Schelling, at least the Schelling of *The Philosophy of Religion*, by means of the implicit presuppositions of the first version of his philosophy itself.[8] We see also that if, for Hegel, God is made in the very course of the evolution at the same time, if we can say this, as He is produced from all eternity in an intemporal domain, perhaps it must be added that this creation makes sense only because God is at first unmade, torn apart at one moment of the evolution. There was an act, at once original cosmic sin and divine sacrifice, a judgment by which God divided himself, the creation of the Son and at the same time creation of the world.[9] It is quite possibly this divine act which reverberates to an inferior degree when through the flood nature is violently separated from man. It is still this act whose echo we encounter in the moral domain, when we see the individual, by his violent emergence out of the uniformity of life, through his division from life, create for himself his own destiny.

To tell the truth, Fichte and Schelling here also had opened the way which later they had to deepen.[10] Thus, in his response to Reinhold, Fichte writes that the essence of the finite is composed of the intuition of the absolute identity of the subjectivity and objectivity; as well it is composed of an intuition of a separation (*Trennung*) of subjectivity and objectivity; and finally the essence of the finite is composed of an analysis of the infinite, an analysis that goes all the way up to infinity. It is this analysis which constitutes temporal life. Xavier Léon, who brought to light in a remarkable way this aspect of Fichte's theories, points out that Fichte seems to borrow from Schelling his expressions. Indeed, through his relation to Schelling, Fichte defines his own thinking, and he endeavors to prove that Schelling admits that there is a foundation of separation that is real entirely by being inconceivable. It seems that there was also a presupposition toward which Fichte's thinking, in a more or less spontaneous fashion, was ascending to. He had become aware of the irrational that was necessary to his very rationalism, which was like the root of this rationalism. For Fichte, the absolute, as he wrote to Schad, is quantified, is divided in knowing and in being. Divisibility, said Fichte in his 1801 *Darstellung*, has its principle in reflection itself; it is the form that defines knowledge itself. The world is born from the divisions of reflection, of quantifiability, which, it is true, is pure possibility. But in one sense, should it not have to be the same for Hegel? This *projectio per hiatum* looked to Fichte therefore like something essential to his philosophy. (Here one should also look at the idea of an *actus individuationis*.) And Gurvitch has insisted correctly on the *Hiatus irrationalis* which Fichte acknowledged, one could say, at the root of things. Fichte had given the idea of this reflection that divides a religious sense in the *Anweisung zum seligen Leben*; what is at issue here is to overcome reflection in order to be united with God.

Schelling also thought that at the origin of the world there is "a division of reflection" that is purely quantitative and formal. This division consists in the infinite series of possible representations of the Absolute; on the basis of this primitive division, the world's epochs develop. The idea of a division, of a fundamental tearing apart, seems essential to Schelling's philosophy, as it will be to that of Friedrich Schlegel.

In his philosophical fragments, Hölderlin illuminates this theory of separation in an interesting way that is quite similar to Hegel's theory:

> The sensibility of the whole therefore increases in the same degree and in the same relation in which the separation into the parts and into their center (where the parts and the whole are at the point of their highest sensibility) increases. The unity, present in intellectual intuition, sensitizes itself insofar as it emerges from itself, insofar as the separation of its parts takes place. These are parts that separate themselves at this very moment only because they feel too united when, in the whole, they are near the center, or because they do not feel that they are united enough, from the viewpoint of perfection, if they are only juxtaposed parts, distanced from the center, or from the viewpoint of life. . . . And here, in the excess of spirit, at the heart of unity and in its effort toward materiality, in the effort of the divisible infinite, the non-organic in which all the organic has to be included, in this effort of the divisible infinite toward separation . . . , in this necessary will of Zeus properly lies the ideal beginning of the real separation.

Zeus is indeed for him the highest thing separable, and it would be curious to compare the Zeus sketched by Hölderlin to Blake's Urizen, the bad understanding that separates, of which Hegel speaks. It is necessary to note also—and this returns us to the idea of the unhappy consciousness—that Hölderlin's editor indicates a variant of the word "separation" in the second sentence of the fragment, and this variant is constituted by the word "suffering." This separation, this suffering, according to Hölderlin, is necessary for self-knowledge. According to Hölderlin, "In order for one to be able to know life, life must present itself in such a way that, in the overabundance of interiority where the opposites change into one another, life separates itself."

What is in question is a very old idea,[11] which is undoubtedly imposed on the thinking of this time through the intermediary of Lessing and Schiller, notably in Schilling's *Theosophy of Julius*. There while moreover apologizing each time that his expressions are sensible and human, Schiller talks about a ripping apart of God, about a separation of Nature that is itself an infinitely divided God. In fact, God is similar to a beam of light, which by striking a prismatic glass, divides into seven dark rays. This idea of separation is at the center of Schiller's aesthetics. Art separates, divides (*trennt, entzweit*) man and nature, Schiller says sounding like a disciple of Rousseau. "Feeling" is characterized by duality. The meditation on Rousseau allows Schiller to rediscover an ancient conception of the mystics and philosophers. If one joins the ideas of the *Theosophy of Julius* with those of the essay on *Naïve and Sentimental Poetry* one manages to conceive the entire world, in relation to the primitive unity, as being in a "sentimental" state. In other words, one manages to reach the idea of the unhappy consciousness.

According to Hegel, this notion is connected to his whole philosophy, and in particular to his theory of the immanence of relations. If God relates to the world, this relation has to have its foundation in God himself. Consequently, the union of God and the world has for a counterpart of its appearance, for its foundation, for its synonym a separation in reality of God from Himself. Therefore alterity, duality, negation, and determination are there as so many names in order to affirm the concrete character of God. The concrete is mediate, and thereby differentiated.

God conceived as a pure and simple substance is an abstraction for Hegel and consequently tends to complete itself, and thereby to separate from Himself, to put a difference between Himself and Himself, to be other than Himself, by means of the process of His own negativity. Through creation—which is not moreover the creation of something which would be purely and simply opposed to itself—through community, God is conscious of Himself.

The idea of the Fichtean "I" made it possible to understand this idea of the fundamental distinction. The "I" of Fichte and the *Grund* of Boehme are the ideas which were united to one another in the thought of Hegel and of Schelling.

The auto-destructive partiality of thought, such that we see in Fichte seems to symbolize for Hegel from that moment on a deeper separation, a divine separation, or if one prefers, a possibility of separation, of which Fichte, as we have seen, had the idea. All of what there is that is real in this separation is its possibility, the separation being reflection and reflection being possibility. We grasp the unique metaphysical root of the idea of the bad infinite, the idea of the *Jenseits* and that of the *Sollen*.

God separates from Himself in order to unite Himself with Himself, and this is why He is subject, why He is Spirit, Hegel will say in the *Phenomenology* (*Phänomenologie*, p. 576) [PS 481/GW IX 424]. Spirit, Subject, and God are qualified by this union of separation and union, of diremption and resumption, of the non-relation and of relation. In other words, God is the *logos*, the *Urteil* that unites just as it rends (*Phänomenologie*, p. 393) [PS 327/GW IX 292]. Spirit, Hegel was already saying in his *First System*, can find itself and can reach the Absolute only through scission.[12] The concept is enriched by dividing itself into its own contrasts. And it is this idea that Hegel will take up when he speaks later on, in his *Logic*, of a judgment (*Urteil*) of the notion: every judgment separates, every separation is judgment. Such is the productive act of alterity. As Heimann says, the judgment will exist for Hegel between the concept and reasoning just as contradiction is between identity and *Ground*.[13]

Essentially there are two things that we can distinguish: this separation that we have spoken about is finally a union; to self-divide is still a way of remaining unified with oneself. Sin, the act of eating the fruit of the tree of knowledge, is at the same time that it is a separation the source of redemption.

Thus, the *Logos* is exteriorized spirit only in order to be internalized spirit once again. "Diremption" absorbs itself somehow back into itself, and this is the true concept of spirit—it is "reconciliation."[14]

The true objectivism merges with a profound subjectivism. And here we hit on one of the essential points of Hegelianism, if it is true that Hegelianism is an attempt to reconcile all oppositions entirely by preserving them, in order to inaugurate an armed peace or a serene war of notions, where there is constantly exchange and succession, and at the same time identity between the negation of contradictories and the fact that they are maintained. That is the mystery of reason which Hegel was making visible in the pages of the *Phenomenology*,[15] when he shows us how the appearance is disjoined and gathered back together. This mystery of reason is the very mystery of love, the joining of that which is itself with that which is not itself.[16] Just as with God, sin is separation and union since it is knowledge. Sin is in a sense the lowest degree of this process of rending and reunification of contraries of which God is the highest degree. In a still very general way, we can say that the ideas of particularity and unhappiness coincide.

We find the prefiguration of this division of God at the beginning of the *Phenomenology*, moreover, when Hegel describes the play of forces in which the solicited force tends to emerge out of itself.

But even more this is life; this is Spirit; this is the essence of man that shows us what the essence of God is. In what does this essence consist, if not in the separation of the self, in its going beyond, in order to return to itself? The separation resides in the notion of man himself. Such is the judgment, that is, the primitive separation of the spirit, the separation that makes up its life.[17]

Now Christianity precisely characterizes itself by this absolute separation that it presupposes. "The infinite in opposition with the finite exists through freedom, and when it separates, separates absolutely."[18]

However, it must be added that Christianity defines itself as well by this constant suppression of the Other, by this disassimilation and reassimilation of the Other which departs from God and returns to God.

If we apply this to the domain of consciousness, we will say that knowledge, which is produced by the separation, would be a falsification if it were only the product of the separation. But if it is true that the stress must be put on the separation and as well on the identity, there is therefore no absolute falsification (*Differenz*, p. 252) [D 161–162/GW IV 68–69] no more than there is an ultimate separation.

Philosophy must be located in the separation as well as in the identity. It must turn the two into metaphysical realities, into absolutes, but also philosophy must realize that they are two things relative to one another.

In his *Spirit of Christianity* (which, by the way, had some similarities with certain thoughts of Fichte), Hegel said that all reflection presupposes something which is not subject to reflection. This is why at the same time as the affirmation of the *Logos*, that is, at the same time as a possibility of separation and a separation which can go to infinity, there is the affirmation of something in which there is no division: God and *Verbum* are separate and are one. The multiplicity of the real is the infinitely realized division. And it is in this sense, according to Hegel, that we say that everything is made by the Son. Hegel here rediscovers the thought of Lessing on Christ, the divided God: the divinity is matter, and the *Verbum* is its form, says Hegel perhaps inspired by the doctrines attributed to David of Dinant. But here form and matter are one. The world is not an emanation of divinity, but rather an emanation of what separates itself in the divinity; it is part of what departs to infinity. At the same, it is what is separated and what separates. Thereby it is life at the same time it is death. What is individual, what is limited, is a branch of the tree of infinite life.

Each part is a whole, a life, and at the same time this life is reflected, is separated into subject and object, into life and into truth. Now to appear and to be reflected, to separate oneself, is one and the same thing (*Differenz*, p. 263, 265) [D 171, 173/GW IV 75, 77]. Oppositions appear; life and light seem to be outside of one another. The *Phenomenology* is essentially a theory of separation insofar as it destroys itself in order to attain reason. And in the *Differenzschrift* Hegel seems to outline the plan of the *Phenomenology*: "every form of Spirit is determined through an opposing form" (p. 265) [D 173/GW IV 76].

The very beginning of philosophy, which is the feeling of a rupture, makes us catch a glimpse of this fundamental schism which projected its appearance outside of the absolute (*Differenz*, p. 172) [D 92-93/GW IV 15]. This feeling of a rupture gave us at the same time this enigmatical philosophical word: "unity."

While protesting against the oppositions that Fichte erects between things and us—oppositions that are no more than the hardening of reason's process of opposition by the understanding, since the understanding is essentially the positing of oppositions—Hegel declares in a passage that resembles those of Hölderlin that "rupture is a necessary fact of life, which is founded upon eternal opposition, and totality is only possible in the highest vitality through its reestablishment outside the highest separation" (*Differenz*, p. 178) [D 95/GW IV 17] [D 98/GW IV 19]. Moreover Hegel strongly acknowledges that reason is the force that posits the opposite subjective and objective totalities, without him coming out as a partisan of Fichte's theory. Hegel sees at the same time in reason the very force which denies separation.

He revisits this idea while speaking about faith, where we see reason as the power of separation and as the power of the negation of separation, but while conserving then in itself the form of separation (*Differenz*, p. 185) [D 103/GW IV 23]. This is why one need only take a step, hardly a step to be able to say that the absolute that is identical to reason is at the origin of separation. "Separation into subjective and into objective is a production of the absolute" (*Differenz*, p. 201) [D 120/GW IV 35].

This separation[19] is the principle of sin, because sin consists in separation, in judgment, but it is at the same time the principle of redemption.

And finally, if it is true that there is a movement of God, eternal producer of the eternal *Verbum*, cannot we, without Hegel having said this explicitly, speak of an unhappy consciousness of God by employing a language that would recall certain Boehmain terms? In any event, in the *Philosophy of History*, Hegel writes, while speaking of the religion of Adonis, that the divine must be understood as spirit, that is, that it must be concrete and must have in itself the moment of negativity which presents itself here as death and the cult of pain: "During the festival of the death and resurrection of Adonis is where the concrete meets consciousness." Hegel also says, "In God the negative and the contradiction come to intuition." At the same time that humanity's consciousness contradicts itself in its unhappiness, it sees the divine consciousness contradicting itself and being itself unhappy.

From the idea of unhappy consciousness, we can return to the idea of negativity, if we seek to transpose the psychology of humanity into the Logic. But, if we transpose the Logic in the language of the *Phenomenology*, that is, of the history of humanity, that is, of the history of God, we can just as well say that negativity is the unhappy consciousness of God because there is a "pure negativity" of God (*Phänomenologie*, p. 585) [PS 488/GW IX 430]. This can hardly be anything other than unhappy consciousness. Thus, we have absolute restlessness, the inequality of absolute Spirit, the creator of the Otherness.[20]

That is to say that one finds in the speculations, which are the embryo of the Hegelian system, the gnosis and the theories of Boehme, the *Grimmigkeit* that Boehme speaks about, the torment of things which is the source of their existence, of their quality (*Qual*, *Quelle*, *Qualität*). And Hegel's philosophy is a lot closer than one first thought to the last philosophy of Schelling.

Before practicing on the subject of the theory of the notion, Hegel's mind was practicing on these ancient speculations. Rosenkranz notes that in 1806, during his course on *Realphilosophie*, Hegel was still calling the pure idea the night of the divine mystery from whose thickness come nature and spirit.[21] The ideas of Schelling and of Boehme easily rejoin one another.

In an 1802 philosophical and lyrical variation, Hegel shows the idea of negativity to be very similar to the wrath of God, making the finitude of creatures appear and disappear. He shows us God, this infinite center, being irritated with the expansion of the nature to which He gave birth, and consuming it. He speaks to us of this divine wrath, making the infinite tremble without rest where there is no present but only a formless seething beyond limits, an infinite pain and a burning flame of this necessary pain so that spirit becomes conscious of itself. And in the *History of Philosophy* he will insist on the analogy between his idea of negativity and the Boehmian theories, although he judges severely, as barbarous, the unreflective character that this philosophy has left to these ideas. It will be necessary, he said in 1802, to subject these conceptions to a function thanks to which we see spirit free itself from them. It will be necessary to transform into knowledge this process by which the creature separates itself from God; it will be necessary to see that this very process is knowledge, spirit itself separating itself by means of reflection, then consuming itself through reflection, in order to turn its pain into the principle of religion and return finally to spirit.

The unhappy consciousness, a man more than anything, came to reveal to us his essence, insofar as his essence is felt through us. And this man is Pascal, but perhaps we can go further than him in the domain of speculation, if with Boehme we return from the pain of the Son to the pain of the Father.[22]

Eckhart's theology and Boehme's speculations came to blend with the Lutheran experience of salvation. Far from believing that the philosophy of Hegel is a purely rational philosophy, we would say that it is an effort toward the rationalization of a background that reason cannot attain. Despite what Hegel sometimes says to us, there are no purely transparent symbols for reason. Light shines in the darkness. The symbols exist—of an opaque and resistant existence—upon which lights come to be projected, lights that make the symbols burn with a somber glare.

What the author of the *Logic* had originally at the bottom of his soul was a Christian vision of the cross and a Boehmian vision of the wrath of God. At the bottom of the soul of this rationalist, there is this double mystery; at the base of the soul of this optimist, there is this double pain. The wrath of God appears as the principle of the dialectic and of this movement of return into itself by which the dialectic is achieved.

The finite will reach happy consciousness only when God, who is the infinite totality, will break this finitude and thereby console and exalt it. Yet, all totality, even the smallest, is, by and large in the course of its life, happy. And if this is so, this very finitude, by which the individual is abstracted from everything, turns the individual precisely into something that is not abstract, a heart that calls to the heart. The result is that what negative there is in him is something absolutely positive

In Hegel's *First System*, we saw obscure monads aspiring toward the God who created them, and this restlessness of the monads was already unhappy consciousness. And by consuming themselves, by working, by complaining, they will go towards joy, toward the moment when all the parts which appear isolated and fixed will dissolve in the whole of life, each one extending itself into its opposite, each one exposing the absolute infinite. What will be at issue for Hegel will be to reach a synthetic view of the unhappiness of the two consciousnesses, divine and human, to gather them into one sole unhappiness. And here still we see the image of the cross and the idea of negativity responding to the same exigency, showing us that the unhappiness of God and the unhappiness of man are one and the same unhappiness.

Unhappy consciousness is also thereby happy consciousness. If nature is the product of God's negativity, then God is the very negativity of nature. And as their unhappiness, God's happiness and man's happiness are one, thanks to this very image of the cross and to this very idea of negativity. This is what Hegel was already declaring at the end of *Glauben und Wissen*: "the pure notion, or the infinite . . . must indicate purely as a moment, but only as a moment of the highest idea, infinite pain, which previously was in the culture only historically" (*Glauben*, p. 157) [FK 190/GW IV 413]. And he sees the Christian affirmation as the foundation of the religion of modern times, particularly in the form that it takes in Luther and in Pascal. God himself is dead, "which is expressed in a form that is only empirical in the words of Pascal: nature is such that it marks everywhere, inside man and outside of man, a lost God." One reaches therefore all at once the ideas of absolute freedom and absolute pain, at the idea "of the speculative Good Friday" (*Glauben*, p. 158) [FK 191/GW IV 414] above the sphere of history and of feeling. What is presented as history must not make us forget that in reality the domain of history is already overcome. It is necessary to keep in mind simultaneously the two ideas of duration and of eternity and see them be reunited in the conception of a duration, of a change, in the eternal.[23] If one celebrates the speculative Good Friday in all its heartbreak, in all its abandonment, in all of the harshness of the death of God, one will no longer see it as the sacrifice of the sensible existence conceived by the disciples of Kant or Fichte, but one will see the deepest sweetness emerge from this harshness, the highest totality, the loftiest idea in its entire seriousness and in its most serene freedom. Happiness is a bird of storms; it is born from unhappiness; it lives in unhappiness; it is the anti-halcyon; it is the storm itself, becoming conscious of itself at the most violent center and likewise in all the twists of its whirlwind.

Such is yet the flame insofar as it constantly changes its substance and conserves it in its permanent form. Movement is rest; the infinite *Verbum* is silence. Such are the absolute movement and the absolute negativity, identical with the satisfied essence of itself and at rest.[24] Such are these Menades for whom the turmoil means that the turmoil of nature is becoming conscious through itself. These Menades line themselves up among the Olympic Gods; they lose nothing of their movement, but form this movement into a peaceful dance, or even a motionless song.

Not only is the pain of the soul the testimony of spirit, not only is pain the affirmation of the belief of the divine apparition that we need, not only does unhappy consciousness have its place in happy consciousness just as all the moments that are overcome find themselves again in the final movement, but yet we can say that unhappy consciousness is the image, only darker, of happy consciousness. Unhappy consciousness is the passage from one opposite to another and thereby somehow the union of them. It is like the reverse reflection of the flame of happy consciousness; it is the consciousness of happiness insoafar as projected in the individual and changing him, and thereby becoming doubled and the consciousness of unhappiness. By wiping clean the mirror in which it reverses itself and in which following Schiller's image it is divided, we see again this straight flame. Through the divine disequilibrium, equilibrium is ratified, and the obscure background becomes transparency itself. Unhappy consciousness is in itself (*nur an sich*) reason. It must simply realize that it is reason (*Phänomenologie*, p. 496) [PS 413/GW IX 366]. And also it must not jealously enclose itself. It must not be like Novalis's heart, perfume which is incessantly enclosed at the heart of the blue flower out of fear that it will vanish.

From then on the immediate becomes mediated, the individual universal, unhappiness happiness. And if this is so, if the true particular is a generality, if the true immediate is mediated, if position and negation imply one another, not only can we say that there is a necessary movement of spirit weaving a fabric of relations, brightening the jewel of the immediate at the very center of relations, but also we can say that we have seen the diamond in what there would be incorruptible in the coal, the diamond with which our eye, to adopt Neo-Platonic language, identifies itself. We have thus attained the concrete universal. The suppression of separation is, in order to take up Schiller's expression in the *Theosophy of Julius*, God's very genesis.

Thus, beyond the properly Christian vision, and beyond the properly Boehmian vision of which we have spoken, there was in Hegel's soul, tightly bound to these two ways of seeing, a third vision, the vision that at the same moment is expressed in certain poems of Blake (under moreover a very different form), the vision that Hegel discovered in the passages cited by Mosheim which he had copied over: "the good man is the unique son of God which the father eternally has engendered. In souls there is something that is not created, and this is reason. All of what the Holy Spirit says about Christ is true of every divine human. All of what belongs to the divine nature belongs to the divine human."[25] Every man is both burning light and flame. In order to love God, one has to be His equal. There is in man a divine spark as the ancient Stoics and the German mystics had seen. Through the intermediary of the Bull of John XXII, and the orthodox historian Mosheim, the thought of Eckhart worked on the Frankfurt theologian.

The moment will come when a universal and truly philosophical religion will appear. Then the true spirit of religion will be revealed, which according to the very laws of history could not show itself in the past moments, but which was contained in them as seeds. Then the third religion will be realized, the second good news which will come to fill in the gaps, the breaks in the text from the first, the eternal Gospel on which certain mystics and intellectuals as Lessing were reflecting (in a way that was moreover quite different), renovating the heretical ideas of the Montanists of the early Church. And the depth of the Christian reconciliation will be one with the beauty of the Greek vision without having to renounce the Boehmian vision and the pride of certain disciples of Eckhart, without having to renounce divine negativity and human affirmation.

Spirit is the force that puts negativity in motion and puts up with it. It is the pain and the force of putting up with pain, at the same time.

It is this coming-and-going, this anabase and this catabase, procession, ecstasy and at the same time interiorization which finally coincide.

God, says Hegel, is absolute wisdom and absolute beatitude, insofar as He is immersed, but mediately, in the process by which the universe is at once at rest and in movement, that is, insofar as He is absolute ideality. And Hegel adds: "the tribunal before which the individual is going to be called, cannot be, precisely because the individual is isolated, an abstract tribunal. God as the judge of the world must, because he is this absolute totality, break the heart; he cannot judge, he can only console." Although this reconciliation takes on for Hegel a nearly ironical appearance in certain passages of the *First System*, or an appearance of forgiveness as in the *Phenomenology*, reconciliation always appears to him as the essential idea of religion.

Thus, evolution is understood for Hegel only because it is a matter of going from unity to unity: "the moment of the reunion cannot coincide with the moment of separation. There are necessary stages between separation and the final union of the infinite notion," necessary stages that, at least according to what Hegel wrote in 1802, cannot be determined through the meaning and direction of the whole.

All of that must not make us forget the realist and classical aspect of Hegelian thought. Unhappy consciousness is consciousness as subject. It is the moment of infinite difference. To turn self-consciousness into a thing, to pass from the subjective to the objective, to escape beyond the romanticism of the *Sehnsucht* to found a classicism of the world—a classicism of the world that is complete precisely because it is incomplete, incomplete because it is complete—such was Hegel's work from this last viewpoint. Spirit must be reality; spirit must be a thing and be identified with things (*Phänomenologie*, p. 504, cf. 496) [PS 419/GW IX 371] [PS 413/GW IX 365–66]. This will turn philosophy into the very expression of Protestantism insofar as it takes its foothold in the subject. But this will be to overcome its stricter forms. It is a matter of creating from reason a religion, from religion reason, to go beyond romanticism while making it classical, to go beyond classicism while making it romantic, to unite romantic subjectivity, restlessness or incessant movement, negativity, and objectivity, the perfect fulfillment of the classical soul, to reach, as we have said, the idea of an infinite development of perfect reason, to sense in divinity itself the theme of essential separation which resounds in the philosophies of the final Schelling and Schopenhauer, to oppose at the same time the triumph of the happy consciousness to the apotheosis of the unhappy consciousness, and to reveal the real and divine tragedy.

The true happiness is not a blank page, a beatitude without suffering. It is the virile happiness. It is Lucifer reascending to the heavens, the particular opening itself and redeemed, under the negative influence of reason, under reason's generality. Thus, the Lutheran theme of humility and triumph is taken up and developed.

Against the philosophies of reflection, Romanticism has placed a value on the idea of the person, but this very idea risked disappearing if one does not reintegrate it into reflection. The person and the state will be concrete universals only if the reflection, which is its moving measure, is put into order around the vital fire.

It is a matter of creating self-consciousness from substance, and from self-consciousness a substance. The double movement meets up in the concrete universal. Substance is self-consciousness because it is the passage toward the opposite, because it is movement. Consciousness being permanence in the midst of the opposition is generality, is substance. But this substance is consciousness for itself: it is spirit.

If one can say that the goal of Hegelianism is to turn the subject into substance by opposing Fichte's first conceptions, then the goal is as well to turn substance into the subject by opposing Schelling. At the same time, it consists in triumphing over all false oppositions that create the unhappiness of consciousness: the opposition of the finite and the infinite, of appearance and essence, of the within and the beyond. The infinite is not opposed to the finite and is not reduced to a vain repetition of the finite. It is comprehended in it, redeemed, sublimated.

The *Phenomenology* in its entirety is, one could say, a movement of disincarnation of the particular, which is explicated through the inverse movement thanks to which the universal was incarnate, and became truly universal by becoming particular, while being incarnate. It is reflection on a trans-substantiation.[26] It is the study of the spirit at work giving birth to itself, revealing itself to itself. The pain of childbirth, the black smoke of the fire from which the Phoenix has arisen is the pain of the aspiration which penetrates all those forms (*Phänomenologie*, p. 566) [PS 472/GW IX 415]. There, Hegel rediscovers one of his first ideas: "just as the anxiety of the one who gives birth is turned into joy, in the same way your worries will transform themselves into bliss." Unhappy consciousness no longer appears then as the movement which follows the religion of beauty, Stoicism and skepticism: it is present in them. The ancient world at the moment of its flowering is a vain aspiration. Comedy is tragedy and the happiness that makes Hölderlin sigh is already in itself, despite the first appearances to which we fixed our attention—the deepest of misfortunes. If we must name an idea that contains all these moments, moments other than revelation of reason, it will be suitable to call it unhappy consciousness (ibid) [PS 473/GW IX 415]. Thus, one cannot exaggerate the generality of this idea. All of what is not the concrete universal, such that primitive Christianity, then Lutheranism, then Hegelianism have defined it, is the unhappiness of consciousness. This idea is a concept in motion that embraces, according to the way we interpret it, a more or less long stretch of history; in the narrowest sense this would be the Middle Ages; in a broader sense the Middle Ages together with Christianity. Extending back farther, it would engulf Judaism and classical antiquity.

The unhappy consciousness is thus the ancient world insofar as it is an abstraction and the vague consciousness that there is something other than abstraction. It is for the same reason the Hebraic world. It is the Christian world in which this double aspiration of the ancient world and the Jewish world comes to transform itself in the cry: "God himself is dead!"

If we project it into modern history, it means the Enlightenment, Kantianism, the reaction against Kantianism. Moreover, there it is this amplification and this reversal of the notions—one of the characteristics of Hegelian thought which at the same time contests theses which initially are opposed, and at the very time that it contests them, conserves from them what in its eyes is their essence.

If we want to translate these ideas into more abstract terms, this consciousness in unhappiness is the very duality of consciousness insofar as it is going to be necessary to the notion of spirit, a duality which still cannot manage to seize its unity. It is the consciousness as subject over and against the object (*Phänomenologie*, p. 590) [PS 492/GW IX 433]. Painful subjectivity comes from the opposition of objectivity, and the object produces the unhappiness of love and of religion. It is thus mediation and negativity.

All the movements of spirit are comparable to this movement of the infant who first places the gods outside of himself, the gods that he fears. He isolates himself from them more and more, but he returns thereby to his own unity, to this unity that was not developed, not evolved and which through its very separation is enriched. He reaches a unity produced by himself, sensed by himself, and he recognizes that the divinity is in himself. The infant recognizes himself as the son of God. He became other for himself only in order to find himself again in himself. As Hölderlin says in *Hyperion*, "at the end, spirit reconciles us with everything. We separate from ourselves only in order to be united more intimately, divinely, pacified with everything, with ourselves. We die to live." And he compares the dissonances of the world to the quarrels of lovers; "the reconciliation is in the middle of the struggle, and all of what is separate is rediscovered."

Abstraction is synonymous with unhappiness; the concrete universal will be for spirit joy. The idea will appear no longer as projected into a foreign being, but as being very close to us, our work, and at the same time the force that creates us and is our substance. The knowledge that appears first as falsification and separation is revelation and union.

In God conceived as triune, we see first the general and indeterminate notion, then particularity opposite other individuals, finally accomplishing in spirit the union of particular and of general, and achieving true individuality. Hegel thus rediscovers this idea of the trinity, of the triangle of triangles, such that under the influence of Baader he conceived it, but here deepened it in a different way.

Furthermore, it is not only true to say that the notion is for Hegel what was the being of the Eastern religions, the beautiful or sublime essence of Greece and Judea, and finally the subject of the Christian religion, it is true likewise to say that for him—the successor to the whole tradition of German mysticism—the notion is at the same time what he would have called the Father, Son, and Holy

Spirit; the notion is the essence, first being in itself, then being outside of itself, and finally knowledge of itself in another, and being for itself. The notion is love, the identity of the Father and of the one that He produced. This unity is Spirit; it is "Spirit insofar as it runs through these three elements of its nature; this movement by which it traverses itself creates its own reality" (*Phänomenologie*, p. 591) [PS 493/GW IX 493]. Thus, above the abstract, above even the dialectical, spirit arrives at the positive, at the "speculative." The study of unhappy consciousness and the reflection on the death of God make us grasp the identity of the speculative with the negative element, dialectic.

As long as consciousness produces only a beyond, which it tries in vain to reach, spirit cannot discover its rest (*Phänomenologie*, p. 575) [PS 480/GW IX 423]. It is too little for itself since it is greater than itself.

As Hegel said in his *First System*: "the highest being has created a world which is for Him made of an aetherial transparency and clarity; but for itself, this world is dark." Obscurity itself must illuminate itself, without losing anything of this original background that it possessed. Unhappy consciousness is cancelled and conserved. It appears close to the faraway shore that forms the horizon, as an island, which, burning in the sun, seems to become a happy cloud.

The wider the gaps, the deeper will have been the abysses, the more they will be filled in a complete fashion. The dissonances of suffering will be resolved. Likewise, the necessary dissonances had to be resolved at the end of *Heinrich von Ofterdingen* or of Empedocles. Schiller said that the peace of divine harmony ascends from the most savage combat. Deeper and deeper reminders of painful memories harmonize with moments of the greatest appeasement, through a sort of paradoxical condensation of duration, as in a great symphony.

At times, Hegel's conception is not very different from that of Goethe. The spirit of nature speaks, in one of Hegel's fragments, in a way quite similar to that in which it would speak to Faust.[27]

But, the Goethian nature, at least at first sight, entails in its vast current all the contradictions and pains without being stopped by them; here in Goethe the separations are finally perhaps only appearances. In contrast, the Hegelian absolute contains "the seriousness, the pain, the endurance, and the labor of the negative" according to the expressions of the Preface to the *Phenomenology,* which we have already cited: it contains oppositions. These are the rocks in the absolute and around which the absolute is thrown in higher and higher waves. The reflections on the antinomies of thought and on the pain of the Christian soul have led Hegel to conceive a more tense Absolute, to take from this absolute a tragic consciousness. Likewise, the Ninth Symphony—whose finale just like the *Phenomenology*'s conclusion finishes with some Schillerian words—has shown the depth of necessary pain at the height of joy. The Hegelian idea of Destiny, born of the reflection on Greek tragedy, deepened through the reflection on the mysteries of religion and philosophy, will effortlessly return to tragedy and will give birth, at least in part, to the conceptions of a Hebbel and a Wagner. If Hebbel has been able to apply Hegelian concepts to tragedy, it is necessary to take account of the fact that these concepts in themselves were tragic concepts.

Like a Caroline de Günderode, who was so representative of what was more profound in German Romanticism, like a Wagner or a Nietzsche, Hegel has tried his hand at a synthesis of joy and unhappiness where these are dissolved or surpassed. Such is therefore one of the ways the problem presented itself to Hegel: how does one become conscious of one's own destiny so that one reaches happiness? We discover here as in Nietzsche the motto of a love of fate. Above the unhappiness of consciousness burns the beauty of the Goethean soul; above the Goethean soul burns the beauty of *Heinrich von Ofterdingen*. But the dark brilliance that one perceives above this sweet glow is Etnean redness, and the reconciliation of Empedocles with his destiny. Empedocles discovers in the underground flames the twinkling of stars; he finds the sparkling aether at the same time as the sparkling Ocean. And his life is illuminated for him by the flame of his own death. Through this pain which intoxicates him, the pain of the midnight, the song of the nightingale in the darkness, man, for Hölderlin, stands taller than the gods. And perhaps, still superior to Empedocles, at least in a sense, is the soul of the poet or the philosopher who sees these movements of this hope and this despair being changed into one another. The soul that observes that the spirit that conquers itself in time possesses itself since always above time, that observes that the drama knotted in time is eternally unknotted in an eternity full of life, in a marriage of centuries such as the one of which Novalis was dreaming, this soul "is spirit, the simple movement of these pure moments."

Everything is infinitely penetrated, Hölderlin said, with pain and joy, with struggle and peace, with form and the absence of form.

(Translated by Christopher Fox and Leonard Lawlor)

Notes

1. Haym had been led to make an analogous remark: "as soon as one attains Christianity, the historical study is suddenly broken. The third part of the *Philosophy of Religion* completely abandons the phenomenological terrain and it exclusively keeps to the metaphysical terrain" (p. 418). Thanks to the idea of the death of Christ, the philosopher jumps from the fact to the idea; the fact as fact here becomes itself the idea (p. 423).
2. TN. Wahl's references to Hegel's *Werke* will be followed, in brackets, by brackets to the current English and German editions. The following English editions will be cited: *Hegel's Phenomenology of Spirit*, trans. A. V. Miller (Oxford: Oxford University Press, 1977) [abbreviated as PS]; *Natural Law*, trans. T. M. Knox (Philadelphia: University of Pennsylvania Press, 1975)

[abbreviated as NL]; *The Difference Between Fichte's and Schelling's Systems of Philosophy*, trans. H. S. Harris and Walter Cerf, (Albany: State University of New York Press, 1977) [abbreviated as D]; and *Faith and Knowledge*, trans. H. S. Harris and Walter Cerf (Albany: State University of New York Press, 1977) [abbreviated as FK]. German references are taken from the *Gesammelte Werke*, Volume 4 (*Jenaer Krisiche Schriften*, which includes Differenzschrift, *Naturrecht*, and *Glauben und Wissen*), edited by Hartmut Buchner and Otto Pöggeler, and Volume 9 (*Phänomenologie des Geistes*), edited by Wolfgang Bonsiepen and Richard Heede. These are cited as GW followed by the volume number.

3. Hegel's thought on this point perhaps can be considered as relying on that of his predecessors. In particular, certain lines of the 1801 dissertation can appear as an deepening of the Kantian essay on negative quantities. Pain is a negation, but it is not nothingness. There are active negations; and the true is the false itself insofar as it shows itself as a nothingness.

   MacTaggart's interpretation presents an intellectualized and "flattened" Hegel. He has diminished as much as possible the specific character of the moment of negativity. He recognizes meanwhile that when it is a matter of crime, of punishment, and reconciliation, or of the death that is necessary to life, one has a sense of the true Hegel.

   There would still be the task of studying what one could call the hierarchy of negatives for Hegel, going from the negative, which is formal indifference and which contains nothing absolute, going as far up as the force of the negativity of reason, while passing through the dividing negations operating in understanding. There would be the task of seeing how, through a continuous degradation or gradation, one can pass from one of these senses to the other, even though they look to be opposites in certain cases.

   Let us add that these separations (the second negative) are necessary to the negativity of reason, to the highest negative. Reflection is necessary to reason, at first because what is negative in it is denied by reason, then because it must in a certain way subsist in reason. Undoubtedly, one can say that what we have called the second negative is the work of the understanding, but this understanding is something essential to the nature of things. If there is in Bergson as in Plotinus a contemporaneous genesis of matter and intelligence, then one can say that there is in Hegel a contemporaneous genesis of negativity and intelligence; or rather they both constitute the very genesis of things. Let us yet add that nothing is purely negative (which is understood, since every stage of consciousness is simultaneously denied and affirmed through the precedent), and that there is an interaction, an indissolubility of the negative and of the positive.

   The spirit which goes from this negation, which is the individual, to this negation, which is the divinity, is the sole positive thing, precisely because it is the absolute negativity, that is, the mediator, the infinite which affirms itself through its negations. And the genuine divinity is identical to it.

For Hegel, negativity, freedom, subjectivity, the processes of the *Aufhebung* are united.

Not only is the *nihil negativum* false, but still, opposed to the pure and simple affirmation, which would be a bad negative, a finite negative, all true affirmation, insofar as it is the negation of a negation is a stage toward the true infinite.

There is a negation, the Fichtean (or so-called Fichtean) negation, for example, which is a separation, which is the imitation, the counterfeit of this rational negation by means of which the infinite is no longer opposed to the finite, but encompasses it. Fichte's philosophy as it is presented at first fixes the processes of negation in a product. It translates a movement of reason in terms of the understanding. From this viewpoint, it is not a philosophy of false becoming, but a philosophy of false being (*Differenz*, p. 173) [D 93/GW IV 15], of being as product (ibid, p. 174) [D 94–95/GW IV 16]. Hegel, as we have noted, caught a glimpse already of what logical importance the idea of becoming had to take, since he wrote (ibid, p. 177) [D 97/GW IV 18] that in it being and non-being are united.

4. The idea that negativity is the very power of the *Aufhebung* is indicated at the end of the *Phenomenology*.
5. Ehrenberg (*Introduction à: Hegel's Erstes System*, [Heidelberg, 1915]) has shown in a brief but interesting way how the Frankfort ideas lost their subjective coloring in order to become the Jena ideas. By following the line of development that he has drawn out, one can say that the idea of the rending of consciousness has become the idea of negativity. And the entire *Phenomenology* appears, according to what Ehrenberg has indicated—which allows us to find once again Royce's theory—as the universalization of the relation found in consciousness.

   From this moment on, the union between individuality and universality, the passage of one of these ideas into its opposite, the negation of the false infinite, the play of forces, this inequality of the essential and the inessential which reconciles itself in equality and identity, the joining of the ideas of religious mediation, of logical mediation, and what one can call psychological mediation, the necessity to which we will have to return, of the idea of a God who separates Himself—these are so many conceptions that are formed in Hegel's mind.
6. Schelling also unites the ideas of ideality and movement.
7. Hegel at first employs the word *Aufheben* simply with the sense of *cancellation* [*supprimer*] (ex. pp. 266 [PS 220/GW IX 201], 268 [PS 222/GW IX 202], 270 [PS 224/ GW IX 204], 276 [PS 229/GW IX 208], 300 [PS 249/GW IX 225], 278–279 [PS 230–232/GW IX 209]). However, a new usage of the

word appears on p. 300 [PS 249/GW IX 225]: "the understanding contradicts sensation; sensation contradicts understanding; as regards the imagination in which both exist and are cancelled." On p. 398, he writes: "fulfilled (*erfüllt*) and at the same time cancelled by itself." The word had from then on has its complete sense, complete and ambiguous. Hegel had been led to this sense by observing that reflection, at the same time that it denies every limited being, by relating it to the absolute, gives to it a consistency precisely in this very act (cf. *Differenz*, p. 178) [D 97–98/GW IV 19], and by seeing that reason cancels the two worlds, that of subject and that of object, in that it unites them. But he saw also that only consequently by uniting them, reflection affirms them as well, since it unites them in the absolute (180) [D 99/GW IV 20]. "Nothing is still in itself, but only insofar as it is posited in the absolute, that is, as identity." One will have then between the absolute and the appearance a relation other than that of negation. Above the principle of contradiction of which tells us that the understanding must always remain the understanding, now an idea is born which shows us that a thing can be at once destroyed and spared.

Then Hegel makes the word *aufheben* (*suprimmer*) harmonize with words which mean: "to conserve" (*in sich schliessen*, p. 89 ; *in sich fassen*, p. 181; *setzen*, p. 188) or "to raise" (*erheben* harmonized with *aufheben*, p. 173, likewise *erhaben*, p. 398; *heraus heben*, p. 87) or "to maintain" (*bestehen*, p. 251). Cf. still, pp. 346–355, 259, 272, 296 and the expression *als aufgehoben gesetzt* (utilized as cancelled) in the *First System* (Lasson edition, *Jenenser Logik*, pp. 75, 86, 96, 117) and *Ein Moment und aufgehoben* (ibid., p. 126). Cf. *Phänomenologie*, pp. 20 [PS 14/GW IX 22], 80 [PS 65/GW IX 69], 86 [PS 70/GW IX 74], 144 [PS 118/GW IX 115], 160 [PS 132/GW IX 126], 586 [PS 488/GW IX 429].

Little by little this word comes to signify what Hegel calls in the *Naturrecht* the now of that which is cancelled. The image of the *plethera*, that of the resurrection of Christ to the right hand of the Father, comes to specify this idea. Likewise, we have the idea of one note conserved within the total harmony.

8. See *Philosophy and Religion* (1804). Note the importance given to the idea of separation from itself and to the idea of possibility in Schelling, as well moreover in Fichte (in the *Anweisung*). Schelling himself has noted the resemblance on this point. Note that Hegel (*Phänomenologie*, p. 581) [PS 484–485/GW IX 426–27] criticizes the Schellingian conception of the Fall.
9. The two creations are identical for Hegel. Furthermore, because Hegel tends to associate the idea of creation with that of sin, we could thus manage to reach an audacious identification of sin and salvation.
10. The discussion which is pursued concerning these ideas between Schelling and Fichte shows how much they have a hard time seeing the point at which

these ideas were diverging. Fichte objects to Schelling for his immanentism and Schelling objects to Fichte for the irrationalist consequences of his philosophy. Fichte is the more Schellingian of the two, and perhaps Schelling's later philosophy will be most directly his heir.

11. It would be necessary to go back to Boehme, all the way to the "titanic struggle" to which Damascius alludes many times, all the way to the Gnostics. Still, this would only be the first stages of a study which would reach perhaps to Orphism, to the cutting up of Zagreus, to Empedocles, and to the primitive cosmogonies. It would be necessary to see how Boehme has connected the ideas of negativity and of separation.
12. H. R. Stirling brought this to light in his *The Secret of Hegel* (London, 1865).
13. B. Heimann, *System und Methode in Hegel's Philosophie* (Leipzig, 1927), p. 356.
14. *Phänomenologie*, pp. 576 [PS 480/GW IX 423], 577 [PS 482/GW IX 424] and 427 [PS 356/GW IX 317].
15. *Phänomenologie*, p. 129 [PS 106/GW IX 104].
16. Ibid, p. 578. [PS 482/GW IX 424].
17. Since we would separate a subject and an attribute, an effect and a cause, in order to reunite them afterwards, in order for us to have within us inside the circle of reflection something analogous to the divine, in order to have the very intuition of the rhythm of God, all we have to do is to pronounce a judgment, to grasp a concept as one and different. Kant's meditation leads us back to Eckhart.
18. Hadlich, *Hegel's Lehren über das Verhältnis von Religion und Philosophie*, (Halle, 1906), p. 314.
19. It would be appropriate to wonder to what extent this Hegelian gnosis harmonizes with Christianity and to what extent it is separate from it. Gross brought to light in an extremely ingenious way these oppositions, in his work *Deutsche Ideaslismus und das Christentum*. Hegel puts the unacceptable idea of creation back into his monism, through the idea of the divine Fall: the creation becomes evil. And on the other hand, sin becomes creation and the principle of redemption. According to Groos, one would witness here a "complete reversal of the Christian dogma." The relations, however, appear to be more complex between Hegelianism and the Christian religion. And yet, it must be said that the creation of the Son and the creation of the world are made identical by Hegel, that he receives from gnosticism the conception of Adam Kadmon, and that his theory looks at times like a gnosis that is no longer mysterious.
20. On this point see Stirling, *Secret*, I, 41: "the 'no' is the principle which creates the distinction." "It is possible that some of Jacob Boehme's cosmogonic ideas are in the background of Hegel."

21. See Rosenkranz, *Hegel's Leben* (Berlin, 1844).
22. One must acknowledge that from the *Phenomenology* onward, Hegel sees only external representations in Boehme's conceptions, p. 582 [PS 485–486/GW IX 427–28].
23. Herder's thought, which was also that of Goethe, according to which the goal is always attained and not attained, intersects with one of the intuitions of mysticism, particularly one of Eckhart's ideas in which he speaks of God's infinite movement and eternal rest.
24. *Phänomenologie,* pp. 372, 400 [PS 310/GW IX 277] [PS 333–334/GW IX 296].
25. What was lacking in Christ's beautiful soul was the audacity, the pride, the bravery of being mantained in the world and of defeating the world. He is posited as an antithesis and not as a synthesis, or this was a synthesis without sufficient force. He was not able to succeed in establishing a religion of the people, but only a religion confined to some individuals or small groups. He did not possess the plentitude of force, although a few of his speeches contains a strange boldness.
26. W. Dilthey, *Die Jugendgeschichte Hegel's* (Berlin, 1905, 1921), p. 81.
27. Dilthey, *Die Jugendgeschichte Hegel's*, p. 196. Goethe and Hegel have the same union of the internal and external, of evolution and law, of movement and rest, the idea of the death of the individual and the permanence of the whole, the union of separation and union.

CHAPTER 2

"The Idea of Death in the Philosophy of Hegel"

—from *Introduction to the Reading of Hegel* (1947; lectures delivered: 1933–34)

Alexandre Kojève

(COMPLETE TEXT OF THE LAST TWO LECTURES OF THE ACADEMIC YEAR 1933–34)*[1]

In a passage of fundamental importance in the Preface to the *Phenomenology* (pp. 19–24),*[2] Hegel outlines the major themes of his philosophy and indicates its principal purpose; he enumerates there the principles that lie at the basis of his thought and the principal consequences that flow from them. An understanding of this passage will provide the key to an understanding of the Hegelian system in its totality and to the *Phenomenology* in particular. In addition, this passage will show clearly the primordial role that the idea of death plays in the philosophy of Hegel.

Hegel begins by indicating what the novel and essential content of his philosophy consists in, according to him.

He says this (p. 19, lines 24–27):

> In my opinion, which can be justified only through the exposition of the System itself, everything depends (es kommt alles darauf an) on this, that one expresses and understands (aufzufassen) the True (Wahre) not [only] as *substance*, but rather just as much as *subject*.

This phrase is directed first of all against Schelling and his conception of the "Absolute" as "Substance." But that Schellingian conception merely reiterates the Spinozist conception, which, in its turn, represents a radical form of traditional—that is, Greek or pagan—ontology. Hegel therefore places his philosophy in opposition to all those that preceded it (with the sole exception of the philosophies of Kant and Fichte and, to a certain extent, that of Descartes). Following Thales and Parmenides, pre-Hegelian philosophers attached themselves exclusively to the notion of "Substance," while forgetting that the notion of "Subject" is just as primordial and irreducible.

Philosophy is not only a truth or a true description; it is rather, or should be, a description of the True. Now if Truth (Wahrheit) is the correct and complete "revelation" (= description) of Being and of the Real through coherent Discourse (Logos), the True (das Wahre) is Being-revealed-through-discourse-in-its-reality. It is not enough therefore for the philosopher to describe Being; he must also describe revealed-Being [l'Etre-révélé] and [must] give an account of the fact of the revelation of Being through Discourse. The philosopher must describe the *totality* of what *is* and exists. Now in fact this totality implies Discourse and in particular philosophical discourse. The philosopher therefore is concerned not only with static-[and-]given-Being (*Sein*) or with the *Substance*, which is the Object of Discourse, but with the *Subject* of Discourse and of philosophy: It is not enough for him to speak of Being that is given to him; he must also speak of himself and [must] explain himself to himself insofar as [he is] speaking of Being and of himself.

In other words, philosophy must explain how and why Being is realized, not only as Nature and as natural World, but also as Man and as historical World. Philosophy may not limit itself to being a Philosophy of nature; it must also be an anthropology; in addition to the ontological bases of natural reality it must investigate those of human reality, which alone is capable of revealing itself through Discourse.

It is by describing the True also as Subject, or in other words, by analyzing the specific characteristics of the human reality, that Hegel discovers the *dialectical* structure of Being and of the Real, and the ontological category of *Negativity* that is at the basis of that dialecticity. And it is in describing the real Dialectic that he discovers the *circularity* of the True and of Truth, and therefore of his philosophy itself.

Hegel says it himself in a passage that follows shortly after the text just cited (p. 20, lines 5–19):

> Further, living Substance [i.e., neither static nor given] is Being which is in truth *Subject*; or, what is the same thing,—[living Substance is Being] which is in truth objectively-real only to the extent that substance is the [dialectical-]movement of the act-of-self-positing [l'acte-de-se-poser-soi-même] (Sich-selbstsetzens) or mediation (Vermittlung) with itself of the act-of-becoming-other-to-itself (Sichander-

> swerdens). As Subject, Substance is pure *Negativity*, *simple-or-undivided* (*einfache*), and by that very token the dichotomy [dédoublement] (Entzweiung) of the simple-or-individual, or the opposing (entgegensetzende) duplication [doublement] (Verdopplung), which is equally (wieder) the negation of that indifferent (gleichgültigen) distinction-or-differentiation (Verschiedenheit) and of its opposite (Gegensatzes). It is only this equality which *re-constitutes* itself, or the reflection within itself in other-ness (Anderssein), which is the True, [and] not the *primordial* (*ursprüngliche*) unifying-unity as such, that is, [the unity-unifying] *immediate* (*unmittelbar*) as such. The True is the becoming of itself, the circle which presupposes its final-term (*Ende*) as its purpose and which has it as [its] beginning, and which is objectively-real only through the realizative-development (Ausführung) and by its final-term.

This very condensed passage implies all the fundamental notions of Hegel's "dialectic" and sums up all there is in his philosophy that is essential and truly new.

If *Substance* conceived as natural static[-and]-given-Being (*Sein*) has Identity (with itself) as its ontological ground, the *Subject* of the Discourse revealing that Being and itself, that is, Man, has Negativity as its ultimate basis. Now the Man who is dominated in his very being by Negativity is not static[-and]-given-Being, but *Action* or the Act-of-positing-itself or of creating itself. And it is objectively-real only as a "dialectical movement," whose result is "mediated" ["médiatisé"] by *negation* of the "given-Being" that serves it as a point of departure. It is Negativity, associated in Being with the Identity of Being, that splits that Being into Object and Subject, in creating [a] Man opposed to Nature. But it is also this same Negativity, realized as human existence in the midst of Nature, that reunites anew the Subject and Object in and through true consciousness, in which Discourse "coincides" with the Being that it reveals. The True, or revealed-Being, is not therefore, as Parmenides and his imitators thought it, the primary and primordial, namely, "immediate" or given and natural identity of being and thought, but [rather, the True is] the *result* of a long active process that begins by *opposing* Man to the Nature of which he speaks and which he "negates" by his action.

The re-establishment of Unity, or the final coincidence of "Substance" and "Subject" is effected in the adequate description of the *totality* of Being and of the Real by "absolute" philosophy (to the elaboration of which is reduced all the human existence of its author—the Wise Man [le Sage]—who ceases therefore to oppose himself actively, as "Subject," to Nature taken as "Substance"). But the totality of the Real implies human reality, which exists only as a creative *movement*. Perfect and definitive adequation of Being (= Substance) and Discourse (= Subject) cannot therefore be effected until the end of times, when the creative movement of Man will have been completed. And that completion is revealed by the fact that Man advances no further and is content to travel again (in his philosophical thought) the road already covered (by his active existence). Thus "absolute" philosophy, or the True in the strong sense of the term, can appear only in the form of a *circular* description of the real Dialectic taken in its totality. That philosophy on the one hand describes the road that leads from the birth of Discourse (= Man) in the heart of Being (= Nature) up to the advent of the Man who will reveal the totality of Being through his Discourse, and on the other hand it [the "absolute" philosophy] is itself this Discourse that reveals the Totality. But that Totality implies the Discourse that reveals it, as well as the process of becoming of this Discourse. Thus, in arriving at the end of the philosophical description, we are thrown back toward its beginning, which is the description of its becoming. The "final-term" of this described becoming is the advent of absolute philosophy. But that advent is also the goal we pursued from the start, because philosophy is not absolute, it does not describe the *totality*, except to the extent that it itself understands itself as describing its own becoming. But this description can be done only from the point of view of absolute philosophy, which is therefore the "beginning" or the origin of all adequate description. This is to say that just like the Totality it describes, absolute philosophy cannot be objectively realized any more than the other [the Totality] except in and through its "development," that is, as the *sum total* of its circular discourse forming an indivisible whole, which reproduces the closed dialectic of reality. It is this circularity of philosophical discourse that guarantees its unsurpassable and unmodifiable *totality*, and therefore its absolute *truth*.

Hegel says it himself (p. 21, lines 3–8), in taking up again (after having written an explanatory note) the idea expressed at the end of the passage cited:

> The True is the Whole [le Tout]. Now the Whole is nothing but the essential-reality (Wesen) which completes-or-perfects-itself through its development. It must be said of the Absolute that it is essentially [a] *result*, that it is only at the *end* what it is in truth; and it is precisely in this that its nature consists, to be [an] objectively-real-entity (Wirkliches), subject or act-of-becoming-itself (Sichselbstwerden).

The True, or Being-revealed-through-discourse, is a *Totality*, that is, the sum-total of a creative or dialectical *movement*, which produces Discourse in the midst of Being. The Absolute or the *totality* of the real is not merely Substance, but rather Subject revealing the real perfectly; however, it is such only at the end of its dialectical (= historical) becoming, which concludes with its own revelation. And this revealing becoming [ce devenir révélateur] signifies that the Totality implies *human* reality, which is not a *given* eternally identical to itself, but a temporally progressive *act* of self-creation [auto-création].

This self-creation of Man is effected through the *negation* of the given (natural and human). The human reality, or the Ego [le Moi], is therefore not a natural or "immediate" reality, but a dialectical or "mediated" reality. To conceive [of] the Absolute as Subject (and that is what is essential, according to Hegel), is therefore to conceive [of] it as implying Negativity and as realizing itself not only as Nature but rather more as [the] Ego or as Man, that is, as creative or historical becoming.

And this is what Hegel says (after a new explanatory note) in the sentence that follows after the passage cited (p. 21, lines 27–31):

> Mediation is nothing other than [an] equality-with-itself (Sichselbstgleichheit) which moves[-dialectically]; or [even further] it is reflection in itself, the constitutive-element (Moment) of the Ego existing-for-itself, pure Negativity, or [when it is] reduced to its pure abstraction,—*simple-or-undivided becoming*.

And Hegel goes on (after a new note) to say this (p. 22, lines 10–11):

> What has just been said can also be expressed by saying that Reason (Vernunft) is a *teleological Action* (*zweckmässiges Tun*).

To say that the Absolute is not only Substance, but also Subject, is to say that the Totality implies Negativity in addition to Identity. It is also to say that Being realizes itself, not only as Nature, but also as Man. And it is to say, finally, that Man—who does not differ essentially from Nature except to the extent that he is Reason (Logos) or coherent Discourse endowed with a meaning that reveals Being—is himself not given-Being, but create-ive Action (= negate-ive of the given). Man is dialectical or historical (= free) movement revealing Being through Discourse only because he lives in function of the *future*, which presents itself to him in the form of a *project* or as a "goal" (Zweck) to be realized through action negate-ive of the given, and because he is not himself real as Man except to the extent that he creates himself through such action as a *work* (Werk).

It is from [this] introduction into ontology of the fundamental category of Negativity or of Action (Tat or Tun, which is the "true being of Man") that flow all the characteristic traits of Hegelian (= "dialectical") philosophy.

From this results, among other things, a consequence we already know of and that Hegel formulates as follows (p. 23, lines 21–24):

> Among the diverse consequences that flow from what has been said, we might take note of that one [which consists in saying] that knowledge is not objectively-real and cannot be exhibited (dargestellt) except as Science or as *System*.

"Science" or "System" signifies in Hegel the adequate, and therefore *circular*, description of the completed or *closed* totality of the real dialectical movement. And in fact, as soon as we introduce Negativity or *create-ive* Action into given-Being, we cannot make any pretense to *absolute*, or *total* and *definitive*, truth except by admitting that the creative dialectical process is *completed*. Now a description of the *completed* dialectical process, that is, of the process that ends up in a term whose negation is no longer the creation of a *new* term [—such a description] can indeed be only *circular*.[1]

And finally, in concluding the passage (pp. 19–24) in which he exposes briefly the essential traits of his System as a whole, Hegel says that we can sum up all that he asserts concerning the dialecticity of Being by saying that the Absolute is *Spirit* (Geist).

Hegel expresses himself as follows (p. 24, lines 7–16 and 27–30):

> [The fact] that the True is objectively-real only as System, or that Substance is essentially Subject, is expressed in the representation (Vorstellung) which speaks of (ausspricht) the Absolute as [being] *Spirit*,—a most sublime concept, and [one] that belongs peculiarly to modern times and to its [Christian] religion. Only spiritual-being (das Geistige) is *objectively-real-entity* (das *Wirkliche*): it is [on the one hand] essential-reality or *entity-existing-in-itself* (Ansichseiende); [it is on the other hand] the entity-which-*relates*-itself [to itself and to others] (das sich *Verhaltende*) and the *specifically-determined-entity* (das *Bestimmte*), *other-being* (*Anderssein*) and *being-for-itself* (*Fürsichsein*); and [it [das Geistige] is finally] the entity-which-remains in itself (in sich selbst Bleibende) in this specific-determination or in its being-outside-itself (Aussersichsein); that is to say that it [das Geistige] is *in and for itself* (*an und für sich*). . . . Spirit which knows-or-is-aware-of itself [as being] thus developed (entwickelt) as Spirit, is *Science*. It [Science] is the objective-reality of Spirit and the realm that it constructs [for] itself in its own element.

To say that the Absolute is Spirit is to affirm the *dialectical* structure of Being and of the Real taken as a whole or as an integral totality. For Spirit is, at the same time, [all of the following:] Being-in-itself (Identity, Thesis, given-Being, Nature), Being-for-itself (Negativity, Antithesis, Action, Man), and Being-in-and-for-itself (Totality, Synthesis, Work, History = "movement"). Being dialectical *totality*, spiritual-entity is objectively-*real*-entity, and it alone is this. For concrete reality implies *everything* that *is*, in whatever manner: [and that means] the natural World as much as the human or historical World and the Universe of discourse. Subject and Object, Thought and Being, Nature and Man are but *abstractions*, when we take them in isolation, just as isolated discourses and particular thingish [chosistes] entities are *abstractions*. Only the *sum total* of Reality, revealed through the *sum total* of Discourse, [only such a sum-total] is an objective-Reality; and this *sum-total* in a double sense—that is, the natural World implying the Man who speaks of it—is precisely what Hegel calls "Spirit."

To study the Real philosophically by conceiving [of] it as Spirit is not, therefore, to limit oneself, as did the Greeks and the philosophical tradition, to the phenomenological, metaphysical, and ontological description of given-Being and of the natural [and] "eternal" Cosmos, but [it is rather] to extend this triple description to the create-ive Action which is Man, and to his historical World. And it is thus alone that the described Real appears as dialectical or "trinitary," namely, as "spiritual."

Now the Man that Hegel has in mind is not the one that the Greeks thought they had perceived and that they bequeathed to philosophical posterity. This pretended Man of the ancient [or Greek] tradition is in fact a purely natural (= identical) being, who has neither freedom (= Negativity), nor history, nor individuality properly speaking. Just like the animal, he can only "represent," in and through his real and active existence, an eternal "idea" or "essence," given once and for all and remaining identical to itself. Just like the life of an animal, his empirical-existence is absolutely determined by the natural place (topos) that he occupies for all time in the midst of a given [and] unchanging Cosmos (his occasional "swervings" being but the effect of "chance"). And if he differs essentially from the animal, it is solely by [virtue of] his thought or his coherent discourse (Logos), whose appearance in the Cosmos, moreover, could never be explained. But this Discourse negates nothing and creates nothing: It is content to reveal the given real (*error* remaining in fact inexplicable). Discourse—that is, Man—is therefore incorporated into given-Being. And what there is, in the final analysis, is this one and unique Being, which thinks itself eternally in its given totality. Or better, as Spinoza will say later, what there is in the final analysis—is [a] God who is Substance.

The Man that Hegel analyzes is on the contrary [that] Man who appears in the Judeo-Christian prephilosophical tradition, the only [one that is] truly anthropological. That tradition has maintained itself in the course of "modern times" in the form of "faith" or "theology," [forms] incompatible with ancient and traditional science or philosophy. And it is that [Judeo-Christian] tradition that transmitted to Hegel the notion of the *free historical Individual* (or of the "Person"), [a notion] that this latter [Hegel] was the first to analyze *philosophically*, by trying to reconcile it with the fundamental notions of the pagan philosophy of Nature.[2] According to that Judeo-Christian tradition, Man differs *essentially* from Nature, and he differs from it, not in his thought alone, but by his very activity. Nature is a "sin" in Man and for Man: He can and must *oppose* himself to it and *negate* it in himself. Even while living in Nature, he does not submit to its laws (miracles!): To the extent that he is opposed to it and negates it, he is independent in the face of it; he is autonomous or *free*. And by living "as a stranger" in the natural World, by being opposed to it and to its laws, he creates there a new World that is his own; a *historical* World, in which man can be "converted" and can become a being radically *other* than what he is as a given natural being (Anderssein). In this *historical* World, and through this *free* "conversion," man is not any sort of representative of an eternal or immutably given "species": He is created, he creates himself, as an *individual* unique of its kind.

When Hegel says that all of his philosophy is nothing else but an attempt to conceive Substance as Subject, he means therefore that that philosophy has for its principal goal to render an account of the existence of Man in the natural World, Man being conceived in the same fashion as the Judeo-Christian anthropological tradition conceives [of] him. And that is precisely why, in the text cited, Hegel makes use of the word "Spirit" in order to sum up the whole of his philosophy. For he is concerned to underscore the Judeo-Christian origin of the *anthropological* notion of "Geist" and to oppose that "modern" notion to the whole ancient or pagan tradition, which is a tradition of the [one] sole "Substance" or of *natural* given-Being (Sein).

But if, according to the cited text, Hegel detaches himself from the pagan philosophical tradition and accepts the Judeo-Christian anthropological tradition, he underlines in this same text [the fact] that he also separates himself from this latter tradition on a point of extreme philosophical importance.

The fact is that the Judeo-Christian anthropological tradition is an essentially religious tradition, namely, theist (and "theological"). To be sure, the Judeo-Christians discovered the "spirituality" (= dialecticity) of Man, which is to say his freedom, his historicity, and his individuality. But for them "spirituality" is realized and manifests itself fully only in the beyond, and Spirit, properly so-called, truly "objectively-real" Spirit, is God: [i.e.,] an infinite and eternal being. Man himself, made in the image of God, is truly "spiritual" only to the extent that he is eternal, and he is eternal or "immortal" by the very fact that he is Spirit. Man *really* transcends the natural World in this sense, that he lives also in a *transcendent* World (and not only in a "transcendental" historical World that is *immanent* to Nature). This [transcendent] World is *beyond* Nature, which among other things implies Man taken in his empirical-existence (Dasein); but this World is said to be more "objective" and still more "real" than the natural World here below. Man penetrates into it after his death, never more to leave it; and he also participates in it while living, by having been in it already before his birth. [Kojève is doubtless referring here to intra-uterine baptism.] To say that Man has an "immortal soul" (which is precisely the Spirit in him) is to admit the reality of that transcendent World; and to admit that reality is to affirm the immortality or the infinitude of Man. Now this [transcendent] World does not depend on Man: It is *given* to him once and for all, being "prior" and essentially immutable in itself. It is on the contrary temporal Man who depends absolutely on this transcendent World: The historical World that Man creates in the here-below is in fact but a reflection in spatio-temporal Nature of the eternal World of the beyond. This eternal World is therefore not properly speaking human: It is *beyond* the free historical individual, just as he is beyond animals and things. This infinite and eternal World is a *divine* World, and its one and unique totality, which is Spirit, is not Man but God. Man gains access to God only *after his death*, and it is then alone that he realizes and fully manifests his "spirituality."

Now according to Hegel "spiritual" or "dialectical" being is necessarily *temporal* and *finite*. The Christian notion of an infinite and eternal Spirit is contradictory in itself: Infinite being is necessarily "natural" given-[and-]static-Being; and created or create-ive, "dynamic," namely, historic or "spiritual" being, is necessarily limited in time, which is to say [that it is] essentially mortal. And the Judeo-Christian tradition did indeed finally take account of the matter. By admitting the immortality of the soul, it admitted the reality of the divine World that is the "natural place" of Man after his death (that death nullifying him as the integrating element of the natural and human World here below). And by the force of the logic of things, Christian thought had to subordinate immortal Man to his eternal infinite transcendent God. It had to give up human freedom and therefore the true historicity and individuality of Man. At one stroke, the three fundamental anthropological (= dialectical) categories were applied literally only to the true Spirit, which is God: For Christian theological thought, Jesus Christ is the only free historical Individual properly speaking, the freedom, historicity, and individuality of the ordinary man being no more than simple effects of divine "grace," that is, [effects] of a trans-human action of the trans-mundane God. But even in applying these categories to the eternal God-Man one runs up against insurmountable difficulties. The Christ is truly autonomous only to the extent that he is God. But being God he can be nothing other than the one and unique Being who thinks himself while remaining eternally identical to himself. Instead of a free historical Individual we have therefore that Substance-Absolute that Parmenides already had in view, that Spinoza rediscovered, and that Schelling revived at the very moment at which Hegel was elaborating his "dialectical" or anthropological philosophy.

Hegel wanted, from the start, to apply to Man the Judeo-Christian notion of free historical Individuality, unknown in pagan antiquity. But in [the course of] philosophically analyzing that "dialectical" notion, he saw it implied finitude or temporality. He understood that Man could not be a free historical individual except on condition of being *mortal* in the proper and strong sense of the term, that is, finite in time and conscious of his finitude. And having understood that, Hegel denied survival: The Man that he has in mind is real only to the extent that he lives and acts in the midst of Nature; outside the natural World he is a pure nothingness.

But to deny survival is in fact to deny God himself. For to say that Man, who *transcends* Nature effectively to the extent that he negates it (by Action), annihilates himself nonetheless as soon as he situates himself *outside* it by dying in it as an animal—to say that is to say that there is *nothing* beyond the natural World. The would-be "transcendent" or "divine" *non*-natural World is in reality only the "transcendental" (or speaking) World of historical human existence, [a world] which does not go beyond the temporal and spatial framework of the natural World. And "God" is objectively real only at the interior of this natural World, where he exists solely in the form of the theological discourse of Man.

Thus, Hegel does not accept the Judeo-Christian anthropological tradition except in a radically secularized or atheistic form. The Spirit-Absolute or the Subject-Substance, of which Hegel speaks, is not God. The Hegelian Spirit is the spatio–temporal totality of the natural World and implies human Discourse revealing this World and itself. Or better, and what is the same thing, Spirit is Man-in-the-World: the mortal Man who lives in a World without God and who speaks of all that exists in it and of all that he creates in it, including himself.

And this is what Hegel says implicitly at the end of the passage cited. He says there that "Spirit" *is* "Science," that "Science" is the only "objective-reality" of Spirit. Now this "Science" is nothing else but Hegelian philosophy, which appeared in the midst of the natural World at the end of the historical becoming of Man. Spirit is therefore nothing other than the spatio–temporal totality of the natural World, to the extent that it is entirely revealed through the discourse of the perfect (= satisfied) man or of the Wise Man [le Sage], this discourse being itself a simple integration of the true meaning of all the discourses spoken by men in the course of History. Or better still: The Spirit that the Judeo-Christians called "God" is in reality Hegelian philosophy, to the extent that the latter is absolutely *true*, that is, to the extent that it reveals correctly and completely *all* that has been, is, and will be.

Now according to Hegel, the discursive revelation of Being is possible only if the revealing or speaking being is essentially finite or mortal. Hegel's Spirit is not therefore truly a "divine" Spirit (because there are no *mortal* gods): It is *human* in the sense that it is a discourse that is immanent to the natural World and that has for its "support" a natural being limited in its existence by time and space.

When Hegel says that the essential content of his whole philosophy can be summed up by saying that it interprets Substance as Subject or [that it] conceives the Absolute as Spirit, that signifies that this philosophy must above all philosophically render an account of itself as a Discourse revealing in a complete and adequate manner the totality of Being and of the Real. It achieves this by explaining how and why Man comes to speak in a coherent fashion of himself and of the World in which he lives and that he creates. And that explanation is a phenomenological, metaphysical, and ontological description of Man understood as free historical Individual. Now to describe Man as a free historical Individual is to describe him [thus]: as "finite" in and through himself, on the ontological level; as "worldly" or spatial and temporal, on the metaphysical level; and as "mortal" on the phenomenological level. On this last level, Man "appears" as a being who is always conscious of his death, [who] often freely accepts it, and, aware of what he is doing, sometimes inflicts it on himself. Thus the "dialectical" or anthropological philosophy of Hegel is in the final analysis *a philosophy of death* (or, what is the same thing: of atheism).

Analysis of the passage of the Preface to the *Phenomenology* in which Hegel outlines the major themes of his philosophy shows clearly the primordial role that the idea of death plays in that philosophy. Acceptance without reserve of the fact of death, or of human finitude conscious of itself, is the ultimate source of all of Hegel's thought, which does no more than draw out all the consequences, even the most ultimate, of the existence of this fact. According to that thought, it is by voluntarily accepting the danger of death in a Struggle for pure prestige that Man appears for the first time in the natural World; and it is by resigning himself to death, by revealing it through his discourse, that Man arrives finally at absolute Knowledge or at Wisdom, in thus completing History. For it is by starting out from the idea of death that Hegel works out his Science or the "absolute" philosophy, which alone is capable of philosophically rendering an account of the fact of the existence in the World of a finite being conscious of its finitude and sometimes disposing of it as it likes.

Thus, Hegel's absolute Knowledge or Wisdom and the conscious acceptance of death understood as complete and definitive annihilation are one and the same. Hegel says it himself in so many words in another passage of the Preface (p. 29 ff.), [which is] of absolutely pivotal importance. And it is only in reading this truly remarkable passage that we grasp the ultimate themes of Hegel's thought, understand its true significance, and take account of all its import.

The text of this passage, can be translated somewhat as follows (p. 29, line 23, to p. 30, line 15):

> The activity (Tätigkeit) of separation (Scheidens) is the force and the work of the *understanding* (*Verstandes*), [that is,] of the power (Macht) [which is] the-most-worthy-of-awe (verwundersamsten) and the greatest [of all], or better still, [of the] absolute [power]. The circle which is at rest [by being] closed in itself and which holds (hält) its constitutive-elements (Momente) as [does a] substance, is immediate relationship (Verhältnis) and consequently not at all (nicht) worthy-of-awe. But [the fact] that the accidental (Akzidentelle) as such separated from its periphery (Umfange), [that] the entity-which-is-bound (Gebundene) and which is objectively-real only in its connection (Zusammenhang) with something-else, achieves an empirical-

> existence (Dasein) of its own and a separate-or-isolated (abgesonderte) freedom, [all that] is [the expression of] the prodigious (ungeheure) power of the Negative; it is the energy of thought (Denkens), of the pure abstract-Ego (Ichs). Death,—if we wish so to call that unreality (Unwirklichkeit)—is what-there-is-that-is-most = terrible (Furchtbarste), and to sustain [maintenir] death is what requires the greatest force. Powerless beauty hates the understanding, because it [the understanding] demands (zumutet) this of it; which it [beauty] is not capable of. Now the life of the Spirit is not [that] life which shudders (scheut) before death and [merely] protects itself (rein bewahrt) from wasting-away (Verwüstung), but [it is] that [life] which supports death and conserves (erhält) itself in it. Spirit achieves its truth only in finding itself in absolute rending (Zerrissenheit). It [Spirit] is not this [prodigious] power by being the Positive which turns away (wegsieht) from the Negative, as when we say of something: this is nothing or [this is] false, and having [thus] gotten rid of it (damit fertig), we pass on therefrom to something else; no, Spirit is that power only to the extent that it contemplates the Negative full in the face (ins Angesicht schaut) [and] abides (verweilt) with it. This abiding-with [séjour-prolongé] (Verweilen) is the magical-force (Zauberkraft) which transposes (umkehrt) the Negative into given-Being (sein).—This [power of Spirit, or this magical-force,] is the same thing as what we called above [p. 19, line 27] the Subject, which, by giving in its [own] element an empirical existence to specific-determination, dialectically-suppresses (aufhebt) abstract Immediateness (Unmittelbarkeit), that is, [an Immediateness] only *existing-as-a-given-being* in general (nur überhaupt *seiende*), and [which] is precisely thereby [par cela même] true-or-genuine [vraie-ou-véritable] (wahrhafte) Substance, [that is,] given-Being or Immediateness which does not have Mediation (Vermittlung) outside it, but which is itself that Mediation.

In order to understand the somewhat enigmatic beginning of this passage, [which is] otherwise perfectly clear and univocal, we must have the following before our minds.

Philosophy is the search for Wisdom, and Wisdom is the fullness of self-consciousness. By aspiring to and in laying claim to Wisdom, Hegel intends therefore, in the last analysis, to take account of himself and to give an accounting of his self [se rendre compte et rendre compte de soi]: [an account, that is,] of what he is and of what he does. Now his activity, the one to which his truly human existence reduces itself, is that of a philosopher or of a Wise Man [un Sage], who reveals by his discourse the being that he himself is and [also the being] that he is not. In philosophizing, Hegel must therefore above all give an account of his own philosophical discourse. Now in [the course of] observing this discourse, Hegel notes that we have here not a question of some passive given, but [rather that it is a matter] of the result of an "activity" which can be called a "labor" ["travail"] and which requires a great "force," provided by what he calls here the "Understanding." He declares therefore that the Understanding is a "power," and he says that it is truly "worthy of awe."

It is apparent that "Understanding" signifies here what is truly and specifically human in Man, because it is the faculty of discourse that distinguishes him from animals and from things. It is also what is essential in every philosopher, whoever he may be, and therefore in Hegel himself. The whole question is to know what it is. Hegel tells us that the Understanding (= Man) is an "*absolute* power," which manifests itself in and through "the activity of *separation*," or even better, as [the] "act-of-*separating*" (Scheiden). But why does he say that?

He says it because the activity of the Understanding, that is, human thought, is essentially *discursive*. Man does not reveal instantaneously, as in a lightning-flash, the totality of the real: He does not grasp that totality in one single concept-word. He reveals one by one, by isolated words or partial discourses, the elements constitutive of the totality, by *separating* them from it in order to be able to do so; and it is only the sum-total of his discourse, extended in time, that can reveal the total, indeed the simultaneous, reality. Now in fact, these elements are *inseparable* from the whole that they constitute, by [virtue of] being bound up among themselves by spatial and temporal, namely, material, interconnections, which are indissoluble. Their *separation* is therefore indeed a "miracle," and the power that effects it well merits being called "absolute."

The absolute force or power of Understanding that Hegel had in mind was in the final analysis nothing but the power or force of *abstraction* that we find in Man.

Whenever we describe any isolated object, we abstract from the rest of the universe. In speaking of "this table" or of "this dog," for example, we speak of them as though they were alone in the world. Now in fact, as real things, the dog and the table occupy at a given moment quite determinate places in the real World, and they cannot be separated from what surrounds them. But man, who isolates them through his thought, can, in that thought, [re-]combine them as he sees fit. He can, for example, place this dog under this table, even if in fact they are separated at this very moment by a distance of a thousand kilometers. Now this power that thought has to separate and recombine things is in effect "absolute," because no real force of connection or repulsion is sufficiently powerful to oppose it. And that power is not at all fictitious or "ideal." For it is in separating and in recombining things in and through his discursive thought that man forms his technical projects, which, once realized through work, really transform the aspect of the natural [and] given World by creating therein a World of culture.

Generally speaking, when we create the *concept* of a real entity, we detach it from its *hic et nunc*. The concept of a thing is that thing itself as [en tant que] detached from its given *hic et nunc*. Thus, the concept "this dog" differs in no respect from the real concrete dog to which it is "related," except that this dog is here and now, while its concept is everywhere and nowhere, always and never. Now, to detach an entity from its *hic et nunc* is to separate it from its "material" support, [which is] determined in a univocal manner by the rest of the given spatio–temporal universe, of which that entity is a part. That is why that entity can be altered or "simplified " as we wish, after it has become a concept. It is thus that this real dog is, as concept, not only "this dog," but beyond that [it is, as concept] "any dog" ["un chien quelconque"], "dog in general," quadruped," "animal," etc., and even simply "Being." And once again that power of *separation*, which is at the source of [all] the sciences, arts, and crafts, is an "absolute" power, against which Nature can oppose no effective resistance.

It is not correct, however, to say that the real entity [which has] become a concept is situated outside time and space. Aristotle was right in pointing out that the platonic "ideas" exist only in "material" spatial and temporal things, of which they are the "essences" or "entelechies." The absolute power of the Understanding goes so far as to *separate* an "essence" from its natural support: The essence "dog" is separated from this dog that runs and barks here and now. But it cannot transport it [the essence] into a world [that is] so to speak "hyper-celestial," beyond space-time. Once detached from its natural support, the "essence" becomes "meaning" or "idea." But the "meaning" does not float in the void: It is necessarily the meaning of a *word* or of a *discourse*—[words or discourses] pronounced, written, or only thought, but existing always in the midst of the spatial and temporal world. The concept is not an "idea" or a "meaning" [merely], but [it is rather] a *word*-having-a-meaning, or a coherent *discourse* (Logos). Thus, the absolute power of the Understanding does not *separate* the essence-idea from its natural support except to attach it, as meaning-idea, to the specific support of a discourse that is itself also [something] here and now (since it is a discourse-endowed-with-a-*meaning* only to the extent that it is comprehended by some *concrete* man).

But it remains no less the case that the *separation* of the "essence" from its *natural* support is not an event that takes place spontaneously in the midst of Nature, but [rather it is] the result of an "activity" of the "Understanding," or of a "labor" that requires a "force" endowed with an "absolute power." Now we can indeed say, with Hegel, that this power is "worthy of awe" and that the principal task of philosophy or of Science is to take account of it.

But the philosophical precursors of Hegel went amiss in [their attempts at] responding to the question posed, [and] in explaining the miracle in question. They saw and posed the problem wrongly. They spoke of the "Subject" in general or of "Thought" as such, in asking themselves how and why Being is also concept, that is, [by asking] why and how it can have a *meaning*; but they forgot to say that there are also discourses endowed with a meaning, [words] that men speak, write, or think in space and time. By thus simplifying the problem they arrived, to be sure, at a result. Parmenides affirms the identity of Being and Thought; Aristotle speaks of a Being that thinks itself eternally in its totality; Spinoza, taking his inspiration from Descartes and [in turn] inspiring Schelling, says that Thought is an attribute of Substance. Hegel does not contest this result of the philosophy that preceded his own. He says only that the relationship between Being and Thought, which that [preceding] philosophy had in view, was nothing very remarkable. In order truly to give an account of the relationship in question, it would have sufficed to identify, with Hegel, Concept and Time; or, what is the same thing, to affirm the *temporality* of Being itself. For the *concept*, or more precisely the *meaning* of Being, differs in no respect from Being itself, except for the absence, in the *meaning*, of the *being* of that Being. And the same holds for the meaning of any thing that *is*, since Being is the integration of *all* that *is*, in such a way that the meaning "Being" is an integration of all meanings in general. The *essence*-meaning of a thing is, as we say, that very thing minus its *existence*. Now the "subtraction" that removes the being from Being is nothing other than Time, which makes Being pass from the present, in which it *is*, into the past, in which it *is not* (is no more), and in which it is therefore only pure *meaning* (or essence without existence). And since this is no *new* Being that *is* in the present, but [rather only] an "old" or *past* Being, we can say that Being is an essence that has acquired [an] existence; or, what is the same thing, [we can say] that the being is not Being solely, but [also] Concept; or, what is again the same thing, [we can say] that Being has a *meaning* to the very extent that it *is* (as Time). In the same way, since it is the same past Being that is in the present and will be in the future (or, *not being* as yet, it is also essence without existence), we can say that Being has a *goal* (this goal, which is the transformation of the future into the present or the grant of existence to essence, which is besides nothing but the transformation of the present into the past, that is, of Being into Concept): [all of] which we can express also by saying that the very being of Being has a meaning; or, what is the same thing [we can say] that Being has a *raison d'être* (that *raison* being the thought of being by Being [la pensée de l'être par l'Etre]). Thus, if Being and Time are but one, we can say that Being coincides with Thought, that it thinks itself eternally, and that Thought is the attribute of its Substance or, if we prefer, [that Thought is] its "goal."

Hegel himself would also agree to putting it that way. Except that for him, this relationship between Being and Thought in the midst of the "sphere" of Parmenides, or of the Aristotelian "Circle" (which Hegel evokes in the text cited), or [in the midst] of the Spinozan and Schellingian "Substance" (of which he speaks as well) [—Hegel would insist that this relationship] has nothing "miraculous" about it. For this relationship is "immediate," says Hegel. Now "immediate" signifies, in Hegel, "natural," or "given." And in fact *this* relationship presupposes no "activity," no "labor," no "force" or "power." For there the "essence" is not *separated* from its "natural" support: The essence of Being subsists in Being itself and in it alone, in the same way as the essence of the dog subsists uniquely in the dog (and that is why there cannot be tables, for example, in *this* Being—that is, [there cannot be any] *artifacts*). There is here neither action nor labor nor power, because given Being remains as it is given, in its immutable identity with itself.

What is "miraculous," on the contrary, is precisely the *separation* that the Understanding effects. For it [the separation] is effectively "against nature." Without the intervention of the Understanding, the essence "dog" would exist only in and through real dogs, which would in return determine it in a univocal manner by their very existence. And that is why we can say that the relationship between the dog and the essence "dog" is "natural" or "immediate." But when, thanks to the absolute power of the Understanding, the essence becomes meaning and is incarnated in a *word*, there is no longer any "natural" relationship between it and its support; otherwise, words that have nothing in common among them insofar as [they are] phonetic or graphic spatio-temporal realities, whatever they may be (dog, chien, Hund, etc.), [—otherwise these words] could not serve as support for one sole and selfsame essence, having all one single and very-same meaning. There has been, therefore, a *negation* here of the given as given (with its "natural" relationships between essence and existence); that is, [there has been] *creation* (of concepts or of word-having-a-meaning, which as words have nothing to do, by themselves, with the meaning that is incarnate in them); in other words [there has been] *action* or *labor*.

Now if the traditional conception of [the conjunction] Being-Thought takes account of the *possibility* of a discourse revealing the meaning of what is, by explaining how and why Being has meaning, it does not say how and why discourse becomes *real*, that is, how and why we manage in fact to "disengage the meaning from the being" and to incarnate it in a collection of words that have nothing in common with that meaning and that have been created out of whole cloth with an eye to that incarnation. Now it is precisely the reality of discourse that is the miracle that philosophy must explain.

What is miraculous, says Hegel, is the fact that some thing that is really *inseparable* from [some] other thing achieves nevertheless a *separate* existence; or better yet—that a simple attribute or "accident" becomes an *autonomous* reality.

Now the essence is a "bound-entity," [tied] to its support, and it is "objectively-real only in its connection with something-other" than itself, that is, with its support. Nevertheless, the Understanding succeeds in *separating* the essence from its natural support and procures for it "an empirical-existence of its own" by incarnating it in a spoken, written, or thought word or discourse. And that "empirical-existence" of its own of the essence that has become meaning is also its "separated-or-isolated freedom." For the meaning embodied in the word and in discourse is no longer subject to the necessity that rules essences bound to their respective natural supports [that are] determined in a univocal manner by their *hic et nunc*. Thus, for example, the meaning embodied in the word "dog" can continue to subsist even after dogs have disappeared from the earth; it can (by being transmitted by radio, for example) overcome obstacles [that would be] insurmountable for a real dog; it [the word] can be placed where there would be no room for the latter [the real dog]; and so forth. And it is this "separated freedom" and the "absolute power" from which it flows that condition the possibility of *error*, for which pre-Hegelian philosophers could never account. For this "Freedom" allows the meaning embodied in words to be combined otherwise than the corresponding essences, bound to their natural supports, would be.

It is this "activity," capable of *disengaging* the meaning from Being, of *separating* essence from existence and of embodying the meaning-essence in discourse [—it is this] that is the miracle for which philosophy (or more precisely, Science and Wisdom) is supposed to account. And it was in [the course of] seeking to account for it that Hegel discovered (or made precise) the fundamental (ontological) category of *Negativity*, which he calls here the "Negative" [le "Négatif"], or the "negative-or-negate-ive-entity' [l'"entité-négative-ou-négatrice"]. This Negativity is "the energy of thought, " which disengages the meaning from Being by separating essence from existence. It [this Negativity] is what is "the energy of the pure abstract-Ego" engendering "thought," that is, the Understanding and its discourse. Now whatever people may sometimes have said, discourse does not fall from heaven, and it does not float in the void, "above the waters." If it [that is, discourse] expresses a "thought" that belongs properly to an "Ego," this Ego has necessarily an empirical-existence in the natural spatio-temporal World, being a *human* Ego. What is an "abstract-Ego" (Ich) on the ontological level (this Ego being the form under which Negativity subsists in Identity or in given-Being) is the human "personal-Ego" (Selbst) on the metaphysical level: It is the Man who "appears," on the phenomenological level, as a free historical *speaking* individual.

The miracle of the existence of discourse, of which philosophy must render an account, is therefore nothing else than the miracle of the existence of Man in the world. And as a matter of fact we can apply to Man himself the passage from Hegel that I have [heretofore] interpreted in reference to Discourse. For Man is *also* a "bound-being" that is "objectively-real only in its connection with something-else": he is nothing without the animal that serves him as support, and he is pure nothingness outside the natural World. Yet nevertheless he *separates* himself from this World and *opposes* himself to it. He creates [for] himself "an empirical-existence of his own," essentially different from every purely natural empirical existence. And he acquires [for] himself "a separate-or-isolated freedom," which permits him to move and to act completely differently from the way in which the animal that incarnates him would have moved and acted, if that animal did not incarnate Negativity and were not therefore an Ego who thinks and who speaks. Endowed with an "absolute power," which becomes in him an effective "force" [which is] "worthy of awe," Man produces, in [or through] "activity," or a "labor" [which is] rational or penetrated by the "Understanding," a real World contrary-to-nature, created by his "separated freedom" for his *own* "empirical-existence"—the technical or cultural, social or historical World.

Therefore, just like the discourses that he utters, Man is not a *given*-Being, nor [is he] the "accident" of a "Substance." He is the *result* of effort by an absolute *power*, and he is that power itself: He is *Negativity* incarnate, or, as Hegel says, "negative-or-negate-ive entity" (das Negative). It is only by comprehending Man as Negativity that we [can] comprehend him in his "miraculous" human specificity, making of him an Ego who thinks and speaks, or who "separates" the essence from its natural or given "connection" with existence.

We know, besides, that on the ontological level, Negativity is actualized as negative or creative *Act* (in order to subsist as "abstract-Ego"). We also know that on the metaphysical level "the *true being* of Man is *his action*," and that it is in it alone that "Individuality is *objectively-real*" (*Phenomenology*, p. 236, lines 25–26). And we know, finally, that on the phenomenological level it is through the action of the *struggle* that Man "manifests" himself for the first time in the World of natural "phenomena, " and that it is in consequence of the action of *labor* that Understanding "appears" in this World with his thought and his words.[3]

Now Negativity, taken in isolation, is pure Nothingness (on the ontological level). This Nothingness nihilates as [the] Action (of the abstract-Ego) in Being. But Action nihilates by annihilating this Being, and therefore [also] by annihilating itself, since without Being it *is* only Nothingness. Negativity therefore is no other thing than the *finitude* of Being (or the presence in it of a genuine future, which will never be its present; and Action [therefore] is essentially *finite*. That is why (on the metaphysical level) the historical World, created by Action, has necessarily a beginning and an end. And the entity that is Action in its very being "appears" (on the phenomenological level) to itself and to others as irremediably *mortal*.

That is why, in the text cited, Hegel can call *Death* the "unreality" that Negativity or the "negative-or-negate-ive-entity" *is*. But if Man is Action, and if Action is Negativity "appearing" as Death, [then] Man is, in his human or speaking existence, only a *death*: [a death] more or less deferred, and conscious of itself.

Therefore: to render an account, philosophically, of Discourse, or of Man as speaking, is to accept without flinching the fact of death, and to describe, on the three philosophical levels [i.e., the ontological, metaphysical, and phenomenological], its significance and import. Now that is precisely what philosophers before Hegel had omitted doing.

Hegel was not surprised at this. For he knew that death "is what is most terrible" and that acceptance of death is "what requires the greatest force." He says that the Understanding requires that acceptance. For the Understanding, through its discourse, reveals the real and reveals itself. And since it [the Understanding] is born of finitude, it is only by thinking death and by speaking of it that it is truly what it is: discourse conscious of itself and of its origin. But Hegel knows also that "powerless beauty" is incapable of bowing to the requirements of the Understanding. The esthete, the romantic, [and] the mystic flee the [very] idea of death and speak of Nothingness itself as of something that *is*.

Now, says Hegel, the "life of the Spirit" is not that [sort of life] "which shudders before death and preserves itself from wasting away, but [rather it is] that [sort of life] which supports death and maintains itself in it." The point is, that Spirit is Being revealed by speech [la parole], and the life of the Spirit is the existence of the philosopher or of the Wise Man [le Sage], conscious of the World and of itself. Now it is only in becoming conscious of his finitude, and therefore of his death, that man truly becomes conscious of himself. For he *is* finite and mortal.

In addition, Spirit "achieves its truth only by finding itself in absolute rending." For once again, Spirit is the Real revealed by Discourse. Now Discourse is born in the Man who opposes himself to Nature, or who negates—in Struggle—the given animal that he is himself, and through Labor, the natural World that is given to him. It is from this "rending" of the Real into Man and Nature that the Understanding and its Discourse are born, which reveal the Real and thus transform it into Spirit. This *opposition*, this conflict between Man and the given Real, manifests itself first by the *erroneous* character of human revelatory [révélateur] discourse, and it is only at the end of times, at the termination of History, that the discourse of the Wise Man *re-joins* reality. For it is [only] then that we can say that "the Spirit re-discovers itself," and that it "achieves its truth," which is the adequate revelation of reality. But it rediscovers itself only in and through that "rending" ["déchirement"] that is manifested in the many forms of error in the course of the historical process. And this process is that of a series of generations that follow each other, that are born, therefore, and [that] die, in time.

It is death that engenders Man in Nature, and it is death that makes him progress to his final destiny, which is that of the Wise Man fully conscious of himself and therefore fully conscious of his own finitude. Thus, Man does not arrive at Wisdom or at the fullness of self-consciousness so long as, in the way of the vulgar, he feigns an ignorance of the Negativity that is the very source of his human existence, and that is manifest in him and to him, not only as struggle and labor, but moreover as death or absolute finitude. The vulgar treat death as something of which one says: "It is nothing, or it is false"; and by turning away from it most quickly, they hasten to pass on to the order of the day.[4] But if the philosopher wants to attain to Wisdom, he must "look the Negative full in the face, and [must] abide with it." And it is in discursive contemplation of Negativity revealing itself through death that the "power" of the Wise Man, conscious of himself, [and] who incarnates Spirit, is manifested. Hegel says that it is this "abiding" with the Negative that is "the magical force that transposes the Negative into given-Being." He alludes, in saying that, to what is, according to him, the birth of Man in the World.[5] For it is in the Struggle [to the death, for pure prestige], that the power of the Negative mani-fests itself [se mani-feste] through the voluntary acceptance of the risk of life (the Master) or through the anguish inspired by the conscious apparition of death (the Slave), [it is only in the Struggle] that Man creates his human being, by thus transforming, as if by "magic," the Nothingness that he is and that is manifest to him and through him as death, into a negate-ive *existence*, of the warrior and of the laborer, creators [both,] of History. It is this "abiding" with death that *real-izes* Negativity and inserts it into the natural World in the form human *being*. And it is by taking up again, in his discourse, this anthropogenetic contact [ce contact anthropogène] with death, that the Wise Man transforms the *nothingness* of an *erroneous* description of Man into the revealed *being* that *truth* is.

This "magical force," Hegel continues, is what he previously (p. 19) called the "Subject," or the "abstract-Ego" of the "Understanding." That is to say that thought and the discourse that reveals the Real are born of the negate-ive Action that real-izes Nothingness by nullifying Being—the given-being of Man in the Struggle, and the given-being of Nature through Labor (which results, moreover, from the real contact with death in the Struggle). This is to say, therefore, that the human being itself is no other thing than that Action; he is [a] death that lives a human life.

The being of man, being thus, if we wish, a deferred death, or an affirmation of Nothingness through the negation of the given—or better yet, *creation*—is not therefore *a given-being*; he is not, like the natural being, the "immediacy *which-exists-as-a-given-being*." On the contrary, he exists humanly only to the extent that he "dialectically-suppresses" or "mediates" that natural "immediacy" through negate-ive Action. That "immediacy" has "mediation outside itself," for it is *Man* who negates or transforms Nature by his Labor and in his Struggles, and it is *human* discourse that reveals it. Man, on the contrary, negates *himself*; it is he *himself* who creates and transforms himself; he is *himself* the "mediation" of given-being through active, and therefore discursive or revelatory, negation. And that is why Man is unique in being a being who reveals Being and who is conscious *of himself*. Or, what is the same thing, the human being, to the extent that he implies the consciousness of and the will for his [own] death, is a being "mediated" by Negation—that is, a *dialectical* being.

Such is the meaning of the cited passage from the Preface to the *Phenomenology*. Interpreted on the ontological level, this passage signifies that it is not the (infinite) *Totality* of Being (or the One-which-is) that reveals itself to itself, but that this Totality is revealed by one of its (limited) *parts*, which also reveals itself. Metaphysically speaking, the passage signifies that Spirit, that is, the Being that reveals itself to itself, is not God, but Man-in-the-World. For the part [of Being] that reveals Being is the *human*, essentially *finite*, being, who creates himself in time through the active negation of Being, and who, being Negation or Negativity, annihilates himself after having *endured*. And this revelation of Being by the temporal and temporary human being is a *discursive* or "dialectical" revelation, which unfolds itself in the time in which it was born and in which it will one day disappear. In this discursive revelation, the human being *relates himself* to the totality of given-Being, first through negate-ive *action* and the *erroneous* discourse that flows from it, but finally through the *adequate* discourse that is born of the passive *contemplation* of the Wise Man who, being "satisfied" by given-Being, ceases to negate it, transform it, and to "disfigure" it, even if this be only in his discourse.

And it is a curious thing, a thing that Hegel does not say in the cited passage, but that follows from the whole of his System: This "satisfaction" (Befriedigung) of the Wise Man, which presupposes his perfect awareness of the World and of himself, does not itself attain its perfection and fullness except in and through the awareness of death.

In effect, Man can be satisfied only in being *aware* of his satisfaction, that is, *aware of himself* as satisfied. Now if Man is essentially finite, he cannot be fully aware of himself except by taking cognizance of his death. It is therefore only by knowing himself to be irremediably *mortal* that the Wise Man can attain the fullness of satisfaction.

Looking at the matter more closely, we realize that this ultimate consequence of Hegelianism is psychologically less paradoxical than it seems at first glance. To be sure, the idea of death does not add to the *well-being* of man; it does not make him *happy*, and procures no *pleasure* for him, nor any *joy*. But it is unique in being able to *satisfy his pride*, that is, in being able to procure for him precisely that "satisfaction" that Hegel has in mind. For Hegelian "satisfaction" is nothing else than the full satisfaction of the human and anthropogenetic desire for Recognition (Anerkennen) of man's desire to see all other men attribute an absolute value to his *free historical individuality* or to his *personhood* [*personnalité*]. Now it is only by being, and by feeling to be, mortal or finite—that is, by existing and feeling himself to exist, in a universe without a beyond and without a God—that Man can affirm and make known his liberty, his historicity, and his individuality, [all] "unique in the world."

The cited passage from the Preface to the *Phenomenology* puts fully in evidence the decisive role that the idea of death plays in the philosophy of Hegel. I would like, nevertheless, to cite a series of other texts that make possible [a further] precision of the Hegelian notion of death. For various reasons, however, I will draw them only from the *Phenomenology* and from earlier writings.

The theme of death appeared already in the fragment on love of 1795, translated in Appendix I (see above, pp. 510 ff.).*[3]

In this fragment love appeared to Hegel as what there is that is most human in man; the "lover" is man viewed as human being. Hegel underlines the essential difference that subsists between the death of man and the [mere] "ending" or "corruption" of a purely natural being; he speaks of a plant—but he could just as well have spoken of an animal or of an inanimate thing. The difference resides in the fact that the end of the natural being is determined by the general laws of nature, that it is imposed in some manner from without by the rest of the universe, by what is "foreign" to the finite being itself. In contrast, the death of man must therefore be understood as an end that is "immanent" or "autonomous," that is, voluntary or willed, and hence, [as] conscious.

In addition, Hegel says that man is *individual* only to the extent that he is mortal. If Spirit (which is called love here) were infinite or immortal, it would be rigorously one. If Spirit realizes itself as multiple, in the form of human beings who differ from one another and of whom each lives an individual life that is his own—[if this be so] it is solely because the human or "spiritual" beings, namely, the "lovers," are mortal.

In the same way, the "autonomy" or the *freedom* of the human being is linked to death. To say of a being that it is "autonomous" is to say that it is mortal.

Finally, the same fragment also contains the idea of the historical survival of man in the here-below. Men are separated and annihilated definitively in and through death; but they live humanly and remain socially united in and through their children (thanks to education and the historical tradition, as we shall see later). The child implies and presupposes the death of the parents; but in spite of the "negation" that separates them, there is [an] "identity" between the generations that succeed each other. And that [identity] is precisely what we call History. Or, if we prefer, it [this process] is the "total," "synthetic," or "dialectical" existence of the human being in which the thesis of the "united" (Identity) and the antithesis of the "separated" (Negativity) coincide in the synthesis of the "re-united" (Totality). The *historicity* (or the dialecticity) of Man is therefore inseparably around to the fact of his death.

All the principal themes of the Hegelian philosophy of death are found therefore already in one of his first writings. And all these themes will be taken up again, rendered more precise, and developed, in the later writings.

The theme of the essential difference between the death of man—which is death properly so called—and the death-corruption of a merely living being is taken up again in the Introduction to the *Phenomenology*.

Hegel says this there (p. 69, lines 12–16):

> What is limited to a natural life cannot by itself go-beyond (hinausgehen) its immediate [or given] empirical-existence (Dasein); but it is driven beyond (hinausgetrieben) this existence by something-else [than itself], and this fact-of-being-wrested[-and-projected-]beyond (Hinausgerissenwerden) is its death.

Once again the "end" of the natural being is presented as an exterior law passively submitted to. The natural being is essentially "given," that is, "static," or "identical" to itself: Any radical change, which is something other than the "development" of its given or innate "nature," is imposed on it from outside and signifies its annihilation. Man, on the contrary, can spontaneously transcend himself and can go by himself beyond his "innate nature," even while remaining what he is, that is, a *human* being. But for the animal that serves him as support, that transcendence signifies death. However, in the *human* animal that death is no longer exterior: He is himself (as man) the cause of his death (as animal). It is only this "autonomous" or "spontaneous" death that can be conscious and also freely accepted or willed (the risk of life). And it is alone[, this conscious dying,] that is truly human, humanizing, or anthropogenetic.

Being a negate-ive being, man would be able to go beyond himself indefinitely (without ceasing to be Man, without having need of becoming a "*Super*-man" [un "*Sur*-homme"]. It is only the end of the anthropophoric *animal* that puts a terminus to human self-transcendence. That is why the death of man is always in some way premature and violent, in contrast to the "natural" death of animals and plants, which have completed the cycle of their evolution. And that is also why human transcendence can be realized as a single and unique History, despite (or because of) the succession of generations, which remain absolutely separated from each other in the plant and animal realm.

Hegel says it in his *Jena Lectures* of 1803–04 (Vol. XIX, last sentence of Note 4 [on p. 222])*[4]:

> The individuals are first of all themselves this death in-the-way-of-becoming (werdende), . . . but in their act-of-becoming-dead (Totwerden) they contemplate at the same time their act-of-becoming-alive. The [human] infant is not, as in the animal relationship, the existent kind [genre], but the parents [recognizing themselves in him . . .].

As we shall see again, it is the self-negate-ive act, that is, [an act that is] free and historical, interrupted by the death of the animal that incarnated it, which prolongs it, which achieves and perfects itself in and through the infant educated or created as human through that very act.

But man would not have been able to negate himself or to transcend himself if he were not finite or mortal. The humanity of man *presupposes* therefore the finitude of the animal that incarnates him, and consequently it presupposes the death of the man himself. And on the other hand, man also *provokes* the death of the animal by transcending, through negate-ive action, his given "nature": In the extreme case, he risks his life and has himself killed without a valid biological reason. We can therefore say that man is a mortal *sickness* of the animal.

And Hegel actually says so.

We find the following passages in the *Lectures* of 1803–04:

> To the extent that the universal system raises the animal at the interior of itself up to the point at which its universal-entity is fixed by opposition (gegen) to its difference [which distinguishes it from all that is not it], exists for itself [and] does not coincide with that difference, it is *sickness* which is posited, in which the animal would [go] beyond itself. [But] to the extent that it cannot organize the universal-entity for itself, without relating it to the animal process, . . . it does no more than to pass into its death [Vol. XIX, p. 174, lines 28–35].—With sickness the animal passes beyond the limit of its nature; but the sickness of the animal is the becoming of the Spirit. *In sickness, the universal-entity . . . has* isolated *itself*; which is what . . . can end only with death, [Vol. XIX, p. 186, lines 12–15 and 18].—The fixed universality of sickness only nullifies the infinitude of opposition (Gegensatzes) and [it] transforms itself (geht über) in death; the universality of Spirit [on the contrary] acts in such a way that the opposition is maintained (bestehen), to the extent that that universality has dialectically-suppressed (aufgehoben) opposition in itself [Vol. XIX, p. 189, lines 4–7].

Sickness and the death of the animal are but an abortive attempt at self-transcendence. Sickness is a discord between the animal and the rest of the natural world; the sick animal is, so to speak, dislodged from its "natural place" (topos), from the *hic et nunc* that fixes its particularity and distinguishes it from everything that is not it. Now to detach [something] from the *hic et nunc* is to universalize [it], to transform [it] into a *general* notion or [into] a concept. But the animal is absolutely determined by its *topos*. To dislodge it therefrom is to nullity it, is to render it sick unto death. For in contrast to Man, the animal cannot "organize the universal in itself, without relating it to the animal process": To put it another way, it [the animal] cannot develop the particular entity that has become a concept by its detachment from its given *hic et nunc* into a universe of discourse (which it will transform by action into a real technical and historical real world). But Man can do so only because the animal that incarnates him is susceptible of being dislodged from its *topos* by sickness and death.

It is through sickness that the animal tries in some way to transcend its given "nature." It does not succeed in this because that transcendence is equivalent, for it, to its nullification. But the success of Man presupposes that attempt, and this is why the sickness that leads to the death of the animal is "the becoming of the Spirit" or of Man. (Spirit is not therefore an eternal and perfect God who incarnates himself, but a sick and mortal animal who transcends himself in time.)

The universality that manifests itself as sickness is "fixed"; which is to say that it is not synthetic, total, or dialectical. It simply destroys the "opposition" of the Particular and the Universal by nullifying the particularity of the animal in and through death. The "universality of the Spirit," by contrast, i.e., that [universality] that manifests itself as human existence, maintains the opposition of the Particular and the Universal, by "dialectically suppressing" these opposites, that is, by synthesizing them in the totality of Individuality. For the *universality* of discourse and of rational action is effectuated in and through the *particularity* of a human individual. But once again, this free historical individuality presupposes the *opposition* of the Particular and the Universal, which is manifested as the sickness and death of animality, which is also that of Man.

That's why Hegel can say, in the *Jena Lectures* of 1805–06 (Vol. XX, p. 164, lines 8–9):*[5]

> The animal dies. [But the] death of the animal [is the] coming to be of [human] consciousness.

In short, Man is the mortal sickness of Nature. And that is why, being necessarily a part of Nature, he is himself essentially mortal.

In the writings of his youth, Hegel attached the *freedom*, the *historicity*, and the *individuality* of Man to death. And this triple theme is also taken up again and made precise in his later writings.

Let us consider, first of all, *freedom*.

In many instances Hegel identifies freedom and Negativity. He does so in a particularly clear way in the *System of Morality* (of 1802?), in which he writes, for example, this:

> The negative-entity (das Negative), which is to say (oder) freedom, which is to say crime [Title of § 2; Vol. VII, p. 450] [p. 446].—That negative-entity, or pure freedom, undertakes (geht auf) therefore the dialectical-suppression (Aufhebung) of the objective-entity in such a way (so), that it . . . makes of the negative-entity the essential-reality (Wesen), negates, as a consequence, reality in its [given] specific-determination (*Bestimmtheit*), but fixes that negation [Vol. VII, p. 452, lines 28–32] [p. 448, lines 28–32].*[6]

Freedom, which is the realization and the manifestation of Negativity, consists therefore in the act of negating the real in its given structure and in maintaining the negation in the form of a work [œuvre] created by that active negation itself. And that freedom, which is Negativity, is the "essential-reality" of Man.

But Negativity taken in itself is no other thing than Nothingness, which can "manifest" itself as death. And Hegel consistently says so in many instances.

Thus for example in the *Lectures* of 1805–06, where he writes in a marginal note (Vol. XX, p. 166, the last three lines of Note 2):

> Its result:—*death*, pure *Negativity*, immediate *Non-being*.

If therefore, on the one hand, freedom is Negativity, and if on the other hand, Negativity is Nothingness and death, there is no freedom without death, and only a mortal being can be free. We can even say that death is the final and authentic "manifestation" of freedom.

Now Hegel by no means shrinks before that consequence; he expressly accepts it, as is shown for example in the following passages, drawn from the *System of Morality* of 1802 and from the *Lectures* of 1803–04:

> This negative Absolute, pure freedom, is in its appearance-or-manifestation (Erscheinung)—death; and through the faculty (Fähigkeit) of death the Subject demonstrates (erweist) itself as free and as absolutely raised above all constraint (Zwang). The Subject is the absolute act-of-constraining (Bezwingung); and because this act is absolute, . . . it is the concept of itself, therefore infinite, and the opposite (Gegenteil) of itself, that is, absolute; and the pure Particularity which is in death, is its proper opposite, [that is] Universality. There is therefore freedom in the act-of-constraining only through the fact that it has for its end (geht auf) purely the dialectical-suppression of a [given] specific-determination . . . , and therefore through the fact that this act, considered in itself, behaves (sich hält) in a purely negative (rein negativ) manner; [Vol. VII, p. 370, lines 10–14, 20–25, 27–28] [p. 366, lines 30–34; p. 366, line 39 – p. 361, line 4; p. 367, lines 7–8].— . . . the supreme abstraction of freedom, that is, the relationship of constraint (Bezwingens) pushed unto its dialectical-suppression, that is, free violent death [Vol. VII, p. 389, lines 17–19] [p. 385, lines 16–19].*[7]—*This simple abs*[*olute*] *point of Consciousness* [= Man] is the absolute-being (absolutsein) of the latter, but [taken] as a negative-or-negate-ive-entity; or [in other words], it is the absolute-being of the individual [taken] as such, as a particular-isolated-entity (Einzelnen). It is the freedom *of its caprice* (*Eigensinns*). The particular (Einzelne) can transform itself (sich machen) in this point; it can, in-an-absolute-

> manner, make abstraction of all, abandon all; it cannot be rendered dependent, [it cannot] be held (gehalten) by anything; it can detach from itself every specific-determination by which it ought to have been grasped (gefasst), and [it can] realize in death its absolute independence and freedom, [it can realize itself therein] as absolutely negative-or-negate-ive Consciousness. But death has in it contradiction in relationship to *life* [Vol. XIX, p. 218, lines 1–12].—Its [= the particular's] particular-isolated (einzelne) freedom is [nothing except] only its caprice,—its death [Vol. XIX, p. 232, last line of Note 2].

It is therefore indeed death—by which is to be understood a death that is voluntary or accepted in full awareness of what is involved—which is the supreme manifestation of freedom at least of the "abstract" freedom of the *isolated* individual. Man could not be free if he were not essentially and voluntarily mortal. Freedom is autonomy in the face of the given, that is, the possibility of *negating* it such as it is given, and it is solely through voluntary death that a man can escape the confinement of *no matter what* given (= imposed) condition of existence. If man were not mortal and if he could not give death to himself without "necessity," he would not escape rigorous determination by the given totality of Being, which in this case would merit being called "God."

The essence of individual freedom is therefore Negativity, which manifests itself in its pure or "absolute" state as death. And this is why, when "pure" or "absolute" freedom is realized on the social level, in the course of the second stage of a genuine Revolution—that is, [a revolution] negate-ive of the social given—it must necessarily manifest itself as a collective violent death or "Terror."

Hegel says so quite clearly in the Section of the *Phenomenology* that is devoted to the analysis of Revolution (p. 418, line 37–p. 419, line 5):

> The unique work and action of general (allgemeinen) Freedom are as a consequence *death*; to wit, a *death* which has no compass (Umfang) nor internal completion-or-accomplishing (Erfüllung), for what is negated [in and through this death] is the non-completed-and-accomplished point of the absolutely free personal-Ego (Selbsts); it is therefore the coldest death and the most pointless, with no more significance-or-importance than the act of cutting a cabbage in two, or than a gulp of water.
>
> [It is] in the flatness of this syllable [that] consists the wisdom of [revolutionary] government, [it is to it that can be reduced] the understanding [which permits] the general will to be accomplished (vollbringen).

In the course of the second stage of the revolution, the revolutionaries who aspire to "absolute freedom" oppose themselves as isolated particulars to the universal incarnated in the State. They oppose themselves to it absolutely, by wanting to negate the given State in an absolute manner, by annihilating it completely. The State cannot therefore maintain itself, the *general* will cannot be accomplished, except on condition that it negate its "particulars" in a manner just as absolute as their affirmation of *themselves* is or would be, through the negation of the *universal* realities. And that is why the "wisdom of the government" manifests itself, in the course of this stage, through the Terror. Now we have seen that death voluntarily faced in a negate-ive struggle is precisely the most authentic realization and manifestation of absolute individual freedom. It is therefore indeed in and through the Terror that this freedom is spread in society, and it cannot be attained in a "tolerant" State, which does not take its citizens seriously enough to guarantee them their political right to death.

Hegel deduces from these analyses that freedom, being essentially Negativity, can neither be realized in its pure state nor willed for itself. *Absolute freedom* (= "non-conformity") is *pure* Negativity, that is, Nothingness and death. Now this latter contradicts life, existence, and being itself. Negativity is something, and not Nothingness, only through Being (= Identity), which it *conserves* even while negating it. Negation (of the given) is *real* only as *creation* (of the new) or [as] accomplished *work* [*œuvre*]. The Revolutionary annihilates himself only to the extent that he succeeds in *conserving* his negate-ive work by attaching it to the identity of being, sustained through [à travers] its negation by memory or tradition.

That is to say that freedom is *realized* only as History, that man can *be* free only to the extent that he is *historical* (= social, = in a state). But inversely, there is no History except where there is freedom, that is, progress or creation, namely, "revolutionary" negation of the given. And since negate-ive freedom implies and presupposes death, only a mortal being can be truly historical.

But History presupposes death, even apart from the fact that it embodies freedom. There is no History except where there is tradition and historical memory on the one hand, and education and resistance to it on the other. Now all this presupposes a succession of generations *which follow each other*, which come into the world and die in it. For the life of children implies necessarily the *death* of the parents.

Hegel says it with a strange brutality in a marginal note to the *Lectures* of 1805–06 (Vol. XX, p. 202, Note 3):

> The savages of North America kill their parents; we do the same thing.

To be sure, the child *educated* by his parents prolongs their social and political action, which is their very being, and he thus assures to them a "survival" in the here-below, which is the only "survival" (albeit limited, in time) that is compatible with freedom. But historical survival conserves the *universality* of individual action, even while nullifying its *particularity*, this nullification being precisely the death of the individual. By educating the child, the parents prepare their own human or historical death, by passing voluntarily from the present to the past.

Hegel says it quite clearly in the *Lectures* of 1803–04 (Vol. XIX, p. 223, lines 18–20, and p. 224, lines 13–22):

> In educating the child, the parents place in him their already-formed (gewordenes) consciousness, and they engender their death. . . .—In education, the *unconscious unity of* the child is dialectically-suppressed; it is articulated in itself, it becomes a *formed-or-educated consciousness*; the consciousness of the parents is the matter dependent on which it forms-or-educates itself. The parents are for the child an obscure unknown presentiment (Ahnen) of itself; they dialectically-suppress the simple-and-individual [and] condensed (gedrungenes) being-at-the-interior-of-itself of the child. What they give to him they lose; they die in him; what they give him is their own consciousness. Consciousness is here the becoming of another consciousness in it, and the parents contemplate, in the becoming of the child, their [own] dialectical-suppression (Aufgehobenwerden).

History is transcendence (in the here-below). It is the "dialectical-suppression" of Man, who "negates" himself (as given) by "conserving" himself (as a *human* being) and is "sublimated" (= progress) through his conservative self-negation. And this "dialectical-movement" implies and presupposes the finitude of what is "moved," that is, the death of the men who create History.

As finitude or temporality and as negativity or freedom, death is therefore doubly the ultimate basis and the first mover [mobile] of History. And that is why the historical process implies necessarily an actualization of death through wars and bloody revolutions.

In the essay on *Natural Right* (of 1802) Hegel affirms resolutely the historical necessity of war (Vol. VII, p. 372, lines 5–8, 16–21, 24–35, and p. 373, lines 21–22) [p. 368, lines 22–26, 33–38; p. 369, lines 1–12, 37–39]:

> The positive-aspect (Positive) of the absolute form [= Man] is the absolute customary-morality (Sittliche), to wit, the habits [l'appartenance] of a people [= State], the particular demonstrating (*erweist*) in a non-ambiguous manner [its] union (Einssein) with the people only in the negative-aspect, through the danger of death [which implies war].—This relationship (Beziehung) of [political] individuality to

> [political, = State] individuality is a relation (Verhältnis), and consequently a double relationship; the one is the positive relationship, the equal [and] tranquil coexistence (Nebeneinanderbestehen) of the two in peace,—the other is the negative relationship, the exclusion of one individuality by the other; and the two relationships are absolutely necessary. . . . Through this second aspect of the relationship is posited the necessity of war for the concrete-form (Gestalt) and the individuality of the customary-moral totality [= the State]. War, [precisely] because there is in it the free possibility not only that isolated-particular specific-determinations might be nullified (vernichtet, but [also] their integrity (Vollständigkeit) [taken] as life, and this for the Absolute itself, that is, for the people [= the State],—[War] preserves the moral (sittliche) health of the people in its indifference in the face of specific determinations and in the face of [their] becoming accustomed to and of the fixation (Festwerden) of these latter, in the same way as the movement of the winds preserves the [waters of] lakes from stagnation, to which a prolonged calm would have committed them, just as a prolonged peace—or even worse (gar) eternal [peace]—[would have committed the people to stagnation] . . .—[for] what is [—as Man—] negative-or-negate-ive by its nature [which is Action], must remain negative-or-negate-ory and must not become something fixed-and-stable (Festes).

And in the *Lectures* of 1805–06 Hegel insists on the fact that it is indeed the presence of death in wars that makes of them the creative agents of History (Vol. XX, p. 261, line 18–p. 262, line 2):

> The soldier-condition and war are the objectively-real sacrifice of the personal-Self, the danger of death for the particular—this contemplation (Anschauung) of its immediate abstract Negativity; in the same way as war is equally the immediate positive personal-Self of the particular . . . in such a way [that in it] each one, as this particular creates itself (macht) as absolute power (Macht), contemplates itself as [being] absolutely free, as universal Negativity [existing] for itself really against an other (Anderes). It is in war that this is permitted (gewährt) to the particular: it is [a] crime [committed] *for the Universal* [= State]; the end [of war is] the conservation [mediated by negation] of the whole [= the State] against the enemy, which is ready to destroy this whole. This alienation (Entäusserung) [of the Particular to the Universal] must have precisely this abstract form, to be deprived-of-individuality; death must be received and given coldly; not by a deliberate [commenté] (statarische) struggle, in which the particular

> perceives the adversary and kills him in an immediate hatred; no, death is given and received in-the-void (leer),—*impersonally*, in consequence of the smoke from the powder [à partir de la fumée de la poudre].

It is therefore indeed murderous war that assures historical freedom and the free historicity of Man. Man is historical only to the extent that he participates actively in the life of the State, and that participation culminates in the voluntary risk of life in a purely political war. Also man is truly historical or human only to the extent that he is a warrior, at least potentially.

Hegel said so in so many words in the *System of Morality* (of 1802?). He again accepts there the irreducible division of society into three "estates" (Stände) or classes: peasants, manufacturers [industriels] and merchants, and the nobility. The first two "estates" work, but they do not struggle and do not risk their lives for the State. The nobility is on the contrary essentially [a] warrior [class], which permits it to lead an authentically human life, even while remaining idle and profiting from the products of the work of the other classes: "their work cannnot be other than that of war, or an educative-formation (Bilden) for this work" (Vol. VII, p. 476, lines 16–18) [p. 472, lines 16–18]. Now it is the nobility and it alone, that real-izes History. The other classes only submit to it, and they can only passively contemplate the historical process incarnated in the political and warlike existence of the nobles.

Hegel says it in highly "metaphysical," even Schellingian language—but nonetheless quite clearly—[in the following] (Vol. VII, p. 476, line 38 – p. 477, line 8) [p. 472, line 38–p. 473, line 8]:

> The first usefulness [of the estate of the warrior nobility] consists in the fact that it is the absolute real moral concrete-form, by constituting thus for them [= the two other estates] the image of the Absolute [= the State] which-exists-as-a-given-being (seienden) and which is moved [-dialectically, = historically, which is] the highest real contemplation that moral nature requires. By their nature, these [non-warrior] estates stop at this contemplation. They do not exist in the absolute concept, by which this [entity], which is posited (gesetztes) for consciousness only as an exterior-entity (Äusseres), would be their own Spirit, absolute [dialectically-]moving itself, which would surmount (überwände) all their differences and [given] specific-determinations. That their moral nature achieves this contemplation,—this advantage is offered them by the first estate [of the warrior nobility].

Later, and notably in the *Phenomenology*, Hegel no longer accepts this "feudal" conception of society. The existence of a class of idle warriors is for him only a transitory historical phenomenon. But the theme of the historical necessity of war is taken up again in the *Phenomenology*.

Hegel says there, among other things, the following (p. 324, lines 10–33):

> On the one hand, the community (Gemeinwesen) can therefore be organized into systems of personal autonomy and of [private] property, [private] right, real and personal; in the same way, the modes of labor for the primarily particular-and-isolated ends of gain and enjoyment, [such modes] [can] be articulated into associations (Zusammenkünften) of their own and [can] become-autonomous. [But] the Spirit of general association [= the State] is *undivided-unity* (*Einfachheit*) and [is] the *negative-or-negate-ive* essential-reality (Wesen) of these systems which isolate themselves. In order not to permit them to take root and to become fixed (festwerden) in this process-of-isolation, which if it happened, the whole would decompose and the Spirit evaporate, the government must shake up the systems from time to time by wars, to injure and disturb thereby the order and the right of autonomy that are granted them (zurechtgemachten), and through the labor imposed [by warfare] to let the individuals know their master, [i.e.,] death, individuals who, by plunging themselves (sich vertiefend) in these systems, get detached from the whole and tend towards inviolable [isolated] *being-for-itself* and the security of the [private] person. Through this dissolution (Auflösung) of the form of the fixed-and-stable-subsistence [du maintien-fixe-et-stable] (Bestehens), the Spirit [= State] removes-the-danger of the fall (Versinken) into natural empirical-existence (Dasein) away from [à partir de] the customary-moral [= historical or human] [empirical-existence], and it conserves and raises up the personal-Self of its consciousness into *freedom* and into its *force*.

To be sure, this text is found in the Section devoted to the analysis of the ancient State (Chapter VI, A, *a*). Now the Master, the citizen of the pagan State, is by definition idle. Not working, he does not "negate" the Nature exterior to him. His truly human activity, i.e., free or negate-ive, is reduced to the negation of his own innate "nature." And that negation culminates in the voluntary risk of life, incurred in the struggle for pure prestige, in a purely political war, stripped of every "vital necessity." The pagan State, in which the citizens are idle warriors, cannot therefore be truly human, i.e., free and historical, except in and through the wars of prestige that it wages from time to time.

The Slave, and the working ex-Slave, can in principle humanize themselves through their labor, without risking their lives. For in working, they "negate" the given and exterior real and, as a consequence, transform themselves. In principle, the State in which the citizens work could therefore renounce wars without decomposing as a State or truly human entity. But in the text cited, Hegel says that in practice a State that is essentially pacifist ceases to be a State properly speaking, and becomes a private industrial and commercial association that has for its supreme goal the well-being of its members, that is, precisely the satisfaction of their "natural," namely, animal, desires. It is therefore, in the last analysis, participation in bloody political struggle that raises man above the animal by making a citizen of him.

However that may be, the final goal of human becoming is, according to Hegel, the synthesis of the warlike existence of the Master and the life of labor of the Slave. The Man who is fully satisfied by his existence, and who achieves precisely thereby the historical evolution of humanity, is the Citizen of the universal and homogeneous State, that is, for Hegel, the worker-soldier of the revolutionary armies of Napoleon. Therefore it is indeed war (for Recognition) that terminates History and carries Man to his perfection (= satisfaction). Thus, Man can perfect himself only to the extent that he is mortal and accepts, with an awareness of what is involved, the risk of life.

Of course, once the universal and homogeneous Empire is established, there are no more wars or revolutions. Man can live in it thenceforth without risking his life. But the truly human existence is then that of the Wise Man, who limits himself to *comprehending* everything, without ever *negating* or *modifying* anything (except for transposing the "essences" of the real into discourse). This existence is therefore neither *free* nor *historical* in the proper sense of these words, in the sense that Hegel himself ascribes to them when he speaks of Man before the end of History. Freedom and historicity properly speaking are inseparable from death: Only a mortal being can be free and historical, provided that it accept the idea and the reality of its death and that it be able to risk its life without any "necessity," in function of an "idea" or "ideal."

In fine, human *individuality* is itself also conditioned by death. We can deduce this by admitting, with Hegel, that one can be individual only by being free, and that one cannot be free without being finite or mortal. But this consequence also flows directly from the Hegelian definition of the Individual.

The Individual, for Hegel, is a synthesis of the Particular and the Universal. *Particularity* would be purely "given," "natural," animal, were it not associated, in human *individuality*, with the *universality* of discourse and of action (the discourse proceeding from the action). Now the action of the particular—and it is always a *particular* that acts—is truly *universal* only if it represents and realizes the "general will" of a "community" (Gemeinwesen), that is, in the last analysis, of a State. It is only by acting as [a] citizen (*against* his particular "private" interest) that [a] man is truly and really universal, even while remaining particular; it is only in and through the State that human individuality is manifested and effectuated, for it is the State that attributes to the *particular* a *universally* recognized reality and value. But action by and for the State culminates in the risk of (particular) life for purely political (= universal) ends; a citizen who refuses to risk his life for the State loses his citizenship, that is, [his] universal recognition. It is therefore in the final analysis because he is able to *die* that [a] man is able to be an *individual*.

Hegel says it in a very clear manner in the *Lectures* of 1803–04 (Vol. XIX, p. 230, line 32 to p. 231, line 10):

> This given-being of the dialectical-suppression (Aufgehobenseins) of the particular totality [that is, of the Citizen, of the individual] is the totality [taken] as absolutely universal, as absolute *Spirit* [= People, = State]. It is the Spirit as absolutely real Consciousness. The particular totality [that is, the individual] contemplates itself [in the State, as citizen,] as an ideal [totality], dialectically suppressed; and it is no longer particular; it is on the contrary for itself this dialectical-suppression of itself, and it [i.e., "the particular totality"] is recognized [as Citizen], it is *universal* [in so much as [en tant que] Citizen] only as [en tant que] that dialectically-suppressed [totality]. The Totality [= the Universal] in so much as [it is] a Particularity [, that is, Individuality,] is posited in (an) itself as a solely possible totality, not-existing-for-itself, solely [as a totality which,] in its subsisting-in-existence (Bestehen), is always ready for death, which has renounced itself, which exists, it is true, as particular totality,—as family, or in [private] property and [personal] enjoyment, but in such a fashion that this [purely particular] relationship [that the family, property, and enjoyment is] is for itself an ideal [relationship] and proves [erweist] itself as [or by] sacrificing itself.

The fact that Individuality implies and presupposes finitude or death can be shown, moreover, in another way.

The Universal is the *negation* of the Particular as Particular. If we want to transform a concrete entity (= a particular) into a concept (= a universal), into a "general notion," we must detach it from the *hic et nunc* of its empirical existence (this dog is here and now, but the concept "this dog" is "everywhere" and "always"). In the same way, if we want to *realize* individuality by transforming the particularity of existence into human universality, we must *really* detach the man from his *hic et nunc*. But for the human *animal* this real detachment is equivalent to death, for in ceasing to exist here and now it no longer exists at all (as *dead*, this dog is also "everywhere" and "always"). Thus, the real penetration of the Universal into the Particular is the completion of the finitude of this latter, that is, its actual death. And if *human* existence can be universal even while remaining particular, that is, if Man can *exist* as an individual, it is solely because the universality of death can be present in him during his lifetime: ideally, in the consciousness that he has of it; and really, through the voluntary risk of life (the consciousness presupposing the risk).

Hegel insists, on several occasions, on the fact that it is death that is the final manifestation and, if we can say it, the "realization," of the Universal in empirical existence. He says so, among other places, in the *Lectures* of 1803–04, in the *Lectures* of 1805–06, and in the *Phenomenology*:

> Death is the aspect of the duplication [dédoublement] of the kind [into particularity and universality] and the perfect liberation of the constitutive-elements [which are the Particular and the Universal]; [death is] the immediate unity of given-Being (Seins), *but in its concept* [it is] *the universal personal-Self* (*Selbst*), *which exists as universal* [Vol. XIX, p. 254, lines 4–8].—In death,—the absolute power, the *master* of the *particular*; that is to say, the common [= universal] will has become pure *given-Being* [which the cadaver of the citizen dead for the State is] [Vol. XX, p. 225, Note 3].—This Universality to which the Particular succeeds as *such*, is pure given-Being, death; . . . Death is the completion-or-perfection (Vollendung) and the supreme work that the individual as such [that is, as Particular] undertakes for the community [= the State, = the Universal]. [*Phenomenology*, p. 231, lines 31–32 and p. 232, lines 6–8].

Thus, the "faculty of death" (Fähigkeit des Todes) is the necessary and sufficient condition, not only of the freedom and historicity of man, but also of his universality, without which he would not be truly individual.

"The true being of Man is his *action*," says Hegel. Now Action in the realization of Negativity, which manifests itself on the "phenomenal" level as death. Which means, as a conscious and voluntary death, that is, *freely* accepted, without any vital *necessity*. Such an acceptance of death is produced when a man consciously risks his life in function solely of the desire for "recognition" (Anerkennen), solely from his "vanity." The desire for recognition is the desire for a *desire*, that is, not for a *given* (= natural) being, but for the presence of the *absence* of such a being. This desire [for recognition] *transcends* therefore the natural given, and to the extent that it *realizes* itself it creates a trans-natural or *human* being. But the desire *realizes* itself only to the extent that it has more power than the natural given being, that is, to the extent that it annihilates it. The being that annihilates itself in function of a desire for recognition disappears, it is true; but its disappearance is that of a *human* being—it is a *death* in the proper sense of the term. And it is this annihilation of the animal that is the creation of Man. Man is himself annihilated, it is true, in his death. But so long as that death endures [*dure*] as a conscious will to risk life with a view to recognition, Man maintains himself in empirical existence as a *human* being, that is, [as] transcendent in relation to *given* being, to Nature.

Man appears therefore (or creates himself) for the first time in the (given) natural World as a combatant in the first bloody Struggle for pure prestige. That is to say that a being cannot constitute itself as human except on condition of being finite or mortal (which means "living"). And that is also to say that a being cannot live humanly except on condition of "realizing" his death: becoming conscious of it, "bearing" it, being capable of facing it voluntarily. To be a Man—is, for Hegel, to be able and to know how to die. "The true being of Man" is therefore, in the final analysis, his death as a *conscious* phenomenon.[6]

The idea of the bloody Struggle for recognition, which engenders the relationship of Mastery and Servitude, appeared in the writings of Hegel around 1802 (*System of Morality*, Vol. VII, pp. 445–447) [pp. 441–443]. But it is above all in the *Lectures* of 1803–04 that Hegel insists at length on this idea. The theme returns in the *Lectures* of 1805–06. And in the *Phenomenology* (1806) the notion of the *anthropogenetic* value of the Struggle and of the Risk of life is definitively evolved and formulated in a perfectly clear manner.

Here are, first of all, some passages drawn from the *Lectures* of 1803–04.

Hegel begins by saying that the simple, purely "natural' *possession* that we observe in the animal becomes essentially human *property*—i.e., a *recognized*, namely juridical, possession—only in and through a struggle to the death engaged in with a view to that recognition. It is not in order to really possess the disputed thing that one risks his life in that struggle for pure prestige; it is in order to gain recognition for his exclusive *right* to the possession. And this right does not become *real*, the "legal person" [le "sujet juridique"] (= specifically human being) is not realized, except in and through this risk, and in the last analysis, in and through death.

Hegel expresses himself as follows:

> The particular is a Consciousness [= Man] only to the extent that each particularity of his possession (Besitzes) and of his given-being appears as attached to his total essential-reality (Wesen), [as] entailed [impliquée] (aufgenommen) in his Indifference, to the extent that he *posits* each constitutive-element (Moment) *as* [what is] *himself*; for this is Consciousness, the ideal-being of the World. Consequently, [even] the loss [lésion] of one of his particularities is infinite; it is an absolute outrage, an outrage to him [taken] as a whole, an outrage to his honor; and a conflict on the basis of any particular thing is a struggle for the whole. The [disputed] thing, [that is,] the specific-determination, is not at all viewed as value, as thing; it is on the contrary entirely nullified, entirely ideal; there is only the fact that it [the thing] is related to me,

> that I am a Consciousness, that the thing has lost its opposition over and against me [by becoming my recognized property]. The two [adversaries], who recognize each other and want to know themselves as being recognized mutually as this totality of particulars, [these two] confront each other as this totality. And the significance-and-importance (Bed[eutung]) that they give mutually to each other is: [a)] that each appear [apparaisse] in the consciousness of the other as the one who excludes him from every *extension* of his particularity [that is, from everything that this latter possesses]; b) that he be, in this, his exclusion [or exclusivity], really [a] totality. Neither can demonstrate it to the other by words, assurances, threats or promise[s]. For language is only the ideal existence of Consciousness, while here objectively-real-entities oppose each other, that is, absolutely-opposed-entities, entities-existing-absolutely-for-themselves, and their relationship is absolutely a practical relationship, [which is] itself objectively-real. The middle-term (Mitte) of their recognition (Anerkennens) must be itself objectively-real. *Consequently*, they *must-necessarily* (*müssen*) *each injure the other* [*se léser l'un l'autre*]; the fact that each one posits itself as exclusive totality in the [sa] particularity of his existence, must-necessarily become objectively-real; outrage is necessary; [Vol. XIX, p. 226, line 6, to p. 227, line 20].—And that conflict must and should (muss und soll) take place, for the fact that the particular as such is Reason (Vern[unft]), [an] Indifference, cannot be known except to the extent that each particularity of his possession and of his given-being is posited in that Indifference [?], and [to the extent] that he relates himself to it [each particularity] as [a] whole. This can be shown only to the extent that he engages (daraufsetzt) all his existence for his [sa] conservation [as proprietor], [that] he absolutely does not subdivide himself [se partage]. And the demonstration is completed solely with death [Vol. XIX, p. 226, Note 3, lines 1–7].

But it is not only in order to gain recognition for his property and to gain recognition for himself as proprietor (= legal subject or person) that a man must risk his life in the struggle to the death for pure prestige. He must do it also in view of the recognition of his reality and of his human value in general. Now for Hegel, Man is humanly *real* and really *human* only to the extent that he is *recognized* as such. It is therefore in order to *be* human and in order to manifest himself or *appear* as such that Man must be able to die and must know how to risk his life.

Hegel explains it as follows:

> Each one can be recognized by the other only to the extent that his manifold appearance (mannigfaltige Erscheinung) is indifferent in him,

[that he] demonstrates himself as infinite in each particularity of his possession and revenges each offence (Verletzung) [by going] as far as the death [of the offender]. And that offence must-necessarily take place, for Consciousness [= Man] must-necessarily have for [its] goal (auf . . . gehen) that recognition; the particulars must-necessarily offend each other mutually, in order to know themselves (erkennen) [and to know] if they are endowed-with-reason [= human]. For Consciousness is essentially such, that the totality of the particular has opposed itself and is the same in that act-of-becoming-other (Anderswerden), that the totality of the particular is in another consciousness, and is the consciousness of the other and that in this latter is precisely this absolute maintaining of its [own] totality that it has for itself; that is to say [that Consciousness is essentially such] that it must be recognized by the other. But the fact my totality, [taken] as [that] of a particular, is in the other consciousness precisely that totality existing-for itself, [that is, the fact] that it is recognized, respected,—I could not know it except through the appearance of the activity (Handelns) of the other in the face of my totality; and by the same token, the other must at the same time appear to me himself as a totality, just as I appeared to him. If they behave negatively [by avoiding each other], if they leave each other mutually [in peace],—then neither one has appeared to the other as [a] totality, nor [has] the given-being of the one [appeared] as a totality in the consciousness of the other, neither [as] presentation (Darstellen), nor [as] recognition. Language, explanations, promise[s], none of these are that recognition; for language is but an ideal middle-term [between the two]: it disappears as it appears, it is not a permanent (bleibendes), or real, recognition [Vol. XIX, p. 226, Note 3, line 15 to the end].—Each particular must posit itself as totality in the consciousness of the other in such a way that he commits against the other, for the conservation of any particularity whatsoever, all its visible [apparaissante] totality, its [very] life; and by the same token, each one must-necessarily have for [its] goal the death of the other. I cannot know myself in the consciousness of the other as that particular totality [that is, as human individual or person] except to the extent that I posit myself in his consciousness as being, in my exclusion [of him], a totality of exclusion [that is, as] having his death as [my] end. In having his death as end, I expose myself to death, I risk my own life. I commit the contradiction of wanting to affirm-or-impose (behaupten) the particularity of my given-being and of my possession; and this affirmation transforms itself into its opposite, [namely, in the fact] that I sacrifice all that possession and possibility of all possession and enjoyment, [in other words] [that I sacrifice] life itself. In positing myself as totality of

particularity, I dialectically-suppress myself as totality of particularity; I want to be recognized in this extension of my existence, in my given-being and [in] my possession; but I transform it in this [sense], that I dialectically-suppress that existence, and I am not recognized in truth as endowed-with-reason [= human], as totality, except to the extent that, by having as end the death of the other, I myself risk my own life and dialectically-suppress that extension of my existence itself, [that is] the totality of my particularity.

This recognition *of the particularity of the totality brings with itself therefore the nothingness of death.* Each one must-necessarily know of the other if he is an absolute Consciousness [= Man]. Each one must-necessarily posit himself in such a relationship over and against the other, that this might come to the light of day; he must-necessarily offend him, and each one can know of the other that he is [a] totality [= individuality or human person] only by forcing him to go to the death (bis auf den Tod treibt); and in the same way, each one shows himself to himself as [being a] totality only by going with himself to the death. If he stops [s'arrête], in himself, this side [en-deça] (innerhalb) of death, if he shows himself to the other only as committing the loss of a part or [even] the totality of the possession, as [risking] [only] wounds [and] not life itself,—he is then for the other, in-an-immediate-manner, a non-totality; he is not absolutely for himself; he becomes the slave of the other. If he stops, in himself, this side of death and ceases the combat (Streit) before the putting to death, then he has not demonstrated himself as totality, nor [has he] recognized the other as such. . . .

This recognition of the particulars is therefore in itself [an] absolute contradiction: recognition is only the given-being of Consciousness, [taken] as totality, in an other Consciousness; but to the extent that the [first] Consciousness becomes objectively-real, it dialectically-suppresses the other Consciousness [by killing it]; thereby the recognition dialectically-suppresses itself. It does not realize itself, but on the contrary ceases to be [= to exist] to the extent that (indem) it is [= exists]. And nonetheless Consciousness is not [= does not exist] at the same time except as an act-of-being-recognized by an other, and it is at the same time Consciousness only as absolute numerical unity (Eins), and [it] must-necessarily be recognized as such; but this signifies that it must-necessarily have as its goal the death of the other and its own, and it is not [= does not exist] except in the objective-reality of death. [Vol. XIX, p. 228, line 17, to p. 229, line 31, and p. 230, lines 7–17.]

Human reality is therefore in the last analysis "the objective-reality of *death*": Man is not only *mortal*; he is *death* incarnate; he *is* his own death. And in contrast to "natural," purely biological death, the death that is Man is a "violent" death, at the same time conscious of itself and voluntary. Human death, the death of man—and consequently all his truly human existence—is therefore, if we prefer, a *suicide*.

Hegel says it in so many words in the *Lectures* of 1805–06 (Vol. XX, p. 211, lines 34–36):[7]

> It appears to Consciousness [= to the man engaged in the Struggle for recognition] [taken] as consciousness, that it has for [its] end the *death* of an other; but [in itself or for us, which is to say, in truth,] it has for [its] end its own death; [it is] suicide, to the extent that it exposes itself to *danger*.

Now it is only in the Struggle for recognition, and solely through the risk of life that this latter implies, that the given (animal) being creates itself as *human* being. It is therefore the very *being* of Man that "appears" or manifests itself as a deferred *suicide* or, as Hegel would say, [a suicide] "mediated" (vermittelt) by the negate-ive Action that engenders a consciousness discursive of the exterior and of itself. Man is a being who commits suicide, or who is at least capable of committing suicide (Fähigkeit des Todes). The human existence of Man is a conscious and voluntary *death* [which is] in the course of coming about [en voie de devenir].

In the *Phenomenology*,[8] Hegel takes up again and refines the theme of the Struggle for recognition. He insists on its *anthropogenetic* character: It is in and through this Struggle alone that Man can create himself starting out from the animal. And Hegel states clearly that what is important in this Struggle is not the will to kill, but that of exposing oneself to the danger of death without any necessity, without being forced to it as an animal. It is through the danger of death voluntarily incurred in the Struggle for pure prestige that one attains the *truth* of Recognition. The "truth"—which is to say the revealed-reality, and therefore the reality itself. Now Man is humanly *real* only to the extent that he is *recognized*. It is therefore the human *reality* itself that is constituted or creates itself in and through the voluntary act of confronting death.

Thus, Hegel maintains and re-enforces in the *Phenomenology* the fundamental idea of the *Lectures* of 1803–04, in which he assimilates the self-creation of Man to the actualization of his death. But he abandons the paradox that he had at first maintained. To be sure, he continues to say that death signifies for man his total and definitive annihilation (cf. *Phenomenology*, p. 145). But he no longer says that the *realization* of Man cannot be entirely accomplished except in actual *death*, that is, precisely through *annihilation*. In the text in question, he says expressly that the mere *risk* of life suffices to real-ize the human being. A being that has voluntarily risked its life, but that has escaped death, can *live* humanly, that is, [can] maintain itself as a man in empirical existence (Dasein) in the midst of the natural World.

And it is precisely through the risk of life that Man comprehends that he is essentially *mortal* in the sense that he cannot *exist* humanly outside the animal that serves as a support for his self -consciousness.

The man who has engaged in the Struggle for recognition must remain alive in order to be able to *live* humanly. But he lives *humanly* only to the extent that he is *recognized* by the other. His adversary must therefore *also* escape death. The combat must cease before the putting to death,—contrary to what Hegel had said in the *Lectures* of 1803–04 (Vol. XIX, p. 229).

In those *Lectures* Hegel allowed for that eventuality. It comes about when one of the two adversaries refuses to risk [his] life and submits to the other, by becoming his Slave, that is, by recognizing him without being recognized in return. But to refuse the risk is to remain within the limits of animality. The Slave is not, therefore, a truly human being, and "recognition" by him cannot, consequently, real-ize the humanity of the recognized. Thus, true recognition can be effected only in and through *death*, which *annihilates* the one who recognizes; therefore the recognition itself [is annihilated] and as a consequence [also] the recognized as recognized—i.e., as a truly human being. Hence the paradox.

In the *Phenomenology* Hegel avoids this paradox by admitting the humanity of the Slave, and therefore the anthropogenetic value of his recognition of the Master. But how does he justify the humanity of the being who has precisely *refused* to subordinate his animal life to the human and anthropogenetic desire for Recognition?

The Master is humanized (is realized as Master, that is, as a specifically human being) through the recognition by the Slave, which he imposes on this latter in accepting the *risk* "against-nature" that the future Slave refuses. As for the Slave himself, he is humanized (is realized as Slave, which is *also* a specifically human mode of being) through the *cognizance* he takes of his essential finitude in experiencing the dread of death, that death appearing to him *in the course of a Struggle for recognition*, that is, as something that is not a purely biological necessity.

Just like the Master, the Slave is conscious of himself, that is, [he is] essentially *human* in his empirical existence. To be sure, at the beginning, at his nascent stage so to speak, the Slave is human only potentially, while the humanity of the Master is "objectively-real," since it is actually recognized. But it remains no less the case that Man creates himself, through the Struggle, at the same time, as Master and Slave, and that the two are specifically human. And they are such, in the last ana1yis, through the fact that they have both been placed in the presence of their death.

The Slave realizes and perfects his humanity in *laboring* in the service of the Master. But this servile or serving Labor [Travail] has an anthropogenetic virtue only to the extent that it is born of the Dread of death and is accompanied by the consciousness of the essential finitude of the one who serves by laboring.

In contrast to the Master, who remains forever fixed in his humanity as Master, the Slave develops and perfects his humanity, [which was] servile at its origin. He raises himself to [the level of] discursive thought and elaborates the abstract notion of freedom; and he creates himself also as a Citizen who is free and ultimately fully *satisfied*, by transforming the given World through the Labor that he performs in the Service of the community. It is therefore he [the Slave-Citizen], and not the Master, who is Man properly speaking, the individual who freely creates History. But we must not forget to notice that Service and Labor are free and creative only to the extent that they are accomplished within [or in terms of] the Dread that is born of the consciousness of death. It is therefore, when all is said and done, this consciousness of death that humanizes Man and constitutes the ultimate basis of his humanity.

If there is to be murder and bloody struggle for recognition, it is in order that there may be "suicide" or *voluntary* risk of life. But this risk itself, which is actualized in the Master, is there in order that there may take place in the Slave the experience of death, which reveals to him his own finitude. And it is life in the presence of death that is "the life of the Spirit," which is to say, a specifically human life, able to attain its perfection or the fullness of satisfaction.

Man is the only being in the world who *knows* that he must die, and we can say that he *is* the consciousness of his death: Truly human existence is an existing consciousness of death, or a death conscious of itself. The perfection of man being the fullness of consciousness of self, and Man being essentially finite in his very being, it is in the conscious acceptance of finitude that human existence culminates. And it is the full (discursive) comprehension of the meaning of death that constitutes that Hegelian Wisdom that completes History by procuring Satisfaction for Man.

For in attaining to Wisdom, Man understands that it is solely his finitude or his death that assures him absolute freedom, by liberating him not only from the given World but also from the eternal and infinite given—which would be God, if Man were not mortal. And the consciousness of this absolute freedom satisfies the infinite pride of Man, which constitutes the very ground of his human existence and which is the ultimate [and] irreducible motive [mobile] of his act of self-creation.

In a general way, Hegelian anthropology is a secularized Christian theology. And Hegel is perfectly aware of it. He repeats on several occasions that everything said by Christian theology is absolutely true, provided that it is applied, not to an imaginary transcendent God, but to real Man, living in the World. The theologian does anthropology without taking account of it. Hegel merely becomes truly conscious of the knowledge called theo-logical, by explaining that its real object is not God, but historical Man, or, as he likes to say, "the Spirit of the people (Volksgeist)."

Among other places, this conception is clearly expressed by Hegel at the end of the *Lectures* of 1805–06 (Vol. XX, p. 268, lines 7–21):

> Religion [in general] is Spirit represented[-as-an-exterior-entity] (vorgestellter): [it is] the personal-Self (Selbst) which does not bring into coincidence (nicht zusammenbringt) its pure consciousness with its objectively-real consciousness, [and] for which the content of the former is opposed [to it], in the latter, as an other-entity [entité-autre]. [In other terms, the Religious [person] is one who does not know that he is speaking in fact of himself when he believes that he is speaking of God]. . . . [The] idea of the absolute [or Christian] Religion is this speculative idea that the personal-Self, [or] the objectively-real-entity, is thought [[la] pensée], [that] essential-reality (Wesen) and given-being (Sein) [are] the same thing. This is put [= expressed] in such a way *that God*, [that is,] *the absolute transcendent* (*jenseitige*) *essential-reality*, [has] *become Man*, this *objectively-real-being* here; but also [it is put in such a way] that this objective-reality is dialectically-suppressed, has become a past [reality], and [that] this God, who is [on the one hand a] [given particular] objective-reality and [on the other hand an] objective reality [which has been] dialectically-suppressed or universal, is the same thing as [a] Spirit-of-the-people; it is only as immediateness [that is, as represented (vorgestellt) as a single man named Jesus] that it is the Spirit of the [Christian] community. *That God is Spirit, this is the content* of that [Christian] religion.

Hegel is therefore in accord with Christianity to the extent of saying that the "Absolute," or the Totality of what *is*, is not Identity, given-Being, Substance, or Nature, but Spirit, that is, Being revealed by the Word [la Parole] or by discursive Reason (Logos). But for the Christian this "absolute" Spirit is a transcendent God, while for Hegel it is Man-in-the-world. And that radical and irreducible difference amounts in the final analysis to this, that the Christian Spirit is eternal and infinite, while the Spirit that Hegel had in mind is essentially finite or mortal. It is by introducing the idea of death that theo-logy is transposed into anthropology. And it is by taking that idea literally, that is, by suppressing the notions of survival and resurrection that we arrive at the *true* or Hegelian anthropology.

Hegel is perfectly aware of this also, and he says so clearly in [the course of] interpreting the evangelical myth in a marginal note, which relates to the passage cited (Vol. XX, p. 268, Note 3, last two lines):

> It is not this man here who dies, but the *divine* [as such]; it is precisely because of that (eben dadurch) that this divine [or this divinity] becomes Man.

Thus, in demonstrating that consciousness, the consciousness of self, the rational will, and discursive reason imply and presuppose finitude or death, Hegel demonstrates that the "absolute Spirit," or the totality of revealed Being, is not an eternal God creating the World out of Nothingness, but *Man*, negating a natural World, given from all eternity, in which he himself is born and dies as historical humanity.

In the final analysis, the God of Christian theology (of ancient or pagan inspiration) is given-Being (Sein), eternally identical to itself, realizing itself and revealing itself in and through a natural World, which only manifests the essence and the power of existing of the Being that *is*. The Man of Hegel, on the contrary, is the Nothingness (*Nichts*) that annihilates given-Being existing as World, and that annihilates itself (as real historical time or History) in and through that annihilation of the given.

The ultimate basis of the natural or "divine" empirical-existence (Dasein) is *given-Being* or the power (Macht) of subsisting eternally in *identity* with itself. The ultimate basis of human empirical-existence, on the contrary, the source and origin of human reality, is *Nothingness* or the power of *Negativity*, which is realized and is [made] manifest only through the transformation of the given *identity* of *being* into [the] create-ive *contradiction* of "dialectical" or historical *becoming*, in which there is existence only in and through Action (which is, if we prefer, the essential-reality or the "essence" of Man), and in which the agent is not what he *is* (as given) and *is* what he is not (from all eternity). If Nature or "God" is the Being that *is* (as real or "physical" Space), Man is the Nothingness that *annihilates* (as Action or real, "historical," Time) by "dialectically supressing" what *is* and by *creating* what is not. This central and ultimate idea of Hegelian philosophy, the idea that the foundation of the source of objective reality (Wirklichkeit) and of human empirical existence (Dasein) is the Nothingness that is manifest or that reveals itself as negate-ive or create-ive Action [which is] free and conscious of itself,—that idea is clearly expressed in a beautiful and "romantic" passage in the *Lectures* of 1805–06, which Hegel delivered at the very moment when he was writing the *Phenomenology*.

Here is that passage (Vol. XX, p. 180, line 24, to p. 181, line 8):

> Man is this night, this empty Nothingness, which contains everything in its undivided-simplicity (Einfachheit): a wealth of an infinite number of representations, of images, no one of which precisely attains to the spirit[dont aucune ne lui vient précisément à l'esprit], or [even more] which are not as really-present (gegenwärtig). It is the night, the interiority-or-intimacy (Innere) of Nature, which exists here:—[i.e.,] [the] *pure personal-Self*. In phantasmagorical representations there is night all around: here there rises up suddenly a head all bloody, there another pale apparition (Gestalt); and they all disappear just as sud-

> denly. It is this night that we perceive when we look into a man's eyes: [we then immerse our gaze] in a night that becomes *terrible* (furchtbar); it is the night of the world which [then] presents itself (hängt entgegen) to us.
>
> *Power* (*Macht*) *to draw images from that night or to let them fall from in autonomous-positing* (*Selbstsetzen*) [that is, free creation], *interior* consciousness, *Action* (*Tun*). It is into this night that is withdrawn [qui s'est retirée] the entity-existing-as-a-being[-which-is-]given (das Seiende); but the [dialectical] movement of this power is equally posited.

The dialectical movement of the power that maintains in Being the Nothingness that Man is,—is History. And that power itself is realized and is manifest as negate-ive or create-ive Action: Action negate-ive of the given that Man himself is, or [the] action of the *Struggle* that creates historical Man; and Action negate-ive of the given that the natural World is, in which the animal lives, or [the] action of *Labor* that creates the cultural World, outside of which Man is only a pure Nothingness, and in which he differs from Nothingness *only for a certain time*.[9]

Notes

Translator's footnotes in the English translation:

*[1] Originally published as Appendix II, "L'idée de la mort dans la philosophie de Hegel," in Kojève's *Introduction à la lecture de Hegel* (Paris: Gallimard, 1947; 5th edition), pp. 527–73.

In the following translation numbered footnotes are Kojève's; the translator uses asterisks. [Bold] brackets represent Kojève's use of brackets; [regular] brackets indicate the translator's insertions. An attempt has been made to reproduce Kojève's punctuation and sentence structure as closely as possible, with the result that those insertions, in French and in English, may annoy the eye even where they do aid in comprehension. In this matter Kojève himself has been the model, and those who are familiar with the gray and cluttered pages of the original will understand. (Parentheses in the text are always Kojève's.)

*[2] References to the *Phenomenology* (which Kojève's text cites as "PhG") are to the Hoffmeister edition of the *Phänomenologie des Geistes* (Hamburg: Felix Meiner, 1952). Where Kojève's page or line numbers do not correspond (he was using a 1937 edition of Hoffmeister), the 1952 edition's equivalents are substituted. So far as *content* is concerned, Kojève's French version of Hegel determines the translation of quoted passages.

*[3] This refers to an earlier section of the book from which the present essay is taken. The "fragment on love" in question can be found in English in *G. W. F. Hegel: Early Theological Writings*, translated by T. M. Knox (Chicago: University of Chicago Press, 1948), pp. 302–08.

*[4] For references to "Vol. XIX," see J. Hoffmeister's edition of *Jenenser Realphilosophie I: Die Vorlesungen von* 1803–04 (Leipzig: Felix Meiner, 1931).

*[5] For references to "Vol. XX," see *Jenaer Realphilosophie*, edited by J. Hoffmeister (Hamburg: Felix Meiner, 1967), a reissue of Hoffmeister's *Jenenser Realphilosophie II* (1931).

*[6] For references to "Vol. VII," see G. Lasson's edition of Hegel's *Schriften zur Politik und Rechtsphilosophie* (Leipzig: Felix Meiner, 1923). Page and line numbers in large brackets refer to this edition; those in small brackets (or in parentheses) are Kojève's originals.

*[7] The preceding passages from "Vol. VII" are not from the *System of Morality* of 1802 but from Hegel's essay "Über die wissenschaftlichen Behandlungsarten des Naturrechts," also of 1802.

Kojève's footnotes in the English translation:

1. According to Hegel *no* truth is possible before the completion of the dialectical (= historical) process. But that consequence is necessary only if we admit the dialecticity of the *totality* of Being. By admitting, on the contrary, that Negativity occurs only in human reality and that *given* Being is ruled only by Identity, we can maintain the traditional notion of truth at least in relation to Nature and to the *past* of Man.
2. As a matter of fact, Hegel was preceded along this way by Descartes (first attempts at a Christian *philosophy*), Kant, and Fichte (Christian philosophers par excellence). But these three attempts at philosophical anthropology failed because their authors did not dare abandon the traditional idea (and in the last analysis "pagan" or "naturalist" [idea]: Identity!) of the *immortality* of Man or of the "soul."—With his notions of "monad" and of "sufficient reason," Leibniz is a precursor of the Hegelian notion of Spirit, that is, of a *totality* [which is] at the same time "subjective" and "objective." But Leibniz did not see the essential difference that obtains between Nature and History, and there is in Leibniz no anthropology properly so-called (i.e., explicit [anthropology]).—As for Hegel himself, he did not succeed in *reconciling* his ("dialectical") anthropology with the traditional ("identical") philosophy of Nature. He refused, rightly, to apply to Man the "naturalistic" categories of the Greeks, and he rejected their pseudo-anthropology. But, wrongly, he also abandoned their philosophy of nature, in trying to apply to the *sum-total* of the real (as much human as natural) his own dialectical categories, which are in fact specifically and exclusively anthropological.

3. Hegel says so, in Section A of Chapter IV of the *Phenomenology*. See above, the translation printed [as] "By Way of Introduction." [That is, "In Place of an Introduction," the first chapter of the English translation of Kojève's *Introduction to the Reading of Hegel*, edited by Allan Bloom, translated by James H. Nichols, Jr. (New York: Basic Books, 1969).] Action reverses the "natural" course of Time in which temporal given-Being or [Being] having a meaning endures. It [i.e., Action] introduces the primacy of the *future* in Time, in which Being *is* and is *given* only in the present. For the present of Action is the realization of a project for the future [d'un projet d'avenir]: In and through Action (or better, *as* Action), the future has a *real presence* in Being. Now the future is *also*, like the past, the nothingness of being [le néant de l'être], that is, its *meaning*. But this meaning was not and is not really attached to present or given existence. That is why it can in some manner be directed away from its "natural" existence (of which it would be the essence) and oriented toward all "artificial" existence, which is that of discourse (of which it will be the meaning). And it is as a *project in discourse* [*projet discursif*] that the future is *really present* as the future. To be sure, the project *realizes* itself in the present, and it is in the past as already *realized*. But the present, and therefore the past, of the project are penetrated and determined by the future, which subsists in it in the form of discourse. The real created by Action is therefore a real revealed by thought or the spoken word [parole]. It is Action (= Man) that creates the World dominated by the future, the World of Science and the arts, in the midst of a natural World dominated by the present (to the extent that the World is inanimate or "material") and by the past (to the extent that the World is living).
4. This theme has been taken up again by Heidegger in *Sein und Zeit*, Vol. I: das Man und das Gerede.
5. Hegel speaks thereof in Section A of Chapter IV [of the *Phenomenology*]. See the translation of that section, printed above [as] "By Way of Introduction." [This note refers to an earlier section of the book, from which the present essay is taken.]
6. Heidegger will say, following Hegel, that human existence (Dasein) is a "life in view of death" (Leben zum Tode). The Christian also used to say it, a long time before Hegel. But for the Christian death is but a passage into the beyond: He does not accept death properly speaking. The Christian man does not place himself face-to-face with Nothingness. He relates himself in his existence to an "other world," which is essentially *given*. There is not therefore in him any "transcendence" (= freedom) in the Hegelian, and Heideggerian, sense of the term.
7. Hegel devotes only two pages there (Vol. XX, pp. 211–213) to the analysis of the Struggle for recognition, and he says there nothing that is truly new.

8. See above the translation with commentary of Section A of Chapter IV, printed [as] "By Way of Introduction" (pp. 18–22) [note from the original edition].
9. Drawn into error by the monistic ontological tradition, Hegel sometimes extends to Nature his analysis of human or historical existence. He says then that *everything* that *is*, is in the last analysis an annihilation of Nothingness (which, obvious1y, has no meaning, and ends up in an indefensible philosophy of nature). He says, for example, in the *Lectures* of 1805–06, in [the course of] developing his philosophy of Nature (Schellingian inspiration): "The shadows are Nothingness; by the same token space and tine are not;—the same way as in general all is Nothingness" (Vol. XX, p. 80, lines 5–6). Heidegger has taken up again the Hegelian themes concerning death; but he neglects the complementary themes concerning Struggle and Labor; thus his philosophy does not succeed in rendering an account of History.—Marx retains the themes of Struggle and Labor, and his philosophy is thus essentially "historicist"; but he neglects the theme of death (even while admitting that man is mortal); that is why he does not see (and even less [do] certain "Marxists") that the Revolution is not only in fact but also essentially and necessarily—bloody (the Hegelian theme of the Terror).

CHAPTER 3

"Husserl, Hegel, Heidegger"

—from *Being and Nothingness: A Phenomenological Essay on Ontology* (1943)

Jean-Paul Sartre

The philosophy of the nineteenth and twentieth centuries seems to have understood that once myself and the Other are considered as two separate substances, we cannot escape solipsism; any union of these substances must in fact be held to be impossible. That is why the examination of modem theories reveals to us an attempt to seize at the very heart of the consciousness a fundamental, transcending connection with the Other which would be constitutive of each consciousness in its very upsurge. But while this philosophy appears to abandon the postulate of the external negation, it nevertheless preserves its essential consequence; that is, the affirmation that my fundamental connection with the Other is realized through *knowledge*.

When Husserl in his *Cartesian Meditations* and in *Formal and Transcendental Logic* attempts to refute solipsism, he believes that he can succeed by showing that a referral to the Other is the indispensable condition for the constitution of a world. Without going into the details of his theory, we shall limit ourselves to indicating his general position. For Husserl the world as it is revealed to consciousness is inter-monadic. The Other is present in it not only as a particular concrete and empirical appearance but as a permanent condition of its unity and of its richness. Whether I consider this table or this tree or this bare wall in solitude or with companions, the Other is always there as a layer of constitutive meanings which belong to the very object which I consider; in short, he is the veritable guarantee of the object's objectivity. And since our psycho-physical self is contemporary with the world, forms a part of the world, and falls with the world under the impact of the phenomenological reduction, the Other appears as necessary to the very constitution of this self. If I am to doubt the existence of my friend Pierre or of others in general, then inasmuch as this existence is on principle outside my experience, I must of necessity doubt also my concrete being, my empirical reality as a professor having this or that tendency, these habits, this particular character. There is no privilege for my self: my empirical Ego and the Other's empirical Ego appear in the world at the same time. The general meaning of "Others" is necessary to the constitution of each one of these "Egos." Thus each object far from being constituted as for Kant, by a simple relation to the *subject*, appears in my concrete experience as polyvalent; it is given originally as possessing systems of reference to an indefinite plurality of consciousnesses; it is *on* the table, *on* the wall that the Other is revealed to me as that to which the object under consideration is perpetually referred—as well as on the occasion of the concrete appearances of Pierre or Paul.

To be sure, these views show progress over the classical positions. It is undeniable that the instrumental-thing from the moment of its discovery refers to a plurality of For-itselfs. We shall have to return to this point. It is also certain that the meaning of "the Other" can not come from the experience nor from a reasoning by analogy effected on the occasion of the experience; on the contrary, it is in the light of the concept of *the Other* that the experience is interpreted. Does that mean that the concept of the Other is *a priori*? This we shall attempt to determine later. But in spite of these undeniable advantages Husserl's theory does not seem to us perceptibly different from Kant's. This is due to the fact that while my empirical Ego is not any more sure than the Other's, Husserl has retained the transcendental subject, which is radically distinct from the Ego and which strongly resembles the Kantian subject. Now what ought to be demonstrated is that it is not the parallelism of the empirical "Egos" which throws doubt on the person but that of the transcendental subjects. This is because actually the Other is *never* that empirical person who is encountered in my experience; he is the transcendental subject to whom this person by nature refers. Thus the true problem is that of the connection of transcendental subjects who are beyond experience. If someone replies that from the start the transcendental subject refers to other subjects *for the constitution* of the noematic whole, it is easy to reply that it refers to them as to *meanings*. The Other here would be a kind of supplementary category which would allow a world to be constituted, not a real being existing beyond this world. Of course the "category" of the Other implies in its very meaning a reference from the other side of the world to a subject, but this reference could be only hypothetical. It has the pure value of the content of a unifying concept; it is valid in and for the world. Its laws are limited to the world, and the Other is by nature outside the world. Furthermore Husserl has removed the very possibility of understanding what can be meant by the extra-mundane *being* of the Other since he defines *being* as the simple indication of an infinite series of operations to be effected. There could be no better way to measure being by knowledge. Now even admitting that knowledge in general measures being, the Other's being is measured in its reality by the knowledge which the Other has of himself, not by that which I have of him. What I must attain is the Other, not as I obtain knowledge of him, but as he obtains knowledge of himself—which is impossible. This would in fact suppose the internal identification of myself with the Other. Thus we find here again that distinction on principle between the Other and myself which does not stem from the exteriority of our bodies but from the simple fact that each of us exists in interiority and that a knowledge valid for interiority can be effected only in interiority which on principle excludes all *knowledge* of the Other as he knows himself—*i.e.*, as he is. Moreover Husserl understood this since he says that "the Other" as he is revealed to our concrete experience is an *absence*. But within Husserl's philosophy, at least, how can one have a full intuition of an absence? The Other is the object of empty intentions, the Other on principle refuses himself to us and flees. The only reality which remains is therefore that of *my* intention; the Other is the empty noema which corresponds to my directing toward the Other, to the extent that he appears concretely in my experience. He is an ensemble of operations of unification and of the constitution of my experience so that he appears as a transcendental concept. Husserl replies to the solipsist that the Other's existence is as sure as that of the world, and Husserl includes in the world my psycho-physical existence. But the solipsist says the same thing: it is as sure, he will say, but no more sure. The existence of the world is measured, he will add, by the knowledge which I have of it; the case will not be otherwise for the existence of the Other.

Formerly I believed that I could escape solipsism by refuting Husserl's concept of the existence of the Transcendental "Ego."[1] At that time I thought that since I had emptied my consciousness of its subject, nothing remained there which was privileged as compared to the Other. But actually although I am still persuaded that the hypothesis of a transcendental subject is useless and disastrous, abandoning it does not help one bit to solve the question of the existence of Others. Even if outside the empirical Ego there is *nothing other* than the consciousness *of* that Ego—that is, a transcendental field without a subject—the fact remains that my affirmation of the Other demands and requires the existence beyond the world of a similar transcendental field. Consequently the only way to escape solipsism would be here again to prove that my transcendental consciousness is in its very being, affected by the extra-mundane existence of other consciousnesses of the same type. Because Husserl has reduced being to a series of meanings, the only conneetion which he has been able to establish between my being and that of the Other is a connection of *knowledge*. Therefore Husserl can not escape solipsism any more than Kant could.

If now instead of observing the rules of chronological succession, we are guided by those of a sort of non-temporal dialectic, we shall find that in the solution which Hegel gives to the problem in the first volume of *The Phenomenology of Mind*, he has made significant progress over Husserl. Here the appearance of the Other is indispensable not to the constitution of the world and of my empirical "Ego" but to the very existence of my consciousness as self-consciousness. In fact as self-consciousness, the Self itself apprehends itself. The equation "Myself = myself" or "I am I" is precisely the expression of this fact. At first this self-consciousness is pure self-identity, pure existence for itself. It has certitude of itself, but this certitude still lacks truth. In fact this certitude would be true only to the extent that its own existence for itself appeared to it as an independent object. Thus self-consciousness is first a syncretic relation without truth between a subject and an object, an object, which is not yet objectified and which is this subject himself. Since the impulse of this consciousness is to realize its concept by becoming conscious of itself in all respects, it tends to make itself valid externally by giving itself objectivity and manifest existence. It is concerned with making the "I am I" explicit and producing itself as an object in order to attain the ultimate stage of development. This state in another sense is naturally the prime mover for the becoming of consciousness; it is self-consciousness in general, which is recognized in other self-consciousnesses and which is identical with them and with itself. The mediator is the *Other*. The Other appears along with myself since self-consciousness is identical with itself by means of the exclusion of every Other. Thus the primary fact is the plurality of consciousnesses, and this plurality is realized in the form of a double, reciprocal relation of exclusion. Here we are then in the presence of that connection by means of an internal negation which was demanded earlier. No external nothingness in-itself separates my consciousness from the Other's consciousness; it is by the very fact of being me that I exclude the Other. The Other is the one who excludes me by being himself, the one whom I exclude by being myself. Consciousnesses are directly supported by one another in a reciprocal imbrication of their being.

This position allows us at the same time to define the way in which the Other appears to me: he is the one who is other than I; therefore he is given as a non-essential object with a character of negativity. But this Other is also a self-consciousness. As such he appears to me as an ordinary object immersed in the being of life. Similarly it is thus that I appear to the Other: as a concrete, sensible, immediate existence. Here Hegel takes his stand on the ground not of a univocal relation which goes from me (apprehended by the *cogito*) to the Other, but of the reciprocal relation which he defines as "the self-apprehension of the one in the other." In fact it is only in so far as each man is opposed to the Other that he is absolutely for himself. Opposite the Other and confronting the Other, each one asserts his right of being individual. Thus the *cogito* itself can not be a point of departure for philosophy; in fact it can be born only in consequence of my appearance for myself as an individual, and this appearance is conditioned by the recognition of the Other. The problem of the Other should not be posited in terms of the *cogito*; on the contrary, the existence of the Other renders the *cogito* possible as the abstract moment when the self is apprehended as an object. Thus the "moment" which Hegel calls *being for the Other* is a necessary stage of the development of self-consciousness; the road of interiority passes through the Other. But the Other is of interest to me only to the extent that he is another Me, a Me-object for Me, and conversely to the extent that he reflects my Me—*i.e.*, is, in so far as I am an object for him. Due to the fact that I must necessarily be an object for myself only over there in the Other, I must obtain from the Other the *recognition* of my being. But if another consciousness must mediate between my consciousness *for itself* and itself, then the being-for-itself of my consciousness—and consequently its being in general—depends on the Other. As I appear to the Other, so I am. Moreover since the Other is such as he appears to me and since my being depends upon the Other, the way in which I appear—that is, the moment of the development of my self-consciousness—depends on the way in which the Other appears to me. The value of the Other's recognition of me depends on the value of my recognition of the Other. In this sense to the extent that the Other apprehends me as bound to a body and immersed in *life*, I am myself only *an Other*. In order to make myself recognized by the Other, I must risk my own life. To risk one's life, in fact, is to reveal oneself as not-bound to the objective form or to any determined existence—as not-bound to life.

But at the same time I pursue the *death* of the Other. This means that I wish to cause myself to be mediated by an Other who is only other—that is, by a dependent consciousness whose essential characteristic is to exist only for another. This will be accomplished at the very moment when I risk my life, for in the struggle against the other I have made an abstraction of my sensible being by *risking* it. On the other hand, the Other prefers life and freedom even while showing that he has not been able to posit himself as not-bound to the objective form. Therefore he remains bound to external things in general; he appears to me and he appears to himself as *non-essential*. He is the *Slave* I am the *Master*; for him it is I who am essence. Thus there appears the famous "Master-Slave" relation which so profoundly influenced Marx. We need not here enter into its details. It is sufficient to observe that the Slave is the truth of the Master. But this unilateral recognition is unequal and insufficient, for the truth of his self-certitude for the Master is a non-essential consciousness; therefore the Master is not certain of *being for himself* as *truth*. In order to attain this truth there is necessary "a moment in which the master does for himself what he does as regards the Other and when the slave does as regards the Other what he does for himself."[2] At this moment there will appear a self-consciousness in general which is recognized in other self-consciousnesses and which is identical with them and with itself.

Thus Hegel's brilliant intuition is to make me depend on the Other *in my being*. I am, he said, a being for-itself which is for-itself only through another.

Therefore the Other penetrates me to the heart. I can not doubt him without doubting myself since "self-consciousness is real only in so far as it recognizes its echo (and its reflection) in another."[3] Since the very doubt implies a consciousness which exists for itself, the Other's existence conditions my attempt to doubt it just as in the work of Descartes my existence conditions systematic doubt. Thus solipsism seems to be put out of the picture once and for all. By proceeding from Husserl to Hegel, we have realized immense progress: first the negation which constitutes the Other is direct, internal, and reciprocal; second, it calls each consciousness to account and pierces it to the deepest part of its being; the problem is posited on the level of inner being, of the universal and transcendental "I;" finally in my essential being I depend on the essential being of the Other, and instead of holding that my being-for-myself is opposed to my being-for-others, I find that being-for-others appears as a necessary condition for my being-for-myself.

Yet in spite of the wide scope of this solution, in spite of the richness and profundity of the detailed insights with which the theory of the Master and the Slave is filled to overflowing, can we be satisfied with it?

To be sure, Hegel has posed the question of the being of consciousnesses. It is being-for-itself and being-for-others which he is studying, and he holds that each consciousness includes the *reality* of the other. Nevertheless it is certain that this ontological problem remains everywhere formulated in terms of knowledge. The mainspring of the conflict of consciousnesses is the effort of each one to transform his self-certitude into *truth*. And we know that this truth can be attained only in so far as my consciousness becomes as *object* for the Other at the same time as the Other becomes an *object* for my consciousness. Thus when idealism asks, "How can the Other be an object for me?" Hegel while remaining on the same ground as idealism replies: if there is in truth a Me for whom the *Other* is an object, this is because there is an *Other* for whom the Me is object. Knowledge here is still the measure of being, and Hegel does not even conceive of the possibility of a being-for-others which is not finally reducible to a "being-as-object." Thus a universal self-consciousness which seeks to disengage itself through all these dialectical phases is by its own admission reducible to a purely empty formula—the "I am I." Yet Hegel writes, "This proposition regarding self-consciousness is void of all content"[4] And in another place he says "[It is] the process of absolute abstraction which consists in surpassing all immediate existence and which results in the purely negative being of consciousness identical with itself." The limiting term of this dialectical conflict, universal self-consciousness, is not enriched in the midst of its avatars; it is on the contrary entirely denuded. It is no more than the "I know that another knows me as me." Of course this is because for idealism absolute being and knowledge are identical. But what does this identification involve?

To begin with, this "I am I," a pure, universal form of identity, has nothing in common with the concrete consciousness which we have attempted to describe in our Introduction. There we established that the being of self-consciousness could not be defined in terms of knowledge. Knowledge begins with *reflection* (*réflexion*) but the game of "the-reflection (*reflet*)-reflecting" is not a subject-object dyad, not even implicitly. Its being does not depend on any transcendent consciousness; rather its mode of being is precisely to be in question for itself. We showed subsequently in the first chapter of Part Two that the relation of the reflection to the reflecting was in no way a relation of identity and could not be reduced to the "Me = Me" or to the "I *am* I" of Hegel. The reflection does not make itself be the reflecting; we are dealing here with a being which nihilates itself in its being and which seeks in vain to dissolve into itself as a *self*. If it is true that this description is the only one which allows us to understand the original fact of consciousness, then we must judge that Hegel has not succeeded in accounting for this abstract doubling of the Me which he gives as equivalent to self-consciousness. Finally we succeeded in getting rid of the pure unreflective consciousness of the transcendental "I" which obscured it and we showed that selfness, the foundation of personal existence, was altogether different from an Ego or from a reference of the Ego to itself. There can be, therefore, no question of defining consciousness in terms of a transcendental ego-ology. In short, consciousness is a concrete being *sui generis*, not an abstract, unjustifiable relation of identity. It is selfness and not the seat of an opaque, useless Ego. Its being is capable of being reached by a transcendental reflection, and there is a *truth* of consciousness which does not depend on the Other; rather the very *being* of consciousness, since it is independent of knowledge, pre-exists its truth. On this plane as for naive realism, being measures truth; for the truth of a reflective intuition is measured by its conformity to being: consciousness was *there* before it was known. Therefore if consciousness is affirmed in the face of the Other, it is because it lays claim to a recognition of its being and not of an abstract truth. In fact it would be ill-conceived to think that the ardent and perilous conflict between master and slave had for its sole stake the recognition of a formula as barren and abstract as the "I am I." Moreover there would be a deception in this very conflict since the end finally attained would be universal self-consciousness, "the intuition of the existing self by the self." Here as everywhere we ought to oppose to Hegel Kierkegaard, who represents the claims of the individual as such. The individual claims his achievement as an individual, the recognition of his concrete being, and of the objective specification of a universal structure. Of course the *rights* which I demand from the Other posit the universality of *self*; respect of persons demands the recognition of my person as universal. But it is my concrete and universal being which flows into this universal and fills it; it is for that *being-there* that I demand rights. The particular is here the support and foundation of the universal; the universal in this case could have no meaning if it did not exist for the purpose of the individual.

This identification of being and knowledge results in a large number of errors or impossibilities. We shall consider them here under *two headings*; that is we shall marshal against Hegel a twofold charge of optimism.

In the first place Hegel appears to us to be guilty of an epistemological optimism. It seems to him that the *truth* of self-consciousness can appear; that is, that an objective agreement can be realized between consciousnesses—by authority of the Other's recognition of me and my recognition of the Other. This recognition can be simultaneous and reciprocal: "I know that the Other knows me as himself." It produces actually and *in truth* the universality of self-consciousness. But the correct statement of the problem of Others renders this passage to the universal impossible. If the Other can in fact refer my "self" to me, then at least at the end of the dialectical evolution there must be a common measure between what I am for him, what he is for me, what I am for myself, what he is for himself. Of course this homogeneity does not exist at the start; Hegel agrees to this. The relation "Master-Slave" is not reciprocal. But Hegel affirms that the reciprocity must be capable of being established. Here at the outset he is creating a confusion—so easy that it seems voluntary—between *being-an-object* and *life*. The Other, he says appears to me as an object. Now the object is *Myself* in the Other. When Hegel wants to define this object-state more exactly, he distinguishes in it three elements: "This self-apprehension by one in the othcr is: (1) The abstract moment of self-identity. (2) Each one, however, has also this particularity, that he manifests himself to the Other as an external object, as an immediately concrete and sensible existence. (3) Each one is absolutely for himself and individual as opposed to the other."[5]

We see that the abstract moment of self-identity is given in the knowledge of the Other. It is given with two other moments of the total structure. But—a curious thing in a philosopher of Synthesis—Hegel did not ask if these three elements did not react on one another in such a way as to constitute a new form resistant to analysis. He defines his point of view in the *Phenomenology of Mind* when he declares that the Other appears first as non-essential (this is the sense of the third moment cited above) and as a "consciousness immersed in the being of life." But here we are dealing with a pure co-existence of the abstract moment and of *life*. It is sufficient therefore that I or the Other risk our life in order that in the very act of offering oneself to danger, we realize the analytical separation of life and consciousness: "What the Other is for each consciousness, each consciousness is for the Other; each consciousness in turn accomplishes in itself by means of its own activity and by means of the activity of the Other, that pure abstraction of being for itself. . . . To present oneself as a pure abstraction of self-consciousness is to reveal oneself as a pure negation of one's objective form, to reveal oneself as not-bound to any determined existence; . . . it is to reveal oneself as not-bound to life."[6] Of course Hegel will say later that by the experience of risk and of the danger of death, self-consciousness learns that life is as essential to it as pure self-consciousness; but this is from a totally different point of view, and the fact still remains that I can always separate, in the Other, the pure *truth* of self-consciousness from his *life*. Thus the slave apprehends the self-consciousness of the master; he is its *truth* although, as we have seen, this truth is still not adequate.[7]

But is it the same thing to say that the Other on principle appears to me as an object and to say that he appears to me as bound to a particular existence, as immersed in *life*? If we remain on the level of pure, logical hypotheses, we shall note first that the Other can in fact be given to a consciousness in the form of an object without that object's being precisely bound to that contingent object which we call a living body. *In fact* our experience presents us only with conscious, living individuals, but *in theory* it must be remarked that the Other is an object for me because he is the Other and not because he appears on the occasion of a body-object; otherwise we should fall back into the illusion of space which we discussed above. Thus what is essential to the Other qua Other is objectivity and not life. Moreover Hegel took this logical affirmation as his point of departure.

But if it is true that the connection between a consciousness and life does not distort the nature of the "abstract moment of self-consciousness" which remains there, immersed, always capable of being discovered, is the case the same for objectivity? In other words, since we know that a consciousness *is* before being known, then is not a known consciousness wholly modified by the very fact that it is known? Is "to appear as an object for a consciousness" still "to be consciousness"? It is easy to reply to this question: the very being of self-consciousness is such that in its being, its being is in question; this means that it is pure interiority. It is perpetually a reference to a *self* which it has to be. Its being is defined by this: that it *is* this being in the mode of being what it is not and of not being what it is. Its being, therefore, is the radical exclusion of all objectivity. I am the one who can not be an object for myself, the one who can not even conceive for myself of existence in the form of an object (save on the plane of the reflective dissociation—but we have seen that reflection is the drama of the being who can not be an object for himself). This is not because of the lack of detachment or because of an intellectual prejudice or of a limit imposed on my knowledge, but because objectivity demands an explicit negation: the object is what I make myself not-be whereas I myself am what I make myself be. I pursue myself everywhere, I can not escape myself, I reapprehend myself from behind. Even if I could attempt to make myself an object, I would already be myself at the heart of that object which I am; and at the very center of that object I should have to be the subject who is looking at it. Moreover this is what Hegel hinted at when he said that the Other's existence is necessary in order for me to be an object for myself. But by holding that self-consciousness is expressed by the "I am I"—*i.e.*, by identifying it with self-knowledge—he failed to derive the consequences of his first affirmations; for he introduced into consciousness something like an object existing potentially to be disengaged without change by the Other. But if to be an object is precisely not-to-be-me, then the fact of being an object for a consciousness radically modifies consciousness not in what it is for itself but in its appearance to the Other. The Other's consciousness is what I can simply contemplate and what because of this fact appears to me as being a pure given instead of being what has to be me. It is what is released to me in universal time (*i.e.*, in the original dispersion of moments) instead of appearing to me within the unity of its own temporalization. For the only consciousness which can appear to me in its own temporalization is *mine*, and it can do so only by renouncing all objectivity. In short the *for-itself* as for-itself can not be known by the Other. The object which I apprehend under the name of the Other appears to me in a radically *other* form. The Other is not a *for-itself* as he appears to me; I do not appear to myself as I am *for-the-Other*. I am incapable of apprehending for myself the self which I am for the Other, just as I am incapable of apprehending on the basis of the *Other-as-object* which appears to me, what the Other is for himself. How then could we establish a universal concept subsuming under the name of self-consciousness, my *consciousness* for myself and (of) myself and my *knowledge* of the Other. But this is not all.

According to Hegel the Other is an object, and I apprehend myself as an object in the Other. But the one of these affirmations destroys the other. In order for me to be able to appear to myself as an object in the Other, I would have to apprehend the Other as subject; that is, to apprehend him in his interiority. But in so far as the Other appears to me as object, my objectivity for him can not appear to me. Of course I apprehend that the Other-as-object *refers to me* by means of intentions and acts, but due to the very fact that he is an object, the Other-as-a-mirror is clouded and no longer reflects anything. These intentions and these acts are things in the world and are apprehended in the Time of the World; they are established and contemplated, their meaning is an object for me. Thus I can only appear to myself as a transcendent quality to which the Other's acts and intentions refer; but since the Other's objectivity destroys my objectivity for him, it is as an internal subject that I apprehend myself as being that to which those intentions and those acts refer. It must be understood that this apprehension of myself by myself is in pure terms of consciousness, not of knowledge; by having to be what I am in form of an ekstatic self-consciousness, I apprehend the Other as an object pointing to me. Thus Hegel's optimism results in failure: between the Other-as-object and Me-as-subject there is no common measure, no more than between self-consciousness and consciousness *of* the Other. I can not know myself *in* the Other if the Other is first an object for me; neither can I apprehend the Other in his true being—that is, in his subjectivity. No universal knowledge can be derived from the relation of consciousnesses. This is what we shall call their ontological separation.

But there is in Hegel another and more fundamental form of optimism. This may be called an ontological optimism. For Hegel indeed truth is truth of the Whole. And he places himself at the vantage point of truth—*i.e.*, of the Whole—to consider the problem of the Other. Thus when Hegelian monism considers the relation of consciousnesses, it does not put itself in any particular consciousness. Although the Whole is to be realized, it is already there as the truth of all which is true. Thus when Hegel writes that every consciousness, since it is identical with itself, is other than the Other, he has established himself in the whole, outside consciousnesses, and he considers them from the point of view of the Absolute. For individual consciousnesses are moments in the whole, moments which by themselves are *unselbständig*, and the whole is a mediator between consciousnesses. Hence is derived an ontological optimism parallel to the epistemological optimism: plurality can and must be surpassed toward the totality. But if Hegel can assert the reality of this surpassing, it is because he has already given it to himself at the outset. In fact he has forgotten his own consciousness; he *is* the Whole, and consequently if he so easily resolves the problem of particular consciousnesses it is because for him there never has been any real problem in this connection. Actually he does not raise the question of the relation between his own consciousness and that of the Other. By effecting completely the abstraction of his own, he studies purely and simply the relation between the consciousnesses of others—*i.e.*, the relation of consciousnesses which are already for him objects whose nature according to him, is precisely that of being a particular type of object,—the subject-object. These consciousnesses from the totalitarian point of view which he has adopted are strictly equivalent to each other although each of them is separated from the rest by a particular privilege.

But if Hegel has forgotten himself, we can not forget Hegel. This means that we are referred back to the *cogito*. In fact, if, as we have established, the being of my consciousness is strictly irreducible to knowledge, then I can not transcend my being toward a reciprocal and universal relation in which I could see my being and that of others as equivalent. On the contrary, I must establish myself *in my being* and posit the problem of the Other in terms of my being. In a word the sole point of departure is the interiority of the *cogito*. We must understand by this that each one must be able by starting out from his own interiority, to rediscover the Other's being as a transcendence which conditions the very being of that interiority. This of necessity implies that the multiplicity of consciousnesses is on principle unsurpassable, for I can undoubtedly transcend myself *toward* a Whole, but I can not establish myself in this Whole so as to contemplate myself and to contemplate the Other. No logical or epistemological optimism can cover the scandal of the plurality of consciousnesses. If Hegel believed that it could, this is because he never grasped the nature of that particular dimension of being which is self-consciousness. The task which an ontology can lay down for itself is to describe this scandal and to found it in the very nature of being, but ontology is powerless to overcome it. It is possible—as we shall see better later—that we may be able to refute solipsism and show that the Other's existence is both evident and certain for us. But even if we could succeed in making the Other's existence share in the apodictic certainty of the *cogito—i.e.*, of my own existence—we should not thereby "surpass" the Other toward any inter-monad totality. So long as consciousnesses exist, the separation and conflict of consciousnesses will remain; we shall simply have discovered their foundation and their true terrain.

What has this long criticism accomplished for us? Simply this: if we are to refute solipsism, then my relation to the Other is first and fundamentally a relation of being to being, not of knowledge to knowledge. We have seen Husserl's failure when on this particular level he measures being by knowledge, and Hegel's when he identifies knowledge and being. But we have equally recognized that Hegel, although his vision is obscured by the postulate of absolute idealism, has been able to put the discussion on its true plane.

In *Sein und Zeit* Heidegger seems to have profited by study of his predecessors and to have been deeply impressed with this twofold necessity: (1) the relation between "human-realities" must be a relation of being; (2) this relation must cause "human-realities" to depend on one another in their essential being. At least his theory fulfills these two requirements. In his abrupt, rather barbaric fashion of cutting Gordian knots rather than trying to untie them, he gives in answer to the question posited a pure and simple *definition*. He has discovered several moments—inseparable except by abstraction—in "being-in-the-world," which characterizes human reality. These moments are "world," "being-in," and "being." He has described the *world* as "that by which human reality makes known to itself what it is;" "being-in" he has defined as *Befindlichkeit* and *Verstand*.[8] We have still to speak of *being*; that is, the mode in which human reality is its being-in-the world. Being, Heidegger tells us, is the *Mit-Sein*—that is, "being-with." Thus human-reality the characteristic of being is that human-reality is its being *with* others. This does not come about by chance. I do not exist *first* in order that subsequently a contingency should make me *encounter* the Other. The question here is of an essential structure of my being. But this structure is not established from outside and from a totalitarian point of view as it was with Hegel. To be sure, Heidegger does not take his departure from the *cogito* in the Cartesian sense of the discovery of consciousness by itself; but the human-reality which is revealed to him and for which he seeks to fix the structures in concepts is his own. "*Dasein ist je meines,*" he writes. It is by making explicit the preontological comprehension which I have of myself that I apprehend being-with-others as an essential characteristic of my being. In short I discover the transcendental relation to the Other as constituting my own being, just as I have discovered that being-in-the-world measures my human-reality. Henceforth the problem of the Other is a false problem. The Other is no longer first a particular existence which I encounter in the world—and which could not be indispensable to my own existence since I existed before encountering it. The Other is the ex-centric limit which contributes to the constitution of my being. He is the test of my being inasmuch as he throws me outside of myself toward structures which at once both escape me and define me; it is this test which originally reveals the Other to me.

Let us observe in addition that the type of connection with the Other has changed. With realism, idealism, Husserl, Hegel, the type of relation between consciousnesses was being-for; the Other appeared to me and even constituted me in so far as he was *for* me or I was *for* him. The problem was the mutual recognition of consciousnesses brought face to face which appeared *in the world* and which confronted each other. "To-be-with" has an altogether different meaning; "with" does not intend the reciprocal relation of recognition and of conflict which would result from the appearance of a human-reality other than mine *in the midst of* the world. It expresses rather a sort of ontological solidarity for the exploitation of this world. The Other is not originally bound to me as an ontic reality appearing in the midst of the world among "instruments" as a type of particular object; in that case he would be already degraded, and the relation uniting him to me could never take on reciprocity. The Other is not an *object*. In his connection with me he remains a human-reality; the being by which he determines me in my being is his pure being apprehended as "being-in-the-world." And we know that the "in" must be understood in the sense of *colo*, *habito*, not of *insum*; to-be-in-the-world is to haunt the world, not to be ensnared in it; and it is in my "being-in-the-world" that the Other determines me. Our relation is not a *frontal* opposition but rather an *oblique* interdependence. In so far as I make a world exist as a complex of instruments which I use for the ends of my human reality, I cause myself to be determined in my being by a being who makes the world exist as a complex of instruments for the ends of his reality. Moreover it is not necessary to understand this being-with as a pure concomitance which is passively received by my being. For Heidegger, to be is to be one's own possibilities; that is, to make oneself be. It is then a mode of being which I make myself be. And it is very true that I am responsible for my being-for the Other in so far as I realize him freely in authenticity or in unauthenticity. It is in complete freedom and by an original choice that, for example, I realize my being-with in the anonymous form of "they." And if I am asked how my "being-with" can exist for-myself, I must reply that through the world I make known to myself what I am. In particular when I am in the unauthentic mode of the "they," the world refers to me a sort of impersonal reflection of my unauthentic possibilities in the form of instruments and complexes of instruments which belong to "everybody" and which belong to me in so far as I am "everybody:" ready-made clothes, common means of transportation, parks, gardens, public places, shelters made for *anyone* who may take shelter there, *etc*. Thus I make myself known as *anybody* by means of the indicative complex of instruments which indicate me as a *Worumwillen*. The unauthentic state—which is my ordinary state in so far as I have not realized my conversion to authenticity—reveals to me my "being-with," not as the relation of one unique personality with other personalities equally unique, not as the mutual connection of "most irreplaceable beings," but as a total interchangeability of the terms of the relation. The determination of the terms is still lacking; I am not opposed to the Other, for I am not "me;" instead we have the social unity of the *they*. To posit the problem on the level of the incommunicability of individual subject was to commit an *ὕστερον πρότερον*,[9] to stand the world on its head. Authenticity and individuality have to be earned: I shall be my own authenticity only if under the influence of the call of conscience (*Ruf des Gewissens*) I launch out toward death with a resolute-decision (*Entschlossenheit*) as toward my own most peculiar possibility. At this moment I reveal myself to myself in authenticity, and I raise others along with myself toward the authentic.

The empirical image which may best symbolize Heidegger's intuition is not that of a conflict but rather a *crew*. The original relation of the Other and my consciousness is not the *you* and *me*; it is the *we*. Heidegger's being-with is not the clear and distinct position of an individual confronting another individual; it is not *knowledge*. It is the mute existence in common of one member of the crew with his fellows, that existence which the rhythm of the oars or the regular movements of the coxswain will render sensible to the rowers and which *will be made manifest* to them by the common goal to be attained, the boat or the yacht to be overtaken, and the entire world (spectators, performance, *etc*.) which is profiled on the horizon. It is on the common ground of this co-existence that the abrupt revelation of my "being-unto-death" will suddenly make me stand out in an absolute "common solitude" while at the same time it raises the others to that solitude.

This time we have indeed been given what we asked for: a being which in its own being implies the Other's being. And yet we can not consider ourselves satisfied. First of all, Heidegger's theory offers us the indication of the solution to be found rather than that solution itself. Even if we should without reservation accept his substitution of "being-with" for "being-for," it would still remain for us a simple affirmation without foundation. Undoubtedly we shall encounter certain empirical states of our being—in particular that to which the Germans give the untranslatable name *Stimmung*[10]—which seem to reveal a co-existence of consciousnesses rather than a relation of opposition. But it is precisely this co-existence which must be explained. Why does it become the unique foundation of our being? Why is it the fundamental type of our relation with others? Why did Heidegger believe that he was authorized to pass from this empirical and ontic establishment of being-with to a position claiming co-existence as the ontological structure of my "being-in-the-world?" And what type of being does this co-existence have? To what extent is the negation which makes the Other *an other* and which constitutes him as non-essential maintained? If we suppress it entirely, are we not going to fall into a monism? And if we are to preserve it as an essential structure of the relation to the Other, then what modification must it undergo in order to lose the character *of opposition* which it had in being-for-others and acquire this character as a connection which creates solidarity and which is the very structure of being-with? And how shall we be able to pass from there to the concrete experience of the Other in the world, as when from my window I see a man walking in the street? To be sure it is tempting to conceive of myself as standing out on the undifferentiated ground of the human by means of the impulse of my freedom, by the choice of my unique possibilities—and perhaps this conception holds an important element of truth. But in this form at least such a view gives rise to serious objections.

First of all, the ontological point of view joins here with the abstract view of the Kantian subject. To say that human reality (even if it is *my* human reality) "is-with" by means of its ontological structure is to say that it is-with by nature—that is, in an essential and universal capacity. Even if this affirmation were proved, it would not enable us to explain any concrete being-with. In other words, the ontological co-existence which appears as the structure of "being-in-the-world" can in no way serve as a foundation to an ontic being-with, such as, for example, the co-existence which appears in my friendship with Pierre or in the couple which Annie and I make. In fact it would be necessary to show that "being-with-Pierre" or "being-with-Annie" is a structure constitutive of my concrete-being. But this is impossible from the point of view which Heidegger has adopted. The Other in the relation "with," taken on the ontological level, can not in fact be concretely determined any more than the directly confronted human-reality of which it is the alter ego; it is an abstract term and hence *unselbständig*, and it does not contain the power of becoming *that* Other—Pierre or Annie. Thus the relation of the *Mit-Sein* can be of absolutely no use to us in resolving the psychological, concrete problem of the recognition of the Other. There are two incommunicable levels and two problems which demand separate solutions.

It may be said that this is only one of the difficulties which Heidegger encounters in passing in general from the ontological level to the ontic level, in passing from "being-in-the-world" in general to my relation with *this* particular instrument, in passing from my being-unto-death, which makes of my death my most essential possibility, to *this* "ontic" death which I shall experience by encountering this or that external existent. But this difficulty can be disguised, if need be, in all other cases since, for example, it is human reality which causes the existence of a world in which a threat of death to human reality is hidden. Better yet, if the world *is*, it is because it is "mortal" in the sense in which we say that a wound is mortal. But the impossibility of passing from one level to the other bursts forth when we meet the problem of the Other. In fact even if in the ekstatic upsurge of its being-in-the-world, human reality makes a world exist, one can not, for all that, say that its being-with causes another human reality to rise up. Of course I am the being by whom "there is" (*es gibt*) being. But are we to say that I am the being by whom "there is" another human-reality? If we understand by that that I am the being for whom there is *for me* another human reality, this is a pure and simple truism. If we mean that I am the being by whom *there are* in general Others, we fall back into solipsism. In fact this human reality "with whom" I am is itself "in-the-world-with-me"; it is the free foundation of a world. (How does this make it *my* world? We can not deduce from the being-with an identity of the worlds "in which" the human realities are.) Human reality is its own possibilities. It is then for itself without having to wait for me to make its being exist in the form of the "there is." Thus I can constitute a world as "mortal," but I can not constitute a human-reality as a concrete being which is its own possibilities. My being-with, apprehended from the standpoint of "my" being, can be considered only as a pure exigency founded in *my* being; it does not constitute the slightest proof of the Other's existence, not the slightest bridge between me and the Other.

More precisely, this ontological relation between me and an abstract Other, due to the very fact that it defines in general my relation to others, is far from facilitating a particular ontic relation between me and Pierre; in fact it renders impossible any concrete connection between my being and a particular Other given in my experience. If my relation with the Other is *a priori,* it thereby exhausts all possibility of relation with others. Empirical and contingent relations can be only the specifications of it, not particular cases. There can be specifications of a law only under two circumstances: either the law is derived inductively from empirical, particular facts, and that is not the case here; or else it is *a priori* and unifies experience, as the Kantian concepts do. Actually in this latter case, its scope is restricted to the limits of experience: I find in things only what I have put into them. Now the act of relating two concrete "beings-in-the-world" can not belong to *my* experience; and it therefore escapes from the domain of *being-with*. But as the law precisely *constitutes* its own domain, it excludes *a priori* every real fact which it has not constructed. The existence of time as an *a priori* form of my sensibility would *a priori* exclude me from all connection with a noumenal time which had the characteristics of a being. Thus the existence of an ontological and hence *a priori* "being-with" renders impossible all ontic connection with a concrete human-reality which would arise *for-itself* as an absolute transcendent. The "being-with," conceived as a structure of my being, isolates me as surely as the arguments for solipsism.

The reason for this is that Heidegger's *transcendence* is a concept in bad faith: it aims, to be sure, at surpassing idealism, and it succeeds in so far as idealism presents us with a subjectivity at rest in itself and contemplating its own images. But the idealism thus surpassed is only a bastard form of idealism, a sort of empirical-critical psychologism. Undoubtedly Heidegger's human-reality "exists outside itself." But this existence outside itself is precisely Heidegger's definition of the *self*. It resembles neither the Platonic [Neo-Platonic?] ekstasis where existence is really alienation, existence in an Other, nor Malebranche's vision in God, our own conception of the ekstasis and of the internal negation. Heidegger does not escape idealism; his flight outside the self, as an *a priori* structure of his being, isolates him as surely as the Kantian reflection on the *a priori* conditions of our experience. In fact what human-reality rediscovers at the inaccessible limit of this flight outside itself is still the self: the flight outside the self is a flight toward the self, and the world appears as the pure distance between the self and the self.

Consequently it would be in vain to look in *Sein und Zeit* for a simultaneous surpassing of all idealism and of all realism. Heidegger's attempt to bring human-reality out of its solitude raises those same difficulties which idealism generally encounters when it tries to found the existence of concrete beings which are similar to us and which as such escape our experience, which even as they are being constituted do not arise from our *a priori*. He seems to escape isolation because he takes the "outside of self" sometimes as being "outside-of-self-toward-self" and sometimes as "outside-self-in-others." But the second interpretation of "outside-of-self," which Heidegger surreptitiously slides in through his devious reasoning, is strictly incompatible with the first. Human-reality at the very heart of its ekstases remains alone. It is here that we can derive a new and valid insight as the result of our critical examination of Heidegger's teaching: Human-reality remains alone because the Other's existence has the nature of a contingent and irreducible fact. We *encounter* the Other; we do not constitute him. And if this fact still appears to us in the form of a necessity, yet it does not belong with those "conditions of the possibility of our experience" or—if you prefer—with the ontological necessity. If the Other's existence is a necessity, it is a "contingent necessity;" that is, it is of the same type as the factual necessity which is imposed on the *cogito*. If the Other is to be capable of being given to us, it is by means of a direct apprehension which leaves to the encounter its character as facticity, just as the *cogito* itself leaves all its facticity to my own thought, a facticity which nevertheless shares in the apodicity of the *cogito* itself—*i.e.*, in its indubitability.

This long exposition of doctrine will not therefore have been useless if it enables us to formulate the necessary and sufficient conditions under which a theory of the existence of others can be valid.

(1) Such a theory can not offer a new *proof* of the existence of others, or an argument better than any other against solipsism. Actually if solipsism is to be rejected, this can not be because it is impossible or, if you prefer, because nobody is truly solipsistic. The Other's existence will always be subject to doubt, at least

if one doubts the Other only in words and abstractly, in the same way that without really being able to conceive of it, I can write, "I doubt my own existence." In short the Other's existence can not be a *probability*. Probability can concern only objects which appear in our experience and from which new effects can appear in our experience. There is probability only if a validation or invalidation of it is at every moment possible. Thus since the Other on principle and in its "For-itself" is outside my experience, the probability of his existence as *Another Self* can never be either validated or invalidated; it can be neither believed nor disbelieved, it can not even be measured; it loses therefore its very being as probability and becomes a pure fictional conjecture. In the same way M. Lalande[11] has effectively shown that an hypothesis concerning the existence of living beings on the planet Mars will remain purely conjectural with no chance of being either true or false so long as we do not have at our disposal instruments or scientific theories enabling us to produce facts validating or invalidating this hypothesis. But the structure of the Other is on principle such that no new experiment will ever be able to be conceived, that no new theory will come to validate or invalidate the hypothesis of his existence, that no instrument will come to reveal new facts inspiring me to affirm or to reject this hypothesis. Therefore if the Other is not immediately present to me, and if his existence is not as sure as my own, all conjecture concerning him is entirely lacking in meaning. But if I do not conjecture about the Other, then, precisely, I affirm him. A theory of the Other's existence must therefore simply question me in my being, must make clear and precise the meaning of that affirmation; in particular, far from inventing a proof, it must make explicit the very foundation of that certainty. In other words Descartes has not *proved* his existence. Actually I have always known that I existed, I have never ceased to practice the *cogito*. Similarly my resistance to solipsism—which is as lively as any I should offer to an attempt to doubt the *cogito*—proves that I have always known that the Other existed, that I have always had a total though implicit *comprehension* of his existence, that this "pre-ontological" comprehension comprises a surer and deeper understanding of the nature of the Other and the relation of his being to my being than all the theories which have been built around it. If the Other's existence is not a vain conjecture, a pure fiction, this is because there is a sort of *cogito* concerning it. It is this *cogito* which we must bring to light by specifying its structures and determining its scope and its laws.

(2) On the other hand, Hegel's failure has shown us that the only point of departure possible is the Cartesian *cogito*. Moreover the *cogito* alone establishes us on the ground of that factual necessity which is the necessity of the Other's existence. Thus what for lack of a better term we called the *cogito* of the Other's existence is merged with my own *cogito*. The *cogito* examined once again, must throw me outside it and onto the Other, just as it threw me outside upon the In-

itself; and this must be done not by revealing to me an *a priori* structure of myself which would point toward an equally *a priori* Other but by disclosing to me the concrete, indubitable presence of a particular, concrete Other, just as it has already revealed to me my own incomparable, contingent but necessary, and concrete existence. Thus we must ask the For-itself to deliver to us the For-others; we must ask absolute immanence to throw us into absolute transcendence. In my own inmost depths I must find not *reasons for believing* that the Other exists but the Other himself as not being me.

(3) What the *cogito* must reveal to us is not the Other-as-object. For a long time now it must have been obvious that what is called an *object* is said to be *probable*. If the Other is an object for me, he refers me to probability. But probability is founded solely on the infinite congruity of our representations. Since the Other is neither a representation nor a system of representations nor a necessary unity of our representations, he can not be probable: he can not *at first* be an object. Therefore if he is *for us*, this can be neither as a constitutive factor of our knowledge of the world nor as a constitutive factor of our knowledge of the self, but as one who "interests" our being, and that not as he contributes *a priori* to constitute our being but as he interests it concretely and "ontically" in the empirical circumstances of our facticity.

(4) If we attempt somehow regarding the Other what Descartes attempted to do for God with that extraordinary "proof by the idea of perfection" which is wholly animated by the intuition of transcendence, then for our apprehension of the Other qua Other we are compelled to reject a certain type of negation which we have called an external negation. The Other must appear to the *cogito* as *not being* me. This negation can be conceived in two ways: either it is a pure, external negation, and it will separate the Other from myself as one substance from another substance—and in this case all apprehension of the Other is by definition impossible; or else it will be an internal negation, which means a synthetic, active connection of the two terms, each one of which constitutes itself by denying that it is the other. This negative relation will therefore be reciprocal and will possess a two fold interiority: This means first that the multiplicity of "Others" will not be a *collection* but a *totality* (in this sense we admit that Hegel is right) since each Other finds his being in the Other.[12] It also means that this Totality is such that it is on principle impossible for us to adopt "the point of view of the whole." In fact we have seen that no abstract concept of consciousness can result from the comparison of my being-for-myself with my object-state for the Other. Furthermore this totality—like that of the For-itself—is a detotalized totality; for since existence-for-others is a radical refusal of the Other, no totalitarian and unifying synthesis of "Others" is possible.

It is in the light of these few observations that we in turn shall now attack the question of The Other.

Notes

1. "La transcendance de l'Ego." 1937.
2. *Phénoménologie de l'Esprit*, p. 148. Edition Cosson.
3. *Propedeutik*, p. 20, first edition of the complete works.
4. *Propedeutik*, p. 20.
5. *Propedeutik*, p. 18.
6. *Phénoménologie de l'Esprit*, 148.
7. *Phénoménologie de l'Esprit*, 148.
8. Tr. Roughly, *Befindlichkeit* is "finitude" and *Verstand* "comprehension."
9. Tr. Correction for *ὑ̓στηρον πρόιηρον*, obviously a misprint.
10. Tr. Literally "pitch" or "tuning." Perhaps the nearest English equivalent is "sympathy" in its original Greek sense of feeling or experiencing *with* someone.
11. *Les théories de l'induction et de l'expérimentation.*
12. *Chaque autrui trouve son être en l'autre.*

CHAPTER 4

"'*Entäusserung*' ('Externalization') as the Central Philosophical Concept of *The Phenomenology of Mind*"

—from *The Young Hegel: Studies in the Relations between Dialectics and Economics* (1948)

Georg Lukács

Before turning to a detailed analysis of the concept of 'externalization' it may be as well to recapitulate briefly the growth of the problem and the history of the concept in Hegel's works. It will be remembered that in his republican phase in Berne the term 'positivity' was used to describe an institution or a complex of ideas standing opposed in lifeless objectivity to the subjectivity, and above all the praxis of man. Even at that early date 'positivity' was used to define the specific character of modern society. At that time, however, Hegel contrasted it rigidly with the 'nonpositive' age of Greek democracy. His philosophy of history culminated in the revolutionary hope that the revival of antiquity in and through the French Revolution would lead to a new era of freedom, and the true hegemony of man, an era without 'positivity'.

The disappointment of these hopes which triggered off the Frankfurt crisis in his thought brought in its wake a more historical and dialectical conception of 'positivity'. Modern institutions were no longer hopelessly 'positive' from the very outset, but instead Hegel became increasingly interested in discovering in detail just how something *became* 'positive', how the relations between man's social praxis and the institutions of society originate, how they decline and how they are transformed in the course of history. This greater concreteness went hand in hand with his study of the intellectual implications of English economic theory, with his deepening interest in the economic problems of capitalism and his growing insight into them. And we have seen also how Hegel gradually began to formulate his own specific concept of dialectics in the course of his own intellectual crisis. The further the process advanced and the more mature Hegel's own philosophy became, the more the concept of 'positivity' receded into the background. It never disappeared entirely, but, increasingly, it came to be used in the sense in which lawyers and theologians speak of positive law or positive theology. The philosophical generality of the Berne and Frankfurt periods vanished. Typically, however, the word 'positive' embodied in Hegel's philosophy could not allow the great age of an institution to be used to justify its further existence. For many years after the Jena period Hegel continued to treat this sort of 'positivity' as the lifeless detritus of history, to be cleared away as soon as possible.

Thus the maturing and deepening of Hegel's philosophy only eliminated the concept of 'positivity', not the problem to which it had referred in Frankfurt, namely the dialectical relation of the praxis of man in society to the objects he has created. It is not necessary to rehearse here the results of our analysis either of the social content or the philosophical terminology of Hegel's Jena period. In the course of his uninterrupted experimentation with terminology, what emerged more and more clearly was that the primal immediacy, the natural, has to be overcome and is overcome in the social praxis of man. It is replaced by a system of institutions created by man in the course of his own labours and endeavours. These labours not only create the institutions of society; they also transform the human subject since they annul his original immediacy, alienating the subject from itself.

In the course of his debate first with subjective idealism and later with objective idealism in its Schellingian form, Hegel developed a new terminology with which to describe these novel ideas and to translate into the general language of philosophy the social phenomena that he had come to understand in his study of history and economics. In this way concepts such as 'mediation' and 'reflection' acquired their specifically Hegelian significance. Likewise, the abstract theory of contradictions and their unity, first formulated in Frankfurt, evolved into the mature theory of the movement of contradictions and their supersession. In the course of this development the terms *Entäusserung* (externalization) and *Entfremdung* (alienation) came to occupy a central position in the Hegelian system. It is difficult to establish the exact chronology here. We noted that the Lectures of 1803–4 still operated to a great extent with Schelling's terminology. In the Lectures of 1805–6 the term *Entäusserung* occurs repeatedly, but is by no means dominant, although in both lecture courses, particularly the later ones, very many of the social and philosophical problems which become the problems of 'externalization' in the *Phenomenology* are already present and given the sort of treatment they receive later, but without being gathered together under the general heading of 'externalization'. Not until the *Phenomenology* do we find the new conceptual system fully worked out and applied.

In themselves there is nothing novel about the terms *Entäusserung* and *Entfremdung*. They are simply German translations of the English word 'alienation'. This was used in works on economic theory to betoken the sale of a commodity, and in works on natural law to refer to the loss of an aboriginal freedom, the handing-over or alienation of freedom to the society which came into being as a result of a social contract. Philosophically, the term *Entäusserung* was first used, to the best of my knowledge, by Fichte for whom it meant both that the positing of an object implied an externalization or alienation of the subject and that the object was to be thought of as an 'externalized' act of reason.[1]

The same problem but with a different terminology turns up in the early works of Schelling. We quote his comments on it since they testify both to his flair for discerning new problems and to his extremism, his tendency to exaggerate his own dialectical insights until they suddenly harden out into sterile dogmas, very much in contrast to Hegel. Schelling uses the term 'to condition' (*bedingen*) to describe what Hegel will later call 'externalization'.

> 'To *condition* is the name we give to the action by virtue of which something becomes a *thing*; *conditioned* (*bedingt*) is what has become a thing (*Ding*). And this makes clear at the same time that no thing can be posited *as a thing by itself*, i.e. an unconditioned thing (*ein unbedingtes Ding*) is a contradiction. For that which is *unconditioned* is something which has not been and cannot be made into a thing.'[2]

There can be no doubt that Schelling is touching upon the same problem with which Hegel had been so profoundly preoccupied. In contrast to Hegel, Schelling easily hits upon an elegant and ingenious solution which 'only' suffers from the slight defect that it opens up a yawning abyss between praxis and the object, thus rendering the entire problem intractable for Schelling himself. However, since these terminological experiments are merely episodes as far as Fichte and Schelling are concerned, episodes which exert no lasting influence on the problems with which they were most deeply concerned, there is no reason to deny Hegel the credit of having developed an original conceptual system in the *Phenomenology,* notwithstanding the use made of certain elements by his predecessors.

In the *Phenomenology* the term 'externalization' is deployed at a very high level of philosophical generality. It has flown far above its original use in economics and social theory. Nevertheless, it is possible to establish with some precision the various meanings given to it by Hegel and which derive from its original use as well as its later philosophical accretions.

We may in fact distinguish three stages in the Hegelian concept of 'externalization'. (1) It refers firstly to the complex subject-object relation inseparably bound up with all work and all human activity of an economic or social kind.

What is involved here is the problem of the objectivity of society, of its development, of the laws governing that development, all this in the general context of the idea that men make their own history themselves. History, then, is regarded as a complex dialectical evolution of the human race, a process rich in contradictions and interactions, propelled by the praxis of socialized individuals. Hegel's achievement in establishing the dialectical relations between subjectivity and objectivity represents a prodigious step forward. On the one hand, it is a great advance on the old materialists who had been unable to reconcile the importance of subjective human praxis with the objectivity of what were largely thought of as 'natural' laws of society (e.g. the climate) and so were unable to move beyond the antinomies resulting from an exaggerated emphasis on one or other of these 'natural' phenomena. On the other hand, it is also a great advance on Kant and Fichte in whose writings necessity and objectivity constitute a world in themselves utterly alien to and different from freedom and praxis. As we have seen, Schelling made efforts to go a step further in his objective-idealist phase but his innovations turned out to be no more than obscure premonitions which were put forward in a declamatory rather than true philosophical manner.

(2) Secondly, there is the specifically capitalist form of 'externalization,' i.e. what Marx would later call 'fetishism'. Naturally, Hegel has no clear insight into what is involved here, if only because his view of the economic base of class conflict does not go beyond an empirical division into rich and poor, and this is not sufficient for him to deduce any significant theoretical conclusions. But he undoubtedly has intimations of the problems arising from the fetishization of objects in capitalist society, and it must be stated that in this respect he stands alone in classical German idealism. Needless to say, the absence of a grounding in economic theory leads him constantly to confuse this class of 'externalized' social objectivity with the first, i.e. he regards many things as the products of social work, of human praxis in general, which are in actuality only the fetish-forms of objectivity specific to capitalism, and vice versa. Despite this defect which is one of the central foci of Marx's criticism there are undoubtedly powerful tendencies in Hegel to explain the fetishized objectivity of socio-economic formations in terms of the social relations between men.

Here, too, idealism leads Hegel badly astray and in the process of reducing social formations to human relations he frequently overlooks the mediating role of things. Frequently, but not invariably. This particular form of idealism occurs, to the best of my knowledge, earlier in Hegel than elsewhere, although it is not uncommon in early attempts to explain fetishized forms of objectivity. It becomes prominent, for example, in the break-up of the Ricardo school. Marx comments on it in his discussion of Hodgskin:

> 'The whole objective world, the "world of commodities", vanishes here as a mere aspect, as the merely passing activity, constantly performed anew, of socially producing men. Compare this "idealism" with the

> crude, material fetishism into which the Ricardian theory develops in the writings "of this incredible cobbler", MacCulloch, where not only the difference between man and animal disappears but even the difference between a living organism and an inanimate object. And then let them say that as against the lofty idealism of bourgeois political economy, the proletarian opposition has been preaching a crude materialism directed exclusively towards the satisfaction of coarse appetites.'[3]

Of course, the profound differences between Hodgskin and Hegel should not be overlooked. Hodgskin is able to draw socialist conclusions from Ricardo's theory of value, albeit confused and contradictory ones. Hegel, as we saw, had not even understood all the problems and contradictions in Adam Smith's theories at the time when he was working on the *Phenomenology*. There can be no question of him deriving socialist ideas from there. And it goes without saying that Hodgskin is and had to be a good deal clearer and more penetrating than Hegel on all such questions. Nevertheless, there is no gain saying that Hegel's thoughts were moving powerfully in this direction and that he was the only thinker concerned to deduce philosophical conclusions from these economic facts.

(3) Thirdly, there is a broad philosophical extension of the concept 'externalization' which then comes to be synonymous with 'thinghood' or objectivity. This is the form in which the history of objectivity is portrayed: objectivity as a dialectical moment in the journey of the identical subject-object on its way back to itself via 'externalization'. Hegel says:

> 'The mind's immediate existence, *conscious life*, has two aspects—cognition and objectivity which is opposed to or negative of the subjective function of knowing. Since it is in the medium of consciousness that mind is developed and brings out its various moments, this opposition between the factors of conscious life is found at each stage in the evolution of mind, and all the various moments appear as modes or forms of consciousness. The scientific statement of the course of this development is a science of the *experience* through which consciousness passes; the substance and its process are considered as the object of consciousness. Consciousness knows and comprehends nothing but what falls within its experience; for what is found in experience is merely spiritual substance, and, moreover, *object* of itself. Mind, however, becomes object, for it consists in the process of becoming an *other to itself*, i.e. an *object for its own self*, and in transcending this otherness.'[4]

The essential tendencies of the mystification involved in the retraction of 'externalization' are already familiar to us. But we know too that by thinking of 'externalization' as a process and by regarding the absolute, the identical subject-object, as the end-product of that process, he opened up entirely new terrain in which to explore the implications of the essential dialectical determinations of objective reality 'so that, ultimately, the Hegelian system represents merely a materialism idealistically turned upside down in method and content.'[5]

It would be a grave error to take Engels' statement to imply that one had merely to turn Hegel the right, i.e. the materialist, way up again. Our investigations have shown that, on the contrary, quite crucial problems have been distorted by the idealist method and that in the treatment of individual issues, important insights continually rub shoulders with idealist distortions, sometimes even in the same sentence. It would also be wrong to focus on the large area opened up to analysis which we have emphasized for the sake of simplicity and clarity, as if all were well on the journey towards the absolute and the idealist mystifications intervened only at the very end. We believe that our earlier concrete analyses have shown such ideas to be misconceived. Here, we must confine ourselves to a statement of the most important problems.

The false equation of 'externalization' and 'thinghood' or objectivity leads Hegel to make quite false distinctions in his definition of nature and society and his attempt to distinguish between them. According to his view both nature and history are 'externalizations' of the spirit. But nature is an eternal externalization, its movement is a pseudo-movement, a movement of the subject; in Hegel's theory nature has no real history.

> 'This last form into which spirit passes, *nature*, is its living immediate process of development. Nature—spirit divested of self (externalized)—is, in its actual existence, nothing but this eternal process of abandoning its (nature's) own independent *subsistence*, and the movement which reinstates subject.'[6]

In contrast to this, 'externalization' in the social praxis of the human race, i.e. in history, is an 'externalization' of the spirit in time, that is to say, there is a real process of becoming and real history. Of course, in the end, as we shall see, even this turns out to be a pseudo-movement, despite Hegel's intentions. About this form of 'externalization', Hegel writes as follows:

> 'The other aspect, however, in which spirit comes into being, *history*, is the process of becoming in terms of knowledge, a *conscious self-mediating process*—spirit externalized and emptied into time. But this form of externalization is, similarly, the emptying of itself by itself; the negative is negative of itself. This way of becoming presents a slow procession and succession of spiritual shapes, a gallery of pictures, each of which is endowed with the entire wealth of spirit, and moves so

slowly just for the reason that the self has to permeate and assimilate all this wealth of its substance. Since its accomplishment consists in spirit knowing *what it is*, in fully *comprehending* its substance, this knowledge means its *concentrating itself on itself* (*Insichgehen*), a state in which spirit leaves its external existence behind and gives its embodiment over to recollection (*Erinnerung*).'[7]

The immediate methodological implications of the distinction between the form assumed by 'externalization' in nature and history is something we have already observed in the *Phenomenology*. In Section B where Hegel focuses on real history, the problems of nature are as good as non-existent. They are treated only in Sections A and C, and in the latter, above all, Hegel's view of the objectivity of nature contributes in no small measure to the mystifications of the problems of dialectics. But over and above that, it spells the end of any real interaction between nature and society, as well as the history of nature during the development of society. As a disciple of the Enlightenment Hegel is by no means ignorant of the relations between nature and society and of those social developments determined by natural conditions (such as the climate). In his later philosophy of history these problems reappear, but only as part of the general introduction to history on the substance of which they do not really impinge.

Even more revealing is the fact that, great dialectician of history though he was, he does not even mention the historical development of nature itself, despite Kant's great discoveries in the field of cosmogony (which, incidentally, remained quite without influence on Kant's own philosophical system and failed to historicize his own view of nature). Nor did the important efforts of some others of his contemporaries, above all Goethe, to introduce the notion of development into the organic world influence him in this direction.

There is, of course, a development of a sort in Hegel's philosophy of nature, but it is precisely not historical: it does not unfold in time. Temporal development is reserved by him for history in the narrower sense, for the history of human society. This is not to deny the existence of contrary tendencies in his work. But they never get beyond the initial stages whereupon they break off abruptly. In the *Jena Logic*, for example, there is an incipient analysis of the earth in evolutionary terms as the theatre of human history. However, the idea that there has been history, but there is none any more, then makes its appearance with a vengeance: according to Hegel by the time human history is launched, the history of the earth is completed and has ceased utterly to develop further. And even while it was still developing the picture Hegel gives of it is highly contradictory. We quote his final summary since this is typical of the whole:

'The present moment reached by the earth in its cycle is one of immobility; it has emerged from its process; in this moment it really is the

> whole, and the character of determinate existence has been stamped on it, a determinate existence, however, which endures, since it is removed from time. . . . The earth, then, as this totality, represents this image of process without the process itself. . . . The living process of the earth is present only in its elements, not in its totality. . . . For this content, then, the process is something in the past; to infuse life into it through time and to represent the moments of its formation as a sequence, does not impinge upon its content.'[8]

Since all of Hegel's statements on this theme are full of contradictions and since we have always found important dialectical and historical discoveries concealed beneath his mystifications it will not come as a surprise to learn that his over-sharp distinction between 'externalization', i.e. objectivity, in nature and in history also has its positive side, and that here too Hegel is on the track of important discoveries. His aim is to clarify the particular character of human existence and he is condemned to do so in an age when the thinkers closest to him in the field of the dialectics of objective idealism (Schelling and Goethe) were excessively preoccupied with nature. It was an age in which the ideas of such men were taken up and exaggerated and developed into a romantic, mystical cult of nature philosophy which threatened to engulf all efforts to achieve a really concrete analysis of the historical development of society in an all-consuming formalist mysticism of the 'eternal' and the 'natural'.

In circumstances such as these it is easy to understand how Hegel came to make such an abrupt distinction between nature and history, and even to make a moral issue of the superiority of spirit over nature. There is a very interesting statement to that effect in the Jena Lectures:

> 'In actual fact the individual spirit can depend on the energy of his own character and can assert his individuality, regardless of nature. His negative attitude towards nature although it differs from himself, scorns its power, and in this scorn he holds nature at arm's length, preserving his freedom. And in fact the individual is only great and free in proportion to the extent of this contempt for nature.'[9]

This extreme expression of Hegel's position should not blind us to the fact that he is speaking here of the individual man who acts and that therefore his observations here do not cancel out or in any sense contradict his polemic against the violation of nature at the hands of the subjective idealism of Fichte.

Marx was fully appreciative of Hegel's attitude here, one which frequently recurs in his later works. Lafargue reports that Milrx often quoted the following remark of Hegel's with approval:

> 'Even the criminal thought of a malefactor has more grandeur and nobility than the wonders of the heavens.'[10]

The aim of such paradoxical formulations is to make a sharp distinction between specific sides of man's social evolution and evolution in nature. And even if Hegel did not take the evolution of nature into account he nevertheless touched upon a fundamental determination of the evolution of society: the idea that men make their own history. Marx too endorses this distinction between the two forms of history, though of course within the context of a true appreciation of their objectivity and unity. Thus, for example, after talking of Darwin's idea of Nature's Technology he calls for a critical history of human technology:

> 'And would not such a history be easier to compile, since, as Vico says, human history differs from natural history in this, that we have made the former, but not the latter?'[11]

This side of human history was correctly intuited by Hegel, as by Vico, even though he failed to recognize, and hence mystified, the other side, the history of nature.

To recognize and to give Hegel the credit for having both constructed a rich and in many respects valid picture of human history and also for having discovered many of the essential determinations of historiography, is not to deny the distortions introduced by the mystificatory aspects of 'externalization'. Here, too, through his conception of the whole Hegel cancels out what he had so laboriously, thoroughly and ingeniously built up in the course of his analysis of the parts. We have already mentioned that the historical process as a whole has a definite goal, one which takes the form of its own self-annulment, its own return into the identical subject-object. Similarly, we have seen that Hegel thinks of history in general as an 'externalization' of spirit into time. Hence the reintegration of history in the absolute subject implies the annulment of time, which in its turn is the consequence of the annulment of objectivity. It is not the case that the dialectical process of history is suspended between two mystical points, with the beginning and end of time defined in terms of religious categories of the creation, etc. In Hegel's scheme, the beginning and end of the historical process coincide, i.e. the end of history is prefigured in its beginning. What we have here, then, is the same negation of a brilliant conception by an unbounded, all-engulfing process of generalization as we found in our discussion of Hegel's teleological ideas. He is quite explicit about this aspect of his historical scheme:

> 'But this substance, which is spirit, is the *development* of itself explicitly to what it is *inherently and implicitly*; and only as this process of reflecting itself into itself is it essentially and in truth *spirit*. It is inherently the movement which is the process of knowledge—the transforming of that *inherent nature* into *explicitness*, of *substance* into *subject*, of the object of *consciousness* into the object of *self-consciousness*, i.e.

> into an object that is at the same time transcended—in other words into the *concept*. This transforming process is a cycle that returns into itself, a cycle that presupposes its beginning, and reaches its beginning only at its end.'[12]

This end, however, is absolute spirit at its peak, as absolute knowledge, as philosophy. History is reduced to a process which is acted out in reality but which reaches its consummation, the goal immanent in it, the nature implicitly contained in it from the very beginning, only in philosophy, in a post-festum commentary on the path leading up to it. This idea is of such overwhelming significance for the view of history in the *Phenomenology* that it occupies a central position in the conclusion of the entire work:

> 'But *recollection* (*Er-innerung*) has conserved that experience, and is the inner being, and, in fact, the higher form of the substance. While, then, this phase of spirit begins all over again its formative development, apparently starting solely from itself, yet at the same time it commences at a higher level. The realm of spirits developed in this way, and assuming definite shape in existence, constitutes a succession, where one detaches and sets loose the other, and each takes over from its predecessor the empire of the spiritual world. The goal of the process is the revelation of the depth of spiritual life, and this is the *absolute concept*. This revelation consequently means superseding its "depth", is its "extension" or *spatial* embodiment, the negation of this inwardly, self-centred ego—a negativity which is its self-relinquishment, its externalization, or its substance: and this revelation is also its *temporal* embodiment, in that this externalization in its very nature relinquishes (externalizes) itself, and so exists at once in its spatial "extension" as well as in its "depth" or the self. The *goal*, which is absolute knowledge or spirit knowing itself as spirit, finds its pathway in the recollection of spiritual forms as they are in themselves and as they accomplish the organization of their spiritual kingdom. Their conservation, looked at from the side of their free existence appearing in the form of contingency, is *history*; looked at from the side of their intellectually comprehended organization, it is the *science of the ways in which knowledge appears*. Both together, or history comprehended (*begriffen*), form at once the recollection and the Golgotha of absolute spirit, the reality, the truth, the certainty of its throne, without which it were lifeless, solitary and alone. Only
>
> The chalice of this realm of spirits
> Foams forth to God his own Infinitude.'[13]

This amounts to the self-annulment of history. History is transformed into the mere realization of a goal inherent in its subject, its spirit from the very outset. At the same time, its immanent reality is also annulled: history does not contain its own real autonomous laws of motion, but on the contrary, the latter only really exist and come into their own in the science that comprehends and annuls history, i.e. in absolute knowledge. But this annuls the whole scheme of history elaborated by objective idealism. The spirit which is supposed to make history and whose very essence is supposed to be the fact that it is the actual driving force, the motor of history, ends up by turning history into a mere simulacrum, as Marx has argued in *The Holy Family*:

> 'Hegel is . . . inconsistent . . . because according to him the absolute spirit makes history only in *appearance*. For as the absolute spirit becomes *conscious* of itself as the creative world-spirit only in the philosopher and *post festum*, its making of history exists only in the consciousness, in the opinion and conception of the philosopher, i.e. in the speculative imagination.'[14]

All this—and we have drawn attention only to the most essential points—is the necessary consequence of Hegel's concept of 'externalization'. It is at this point that the young Marx's great criticism of Hegel's central dilemma intervenes in the debate. This criticism is one of the crucial texts in the process of turning the idealist dialectic into a materialist one and in the criticism of Hegelian idealism. At the same time it is a *locus classicus* establishing continuity between the dialectical heritage and the new science of dialectical materialism.

In the *Economic and Philosophic Manuscripts* of 1844 Marx provides a comprehensive and systematic criticism of the Hegelian dialectic.[15] This criticism has two methodological characteristics of interest to us.

(1) In the first place, it concentrates on *The Phenomenology of Mind*, and within this, on Hegel's conception of 'externalization' and its supersession. This emphasis, meaningful in itself, can also be explained by reference to the polemical needs of the period, since the subjectivization of Hegelian philosophy carried out by the Young Hegelians, Bruno Bauer and Max Stirner in particular, was based largely on the *Phenomenology* and extends its mystification into realms not dreamed of by Hegel. The philosophical annihilation of this Left-Hegelianism was an important premise both of the new science of dialectical materialism and also of the theoretical and practical programme of the workers' party then in the process of formation. Marx's arguments here, then, are in a sense preparatory to the *Communist Manifesto*.

On the other hand, as we shall see, the critique of Hegel's concept of 'externalization' forms an important element of Feuerbach's criticism of Hegel and hence of the great shift from idealism to materialism that took place in Germany in the 1840s. Feuerbach's criticism is a concentrate of the virtues as well as the defects and limitations of Feuerbach's materialism. Marx's critique of Hegel's 'externalization' shows him entering into possession of the Feuerbachian heritage and at the same time we see him transcending the old materialism dialectically and leaving it behind.

(2) The second important characteristic of Marx's critique is that for the first time in Germany since Hegel himself it combines economic and philosophical perspectives in its treatment of the problems of society and philosophy. Needless to say, this functions at an incomparably higher level in Marx than in Hegel, and this is as true of the philosophical as of the economic aspect. Philosophically, as we know, the problem is the replacement of idealist by materialist dialectics. The critique of idealism here is based on a much greater knowledge of economics than was available to Hegel. Marx's economic observations already contain a *socialist critique* of the ideas of the classics of economic theory. (The brilliant essay of the young Engels in the *Deutsch-Französische Jahrbücher* had already appeared a little earlier.) And it is only this socialist criticism of capitalist economics and its scientific formulation in the works of the classics of economic theory that makes it possible to discover the real dialectical movement in the actual life of the economy, in the economic praxis of man. The rapid progress made by the young Marx and Engels in their study of the real dialectics of economic life soon laid the foundations for the criticism of the ideas which had sought to grasp that life: the classics of economic theory, on the one hand, and Hegel, on the other.

Thus Marx's emphasis on 'externalization' as the central concept of the *Phenomenology* and of idealist dialectics in general was not the result of an arbitrary decision. Hegel's inspired guess on the basis of very incomplete knowledge of economics enabled him to see that 'externalization', alienation, was a fundamental fact of life, and *for that reason* he put it in the centre of philosophy. Marx's critique of Hegel proceeds from a more profound and accurate grasp of the *economic realities*. That is to say, it was first necessary to gain an understanding of the fundamental facts of economics on the basis of a socialist critique of the alienation of labour under capitalism before it became possible to assess the rights and wrongs, the essential truths and the mystifications of Hegel's interpretation of them.

The one-sidedness of Feuerbach's criticism of Hegel is due in great measure to the fact that he analysed and overcame Hegel's 'externalization' only in its ultimate philosophical consequences. He had no conception whatever of the process that led from reality itself to the philosophical conception and that threw up such a contradictory reflection in his philosophy. That is to say, he had no inkling of the connections between economics and philosophy. Hence his criticism remained one-sided, incomplete and abstract. Hence, too, despite his materialist opposition to Hegel's idealism, he was not really able to overcome the limitations and defects of Hegel's thought, for these ultimately were social and not philosophical; as we shall see they were closely bound up with the nature of bourgeois society.

The bond between economics and philosophy is, then, a profound necessity: it is the precondition for any real refutation of Hegel's idealist dialectic and for any further advance. For that reason it would be superficial to imagine that Marx's concern with Hegel begins only in the last portion of the Manuscript which contains the critique of the *Phenomenology*. The four preceding sections on economics, which do not expressly concern themselves with Hegel at all, are nevertheless the foundation on which that criticism is built: they provide the economic clarification of the real nature of alienation. We shall quote only a few of Marx's salient definitions. Marx takes as his point of departure the real facts of capitalist economics. He rejects every type of economic Robinsonade out of hand. For the latter explain the division of labour, exchange etc., just as theology explains the origin of evil by means of the Fall, i.e. by assuming the existence of the very thing whose origins it is supposed to explain. On the basis of an analysis of the actual facts of capitalist economics Marx gives this definition of alienation as it is created in the labour process:

> 'This fact expresses merely that the object which labour produces—labour's product—confronts it as *something alien*, as a *power independent* of the producer. The product of labour is labour which has been embodied in an object, which has become material: it is the *objectification* of labour. Labour's realization is its objectification. In the sphere of political economy this realization of labour appears as *loss of realization* for the workers; objectification as *loss of the object* and *bondage to it*; appropriation as *alienation*, as *externalization*. . . . All these consequences result from the fact that the worker is related to the *product of his labour* as to an *alien* object.'[16]

Hegel is not even mentioned here by name and no philosophical inference is drawn from this economic analysis. But even a cursory glance is enough to reveal that these apparently descriptive remarks in fact contain a fundamental critique of Hegel's philosophy. For alienation is sharply distinguished from objective reality, from objectification in the act of labour. The latter is a characteristic of work in general and of the relation of human praxis to the objects of the external world; the former is a consequence of the social division of labour under capitalism, of the emergence of the so-called free worker who has to work with the means of production belonging to another and for whom, therefore, these means of production as well as his own product exist as an independent, alien power.

Now when we examine the process of labour itself, this fundamental aspect of capitalist society appears to be doubly intensified and concentrated in the person of the worker. Marx emphasizes here above all

> 'the fact that labour is *external* to the worker, i.e. it does not belong to his essential being; that in his work, therefore, he does not affirm himself but denies himself, does not feel content but unhappy, does not develop freely his physical and mental energy but mortifies his body and ruins his mind. The worker therefore only feels himself outside his work, and in his work feels outside himself. He is at home when he is not working, and when he is working he is not at home.'

This results in the inversion of all human values:

> 'What is animal becomes human and what is human becomes animal. Certainly, eating, drinking, procreating, etc. are also genuinely human functions. But abstractly taken, separated from the sphere of all other human activity and turned into sole and ultimate ends, they are animal functions.'[17]

In this way alienation permeates the entire subjective and objective reality of human life. Objectively, the product of labour appears as an alien thing ruling over man; subjectively, the process of labour is a self-alienation corresponding to the alienation of the thing described above.

From these premises, all of which without exception are the product of a close examination of economic realities, he comes to the following conclusions about the relation of the individual to the species in capitalist society:

> 'In alienating from man (1) nature, and (2) himself, his own active functions, his life activity, alienated labour alienates the *species* from man. . . . Firstly, it alienates the life of the species and individual life, and secondly it makes individual life in its abstract form the purpose of the life of the species, likewise in its abstract and alienated form.'[18]

It is obvious that such insights into the alienation of labour with all its human and social consequences could only be obtained through a socialist criticism of capitalism. This circumstance enables us to appreciate the full implications of Marx's statement that Hegel does indeed stand on the heights of classical economic theory and that he has a genuine understanding of work as the process by which man creates himself, but that he has no insight into the negative aspects of work in capitalist society since he only considers its positive sides. Marx's whole criticism of the fundamental concepts of the *Phenomenology* is based on this assertion: since Hegel does not see the negative aspects of work, he becomes guilty of false distinctions and false syntheses, of the mystifications of idealism. The discovery of the true dialectics of labour in capitalist society is the precondition for a materialist critique of the philosophy which developed a one-sided view of labour and made it into the foundation of a general philosophy of the evolution of the human race.

We have already referred to Marx's comment that Hegel's philosophy contains a tendency towards an 'uncritical idealism'. This 'uncritical idealism' is expressed—and here we are already poised at the centre of the critique of the *Phenomenology*—in Hegel's view of what philosophy is. Hegel speaks of 'externalization' and its annulment by philosophy. He does not suspect, however, that the philosophy which is supposed to annul 'externalization' is itself an egregious instance of 'externalization':

> '. . . the philosophic mind is nothing but the alienated mind of the world thinking within its self-estrangement—i.e., comprehending itself abstractly. *Logic* (mind's *coin of the realm*, the speculative or *thought-value* of man and nature—their essence grown totally indifferent to all real determinateness, and hence their unreal essence) is *externalized thinking*, and therefore thinking which abstracts from real man: *abstract* thinking.'[19]

Hegel does not perceive this and by failing to notice that alienated thought is alienated and by regarding it, indeed, as the very instrument by which alienation can be annulled, he succumbs to an uncritical idealism and turns the true pattern of alienation on its head. Consistently with this, Hegelian idealism identifies man with his self-consciousness.

> 'All alienation of human essence is therefore *nothing but alienation of self-consciousness*. The alienation of self-consciousness is not regarded as an *expression* of the *real* alienation of the human being—its expression reflected in the realm of knowledge and thought. Instead, the *real* alienation—that which appears real—is according to its *innermost*, hidden nature (a nature first brought to light by philosophy) nothing but the *manifestation* of the estrangement of the real essence of man, of *self-consciousness*. The science which comprehends this is therefore called *Phenomenology*. All reappropriation of the alienated objective essence appears, therefore, as a process of incorporation into self-consciousness: The man who takes hold of his essential being is *merely* the self-consciousness which takes hold of objective essences. Return of the object into the self is therefore the reappropriation of the object.'[20]

Marx's critical comments show succinctly how the false identification of man and self-consciousness necessarily springs from a false view of alienation in society. On the subjective side, there is the mistaken identification of man and self-consciousness demonstrated and criticized by Marx; on the objective side, there is the equation of alienation and objectification in general.

In his discussion of economics Marx, drawing on his knowledge of the empirical evidence, distinguishes sharply between objectification in work in general and the alienation of subject and object in the *capitalist form* of work. Armed with this distinction he can expose Hegel's erroneous equation. He proffers the following criticism of the methodological foundations of the *Phenomenology*:

> 'It is not the fact that the human being *objectifies himself inhumanly*, in opposition to himself, but the fact that he *objectifies himself* in *distinction* from and in *opposition* to abstract thinking, that constitutes the essence of the alienation and the thing to be superseded.'[21]

Hegel's false problem, with which we are now thoroughly familiar from our discussion of the *Phenomenology* and its antecedents, is followed by the equally false culmination of his philosophy in the annulment of objectivity:

> 'The task, therefore, is to surmount the *object of consciousness*. *Objectivity* as such is regarded as an *alienated* human relationship which does not correspond to the *essence of man*, to self-consciousness. The *reappropriation* of the objective essence of man, begotten in the form of alienation as something alien, therefore not only as the annulment of *alienation*, but of *objectivity* as well. Man, that is to say, is regarded as a *non-objective*, *spiritual* being.'[22]

We can see quite clearly here how the false idealist problem with its equally false idealist solution springs necessarily from Hegel's no less necessarily one-sided and incomplete interpretation of capitalist society. It is no less clear that this, the highest form of idealist dialectics, can only be wholly superseded if and when a socialist critique of capitalist economics has been rendered practicable by the emergent possibility of a real annulment of capitalist alienation.

Marx now goes on to oppose a materialist theory of objectivity to the idealist theory of the annulment of objectivity. It must be noted right away, and we shall return to it later, that Marx's materialist theory explains both capitalist alienation and its annulment and for that reason is in a position to give a more complete and comprehensive refutation of Hegel's idealism than was Feuerbach. Since Feuerbach had paid no heed to this social problem he failed to register the valid aspects of the Hegelian theory and furthermore he fell into the same errors as Hegel himself, though starting from an opposed point of view. The quintessence of Marx's materialist theory of objectivity is as follows:

> 'Whenever real, corporeal *man*, man with his feet firmly on the solid ground, man exhaling and inhaling all the forces of nature, *establishes* his real, objective *essential powers* as alien objects by his externalization, it is not the *act of positing* which is the subject in this process: it is the subjectivity of *objective* essential powers, whose action, therefore, must also be something *objective*. An objective being acts objectively, and he would not act objectively if the objective did not reside in the very nature of his being. He creates or establishes only *objects*, *because* he is established by objects—because at bottom he is *nature*. In the act of establishing, therefore, this objective being does not fall from his state of "pure activity" into a *creating of the object*; on the contrary, his *objective* product only confirms his *objective* activity, establishing his activity as the activity of an objective, natural being. . . . *To be* objective, natural and sensuous, and at the same time to have object nature and sense outside oneself, or oneself to be object, nature and sense for a third party, is one and the same thing. . . . An unobjective being is a nullity—an *un-being*.'[23]

Thus Marx's materialist criticism of Hegel's idealism is based on his account of the real premises of human thought and human praxis, as opposed to the alleged absence of premises in absolute idealism. The comparison also exposes the real premises of absolute idealism. In this sense, too, then, materialist dialectics are the truth of objective idealism. They not only annihilate it critically, but also deduce the source of its mistakes and use this discovery to clear the way for its real supersession, i.e. to an annulment which also conserves its essential and valid insights. By opposing the real premises of philosophy, the real facts of existence (of nature, economics and history) to the mystified premises of objective idealism, and by inferring the correct philosophical conclusions from the accurate dialectical reflection of these facts, Marx reveals that both the 'uncritical idealism' and the 'uncritical positivism' of Hegel are the necessary consequence of his social existence. It then becomes plain 'of its own accord' how and why Hegel was able to work within the framework of these idealist mystifications and to make so many discoveries not just about economics and history but also about the dialectical laws of objective reality in general; it becomes plain, in short, how Hegelian dialectics were able to serve as the immediate prototype of materialist dialectics. The decisive factor, as we have observed, was that Hegel thought of work as the self-creating process of man, of the human species.

It is on the basis of this recognition that Marx formulates his most penetrating criticism, focusing unerringly on the points at which Hegel's insights are distorted by the mystical form in which they appear. We have already quoted Marx's criticism that the course of history is really only an apparent movement in Hegel.

Our point then was that the annulment of objectivity in absolute knowledge had the consequence that the Hegelian 'bearer' of history, the absolute spirit, did not really make history as Hegel imagined, but only seemed to do so. Proceeding from the criticism of Hegel's theory of objectivity Marx now mounts a frontal attack on the mystifications in the entire theory of a 'bearer' of history, which is itself the foundation of the idealist mystification of history itself.

> 'This process must have a bearer, a subject. But the subject first emerges as a result. This result—the subject knowing itself as absolute self-consciousness—is therefore *God—absolute spirit—the self-knowing and self-manifesting idea*. Real man and real nature become mere predicates—symbols of this esoteric, unreal man and of this unreal nature. Subject and predicate are therefore related to each other in absolute reversal—a *mystical subject-object* or a *subjectivity reaching beyond the object*—the *absolute subject* as a *process*, as *subject alienating itself* and returning from alienation into itself, but at the same time retracting this alienation into itself, and the subject as this process; a pure *restless* revolving within itself.'[24]

Real history, according to Hegel, is thus made to depend on an abstract, imaginary, mystificatory 'bearer' which, it goes without saying, can only 'make' history in an abstract, imaginary, mystificatory fashion. The real process, the real determinants of the process can only, as it were, sneak in through the back door. The fact that they dominate the particular, concrete stages of history is what creates that contradictory image which we have now analysed at length.

More than a decade later, Marx returns to the same question, no longer in the context of a critique of the *Phenomenology*, but instead as part of a comprehensive assessment of the philosophical foundations of Hegel's idealism as a whole. In the great Introduction to the *Contribution to the Critique of Political Economy* Marx analyses the various complementary and interconnected modes of reflecting, of coming to grips with objective reality, and in the course of his discussion he compares the real, materialist approach with Hegelian illusions:

> 'The concrete concept is concrete because it is a synthesis of many definitions, thus representing the unity of diverse aspects. It appears, therefore, in reasoning as a summing-up, a result, and not as the starting point, although it is the real point of origin, and thus also the point of origin of perception and imagination. The first procedure attenuates meaningful images to abstract definitions, the second leads from abstract definitions by way of reasoning to the reproduction of the concrete situation. Hegel accordingly conceived the illusory idea that the real world is the result of thinking which causes its own synthesis, its

> own deepening and its own movement; whereas the method of advancing from the abstract to the concrete is simply the way in which thinking assimilates the concrete and reproduces it as a concrete mental category. This is, however, by no means the process of evolution of the concrete world itself.'[25]

This, then, is Marx's critique of Hegel in its maturest form.

This comprehensive analysis of Hegel's conception of alienation makes it possible for Marx to provide a materialist critique of that other fundamental concept, supersession. Once again, it is important to bear in mind that when Marx subjects idealist dialectics to criticism and transcends it critically, importing its valuable elements into materialist dialectics, he is *exclusively* concerned with idealism in its Hegelian form. Thus in the problem under discussion Marx utterly ignores Schelling's definition of 'supersession': the destruction of the annulled determinations, their annihilation through their elevation into the absolute. Nor does he so much as mention the Kantian variant of agnostic antinomy. Marx regards Hegelian dialectics as the complete and definitive answer to all earlier versions. Accordingly it is with the Hegelian conception that he takes issue, i.e. with that highest form of 'supersession' in which the annulled determinations are not simply negated but also conserved at a higher level, a 'supersession' in which otherness is not annihilated in the absolute but finds its existence and its relative justification respected. Hegel's definition of 'externalization', unlike that of Schelling, has a positive connotation since it creates objectivity, and it is this that Marx takes as his point of departure, taking it as read that the discussions of Hegel with his predecessors had been resolved in Hegel's favour. Marx goes on to examine the defects of Hegel's version of 'supersession' and comes to this conclusion:

> 'On the other hand, says Hegel, there is here at the same time this other moment, that consciousness has just as much annulled and reabsorbed this externalization and objectivity, being thus *at home* in its *other-being as such*.
>
> 'In this discussion are brought together all the illusions of speculation.
>
> '*First of all*, consciousness, self-consciousness is *at home in its other being as such*. . . . This implies for one thing that consciousness (knowing as knowing, thinking as thinking) pretends to be directly the other of itself—to be the world of sense, the real world, life. . . . This aspect is contained herein, inasmuch as mere consciousness takes offence not at alienated objectivity, but at *objectivity as such*.
>
> '*Secondly*, this implies that self-conscious man, in so far as he has recognized and annulled and superseded the spiritual world (or his

> world's spiritual, general mode of being) as self-alienation, nevertheless again confirms this in its alienated shape and passes it off as his true mode of being—re-establishes it, and pretends to be *at home in his other-being as such*. Thus, for instance, after annulling and superseding religion, after recognizing religion to be a product of self-alienation, he yet finds confirmation of himself in *religion as religion*. Here is the root of Hegel's false positivism, or of his merely apparent criticism: this is what Feuerbach designated as the positing, negating and re-establishing of religion or theology—but it has to be grasped in more general terms. Thus reason is at home in unreason as unreason. The man who has recognized that he is leading an alienated life in politics, law etc., is leading his true human life in this alienated life as such. Self-affirmation, in *contradiction* with itself—in contradiction both with the knowledge of and with the essential being of the object—is thus true *knowledge* and *life*.
>
> 'There can therefore no longer be any question of an act of accommodation on Hegel's part *vis-à-vis* religion, the state, etc., since this lie is the lie of his principle.'[26]

Here, then, we have the profoundest criticism precisely of Hegel's most positive and significant ideas. Marx exposes the ultimate philosophical implications of Hegel's position *vis-à-vis* capitalist society in so far as these are reflected in the abstract problems arising from the dialectical structure of his philosophy. We have ourselves drawn attention to some of these contradictions and have shown how they have their roots in the society of his age, as well as in his attitude towards it. Now we see the purely philosophical consequences to which these social contradictions had to lead and did lead in actual fact. Now, too, we can see that all criticism of Hegel's ambiguous stance on problems of religion, the state etc., that was based on a dualism between his esoteric and exoteric philosophy was bound to miss the central problems. This is so regardless of the fact that subjectively, as we saw, Hegel was from time to time not unaware of such a cleavage in his thought; for the contradictions, the problematic nature of his philosophy, reach into the very centre even of his exoteric ideas. Of course, it is and will remain for the student of the history of philosophy to establish where, when and how in particular questions Hegel made any concessions to the society of his day. But any such historical analysis must make it quite clear that whatever answers it comes up with will not touch the central issue of the problematic nature of the Hegelian dialectic.[27]

The profundity of Marx's criticism is apparent from the way in which it moves from the problems of actual life to the most abstract questions of the Hegelian dialectics, solves them finally in terms of dialectical materialism and then moves on at once, finding an immediate connection with the problems of real life. What we are concerned with here is the central problem of the whole philosophy of Hegel, what Engels called the contradiction between method and system.

This contradiction embraces further contradictory attitudes on the question of human progress and, specifically, on the question of the position of capitalism in history in general, and in German history in particular. The question of supersession is on the one hand one of the ultimate and most abstract components of the dialectic, but on the other hand it is of the greatest importance for his philosophy of history and society. The mixture of progressive and reactionary tendencies in Hegel crystallizes out in the contradictions contained in the dialectical process of supersession, contradictions which have been analysed and criticized by Marx in the passages just quoted.

The socialist critique of 'externalization' has exposed the real alienation contained in the capitalist form of work, an alienation that has to be annulled in reality. Expressing this critique in general philosophical terms, we see that since the Hegelian concept of 'externalization' implies that consciousness is at home in its other-being as such, it *eo ipso* contains an important reactionary element, a vindication of what exists even if it has been overcome historically. The fact that Hegel also exhibits the opposite tendency and repeatedly follows it up simply confirms the accuracy of Marx's and Engels' diagnosis of an indissoluble contradiction between system and method.

This contradiction and the tendencies contained within it played a crucial role in the great ideological debates of the 1840s which prepared the ground for democratic revolution. What we find there are two different interpretations of Hegel's views, both of which lead to political passivity, to the non-comprehension of the concrete problems of the democratic revolution and beyond that—in theory—of revolution in general. The general significance of these problems far exceeds the importance of the debates of the 1840s, for the misconceptions we are concerned with are rooted in capitalism and it is only their intellectual form that is determined by the arguments surrounding Hegel's view of dialectical supersession. The first of these views is the direct continuation of Hegelian idealism; it involves the further subjectivization, the exaggeration of Hegel's idealistic misconceptions by the Young Hegelians. The other tendency arises from the epistemologically correct but abstract and one-sided critique of Hegel's supersession by Feuerbach himself.

Let us begin with the first position. Since, according to Hegel, 'externalization' is ultimately the 'externalization' of consciousness, it ought to be superseded *exclusively* by consciousness, *within* consciousness. In Hegel himself the identity of absolute knowledge and the philosopher who possesses it remained in the half-light. His objectivism prevented him from making this identity into a simple personal union. But the tendency was nevertheless implicit in his position. Once again it was Heinrich Heine who with irony and self-irony took the matter to its logical conclusion:

> 'I was never an abstract thinker and I accepted the synthesis of Hegel's doctrine without questioning it, since its consequences flattered my conceit. I was young and proud and it pleased my vanity when I learned from Hegel that the God residing in Heaven was not God, as my grandmother imagined, but that I, living here on earth, was he.'[28]

What Heine said ironically was taken up in Bruno Bauer's *Philosophy of Self-Consciousness* and turned into a philosophical and political doctrine which exercised a dangerous and pernicious influence on the left-wing German intelligentsia, as well as on the emergent proletarian party (via the detour of 'True Socialism').

If we examine Marx's penetrating criticism of Bauer's view in *The Holy Family*, we can see how it grows directly out of his criticism of Hegel's view of 'supersession'. We should note, however, that Bauer's intellectual arrogance, his overweening contempt for the action of the masses in history is something that has grown out of Hegel's philosophy and his view of history, but it appears in Bauer without Hegel's important progressive and realistic tendencies and instead it takes Hegel's idealism to an extreme of subjectivity. Marx discusses Bauer's view in these terms:

> 'The enemies of progress *outside* the mass are precisely those *products* of *self-debasement*, *self-rejection* and *self-alienation* of the *mass* which have been endowed with independent being and a life of their *own*. The mass therefore rises against its own deficiency when it rises against the independently existing *products* of its *self-debasement* just as man, turning against the existence of God, turns against his *own religiosity*. But as those practical self-alienations of the mass exist in the real world in an external way, the mass must fight them in an *external* way. It must by no means consider these products of its self-alienation as mere *ideal* fancies, mere *externalizations of self-consciousness*, and must not wish to abolish *material* alienation by a purely *inward spiritual* action. As early as 1789 Loustalot's journal gave the motto:
>
> The great appear great in our eyes
> Only because we kneel.
> Let us rise!
>
> 'But to rise it is not enough to do so *in thought* and to leave hanging over our *real sensual* head the *real palpable* yoke that cannot be subtilized away with ideas. Yet Absolute Criticism has at least learnt from Hegel's *Phenomenology* the art of changing *real objective* chains that exist *outside me* into *mere ideal*, mere *subjective* chains existing *in*

> *me*, and thus to change all *exterior* palpable struggles into pure struggles of thought.'[29]

It is not necessary to provide further evidence in support of the proposition that Bauer's ideology grows out of Hegel's 'externalization' and its supersession. Nor of the political danger inherent in such views, to say nothing of the persistence of the ideology of passivity among an arrogant intelligentsia in capitalist societies, an ideology which endures to this day, though of course it has long ceased to base itself on Hegelian philosophy. But Hegelianism does lend itself to such use, as we can see not just from the history of the 1840s but also—and in particularly extreme and grotesque forms—in the neo-Hegelianism of the Imperialist age.

To turn to the second form, viz. Feuerbach's critique of the Hegelian dialectic, it is important to consider Marx's attitude. Marx thinks that what was important and original in Feuerbach's analysis was that he showed how Hegel's supersession in fact entailed the reinstatement of what had been superseded. We have already quoted the crucial passage from his critique in another context (p. 518f.). Marx praised Feuerbach for proving that Hegel's philosophy amounted to a reinstatement of religion. Furthermore, he admired Feuerbach's advance to a true materialism and, lastly, his critique of supersession, of the negation of negation. We shall confine ourselves to this latter point. Feuerbach was right

> 'in opposing to the negation of the negation, which claims to be the absolute positive, the self-supporting positive, positively based on itself.'[30]

This positive represents the priority of existence over consciousness. According to Feuerbach the process of supersession in Hegel's dialectic inverts the relation of existence to consciousness. He goes on to show how this idealist inversion leads to the reinstatement of religion by philosophy. Marx summarizes Feuerbach's position in this way:

> 'Feuerbach thus conceives the negation of the negation *only* as a contradiction of philosophy with itself—as the philosophy which affirms theology (the transcendental, etc.) after having denied it and which it therefore affirms in opposition to itself.'[31]

Marx accepts this, the materialist side of Feuerbach's criticism, but he immediately qualifies his praise by pointing out its one-sidedness. This consists, on the one hand, in the fact that Feuerbach treats 'externalization' purely as a philosophical problem so that he too sticks fast in abstraction (cf. Marx's and Engels' later criticism of the abstractness of Feuerbach's 'man'). On the other hand, Feuerbach's materialist view of reality is not dialectical so that he overlooks Hegel's real insights because of their idealist form and so rejects the whole of Hegel's dialectic, the good along with the bad. Thus as Marx emphasizes in the last quotation, Feuerbach can only see the weaknesses of Hegel's idealism in the negation of the negation, 'which he directly and immediately confronts with the position of sense-certainty based on itself'.

Feuerbach's self-imposed restriction to epistemology is the source of his abstractness; the direct, conscious exclusion of all mediations does away with Hegel's dialectics as well as his idealism. This is why Feuerbach ignores the most important and crucial determinations of Hegel's philosophy. Marx adds:

> 'But because Hegel has conceived the negation of the negation, from the point of view of the positive relation inherent in it, as the true and only positive, and from the point of view of the negative relation inherent in it as the only true act and self-realizing act of all being, he has only found the *abstract*, *logical*, *speculative* expression for the movement of history; which is not yet the *real* history of man—of man as a given subject, but only man's *act of creation*—the story of man's origin.'[32]

Thus the socialist criticism of capitalism discerns in Hegel's *Phenomenology* some of the essential and correct definitions of the process that Marx was later to call the 'pre-history' of mankind. Feuerbach, however, is no less imprisoned within the horizon of the bourgeoisie than Hegel, albeit from a very different standpoint, and so he can only deal with Hegel's thought in terms of an absolute Either/Or. In his account of the *Phenomenology*, Marx refers to a number of passages where Hegel correctly understood certain specific features of the 'pre-history' of mankind. And he shows, further, that although the concepts of alienation and supersession are distorted by idealism and given a reactionary colouring in Hegel, they are not utterly false, as Feuerbach believed, but are a one-sided reflection of reality, deformed and inhibited by the capitalist perspective, whose correct intuitions, however, were worthy of preservation:

> 'The *Phenomenology* is, therefore, a hidden and mystifying criticism—still to itself obscure; but inasmuch as it grasps steadily man's *alienation*, even though man only appears in the shape of mind, there lie concealed in it *all* the elements of criticism, already *prepared* and *elaborated* in a manner often rising far above the Hegelian standpoint. The Unhappy Consciousness, the Honest Consciousness, the struggle of the Noble and Base Consciousness, etc. etc.,—these separate sections contain, but as yet in an alienated form, the *critical* elements of whole spheres such as religion, the state, civil life, etc.'[33]

Thus Marx's really comprehensive criticism of Hegel's dialectic grows into a criticism of Feuerbach's one-sided and myopic judgment of Hegel, and that leads to a criticism of Feuerbach's metaphysical materialism and of his rejection of dialectics. The point of interest to us is that in the debates of the 1840s the Feuerbachian critique of Hegel's idealism had very dangerous political repercussions. For although Feuerbach's critique of the negation of the negation is based on the immediate sensuousness of material life, he is unable to grasp the dialectical movement within that material life. As Marx points out in the *Theses on Feuerbach* he is unable to comprehend sensuousness in its practical implications.

> 'The chief defect of all hitherto existing materialism (that of Feuerbach included) is that the thing, reality, sensuousness, is conceived only in the form of the *object or of contemplation*, but not as *sensuous human activity*, *practice*, not subjectively. Hence, in contradistinction to materialism, the *active* side was developed abstractly by idealism—which of course does not know real, sensuous activity as such. Feuerbach wants sensuous objects, really distinct from the thought objects, but he does not conceive human activity itself as *objective* activity. Hence, in *Das Wesen des Christentums*, he regards the theoretical attitude as the only genuine human attitude, while practice is conceived and fixed only in its dirty-Jewish manifestation. Hence he does not grasp the significance of "revolutionary", of "practical-critical" activity.'[34]

This makes it very clear that the analysis of economic concepts, the precise distinction between objectivity and alienation in human praxis prepared the ground for a critique not only of Hegel's idealism but also of Feuerbach's mechanical materialism.

It is important to give a brief account of the implications of Feuerbach's position in the ideological and political struggles of the 1840s. Engels has provided a clear definition (and trenchant criticism) of the crucial aspect of Feuerbach's stance *vis-à-vis* the real world. He quotes the following passage from Feuerbach's *Philosophy of the Future*:

> 'Existence is not a general concept which can be separated from things. . . . Existence is the positing of essence. *My essence is my existence*. . . . Even language identifies existence and essence. Only in human life is existence divorced from essence—*but only in exceptional, unhappy cases*; it happens that a person's essence is not in the place where he exists, but just because of this division his soul is not truly in the place where the body really is. *You are* there only where your heart is! But all things—*apart from abnormal cases*—are glad to be in the place where they are, and are glad to be what they are.'[35]

Engels then delivers the following scathing commentary on this passage, drawing out the necessary political implications, implications certainly unwelcome to Feuerbach, who subjectively was a sincere revolutionary democrat, but which flow inevitably from his liquidation of the Hegelian dialectic, from the elimination of all mediating determinations and relations, from his return to immediacy—all of which reflects the fact that he was unable to overcome his built-in preconceptions and look the economic and social realities of capitalism squarely in the face. Objectively, as Engels shows, his blindness on this score could have the effect of turning him into an apologist for reactionary conditions.

> 'A fine panegyric upon the existing state of things. Exceptional cases and a few abnormal cases apart, when you are seven years old you are glad to become a door-keeper in a coal-mine and to remain alone in the dark for fourteen hours a day, and because it is your existence, therefore it is also your essence. . . . It is your "essence" to be subservient to a branch of labour.'[36]

Engels' criticism helps to explain why the radical and sometimes even socialist intellectuals of the 1840s who looked to Feuerbach to provide them with a philosophical foundation for their political radicalism, were as unsuccessful as those who attempted to use Hegel for the same purposes. A close examination of Feuerbach's position would reveal that such conscious or unconscious apologias for the existing order of things on the basis of the immediate philosophical identity of existence and essence have—*mutatis mutandis*—continued to play a part in the defence of reactionary conditions and still do so today long after Feuerbach and quite independently of him.

It was necessary to point to the political consequences of the ideological conflicts of the 1840s to make it clear how Marx's criticism of Hegel's idealist dialectics grows out of the socialist critique of capitalism and into the preparatory phase of the 1848 Revolution, and beyond that to all the democratic and proletarian revolutions of the future. The internal movement of Marx's criticism shows how wrong it would be to consider these problems purely as problems of philosophy even in Hegel. Not the least of Feuerbach's defects is that his approach to Hegel was confined to the purely epistemological and philosophical plane while the dialectical interaction of such problems with the problems of society, of man's social and economic praxis, were as good as non-existent for him. The superiority of Hegel's philosophy over Feuerbach's (in a certain sense, in certain areas)—despite his idealism—is precisely that Hegel did strive, if often in vain, to make these connections the basis of his dialectics. It is for this reason that his dialectics is a watershed in the history of philosophy: it is the highest form of idealist dialectics and so of bourgeois philosophy in general and hence it is the mediating link capable of forming a *direct* connection with dialectical materialism.

Lenin was not able to consult the Marxian Manuscripts which we have now discussed at length and so could not know of the connections established there between economics and dialectics in the course of his critique of Hegel. Nevertheless, he had a clear view of what these connections entailed. We have already quoted his comment that there was a *direct* link between Marx and Hegel (p. 352). His remark insists on a point that was wholly neglected during the period of the Second International even though Marx and Engels lost no opportunity—in prefaces, comments and letters, etc.—to draw attention to the importance of Hegel and to urge the study of his philosophy as an indispensable prerequisite for the understanding of dialectical materialism. These exhortations were utterly ignored by the most important and honest theoreticians of the period. Not even Plekhanov who, unlike Mehring and Lafargue, had made an intensive study of Hegel, had the least idea of the connections, the profound methodological links between economics and dialectics.

Following Marx, Lenin was the first to re-establish them. It would be a gross over-simplification to imagine that Lenin's critical commentary of Hegel's *Logic* should be confined to epistemology in the narrower sense. Even when he is talking about problems of knowledge Lenin is always concerned, as we saw in his remarks on teleology, with the great, universal perspectives of Marxism. In his critical comments on Hegel, therefore, he continually returns to this decisive question.

We shall illustrate this briefly, confining ourselves to a few of Lenin's most important statements:

> 'It is impossible completely to understand Marx's *Capital*, and especially its first chapter, without having thoroughly studied and understood the *whole* of Hegel's *Logic*. Consequently, half a century later none of the Marxists understood Marx!!'[37]

And elsewhere:

> 'If Marx did not leave behind him a *Logic* (with a capital letter), he did leave the *logic* of *Capital*, and this ought to be utilized to the full in this question [i.e. the question of dialectics—G. L.]. In *Capital*, Marx applied to a single science logic, dialectics and the theory of knowledge of materialism (three words are not needed: it is one and the same thing) which has taken everything valuable in Hegel and developed it further.'[38]

These comments are to be found, characteristically enough, in the midst of Lenin's analysis of the plan of Hegel's dialectics and they are followed, no less characteristically, by his observations on Marx's dialectical application of the categories of economics in *Capital*. Lenin thus demonstrates, as Marx had done before him, how philosophical problems are to be tackled and solved in dialectical materialism. The 'Lenin period' of philosophical development initiated by Stalin ought to extend these methods to every aspect of philosophy so that philosophical praxis will finally be able to eradicate the traditions of the Second International.

The 'Lenin period' of philosophy must also devote itself to the problems of history, it goes without saying. The present study was designed to make a contribution to this aspect. It aimed to explore the impact of the contradictions of capitalist society in the highest expression of bourgeois philosophy, on Hegel's idealist dialectics. We hoped to show this connection in all its social and philosophical complexity, and in particular to reveal how the origins and development of the dialectic were influenced by the intellectual reflection of these contradictions in the classical economic theory of England and by their actual explosion in the French Revolution. Moreover, we have been concerned to show the effects—for good and evil—that resulted from the circumstance that these French and English events, both real and ideological, were brought together into a dialectical method and an idealist system in the mind of a man living in the socially and economically backward nation of Germany.

Only this approach has enabled us to treat the relation between Hegel and his predecessors in a manner that could dispense with the schematic method, the violations and factual distortions current in bourgeois histories of philosophy, traces of which are not uncommon in the treatment of such questions by Marxists. We believe that we have been able to show that both Hegel's independence of his important contemporaries and forerunners and also his involuntary agreement with them are to be explained in terms of these problems of the nature of society.

This is not merely an historical question, not merely an issue of importance to the so-called Hegel scholars (even though they have become important and topical in consequence of the recent Fascist and Fascistoid distortions of history). An understanding of the real causes of the greatness and the limitations of the Hegelian dialectic also results in the clarification of the relation of Marx to Hegel, and the concretization of the historical heritage of Hegelianism as critically sifted and preserved in Marxism. For if one thing is clear, it is that Marx was always concerned with the *real* Hegel. In the midst of his polemics he always makes a clear distinction between Hegel with all his limitations, and whatever his disciples and followers have made of him. Between Marx's criticism and our age there lies almost a century whose 'achievement' in this respect consists in the distortion of our image of the real Hegel, a distortion which up to now has not been made good in any Marxist study of Hegel or any attempt to excavate the real Hegel from the rubble. The ideas with which even the majority of philosophically educated readers approach Hegel are, even without their knowing it, profoundly influenced by these bourgeois falsifications. And the far-reaching implications of the critical comments of Marx, Engels, Lenin and Stalin can only be properly understood and utilized if we know the *real* object of their criticism, i.e. if we know the *real* Hegel.

Only in the context of this situation can the *philosophical* significance of Hegel's economic studies and ideas become fully apparent. Contradictory and imperfect though Hegel's views may have been, and we have analysed the contradictions inherent in them at length, it is undoubtedly no accident that the man who completed the edifice of idealist dialectics was the *only* philosopher of the age to have made a *serious* attempt to get to grips with the economic structure of capitalist society. Rather is it the case that the *specific* form of dialectics evolved by him grew out of his preoccupation with the problems of capitalism and of economics.

We repeat: the mere form of a unity of opposites, of contradictions, can be found everywhere in the modern era from Nicholas of Cusa and Giordano Bruno onwards. But as far as the *decisive* questions of dialectics are concerned, even Schelling's philosophy, the most highly developed philosophy of dialectics before Hegel, does not really advance matters further than they. The specifically Hegelian categories, whose emergence and problematic nature we have studied, were the first to elaborate the essential determinations to the point where the materialist dialectics of Marx could take over—criticizing Hegel and turning him the right way up, but nevertheless taking up *directly* where he had left off. The unique importance of Marx's critique of Hegel consists in the fact that it locates the achievement and the limitations of his dialectics in the accuracy and the defects of his grasp of the contradictions and the laws of motion of capitalist society and its economics.

Only from this vantage-point can Hegel's historical achievement be seen for what it is. Every thinker is, as Hegel remarks, the child of his age; as such he takes up where his predecessors left off. But if we wish to establish the greatness and the achievement of a thinker we must inquire how far he was dependent on his predecessors for the methods and the substance of his thought and how far he was able to test them against reality and develop them further, in short, we must determine to what extent his thought is based on reality and to what extent he remains bound by the philosophical traditions and horizons of his predecessors.

This is the qualitative distinction between Fichte and Schelling on the one hand and Hegel on the other (to say nothing of the lesser thinkers of the age, who, however, are themselves real giants when put by the side of the so-called 'great' minds of contemporary bourgeois philosophy). Obviously, the philosophies of Fichte and Schelling were determined by objective social reality, both in their assumptions and in their general lines. Philosophically speaking, however, they remain imprisoned within the framework of Kantianism, and even though Schelling, for instance, takes the step from subjective to objective idealism he remains unable to break out of that framework; all he can do is try new combinations within it, and although he declares his intentions of going beyond Kant, his real advance is proclaimed and asserted rather than genuinely realized in philosophical terms.

Hegel is the only philosopher of the period following Kant to make a truly original approach to the problems of the age. We have explored his early beginnings in detail and have seen how all the problems of dialectics grew out of his reflections on the two great world-historical facts of the age: the French Revolution and the Industrial Revolution in England. Only in the course of the concrete elaboration of his system did Hegel begin to take issue with his predecessors. Moreover, right from the start, his preoccupation with them was critical, bursting the framework of the Kantian system. Similarities with his forerunners can be found only occasionally, where the social condition of Germany forced his thought into narrow-minded and even philistine channels.

Historically, only one figure may be placed on a par with Hegel: Goethe. It is not just a coincidence that the preparatory stages of the *Phenomenology* provide evidence of a long and detailed preoccupation with Goethe's *Faust*. Both works express a similar aspiration: to provide an encyclopaedic account of the development of mankind to the point reached in the present, and to portray that development in its immanent movement, in terms of its own laws. It was not for nothing that Pushkin referred to *Faust* as an 'Iliad of the modern world' and Schelling's witty description of his philosophy of spirit as the homecoming of spirit, as an 'Odyssey of the spirit' is an epithet better applied to the *Phenomenology* than to any work of Schelling's.

Goethe and Hegel lived at the beginning of the last great tragic period of bourgeois development. Both could see the insoluble contradictions of bourgeois society opening up on the horizon, both could see how history was creating an abyss between the individual and the species. Their greatness lay, on the one hand, in their fearless confrontation of these contradictions and in their efforts to express them at the highest level of philosophy or poetry. On the other hand, they both lived at the beginning of the period, so that both were able—though not always without artificiality or inconsistency—to create lasting images of the generic experience of mankind and the development of man's generic consciousness, images which were comprehensive and large in scope, yet penetrating and true in detail. In this respect, *Wilhelm Meister* and *Faust* are documents of man's development which are just as immortal as the *Phenomenology*, the *Logic* and the *Encyclopaedia*. Of course, these profound affinities should not blind us to their differences: Goethe was much more at home in nature than was Hegel, he was closer to materialism, but equally he was unable to respond to some of Hegel's most important dialectical discoveries. A detailed history of the epoch would have to deal fully with these differences. They are of the greatest importance since only when they have been clarified will it be possible to obtain a really clear picture of the internal contradictions in the progressive currents of the period.

For our purposes, however, it is enough to establish the parallel between the two men. We do not need to chart in detail the complex dialectic that made Goethe's treatment of the problems of capitalist society partly more realistic and perceptive about the future, partly less dialectical and less sensitive to contradictions than Hegel's. It is enough for us to point out that fundamental to them both was the principle of human labour as the key to the self-creation of man. This idea appears as early as the Prometheus Fragment of the young Goethe, though not yet in a consciously economic form and—revealingly, from the point of view of the differences between Goethe and Hegel—with a marked anti-religious bias. In Goethe's greatest works, however, the self-creation of man through work is closely connected with the relation of man to capitalist society and ends in a humanist critique of capitalism. This critique does not lose sight of the idea of human progress for a single instant and so prefers to move 'amidst the manure of the contradictions' than to make concessions to any reactionary romanticism. It would be ridiculous and pedantic to attempt to draw any mechanical parallels between Goethe's literary works and the philosophy of Hegel. But the road on which Goethe discovers his *Faust* or *Wilhelm Meister* is, broadly speaking, the same as that of the spirit in Hegel's *Phenomenology*.[39]

Notes

1. For the first meaning cf. *Die Grundlagen der gesamten Wissenschaftslehre*, 1794, *Werke,* Stuttgart and Augsburg, 1858, Vol. I, p. 360; for the second cf. *Darstellung der Wissenschaftslehre*, 1801, ibid., *Werke,* Vol IV, p 73.
2. *Werke*, Vol I, p. 166.
3. *Theories of Surplus Value*, Vol III, London, 1972, p. 267.
4. *The Phenomenology of Mind*, trans. J. B. Baillie, London, 1964, p. 96.
5. Engels, *Feuerbach*, in *Selected Works*, Moscow and London, 1950, Vol II, p. 336.
6. *The Phenomenology of Mind*, p. 807.
7. Ibid., p. 807.
8. *Jena Logic*, ed. G. Lasson, Leipzig, 1923, pp. 320ff.
9. Rosenkranz, *Life of Hegel*, Berlin, 1844, p. 187.
10. *Reminiscences of Marx and Engels*, Moscow, n.d., p. 76.
11. *Capital*, Vol I, Moscow and London, 1962, p 372.
12. *The Phenomenology of Mind*, p. 801.

13. Ibid., p. 808. The verse at the end is a free adaptation of the concluding lines of Schiller's poem *Friendship* and also the poem *God* from the *Philosophical Letters*.
14. *The Holy Family*, Moscow and London, 1956, pp 115–16.
15. On what follows cf. my study. 'Zur philosophischen Entwicklung des jungen Marx', in *Deutsche Zeitschrift für Philosophie*, No. 2/II/1954.
16. *Economic and Philosophic Manuscripts of 1844*, trans. M. Milligan, London, 1970, p. 108.
17. Ibid., pp. 110–11.
18. Ibid., pp. 112–13.
19. Ibid., p. 174.
20. Ibid., pp. 178–9.
21. Ibid., p. 175.
22. Ibid., p. 178.
23. Ibid., pp. 180–2.
24. Ibid., p. 188.
25. *Contribution to the Critique of Political Economy*, London, 1971, p. 206.
26. *Economic and Philosophic Manuscripts of 1844*, pp 184–5.
27. In my article 'Zur philosophischen Entwicklung des jungen Marx', *Deutsche Zeitschrift für Philosophie*, No. 2/II/1954, I have shown that Marx consistently rejected the Young-Hegelian distinction between Hegel's esoteric and exoteric line from his *Dissertation* on, and that he regarded attempts to explain away the exoteric line in terms of an accommodation to society as superficial.
28. *Werke*, ed. Elster, Vol VI, p. 48.
29. *The Holy Family*, p. 111.
30. *Economic and Philosophic Manuscripts of* 1844, p 172.
31. Ibid., p. 172.
32. Ibid., p. 173.
33. Ibid., p. 176.
34. *The German Ideology*, London, 1965, p. 659.
35. *Werke*, Vol. II, p. 311.
36. *The German Ideology*, p. 675.
37. Lenin, *Philosophical Notebooks*, p. 180.
38. Ibid., p. 319.
39. I have discussed the parallels between *Faust* and the *Phenomenology* at length in my book, *Goethe and his Age*, London 1968, pp. 157–255.

CHAPTER 5

"Hegel's Existentialism"

—from *Sense and Non-Sense* (1948)

Maurice Merleau-Ponty

Jean Hyppolite, who first became known through his annotated translation of the *Phénoménologie de l'esprit*, has since published his *Genèse et structure de la Phénoménologie de l'esprit*, which is bound to mark a decisive step in French studies of Hegel.[2] All the great philosophical ideas of the past century—the philosophies of Marx and Nietzsche, phenomenology, German existentialism, and psychoanalysis—had their beginnings in Hegel; it was he who started the attempt to explore the irrational and integrate it into an expanded reason which remains the task of our century. He is the inventor of that Reason, broader than the understanding, which can respect the variety and singularity of individual consciousnesses, civilizations, ways of thinking, and historical contingency but which nevertheless does not give up the attempt to master them in order to guide them to their own truth. But, as it turns out, Hegel's successors have placed more emphasis on what they reject of his heritage than on what they owe to him. If we do not despair of a *truth* above and beyond divergent points of view, if we remain dedicated to a new classicism, an organic civilization, while maintaining the sharpest sense of subjectivity, then no task in the cultural order is more urgent than re-establishing the connection between on the one hand, the thankless doctrines which try to forget their Hegelian origin and, on the other, that origin itself. That is where their common language can be found and a decisive confrontation can take place. Not that Hegel himself offers the truth we are seeking (there are several Hegels, and even the most objective historian will be led to ask which of them went furthest), but all our antitheses can be found in that single life and work. There would be no paradox involved in saying that interpreting Hegel means taking a stand on all the philosophical, political, and religious problems of our century. The great interest of Hyppolite's lecture is that, as far as existentialism is concerned, it begins the translation which will illuminate the discussions of our time. As is quite natural, the historian tempered the philosopher every step of the way. Since our own aims are non-historical, let us follow this lecture freely rather than textually, to disagree occasionally and constantly to comment.

Kierkegaard, the first to use "existence" in the modem sense of the word, deliberately set himself up in opposition to Hegel. The Hegel he had in mind was the late Hegel, who treated history as the visible development of a logical system, who sought in the relationships between ideas the final explanation of events, and who subordinated the individual experience of life to the life appropriate to ideas, as to a destiny. This Hegel of 1827 offers us nothing but a "palace of ideas," to use Kierkegaard's phrase, where all historical antitheses are overcome, but only by thought. Kierkegaard is right in objecting that mere thought is not enough to enable the individual to overcome the contradictions facing him, that he is faced with dilemmas neither term of which he can accept. This last Hegel has understood everything except his own historical situation; he has taken everything into account except his own existence, and the synthesis he offers is no true synthesis precisely because it pretends ignorance of being the product of a certain individual and a certain time. Kierkegaard's objection, which is in profound agreement with that of Marx, consists in reminding the philosopher of his own inherence in history: where are you speaking from when you judge the world's development and declare that it attains perfection in the Prussian state, and how can you pretend to be outside all situations? Here the reminder of the thinker's own existence and subjectivity merges with the recall to history.

But if the Hegel of 1827 may be criticized for his idealism, the same cannot be said of the Hegel of 1807. The *Phénoménologie de l'esprit* is a history not only of ideas but of all the areas which reveal the mind at work: customs, economic structures, and legal institutions as well as works of philosophy. It is concerned with recapturing a total sense of history, describing the inner workings of the body social, not with explaining the adventures of mankind by debates among philosophers. *Absolute knowledge*, the final stage in the evolution of the spirit as phenomenon wherein consciousness at last becomes equal to its spontaneous life and regains its self-possession, is perhaps not a philosophy but a way of life. It is a militant philosophy that we find in the *Phénoménologie de l'esprit*, not as yet a victorious one. (And besides, up until the *Principes de la philosophie du droit,* Hegel clearly states that philosophers do not create history but always give voice to a situation already established in the world before their appearance on the scene.)[3] The real debate between Marx and Hegel has nothing to do with the relationship of ideas to history; rather, it involves the conception of historical movement, which ends for the Hegel of 1827 in a hierarchical society whose meaning is accessible to none except the philosopher but which the Hegel of 1807 perhaps saw culminating in a genuine reconciliation between men.

What is certain in any case is that the *Phénoménologie de l'esprit* does not try to fit all history into a framework of pre-established logic but attempts to bring each doctrine and each era back to life and to let itself be guided by their internal logic with such impartiality that all concern with system seems forgotten. The introduction states that the philosopher should not put himself in the place of human experiences; his task is simply to collect and decipher these experiences as history makes them available. It is in this sense that we can begin to speak of "Hegelian existentialism," since he does not propose to connect concepts but to reveal the immanent logic of human experience in all its sectors. The question is no longer limited, as it was in the *Critique de la raison pure théorique*, to discovering what conditions make scientific experience possible but is one of knowing in a general way how moral, aesthetic, and religious experiences are possible, of describing man's fundamental situation in the face of the world and other men, and of understanding religions, ethics, works of art, economic and legal systems as just so many ways for man to flee or to confront the difficulties of his condition.[4] Experience here no longer simply means our entirely contemplative contact with the sensible world as it did in Kant; the word reassumes the tragic resonance it has in ordinary language when a man speaks of what he has lived through. It is no longer a laboratory test but is a trial of life.

To be more exact, Hegel's thought is existentialist in that it views man not as being from the start a consciousness in full possession of its own clear thoughts but as a life which is its own responsibility and which tries to understand itself. All of the *Phénoménologie de l'esprit* describes man's efforts to reappropriate himself. At every period of history he starts from a subjective "certainty," makes his actions conform to the directions of that certainty, and witnesses the surprising consequences of his first intention, discovering its objective "truth." He then modifies his project, gets under way once more, again becomes aware of the abstract qualities of his new project, until subjective certainty finally equals objective truth and in the light of consciousness he becomes fully what he already obscurely was. As long as this last stage of history remains unattained—and should it ever be reached, man, deprived of movement, would be like an animal—man, as opposed to the pebble which is what it is, is defined as a place of unrest *(Unruhe),* a constant effort to get back to himself, and consequently by his refusal to limit himself to one or another of his determinations. "Consciousness . . . therefore immediately becomes the act of surpassing the limit and, when it has incorporated this limit into itself, of surpassing itself. . . . Consciousness thus suffers at its own hand the violence by which it spoils all limited satisfactions. Feeling this violence, anxiety may well shrink before the truth, may aspire and tend to save the very thing which is threatened with loss, but there is no calming this anxiety: its attempt to sink into a thoughtless inertia is in vain. . . ."[5] Whatever relationships may be shown to exist between consciousness and the body or brain, all the discoveries of phrenology will not suffice to make consciousness a *bone,* for a bone is still a thing or a being, and if the only components of the world were things or beings, there would not be even a semblance of what we call man—that is, a being which is not, which denies things, an existence without an essence.

Today this idea is trite, but it regains its force if one applies it, as did Hegel, to the relationships between life and our consciousness of it. Of course, all we say about life has to do in reality with consciousness of life, since we who talk about it are conscious of it. However, consciousness re-appropriates as its own limit and source what preconscious life would have been. It would have been a force which disperses itself wherever it acts, a "dying and becoming" which would not even be aware of itself as such. For there to be consciousness of life, that dispersion would have to be ended; it would have to become total and aware of itself—which is in principle impossible for life. An absence of being would have to come into the world, a nothingness from which being would be visible, such that consciousness of life, taken radically, is consciousness of death. Even the doctrines which would imprison us in our racial or local peculiarities and hide our humanity from us can only do so—since they are doctrines and propaganda—by forsaking the immediate life and borrowing shamefully from consciousness of death. Nazi ideology is not to be reproached for reminding men of the tragic but for using the tragic and the vertigo of death to give a semblance of force to prehuman instincts; in short, for obscuring the awareness of death. To be aware of death and to think or reason are one and the same thing, since one thinks only by disregarding what is characteristic of life and thus by conceiving death.

Man cannot be made unaware of death except by being reduced to the state of an animal, and then he would be a poor animal if he retained any part of his consciousness, since consciousness implies the ability to step back from any given thing and to deny it. An animal can quietly find contentment in life and can seek salvation in reproduction; man's only access to the universal is the fact that he exists instead of merely living. This is the price he pays for his humanity, and it is the reason why the idea of the sound man is a myth, closely related to Nazi myths. "Man is the sick animal," said Hegel in an old text of his *Realphilosophie* published by Hoffmeister. Life can only be thought of as revealed to a consciousness of life which denies it.

All consciousness is therefore unhappy, since it knows it is a secondary form of life and misses the innocence from which it senses it came. Judaism's historical mission has been to spread this sense of separation throughout the entire world, and, as Hyppolite said to his students during the war, we are all Jews to the extent that we care about the universal, refuse to resign ourselves to merely being, and want to exist.

Consciousness of death is, however, neither a dead-end nor an outer limit. There are two ways of thinking about death: one pathetic and complacent, which butts against our end and seeks nothing in it but the means of exacerbating violence; the other dry and resolute, which integrates death into itself and turns it into a sharper awareness of life. The young Hegel speaks more willingly of death; the older Hegel prefers to speak of negativity. The Hegel of the *Phénoménologie* juxtaposes the pathetic and logical vocabularies and makes us understand what role consciousness of death plays in the advent of humanity. Death is the negation of all particular given beings, and consciousness of death is a synonym for consciousness of the universal, but it is only an empty or abstract universal as long as we remain at this point. We cannot in fact conceive nothingness except against a ground of being (or, as Sartre says, against the world). Therefore, any notion of death which claims to hold our attention is deceiving us, since it is in fact surreptitiously using our consciousness of being. To plumb our awareness of death, we must transmute it into life, "interiorize" it, as Hegel said. The abstract universal which starts out opposed to life must be made concrete. There is no being without nothingness, but nothingness can exist only in the hollow of being, and so consciousness of death carries with it the means for going beyond it.

The only experience which brings me close to an authentic awareness of death is the experience of contact with another, since under his gaze I am only an object just as he is merely a piece of the world under my own. Thus each consciousness seeks the death of the other which it feels dispossesses it of its constitutive nothingness. But I do not feel threatened by the presence of another unless I remain aware of my subjectivity at the very moment his gaze is reducing me to an object; I do not reduce him to slavery unless he continues to be present to me as consciousness and freedom precisely when he is an object in my eyes. We cannot be aware of the conflict unless we are aware of our reciprocal relationship and our common humanity. We do not deny each other except by mutual recognition of our consciousness. That negation of everything and of others which I am is completed only by reduplicating itself through another's negation of it. And just as my consciousness of myself as death and nothingness is deceitful and contains an affirmation of my being and my life, so my consciousness of another as an enemy comprises an affirmation of him as an equal. If I am negation, then by following the implication of this universal negation to its ultimate conclusion, I will witness the self-denial of that very negation and its transformation into coexistence. By myself I cannot be free, nor can I be a consciousness or a man; and that other whom I first saw as my rival is a rival only because he is myself. I discover myself in the other, just as I discover consciousness of life in consciousness of death, because I am from the start this mixture of life and death, solitude and communication, which is heading toward its resolution.

Domination, sadism, and violence destroy themselves just as consciousness of death goes beyond itself. If each participant in the duel of consciousnesses, of fraternal enemies, succeeded in fatally wounding the other, nothing would be left; there would not even be a place for that hatred of the other and that affirmation of self which is the principle behind the struggle. Thus, the man with the most exact awareness of the human situation is not the master (since the master pretends ignorance of the foundation of being and communication underlying the play of his despair and pride) but the slave. The slave has been truly afraid, has given up trying to conquer by the sword, and he is the only one with experience of death because he alone has known the love of life. The master wants to exist for no one but himself, but in fact he seeks recognition of his mastery from someone and so is weak in his strength. The slave consents to exist only for others, but nevertheless it is he who chooses to go on living on these terms, and he therefore has strength in his weakness. Since he is better acquainted with man's vital core than the master, it is he who will finally have the only possible mastery—at the expense of nature, not of other people. His life is more frankly rooted in the world than is the master's, which is precisely why he knows better than the master what death means: he has really experienced anxiety, the "fluidification of everything stable." Human existence, which had been risk and guilt, becomes history through him, and mankind's successive decisions can be concentrated in one single act by which consciousness is made whole, and God becomes man or, if you prefer, man becomes God.

This is where Hegel's thought abandons its initial pessimism. Learning the truth about death and struggle is the long maturation process by which history overcomes its contradictions and fulfills the promise of humanity—present in the consciousness of death and in the struggle with the other—in the living relationship among men. This is also where Hegel stops being an existentialist, Hyppolite adds. Whereas for Heidegger we exist for the sake of death and the awareness of death remains fundamental to philosophy as well as to behavior, Hegel transmutes death into a higher form of life. He therefore moves from the individual to history, whereas for Sartre there can be no remedy for the contradictions of the *for itself* and the *for others*, with the result that his dialectic is truncated. One might say that in this sense the *Phénoménologie de l'esprit* makes possible a Communist philosophy of the party or a philosophy of the Church rather than a philosophy of the individual such as existentialism. It is true, adds Hyppolite again, that there are other ways of understanding existentialism. This last statement seems the most accurate, since we should note that, even in Heidegger, consciousness of death is not authentic life; the only attitude which does not deceive us is the one which also has a place for the fact of our existence. The decision we must make is to accept death, but that cannot be separated from the decision to live and to get a new grip on our fortuitous existence. As for the existence of the other and the historicity which results, Heidegger does not deny it. It has apparently been forgotten that the last part of *Sein und Zeit* is devoted to the notion of history.[6] One might even say that what Heidegger lacks is not historicity but, on the contrary, an affirmation of the individual: he does not mention that struggle of consciousnesses and that opposition of freedoms without which coexistence sinks into anonymity and everyday banality. It is even more certain that French existentialists are not arrested at an awareness of death. "My death interrupts my life only when I die, and that only from the point of view of others. Death does not exist for me while I am alive; my project goes right through it without meeting any obstacles. The full impetus of my transcendence runs into no barriers; it alone determines when it shall run down, like the sea which strikes against a smooth shore and stops at a certain point, to go no further."[7] And so I live not for death but forever, and likewise, not for myself alone but with other people. A more complete definition of what is called existentialism than we get from talking of anxiety and the contradictions of the human condition might be found in the idea of a universality which men affirm or imply by the mere fact of their being and at the very moment of their opposition to each other, in the idea of a reason immanent in unreason, of a freedom which comes into being in the act of accepting limits and to which the least perception, the slightest movement of the body, the smallest action, bear incontestable witness.

Notes

1. Concerning J. Hyppolite's lecture of the same title, delivered on Feb. 16, 1947, to l'Institut d'Etudes germaniques.
2. English translation of Hegel's *Phänomenologie des Geistes* by J.B. Baillie, *Phenomenology of Mind* (New York, 1931).—Trans.
3. English translation of Hegel's *Grundlinien der Philosophie des Rechts* by T. M. Knox, *Philosophy of Right* (Oxford, 1945).—Trans.
4. English translation of Kant's *Kritik der reinen Vernunft* by Norman Kemp-Smith, *Critique* of *Pure Reason* (London, 1933).—Trans.
5. *Phénoménologie de l'esprit*, trans. J. Hyppolite, Introduction, p. 71.
6. English translation of Heidegger's *Sein und Zeit* by J. Macquarrie and E. Robinson, *Being and Time* (London, 1962).—Trans.
7. Simone de Beauvoir, *Pyrrhus et Cinéas*, p. 61.

CHAPTER 6

"Literature and the Right to Death"

—from *The Work of Fire* (1949)

Maurice Blanchot

One can certainly write without asking why one writes. As a writer watches his pen form the letters, does he even have a right to lift it and say to it: "Stop! What do you know about yourself? Why are you moving forward? Why can't you see that your ink isn't making any marks, that although you may be moving ahead freely, you're moving through a void, that the reason you never encounter any obstacles is that you never left your starting place? And yet you write—you write on and on, disclosing to me what I dictate to you, revealing to me what I know; as others read, they enrich you with what they take from you and give you what you teach them. Now you have done what you did not do; what you did not write has been written: you are condemned to be indelible."

Let us suppose that literature begins at the moment when literature becomes a question. This question is not the same as a writer's doubts or scruples. If he happens to ask himself questions as he writes, that is his concern; if he is absorbed by what he is writing and indifferent to the possibility of writing it, if he is not even thinking about anything, that is his right and his good luck. But one thing is still true: as soon as the page has been written, the question which kept interrogating the writer while he was writing—though he may not have been aware of it—is now present on the page; and now the same question lies silent within the work, waiting for a reader to approach—any kind of reader, shallow or profound; this question is addressed to language, behind the person who is writing and the person who is reading, by language which has become literature.

This concern that literature has with itself may be condemned as an infatuation. It is useless for this concern to speak to literature about its nothingness, its lack of seriousness, its bad faith; this is the very abuse of which it is accused. Literature professes to be important while at the same time considering itself an object of doubt. It confirms itself as it disparages itself. It seeks itself: this is more than it has a right to do, because literature may be one of those things which deserve to be found but not to be sought.

Perhaps literature has no right to consider itself illegitimate. But the question it contains has, properly speaking, nothing to do with its value or its rights. The reason the meaning of this question is so difficult to discover is that the question tends to turn into a prosecution of art and art's capacities and goals. Literature is built on top of its own ruins: this paradox has become a cliché to us. But we must still ask whether the challenge brought against art by the most illustrious works of art in the last thirty years is not based on the redirection, the displacement, of a force laboring in the secrecy of works and loath to emerge into broad daylight, a force the thrust of which was originally quite distinct from any deprecation of literary activity or the literary Thing.

We should point out that as its own negation, literature has never signified the simple denunciation of art or the artist as mystification or deception. Yes, literature is unquestionably illegitimate, there is an underlying deceitfulness in it. But certain people have discovered something beyond this: literature is not only illegitimate, it is also null, and as long as this nullity is isolated in a state of purity, it may constitute an extraordinary force, a marvelous force. To make literature become the exposure of this emptiness inside, to make it open up completely to its nothingness, realize its own unreality—this is one of the tasks undertaken by surrealism. Thus we are correct when we recognize surrealism as a powerful negative movement, but no less correct when we attribute to it the greatest creative ambition, because if literature coincides with nothing for just an instant, it is immediately everything, and this everything begins to exist: what a miracle!

It is not a question of abusing literature, but rather of trying to understand it and to see why we can only understand it by disparaging it. It has been noted with amazement that the question "What is literature?" has received only meaningless answers. But what is even stranger is that something about the very form of such a question takes away all its seriousness. People can and do ask, "What is poetry?" "What is art?" and even "What is the novel?" But the literature which is both poem and novel seems to be the element of emptiness present in all these serious things, and to which reflection, with its own gravity, cannot direct itself without losing its seriousness. If reflection, imposing as it is, approaches literature, literature becomes a caustic force, capable of destroying the very capacity in itself and in reflection to be imposing. If reflection withdraws, then literature once again becomes something important, essential, more important than the philosophy, the religion, or the life of the world which it embraces. But if reflection, shocked by this vast power, returns to this force and asks it what it is, it is immediately penetrated by a corrosive, volatile element and can only scorn a Thing so vain, so vague, and so impure, and in this scorn and this vanity be consumed in turn, as the story of Monsieur Teste has so clearly shown us.

It would be a mistake to say that the powerful negative contemporary movements are responsible for this volatizing and volatile force which literature seems to have become. About one hundred fifty years ago, a man who had the highest idea of art that anyone can have—because he saw how art can become religion and religion, art—this man (called Hegel) described all the ways in which someone who has chosen to be a man of letters condemns himself to belong to the "animal kingdom of the mind."[1] From his very first step, Hegel virtually says, a person who wishes to write is stopped by a contradiction: in order to write, he must have the talent to write. But gifts, in themselves, are nothing. As long as he has not yet sat down at his table and written a work, the writer is not a writer and does not know if he has the capacity to become one. He has no talent until he has written, but he needs talent in order to write.

This difficulty illuminates, from the outset, the anomaly which is the essence of literary activity and which the writer both must and must not overcome. A writer is not an idealistic dreamer, he does not contemplate himself in the intimacy of his beautiful soul, he does not submerse himself in the inner certainty of his talents. He puts his talents to work; that is, he needs the work he produces in order to be conscious of his talents and of himself. The writer only finds himself, only realizes himself, through his work; before his work exists, not only does he not know who he is, but he is nothing. He exists only as a function of the work; but then how can the work exist? "An individual," says Hegel, "cannot know what he [really] is until he has made himself a reality through action. However, this seems to imply that he cannot determine the *End* of his action until he has carried it out; but at the same time, since he is a *conscious* individual, he must have the action in front of him beforehand as *entirely his* own, i.e., as an *End*."[2] Now, the same is true for each new work, because everything begins again from nothing. And the same is also true when he creates a work part by part: if he does not see his work before him as a project already completely formed, how can he make it the conscious end of his conscious acts? But if the work is already present in its entirety in his mind and if this presence is the essence of the work (taking the words, for the time being, to be inessential), why would he realize it any further? Either as an interior project it is everything it ever will be, and from that moment the writer knows everything about it that he can learn, and so will leave it to lie there in its twilight, without translating it into words, without writing it—but then he won't ever write; and he won't be a writer. Or, realizing that the work cannot be planned, but only carried out, that it has value, truth, and reality only through the words which unfold it in time and inscribe it in space, he will begin to write, but starting from nothing and with nothing in mind—like a nothingness working in nothingness, to borrow an expression of Hegel's.

In fact, this problem could never be overcome if the person writing expected its solution to give him the right to begin writing. "For that very reason," Hegel remarks, "he has to start immediately, and, whatever the circumstances, without further scruples about beginning, means, or End, proceed to action."[3] This way, he can break the circle, because in his eyes the circumstances under which he begins to write become the same thing as his talent, and the interest he takes in writing, and the movement which carries him forward, induce him to recognize these circumstances as his own, to see his own goal in them. Valéry often reminded us that his best works were created for a chance commission and were not born of personal necessity. But what did he find so remarkable about that? If he had set to work on *Eupalinos* of his own accord, what reasons would he have had for doing it? That he had held a piece of shell in his hand? Or that opening a dictionary one morning, he happened to read the name Eupalinos in *La Grande Encyclopédie*? Or that he wanted to try dialogue as a form and happened to have on hand a piece of paper that lent itself to that form? One can imagine the most trivial circumstance as the starting point of a great work; nothing is compromised by that triviality: the act by which the author makes it into a crucial circumstance is enough to incorporate it into his genius and his work. In this sense, the publication *Architectures*, which commissioned *Eupalinos* from Valéry, was really the form in which he originally had the talent to write it: that commission was the beginning of that talent, was that talent itself, but we must also add that that commission only became real, only became a true project through Valéry's existence, his talent, his conversations in the world, and the interest he had already shown in this sort of subject. Every work is an occasional work: this simply means that each work has a beginning, that it begins at a certain moment in time and that that moment in time is part of the work, since without it the work would have been only an insurmountable problem, nothing more than the impossibility of writing it.

Let us suppose that the work has been written: with it the writer is born. Before, there was no one to write it; starting from the book, an author exists and merges with his book. When Kafka chances to write the sentence "He was looking out the window," he is—as he says—in a state of inspiration such that the sentence is already perfect. The point is that he is the author of it—or rather that, because of it, he is an author: it is the source of his existence, he has made it and it makes him, it is himself and he is completely what it is. This is the reason for his joy, his pure and perfect joy. Whatever he might write, "the sentence is already perfect." This is the reason for his joy, his pure and perfect joy. This is the strange and profound certainty which art makes into a goal for itself. What is written is neither well nor badly written, neither important nor frivolous, memorable nor forgettable: it is the perfect act through which what was nothing when it was inside emerges into the monumental reality of the outside as something which is necessarily true, as a translation which is necessarily faithful, since the person it translates exists only through it and in it. One could say that this certainty is in some sense the writer's inner paradise and that *automatic writing* has been only one way of making this golden age real—what Hegel calls the pure joy of passing from the night of possibility into the daytime of presence—or again, the certainty that what bursts into the light is none other than what was sleeping in the night. But what is the result of this? The writer who is completely gathered up and enclosed in the sentence "He was looking out the window" apparently cannot be asked to justify this sentence, since for him nothing else exists. But at least the sentence exists, and if it really exists to the point of making the person who wrote it a writer, this is because it is not just his sentence, but a sentence that belongs to other people, people who can read it—it is a universal sentence.

At this point, a disconcerting ordeal begins. The author sees other people taking an interest in his work, but the interest they take in it is different from the interest that made it a pure expression of himself, and that different interest changes the work, transforms it into something different, something in which he does not recognize the original perfection. For him the work has disappeared, it has become a work belonging to other people, a work which includes them and does not include him, a book which derives its value from other books, which is original if it does not resemble them, which is understood because it is a reflection of them. Now the writer cannot disregard this new stage. As we have seen, he exists only in his work, but the work exists only when it has become this public, alien reality, made and unmade by colliding with other realities. So he really is inside the work, but the work itself is disappearing. This is a particularly critical moment in the experiment. All sorts of interpretations come into play in getting beyond it. The writer, for example, would like to protect the perfection of the written Thing by keeping it as far away from life outside as possible. The work is what he created, not the book that is being bought, read, ground up, and praised or demolished in the marketplace of the world. But then where does the work begin, where does it end? At what moment does it come into existence? Why make it public if the splendor of the pure self must be preserved in the work, why take it outside, why realize it in words which belong to everyone? Why not withdraw into an enclosed and secret intimacy without producing anything but an empty object and a dying echo? Another solution—the writer himself agrees to do away with himself: the only one who matters in the work is the person who reads it. The reader makes the work; as he reads it, he creates it; he is its real author, he is the consciousness and the living substance of the written thing; and so the author now has only one goal, to write for that reader and to merge with him. A hopeless endeavor. Because the reader has no use for a work written for him, what he wants is precisely an alien work in which he can discover something unknown, a different reality, a separate mind capable of transforming him and which he can transform into himself. An author who is writing specifically for a public is not really writing: it is the public that is writing, and for this reason the public can no longer be a reader; reading only appears to exist, actually it is nothing. This is why works created to be read are meaningless: no one reads them. This is why it is dangerous to write for other people, in order to evoke the speech of others and reveal them to themselves: the fact is that other people do not want to hear their own voices; they want to hear someone else's voice, a voice that is real, profound, troubling like the truth.

A writer cannot withdraw into himself, for he would then have to give up writing. As he writes, he cannot sacrifice the pure night of his own possibilities, because his work is alive only if that night—and no other—becomes day, if what is most singular about him and farthest removed from existence as already revealed now reveals itself within shared existence. It is true that the writer can try to justify himself by setting himself the task of writing—the simple operation of writing, made conscious of itself quite independently of its results. As we know, this was Valéry's way of saving himself. Let us accept this. Let us accept that a writer may concern himself with art as pure technique, with technique as nothing more than the search for the means by which what was previously not written comes to be written. But if the experiment is to be a valid one, it cannot separate the operation from its results, and the results are never stable or definitive, but infinitely varied and meshed with a future which cannot be grasped. A writer who claims he is concerned only with how the work comes into being sees his concern get sucked into the world, lose itself in the whole of history; because the work is also made outside of him, and all the rigor he put into the consciousness of his deliberate actions, his careful rhetoric, is soon absorbed into the workings of a vital contingency which he cannot control or even observe. Yet his experiment is not worthless: in writing, he has put himself to the test as a nothingness at work, and after having written, he puts his work to the test as something in the act of disappearing. The work disappears, but the fact of disappearing remains and appears as the essential thing, the movement which allows the work to be realized as it enters the stream of history, to be realized as it disappears. In this experiment, the writer's real goal is no longer the ephemeral work but something beyond that work: the truth of the work, where the individual who writes—a force of creative negation—seems to join with the work in motion through which this force of negation and surpassing asserts itself.

This new notion, which Hegel calls the Thing Itself, plays a vital role in the literary undertaking. No matter that it has so many different meanings: it is the art which is above the work, the ideal that the work seeks to represent, the World as it is sketched out in the work, the values at stake in the creative effort, the authenticity of this effort; it is everything which, above the work that is constantly being dissolved in things, maintains the model, the essence, and the spiritual truth of that work just as the writer's freedom wanted to manifest it and can recognize it as its own. The goal is not what the writer makes but the truth of what he makes. As far as this goes, he deserves to be called an honest, disinterested conscience—

the honest man. But here we run into trouble: as soon as honesty comes into play in literature, imposture is already present. Here bad faith is truth, and the greater the pretension to morality and seriousness, the more surely will mystification and deceit triumph. Yes, literature is undoubtedly the world of values, since above the mediocrity of the finished works everything they lack keeps appearing as their own truth. But what is the result of this? A perpetual enticement, an extraordinary game of hide-and-seek in which the writer claims as an excuse that what he has in mind is not the ephemeral work but the spirit of that work and of every work—no matter what he does, no matter what he has not been able to do, he adapts himself to it, and his honest conscience derives knowledge and glory from it. Let us listen to that honest conscience; we are familiar with it because it is working in all of us. When the work has failed, this conscience is not troubled: it says to itself, "Now it has been fully completed, for failure is its essence; its disappearance constitutes its realization," and the conscience is happy with this; lack of success delights it. But what if the book does not even manage to be born, what if it remains a pure nothing? Well, this is still better: silence and nothingness are the essence of literature, "the Thing Itself." It is true: the writer is willing to put the highest value on the meaning his work has for him alone. Then it does not matter whether the work is good or bad, famous or forgotten. If circumstances neglect it, he congratulates himself, since he wrote it only to negate circumstances. But when a book that comes into being by chance, produced in a moment of idleness and lassitude, without value or significance, is suddenly made into a masterpiece by circumstantial events, what author is not going to take credit for the glory himself, in his heart of hearts, what author is not going to see his own worth in that glory, and his own work in that gift of fortune, the working of his mind in providential harmony with his time?

A writer is his own first dupe, and at the very moment he fools other people he is also fooling himself. Listen to him again: now he states that his function is to write for others, that as he writes he has nothing in mind but the reader's interest. He says this and he believes it. But it is not true at all. Because if he were not attentive first and foremost to what *he* is doing, if he were not concerned with literature as his own action, he could not even write: he would not be the one who was writing—the one writing would be no one. This is why it is futile for him to take the seriousness of an ideal as his guarantee, futile for him to claim to have stable values: this seriousness is not his own seriousness and can never settle definitively where he thinks he is. For example: he writes novels, and these novels imply certain political statements, so that he seems to side with a certain Cause. Other people, people who directly support the Cause, are then inclined to recognize him as one of themselves, to see his work as proof that the Cause is really his cause, but as soon as they make this claim, as soon as they try to become involved in this activity and take it over, they realize that the writer is not on their side, that he is only on his own side, that what interests him about the

Cause is the operation he himself has carried out—and they are puzzled. It is easy to understand why men who have committed themselves to a party, who have made a decision, distrust writers who share their views; because these writers have also committed themselves to literature, and in the final analysis literature, by its very activity, denies the substance of what it represents. This is its law and its truth. If it renounces this in order to attach itself permanently to a truth outside itself, it ceases to be a literature and the writer who still claims he is a writer enters into another aspect of bad faith. Then must a writer refuse to take an interest in anything, must he turn his face to the wall? The problem is that if he does this, his equivocation is just as great. First of all, looking at the wall is also turning toward the world; one is making the wall into the world. When a writer sinks into the pure intimacy of a work which is no one's business but his own, it may seem to other people—other writers and people involved in other activities—that at least they have been left at peace in their Thing and their own work. But not at all. The work created by this solitary person and enclosed in solitude contains within itself a point of view which concerns everyone, implicitly passing judgment on other works, on the problems of the times, becoming the accomplice of whatever it neglects, the enemy of whatever it abandons, and its indifference mingles hypocritically with everyone's passion.

What is striking is that in literature, deceit and mystification not only are inevitable but constitute the writer's honesty, whatever hope and truth are in him. Nowadays people often talk about the sickness of words, and we even become irritated with those who talk about it, and suspect them of making words sick so they can talk about it. This could be the case. The trouble is that this sickness is also the words' health. They may be torn apart by equivocation, but this equivocation is a good thing—without it there would be no dialogue. They may be falsified by misunderstanding—but this misunderstanding is the possibility of our understanding. They may be imbued with emptiness—but this emptiness is their very meaning. Naturally, a writer can always make it his ideal to call a cat a cat. But what he cannot manage to do is then believe that he is on the way to health and sincerity. On the contrary, he is causing more mystification than ever, because the cat is not a cat, and anyone who claims that it is has nothing in mind but this hypocritical violence: Rolet is a rascal.[4]

There are many reasons for this imposture. We have just been discussing the first reason: literature is made up of different stages which are distinct from one another and in opposition to one another. Honesty, which is analytical because it tries to see clearly, separates these stages. Under the eyes of honesty pass in succession the author, the work, and the reader; in succession the art of writing, the thing written, and the truth of that thing or the Thing Itself; still in succession, the writer without a name, pure absence of himself, pure idleness, then the writer who is work, who is the action of a creation indifferent to what it is creating, then the writer who is the result of this work and is worth something because of this result and not because of the work, as real as the created thing is real, then the writer who is no longer affirmed by this result but denied by it, who saves the ephemeral work by saving its ideal, the truth of the work, etc. The writer is not simply one of these stages to the exclusion of the others, nor is he even all of them put together in their unimportant succession, but the action which brings them together and unifies them. As a result, when the honest conscience judges the writer by immobilizing him in one of these forms, when, for instance, it attempts to condemn the work because it is a failure, the writer's other honesty protests in the name of the other stages, in the name of the purity of art, which sees its own triumph in the failure—and likewise, every time a writer is challenged under one of his aspects, he has no choice but to present himself as someone else, and when addressed as the author of a beautiful work, disown that work, and when admired as an inspiration and a genius, see in himself only application and hard work, and when read by everyone, say: "Who can read me? I haven't written anything." This shifting on the part of the writer makes him into someone who is perpetually absent, an irresponsible character without a conscience, but this shifting also forms the extent of his presence, of his risks and responsibility.

The trouble is that the writer is not only several people in one, but each stage of himself denies all the others, demands everything for itself alone, and does not tolerate any conciliation or compromise. The writer must respond to several absolute and absolutely different commands at once, and his morality is made up of the confrontation and opposition of implacably hostile rules.

One rule says to him: "You will not write, you will remain nothingness, you will keep silent, you will not know words."

The other rule says: "Know nothing but words."

"Write to say nothing."

"Write to say something."

"No works; rather, the experience of yourself, the knowledge of what is unknown to you."

"A work! A real work, recognized by other people and important to other people."

"Obliterate the reader."

"Obliterate yourself before the reader."

"Write in order to be true."

"Write for the sake of truth."

"Then be a lie, because to write with truth in mind is to write what is not yet true and perhaps never will be true."

"It doesn't matter, write in order to act."

"Write—you who are afraid to act."

"Let freedom speak in you."

"Oh! do not let freedom become a word in you."

Which law should be obeyed? Which voice should be listened to? But the writer must listen to them all! What confusion! Isn't clarity his law? Yes, clarity, too. He must therefore oppose himself, deny himself even as he affirms himself, look for the deepness of the night in the facility of the day, look in the shadows which never begin, to find the sure light which cannot end. He must save the world and be the abyss, justify existence and allow what does not exist to speak; he must be at the end of all eras in the universal plenitude, and he is the origin, the birth of what does nothing but come into being. Is he all that? Literature is all that, in him. But isn't all that what literature would *like* to be, what in reality it is not? In that case, literature is nothing. But is it nothing?

Literature is not nothing. People who are contemptuous of literature are mistaken in thinking they are condemning it by saying it is nothing. "All that is only literature." This is how people create an opposition between action, which is a concrete initiative in the world, and the written word, which is supposed to be a passive expression on the surface of the world; people who are in favor of action reject literature, which does not act, and those in search of passion become writers so as not to act. But this is to condemn and to love in an abusive way. If we see work as the force of history, the force that transforms man while it transforms the world, then a writer's activity must be recognized as the highest form of work. When a man works, what does he do? He produces an object. That object is the realization of a plan which was unreal before then: it is the affirmation of a reality different from the elements which constitute it and it is the future of new objects, to the extent that it becomes a tool capable of creating other objects. For example, my project might be to get warm. As long as this project is only a desire, I can turn it over every possible way and still it will not make me warm. But now I build a stove: the stove transforms the empty ideal which was my desire into something real; it affirms the presence in the world of something which was not there before, and in so doing, denies something which was there before; before, I had in front of me stones and cast iron; now I no longer have either stones or cast iron, but instead the product of the transformation of these elements—that is, their denial and destruction—by work. Because of this object, the world is now different. All the more different because this stove will allow me to make other objects, which will in turn deny the former condition of the world and prepare its future. These objects, which I have produced by changing the states of things, will in turn change me. The idea of heat is nothing, but actual heat will make my life a different kind of life, and every new thing I am able to do from now on because of this heat will also make me someone different. Thus is history formed, say Hegel and Marx—by work which realizes being in denying it, and reveals it at the end of the negation.[5]

But what is a writer doing when he writes? Everything a man does when he works, but to an outstanding degree. The writer, too, produces something—a work in the highest sense of the word. He produces this work by transforming natural and human realities. When he writes, his starting point is a certain state of language, a certain form of culture, certain books, and also certain objective elements—ink, paper, printing presses. In order to write, he must destroy language in its present form and create it in another form, denying books as he forms a book out of what other books are not. This new book is certainly a reality: it can be seen, touched, even read. In any case, it is not nothing. Before I wrote it, I had an idea of it, at least I had the project of writing it, but I believe there is the same difference between that idea and the volume in which it is realized as between the desire for heat and the stove which makes me warm. For me, the written volume is an extraordinary, unforeseeable innovation—such that it is impossible for me to conceive what it is capable of being without writing it. This is why it seems to me to be an experiment whose effects I cannot grasp, no matter how consciously they were produced, and in the face of which I shall be unable to remain the same, for this reason: in the presence of something other, I become other. But there is an even more decisive reason: this other thing—the book—of which I had only an idea and which I could not possibly have known in advance, is precisely myself become other.

The book, the written thing, enters the world and carries out its work of transformation and negation. It, too, is the future of many other things, and not only books: by the projects which it can give rise to, by the undertakings it encourages, by the totality of the world of which it is a modified reflection, it is an infinite source of new realities, and because of these new realities existence will be something it was not before.

So is the book nothing? Then why should the act of building a stove pass for the sort of work which forms and produces history, and why should the act of writing seem like pure passivity which remains in the margins of history and which history produces in spite of itself? The question seems unreasonable, and yet it weighs on the writer and its weight is crushing. At first sight one has the impression that the formative power of written works is incomparably great; one has the impression that the writer is endowed with more power to act than anyone else since his actions are immeasurable, limitless: we know (or we like to believe) that one single work can change the course of the world. But this is precisely what makes us think twice. The influence authors exert is very great, it goes infinitely far beyond their actions, to such an extent that what is real in their actions does not carry over into their influence and that tiny bit of reality does not contain the real substance that the extent of their influence would require. What is an author capable of? Everything—first of all, everything: he is fettered, he is enslaved, but as long as he can find a few moments of freedom in which to write, he is *free* to create a world without slaves, a world in which the slaves become the masters and formulate a new law; thus, by writing, the chained man immediately obtains freedom for himself and for the world; he denies everything he is, in order to become everything he is not. In this sense, his work is a prodigious act, the greatest and most important there is. But let us examine this more closely. Insofar as he *immediately* gives himself the freedom he does not have, he is neglecting the actual conditions for his emancipation, he is neglecting to do the real thing that must be done so that the abstract idea of freedom can be realized. His negation is *global*. It not only negates his situation as a man who has been walled into prison but bypasses time that will open holes in these walls; it negates the negation of time, it negates the negation of limits. This is why this negation negates nothing, in the end, why the work in which it is realized is not a truly negative, destructive act of transformation, but rather the realization of the inability to negate anything, the refusal to take part in the world; it transformed the freedom which would have to be embodied in things in the process of time into an ideal above time, empty and inaccessible.

A writer's influence is linked to this privilege of being master of everything. But he is only master of everything, he possesses only the infinite; he lacks the finite, limit escapes him. Now, one cannot act in the infinite, one cannot accomplish anything in the unlimited, so that if a writer acts in quite a real way as he produces this real thing which is called a book, he is also discrediting all action by this action, because he is substituting for the world of determined things and defined work a world in which *everything* is *instantly* given and there is nothing left to do but read it and enjoy it.

In general, the writer seems to be subjected to a state of inactivity because he is the master of the imaginary, and those who follow him into the realm of the imaginary lose sight of the problems of their true lives. But the danger he represents is much more serious. The truth is that he ruins action, not because he deals with what is unreal but because he makes *all* of reality available to us. Unreality begins with the whole. The realm of the imaginary is not a strange region situated beyond the world, it is the world itself, but the world as entire, manifold, the world as a whole. That is why it is not in the world, because it is the world, grasped and realized in its entirety by the global negation of all the individual realities contained in it, by their disqualification, their absence, by the realization of that absence itself, which is how literary creation begins, for when literary creation goes back over each thing and each being, it cherishes the illusion that it is creating them, because now it is seeing and naming them from the starting point of *everything*, from the starting point of the *absence* of everything, that is, from nothing.

Certainly that literature which is said to be "purely imaginative" has its dangers. First of all, it is not pure imagination. It believes that it stands apart from everyday realities and actual events, but the truth is that it has stepped aside from them; it is that distance, that remove from the everyday which necessarily takes the everyday into consideration and describes it as separateness, as pure strangeness. What is more, it makes this distance into an absolute value, and then this separateness seems to be a source of general understanding, the capacity to grasp everything and attain everything immediately, for those who submit to its enchantment enough to emerge from both their life, which is nothing but limited understanding, and time, which is nothing but a narrow perspective. All this is the lie of a fiction. But this kind of literature has on its side the fact that it is not trying to deceive us: it presents itself as imaginary; it puts to sleep only those who want to go to sleep.

What is far more deceitful is the literature of action. It calls on people to do something. But if it wants to remain authentic literature, it must base its representation of this "something to do," this predetermined and specific goal, on a world where such an action turns back into the unreality of an abstract and absolute value. "Something to do," as it may be expressed in a work of literature, is never more than "everything remains to be done," whether it presents itself as this "everything," that is, as an absolute value, or whether it needs this "everything," into which it vanishes, to justify itself and prove that it has merit. The language of a writer, even if he is a revolutionary, is not the language of command. It does not command, it presents; and it does not present by causing whatever it portrays to be present, but by portraying it behind everything, as the meaning and the absence of this everything. The result is either that the appeal of the author to the reader is only an empty appeal, and expresses only the effort which a man cut off from the world makes to reenter the world, as he stands discreetly at its periphery—or that the "something to do," which can be recovered only by starting from absolute values, appears to the reader precisely as that which cannot be done or as that which requires neither work nor action in order to be done.

As we know, a writer's main temptations are called stoicism, skepticism, and the unhappy consciousness. These are all ways of thinking that a writer adopts for reasons he believes he has thought out carefully, but which only literature has thought out in him. A stoic: he is the man of the universe, which itself exists only on paper, and, a prisoner or a poor man, he endures his condition stoically because he can write and because the one minute of freedom in which he writes is enough to make him powerful and free, is enough to give him not his own freedom, which he derides, but universal freedom. A nihilist, because he does not simply negate this and that by methodical work which slowly transforms each thing: he negates everything at once, and he is obliged to negate everything, since he deals only with everything. The unhappy consciousness! It is only too evident that this unhappiness is his most profound talent, since he is a writer only by virtue of his fragmented consciousness divided into irreconcilable moments called inspiration—which negates all work; work—which negates the nothingness of genius; the ephemeral work—in which he creates himself by negating himself; the work as everything—in which he takes back from himself and from other people everything which he seems to give to himself and to them. But there is one other temptation.

Let us acknowledge that in a writer there is a movement which proceeds without pause, and almost without transition, from nothing to everything. Let us see in him that negation that is not satisfied with the unreality in which it exists, because it wishes to realize itself and can do so only by negating something real, more real than words, more true than the isolated individual in control: it therefore keeps urging him toward a worldly life and a public existence in order to induce him to conceive how, even as he writes, he can become that very existence. It is at this point that he encounters those decisive moments in history when everything seems put in question, when law, faith, the State, the world above, the world of the past—everything sinks effortlessly, without work, into nothingness. The man knows he has not stepped out of history, but history is now the void, the void in the process of realization; it is *absolute* freedom which has become an event. Such periods are given the name Revolution. At this moment, freedom aspires to be realized in the *immediate* form of *everything* is possible, everything can be done. A fabulous moment—and no one who has experienced it can completely recover from it, since he has experienced history as his own history and his own freedom as universal freedom. These moments are, in fact, fabulous moments: in them, fable speaks; in them, the speech of fable becomes action. That the writer should be tempted by them is completely appropriate. Revolutionary action is in every respect analogous to action as embodied in literature: the passage from nothing to everything, the affirmation of the absolute as event and of every event as absolute. Revolutionary action explodes with the same force and the same facility as the writer who has only to set down a few words side by side in order to change the world. Revolutionary action also has the same demand for purity, and the certainty that everything it does has absolute value, that it is not just any action performed to bring about some desirable and respectable goal, but that it is itself the ultimate goal, the Last Act. This last act is freedom, and the only choice left is between freedom and nothing. This is why, at that point, the only tolerable slogan is Freedom or Death. Thus the Reign of Terror comes into being. People cease to be individuals working at specific tasks, acting here and only now: each person is universal freedom, and universal freedom knows nothing about elsewhere or tomorrow, or work or a work accomplished. At such times there is nothing left for anyone to do, because everything has been done. No one has a right to a private life any longer, everything is public, and the most guilty person is the suspect—the person who has a secret, who keeps a thought, an intimacy to himself. And in the end no one has a right to his life any longer, to his actually separate and physically distinct existence. This is the meaning of the Reign of Terror. Every citizen has a right to death, so to speak: death is not a sentence passed on him, it is his most essential right; he is not suppressed as a guilty person—he needs death so that he can proclaim himself a citizen, and it is in the disappearance of death that freedom causes him to be born. Where this is concerned, the French Revolution has a clearer meaning than any other revolution. Death in the Reign of Terror is not simply a way of punishing seditionaries; rather, since it becomes the unavoidable, in some sense the desired lot of everyone, it appears as the very operation of freedom in free men. When the blade falls on Saint-Just and Robespierre, in a sense it executes no one. Robespierre's virtue, Saint-Just's relentlessness, are simply their existences already suppressed, the anticipated presence of their deaths, the decision to allow freedom to assert itself completely in them and through its universality to negate the particular reality of their lives. Granted, perhaps they caused the Reign of Terror to take place. But the Terror they personify does not come from the death they inflict on others but from the death they inflict on themselves. They bear its features, they do their thinking and make their decisions with death sitting on their shoulders, and this is why their thinking is cold, implacable; it has the freedom of a decapitated head. The Terrorists are those who desire absolute freedom and are fully conscious that this constitutes a desire for their own death, they are conscious of the freedom they affirm, as they are conscious of their death, which they realize, and consequently they behave during their lifetimes not like people living among other living people but like beings deprived of being, like universal thoughts, pure abstractions beyond history, judging and deciding in the name of all of history.

Death as an event no longer has any importance. During the Reign of Terror individuals die and it means nothing. In the famous words of Hegel, "It is thus the coldest and meanest of all deaths, with no more significance than cutting off a head of cabbage or swallowing a mouthful of water."[6] Why? Isn't death the achievement of freedom—that is, the richest moment of meaning? But it is also only the empty point in that freedom, a manifestation of the fact that such a freedom is still abstract, ideal (literary), that it is only poverty and platitude. Each person dies, but everyone is alive, and that really also means everyone is dead. But "is dead" is the positive side of freedom which has become the world: here, being is revealed as absolute. "Dying," on the other hand, is pure insignificance, an event without concrete reality, one which has lost all value as a personal and interior drama because there is no longer any interior. It is the moment when *I die* signifies to me as I die a banality which there is no way to take into consideration: in the liberated world and in these moments when freedom is an absolute apparition, dying is unimportant and death has no depth. The Reign of Terror and revolution—not war—have taught us this.

The writer sees himself in the Revolution. It attracts him because it is the time during which literature becomes history. It is his truth. Any writer who is not induced by the very fact of writing to think, "I am the revolution, only freedom allows me to write," is not really writing. In 1793 there is a man who identifies himself completely with revolution and the Reign of Terror. He is an aristocrat clinging to the battlements of his medieval castle, a tolerant man, rather shy and obsequiously polite: but he writes, all he does is write, and it does not matter that freedom puts him back into the Bastille after having brought him out, he is the one who understands freedom the best, because he understands that it is a time when the most insane passions can turn into political realities, a time when they have a right to be seen, and are the law. He is also the man for whom death is the greatest passion and the ultimate platitude, who cuts off people's heads the way you cut a head of cabbage, with such great indifference that nothing is more unreal than the death he inflicts, and yet no one has been more acutely aware that death is sovereign, that freedom is death. Sade is the writer par excellence, he combines all the writer's contradictions. Alone: of all men he is the most alone, and yet at the same time a public figure and an important political personage; forever locked up and yet absolutely free, theoretician and symbol of absolute freedom. He writes a vast body of work, and that work exists for no one. Unknown: but what he portrays has an immediate significance for everyone. He is nothing more than a writer, and he depicts life raised to the level of a passion, a passion which has become cruelty and madness. He turns the most bizarre, the most hidden, the most unreasonable kind of feeling into a universal affirmation, the reality of a public statement which is consigned to history to become a legitimate explanation of man's general condition. He is, finally, negation itself: his oeuvre is nothing but the work of negation, his experience the action of a furious negation, driven to blood, denying other people, denying God, denying nature, and, within this circle in which it runs endlessly, reveling in itself as absolute sovereignty.

Literature contemplates itself in revolution, it finds its justification in revolution, and if it has been called the Reign of Terror, this is because its ideal is indeed that moment in history, that moment when "life endures death and maintains itself in it" in order to gain from death the possibility of speaking and the truth of speech. This is the "question" that seeks to pose itself in literature, the "question" that is its essence. Literature is bound to language. Language is reassuring and disquieting at the same time. When we speak, we gain control over things with satisfying ease. I say, "This woman," and she is immediately available to me, I push her away, I bring her close, she is everything I want her to be, she becomes the place in which the most surprising sorts of transformations occur and actions unfold: speech is life's ease and security. We cannot do anything with an object that has no name. Primitive man knows that the possession of words gives him mastery over things, but for him the relationship between words and the world is so close that the manipulation of language is as difficult and as fraught with peril as contact with living beings: the name has not emerged from the thing, it is the inside of the thing which has been dangerously brought out into the open and yet it is still the hidden depths of the thing; the thing has therefore not yet been named. The more closely man becomes attached to a civilization, the more he can manipulate words with innocence and composure. Is it that words have lost all relation to what they designate? But this absence of relation is not a defect, and if it is a defect, this defect is the only thing that gives language its full value, so that of all languages the most perfect is the language of mathematics, which is spoken in a rigorous way and to which no entity corresponds.

I say, "This woman." Hölderlin, Mallarmé, and all poets whose theme is the essence of poetry have felt that the act of naming is disquieting and marvelous. A word may give me its meaning, but first it suppresses it. For me to be able to say, "This woman," I must somehow take her flesh-and-blood reality away from her, cause her to be absent, annihilate her. The word gives me the being, but it gives it to me deprived of being. The word is the absence of that being, its nothingness, what is left of it when it has lost being—the very fact that it does not exist. Considered in this light, speaking is a curious right. In a text dating from before *The Phenomenology*, Hegel, here the friend and kindred spirit of Hölderlin, writes: "Adam's first act, which made him master of the animals, was to give them names, that is, he annihilated them in their existence (as existing creatures)."[7] Hegel means that from that moment on, the cat ceased to be a uniquely real cat and became an idea as well. The meaning of speech, then, requires that before any word is spoken, there must be a sort of immense hecatomb, a preliminary flood plunging all of creation into a total sea. God had created living things, but man had to annihilate them. Not until then did they take on meaning for him, and he in turn created them out of the death into which they had disappeared; only instead of beings (*êtres*) and, as we say, existants (*existants*), there remained only being (*l'être*), and man was condemned not to be able to approach anything or experience anything except through the meaning he had to create. He saw that he was enclosed in daylight, and he knew this day could not end, because the end itself was light, since it was from the end of beings that their meaning—which is being—had come.

Of course my language does not kill anyone. And yet, when I say, "This woman," real death has been announced and is already present in my language; my language means that this person, who is here right now, can be detached from herself, removed from her existence and her presence, and suddenly plunged into a nothingness in which there is no existence or presence; my language essentially signifies the possibility of this destruction; it is a constant, bold allusion to such an event. My language does not kill anyone. But if this woman were not really capable of dying, if she were not threatened by death at every moment of her life, bound and joined to death by an essential bond, I would not be able to carry out that ideal negation, that deferred assassination which is what my language is.

Therefore it is accurate to say that when I speak, death speaks in me. My speech is a warning that at this very moment death is loose in the world, that it has suddenly appeared between me, as I speak, and the being I address: it is there between us as the distance that separates us, but this distance is also what prevents us from being separated, because it contains the condition for all understanding. Death alone allows me to grasp what I want to attain; it exists in words as the only way they can have meaning. Without death, everything would sink into absurdity and nothingness.

This situation has various consequences. Clearly, in me, the power to speak is also linked to my absence from being. I say my name, and it is as though I were chanting my own dirge: I separate myself from myself, I am no longer either my presence or my reality, but an objective, impersonal presence, the presence of my name, which goes beyond me and whose stonelike immobility performs exactly the same function for me as a tombstone weighing on the void. When I speak, I deny the existence of what I am saying, but I also deny the existence of the person who is saying it: if my speech reveals being in its nonexistence, it also affirms that this revelation is made on the basis of the nonexistence of the person making it, out of his power to remove himself from himself, to be other than his being. This is why, if true language is to begin, the life that will carry this language must have experienced its nothingness, must have "trembled in the depths; and everything in it that was fixed and stable must have been shaken." Language can begin only with the void; no fullness, no certainty can ever speak; something essential is lacking in anyone who expresses himself. Negation is tied to language. When I first begin, I do not speak in order to say something; rather, a nothing demands to speak, nothing speaks, nothing finds its being in speech, and the being of speech is nothing. This formulation explains why literature's ideal has been the following: to say nothing, to speak in order to say nothing. That is not the musing of a high-class kind of nihilism. Language perceives that its meaning derives not from what exists but from its own retreat before existence, and it is tempted to proceed no further than this retreat, to try to attain negation in itself and to make everything of nothing. If one is not to talk about things except to say what makes them nothing, then to say nothing is really the only hope of saying everything about them.

A hope which is naturally problematic. Everyday language calls a cat a cat, as if the living cat and its name were identical, as if it were not true that when we name the cat, we retain nothing of it but its absence, what it is not. Yet for a moment everyday language is right, in that even if the word excludes the existence of what it designates, it still refers to it through the thing's nonexistence, which has become its essence. To name the cat is, if you like, to make it into a non-cat, a cat that has ceased to exist, has ceased to be a living cat, but this does not mean one is making it into a dog, or even a non-dog. That is the primary difference between common language and literary language. The first accepts that once the nonexistence of the cat has passed into the word, the cat itself comes to life again fully and certainly in the form of its idea (its being) and its meaning: on the level of being (idea), the word restores to the cat all the certainty it had on the level of existence. And in fact that certainty is even much greater: things can change if they have to, sometimes they stop being what they are—they remain hostile, unavailable, inaccessible; but the being of these things, their idea, does not change: the idea is definitive, it is sure, we even call it eternal. Let us hold on to words, then, and not revert back to things, let us not let go of words, not believe they are sick. Then we shall be at peace.

Common language is probably right, this is the price we pay for our peace. But literary language is made of uneasiness; it is also made of contradictions. Its position is not very stable or secure. On the one hand, its only interest in a thing is in the meaning of the thing, its absence, and it would like to attain this absence absolutely in itself and for itself, to grasp in its entirety the infinite movement of comprehension. What is more, it observes that the word "cat" is not only the nonexistence of the cat but a nonexistence made *word*, that is, a completely determined and objective reality. It sees that there is a difficulty and even a lie in this. How can it hope to have achieved what it set out to do, since it has transposed the unreality of the thing into the reality of language? How could the infinite absence of comprehension consent to be confused with the limited, restricted presence of a single word? And isn't everyday language mistaken when it tries to persuade us of this? In fact, it is deceiving itself and it is deceiving us, too. Speech is not sufficient for the truth it contains. Take the trouble to listen to a single word: in that word, nothingness is struggling and toiling away, it digs tirelessly, doing its utmost to find a way out, nullifying what encloses it—it is infinite disquiet, formless and nameless vigilance. Already the seal which held this nothingness within the limits of the word and within the guise of its meaning has been broken; now there is access to other names, names which are less fixed, still vague, more capable of adapting to the savage freedom of the negative essence—they are unstable groups, no longer terms but the movement of terms, an endless sliding of "turns of phrase" which do not lead anywhere. Thus is born the image that does not directly designate the thing but, rather, what the thing is not; it speaks of a dog instead of a cat. This is how the pursuit begins in which all of language, in motion, is asked to give in to the uneasy demands of one single thing that has been deprived of being and that, after having wavered between each word, tries to lay hold of them all again in order to negate them all at once, so that they will designate the void as they sink down into it—this void which they can neither fill nor represent.

Even if literature stopped here, it would have a strange and embarrassing job to do. But it does not stop here. It recalls the first name which would be the murder Hegel speaks of. The "existant" was called out of its existence by the word, and it became being. This *Lazare, veni foras* summoned the dark, cadaverous reality from its primordial depths and in exchange gave it only the life of the mind. Language knows that its kingdom is day and not the intimacy of the unrevealed; it knows that in order for the day to begin, for the day to be that Orient which Hölderlin glimpsed—not light that has become the repose of noon but the terrible force that draws beings into the world and illuminates them—something must be left out. Negation cannot be created out of anything but the reality of what it is negating; language derives its value and its pride from the fact that it is the achievement of this negation; but in the beginning, what was lost? The torment of language is what it lacks because of the necessity that it be the lack of precisely this. It cannot even name it.

Whoever sees God dies. In speech what dies is what gives life to speech; speech is the life of that death, it is "the life that endures death and maintains itself in it." What wonderful power. But something was there and is no longer there. Something has disappeared. How can I recover it, how can I turn around and look at what exists *before*, if all my power consists of making it into what exists *after*? The language of literature is a search for this moment which precedes literature. Literature usually calls it existence; it wants the cat as it exists, the pebble *taking the side of things*, not man but the pebble, and in this pebble what man rejects by saying it, what is the foundation of speech and what speech excludes in speaking, the abyss, Lazarus in the tomb and not Lazarus brought back into the daylight, the one who already smells bad, who is Evil, Lazarus lost and not Lazarus saved and brought back to life. *I say a flower*! But in the absence where I mention it, through the oblivion to which I relegate the image it gives me, in the depths of this heavy word, itself looming up like an unknown thing, I passionately summon the darkness of this flower, I summon this perfume that passes through me though I do not breathe it, this dust that impregnates me though I do not see it, this color which is a trace and not light. Then what hope do I have of attaining the thing I push away? My hope lies in the materiality of language, in the fact that words are things, too, are a kind of nature—this is given to me and gives me more than I can understand. Just now the reality of words was an obstacle. Now, it is my only chance. A name ceases to be the ephemeral passing of nonexistence and becomes a concrete ball, a solid mass of existence; language, abandoning the sense, the meaning which was all it wanted to be, tries to become senseless. Everything physical takes precedence: rhythm, weight, mass, shape, and then the paper on which one writes, the trail of the ink, the book. Yes, happily language is a thing: it is a written thing, a bit of bark, a sliver of rock, a fragment of clay in which the reality of the earth continues to exist. The word acts not as an ideal force but as an obscure power, as an incantation that coerces things, makes them *really* present outside of themselves. It is an element, a piece barely detached from its subterranean surroundings: it is no longer a name, but rather one moment in the universal anonymity, a bald statement, the stupor of a confrontation in the depths of obscurity. And in this way language insists on playing its own game without man, who created it. Literature now dispenses with the writer: it is no longer this inspiration at work, this negation asserting itself, this idea inscribed in the world as though it were the absolute perspective of the world in its totality. It is not beyond the world, but neither is it the world itself: it is the presence of things before the *world* exists, their perseverance after the world has disappeared, the stubbornness of what remains when everything vanishes and the dumbfoundedness of what appears when nothing exists. That is why it cannot be confused with consciousness, which illuminates things and makes decisions; it *is my* consciousness *without me*, the radiant passivity of mineral substances, the lucidity of the depths of torpor. It is not the night, it is the obsession of the night; it is not the night but the consciousness of the night, which lies awake watching for a chance to surprise itself and because of that is constantly being dissipated. It is not the day, it is the side of the day that day has rejected in order to become light. And it is not death either, because it manifests existence without being, existence which remains below existence, like an inexorable affirmation, without beginning or end—death as the impossibility of dying.

By turning itself into an inability to reveal anything, literature is attempting to become the revelation of what revelation destroys. This is a tragic endeavor. Literature says, "I no longer represent, I am; I do not signify, I present." But this wish to be a thing, this refusal to mean anything, a refusal immersed in words turned to salt; in short, this destiny which literature becomes as it becomes the language of no one, the writing of no writer, the light of a consciousness deprived of self, this insane effort to bury itself in itself, to hide itself behind the fact that it is visible—all this is what literature now manifests, what literature now shows. If it were to become as mute as a stone, as passive as the corpse enclosed behind that stone, its decision to lose the capacity for speech would still be legible on the stone and would be enough to wake that bogus corpse.

Literature learns that it cannot go beyond itself toward its own end: it hides, it does not give itself away. It knows it is the movement through which whatever disappears keeps appearing. When it names something, whatever it designates is abolished; but whatever is abolished is also sustained, and the thing has found a refuge (in the being which is the word) rather than a threat. When literature refuses to name anything, when it turns a name into something obscure and meaningless, witness to the primordial obscurity, what has disappeared in this case—the meaning of the name—is really destroyed, but signification in general has appeared in its place, the meaning of the meaninglessness embedded in the word as expression of the obscurity of existence, so that although the precise meaning of the terms has faded, what asserts itself now is the very possibility of signifying, the empty power of bestowing meaning—a strange impersonal light.

By negating the day, literature re-creates day in the form of fatality; by affirming the night, it finds the night as the impossibility of the night. This is its discovery. When day is the light of the world, it illuminates what it lets us see: it is the capacity to grasp, to live, it is the answer "understood" in every question. But if we call the day to account, if we reach a point where we push it away in order to find out what is prior to the day, under it we discover that the day is already present, and that what is prior to the day is still the day, but in the form of an inability to disappear, not a capacity to make something appear: the darkness of necessity, not the light of freedom. The nature, then, of what is prior to the day, of prediurnal existence, is the dark side of the day, and that dark side is not the undisclosed mystery of its beginning but its inevitable presence—the statement "There is no day," which merges with "There is already day," its appearance coinciding with the moment when it has not yet appeared. In the course of the day, the day allows us to escape from things, it lets us comprehend them, and as it lets us comprehend them, it makes them transparent and as if null—but what we cannot escape from is the day: within it we are free, but it, itself, is fatality, and day in the form of fatality is the being of what is prior to the day, the existence we must turn away from in order to speak and comprehend.

If one looks at it in a certain way, literature has two slopes. One side of literature is turned toward the movement of negation by which things are separated from themselves and destroyed in order to be known, subjugated, communicated. Literature is not content to accept only the fragmentary, successive results of this movement of negation: it wants to grasp the movement itself and it wants to comprehend the results in their totality. If negation is assumed to have gotten control of everything, then real things, taken one by one, all refer back to that unreal whole which they form together, to the world which is their meaning as a group, and this is the point of view that literature has adopted—it looks at things from the point of view of this still *imaginary* whole which they would *really* constitute if negation could be achieved. Hence its non-realism—the shadow which is its prey. Hence its distrust of words, its need to apply the movement of negation to language itself and to exhaust it by realizing it as that totality on the basis of which each term would be nothing.

But there is another side to literature. Literature is a concern for the reality of things, for their unknown, free, and silent existence; literature is their innocence and their forbidden presence, it is the being which protests against revelation, it is the defiance of what does not want to take place outside. In this way, it sympathizes with darkness, with aimless passion, with lawless violence, with everything in the world that seems to perpetuate the refusal to come into the world. In this way, too, it allies itself with the reality of language, it makes language into matter without contour, content without form, a force that is capricious and impersonal and says nothing, reveals nothing, simply announces—through its refusal to say anything—that it comes from night and will return to night. In itself, this metamorphosis is not unsuccessful. It is certainly true that words are transformed. They no longer *signify* shadow, earth, they no longer represent the absence of shadow and earth which is meaning, which is the shadow's light, which is the transparency of the earth: opacity is their answer; the flutter of closing wings is their speech; in them, physical weight is present as the stifling density of an accumulation of syllables that has lost all meaning. The metamorphosis has taken place. But beyond the change that has solidified, petrified, and stupefied words two things reappear in this metamorphosis: the meaning of this metamorphosis, which illuminates the words, and the meaning the words contain by virtue of their apparition as things or, if it should happen this way, as vague, indeterminate, elusive existences in which nothing appears, the heart of depth without appearance. Literature has certainly triumphed over the meaning of words, but what it has found in words considered apart from their meaning is meaning that has become thing: and thus it is meaning detached from its conditions, separated from its moments, wandering like an empty power, a power no one can do anything with, a power without power, the simple inability to cease to be, but which, because of that, appears to be the proper determination of indeterminate and meaningless existence. In this endeavor, literature does not confine itself to rediscovering in the interior what it tried to leave behind on the threshold. Because what it finds, as the interior, is the outside which has been changed from the outlet it once was into the impossibility of going out—and what it finds as the darkness of existence is the being of day which has been changed from explicatory light, creative of meaning, into the aggravation of what one cannot prevent oneself from understanding and the stifling obsession of a reason without any principle, without any beginning, which one cannot account for. Literature is that experience through which the consciousness discovers its being in its inability to lose consciousness, in the movement whereby, as it disappears, as it tears itself away from the meticulousness of an I, it is re-created beyond unconsciousness as an impersonal spontaneity, the desperate eagerness of a haggard knowledge which knows nothing, which no one knows, and which ignorance always discovers behind itself as its own shadow changed into a gaze.

One can, then, accuse language of having become an interminable resifting of words instead of the silence it wanted to achieve. Or one can complain that it has immersed itself in the conventions of literature when what it wanted was to be absorbed into existence. That is true. But this endless resifting of words without content, this continuousness of speech through an immense pillage of words, is precisely the profound nature of a silence that talks even in its dumbness, a silence that is speech empty of words, an echo speaking on and on in the midst of silence. And in the same way literature, a blind vigilance which in its attempt to escape from itself plunges deeper and deeper into its own obsession, is the only rendering of the obsession of existence, if this itself is the very impossibility of emerging from existence, if it is being which is always flung back into being, that which in the bottomless depth is already at the bottom of the abyss, a recourse against which there is no recourse.[8]

Literature is divided between these two slopes. The problem is that even though they are apparently incompatible, they do not lead toward distinctly different works or goals, and that an art which purports to follow one slope is already on the other. The first slope is meaningful prose. Its goal is to express things in a language that designates things according to what they mean. This is the way everyone speaks; and many people write the way we speak. But still on this side of language, there comes a moment when art realizes that everyday speech is dishonest and abandons it. What is art's complaint about everyday speech? It says it lacks meaning: art feels it is madness to think that in each word some thing is completely present through the absence that determines it, and so art sets off in quest of a language that can recapture this absence itself and represent the endless movement of comprehension. We do not need to discuss this position again, we have described it at length already. But what can be said about this kind of art? That it is a search for a pure form, that it is a vain preoccupation with empty words? Quite the contrary: its only concern is true meaning; its only preoccupation is to safeguard the movement by which this meaning becomes truth. To be fair, we must consider it more significant than any ordinary prose, which only subsists on false meanings: it represents the world for us, it teaches us to discover the total being of the world, it is the work of the negative in the world and for the world. How can we help admiring it as preeminently active, lively, and lucid art? Of course we must. But then we must appreciate the same qualities in Mallarmé, who is the master of this art.

Mallarmé is on the other slope of literature, too. In some sense all the people we call poets come together on that slope. Why? Because they are interested in the reality of language, because they are not interested in the world, but in what things and beings would be if there were no world; because they devote themselves to literature as to an impersonal power that only wants to be engulfed and submerged. If this is what poetry is like, at least we will know why it must be withdrawn from history, where it produces a strange insectlike buzzing in the margins, and we will also know that no work which allows itself to slip down this slope toward the chasm can be called a work of prose. Well, what is it, then? Everyone understands that literature cannot be divided up, and that if you choose exactly where your place in it is, if you convince yourself that you really are where you wanted to be, you risk becoming very confused, because literature has already insidiously caused you to pass from one slope to the other and changed you into something you were not before. This is its treachery; this is also its cunning version of the truth. A novelist writes in the most transparent kind of prose, he describes men we could have met ourselves and actions we could have performed; he says his aim is to express the reality of a human world the way Flaubert did. In the end, though, his work really has only one subject. What is it? The horror of existence deprived of the world, the process through which whatever ceases to be continues to be, whatever is forgotten is always answerable to memory, whatever dies encounters only the impossibility of dying, whatever seeks to attain the beyond is always still here. This *process* is day which has become fatality, consciousness whose light is no longer the lucidity of the vigil but the stupor of lack of sleep, it is existence without being, as poetry tries to recapture it behind the meaning of words, which reject it.

Now here is a man who does more observing than writing: he walks in a pine forest, looks at a wasp, picks up a stone. He is a sort of scholar, but this scholar fades away in the face of what he knows, sometimes in the face of what he wants to know; he is a man who learns for the sake of other men: he has gone over to the side of objects, sometimes he is water, sometimes a pebble, sometimes a tree, and when he observes things, he does it for the sake of things, and when he describes something, it is the thing itself that describes itself. Now, this is the surprising aspect of the transformation, because no doubt it is possible to become a tree, and is there any writer who could not succeed in making a tree talk? But Francis Ponge's tree is a tree that has observed Francis Ponge and that describes itself as it imagines Ponge might describe it. These are strange descriptions. Certain traits make them seem completely human: the fact is that the tree knows the weakness of men who only speak about what they know; but all these metaphors borrowed from the picturesque human world, these images which form an image, really represent the way things regard man, they really represent the singularity of human speech animated by the life of the cosmos and the power of seeds; this is why other things slip in among these images, among certain objective notions—because the tree knows that science is a common ground of understanding between the two worlds: what slip in are vague recollections rising from deep down in the earth, expressions that are in the process of metamorphosing, words in which a thick fluidity of vegetable growth insinuates itself under the clear meaning. Doesn't everyone think he understands these descriptions, written in perfectly meaningful prose? Doesn't everyone think they belong to the clear and human side of literature? And yet they do not belong to the world but to the underside of the world; they do not attest to form but to lack of form, and they are clear only to a person who does not penetrate them, the opposite of the oracular words of the tree of Dodona—another tree—which were obscure but concealed a meaning: these are clear only because they hide their lack of meaning. Indeed, Ponge's descriptions begin at that hypothetical moment after the world has been achieved, history completed, nature almost made human, when speech advances to meet the thing and the thing learns to speak. Ponge captures this touching moment when existence, which is still mute, encounters speech at the edge of the world, speech which as we know, is the murderer of existence. From the depths of dumbness, he hears the striving of an antediluvian language and he recognizes the profound work of the elements in the clear speech of the concept. In this way he becomes the will that mediates between that which is rising slowly to speech and speech which is descending slowly to the earth, expressing not existence as it was before the day but existence as it is after the day: the world of the end of the world.

Where in a work lies the beginning of the moment when the words become stronger than their meaning and the meaning more physical than the word? When does Lautréamont's prose lose the name of prose? Isn't each sentence understandable? Isn't each group of sentences logical? And don't the words say what they mean? At what moment, in this labyrinth of order, in this maze of clarity, did meaning stray from the path? At what turning did reason become aware that it had stopped "following," that something else was continuing, progressing, concluding in its place, something like it in every way, something reason thought it recognized as itself, until the moment it woke up and discovered this other that had taken its place? But if reason now retraces its steps in order to denounce the intruder, the illusion immediately vanishes into thin air, reason finds only itself there, the prose is prose again, so that reason starts off again and loses its way again, allowing a sickening physical substance to replace it, something like a walking staircase, a corridor that unfolds ahead—a kind of reason whose infallibility excludes all reasoners, a logic that has become the "logic of things." Then where is the work? Each moment has the clarity of a beautiful language being spoken, but the work as a whole has the opaque meaning of a thing that is being eaten and that is also eating, that is devouring, being swallowed up, and re-creating itself in a vain effort to change itself into nothing.

Lautréamont is not a true writer of prose? But what is Sade's style, if it isn't prose? And does anyone write more clearly than he does? Is there anyone less familiar than he—who grew up in the least poetic century—with the preoccupations of a literature in search of obscurity? And yet in what other work do we hear such an impersonal, inhuman sound, such a "gigantic and haunting murmur" (as Jean Paulhan says)? But this is simply a defect! The weakness of a writer who cannot be brief! It is certainly a serious defect—literature is the first to accuse him of it. But what it condemns on one side becomes a merit on the other; what it denounces in the name of the work it admires as an experience, what seems unreadable, is really the only thing worth being written. And at the end of everything is fame; beyond, there is oblivion; farther beyond, anonymous survival as part of a dead culture; even farther beyond, perseverance in the eternity of the elements. Where is the end? Where is that death which is the hope of language? But language is *the life that endures death and maintains itself in it*.

If we want to restore literature to the movement which allows all its ambiguities to be grasped, that movement is here: literature, like ordinary speech, *begins* with the *end*, which is the only thing that allows us to understand. If we are to speak, we must see death, we must see it behind us. When we speak, we are leaning on a tomb, and the void of that tomb is what makes language true, but at the same time void is reality and death becomes being. There is being—that is to say, a logical and expressible truth—and there is a world, because we can destroy things and suspend existence. This is why we can say that there is being because there is nothingness: death is man's possibility, his chance, it is through death that the future of a finished world is still there for us; death is man's greatest hope, his only hope of being man. This is why existence is his only real dread, as Emmanuel Lévinas has clearly shown;[9] existence frightens him, not because of death, which could put an end to it, but because it excludes death, because it is still there underneath death, a presence in the depths of absence, an inexorable day in which all days rise and set. And there is no question that we are preoccupied by dying. But why? It is because when we die, we leave behind not only the world but also death. That is the paradox of the last hour. Death works with us in the world; it is a power that humanizes nature, that raises existence to being, and it is within each one of us as our most human quality; it is death only in the world—man knows death only because he is man, and he is man only because he is death in the process of becoming. But to die is to shatter the world; it is the loss of the person, the annihilation of the being; and so it is also the loss of death, the loss of what in it and for me made it death. As long as I live, I am a mortal man, but when I die, by ceasing to be a man I also cease to be mortal, I am no longer capable of dying, and my impending death horrifies me because I see it as it is: no longer death but the impossibility of dying.

Certain religions have taken the impossibility of death and called it immortality. That is, they have tried to "humanize" the very event which signifies "I cease to be a man." But it is only the opposite thrust that makes death impossible: through death I lose the advantage of being mortal, because I lose the possibility of being man; to be man beyond death could only have this strange meaning—to be, in spite of death, still capable of dying, to go on as though nothing had happened, with death as a horizon and the same hope—death which would have no outcome beyond a "go on as though nothing had happened," etc. This is what other religions have called the curse of being reborn: you die, but you die badly because you have lived badly, you are condemned to live again, and you live again until, having become a man completely, in dying you become a truly blessed man—a man who is really dead. Kafka inherited this idea from the Cabala and Eastern traditions. A man enters the night, but the night ends in awakening, and there he is, an insect. Or else the man dies, but he is actually alive; he goes from city to city, carried along by rivers, recognized by some people, helped by no one, the mistake made by old death snickering at his bedside; his is a strange condition, he has forgotten to die. But another man thinks he is alive, when the fact is, he has forgotten his death, and yet another, knowing he is dead, struggles in vain to die; death is over there, the great unattainable castle, and life was over there, the native land he left in answer to a false summons; now there is nothing to do but to struggle, to work at dying completely, but if you struggle, you are still alive; and everything that brings the goal closer also makes the goal inaccessible.

Kafka did not make this theme the expression of a drama about the next world, but he did try to use it to capture the present fact of our condition. He saw in literature the best way of trying to find a way out for this condition, not only of describing it. This is high praise, but does literature deserve it? It is true that there is powerful trickery in literature, a mysterious bad faith that allows it to play everything both ways and gives the most honest people an unreasonable hope of losing and yet winning at the same time. First of all, literature, too, is working toward the advent of the world; literature is civilization and culture. In this way, it is already uniting two contradictory movements. It is negation, because it drives the inhuman, indeterminate side of things back into nothingness; it defines them, makes them finite, and this is the sense in which literature is really the work of death in the world. But at the same time, after having denied things in their existence, it preserves them in their being; it causes things to have a meaning, and the negation which is death at work is also the advent of meaning, the activity of comprehension. Besides this, literature has a certain privilege: it goes beyond the immediate place and moment, and situates itself at the edge of the world and as if at the end of time, and it is from this position that it speaks about things and concerns itself with men. From this new power, literature apparently gains a superior authority. By revealing to each moment the whole of which it is a part, literature helps it to be aware of the whole that it is not and to become another moment that will be a moment within another whole, and so forth; because of this, literature can be called the greatest ferment in history. But there is one inconvenient consequence: this whole which literature represents is not simply an idea, since it is *realized* and not formulated abstractly—but it is not realized in an objective way, because what is real in it is not the whole but the particular language of a particular work, which is itself immersed in history; what is more, the whole does not present itself as real but as fictional, that is, precisely as whole, as everything: perspective of the world, grasp of that *imaginary* point where the world can be seen in its entirety. What we are talking about, then, is a view of the world which realizes itself as unreal using language's peculiar reality. Now, what is the consequence of this? As for the task which is the world, literature is now regarded more as a bother than as a serious help; it is not the result of any true work, since it is not reality but the realization of a point of view which remains unreal; it is foreign to any true culture, because culture is the work of a person changing himself little by little over a period of time, and not the immediate enjoyment of a fictional transformation which dispenses with both time and work.

Spurned by history, literature plays a different game. If it is not really in the world, working to make the world, this is because its lack of being (of intelligible reality) causes it to refer to an existence that is still inhuman. Yes, it recognizes that this is so, that in its nature there is a strange slipping back and forth between being and not being, presence and absence, reality and nonreality. What is a work? Real words and an imaginary story, a world in which everything that happens is borrowed from reality, and this world is inaccessible; characters who are portrayed as living—but we know that their life consists of not living (of remaining a fiction); pure nothingness, then? But the book is there, and we can touch it, we read the words and we cannot change them; is it the nothingness of an idea, then, of something which exists only when understood? But the fiction is not understood, it is experienced through the words with which it is realized, and for me, as I read it or write it, it is more real than many real events, because it is impregnated with all the reality of language and it substitutes itself for my life simply by existing. Literature does not act: but what it does is plunge into this depth of existence which is neither being nor nothingness and where the hope of doing anything is completely eliminated. It is not explanation, and it is not pure comprehension, because the inexplicable emerges in it. And it expresses without expressing, it offers its language to what is murmured in the absence of speech. So literature seems to be allied with the strangeness of that existence which being has rejected and which does not fit into any category. The writer senses that he is in the grasp of an impersonal power that does not let him either live or die: the irresponsibility he cannot surmount becomes the expression of that death without death which awaits him at the edge of nothingness; literary immortality is the very movement by which the nausea of a survival which is not a survival, a death which does not end anything, insinuates itself into the world, a world sapped by crude existence. The writer who writes a work eliminates himself as he writes that work and at the same time affirms himself in it. If he has written it to get rid of himself, it turns out that the work engages him and recalls him to himself, and if he writes it to reveal himself and live in it, he sees that what he has done is nothing, that the greatest work is not as valuable as the most insignificant act, and that his work condemns him to an existence that is not his own existence and to a life that has nothing to do with life. Or again he has written because in the depths of language he heard the work of death as it prepared living beings for the truth of their name: he worked for this nothingness and he himself was a nothingness at work. But as one realizes the void, one creates a work, and the work, born of fidelity to death, is in the end no longer capable of dying; and all it brings to the person who was trying to prepare an unstoried death for himself is the mockery of immortality.

Then where is literature's power? It plays at working in the world, and the world regards its work as a worthless or dangerous game. It opens a path for itself toward the obscurity of existence and does not succeed in pronouncing the "Never more" which would suspend its curse. Then where is its force? Why would a man like Kafka decide that if he had to fall short of his destiny, being a writer was the only way to fall short of it truthfully? Perhaps this is an unintelligible enigma, but if it is, the source of the mystery is literature's right to affix a negative or positive sign indiscriminately to each of its moments and each of its results. A strange right—one linked to the question of ambiguity in general. Why is there ambiguity in the world? Ambiguity is its own answer. We cannot answer it except by rediscovering it in the ambiguity of our answer, and an ambiguous answer is a question about ambiguity. One of the ways it reduces us is by making us want to clear it up, a struggle that is like the struggle against evil Kafka talks about, which ends in evil, "like the struggle with women, which ends in bed."

Literature is language turning into ambiguity. Ordinary language is not necessarily clear, it does not always say what it says; misunderstanding is also one of its paths. This is inevitable. Every time we speak, we make words into monsters with two faces, one being reality, physical presence, and the other meaning, ideal absence. But ordinary language limits equivocation. It solidly encloses the absence in a presence, it puts *a term* to understanding, to the indefinite movement of comprehension; understanding is limited, but misunderstanding is limited, too. In literature, ambiguity is in some sense abandoned to its excesses by the opportunities it finds and exhausted by the extent of the abuses it can commit. It is as though there were a hidden trap here to force ambiguity to reveal its own traps, and as though in surrendering unreservedly to ambiguity, literature were attempting to keep it—out of sight of the world and out of the thought of the world—in a place where it fulfills itself without endangering anything. Here ambiguity struggles with itself. It is not just that each moment of language can become ambiguous and say something different from what it is saying, but that the general meaning of language is unclear: we do not know if it is expressing or representing, if it is a thing or means that thing; if it is there to be forgotten or if it only makes us forget it so that we will see it; if it is transparent because what it says has so little meaning or clear because of the exactness with which it says it, obscure because it says too much, opaque because it says nothing. There is ambiguity everywhere: in its trivial exterior—but what is most frivolous may be the mask of the serious; in its disinterestedness—but behind this disinterestedness lie the forces of the world, and it connives with them without knowing them, or again, ambiguity uses this disinterestedness to safeguard the absolute nature of the values without which action would stop or become mortal; its unreality is therefore both a principle of action and the incapacity to act, in the same way that the fiction in itself is truth and also indifference to truth; in the same way that if it allies itself with morality, it corrupts itself, and if it rejects morality, it still perverts itself; in the same way that it is nothing if it is not its own end, but it cannot have its end in itself, because it is without end, it ends outside itself, in history, etc.

All these reversals from *pro* to *contra*—and those described here—undoubtedly have very different causes. We have seen that literature assigns itself irreconcilable tasks. We have seen that in moving from the writer to the reader, from the labor to the finished work, it passes through contradictory moments and can only place itself in the affirmation of all the opposing moments. But all these contradictions, these hostile demands, these divisions and oppositions, so different in origin, kind, and meaning, refer back to an ultimate ambiguity whose strange effect is to attract literature to an unstable point where it can indiscriminately change both its meaning and its sign.

This ultimate vicissitude keeps the work in suspense in such a way that it can choose whether to take on a positive or a negative value and, as though it were pivoting invisibly around an invisible axis, enter the daylight of affirmations or the backlight of negations, without its style, genre, or subject being accountable for the radical transformation. Neither the content of the words nor their form is involved here. Whether the work is obscure or clear, poetry or prose, insignificant or important, whether it speaks of a pebble or of God, there is something in it that does not depend on its qualities and that deep within itself is always in the process of changing the work from the ground up. It is as though in the very heart of literature and language, beyond the visible movements that transform them, a point of instability were reserved, a power to work substantial metamorphoses, a power capable of changing everything about it without changing anything. This instability can appear to be the effect of a disintegrating force, since it can cause the strongest, most forceful work to become a work of unhappiness and ruin, but this disintegration is also a form of construction, if it suddenly causes distress to turn into hope and destruction into an element of the indestructible. How can such imminence of change, present in the depths of language quite apart from the meaning that affects it and the reality of that language, nevertheless be present in that meaning and in that reality? Could it be that the meaning of a word introduces something else into the word along with it, something which, although it protects the precise signification of the word and does not threaten that signification, is capable of completely modifying the meaning and modifying the material value of the word? Could there be a force at once friendly and hostile hidden in the intimacy of speech, a weapon intended to build and to destroy, which would act behind signification rather than upon signification? Do we have to suppose a meaning for the meaning of words that, while determining that meaning, also surrounds this determination with an ambiguous indeterminacy that wavers between yes and no?

But we cannot suppose anything: we have questioned this meaning of the meaning of words at length, this meaning which is as much the movement of a word toward its truth as it is its return through the reality of language to the obscure depths of existence; we have questioned this absence by which the thing is annihilated, destroyed in order to become being and idea. It is *that life which supports death and maintains itself in it*—death, the amazing power of the negative, or freedom, through whose work existence is detached from itself and made significant. Now, nothing can prevent this power—at the very moment it is trying to understand things and, in language, to specify words—nothing can prevent it from continuing to assert itself as continually differing possibility, and nothing can stop it from perpetuating an irreducible *double meaning*, a choice whose terms are covered over with an ambiguity that makes them identical to one another even as it makes them opposite.

If we call this power negation or unreality or death, then presently death, negation, and unreality, at work in the depths of language, will signify the advent of truth in the world, the construction of intelligible being, the formation of meaning. But just as suddenly, the sign changes: meaning no longer represents the marvel of comprehension, but instead refers us to the nothingness of death, and intelligible being signifies only the rejection of existence, and the absolute concern for truth is expressed by an incapacity to act in a real way. Or else death is perceived as a civilizing power which results in a comprehension of being. But at the same time, a death that results in being represents an absurd insanity, the curse of existence—which contains within itself both death and being and is neither being nor death. Death ends in being: this is man's hope and his task, because nothingness itself helps to make the world, nothingness is the creator of the world in man as he works and understands. Death ends in being: this is man's laceration, the source of his unhappy fate, since by man death comes to being and by man meaning rests on nothingness; the only way we can comprehend is by denying ourselves existence, by making death *possible*, by contaminating what we comprehend with the nothingness of death, so that if we emerge from being, we fall outside the possibility of death, and the way out becomes the disappearance of every way out.

This original double meaning, which lies deep inside every word like a condemnation that is still unknown and a happiness that is still invisible, is the source of literature, because literature is the form in which this double meaning has chosen to show itself behind the meaning and value of words, and the question it asks is the question asked by literature.

Notes

1. In this argument, Hegel is considering human work in general. It should be understood that the remarks which follow are quite remote from the text of the *Phenomenology* and make no attempt to illuminate it. The text can be read in Jean Hippolyte's translation and pursued further through his important book, *Origin and Structure of Hegel's 'Phenomenology of the Spirit.'*
2. Hegel, *Phenomenology of Spirit*, trans. A. V. Miller (Oxford University Press, 1977, p. 240); chap. V, sec. Ia, "The spiritual animal kingdom and deceit or the 'matter in hand' itself."—TRANS.
3. Ibid.—TRANS.
4. Blanchot is referring to a remark made by Nicolas Boileau (1637–1711) in his first *Satire*: "J'appelle un chat un chat et Rolet un fripon" ("I call a cat a cat and Rolet a rascal"). Rolet was a notorious figure of the time.—TRANS.

5. Alexandre Kojève offers this interpretation of Hegel in his *Introduction to the Reading of Hegel* (Readings on *The Phenomenology of the Spirit*, selected and published by Raymond Queneau).
6. Hegel, *Phenomenology of the Spirit*, p. 360.—TRANS.
7. From a collection of essays titled *System of 1803–1804*. A. Kojève, in his *Introduction to the Reading of Hegel*, interpreting a passage from the *Phenomenology*, demonstrates in a remarkable way how for Hegel comprehension was equivalent to murder.
8. In his book *Existence and Existents*, Emmanuel Lévinas uses the term *il y a* ("there is") to throw some "light" on this anonymous and impersonal flow of being that precedes all being, being that is already present in the heart of disappearance, that in the depths of annihilation still returns to being, being as the fatality of being, nothingness as existence: when there is nothing, *il y a being*. See also *Deucalion I*. (*Existence and Existents*, trans. A. Lingis, Boston: Kluwer, 1978).—TRANS.
9. He writes, "Isn't dread in the face of being—horror of being—just as primordial as dread in the face of death? Isn't fear of being just as primordial as fear for one's being? Even more primordial, because one could account for the latter by means of the former" (*Existence and Existents*).

CHAPTER 7

"The Negro and Hegel"

—from *Black Skin, White Masks* (1952)

Frantz Fanon

> *Self-consciousness exists* in itself *and* for itself, *in that and by the fact that it exists for another self-consciousness; that is to say, it* is *only by being acknowledged or recognized.*
>
> —Hegel, *The Phenomenology of Mind*

Man is human only to the extent to which he tries to impose his existence on another man in order to be recognized by him. As long as he has not been effectively recognized by the other, that other will remain the theme of his actions. It is on that other being, on recognition by that other being, that his own human worth and reality depend. It is that other being in whom the meaning of his life is condensed.

There is not an open conflict between white and black. One day the White Master, *without conflict*, recognized the Negro slave.

But the former slave wants to *make himself recognized*.

At the foundation of Hegelian dialectic there is an absolute reciprocity which must be emphasized. It is in the degree to which I go beyond my own immediate being that I apprehend the existence of the other as a natural and more than natural reality. If I close the circuit, if I prevent the accomplishment of movement in two directions, I keep the other within himself. Ultimately, I deprive him even of this being-for-itself.

The only means of breaking this vicious circle that throws me back on myself is to restore to the other, through mediation and recognition, his human reality, which is different from natural reality. The other has to perform the same operation. "Action from one side only would be useless, because what is to happen can only be brought about by means of both. . . ."; "*they recognize themselves as mutually recognizing each other*."[1]

In its immediacy, consciousness of self is simple being-for-itself. In order to win the certainty of oneself, the incorporation of the concept of recognition is essential. Similarly, the other is waiting for recognition by us, in order to burgeon into the universal consciousness of self. Each consciousness of self is in quest of absoluteness. It wants to be recognized as a primal value without reference to life, as a transformation of subjective certainty (*Gewissheit)* into objective truth (*Wahrheit*).

When it encounters resistance from the other, self-consciousness undergoes the experience of *desire*—the first milestone on the road that leads to the dignity of the spirit. Self-consciousness accepts the risk of its life, and consequently it threatens the other in his physical being. "It is solely by risking life that freedom is obtained; only thus is it tried and proved that the essential nature of self-consciousness is not *bare existence*, is not the merely immediate form in which it at first makes its appearance, is not its mere absorption in the expanse of life."[2]

Thus human reality in-itself-for-itself can be achieved only through conflict and through the risk that conflict implies. This risk means that I go beyond life toward a supreme good that is the transformation of subjective certainty of my own worth into a universally valid objective truth.

As soon as I *desire* I am asking to be considered. I am not merely here-and-now, sealed into thingness. I am for somewhere else and for something else. I demand that notice be taken of my negating activity insofar as I pursue something other than life; insofar as I do battle for the creation of a human world—that is, of a world of reciprocal recognitions.

He who is reluctant to recognize me opposes me. In a savage struggle I am willing to accept convulsions of death, invincible dissolution, but also the possibility of the impossible.[3]

The other, however, can recognize me without struggle: "The individual, who has not staked his life, may, no doubt, be recognized as a *person*, but he has not attained the truth of this recognition as an independent self-consciousness."[4]

Historically, the Negro steeped in the inessentiality of servitude was set free by his master. He did not fight for his freedom.

Out of slavery the Negro burst into the lists where his masters stood. Like those servants who are allowed once every year to dance in the drawing room, the Negro is looking for a prop. The Negro has not become a master. When there are no longer slaves, there are no longer masters.

The Negro is a slave who has been allowed to assume the attitude of a master.

The white man is a master who has allowed his slaves to eat at his table.

One day a good white master who had influence said to his friends, "Let's be nice to the niggers. . . ."

The other masters argued, for after all it was not an easy thing, but then they decided to promote the machine-animal-men to the supreme rank of *men.*

Slavery shall no longer exist on French soil.

The upheaval reached the Negroes from without. The black man was acted upon. Values that had not been created by his actions, values that had not been born of the systolic tide of his blood, danced in a hued whirl round him. The upheaval did not make a difference in the Negro. He went from one way of life to another, but not from one life to another. Just as when one tells a much improved patient that in a few days he will be discharged from the hospital, he thereupon suffers a relapse, so the announcement of the liberation of the black slaves produced psychoses and sudden deaths.

It is not an announcement that one hears twice in a lifetime. The black man contented himself with thanking the white man, and the most forceful proof of the fact is the impressive number of statues erected all over France and the colonies to show white France stroking the kinky hair of this nice Negro whose chains had just been broken.

"Say thank you to the nice man," the mother tells her little boy . . . but we know that often the little boy is dying to scream some other, more resounding expression. . . .

The white man, in the capacity of master,[5] said to the Negro, "From now on you are free."

But the Negro knows nothing of the cost of freedom, for he has not fought for it. From time to time he has fought for Liberty and Justice, but these were always white liberty and white justice; that is, values secreted by his masters. The former slave, who can find in his memory no trace of the struggle for liberty or of that anguish of liberty of which Kierkegaard speaks, sits unmoved before the young white man singing and dancing on the tightrope of existence.

When it does happen that the Negro looks fiercely at the white man, the white man tells him: "Brother, there is no difference between us." And yet the Negro *knows* that there is a difference. He *wants* it. He wants the white man to turn on him and shout: "Damn nigger." Then he would have that unique chance—to "show them. . . ."

But most often there is nothing—nothing but indifference, or a paternalistic curiosity.

The former slave needs a challenge to his humanity, he wants a conflict, a riot. But it is too late: The French Negro is doomed to bite himself and just to bite. I say "the French Negro," for the American Negro is cast in a different play. In the United States, the Negro battles and is battled. There are laws that, little by little, are invalidated under the Constitution. There are other laws that forbid certain forms of discrimination. And we can be sure that nothing is going to be given free.

There is war, there are defeats, truces, victories.

"The twelve million black voices"[6] howled against the curtain of the sky. Torn from end to end, marked with the gashes of teeth biting into the belly of interdiction, the curtain fell like a burst balloon.

On the field of battle, its four corners marked by the scores of Negroes hanged by their testicles, a monument is slowly being built that promises to be majestic.

And, at the top of this monument, I can already see a white man and a black man *hand in hand*.

For the French Negro the situation is unbearable. Unable ever to be sure whether the white man considers him consciousness in-itself-for-itself, he must forever absorb himself in uncovering resistance, opposition, challenge.

This is what emerges from some of the passages of the book that Mounier has devoted to Africa.[7] The young Negroes whom he knew there sought to maintain their alterity. Alterity of rupture, of conflict, of battle.

The self takes its place by opposing itself, Fichte said. Yes and no.

I said in my introduction that man is a *yes*. I will never stop reiterating that.

Yes to life. *Yes* to love. *Yes* to generosity.

But man is also a *no*. *No* to scorn of man. *No* to degradation of man. *No* to exploitation of man. *No* to the butchery of what is most human in man: freedom.

Man's behavior is not only reactional. And there is always resentment in a *reaction*. Nietzsche had already pointed that out in *The Will to Power*.

To educate man to be *actional*, preserving in all his relations his respect for the basic values that constitute a human world, is the prime task of him who, having taken thought, prepares to act.

Notes

1. G. W. F. Hegel, *The Phenomenology of Mind,* trans. by J. B. Baillie, 2nd rev. ed. (London, Allen and Unwin, 1949), pp. 230, 231.
2. *Ibid*, p. 233.
3. When I began this book, I wanted to devote one section to a study of the death wish among Negroes. I believed it necessary because people are forever saying that Negroes never commit suicide.

   M. Achille did not hesitate to maintain this in a lecture, and Richard Wright, in one of his stories, has a white character say, "If I were a Negro I'd kill myself . . . ," in the sense that only a Negro could submit to such treatment without feeling drawn to suicide.

   Since then, M. Deshaies has taken the question of suicide as the subject of his thesis. He demonstrates that the studies by Jaensch, who contrasted the disintegrated-personality "type" (blue eyes, white skin) to the integrated-personality "type" (brown eyes and skin), are predominantly specious.

According to Durkheim, Jews never committed suicide. Now it is the Negroes. Very well: "The Detroit municipal hospital found that 16.6 percent of its suicide cases were Negroes, although the proportion of Negroes in the total population is only 7.6 percent. In Cincinnati, the number of Negro suicides is more than double that of whites; this may result in part from the amazing sexual disparity among Negro suicides: 358 women against 76 men." (Gabriel Deshaies, *Psychologie du suicide*, note 23.)

4. Hegel, *op. cit.*, p. 233.
5. I hope I have shown that here the master differs basically from the master described by Hegel. For Hegel there is reciprocity; here the master laughs at the consciousness of the slave. What he wants from the slave is not recognition but work.

   In the same way, the slave here is in no way identifiable with the slave who loses himself in the object and finds in his work the source of his liberation.

   The Negro wants to be like the master.

   Therefore he is less independent than the Hegelian slave.

   In Hegel the slave turns away from the master and turns toward the object.

   Here the slave turns toward the master and abandons the object.
6. In English in the original. (Translator's note.)
7. Emmanuel Mounier, *L'eveil de l'Afrique noire* (Paris, Éditions du Seuil, 1948).

CHAPTER 8

"Logic and Existence"

—from *Logic and Existence* (1953)

Jean Hyppolite

We can extend Hegel's philosophy in two different directions. One direction leads to the deification of Humanity; the other, the one that we have followed in this work, leads to the Absolute's self-knowledge across man. In each of these cases, the term Existence, applied to human reality, has a different sense. Perhaps it would not be useless to outline briefly these senses.

Hegel, it is said, *engendered* (*genuit*) *Feuerbach, who engendered* (*genuit*) *Marx,* and this historical relationship is significant. Hegel is the author of the *Phenomenology* just as much as he is the author of the *Science of Logic,* the author of the *Philosophy of History* just as much as he is the author of the conclusion of the *Encyclopaedia*. Consequently, the absolute Idea, which actualizes itself in history, this sense of human history, can appear not as the revelation of an absolute spirit, but as the realization of Humanity. Christian religion is revealed or manifest religion. What is revealed in it "is that the divine nature is the same as human nature" (PH §759). Religion, however, is still *representation*; it presents this identity as not being our work, but the work of a mediator. Reconciliation, the transfiguration of the world, is not actual in religion. The religious spirit is still alienated from itself. Only philosophy, as concept, sublates all transcendence. Self-consciousness surmounts all alienation; and, without retreating into a vain subjectivity, it thinks itself in all content, in all objectivity. Nature and history are the presentation of the Absolute in space and time, but this Absolute thinks itself as the *Logos*; it knows itself. This *Logos* is not a divine understanding which would exist somewhere else in another world. It is the light of Being in human reality.

The religious spirit therefore is still affected with a diremption. Its self-consciousness is not reconciled with its consciousness.

> Its reconciliation, therefore, is in its heart, but its consciousness is still divided against itself and its actual world is disrupted. What enters its consciousness as the in-itself, or the side of pure mediation, is a reconciliation that lies in the beyond: but what enters it as present, as the side of immediacy and Dasein, is the world which has still to await its transfiguration. The world is indeed in itself reconciled with essence, and regarding essence it is known, of course, that it recognizes the object as no longer alienated from it but as identical with it in its love. But for self-consciousness, this immediate presence still has not the shape of spirit. (PH §787)

Religion presents what is already there as a "beyond." It does not conceive itself; it experiences the identity but does not think it. However, the *Phenomenology of Spirit* constantly criticizes the illusion of another world, and this critique takes the form of the critique of *alienation.* This concept appears as the key concept of the *Phenomenology of Spirit.* Alienation is indeed the concept to which Feuerbach and Marx will fasten themselves. Not only will they extend the Hegelian critique, in the form of a critique of religion, but also they will try to show that speculative philosophy, Hegel's absolute knowledge, is itself also a form of alienation, a substitute for religion. Man believes in another world in order to escape from the hostility of the one in which he lives; he projects into the "beyond" his own essence because his essence is not realized in this world. History is, however, the realization of the universal "divine man." It is Hegel himself who has turned history into a genesis of man. Why speak then of absolute spirit? "Absolute spirit," Feuerbach says, "is man." Marx pushes the critique of religion and of absolute knowledge found in Feuerbach farther. In his *1844 Manuscripts,* which are written in the margins of the *Phenomenology of Spirit* and the works of economists, he proposes to replace the term "self-consciousness" with the term "man," and thereby to demystify Hegelianism.

This replacement, however, transforms all of Hegel's philosophy. What the *Phenomenology* unveils to us across "conceived history" is the existence of an universal self-consciousness which is "the ether of the life of spirit." This self-consciousness is not human self-consciousness, but Being's self-consciousness across human reality. Absolute knowledge is not an anthropology (one need only read Hegel's *Logic* in order to realize this); it is the knowledge which has sublated the opposition of self and being, but this absolute knowledge is what appears in history. Consequently, why not turn this revelation into a genuine end of history? Why not make this end of history coincide with the realization of the human essence? In order to bring about this coincidence, one need only unveil the deception which consists in explaining nature by the Logos and not the Logos by nature. More penetrating than that of Feuerbach, the whole Marxist critique amounts to showing, by interpreting every objectification as an alienation and every alienation as an objectification, the confusion which victimizes Hegel.

In order to show this, one has to place the Hegelian system back on its feet. This system defines the Absolute as mediation, as the mutual relation of the Logos and nature, but nature is first and the Logos only an abstraction. Marx moreover does not wonder how this abstraction is possible and how nature can reveal itself as sense, abstract itself from itself, and think itself. He takes up Feuerbach's argumentation which opposes the sensible world to the abstraction of being. What the Logic reveals in fact is that what is at issue is only an abstraction, and that it is necessary to emerge from it in order to rediscover finally intuition and carnal nature.

> The abstract idea which becomes direct intuition is absolutely nothing other than the abstract thought which renounces itself and decides to become intuition. This entire transition from the Logic to the Philosophy of nature is nothing other than the transition—so difficult to establish for the abstract thinker and for that very reason described by him in a way just as strange—from abstraction to intuition. The mystical feeling, what pushes the philosophers from abstract thought to intuition, is boredom, the living desire of a content. Man alienated from himself is also the thinker alienated from his being, that is, from natural and human being. (MM 190)

It is necessary therefore to start from the natural and human being, from man produced by nature and objectifying himself in nature through work. By substituting the term "man" for the term "self-consciousness" one discovers a valuable description of the human condition in the *Phenomenology*. One discovers there this fundamental idea: "to consider the proper production of man as a process . . . to conceive therefore the essence of work, and to see in objective man, in true man because real, the result of his own work" (MM 177). Man reproduces and produces himself by increasing himself. He engenders his own history, and Hegel has laid the foundations of this philosophy of history, which is a philosophy of man grappling with nature and with his own species being. Universal self-consciousness is the realization, through the intermediary of the struggle for recognition, of human species being, what we used to call the essence of man. It is clear that Marx replaces the Hegelian absolute Idea with this species being, this essence of man. History is therefore the realization of Humanity. The Hegelian universal is immanent to each human individual, as ideal totality, "as the subjective existence of society thought and felt for itself." The individual dies because he is inadequate to this universal. "Death appears as a hard victory of the species over the individual and seems to contradict the unity of the species, but the determined individual is only a determined species being, and as such he is mortal" (MM 138). This humanity emerges from nature and transforms it in order to give it a human face:

> Just as society itself produces man as man, society is produced by him. As for their content, activity and spirit, according to their mode of existence, are equally social, social activity and social spirit. The human being of nature exists only for the social man, for it is only there that nature exists for him as a connection with man, as existence for others and as existence of others for him. It is only there that his natural existence became for him his human existence and that nature became for him human. Society is therefore the achieved consubstantiality of man with nature, the true resurrection of nature, the realization of the naturalism of man and of the humanism of nature. (MM 137)

The Hegelian idea therefore becomes the idea of concrete and social man, and history is this monumental genesis of man; from Hegel, Marx retains this genetic conception of history, not according to the model of a natural history which would not be our history, but according to the model of a comprehensive creation of the self by the self. This production is not a fact of nature like others; it is—despite certain of Marx's overly objective expressions—the Absolute which is subject, the divine universal man, the God who makes himself instead of the God contemplated in heaven:

> Man appropriates his universal being in a universal manner, that is, as total man. Each of his human relations to the world—seeing, hearing, smelling, tasting, thinking, observing, experiencing, wanting, acting, loving—in short, all the organs of his individual being, like those organs which are directly social in their form, are in their objective orientation or in their orientation to the object, the appropriation of that object, the appropriation of human reality. The way in which the organs behave in relation to the object is the manifestation of human reality. This manifestation is as varied as the determinations and human activities, human activity and human suffering, for suffering taken in the human sense is a proper joy of man. (MM 139)

Hegel, however, has confused *objectification* and *alienation*. In objectification, he has seen an alienation of the Logos. Nature is in this way the Other of the Logos; Hegel has transposed a particular process of history into speculative philosophy and just by that he is condemned, condemned to misunderstand nature and falsify history. He has misunderstood nature because, instead of starting from it, he has seen there a relative, non-originary term. Hegel has falsified history, because to overcome alienation became for him identical to overcoming objectification. And, since he could not make the sublation of nature the issue without mystification, the sublation of alienation is reduced for him to speculative philosophy, to self-consciousness rediscovering itself in its alienation. In fact, the alienation specific to history is not thereby sublated. The worker continues to see the products of his work, and even his own work as being alien to himself. The capitalist continues to be prey to a mechanism which he believes himself to direct. Alienation is not objectification. Objectification is natural. It is not a way for consciousness to make itself alien to itself, but a way to express itself naturally:

> An objective being acts objectively and he would not act objectively if the objective were not to be found in the determination of its being. He creates and posits objects only because he is posited by objects, because, from the beginning, he is nature. In the act of positing, he does not therefore emerge from his pure activity in order to create the object, but his objective product presents simply his objective activity, his activity as the activity of a natural objective being. We see here that consistent naturalism or humanism differs from idealism as well as from materialism, and is at the same time the truth which unites them both. We see at the same time that naturalism alone is capable of understanding universal history. (MM 180-81)

This history, however, indeed became an alienation insofar as it has engendered—as a necessary moment—capital, the development of value out of value. Thereby, the objectification of man became—moreover for his greatest future good—an alienation. "Alienation appears as well in this sense, that my means of subsistence is that of another, that the object of my desire is the inaccessible good of another, that everything is itself something belonging to another, and finally that (and this holds equally for the capitalist) overall an inhuman power dominates" (MM 115). The alienation of man in history is capitalism, and not the objectification of man which is the extension of his nature. This is why the history that comprehends the genesis of this alienation, on the basis of social work and the mutual relation of men, discovers also the means of their liberation, communism, which "as fully developed naturalism, equals humanism, and as fully developed humanism equals naturalism; it is the true solution of the antagonism between man and man, the true solution of the strife between origin and being, between objectification and subjectification, between freedom and necessity, between the individual and the species. Communism is the riddle of history solved and it knows itself to be this solution" (MM 135).

Marx praises Feuerbach: "(1) For having provided the proof that philosophy is nothing else but religion rendered into thought and expounded by thought, hence equally to be condemned as another form and manner of existence of the alienation of the being of man; (2) For having established true materialism and real science since Feuerbach also makes the social relationship of 'man to man' the basic principle of the theory; (3) For having opposed to the negation of the negation, which claims to be the absolute positive, the self-supporting positive, positively based on itself" (MM 172). Undoubtedly the whole debate is concentrated on this last point. For the negation of the negation, it is necessary to substitute the first positivity of nature; it is necessary to understand man objectifying himself on the basis of this positivity. Let us not discuss this principle which is self-supporting, because the position of nature is really more than nature; all of us would be harmonized by means of this self-foundation. There is however a negation in history, an alienation; but it holds only for history and it is up to history to resolve this problem that it poses. Marx adds this historical dimension to Feuerbach. He rediscovers then, more or less, Hegelian dialectic in the concrete conflicts of history, but he refuses to reduce the positive to the negation of the negation. The distinction is important. The Absolute, for Hegel, will never be an immobile synthesis. His position will always contain negation, the tension of opposition; but Marx, like empiricism, starts from the positive, from the immediacy which is not in itself a negation, from nature. Human objectification is not for him an alienation, because the determined object is not a negation; it is first. History then has created the conflicts and will put an end to them. We could already wonder about the source of this negation in history; why we do not remain just in nature? Undoubtedly, the response would be to speak of human nature, which did not stay put within pure nature, but which overcame itself, which created itself and continues to create itself. When we read *Capital,* we have the impression of a will to power which has built up a world, which increases value from value itself. Without, however, insisting on this ambiguous term of the will to power (there is in Hegel a struggle for pure prestige as the condition of history), one has to speak of a negativity in human self-consciousness, an existence which does not let itself be engulfed in objectivity, an existence which therefore is discovered alienated in every determination, in every manner of being in the world. We rediscover on this new level the problem of the origin of negation which we have already encountered in considering empirical reflection and critical reflection.

One is quickly tempted to grant to Marx that nature is first there in its positivity, that one has to begin with it, that the Logos is only an abstraction (but what does this abstraction mean?), that man objectifies himself by means of nature and that alienation is a secondary process, essential in order to explain our history up to the present, but, in the final account, destined to disappear. Human nature will then present itself after the resolution of historical conflicts. Positivity is first, positivity will be last, and this positivity must have no fissures in it, nothing negative. Despite being a philosophy of history, Hegelianism preserves in its immanence the negation at the heart of every position; in actual history, there is a real negation, but the Logos comprehends this negation since negation is ontological. The Logos is the thought of itself and of all actuality.

For Marx however, what is the source of this real negativity, this prodigious historical growth, an edification whose *utility* in the strict sense could not be explained? What is human existence such that it engenders this history? One has to admit that Hegel went a lot farther than Marx on this point. While remaining in anthropology, he opened perspectives that Marx neglected, and these perspectives bear precisely on the fact that for him every determinate objectification is an alienation. He discovered this dimension of pure subjectivity *which* is *nothingness*. The ground of self-consciousness is what, in nature, presents itself as disappearance and death. Negation is indeed in nature, in particular in life, but it is there as the concept for the spirit who discovers it; animals die but know nothing of it; negation is external because it is internal. Therefore, by comprehending death, man attains this supreme freedom or rather suspects it in himself, because it always sustains his determinations: "Man is the being who is not what he is and is what he is not," an always future hollow. Death is the revelation of absolute negativity, because man, as pure self-consciousness, exists this nothingness (*existe ce néant*). By apprehending death, man becomes the supreme abstraction which was nature's interiority, its nothingness, its detachment from every Dasein, from every determination:

> For this consciousness has precisely felt this anxiety, not of this or that particular thing or just at odd moments, but its whole being has been seized with anxiety; for it has experienced the fear of death, the absolute master. In this anxiety, it has been intimately dissolved, has trembled in every fiber of its being, and everything solid and stable has been shaken to its foundations. But this pure universal movement, the absolute melting away of everything stable, is the simple, essential nature of self-consciousness, absolute negativity, pure being for itself, which consequently is implicit in this consciousness. (PH §194)

This melting away of everything stable is the negation of the negation, because everything stable is for man a negation, a self-limitation. In Marx, the proletariat is the comprehension of human alienation and this comprehension is its existence. By discovering self-consciousness' alienation, Hegel extends this term to every objectification. However, being-for-itself cannot not objectify itself; it is always there in the world and "the individual is what his world is." He is there for others and this for-others is the limit over which his subjectivity cannot go. "Each individual is first for the other in the manner of any object whatsoever." Each refuses to be only his work, to coincide with this appearance for the other which he cannot realize completely. Each is beyond his expression and this "beyond" is only immanent negativity. At the heart of this inevitable objectification, consciousness sublates itself. If objectification were not an alienation, history would stop, being-for-itself as such would disappear. Hegel described the alienation of consciousness in natural life as well as in the Wealth and Dominion which constitute social powers:

> Dominion and Wealth are the supreme ends of its [the self's] exertions, it knows that through renunciation and sacrifice it forms itself into the universal, attains to the possession of it, and in this possession is universally recognized and accepted: dominion and wealth are the real and acknowledged powers. However this recognition and acceptance is itself vain; and just by taking possession of dominion and wealth, it knows them to be without a self of their own, knows rather that it is the power over them, while they are vain things. (PH §526)

In the dialectical beginning of history, there is unlimited desire for recognition, the desire of the desire of the other, a groundless power (groundless because it lacks a first positivity). Hegel has shown the specific character of the alienation of self-consciousness in Wealth, and the sundered world that results from it:

> Its object is a being-for-self, i.e., its own being-for-self; but, because it has an object, it is at the same time *ipso facto* an alien reality which has its own being-for-self, which has a will of its own; i.e., it sees itself in the power of an alien will on which it is dependent for possession of its own self. . . . The self sees its self-certainty as such to be completely devoid of essence, sees that its pure personality is absolutely not a personality. The spirit of its gratitude is, therefore, the feeling of the most profound dejection as well as of extreme rebellion. When the pure "I" beholds itself outside of itself and rent asunder and is destroyed, then everything that has continuity and universality, everything that is called law, good, and right, is at the same time rent asunder and destroyed. All similarity dissolves away, for the utmost disparity now occupies the scene; what is absolutely essential is now absolutely unessential, being-for-self is now external to itself: the pure ego itself is absolutely disrupted. (PH §516, §517)

Existence appears therefore as freedom, which sub-tends all the particular shapes of self-consciousness. Self-consciousness always sublates the shapes, never stays at the place at which we would like to attain it or fix it. Nevertheless, this sublation has a sense; when we replace "the aspect of free Dasein, presenting itself in the form of contingency, history," with "the aspect of the conceptual organization of these shapes or the *Phenomenology*" (PH §808), we see them engender one another in a conceived history which, in temporal dispersion, incarnates this supreme sublation that is the absolute Idea. In fact, self-consciousness cannot retreat into this complete freedom—the mere form of subjectivity—without dissolving itself. This freedom is the supreme abstraction; when self-consciousness retreats from every determination, it stops acting, stops making itself, it stops being-in-the-world or being-there (*être-là*, Dasein). Its being is its nothingness; it vanishes, "its light dies away little by little within it and it vanishes like a shapeless vapor that dissolves into thin air" (PH §658). Nothingness is there only as the nothingness of a particular determination of which nothingness is the soul and the sublation. Nothingness presents itself as negativity. Hegelian dialectic is not the dissolution of all the determinations, like skepticism, but their mediation. Being-for-itself must consent to mediation, to the history which thinks itself as common work, the work of all and each. This work thinks itself by making itself; this work is the history of finite, *objective* spirit, and there is a philosophy of history because it is impossible to conceive history, at least retrospectively, without determining it as sense. It is here that Hegelianism presents almost insurmountable difficulties. What is the relation between absolute knowledge, the Logos, and this philosophy of history? For Hegel, is the common work Humanity? We can respond to the second question quite clearly. Humanity as such is not the supreme end for Hegel. When man is reduced to himself, he is lost; this is how he is in Greek comedy and in the *Aufklärung*. He makes use of his freedom in order to retreat into abstract self-certainty, but this certainty is contentless and gives itself an empirical, a finite project. Man is an intersection; he is not a natural Dasein which would have a primordial positivity. To connect abstract self-certainty to this natural Dasein is to be condemned "to know only what is finite, and, moreover, knowing it as truth, and thinking that this knowledge of the finite as true is the highest knowledge attainable" (PH §562). Man then is defined by this last platitude: "Just as everything is useful to man, so man is useful too, and his vocation is to make himself a member of the group, of use for the common good and serviceable to all. The extent to which he looks after his own interests must also be matched by the extent to which he serves others, so far is he taking care of himself: one hand washes the other. But wherever he finds himself, there he is in the right place; he makes use of others and is himself made use or" (PH §560). Here Hegel anticipates Nietzsche. Humanistic reflection is the fall into the "the human, all-too-human." Perhaps even one can say that this reflection, which turns the human project into the Absolute, results at the reverse of what it claims to attain. Hegel indeed speaks of history having a sense, the absolute Idea, but this idea is not man. It is not the rational project of the individual. On the contrary, the individual learns to recognize a certain necessity in the destiny of history:

> The individual self must discover himself in all of what he plans and does: even the pious individual wishes to be saved and happy. This

> pole of the antithesis, existing for itself, is—in contrast with absolute essence, the universal—a particular which knows and wills particularity. In short, it plays its part in the region of mere phenomena. This is the sphere of particular purposes in effecting which individuals exert themselves on behalf of their individuality—give it full play and objective realization. This is the sphere of happiness and its opposite. Happy is he who has made his existence conform to his character, to his will and to his fancy, and so enjoys himself in his existence. World history is not the theatre of happiness. Periods of happiness are blank pages in it. (HI 26)

Existence, however, as mere sublation, as the impossible adventure of man, is also an impasse. It defines man by the freedom of being-for-itself which is simultaneously always opposed to being-in-itself and always related to it. Man does not possess the freedom that allows him to wander from one determination to another or to be dissolved in abstract nothingness; rather, freedom possesses man. Nothingness is not then between the for-itself and the in-itself; it is the very nothingness of being or the being of nothingness. It opens to man, not the mere real negativity that makes history objective, but the dimension of the universal at the heart of which all sense is determined and engendered. Through this freedom, which Hegel says is immanent to all history, which Hegel says is the absolute Idea of history (and of course, equivocity is evident in the relation of the philosophy of history to the Logos in Hegel, and in this very term "freedom"), man does not conquer himself as man, but becomes the house (*la demeure*) of the Universal, of the Logos of Being, and becomes capable of Truth. In this opening which allows the existents of Nature, and history itself, to be clarified, to be conceived, Being comprehends itself as this eternal self-engendering; it is Logic in Hegel's sense, absolute knowledge. Man then *exists* as the natural Dasein in which being's universal self-consciousness appears. Man is the trace of this self-consciousness, but an indispensable trace without which self-consciousness would not be. Logic and Existence are here joined, if Existence is this human freedom which is the universal, the light of sense. In this Logos, everything has a sense, and the very sense of sense. We then have to return to our first question: what is the relation between absolute knowledge, the Logos, and the philosophy of history? Hegel's own response is ambiguous, perhaps different in the *Phenomenology* and in the *Encyclopaedia*. This ambiguity explains the radical differences among his disciples. One has to note, however, that, like nature, history is a presentation of the complete alienation of the Logos, a presentation that the Logos also expounds in itself: "The self-knowing spirit knows not only itself but also the negative of itself . . . spirit displays the process of its becoming spirit in the form of free contingent happening, intuiting its pure self as time outside of it, and equally its Being as space" (PH §807). But space is the indifference of determinations. Time is negativity, the pure restlessness of difference. In time, alienation alienates itself: "The negative is the negative of itself" (PH §808). Thus history is the objectivity of spirit's becoming, its temporal incarnation (*its sense, without being yet the sense of sense*).

However, absolute knowledge is the ground of the knowledge that appears in history, and history opens this dimension; history is the place of passage from temporal objective spirit to absolute spirit and to the Logos. History is the appearance of freedom, that is, the appearance of the concept through which man has access to the eternal sense. This sense, however, is not another world behind history. The Logos is there; it comprehends itself and comprehends also this nature and this history. This self-comprehension is not a plan similar to a human plan. Hegelian logic sublates every human and *moral view* of the world. Being is grounded in itself. It is because it is possible; but it is possible because it is. History's real negativity is there, and comprehends itself as the negativity of being in the Logos. The issue is not one of justifying being, because every justification is a justification of sense, and the question of Sense and Being is the Logos itself. History does not produce the Logos, the self-knowledge of the Absolute, as we produce an effect according to a plan conceived in advance. Philosophy is not a conscious end, but man *exists* because he is a philosopher.

This passage from history to absolute knowledge, the passage from the temporal to the eternal, is Hegelianism's most obscure dialectical synthesis; history is self-creating, like the Logos, but this creation is there temporal, here eternal. The Logos is not an essence. It is the element in which being and sense reflect one another, where being appears as sense and sense as being. The Logos is absolute genesis, and time is the image of this mediation, not the reverse. Time is the concept, but the concept in its immediate Dasein because time is the exstasis of difference, which in the Logos presents itself as the internal movement of determinations, temporality as eternal. The Hegelian eternity is not an eternity before time, but the mediating thought which presupposes itself absolutely in time. This is why history's objective spirit becomes absolute spirit; this is a becoming which seems to us difficult to conceive as an epoch of world history: "But the spirit which thinks world history, stripping off at the same time those limitations of the several national spirits and its own temporal restrictions, lays hold of its concrete universality, and rises to apprehend absolute spirit, as the eternally actual truth in which the contemplative reason enjoys freedom, while the necessity of nature and the necessity of history are only ministrant to its revelation and the vessels of its honor" (ES §552). The leading difficulty of Hegelianism is the relation of the *Phenomenology* and the *Logic*. Today we would speak of anthropology and ontology. The one studies the properly human reflection, the other the absolute reflection that passes through man. In the *Phenomenology,* Hegel believed himself able to comprehend human reflection in the light of absolute knowledge (the work's "for us"), and it seems to us that the principle of this comprehension is contained in the meaning of the Hegelian ontology. He, however, believed himself able to exhibit human consciousness's becoming-absolute-knowledge, as if this becoming were a history. History is indeed the place of this passage, but this passage is not itself a *historical fact*. And then there is forgetfulness and memory. Existence, the relation of man to the Logos, indeed puts the Logos back where it was at the beginning:

"Mais rendre la lumière suppose d'ombre une morne moitié."[1]

Abbreviations

At times, we have altered the standard English translations in order to make them consistent with Hyppolite's commentary.

ES *Hegel's Philosophy of Mind: Being Part Three of the Encyclopedia of Philosophical Sciences (1830)*, tr. William Wallace (London: Oxford University Press, 1971).

HI *The Philosophy of History*, tr. J. Sibree (New York: Dover, 1956).

PH *Hegel's Phenomenology of Spirit*, tr. A.V. Miller (New York: Oxford University Press, 1977).

Other text cited:

MM Karl Marx, *Economic and Philosophic Manuscripts of 1844*, tr. Martin Mulligan (New York: International, 1976).

Notes

1. This quote comes from Paul Valéry, "La Cimitière Marin," in *Oeuvres de Paul Valéry*, 1: 148. English translation by David Paul in *Paul Valery: An Anthology*: "But to reflect the light / Bespeaks another half of mournful shade" (p. 271).—TR.

CHAPTER 9

"Hegel, Death and Sacrifice"[1]

—(1955)

Georges Bataille

> The animal dies. But the death of the animal is the becoming of consciousness.

I. DEATH

Man's Negativity

In the *Lectures* of 1805–1806, at the moment of his thought's full maturity, during the period when he was writing *The Phenomenology of Spirit*, Hegel expressed in these terms the black character of humanity:

"Man is that night, that empty Nothingness, which contains everything in its undivided simplicity: the wealth of an infinite number of representations, of images, not one of which comes precisely to mind, or which [moreover], are not [there] insofar as they are really present. It is the night, the interiority—or—the intimacy of Nature which exists here: [*the*] pure personal-Ego. In phantasmagorical representations it is night on all sides: here suddenly surges up a blood-spattered head; there, another, white, apparition; and they disappear just as abruptly. That is the night that one perceives if one looks a man in the eyes: then one is delving into a night which becomes terrible; it is the night of the world which then presents itself to us."[2]

Of course, this "beautiful text," where Hegel's Romanticism finds expression, is not to be understood loosely. If Hegel was a romantic, it was perhaps in a *fundamental* manner (he was at any rate a romantic at the beginning—in his youth—, when he was a commonplace revolutionary), but he did not see in

Romanticism the method by which a proud spirit deems itself capable of subordinating the real world to the arbitrariness of its own dreams. Alexandre Kojève, in citing them, says of these lines that they express "the central and final idea of Hegelian philosophy," which is "the idea that the foundation and the source of human objective reality (*Wirklichkeit*) and empirical existence (*Dasein*) are the Nothingness which manifests itself as negative or creative Action, free and self-conscious."

To permit access to Hegel's disconcerting world, I have felt obliged to mark, by a careful examination, both its violent contrasts and its ultimate unity.

For Kojève, "the 'dialectical' or anthropological philosophy of Hegel is in the final analysis a *philosophy of death* (or, which is the same thing, of atheism)" (K, 537; TEL, 539).

But if man is "death living a human life" (K, 548; TEL, 550), man's negativity, given in death by virtue of the fact that man's death is essentially voluntary (resulting from risks assumed without necessity, without biological reasons), is nevertheless the principle of action. Indeed, for Hegel, Action is Negativity, and Negativity Action. On the one hand, the man who negates Nature—by introducing into it, like a flip-side, the anomaly of a "pure, personal ego"—is present within that Nature's heart like a night within light, like an intimacy within the exteriority of those things which are *in themselves*—like a phantasmagoria in which nothing takes shape but to evanesce, nothing appears but to disappear, where nothing exists except absorbed without respite in the *annihilation* of time, from which it draws the beauty of a dream. But there is a complementary aspect: this negation of Nature is not merely given in consciousness—where that which exists *in itself* appears (but only to disappear)—; this negation is exteriorized, and in being exteriorized, really (*in itself*) changes the reality of Nature. Man works and fights; he transforms the given; he transforms Nature and in destroying it he creates a world, a world which was not. On the one hand there is poetry, the destruction that has surged up and diluted itself, a *blood-spattered* head; on the other hand there is Action, work, struggle. On the one hand, "pure Nothingness," where man "differs from Nothingness only *for a certain time*" (K, 573; TEL, 575). On the other, a historical World, where man's Negativity, that Nothingness that gnaws him from within, creates the whole of concrete reality (at once object and subject, real world changed or unchanged, man who thinks and changes the world).

Hegel's Philosophy is a Philosophy of Death—or of Atheism[3]

The essential—and the original—characteristic of Hegelian philosophy is to describe the totality of what is; and, consequently, at the same time that it accounts for everything which appears before our eyes, to give an integrated account of the thought and language which express—and reveal—that appearance.

"In my opinion," says Hegel, "Everything depends on one's expressing and understanding Truth not (only) as substance, but also as subject."[4]

In other words, natural knowledge is incomplete, it does not and cannot envisage any but abstract entities, isolated from a whole, from an indissoluble totality, which alone is concrete. Knowledge must at the same time be anthropological: "in addition to the ontological bases of natural reality," Kojève writes, "[knowledge] must find those of human reality, which alone is capable of being revealed through Discourse" (K, 528; TEL, 530). Of course, this anthropology does not envisage Man as do the modern sciences but as a movement impossible to isolate from the heart of the totality. In a sense, it is actually a theology, where man has taken the place of God.

But for Hegel, the human reality which he places at the heart, and center, of the totality is very different from that of Greek philosophy. His anthropology is that of the Judeo-Christian tradition, which emphasizes Man's *liberty*, *historicity*, and *individuality*. Like Judeo-Christian man, the Hegelian man is a spiritual (i.e., "dialectical") being. Yet, for the Judeo-Christian world, "spirituality" is fully realized and manifest only in the hereafter, and Spirit properly speaking, truly "objectively real" Spirit, is God: "an infinite and eternal being." According to Hegel, the "spiritual" or "dialectical" being is "necessarily *temporal* and finite." This means that death alone assures the existence of a "spiritual" or "dialectical" being, in the Hegelian sense. If the animal which constitutes man's natural being did not die, and—what is more—if death did not dwell in him as the source of his anguish—and all the more so in that he seeks it out, desires it and sometimes freely chooses it—there would be no man or liberty, no history or individual. In other words, if he revels in what nonetheless frightens him, if he is the being, identical with himself, who risks (identical) being itself, then man is truly a Man: he separates himself from the animal. Henceforth he is no longer, like a stone, an immutable given, he bears within him *Negativity*; and the force, the violence of negativity cast him into the incessant movement of history, which changes him and which alone realizes the totality of the concrete real through time. Only history has the power to finish what is, to finish it in the passage of time. And so the idea of an eternal and immutable God is in this perspective merely a provisional end, which survives while awaiting something better. Only completed history and the spirit of the Sage (of Hegel)—in whom history revealed, then revealed in full, the development of being and the totality of its becoming—occupy a sovereign position, which God only provisionally occupies, as a regent.

The Tragi-Comic Aspect of Man's Divinity

This way of seeing things can with justice be considered comic. Besides, Hegel never expressed it explicitly. The texts where it is *implicitly* affirmed are ambiguous, and their extreme difficulty ultimately kept them from full consideration. Kojève himself is circumspect. He does not dwell on them and avoids drawing precise conclusions. In order to express appropriately the situation Hegel got himself into, no doubt involuntarily, one would need the tone, or at least, in a restrained form, the horror of tragedy. But things would quickly take on a comic appearance.

Be that as it may, to pass through death is so absent from the divine figure that a myth situated in the tradition associated death, and the agony of death, with the eternal and unique God of the Judeo-Christian sphere. The death of Jesus partakes of comedy to the extent that one cannot unarbitrarily introduce the forgetting of his eternal divinity—which is his—into the consciousness of an omnipotent and infinite God. Before Hegel's "absolute knowledge," the Christian myth was already based precisely on the fact that nothing divine is possible (in the pre-Christian sense of *sacred*) which is finite. But the vague consciousness in which the (Christian) myth of the death of God took form differed, nonetheless, from that of Hegel: in order to misrepresent a figure of God that limited the infinite as the totality, it was possible to add on, in contradiction with its basis, a movement toward the finite.

Hegel was able—and it was necessary for him—to add up the sum (the Totality) of the movements which were produced in history. But humor, it seems, is incompatible with work and its necessary assiduity. I shall return to this subject; I have merely, for the moment, shuffled cards. . . . It is difficult to pass from a humanity humiliated by divine grandeur to that . . . of the apotheosized and sovereign Sage, his pride swollen with human vanity.

A Fundamental Text

In what I have written up to this point, only one necessity emerges in a precise fashion: there can be authentic Wisdom (absolute Wisdom, or in general anything approaching it) only if the Sage raises himself, if I can put it this way, to the height of death, at whatever anguish to him.

A passage from the preface to the *Phenomenology of Spirit*[5] forcefully expresses the necessity of such an attitude. There is no doubt from the start of the "capital importance" of this admirable text, not only for an understanding of Hegel, but in all regards.

"Death," writes Hegel, "—if we wish so to name that unreality—is the most terrible thing there is and to uphold the work of death is the task which demands the greatest strength. Impotent beauty hates this awareness, because understanding makes this demand of beauty, a requirement which beauty cannot fulfill. Now, the life of Spirit is not that life which is frightened of death, and spares itself destruction, but that life which assumes death and lives with it. Spirit attains its truth only by finding itself in absolute dismemberment. It is not that (prodigious) power by being the Positive that turns away from the Negative, as when we say of something: this is nothing or (this is) false and, having (thus) disposed of it, pass from there to something else; no, Spirit is that power only to the degree in which it contemplates the Negative face to face (and) dwells with it. This prolonged sojourn is the magical force which transposes the negative into given-Being."

The Human Negation of Nature and of the Natural Being of Man

In principle, I ought to have started the passage just cited at an earlier point. I did not want to weigh this text down by giving the "enigmatic" lines which precede it. But I shall sketch out the sense of the omitted lines by restating Kojève's interpretation, without which the consequences, in spite of an appearance of relative clarity, would remain closed to us.

For Hegel, it is both fundamental and altogether worthy of astonishment that human understanding (that is, language, discourse) should have had the force (an incomparable force) to separate its constitutive elements from the Totality. These elements (this tree, this bird, this stone) are in fact inseparable from the whole. They are "bound together by spatial and temporal, indeed material, bonds which are indissoluble." Their separation implies the human Negativity toward Nature of which I spoke, without pointing out its decisive consequences. For the man who negates nature could not in any way live outside of it. He is not merely a man who negates Nature, he is first of all an animal, that is to say the very thing he negates: he cannot therefore negate Nature without negating himself. The intrinsic totality of man is reflected in Kojève's bizarre expression, that totality is first of all Nature (natural being), it is "the anthropomorphic animal" (Nature, the animal indissolubly linked to the whole of Nature, and which supports Man). Thus human Negativity, Man's effective desire to negate Nature in destroying it—in reducing it to his own ends, as when, for example, he makes a tool of it (and the tool will be the model of an object isolated from Nature)—cannot stop at Man himself; insofar as he is Nature, Man is exposed to his own Negativity. To negate Nature is to negate the animal which props up Man's Negativity. It is undoubtedly not the understanding, breaker of Nature's unity, which seeks man's death, and yet the separating Action of the understanding implies the monstrous energy of thought, of the "pure abstract I," which is essentially opposed to fusion, to the inseparable character of the elements—constitutive of the whole—which firmly upholds their separation.

It is the very separation of Man's being, it is his isolation from Nature, and, consequently, his isolation in the midst of his own kind, which condemn him to disappear definitively. The animal, negating nothing, lost in a global animality to which it offers no opposition—just as that animality is itself lost in Nature (and in the totality of all that is)—does not truly disappear. . . . No doubt the individual fly dies, but today's flies are the same as those of last year. Last year's have died? . . . Perhaps, but *nothing* has disappeared. The flies remain, equal to themselves like the waves of the sea. This seems contrived: a biologist can separate a fly from the swarm, all it takes is a brushstroke. But he separates it *for himself*, he does not separate it for the flies. To separate itself from the others a fly would need the monstrous force of the understanding; then it would name itself and do what the understanding normally effects by means of language, which alone founds the separation of elements and by founding it founds itself on it, within a world formed of separated and denominated entities. But in this game the human animal finds death; it finds precisely human death, the only one which frightens, which freezes—but which only frightens and transfixes the man who is absorbed in his future disappearance, to the extent that he is a separated and irreplaceable being. The only true death supposes separation and, through the discourse which separates, the consciousness of being separated.

"Impotent Beauty Hates the Understanding"

Up to this point, Hegel's text presents a *simple* and *common* truth, but one enunciated in a philosophical manner which is, properly speaking, sibylline. In the passage from the Preface cited above, Hegel, on the contrary, affirms and describes a *personal* moment of violence—Hegel, in other words the Sage, to whom an absolute Knowledge has conferred definitive satisfaction. This is not an unbridled violence. What Hegel unleashes here is not the violence of Nature, it is the energy, or the violence, of the Understanding—the Negativity of the Understanding—opposing itself to the pure beauty of the dream, which cannot act, which is impotent.

Indeed, the beauty of the dream is on that side of the world where nothing is yet separated from what surrounds it, where each element, in contrast to the abstract objects of the Understanding, is given concretely, in space and time. But beauty cannot *act*. It can only be and preserve itself. Through action it would no longer exist, since action would first destroy what beauty is: beauty, which seeks nothing, which is, which refuses to move itself but which is disturbed by the force of the Understanding. Moreover, beauty does not have the power to respond to the request of the Understanding, which asks it to uphold and preserve the work of *human* death. Beauty is incapable of it, in the sense that to uphold that work, it would be engaged in Action. Beauty is sovereign, it is an end, or it is not: that is why it is not susceptible to acting, why it is, even in principle, powerless and why it cannot yield to the active negation of the Understanding, which changes the world and itself becomes other than it is.[6]

This beauty without consciousness of itself *cannot therefore* really—but not for the same reason as life, which "recoils in horror from death and wants to save itself from annihilation"—bear death and preserve itself in it. This impotent beauty at least suffers from feeling the breakup of the profoundly indissoluble Totality of what is (of the concrete-real). Beauty would like to remain the sign of an accord of the real with itself. It cannot become conscious Negativity, awakened in dismemberment, and the lucid gaze, absorbed in the Negative. This latter attitude presupposes the violent and laborious struggle of Man against Nature and is its end. That is the historic struggle where Man constitutes himself as "Subject" or as "abstract I" of the "Understanding," as a separated and named being.

"That is to say," Kojève clarifies, "that thought and the discourse which reveals the real are born of the negative Action which actualizes Nothingness by annihilating Being: the given being of Man (in the Struggle) and the given being of Nature (through Work—which results, moreover, from the real contact with death in the Struggle.) That is to say, therefore, that the human being himself is none other than that Action: he is death which lives a human life" (K, 548; TEL, 550).

I want to insist on the continual connection between an abyssal aspect and a tough, down-to-earth aspect in this philosophy, the only one having the ambition to be complete. The divergent possibilities of opposed human figures confront each other and assemble in it: the figure of the dying man and of the proud one, who turns from death, the figure of the master and that of the man pinned to his work, the figure of the revolutionary and that of the skeptic, whose egotistical interest limits desire. This philosophy is not only a philosophy of death. It is also one of class struggle and work.

But within the limits of this study I do not intend to envisage this other side. I would like to compare that Hegelian doctrine of death with what we know about "sacrifice."

II. SACRIFICE

Sacrifice, on the one hand, and on the other, the Gaze of Hegel Absorbed in Death and Sacrifice

I shall not speak of the interpretation of sacrifice which Hegel gives in the chapter of the *Phenomenology* devoted to Religion.[7] It no doubt makes sense in the development of the chapter, but it strays from the essential and, from the point of view of the theory of sacrifice, it is, in my opinion, of less interest than the implicit representation which is given in the text of the Preface and which I shall continue to analyze.

Concerning sacrifice, I can essentially say that, on the level of Hegel's philosophy, Man has, in a sense, revealed and founded human truth by sacrificing; in sacrifice he destroyed the animal[8] in himself, allowing himself and the animal to survive only as that noncorporeal truth which Hegel describes and which makes of man—in Heidegger's words—a being unto death (*Sein zum Tode*), or—in the words of Kojève himself—"death which lives a human life."

Actually, the problem of Hegel is given in the action of sacrifice. In sacrifice, death, on the one hand, essentially strikes the corporeal being; and on the other hand, it is precisely in sacrifice that "death lives a *human* life." It should even be said that sacrifice is the precise response to Hegel's requirement, the original formulation of which I repeat:

"Spirit attains its truth only by finding itself in absolute dismemberment. It does not attain that (prodigious) power by being the Positive that turns away from the Negative . . . no, Spirit is that power only in the degree to which it contemplates the Negative face to face [and] dwells with it . . ."

If one takes into account the fact that the institution of sacrifice is practically universal, it is clear that Negativity, incarnated in Man's death, not only is the arbitrary construction of Hegel, but also that it has played a role in the spirit of the simplest men, without any common grounds comparable to those which are regulated once and for all by the ceremonies of a Church—but nonetheless in a univocal manner. It is striking to see that across the world a communal *Negativity* has maintained a strict parallelism in the development of rather stable institutions, which have the same form and the same effects.

Whether He Lives or Dies, Man Cannot Immediately Know Death

I shall speak later of the profound differences between the man of sacrifice, acting in ignorance (unconscious) of the full scope of what he is doing, and the Sage (Hegel) surrendering to the implications of a Knowledge which, in his own eyes, is absolute.

Despite these differences, the question of manifesting the Negative still remains (and still under a concrete form, i.e., at the heart of the Totality, whose constitutive elements are inseparable). The privileged manifestation of Negativity is death, but death, in fact, reveals nothing. In theory, it is his natural, animal being whose death reveals Man to himself, but the revelation never takes place. For when the animal being supporting him dies, the human being himself ceases to be. In order for Man to reveal himself ultimately to himself, he would have to die, but he would have to do it while living—watching himself ceasing to be. In other words, death itself would have to become (self-) consciousness at the very moment that it annihilates the conscious being. In a sense, this is what takes place (what at least is on the point of taking place, or which takes place in a fugitive, ungraspable manner) by means of a subterfuge. In the sacrifice, the sacrificer identifies himself with the animal that is struck down dead. And so he dies in seeing himself die, and even, in a certain way, by his own will, one in spirit with the sacrificial weapon. But it is a comedy!

At least it would be a comedy if some other method existed which could reveal to the living the invasion of death: that finishing off of the finite being, which *his* Negativity—which kills him, *ends* him and definitively suppresses him—accomplishes alone and which it alone can accomplish. For Hegel, *satisfaction* can only take place, desire can be appeased only in the consciousness of death. If it were based on the exclusion of death, satisfaction would contradict that which death designates, if the satisfied being who is not conscious, not utterly conscious, of what in a constitutive manner he is, i.e., mortal, were eventually to be driven from satisfaction by death. That is why the consciousness that he has *of himself* must reflect (must mirror) the movement of negativity which creates him, which makes a man of him for the very reason that it will one day kill him.

He will be killed by his own negativity, but for him, thereafter, there will be nothing left; his is a creative death, but if the consciousness of death—of the marvelous magic of death—does not touch him before he dies, during his life it will seem that death is not destined to reach him, and so the death awaiting him will not give him a *human* character. Thus, at all costs, man must live at the moment that he really dies, or he must live with the impression of really dying.

Knowledge of Death Cannot Do Without a Subterfuge: Spectacle

This difficulty proclaims the necessity of *spectacle,* or of *representation* in general, without the practice of which it would be possible for us to remain alien and ignorant in respect to death, just as beasts apparently are. Indeed, nothing is less animal than fiction, which is more or less separated from the real, from death.

Man does not live by bread alone, but also by the comedies with which he willingly deceives himself. In Man it is the animal, it is the natural being, which eats. But Man takes part in rites and performances. Or else he can read: to the extent that it is sovereign—authentic—, literature prolongs in him the haunting magic of performances, tragic or comic.

In tragedy,[9] at least, it is a question of our identifying with some character who dies, and of believing that we die, although we are alive. Furthermore, pure and simple imagination suffices, but it has the same meaning as the classic subterfuges, performances, or books, to which the masses have recourse.

Agreement and Disagreement between Naive Behaviors and Hegel's Lucid Reaction

By associating it with sacrifice and, thereby, with the primary theme of *representation* (in art, in festivals, in performances), I have sought to demonstrate that Hegel's reaction is fundamental human behavior. It is not a fantasy or a strange attitude, it is *par excellence* the expression endlessly repeated by tradition. It is not Hegel alone, it is all of humanity which everywhere always sought, obliquely, to seize what death both gave and took away from humanity.

Between Hegel and the man of sacrifice there nevertheless remains a profound difference. Hegel was *conscious* of his representation of the Negative: he situated it, lucidly, in a definite point of the "coherent discourse" which revealed him to himself. That Totality included the discourse which reveals it. The man of sacrifice, who lacked a discursive consciousness of what he did, had only a "sensual" awareness, i.e., an obscure one, reduced to an unintelligible emotion. It is true that Hegel himself, beyond discourse, and in spite of himself (in an "absolute dismemberment,") received the shock of death even more violently. More violently, above all, for the primary reason that the broad movement of discourse extended its reach beyond limits, i.e., within the framework of the Totality of the real. Beyond the slightest doubt, for Hegel, the fact that he was still alive was simply an aggravation. The man of sacrifice, on the other hand, maintains his life essentially. He maintains it not only in the sense that life is necessary for the representation of death, but [also in the sense that] he seeks to *enrich* it. But from an external perspective, the palpable and *intentional* excitement of sacrifice was of greater interest than the *involuntary* sensitivity of Hegel. The excitement of which I speak is well-known, is definable; it is *sacred* horror: the richest and the most agonizing experience, which does not limit itself to dismemberment but which, on the contrary, opens itself, like a theatre curtain, onto a realm beyond this world, where the rising light of day transfigures all things and destroys their limited meaning.

Indeed, if Hegel's attitude opposes learned consciousness and the limitless organization of a discursive thinking to the naiveté of sacrifice, still that consciousness and that organization remain unclear on one point; one cannot say that Hegel was unaware of the "moment" of sacrifice; this "moment" is included, implicated in the whole movement of the *Phenomenology*—where it is the Negativity of death, insofar as it is assumed, which makes a man of the human animal. But because he did not see that sacrifice in itself bore witness to the *entire* movement of death,[10] the final experience—the one peculiar to the Sage—described in the Preface to the *Phenomenology* was at first *initial* and *universal*—he did not know to what extent he was right—with what precision he described the intimate movement of Negativity; he did not clearly separate death from the feeling of sadness to which naive experience opposes a sort of shunting yard of the emotions.

Pleasure and the Sadness of Death

It was precisely the univocal character of death for Hegel that inspired the following commentary from Kojève, which applies, again, to the passage from the Preface: (K, 549; TEL, 551). "Certainly, the idea of death does not heighten the *well-being* of Man; it does not make him *happy* nor does it give him any pleasure." Kojève wondered in what way satisfaction results from a familiarity with the Negative, from a *tête-à-tête* with death. He believed it his duty, out of decency, to reject vulgar satisfaction. The fact that Hegel himself said, in this respect, that Spirit "only attains it truth by finding itself in absolute dismemberment" goes together, in principle, with Kojève's Negation. Consequently, it would even be superfluous to insist. . . . Kojève simply states that the idea of death "is alone capable of satisfying man's pride." . . . Indeed, the desire to be "recognized," which Hegel places at the origin of historical struggles, could be expressed in an intrepid attitude, of the sort that shows a character to its best advantage. "It is only," says Kojève, "in being or in becoming aware of one's mortality or finitude, in existing and in feeling one's existence in a universe without a beyond or without a God, that Man can affirm his liberty, his historicity and his individuality—'unique in all the world'—and have them be recognized. (Ibid.). But if Kojève sets aside vulgar satisfaction—happiness—he now also sets aside Hegel's "absolute dismemberment": indeed, such dismemberment is not easily reconciled with the desire for recognition.

Satisfaction and dismemberment coincide, however, in one point, but here they harmonize with *pleasure*. This coincidence takes place in "sacrifice"; it is generally understood as the *naive form of life*, as every existence in present time, which manifests what Man *is*: the novelty which he signifies in the world after he has become *Man*, on the condition that he has satisfied his "*animal*" needs.

At any rate, *pleasure*, or at least sensual pleasure, is such that in respect to it Kojève's affirmation would be difficult to uphold: the idea of death helps, in a certain manner and in certain cases, to multiply the pleasures of the senses. I go so far as to believe that, under the form of defilement, the world (or rather the general imagery) of death is at the base of erotism. The feeling of sin is connected in lucid consciousness to the idea of death, and *in the same manner* the feeling of sin is connected with pleasure.[11] There is in fact no *human* pleasure without some irregularity in its circumstances, without the breaking of an interdiction—the simplest, and the most powerful of which, is currently that of nudity.

Moreover, possession was associated in its time with the image of sacrifice; it was a sacrifice in which woman was the victim. . . . That association from ancient poetry is very meaningful; it refers back to a precise state of sensibility in which the sacrificial element, the feeling of sacred horror itself, joined, in a weakened state, to a tempered pleasure; in which, too, the taste for sacrifice and the emotion which it released seemed in no way contrary to the ultimate uses of pleasure.

It must be said too that sacrifice, like tragedy, was an element of a celebration; it bespoke a blind, pernicious joy and all the danger of that joy, and yet this is precisely the principle of *human joy*; it wears out and threatens with death all who get caught up in its movement.

Gay Anguish, Anguished Gaiety

To the association of death and pleasure, which is not a given, at least is not an immediate given in consciousness, is obviously opposed the sadness of death, always in the background of consciousness. In principle, *consciously*, humanity "recoils in horror before death." In principle, the destructive effects of Negativity have Nature as their object. But for Man's Negativity to drive him into a confrontation with danger, for him to make of himself, or at least of the animal, of the natural being that he is, the object of his destructive negation, the banal prerequisite is his unconsciousness of the cause and the effects of his actions. Now, it was essential for Hegel to *gain consciousness* of Negativity as such, to capture its horror—here the horror of death—by upholding and by looking the work of death right in the face.

Hegel, in this way, is less opposed to those who "recoil" than to those who say: "it is nothing." He seems to distance himself most from those who react with gaiety.

I want to emphasize, as clearly as possible, after their similarity, the opposition between the naive attitude and that of the—*absolute*—Wisdom of Hegel. I am not sure, in fact, that of the two attitudes the more naive is the less *absolute*.

I shall cite a paradoxical example of a gay reaction in the face of the work of death.

The Irish and Welsh custom of the "wake" is little known but was still practiced at the end of the last century. It is the subject of Joyce's last work,[12] *Finnegans Wake*—the deathwatch of Finnegan (however, the reading of this famous novel is difficult at best). In Wales, the coffin was placed *open*, standing at the place of honor of the house. The dead man would be dressed in his finest suit and top hat. His family would invite all of his friends, who honored the departed all the more the longer they danced and the deeper they drank to his health. It is the death of an *other*, but in such instances, the death of the other is always the image of one's own death. Only under one condition could anyone so rejoice; with the presumed agreement of the dead man—who is an other—, the dead man that the drinker in his turn will become shall have no other meaning than his predecessor.

This paradoxical reaction could be considered a response to the desire to deny *the existence of death*. A logical desire? Not in the least, I think. In Mexico today, death is commonly envisaged on the same level as the amusements that can be found at festivals: skeleton puppets, skeleton candies, skeleton merry-go-rounds—but this custom is associated with an intense cult of the dead, a visible obsession with death.[13]

If I envisage death gaily, it is not that I too say, in turning away from what is frightening: "it is nothing" or "it is false." On the contrary, gaiety, connected with the work of death, causes me anguish, is accentuated by my anguish, and in return exacerbates that anguish: ultimately, gay anguish, anguished gaiety cause me, in a feverish chill,[14] "absolute dismemberment," where it is my joy that finally tears me apart, but where dejection would follow joy were I not torn all the way to the end, immeasurably.

There is one precise opposition that I would like to bring out fully: on the one hand Hegel's attitude is less whole than that of naïve humanity, but this is meaningless unless, reciprocally, one sees that the naïve attitude is powerless to maintain itself without subterfuge.

Discourse Gives Useful Ends to Sacrifice "Afterwards"

I have linked the meaning of sacrifice to Man's behavior once his animal needs have been satisfied: Man differs from the natural being which he also is; the sacrificial gesture is what he humanly is, and the spectacle of sacrifice then makes his humanity manifest. Freed from animal need, man is sovereign: he does what be pleases—his pleasure. Under these conditions he is finally able to make a rigorously autonomous gesture. So long as he needed to satisfy animal needs, he had to act with an end in view (he had to secure food, protect himself from the cold). This supposes a servitude, a series of acts subordinated to a final result: the natural, animal satisfaction without which Man properly speaking, sovereign Man, could not subsist. But Man's intelligence, his *discursive thought*, developed as functions of servile labor. Only sacred, poetic words, limited to the level of impotent beauty, have retained the power to manifest full sovereignty. Sacrifice, consequently, is a *sovereign, autonomous* manner of being only to the extent that it is uninformed by *meaningful* discourse. To the extent that discourse informs it, what is *sovereign* is given in terms of *servitude*. Indeed by definition what is *sovereign* docs not *serve*. But simple discourse must respond to the question that discursive thought asks concerning the meaning that each thing must have on the level of utility. In principle, each thing is there to *serve* some purpose or other. Thus the simple manifestation of Man's link to annihilation, the pure revelation of Man to himself (at the moment when death transfixes his attention) passes from sovereignty to the primacy of servile ends. Myth, associated with ritual, had at first the impotent beauty of poetry, but discourse concerning sacrifice slipped into vulgar, self-serving interpretation. Starting with effects naively imagined on the level of poetry, such as the appeasing of a god or the purity of beings, the end of meaningful discourse became the abundance of rain or the city's well-being. The substantial work of Frazer, who recalls those forms of sovereignty that were the most *impotent* and, apparently, the least propitious for happiness, generally tends to reduce the meaning of the ritual act to the same purposes as labor in the fields, and to make of sacrifice an agrarian rite. Today that thesis of the *Golden Bough* is discredited, but it seemed reasonable insofar as the same people who sacrificed inscribed sovereign sacrifice within the frame of a language of plowmen. It is true that in a very arbitrary manner, which never merited the credence of rigorous reason, these people attempted, and must have labored to submit sacrifice to the laws of action, laws to which they themselves were submitted, or labored to submit themselves.

Impotence of the Sage to Attain Sovereignty on the Basis of Discourse

Thus, the sovereignty of sacrifice is not absolute either. It is not absolute to the extent that the institution maintains within the world of efficacious activity a form whose meaning is, on the contrary, sovereign. A slippage cannot fail to occur, to the benefit of servitude.

If the attitude of the Sage (Hegel) is not, for its part, sovereign, at least things function in the opposite direction; Hegel did not distance himself and if he was unable to find authentic sovereignty, he came as near to it as he could. What separated him from it would even be imperceptible were we not able to glimpse a richer image through these alterations of meaning, which touch on sacrifice and which have reduced it from an *end* to a simple *means*. The key to a lesser rigorousness on the part of the Sage is the fact, not that discourse engages his sovereignty within a frame that cannot suit him and which atrophies it, but precisely the opposite: sovereignty in Hegel's attitude proceeds from a movement which *discourse* reveals and which, in the Sage's spirit, is never separated from its revelation. It can never, therefore, be fully *sovereign*; the Sage, in fact, cannot fail to subordinate it to the goal of a Wisdom which supposes the completion of discourse. Wisdom alone *will be* full autonomy, the sovereignty of being. . . . At least it *would be* if we could find sovereignty by searching for it: and, in fact, if I search for it, I am undertaking the project of being-sovereignly: but the *project* of being-sovereignly presupposes a servile being! What nonetheless assures the sovereignty of the moment described is the "absolute dismemberment" of which Hegel speaks, the rupture, for a time, of discourse. But that rupture itself is not sovereign. In a sense it is an accident in the ascent. Although the two sovereignties, the naive and the sage ones, are both sovereignties of death, beyond the difference between a decline at birth (between a gradual alteration and an imperfect manifestation), they differ on yet another precise point: on Hegel's part, it is precisely a question of an accident. It is not a stroke of fate, a piece of bad luck, which would be forever deprived of sense. Dismemberment is, on the contrary, full of meaning. ("*Spirit only attains its truth*," writes Hegel (but it is my emphasis), "by finding itself in absolute dismemberment.") But this meaning is unfortunate. It is what limited and impoverished the revelation which the Sage drew from lingering in the regions where death reigns. He welcomed sovereignty as a weight, which he let go. . .

Do I intend to minimize Hegel's attitude? But the contrary is true! I want to show the incomparable scope of his approach. To that end I cannot veil the very minimal (and even inevitable) part of failure.

To my mind, it is rather the exceptional certainty of that approach which is brought out in my associations. If he failed, one cannot say that it was the result of an error. The meaning of the failure itself differs from that of the failure which caused it: the error alone is perhaps fortuitous. In general, it is as an authentic movement, weighty with sense, that one must speak of the "failure" of Hegel.

Indeed, man is always in pursuit of an authentic sovereignty. That sovereignty, apparently, was, in a certain sense, originally his, but doubtless that could not then have been in a *conscious* manner, and so in a sense it was not his, it escaped him. We shall see that in a number of ways he continued to pursue what forever eluded him. The essential thing is that one cannot attain it consciously and seek it, because seeking distances it. And yet I can believe that nothing is given us that is not given in that equivocal manner.

Notes

1. Excerpt from a study on the—fundamentally Hegelian—thought of Alexandre Kojève. This thought seeks, so far as possible, to be Hegel's thought, such a contemporary spirit, knowing what Hegel did not know (knowing, for example, the events that have occurred since 1917 and, as well, the philosophy of Heidegger), could grasp it and develop it. Alexandre Kojève's originality and courage, it must be said, is to have perceived the impossibility of going any further, the necessity, consequently, of renouncing the creation of an original philosophy and, thereby, the interminable starting-over which is the avowal of the vanity of thought. This essay was first published in *Deucalion* 5 (1955). With permission of Editions Gallimard © 1988.
2. G. W. F. Hegel, *Jenenser Philosophie des Geistes* in *Sämtliche Werke,* ed. Johannes Hoffmeister, (Leipzig: Felix Meiner, 1931), vol. 20 180–81. Cited by Kojève in *Introduction to the Reading of Hegel*, (Paris: Gallimard, 1947), 573. (TEL edition [Paris: Gallimard, 1980], 575.) Henceforth cited in the text, as K; TEL).
3. In this paragraph, and the following, I repeat in a different form what has been said by Alexandre Kojève. But not only in a different form; essentially

I have to develop the second part of that sentcnce, which is, at first glance, difficult to comprehend in its concrete aspect: "The being or the annihilation of the 'Subject' is the temporalizing annihilation of Being, which must be *before* the annihilated being: the being of the 'Subject' necessarily has, therefore, a beginning. And being the (temporal) annihilation of the nothingness in Being, being nothingness which nihilates (insofar as Time), the "Subject" is essentially negation of itself: therefore it has an end." In particular, I have followed for this (as I have already done in the preceding paragraph) the part of *Introduction to the Reading of Hegel* which concerns parts 2 and 3 of the present study, i.e., Appendix II, "The Idea of Death in the Philosophy of Hegel," Kojève, 527–73. (TEL, 529–75.) [Translator's note: This appendix, from which all of Bataille's references to Kojève are taken, remains untranslatcd in English; it is not included in Allan Bloom's reedition (and abridgment) of Kojève's *Introduction to the Reading of Hegel* (New York: Basic Books, 1969).]

4. Cf., G. W. F. Hegel, *The Phenomenology of Spirit*, trans. A. V. Miller (Oxford: Oxford University Press, 1977), 9–10. In his footnotes, Bataille attributes the French versions he uses of Hegel to Jean Hyppolite's translation of *The Phenomenology of Spirit* and often also cites the pages from *Introduction à la lecture* de *Hegel* where Alexandre Kojève quotes the same passages. However, Kojève's version differs from that of Hyppolite and Bataille's from both. It is the latter that I have translated. Page references will hereafter be given to the English translation by A. V. Miller, which is often at significant variance with the quotations as I have rendered them. [Translator's note.]
5. Cf., Hegel, *The Phenomenology of Spirit*, trans. A. V. Miller, 19. Cited by Kojève, 538–39. (TEL, 540–41.) Kojève, Hyppolite, and Bataille all translate the German "Zerrissenheit" by "déchirement," which I in turn have given as "dismemberment," the same word which appears in Miller's translation of Hegel. It is important to note that the word "déchirement" has the meanings of "shredding" and "tearing" and, unlike "dismemberment," does not imply a disarticulation into predetermined units. In *L'Expérience intérieure*, for example, Bataille speaks of himself as left in "*lambeaux*" (shreds, as of cloth or paper) which his "inability to respond *achevait de . . . déchirer*." (Paris: Gallimard, 1954), 19). [Translator's note.]
6. Here my interpretation differs slightly from Kojève's (146 [TEL, 148]). [Translator's note: this passage too is missing from Bloom's abridgment of Kojève, which starts only with the lectures given in 1937–38. (The passage in question is from the 1936–37 lectures.)] Kojève simply states that "impotent beauty is incapable of bending to the requirements of the Understanding. The esthete, the romantic, the mystic, flee the idea of death and speak of Nothingness itself as something which *is*." In particular, he admirably

describes the mystic in this way. But the same ambiguity is found in philosophers (in Hegel, in Heidegger), at least ultimately. In truth, Kojève seems to me wrong not to have envisaged, beyond classical mysticism, a "conscious mysticism," conscious of making a Being from Nothingness, and, in addition, defining that impasse as a Negativity which would no longer have a field of action (at the end of history). The atheistic mystic, *self-conscious*, conscious of having to die and to disappear, would live, as Hegel *obviously said concerning himself*, "in absolute dismemberment"; but, for him, it is only the matter of a certain period: unlike Hegel, he would never come out of it, "contemplating the Negative right in the face," but never being able to transpose it into Being, refusing to do it and maintaining himself in ambiguity.

7. The *Phenomenology of Spirit*, chapter 8: Religion, B.: Religion in the form of Art, a) The abstract work of art (434–35). In these two pages, Hegel dwells on the disappearance of *objective essence*, but without developing its consequences. On the second page Hegel limits himself to considerations proper to "aesthetic religion" (the religion of the Greeks).
8. Still, although animal sacrifice seems to predate human sacrifice, there is nothing to prove that the choice of an animal signifies the unconscious desire to oppose the animal as such; man is only opposed to corporeal being, the being that is given. He is, furthermore, just as opposed to the plant.
9. I discuss comedy further on.
10. Perhaps for lack of a Catholic religious experience. I imagine Catholicism closer to pagan experience; I mean to a universal religious experience from which the Reformation distanced itself. Perhaps a profound Catholic piety could alone have introduced the inward sense without which the phenomenology of sacrifice would be impossible. Modern knowledge, much more extensive than that of Hegel's time, has assuredly contributed to the solution of that fundamental enigma (why, without any plausible reason, *has humanity in general* "sacrificed"?), but I seriously believe that a correct phenomenological description could only be based on at least a Catholic *period*.

    —But at any rate, Hegel, hostile to *being* which does nothing,—to what simply *is*, and is not *Action*,—was more interested in military death; it is through such death that he perceived the theme of sacrifice (but he himself uses the word in a moral sense): "The state-of-the-soldier," he states in his *Lectures* of 1805–06, "and war are the objectively real sacrifice of the personal-I, the danger of death for the particular,—that contemplation of his abstract immediate Negativity . . ." (in Hegel, *Sämtliche Werke*, vol. 20, 261–62. Cited by Kojève in *Introduction to the Reading of Hegel*, 558 [TEL, 560]). Nonetheless, religious sacrifice has, even from Hegel's point of view, an essential signification.

11. This is at least possible and, if it is a matter of the most common interdictions, banal.
12. On the subject of this obscure book, *vide* E. Jolas, "Elucidation du monomythe de James Joyce" in *Critique* (July 1948): 579–95.
13. This came out in the documentary which Eisenstein drew from his work for a long film: *¡Viva Mexico!* The crux of this film dealt with the bizarre practices which I have discussed.
14. Reading "chaud et froid" for "chaud-froid," which means a dish prepared hot but served cold.

CHAPTER 10

"The Subversion of the Subject and the Dialectic of Desire in the Freudian Unconscious"

—from *Écrits* (1966; lecture delivered: 1960)

Jacques Lacan

This text represents my contribution to a conference entitled 'La Dialectique', held at Royaumont 19–23 September, 1960. The conference was organized by the 'Colloques philosophiques intemationaux', and I was invited to participate by Jean Wahl.

This conference preceded by a month the Congrès de Bonneval, at which I delivered my text, *Position de l'inconscient*. The later text was very much a development of this (earlier) one, and its publication serves to demonstrate that my teaching has always been ahead of my published work.

(The graph reproduced here first appeared in my seminar on the formations of the unconscious. It was worked out with particular relation to the structure of the witticism, which, to the surprise of my audience, I took as a point of departure. An account of this seminar, which took place in the first term of the year 1957–58, appeared, together with the graph, in a number of the *Bulletin de psychologie*.)

The praxis that we call psychoanalysis is constituted by a structure. An audience like the one here today—an audience that we presume to be aware of philosophical problems—cannot ignore this structure.

The notion that to be a philosopher means being interested in what everyone is interested in without knowing it has the interesting peculiarity that its pertinence does not imply that it can be verified. For it can be put to the test only by everyone becoming a philosopher.

I say its philosophical pertinence, for such, in the last resort, is the schema that Hegel gave us of History in *The Phenomenology of Mind*.

Summarizing it in this way is to provide us with a mediation that facilitates the situating of the subject—namely, in relation to knowledge.

It is also easy to demonstrate the ambiguity of such a relation.

The same ambiguity is manifested in the effects of science in the world today.

The scientist, too, is a subject, and one particularly qualified in his constitution, as is shown by the fact that science did not come into the world of its own accord (its birth was not without its vicissitudes, and it was preceded by a number of failures—by abortion or premature birth).

Now this subject who must know what he is doing, or so one presumes, does not know what, in the effects of science, is already, in fact, of interest to everyone. Or so it would appear in the world of today, where everyone finds himself at the same level as the scientist as far as ignorance on this point is concerned.

This fact alone justifies us in speaking of a subject of science—a notion to which an epistemology that can be said to display more promise than success hopes to be equal.

Hence, let it be noted, my entirely didactic reference to Hegel, by which I wished to say something, for the purposes of the training that I have in mind, about the question of the subject, in so far as that question is properly subverted by psychoanalysis.

What qualifies me to proceed in this direction is obviously my experience of this praxis. What has decided me to do so, those who follow my teaching will bear this out, is a theoretical nullity coupled with abuses in the way in which it is passed on, which, while presenting no danger to the praxis itself, result, in either case, in a total absence of scientific status. To pose the question of the minimum conditions required for such a status was not perhaps a dishonest departure. This departure has taken us a long way.

I am not dealing here with anything so broad in scope as a radical questioning of social bases; I do not intend, in particular, to dwell on the conclusions that I have been forced to draw about the notorious deviations in analytic praxis that are perpetrated in the name of psychoanalysis in Britain and America.

What I will try to define is subversion proper, and I apologize to this gathering, whose quality I have already acknowledged, for being unable to do more in its presence than in its absence, that is, to take it as the very pivot of my demonstration, even though it is up to me to justify this latitude with regard to it.

Yet I shall use it in order to take as given the fact that empiricism cannot constitute the foundations for a science.

At a second stage, we encounter what has already been constituted, by virtue of a scientific label, under the name of psychology.

A label that I would reject—precisely because, as I will show, the function of the subject, as it is established in Freudian experience, disqualifies from the outset what, under cover of the term 'psychology', however one dresses up its premises, merely perpetuates an academic framework.

Its criterion is the unity of the subject, which is one of the presuppositions of this sort of psychology, it being even taken as symptomatic that its theme is always more emphatically isolated, as if it were a question of the return of a certain subject of knowledge (*connaissance*), or as if the psychical had to obtain its credentials as a double of the physical organism.

We must take as our standard here the idea in which a whole body of traditional thought comes together to validate a term, 'state of knowledge' (*état de la connaissance*), that is not without foundation. Whether it is a question of the states of enthusiasm described by Plato, the Buddhist degrees of *samadhi,* or the *Erlebnis*, the experience obtained under the influence of hallucinogenic drugs, it is necessary to know how much of these is authenticated by any theory.

Authenticated in the register of the connaturality implied in knowledge (*connaissance*).

It is clear that Hegelian knowledge (*savoir*), in the logicizing *Aufhebung* on which it is based, sets as little store by these states in themselves as modern science, which can recognize in them an object of experience, in the sense of an opportunity to define certain co-ordinates, but in no way an ascesis that might, let us say, be epistemogenic or noophoric.

It is certainly on this account that reference to them is pertinent to my approach.

For I suppose my listeners are sufficiently informed about Freudian practice to grasp that such states play no part in it—but what is not fully appreciated is the fact that the practitioners of this supposedly depth psychology do not think of using them to obtain illumination, for example, do not even attribute to these states any value in relation to the direction indicated by such a depth psychology.

For that is the meaning, which is not insisted on, of that distance from which Freud proceeds when it comes to hynoid states, even when it is merely a question of explaining the phenomena associated with hysteria. The stupifying fact is that Freud prefers the discourse of the hysteric. What I have called 'fruitful moments' (*moments féconds*) in my mapping of paranoiac knowledge (*connaissance*) is not a Freudian reference.

I have some difficulty in getting a hearing in circles infatuated with the most incredible illogicality for what is involved in questioning the unconscious as I do, that is to say, to the point at which it gives a reply that is not some sort of transport of delight, or flat rejection, but rather that 'it says why'.

If we take the subject anywhere it is to a deciphering that already presupposes this sort of logic in the unconscious: in which, for example, an interrogative voice, even the development of an argument, is recognized.

The whole psychoanalytic tradition supports the view that the analyst's voice can intervene only if it enters at the right place, and that if it enters too early it merely produces a closing up of communication.

In other words, psychoanalysis that is sustained by its allegiance to Freud cannot in any circumstances offer itself as a 'rite of passage' to some archetypal, or in any sense ineffable, experience: the day when anyone expresses a view of this order that is not simply a dead loss will be the day when all limits have been abolished. And we are still a long way from that.[1]

This is merely an approach to our subject. For it is a question of grasping more precisely what Freud in his doctrine himself articulates as constituting a 'Copernican' step.

Is it enough that a privilege should be consigned to it, namely the one that put the earth in the central place? The subsequent dislodging of man from a similar place by the triumph of the idea of evolution gives one the feeling that this would involve a gain that would be confirmed by its consistency.

But can one be sure that this is a gain, that it is real progress? Does nothing make it appear that the other truth, if we may so term revealed truth, is seriously affected as a result? Do we not believe that, by exalting the centre, heliocentrism is no less of a lure than seeing the earth as the centre of the Universe, and that the fact of the ecliptic no doubt provided a more stimulating model of our relations with the true, before it lost much of its interest by being no more than the earth nodding its assent?

In any case, it is not because of Darwin that men believe themselves to be any the less the top dogs in creation, for it is precisely of this that he convinces them.

The linguistically suggestive use of Copernicus' name has more hidden resources that touch specifically on what has just slipped from my pen as the relation to the true, namely, the emergence of the ellipse as being not unworthy of the locus from which the so-called higher truths take their name. The revolution is no less important for concerning only the 'celestial revolutions'.

To stop at this stage no longer means simply revoking some idiotic notion deriving from the religious tradition, which, as can be seen well enough, is none the worse for it, but rather of binding more closely the régime of knowledge to the régime of truth.

For if the work of Copernicus, as others have remarked before, is not as Copernican as is customarily believed, it is in this that the doctrine of double truth continues to offer shelter to a knowledge that until that time, it must be said, had every appearance of being quite content with it.

So here we are at this sensitive frontier between truth and knowledge; and it might be said after all that, at first sight, our science certainly seems to have re-adopted the solution of closing the frontier.

Yet if the historical birth of science is still a sufficiently burning question for us to be aware that at that frontier a shift took place, it is perhaps there that psychoanalysis is marked out to represent an earthquake yet to come.

For let us look again from this angle at the service we expected from Hegel's phenomenology, for it represents an ideal solution—a solution, one might say, involving a permanent revisionism, in which truth is in a state of constant re-absorption in its own disturbing element, being in itself no more than that which is lacking for the realization of knowledge. The antinomy that the Scholastic tradition posed as a matter of principle is here taken to be resolved by virtue of being imaginary. Truth is nothing other than that which knowledge can apprehend as knowledge only by setting its ignorance to work. A real crisis in which the imaginary is resolved, thus engendering a new symbolic form, to use my own categories. This dialectic is convergent and attains the conjuncture defined as absolute knowledge. As such it is deduced, it can only be the conjunction of the symbolic with a real of which there is nothing more to be expected. What is this real, if not a subject fulfilled in his identity to himself? From which, one can conclude that this subject is already perfect in this regard, and is the fundamental hypothesis of this whole process. He is named, in effect, as being the substratum of this process; he is called the *Selbstbewusstsein*, the being conscious of self, the fully conscious self.

I would to heaven it were so, but the history of science itself—I mean our science, from its inception, say, in Greek mathematics—presents itself rather in the form of détours that comply very little with this immanentism. In fact, the theories—and let us not be misled by any re-absorption of the limited theory into the generalized theory—do not, in any way, fit together according to the thesis/antithesis/synthesis dialectic.

Indeed, a number of cracks to be heard confusedly in the great consciousnesses responsible for some of the outstanding changes in physics remind us that, after all, for this knowledge as for others it is elsewhere that the hour of truth must strike.

And why would we not see that the astonishing consideration shown to the din emerging from psychoanalysis in science may be due to the theoretical hope psychoanalysis offers—a hope that is not only the result of confusion?

Of course, I am not referring to that extraordinary lateral transference, by which the categories of a psychology that re-invigorates its menial tasks with social exploitation acquire a new strength in psychoanalysis. For the reason already given, I regard the fate of psychology as signed and sealed.

In any case, my double reference to Hegel's absolute subject and to the abolished subject of science provides the illumination necessary to an accurate formulation of Freud's dramatism: the re-entry of truth into the field of science at the same time as it gains recognition in the field of its praxis: repressed, it reappears.

Who cannot see the distance that separates the unhappy consciousness—of which, however strongly it is engraven in Hegel, it can be said that it is still no more than the suspension of a corpus of knowledge—from the 'discontents of civilization' in Freud, even if it is only in a mere phrase, uttered as if disavowed, that marks for us what, on reading it, cannot be articulated otherwise than the 'skew' relation[2] that separates the subject from sexuality?

There is nothing, then, in our expedient for situating Freud that owes anything to the judicial astrology in which the psychologist dabbles. Nothing that proceeds from quality, or even from the intensive, or from any phenomenology from which idealism may draw reassurance. In the Freudian field, in spite of the words themselves, consciousness is a feature as inadequate to ground the unconscious in its negation (that unconscious dates from St Thomas Aquinas) as the affect is unsuited to play the role of the protopathic subject, since it is a service that has no holder.

Since Freud the unconscious has been a chain of signifiers that somewhere (on another stage, in another scene, he wrote) is repeated, and insists on interfering in the breaks offered it by the effective discourse and the cogitation that it informs.

In this formula, which is mine only in the sense that it conforms as closely to Freud's text as to the experience that it opened up, the crucial term is the signifier, brought back to life from the ancient art of rhetoric by modern linguistics, in a doctrine whose various stages cannot be traced here, but of which the names of Ferdinand de Saussure and Roman Jakobson will stand for the dawn and its present-day culmination, not forgetting that the pilot science of structuralism in the West has its roots in Russia, where formalism first flourished. 'Geneva 1910' and 'Petrograd 1920' suffice to explain why Freud lacked this particular tool. But this defect of history makes all the more instructive the fact that the mechanisms described by Freud as those of 'the primary process', in which the unconscious assumes its rule, correspond exactly to the functions that this school believes determines the most radical aspects of the effects of language, namely metaphor and metonymy—in other words, the signifier's effects of substitution and combination on the respectively synchronic and diachronic dimensions in which they appear in discourse.

Once the structure of language has been recognized in the unconscious, what sort of subject can we conceive for it?

We can try, with methodological rigour, to set out from the strictly linguistic definition of the I as signifier, in which there is nothing but the 'shifter' or indicative, which, in the subject of the statement, designates the subject in the sense that he is now speaking.

That is to say, it designates the subject of the enunciation,[3] but it does not signify it. This is apparent from the fact that every signifier of the subject of the enunciation may be lacking in the statement, not to mention the fact that there are those that differ from the I, and not only what is inadequately called the cases of the first person singular, even if one added its accommodation in the plural invocation, or even in the *Self* (*Soi*) of auto-suggestion.

I think, for example, that I recognized the subject of the enunciation in the signifier '*ne*', which grammarians call the expletive, a term that already prefigures the incredible opinion of those, and they are to be found among the best, who regard its form as being a matter of mere chance. May the weight that I give it persuade them to think again, before it becomes obvious that they have missed the point (*avant qu'il* ne *soit avéré qu'ils n'y comprennent rien*)—take out that *ne* and my enunciation loses its attack, *Je* eliding me into the impersonal. But I fear that in this way they will come to curse me (*je crains ainsi qu'ils* n'*en viennent à me honnir*)—slide over that *n'* and its absence, reducing the alleged fear of a declaration of my repugnance to a timid assertion, reduces the emphasis of my enunciation by situating me in the statement.

But if I say '*tue*' [the 3rd person singular of *tuer*, to kill and the past participle of *se taire*, to fall, or remain, silent], because they bore me to death, where am I situated if not in the '*tu*' [the familiar form of 'you'] from which I eye them?

Don't go into a sulk, I am merely referring obliquely to what I am reluctant to cover with the distorting map of clinical medicine.

Namely, the right way to reply to the question, 'Who is speaking?', when it is the subject of the unconscious that is at issue. For this reply cannot come from that subject if he does not know what he is saying, or even if he is speaking, as the entire experience of analysis has taught us.

It follows that the place of the 'inter-said' (*inter-dit*), which is the 'intrasaid' (*intra-dit*) of a between-two-subjects, is the very place in which the transparency of the classical subject is divided and passes through the effects of 'fading'[4] that specify the Freudian subject by its occultation by an ever purer signifier: that these effects lead us to the frontiers at which slips of the tongue and witticisms, in their collusion, become confused, even where elision is so much the more allusive in tracking down presence to its lair, that one is surprised that the *Dasein* hunt hasn't done better out of it.

Lest the hunt be in vain for us analysts, we must bring everything back to the function of the cut in discourse, the strongest being that which acts as a bar between the signifier and the signified. There the subject that interests us is surprised, since by binding himself in signification he is placed under the sign of the pre-conscious. By which we would arrive at the paradox of conceiving that the discourse in an analytic session is valuable only in so far as it stumbles or is interrupted: if the session itself were not instituted as a cut in a false discourse, or rather, to the extent that the discourse succeeds in emptying itself as speech, in being no more than Mallarmé's worn coinage that is passed from hand to hand 'in silence'.

This cut in the signifying chain alone verifies the structure of the subject as discontinuity in the real. If linguistics enables us to see the signifier as the determinant of the signified, analysis reveals the truth of this relation by making 'holes' in the meaning of the determinants of its discourse.

It was along this line of approach that Freud was able to carry out the imperative, which he brought to a level of sublimity worthy of the pre-Socratics in the formulation, '*Wo es war, soll Ich werden*', which I have commented upon several times already, and which I will now try to present in a different light.

To take one step at a time in Freud's grammar: 'there where it was . . .' (*là où ce fut . . .*), which means what? If it were only that which had been (in an aoristic, indefinite form), how can I come there in order to make myself be there, to state it now?

But the French says: '*Là où c'était . . .*' Let us make use of the benefit that French gives us of a distinct imperfect.[5] There where it was just now, there where it was for a while, between an extinction that is still glowing and a birth that is retarded, 'I' can come into being and disappear from what I say.

An enunciation that denounces itself, a statement that renounces itself, ignorance that dissipates itself, an opportunity that loses itself, what remains here if not the trace of what *must* be in order to fall from being?

A dream described by Freud in his article, 'Formulations on the Two Principles of the Mental Functioning',[6] gives us, with all the pathos that the figure of a dead father returning as a ghost would be invested, the sentence: 'He did not know that he was dead.'

I have already taken the pretext of this sentence to illustrate the relation of the subject to the signifier—a relation that is embodied in an enunciation (*énonciation*) whose being trembles with the vacillation that comes back to it from its own statement (*enoncé*).

If the figure of the dead father survives only by virtue of the fact that one does not tell him the truth of which he is unaware, what, then, is to be said of the *I*, on which this survival depends?

He did not know . . . A little more and he'd have known. Oh! let's hope that never happens! Rather than have him know, *I*'d die. Yes, that's how *I* get there, there where it was: who knew, then, that *I* was dead?

Being of non-being, that is how *I* as subject comes on the scene, conjugated with the double aporia of a true survival that is abolished by knowledge of itself, and by a discourse in which it is death that sustains existence.

Are we to weigh this being against that, which Hegel as subject has forged, of being the subject who treats of history in the discourse of absolute knowledge?

We remember that he admits to having experienced the temptation of madness. And is our way not that which overcomes that temptation, in going as far as the truth of the vanity of this discourse?

Let us not advance our doctrine on madness at this point. For this eschatological excursion is here only to designate the gap that separates those two relations of the subject to knowledge, the Freudian and the Hegelian.

And to show that there is no firmer root than the modes that distinguish the dialectic from desire.

For in Hegel it is desire (*Begierde*) that is given the responsibility for that minimum connexion with ancient knowledge (*connaissance*) that the subject must retain if truth is to be immanent in the realization of knowledge (*savoir*). Hegel's 'cunning of reason' means that, from beginning to end, the subject knows what he wants.

It is here that Freud reopens the junction between truth and knowledge to the mobility out of which revolutions come.

In this respect: that desire becomes bound up with the desire of the Other, but that in this loop lies the desire to know.

Freud's biologism has nothing to do with the moralistic abjection that wafts up from the psychoanalytic kitchen.

And you have to be made to live the death instinct, which is held in such abomination there, if you are to catch the true tone of Freud's biology. For to ignore the death instinct in his doctrine is to misunderstand that doctrine entirely.

From the approach that we have indicated, the reader should recognize in the metaphor of the return to the inanimate (which Freud attaches to every living body) that margin beyond life that language gives to the human being by virtue of the fact that he speaks, and which is precisely that in which such a being places in the position of a signifier, not only those parts of his body that are exchangeable, but this body itself. Thus it becomes apparent that the relation of the object to the body is in no way defined as a partial identification that would have to be totalized in such a relation, since, on the contrary, this object is the prototype of the significance of the body as that which for being is at stake.

At this point, I take up the challenge that is offered to me when what Freud calls *Trieb* is translated as 'instinct'. 'Drive' would seem to translate the German word quite well in English, but is avoided in the *Standard Edition*. In French, my last resort would be '*dérive*', if I were unable to give the bastard term '*pulsion*' the necessary forcefulness.

And so we insist on promoting instinct, whether grounded or not in biological observation, to a place among the modes of knowledge (*connaissance*) required by nature of the living being so that he may satisfy his needs. Instinct is then defined as knowledge (*connaissance*) that has the astonishing property of being unable to be knowledge (*un savoir*). But in Freud it is a question of something quite different, which is a *savoir*, certainly, but one that involves not the least *connaissance*, in that it is inscribed in a discourse, of which, like the 'messenger-slave' of ancient usage, the subject who carries under his hair the codicil that condemns him to death knows neither the meaning nor the text, nor in what language it is written, nor even that it had been tatooed on his shaven scalp as he slept.

This story hardly exaggerates the little physiology that is of interest to the unconscious.

It will be appreciated by the counter-proof of the contribution made by psychoanalysis to physiology since its inception: this contribution is nil, even where the sexual organs are concerned. No amount of fabulation will alter this balance-sheet.

For, of course, psychoanalysis involves the real of the body and the imaginary of its mental schema. But to recognize their scope in the perspective that is authorized by development, we must first perceive that the more or less departmented integrations that appear to order it, function in it above all like heraldic elements, like the body's coat-of-arms. This is confirmed by the use one makes of it to read children's drawings.

What we have here is the principle—we shall return to it later—of the paradoxical privilege possessed by the phallus in the dialectic of the unconscious, without the theory produced by the part-object being a sufficient explanation of it.

Need I now say that if one understands what sort of support we have sought in Hegel to criticize a degradation of psychoanalysis so inept that it can find no other claim to interest than being the psychoanalysis of today, it is inadmissible that I should be thought of as having been lured by a purely dialectical exhaustion of being. Nor can I regard a particular philosopher[7] as being responsible when he authorizes this misunderstanding.

For far from ceding to a logicizing reduction where it is a question of desire, I find in its irreducibility to demand the very source of that which also prevents it from being reduced to need. To put it elliptically: it is precisely because desire is articulated that it is not articulable, I mean in the discourse best suited to it, an ethical, not a psychological discourse.

I must now develop much further for you the topology that I have elaborated in my teaching over the past five years, that is, introduce a certain diagram, which, I should warn you, also serves purposes other than the use that I am going to make of it here, having been constructed and completed quite openly in order to map in its arrangement the most broadly practical structure of the data of our experience. It will serve here to show where desire, in relation to a subject defined in his articulation by the signifier, is situated.

This is what might be said to be its elementary cell (cf. *Graph I*). In it is articulated what I have called the 'anchoring point' (*point de capiton*), by which the signifier stops the otherwise endless movement *(glissement)* of the signification. The signifying chain is regarded as being supported by the vector

Graph I

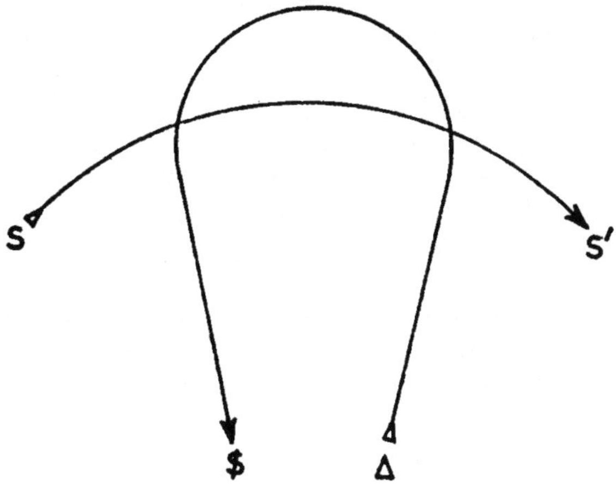

$\overrightarrow{S.S.'}$—even without entering into the subtleties of the retrograde direction in which its double intersection with the vector $\overrightarrow{\Delta.\$}$ occurs. Only in this vector does one see the fish it hooks, a fish less suitable in its free movement to represent what it withholds from our grasp than the intention that tries to bury it in the mass of the pre-text, namely, the reality that is imagined in the ethological schema of the return of need.

The diachronic function of this anchoring point is to be found in the sentence, even if the sentence completes its signification only with its last term, each term being anticipated in the construction of the others, and, inversely, sealing their meaning by its retroactive effect.

But the synchronic structure is more hidden, and it is this structure that takes us to the source. It is metaphor in so far as the first attribution is constituted in it—the attribution that promulgates 'the dog goes miaow, the cat goes woof-woof',[8] by which the child, by disconnecting the animal from its cry, suddenly raises the sign to the function of the signifier, and reality to the sophistics of signification, and by contempt for verisimilitude, opens up the diversity of objectifications of the same thing that have to be verified.

Does this possibility require the topology of a four-cornered game? That is the sort of question that looks innocent enough, but which may give some trouble, if the subsequent construction must be dependent on it.

I will spare you the various stages by giving you at one go the function of the two points of intersection in this simplified graph. The first, connoted O, is the locus of the signifier's treasure, which does not mean the code's treasure, for it is not that the univocal correspondence of a sign with something is preserved in it, but that the signifier is constituted only from a synchronic and enumerable collection of elements in which each is sustained only by the principle of its opposition to each of the others. The second, connoted *s*(O), is what may be called the punctuation in which the signification is constituted as finished product.

Observe the dyssymetry of the one, which is a locus (a place, rather than a space), to the other, which is a moment (a rhythm, rather than a duration).

Both participate in this offering to the signifier that is constituted by the hole in the real, the one as a hollow for concealment, the other as a boring-hole to escape from.

The subjection of the subject to the signifier, which occurs in the circuit that goes from *s*(O) to O and back from O to *s*(O) is really a circle, even though the assertion that is established in it—for lack of being able to end on anything other than its own scansion, in other words, for lack of an act in which it would find its certainty—refers only to its own anticipation in the composition of the signifier, in itself insignificant.

To be possible, the squaring of this circle only requires the completion of the signifying battery set up in O, henceforth symbolizing the locus of the Other. It then becomes apparent that this Other is simply the pure subject of modern games theory, and as such perfectly accessible to the calculation of conjecture, even though the real subject, in order to govern his own calculation, must leave out of account any so-called subjective aberration, in the common, that is, the psychological, acceptation of the term, and concern himself only with the inscription of an exhaustible combinatory.

Yet such a squaring is impossible, but only by virtue of the fact that the subject is constituted only by subtracting himself from it and by decompleting it essentially in order, at one and the same time, to have to depend on it and to make it function as a lack.

The Other as previous site of the pure subject of the signifier holds the master position, even before coming into existence, to use Hegel's term against him, as absolute Master. For what is omitted in the platitude of modern information theory is the fact that one can speak of code only if it is already the code of the Other, and that is something quite different from what is in question in the message, since it is from this code that the subject is constituted, which means that it is from the Other that the subject receives even the message that he emits. And the notations O and *s*(O) are justified.

Code messages or message codes will be distinguished in pure forms in the subject of psychosis, the subject who is satisfied with that previous Other.

Observe, in parentheses, that this Other, which is distinguished as the locus of Speech, imposes itself no less as witness to the Truth. Without the dimension that it constitutes, the deception practised by Speech would be indistinguishable from the very different pretence to be found in physical combat or sexual display.

Pretence of this kind is deployed in imaginary capture, and is integrated into the play of approach and rejection that constituted the original dance, in which these two vital situations find their rhythm, and in accordance with which the partners ordered their movements—what I will dare to call their 'dancity' (*dansité*). Indeed, animals, too, show that they are capable of such behaviour when they are being hunted; they manage to put their pursuers off the scent by making a false start. This can go so far as to suggest on the part of the game animal the nobility of honoring the element of display to be found in the hunt. But an animal does not pretend to pretend. He does not make tracks whose deception lies in the fact that they will be taken as false, while being in fact true ones, ones, that is, that indicate his true trail. Nor does an animal cover up its tracks, which would be tantamount to making itself the subject of the signifier.

All this has been articulated in a confused way even by professional philosophers. But it is clear that Speech begins only with the passage from 'pretence' to the order of the signifier, and that the signifier requires another locus—the locus of the Other, the Other witness, the witness Other than any of the partners—for the Speech that it supports to be capable of lying, that is to say, of presenting itself as Truth.

Thus it is from somewhere other than the Reality that it concerns that Truth derives its guarantee: it is from Speech. Just as it is from Speech that Truth receives the mark that establishes it in a fictional structure.

The first words spoken (*le dit premier*) stand as a decree, a law, an aphorism, an oracle; they confer their obscure authority upon the real other.

Take just one signifier as an emblem of this omnipotence, that is to say of this wholly potential power (*ce pouvoir tout en puissance*), this birth of possibility, and you have the unbroken line (*trait unaire*) which, by filling in the invisible mark that the subject derives from the signifier, alienates this subject in the primary identification that forms the ego ideal.

This is inscribed in the notation I(O), which, at this stage, I must substitute for the $, the barred S of the retrograde vector, bringing its tip back to its starting point (cf. *Graph II*).

This is a retroversion effect by which the subject becomes at each stage what he was before and announces himself—he will have been—only in the future perfect tense.

At this point the ambiguity of a failure to recognize that is essential to knowing myself (*un méconnaître essentiel au me connaître*) is introduced. For, in this 'rear view' (*rétrovisée*), all that the subject can be certain of is the anticipated image coming to meet him that he catches of himself in his mirror. I shall not return here to the function of my 'mirror stage', that first strategic point that I developed in opposition to the favour accorded in psychoanalytic theory to the supposedly *autonomous ego*. The academic restoration of this 'autonomous ego' justified my view that a misunderstanding was involved in any attempt to

Graph II

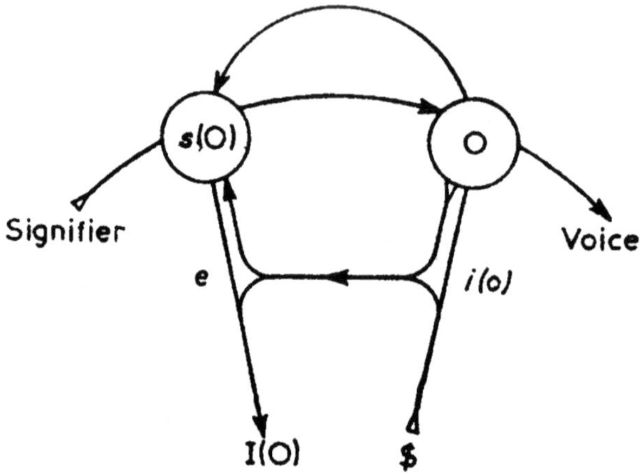

strengthen the ego in a type of analysis that took as its criterion of 'success' a successful adaptation to society—a phenomenon of mental abdication that was bound up with the ageing of the psychoanalytic group in the diaspora of the war, and the reduction of a distinguished practice to a label suitable to the 'American way of life'.[9]

In any case, what the subject finds in this altered image of his body is the paradigm of all the forms of resemblance that will bring over on to the world of objects a tinge of hostility, by projecting on them the manifestation of the narcissistic image, which, from the pleasure derived from meeting himself in the mirror, becomes when confronting his fellow man an outlet for his most intimate aggressivity .

It is this image that becomes fixed, the ideal ego, from the point at which the subject stops as ego ideal. From this point on, the ego is a function of mastery, a play of presence, of bearing (*prestance*), and of constituted rivalry. In the capture to which it is subjected by its imaginary nature, the ego masks its duplicity, that is to say, the consciousness in which it assures itself of an incontestable existence (a naivety to be found in the meditation of a Fénelon) is in no way immanent in it, but, on the contrary, is transcendent, since it is supported by the unbroken line of the ego ideal (which the Cartesian *cogito* did not fail to recognize[10]). As a result, the transcendental ego itself is relativized, implicated as it is in the *méconnaissance* in which the ego's identifications take root.

This imaginary process, which begins with the specular image and goes on to the constitution of the ego by way of subjectification by the signifier, is signified in our graph by the vector $i(\overrightarrow{o}).e$, which is one-way, but which is doubly articulated, once in a short circuit over $\$.I(\overrightarrow{O})$, and again in a return direction over

$s(\overrightarrow{O).O}$. This shows that the ego is only completed by being articulated not as the *I* of discourse, but as a metonymy of its signification (what Damourette and Pichon take as the 'alloyed' (*étoffé*) person, as opposed to the 'purified' (*subtile*) person, the latter being no more than the function designated above as the 'shifter').

The promotion of consciousness as being essential to the subject in the historical after-effects of the Cartesian *cogito* is for me the deceptive accentuation of the transparency of the I in action at the expense of the opacity of the signifier that determines the I; and the sliding movement (*glissement*) by which the *Bewusstsein* serves to cover up the confusion of the *Selbst* eventually reveals, with all Hegel's own rigour, the reason for his error in *The Phenomenology of Mind*.

The very movement that shifts the axis of the phenomenon of mind towards the imaginary relation to the other (that is to say, to the counterpart connoted by the small 'o', the *objet petit* a), reveals its effect: namely, the aggressivity that becomes the beam of the balance on which will be centred the decomposition of the equilibrium of counterpart to counterpart in the Master-Slave relationship, a relationship that is pregnant with all the cunning tricks (*ruses*) by which reason sets its impersonal reign in motion.

I can now show what is concealed in this initial enslavement—a mythical, rather than a real genesis, no doubt—of the 'roads to freedom' precisely because I have revealed it as never before.

The struggle that establishes this initial enslavement is rightly called a struggle of pure prestige, and the stake, life itself, is well suited to echo that danger of the generic prematuration of birth, which Hegel was unaware of, and which I see as the dynamic origin of specular capture.

But precisely because it is drawn into the function of the stakes—a more honest wager than Pascal's, though it is also a question of poker, since there is a limit on how high one can raise the bid—death shows by the same token what is elided from a prior rule, and from the ultimate rule. For, in the end, the loser must not perish if he is to become a slave. In other words, the pact is everywhere anterior to the violence before perpetuating it, and what I call the symbolic dominates the imaginary, which is why one may ask oneself whether murder is the absolute Master.

For it is not enough to decide on the basis of its effect—Death. It still remains to be decided which death,[11] that which is brought by life or that which brings life.

Without detracting from the Hegelian dialectic by an accusation of inadequacy, which has often been laid against it on the question of what bound the society of masters together, I simply wish at this point to stress what, on the basis of my own experience, is self-evidently symptomatic, that is to say, as installation in repression. This is properly the theme of the Cunning (*Ruse*) practised by reason—and the fact that it is erroneous, as I pointed out above, in no way diminishes its attraction. The work to which the slave is subjected and the pleasure that he renounces out of fear of death, we are told, will be precisely the way through which he will achieve freedom. There can be no more obvious lure than this, politically or psychologically. *Jouissance* comes easily to the slave, and it will leave the work in bondage.

The cunning of reason is an attractive notion because it echoes with a personal myth that is very familiar to the obsessional neurotic, and whose structure is often found among the *intelligentsia*. But even if the obsessional avoids the bad faith of the professor, he cannot easily deceive himself that it is his work that must make *jouissance* possible for him. Paying very properly unconscious homage to the history written by Hegel, he often finds his alibi in the death of the Master. But what about this death? He quite simply waits for it.

In fact, it is from the locus of the Other where he installs himself that he follows the game, thus rendering any risk inoperant, especially the risk of any contest, in a 'consciousness-of-self' for which death is present only in jest.

So philosophers should not make the mistake of thinking that they can take little account of the irruption that Freud's views on desire represented.

And this under the pretext that demand, together with the effects of frustration, has submerged everything that reaches them from a practice that has declined into educative banality that cannot be revived even by such a sell-out.

Yes, the enigmatic traumas of the Freudian discovery are now merely repressed desires. Psychoanalysis is nourished by the observation of children and by the infantilism of the observations. I will not bore you with case-histories, edifying as they all no doubt are—though they are hardly noted for their humour, their authors being too concerned with their 'responsibilities' to leave any room for the irremediably ridiculous side to the relations that the unconscious maintains with its linguistic roots.

Yet it is impossible, for those who claim that it is through the welcome accorded to demand that incompatibility is introduced into the needs that are supposed to lie at the origin of the subject, to ignore the fact that there is no demand that does not in some sense pass through the defiles of the signifier.

And if the somatic *ananke* of man's powerlessness for some time after birth to move of his own accord, and *a fortiori* to be self-sufficient, ensures that he will be grounded in a psychology of dependence, how can that *ananke* ignore the fact that this dependence is maintained by a world of language, precisely because by and through language needs are diversified and reduced to a point at which their scope appears to be of a quite different order, whether in relation to the subject or to politics? To sum up: to the point that these needs have passed over into the register of desire, with all that this brings in terms of an obligation to confront our new experience with its paradoxes, which have always interested the moralist, with that mark of the infinite that theologians find in it, even with the precariousness of its status, as expressed in its most extreme form by Sartre: desire, a useless passion.

What psychoanalysis shows us about desire in what might be called its most natural function, since on it depends the propagation of the species, is not only that it is subjected, in its agency, its appropriation, its normality, in short, to the accidents of the subject's history (the notion of trauma as contingency), but also that all this requires the co-operation of structural elements, which, in order to intervene, can do very well without these accidents, whose effects, so unharmonious, so unexpected, so difficult to reduce, certainly seem to leave to experience a remainder that drove Freud to admit that sexuality must bear the mark of some unnatural split (*fêlure*).

It would be wrong to think that the Freudian myth of the Oedipus complex had put an end to theology on the matter. For it is not enough to wave the flag of sexual rivalry. It would be better to read what Freud has to say about its co-ordinates; for they amount to the question with which he himself set out: 'What is a Father?'

'It is the dead Father', Freud replies, but no one listens, and, concerning that part of it that Lacan takes up again under the heading 'Name-of-the-Father', it is regrettable that so unscientific a situation should still deprive him of his normal audience.[12]

Yet analytic reflexion has centred vaguely on the problematic *méconnaissance* on the part of certain primitive peoples of the function of the progenitor, and psychoanalysts have argued, under the contraband banner of 'culturalism', over the forms of an authority of which it cannot even be said that any sector of anthropology has provided a definition of any scope.

Will we have to be overtaken by the practice, which may in the course of time become common practice, of artificially inseminating women who have broken the phallic bounds with the sperm of some great man, before a verdict on the paternal function can be dragged out of us?

Yet the Oedipus complex cannot run indefinitely in forms of society that are more and more losing the sense of tragedy.

Let us set out from the conception of the Other as the locus of the signifier. Any statement of authority has no other guarantee than its very enunciation, and it is pointless for it to seek it in another signifier, which could not appear outside this locus in any way. Which is what I mean when I say that no metalanguage can be spoken, or, more aphoristically, that there is no Other of the Other. And when the Legislator (he who claims to lay down the Law) presents himself to fill the gap, he does so as an imposter.

But there is nothing false about the Law itself, or about him who assumes its authority.

The fact that the Father may be regarded as the original representative of this authority of the Law requires us to specify by what privileged mode of presence he is sustained beyond the subject who is actually led to occupy the place of the Other, namely, the Mother. The question, therefore, is pushed still further back.

It will seem odd, no doubt, that in opening up the immeasurable space that all demand implies, namely, that of being a request for love, I should not leave more play to the question; but should concentrate it on that which is closed this side of it, by the very effect of demand, in order to give desire its proper place.

Indeed, it is quite simply, and I will say later in what way, as desire of the Other that man's desire finds form, but it does so in the first instance by representing need only by means of a subjective opacity.

I will now explain by what bias this opacity produces, as it were, the substance of desire.

Desire begins to take shape in the margin in which demand becomes separated from need: this margin being that which is opened up by demand, the appeal of which can be unconditional only in regard to the Other, under the form of the possible defect, which need may introduce into it, of having no universal satisfaction (what is called 'anxiety'). A margin which, linear as it may be, reveals its vertigo, even if it is not trampled by the elephantine feet of the Other's whim. Nevertheless, it is this whim that introduces the phantom of the Omnipotence, not of the subject, but of the Other in which his demand is installed (it is time this idiotic cliché was, once and for all, put back in its place), and with this phantom the need for it to be checked by the Law.

But I will stop there and return to the status of the desire that presents itself as autonomous in relation to this mediation of the Law, for the simple reason that it originates in desire, by virtue of the fact that by a strange symmetry it reverses the unconditional nature of the demand for love, in which the subject remains in subjection to the Other, and raises it to the power of absolute condition (in which 'absolute' also implies 'detachment').

For the gain obtained over anxiety with regard to need, this detachment is successful in its first, humblest form, that in which it was detected by a certain psychoanalyst in the course of his pediatric practice, and which is called 'the transitional object', in other words, the bit of 'nappie' or the beloved bit of material that the child never allows to leave his lips or hand.

This is no more than an emblem, I say; the representative of representation in the absolute condition is at home in the unconscious, where it causes desire according to the structure of the phantasy that I will now extract from it.

For it is clear that the state of nescience in which man remains in relation to his desire is not so much a nescience of what he demands, which may after all be circumscribed, as a nescience as to where he desires.

This is what I mean by my formula that the unconscious is '*discours de l' Autre*' (discourse of the Other), in which the *de* is to be understood in the sense of the Latin *de* (objective determination): *de Alio in oratione* (completed by: *tua res agitur*).

But we must also add that man's desire is the *désir de l'Autre* (the desire of the Other) in which the *de* provides what grammarians call the 'subjective determination', namely that it is *qua* Other that he desires (which is what provides the true compass of human passion).

That is why the question *of* the Other, which comes back to the subject from the place from which he expects an oracular reply in some such form as '*Che vuoi?*', 'What do you want?', is the one that best leads him to the path of his own desire—providing he sets out, with the help of the skills of a partner known as a psychoanalyst, to reformulate it, even without knowing it, as 'What does he want of me?'

It is this superimposed level of the structure that will bring my graph (cf. *Graph III*) to completion, first by introducing into it as the drawing of a question-mark placed in the circle of the capital O of the Other, symbolizing by a confusing homography the question it signifies.

Of what bottle is this the opener? Of what reply is it the signifier, the universal key?

It should be noted that a clue may be found in the clear alienation that leaves to the subject the favour of stumbling upon the question of its essence, in that he cannot fail to recognize that what he desires presents itself to him as what he does not want, the form assumed by the negation in which the *méconnaissance* of which he himself is unaware is inserted in a very strange way—a *méconnaissance* by which he transfers the permanence of his desire to an ego that is nevertheless intermittent, and, inversely, protects himself from his desire by attributing to it these very intermittences.

Of course, one may be surprised by the extent of what is accessible to consciousness-of-self, providing one has learnt it elsewhere—which is certainly the case here.

For in order to rediscover the pertinence of all this, a fairly detailed study is required—a study that can only take place in the analytic experience—that would enable us to complete the structure of the phantasy by linking it essentially, whatever its occasional elisions may be, to the condition of an object (the privilege of which I have done no more than touch on above in terms of diachrony), the moment of a 'fading'[13] or eclipse of the subject that is closely bound up with the *Spaltung* or splitting that it suffers from its subordination to the signifier.

This is what is symbolized by the sigla ($\$\Diamond o$), which I have introduced in the form of an algorithm; and it is no accident that it breaks the phonematic element constituted by the signifying unity right down to its literal atom. For it is created to allow a hundred and one different readings, a multiplicity that is admissible as long as the spoken remains caught in its algebra.

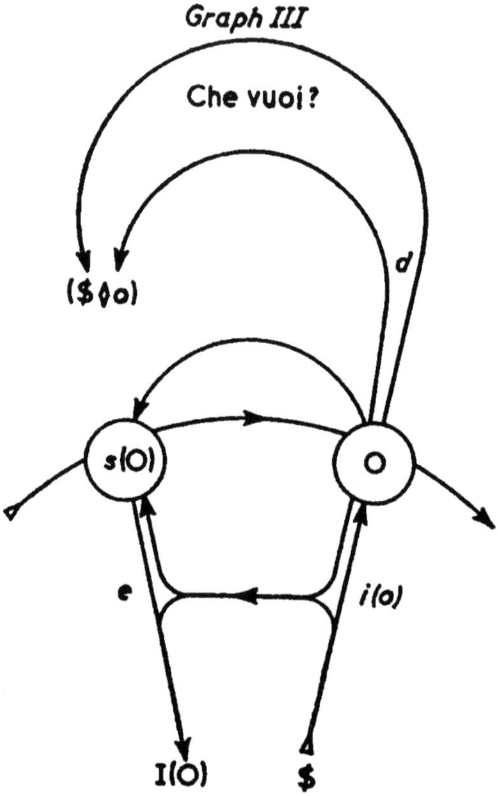

This algorithm and the analogues of it used in the graph in no way contradict what I said earlier about the impossibility of a metalanguage. They are not transcendent signifiers; they are the indices of an absolute signification, a notion which, without further commentary, will seem appropriate, I hope, to the condition of the phantasy.

On to the phantasy presented in this way, the graph inscribes that desire governs itself, which is similar to the relation between the ego and the body image, except that it still marks the inversion of the *méconnaissances* on which each is based. Thus the imaginary way, through which I must pass in analysis, and where the unconscious was *itself*,[14] is closed.

Let us say, borrowing the metaphor used by Damourette and Pichon about the grammatical 'I' and applying it to a subject to which it is better suited, that the phantasy is really the 'stuff' of the 'I' that is originally repressed, because it can be indicated only in the 'fading' of the enunciation.

So our attention is now drawn to the subjective status of the signifying chain in the unconscious, or rather in primal repression (*Urverdrängung*).

In our deduction it is easier to understand why it was necessary to question oneself regarding the function that supports the subject of the unconscious, to grasp that it is difficult to designate that subject anywhere as subject of a statement, and therefore as the articulator, when he does not even know that he is speaking. Hence the concept of drive, in which he is designated by an organic, oral, anal, etc., mapping that satisfies the requirement of being all the farther away from speaking the more he speaks.

But although our completed graph enables us to place the drive as the treasure of the signifiers, its notation as ($◊D) maintains its structure by linking it with diachrony. It is that which proceeds from demand when the subject disappears in it. It is obvious enough that demand also disappears, with the single exception that the cut remains, for this cut remains present in that which distinguishes the drive from the organic function it inhabits: namely, its grammatical artifice, so manifest in the reversions of its articulation to both source and object—Freud is unfailingly illuminating on this matter.

The very delimitation of the 'erogenous zone' that the drive isolates from the metabolism of the function (the act of devouring concerns other organs than the mouth—ask one of Pavlov's dogs) is the result of a cut (*coupure*) expressed in the anatomical mark (*trait*) of a margin or border—lips, 'the enclosure of the teeth', the rim of the anus, the tip of the penis, the vagina, the slit formed by the eyelids, even the horn-shaped aperture of the ear (I am avoiding embryological details here). Respiratory erogeneity has been little studied, but it is obviously through the spasm that it comes into play.

Observe that this mark of the cut is no less obviously present in the object described by analytic theory: the mamilla, faeces, the phallus (imaginary object), the urinary flow. (An unthinkable list, if one adds, as I do, the phoneme, the gaze, the voice—the nothing.) For is it not obvious that this feature, this partial feature, rightly emphasized in objects, is applicable not because these objects are part of a total object, the body, but because they represent only partially the function that produces them?

These objects have one common feature in my elaboration of them—they have no specular image, or, in other words, alterity.[15] It is what enables them to be the 'stuff', or rather the lining, though not in any sense the reverse, of the very subject that one takes to be the subject of consciousness. For this subject, who thinks he can accede to himself by designating himself in the statement, is no more than such an object. Ask the writer about the anxiety that he experiences when faced by the blank sheet of paper, and he will tell you who *is* the turd of his phantasy.

It is to this object that cannot be grasped in the mirror that the specular image lends its clothes. A substance caught in the net of the shadow, and which,

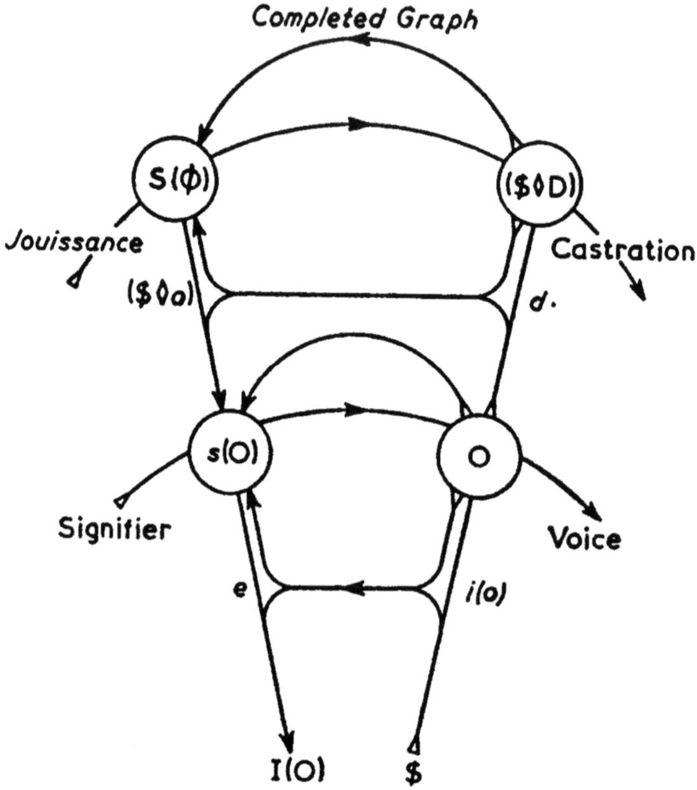

robbed of its shadow-swelling volume, holds out once again the tired lure of the shadow as if it were substance.[16]

What the graph now offers us is situated at the point at which every signifying chain prides itself on looping its signification. If we are to expect such an effect from the unconscious enunciation, it is to be found here in S(Ø), and read as: signifier of a lack in the Other, inherent in its very function as the treasure of the signifier. And this is so even though the Other is required (*che vuoi*) to respond to the value of this treasure, that is to say, to reply, from its place in the lower chain certainly, but also in the signifiers that constitute the upper chain, in terms of drive, in other words.

The lack referred to here is indeed that which I have already formulated: that there is no Other of the Other. But is this mark made by the Unbeliever of the truth really the last word that is worth giving in reply to the question, 'What does the Other want of me?', when we, the analysts, are its mouthpiece? Surely not, and precisely because there is nothing doctrinal about our office. We are answerable to no ultimate truth; we are neither for nor against any particular religion.

It is already quite enough that at this point I had to situate the dead Father in the Freudian myth. But a myth is not enough to support a rite, and psychoanalysis is not the rite of the Oedipus complex—a point that I shall develop later.

No doubt the corpse is a signifier, but Moses's tomb is as empty for Freud as that of Christ was for Hegel. Abraham revealed his mystery to neither of them.

Personally, I will begin with what is articulated in the sigla S(Ø) by being first of all a signifier. My definition of a signifier (there is no other) is as follows: a signifier is that which represents the subject for another signifier. This signifier will therefore be the signifier for which all the other signifiers represent the subject: that is to say, in the absence of this signifier, all the other signifiers represent nothing, since nothing is represented only *for* something else.

And since the battry of signifiers, as such, is by that very fact complete, this signifier can only be a line (*trait*) that is drawn from its circle without being able to be counted part of it. It can be symbolized by the inherence of a (–1) in the whole set of signifiers.

As such it is inexpressible, but its operation is not inexpressible, for it is that which is produced whenever a proper noun is spoken. Its statement equals its signification.

Thus, by calculating that signification according to the algebraic method used here, namely:

$$\frac{\text{S (signifier)}}{\text{s (signified)}} = \text{s (the statement), with S} = (-1)\text{, produces: s} = \sqrt{-1}$$

This is what the subject lacks in order to think himself exhausted by his *cogito*, namely, that which is unthinkable for him. But where does this being, who appears in some way defective in the sea of proper nouns, originate?

We cannot ask this question of the subject as 'I'. He lacks everything needed to know the answer, since if this subject 'I' was dead, he would not, as I said earlier, know it. He does not know, therefore, that I am alive. How, therefore, will 'I' prove to myself that I am?

For I can only just prove to the Other that he exists, not, of course, with the proofs for the existence of God, with which over the centuries he has been killed off, but by loving him, a solution introduced by the Christian *kerygma*. Indeed, it is too precarious a solution for me even to think of using it as a means of circumventing our problem, namely: 'What am "I"?'

'I' am in the place from which a voice is heard clamouring 'the universe is a defect in the purity of Non-Being'.

And not without reason, for by protecting itself this place makes Being itself languish. This place is called *Jouissance*, and it is the absence of this that makes the universe vain.

Am I responsible for it, then? Yes, probably. Is this *Jouissance*, the lack of which makes the Other insubstantial, mine, then? Experience proves that it is usually forbidden me, not only, as certain fools believe, because of a bad arrangement of society, but rather because of the fault (*faute*) of the Other if he existed: and since the Other does not exist, all that remains to me is to assume the fault upon 'I', that is to say, to believe in that to which experience leads us all, Freud in the vanguard, namely, to original sin. For even if we did not have Freud's express, and sorrowful avowal, the fact would remain that the myth Freud gave us—the latest-born myth in history—is no more use than that of the forbidden apple, except for the fact, and this has nothing to do with its power as myth, that, though more succinct, it is distinctly less oppressive (*crétinisant*).

But what is not a myth, and which Freud nevertheless formulated soon after the Oedipus complex, is the castration complex.

In the castration complex we find the major mainspring of the very subversion that I am trying to articulate here by means of its dialectic. For this complex, which was unknown as such until Freud introduced it into the formation of desire, can no longer be ignored in any reflexion on the subject.

There can be little doubt that in psychoanalysis, far from there having been any attempt to carry its articulation further, it has been employed precisely in order to avoid any explanation of it. This is why this great Samson-like body has been reduced to turning the grinding wheel for the Philistines of general psychology.

Certainly there is in all this what is called a bone. Though it is precisely what is suggested here, namely, that it is structural of the subject, it constitutes in it essentially that margin that all thought has avoided, skipped over, circumvented, or blocked whenever it seems to succeed in being sustained by a circle, whether that circle be dialectical or mathematical.

This is why I am so anxious to guide my students over the places where logic is disconcerted by the disjunction that breaks through from the imaginary to the symbolic, not in order to enjoy the paradoxes that are produced in such a disjunction, nor to point out some 'crisis' in thought, but, on the contrary, to bring their false brilliance back to the gap that they designate, which I always find instructive, and above all to try to work out the method of a sort of calculation, the inappropriation of which as such would spoil the secret.

Such is the phantom of the cause, which I have followed in the purest symbolization of the imaginary through the alternation of the similar and the dissimilar.[17]

Let us observe carefully, therefore, what it is that objects to conferring on our signifier S(Ø) the meaning of *Mana* or of any of its cognates. The fact is we cannot be content to articulate it from the poverty of the social fact, even if this is tracked down in some supposed total fact.

No doubt Claude Lévi-Strauss, in his commentary on Mauss, wished to recognize in it the effect of a zero symbol. But it seems to me that what we are dealing with here is rather the signifier of the lack of this zero symbol. That is why, at the risk of incurring a certain amount of opprobrium, I have indicated to what point I have pushed the distortion of the mathematical algorithm in my use of it: the symbol $\sqrt{-1}$, which is still written as '*i*' in the theory of complex numbers, is obviously justified only because it makes no claim to any automatism in its later use.

But we must insist that *jouissance* is forbidden to him who speaks as such, although it can only be said between the lines for whoever is subject of the Law, since the Law is grounded in this very prohibition.

Indeed, the Law appears to be giving the order, '*Jouis!*', to which the subject can only reply '*J'ouis*' (I hear), the *jouissance* being no more than understood.

But it is not the Law itself that bars the subject's access to *jouissance*—rather it creates out of an almost natural barrier a barred subject. For it is pleasure that sets the limits on *jouissance*, pleasure as that which binds incoherent life together, until another, unchallengeable prohibition arises from the regulation that Freud discovered as the primary process and appropriate law of pleasure.

It has been said that in this discovery Freud merely followed the course already being pursued by the science of his time, indeed, that it belonged to a long-standing tradition. To appreciate the true audacity of his step, we have only to consider his recompense, which was not slow in coming: failure over the heteroclite nature of the castration complex.

It is the only indication of that *jouissance* of its infinitude that brings with it the mark of its prohibition, and, in order to constitute that mark, involves a sacrifice: that which is made in one and the same act with the choice of its symbol, the phallus.

This choice is allowed because the phallus, that is, the image of the penis, is negativity in its place in the specular image. It is what predestines the phallus to embody *jouissance* in the dialectic of desire.

We must distinguish, therefore, between the principle of sacrifice, which is symbolic, and the imaginary function that is devoted to that principle of sacrifice, but which, at the same time, masks the fact that it gives it its instrument.

The imaginary function is that which Freud formulated to govern the investment of the object as narcissistic object. It was to this point that I returned myself when I showed that the specular image is the channel taken by the transfusion of the body's libido towards the object. But even though part of it remains preserved from this immersion, concentrating within it the most intimate aspect of autoeroticism, its position at the 'tip' of the form predisposes it to the phantasy of decrepitude in which is completed its exclusion from the specular image and from the prototype that it constitutes for the world of objects.

Thus the erectile organ comes to symbolize the place of *jouissance*, not in itself, or even in the form of an image, but as a part lacking in the desired image: that is why it is equivalent to the $\sqrt{-1}$ of the signification produced above, of the *jouissance* that it restores by the coefficient of its statement to the function of lack of signifier (–1).

If its role, therefore, is to bind the prohibition of *jouissance*, it is nevertheless not for these formal reasons, but because their supersession (*outrepassement*) signifies that which reduces all desired *jouissance* to the brevity of auto-eroticism: the paths laid out by the anatomical conformation of the speaking being, that is, the already perfected hand of the monkey, have not, in effect, been ignored in a certain philosophical ascesis as paths of a wisdom that has wrongly been termed cynical. Certain individuals, obsessed no doubt by this memory, have suggested to me that Freud himself belongs to this tradition: the technique of the body, as Mauss calls it. The fact remains that analytic experience demonstrates the original character of the guilt that its practice induces.

Guilt that is bound up with the recall of *jouissance* that is lacking in the office rendered to the real organ, and consecration of the function of the imaginary signifier to strike the objects of prohibition.

This, indeed, is the radical function for which a more primitive stage in the development of psychoanalysis found more accidental (educative) causes, just as it inflected towards the trauma the other forms in which it had the merit of interesting itself, namely, those relating to the sacralization of the organ (circumcision).

The passage from the ($-\phi$) (small phi) of the phallic image from one side to the other of the equation, from the imaginary to the symbolic, renders it positive in any case, even if it fulfils a lack. Although a support of the (–1) , it becomes Φ (capital phi), the symbolic phallus that cannot be negated, the signifier of *jouissance*. And it is this character of the Φ that explains both the particularities of the woman's approach to sexuality, and that which makes the male sex the weak sex in the case of perversion.

I will not deal with the question of perversion here, in as much as it accentuates to some extent the function of desire in the man, in so far as he sets up dominance in the privileged place of *jouissance*, the object *o* of the phantasy (*objet petit* a), which he substitutes for the Ø. Perversion adds a reabsorption of the ϕ that would scarcely appear original if it did not interest the Other as such in a very particular way. Only my formulation of phantasy enables us to reveal that the subject here makes himself the instrument of the Other's *jouissance*.

It is all the more important for philosophers to grasp the relevance of this formula in the case of the neurotic, precisely because the neurotic falsifies it.

Indeed, the neurotic, whether hysteric, obsessional, or, more radically, phobic, is he who identifies the lack of the Other with his demand, Φ with D.

As a result, the demand of the Other assumes the function of an object in his phantasy, that is to say, his phantasy (my formulae make it possible to know this phantasy immediately) is reduced to the drive ($\$\lozenge D$). That is why it was possible to draw up the catalogue of drives in the case of the neurotic.

But this prevalence given by the neurotic to demand, which, for an analysis declining into facility, shifted the whole treatment towards the handling of frustration, conceals its anxiety from the desire of the Other, anxiety that is impossible not to recognize when it is covered only by the phobic object, but more difficult to understand in the case of the other two neuroses, when one is not in possession of the thread that makes it possible to present the phantasy as desire of the Other. One then finds its two terms shattered, as it were: the first, in the case of the obsessional, in as much as he denies the desire of the Other in forming his phantasy by accentuating the impossibility of the subject vanishing, the second, in the case of the hysteric, in as much as desire is maintained only through the lack of satisfaction that is introduced into it when he eludes himself as object.

These features are confirmed by the fundamental need of the obsessional neurotic to stand in the place of the Other, and by the disbelieving side of hysterical intrigue.

In fact, the image of the ideal Father is a phantasy of the neurotic. Beyond the Mother, the real Other of demand, whose desire (that is, her desire) one wishes she would assuage, there stands out the image of a father who would close his eyes to desires. The true function of the Father, which is fundamentally to unite (and not to set in opposition) a desire and the Law, is even more marked than revealed by this.

The neurotic's wished-for Father is clearly the dead Father. But he is also a Father who can perfectly master his desire—and the same can be said of the subject.

This is one of the dangers that analysis must avoid, the interminable aspect of the transference principle.

That is why a calculated vacillation of the analyst's 'neutrality' may be more valuable for a hysteric than any amount of interpretation—though there is always a danger of frightening the patient. Provided, of course, that this fright does not lead to a breaking off of the analysis, and that he becomes convinced by what follows that the analyst's desire was in no way involved. This, of course, is not a piece of technical advice, but a view that is opened up to the question of the analyst's desire for those who would not otherwise know about it: how the analyst must preserve for the other the imaginary dimension of his non-mastery, of his necessary imperfection, is as important a matter to settle as the intentional consolidation in him of his ignorance of each subject who comes to him for analysis, of an ever renewed ignorance that prevents anyone becoming a 'case'.

To return to phantasy, let us say that the pervert imagines himself to be the Other in order to ensure his *jouissance*, and that it is what the neurotic reveals when he imagines himself to be a pervert—in his case, to assure himself of the existence of the Other.

It is this that gives the meaning of the perversion that is supposed to lie in the very principle of neurosis. The perversion is in the unconscious of the neurotic as phantasy of the Other. But this does not mean that in the case of the pervert the unconscious is 'open ended'. He, too, after his fashion, defends himself in his desire. For desire is a defence (*défense*), a prohibition (*défense*) against going beyond a certain limit in *jouissance*.

In its structure as I have defined it, the phantasy contains the (–ø), the imaginary function of castration under a hidden form, reversible from one of its terms to the other. That is to say, like a complex number, it imaginarizes (if I may use such a term) alternatively one of these terms in relation to the other.

Included in the *objet a* is the *ἄγαλμα*, the inestimable treasure that Alcibiades declares is contained in the rustic box that for him Socrates's face represents. But let us observe that it bears the sign (–). It is because he has not seen Socrates's prick, if I may be permitted to follow Plato, who does not spare us the details, that Alcibiades the seducer exalts in him the *ἄγαλμα,* the marvel that he would like Socrates to cede to him in avowing his desire: the division of the subject that he bears within himself being admitted with great clarity on this occasion.

Such is the woman concealed behind her veil: it is the absence of the penis that turns her into the phallus, the object of desire. Draw attention to this absence in a more precise way by getting her to wear a pretty wig and fancy dress, and you, or rather she, will have plenty to tell us about: the effect is guaranteed 100 per cent, for men who go straight to the point.

Thus by showing his object as castrated, Alcibiades presents himself as he who desires—a fact that does not escape Socrates's attention—for someone else who is present, Agathon, whom Socrates, the precursor of psychoanalysis, and confident of his position in this fashionable gathering, does not hesitate to name as the object of the transference, placing in the light of an interpretation a fact that many analysts are still unaware of: that the love-hate effect in the analytic situation is to be found elsewhere.

But Alcibiades is certainly not a neurotic. It is even because he is *par excellence* he who desires, and he who goes as far as he can along the path of *jouissance*, that he can thus (with the help of a certain amount of drink) produce in the eyes of all the central articulation of the transference, made present by the object adorned with his reflexions.

Nevertheless, he projected Socrates into the ideal of the perfect Master, whom, through the action of (–ø), he has completely imaginarized.

In the case of the neurotic, the (–ø), slides under the $ of the phantasy, to the advantage of the imagination that is peculiar to it, that of the ego. For the neurotic has been subjected to imaginary castration from the beginning; it is castration that sustains this strong ego, so strong, one might say, that its proper name is an inconvenience for it, since the neurotic is really Nameless.

Yes, it is beneath this ego, which certain analysts choose to strengthen still more, that the neurotic hides the castration that he denies.

But, contrary to appearances, he clings to it.

What the neurotic does not want, and what he strenuously refuses to do, until the end of the analysis, is to sacrifice his castration to the *jouissance* of the Other by allowing it to serve that *jouissance*.

And, of course, he is not wrong, for although, at bottom, he feels himself to be what is most vain in existing, a Want-to-be (*un Manque-à-etre*) or a Too-much-of-it (*un En-Trop*), why should he sacrifice his difference (anything but that) to the *jouissance* of an Other, which, let us remember, does not exist. Yes, but if by some chance it did exist, he would 'enjoy' it (*il en jouirait*). And that is what the neurotic does not want. For he imagines that the Other demands his castration.

What analytic experience shows is that, in any case, it is castration that governs desire, whether in the normal or the abnormal

Providing it oscillates alternately between $ and *o* in the phantasy, castration turns phantasy into that supple, yet inextensible chain by which the arrest of the object-investment, which can hardly go beyond certain natural limits, takes on the transcendental function of ensuring the *jouissance* of the Other, which passes this chain on to me in the Law.

To whomsoever really wishes to confront this Other, there opens up the way of experiencing not only his demand, but also his will. And then: either to realize oneself as object, to turn oneself into a mummy, as in some Buddhist initiation rite, or to satisfy the will to castration inscribed in the Other, which culminates in the supreme narcissism of the Lost Cause (this is the way of Greek tragedy, which Claudel rediscovers in a Christianity of despair).

Castration means that *jouissance* must be refused, so that it can be reached on the inverted ladder (*l'échelle renversée*) of the Law of desire.

I won't go any further here.

This article is now appearing for the first time: an unexpected shortage of the funds that are usually lavished on the publication, even in their entirety, of such 'round-table' conferences having left it in abeyance, together with all the fine things that adorned this one.

I should mention, for the record, that the 'Copernican' development was added later, and that the end of the article, on castration, was never delivered owing to lack of time, and was replaced in fact by a few remarks on the machine in the modem sense of the word, from which the relation of the subject to the signifier can be materialized.

From the fellow feeling natural in any discussion, I should not like to exclude that which was aroused in me by a particular disagreement. The term 'a-human' which someone wished to attribute to what I said did not cause me the least distress, since the element of the new that the category implies gave me, on the contrary, a certain pleasure. I noted with no less interest the crackling that followed soon afterwards at the word 'hell', since the voice that pronounced it gave it, owing to the speaker's declared allegiance to Marxism, a certain piquancy. I must admit that I am partial to a certain form of humanism, a humanism that comes from an area where, although it is not used with any less cunning than elsewhere, nevertheless has a certain quality of candour about it: 'When the miner comes home, his wife rubs him down . . .' I am left defenceless against such things.

In a private conversation someone asked me (this was how he put it) whether to speak for the blackboard did not imply belief in an eternal scribe. Such a belief is not necessary, I replied, to him who knows that all discourse has its effect through the unconscious.

Notes

1. Or even from attempting to interest people, under the heading of *Psi* phenomena, in telepathy, or in the whole Gothic psychology that a Myers is capable of reviving. The most vulgar quack will be able to uncross the field in which Freud has contained him in advance, by presenting what he accepts of these phenomena as requiring translation, in the strict sense of the term, into contemporary forms of discourse.

   Even when prostituted, psychoanalytic theory remains prudish (a well-known characteristic of the brothel). As we say since Sartre, she's a respectable girl [*une respectueuse*, a reference to Sartre's play, *La putain respectueuse*—Tr.]: she won't walk in any old street (note added, 1966).
2. The original reads: 'le rapport de travers (en anglais on dirait: skew) . . .' [Tr.].
3. I have translated *énoncé* as 'statement' and *énonciation* as 'enunciation', the former referring to the actual words uttered, the second to the act of uttering them [Tr.].
4. English in the original [Tr.].

5. The English 'was' translates the French '*fut*' (*passé simple*, past historic) and *était* (*imparfait*, imperfect) [Tr.].
6. *G. W.*, VIII: 237–8; *Standard Edition*, 12: 225–6.
7. I am referring here to the friend who invited me to this conference, having, some months before, revealed to me the reservations that he derived from his personal ontology against 'psychoanalysts' who were too 'Hegelian' for his liking, as if anyone except myself in that assembly could be accused of this.

   This in the confusion of pages from his journal cast to the four winds (no doubt by accident) that had snatched them from him.

   At which I made him agree that, in order to interest this ontology of his in the, even entertaining, terms in which he clothed it in familiar notes, I found its 'certainly not, but perhaps' procedure doomed to mislead.
8. '*Le chien fait miaou, le chat fait oua-oua*'. A nursery song in which various animals are attributed with the wrong sound [Tr.].
9. I leave this paragraph only as a monument to a battle long since forgotten (note added, 1962: where was my head?).
10. The words in brackets have been added, with a view to pinpointing later developments on identification (1962).
11. This, too, refers to what I said in my seminar, 'L'Éthique de la psychanalyse' (1959–60), on the second death. Like Dylan Thomas, I don't want there to be two. But is the Absolute Master, therefore, the only one that remains?
12. That I should have said this at the time, even in more vigorous terms, in this détour, serves as a meeting-point by virtue of the fact that, three years later, on the subject of the Name-of-the-Father, I took the opportunity of abandoning the theses that I had promised in my seminar, on account of the permanence of this situation.
13. English in the original [Tr.].
14. 'là où s'était', thus making the verb 'to be' reflexive—an allusion to Lacan's gloss on Freud's '*Wo es war soll Ich werden*' [Tr.].
15. Which I have since justified by means of a topological model borrowed from surface ilieory in *analysis situs* (note added 1962).
16. In French, '*proie*' is usually 'prey', but it is also used in the phrase '*lâcher la proie pour l'ombre*' ('to drop the substance for the shadow') [Tr.].
17. More recently, in the opposite direction, in the attempt to make homologous surfaces topologically defined in the terms employed here in the subjective articulation. Cf. the simple refutation of the supposed paradox 'I am lying' (note added 1962).

CHAPTER 11

"World Spirit and Natural History: An Excursion to Hegel"

—from *Negative Dialectics* (1966)

Theodor W. Adorno

THE SUPRAMUNDANE CHARACTER OF THE HEGELIAN WORLD SPIRIT

By Hegel, however, notably by the Hegel of *Philosophy of History* and *Philosophy of Law*, the historical objectivity that happened to come about is exalted into transcendence: "This universal substance is not the mundane; the mundane impotently strives against it. No individual can get beyond this substance; he can differ from other individuals, but not from the popular spirit."[1]

The opposite of the "mundane," the identity to which the particular entity is unidentically doomed, would thus be supramundane. There is a grain of truth even to such ideology: the critic of his own popular spirit is also chained to what is commensurable to him, as long as mankind is splintered into nations. In the recent past the greatest, though mostly disparagingly garbed model of this has been the constellation between Karl Kraus and Vienna. But to Hegel, as always when he meets with something contrary, things are not that dialectical. The individual, he goes on, "may have more *esprit* than many others, but he cannot surpass the popular spirit. *Les esprits* are merely those who know about their people's spirit and know how to go by it."[2] With a malice that one cannot fail to hear in the use of the word *esprit*, the relationship is described far beneath the level of the Hegelian conception. "To go by it" would be literally nothing but to adjust. Like one confessing compulsively, Hegel deciphers his previously taught affirmative identity as a continuing break and postulates the submission of the weak to the more powerful. Euphemisms such as that in *Philosophy of History*, that in the course of world history "some individuals have been hurt,"[3] are involuntary approaches to a sense of nonreconcilement, and the trumpet call "Duty is the individual's liberation to substantial freedom"[4]—a common property of German thought, by the way—already defies distinction from its parody in the doctor scene from Büchner's *Woyzeck*.

What Hegel puts into philosophy's mouth is "that no power surpasses that of the good, of God, and keeps him from prevailing; that God is borne out; that world history represents nothing but the plan of Providence. God rules the world; the content of his rule, the execution of his plan, is world history; to comprehend this plan is the philosophy of world history; and its premise is that the ideal is accomplished, that only that which is in line with the idea has reality."[5] The world spirit seems to have worked in pretty cunning fashion when Hegel, as if to crown his edifying homily—to use Arnold Schönberg's phrase—apes Heidegger in advance: "For reason is the perceiving of the divine work."[6] The omnipotent thought has to abdicate and to make itself complaisant as mere perceiving.

To gild the heteronomy of the substantially universal, Hegel mobilizes Greek conceptions this side of experienced individuality. In such passages he vaults all historic dialectics and unhesitatingly proclaims that morality's form in Antiquity, the form which was first that of official Greek philosophy and then the one of German *Gymnasien*, is its true form: "For the morality of the state is not the moralistic, reflected one in which one's own convictions hold sway; this is more accessible to the modern world, while the true morality of Antiquity has its roots in every man's stand by his duty."[7]

The objective spirit takes revenge on Hegel. As memorial orator of Spartanism he anticipates the jargon of intrinsicality by a hundred years, with the term "stand by his duty." He stoops to offering victims decorative comfort without touching on the substantiality of the condition whose victims they are. What spooks there, behind his superior declarations, had previously been petty cash in the bourgeois till of Schiller, in whose "Song of the Bell" the *pater familias* burned out of house and home is not only sent wandering, i.e., begging, but told to do it merrily, to boot; for a nation—said to be worthless otherwise—Schiller prescribes joy in committing its all to its honor. The terror of good cheer internalizes the *contrainte sociale*.

Such exaggeration is not a poetic luxury. The idealistic social pedagogue must do something extra, since without the performance of additional and irrational identification it would be all too flagrant that the universal robs the particular of what it is being promised. Hegel associates the power of the universal with the esthetically formal concept of greatness: "These are a people's great men; they guide the people in accordance with the universal spirit. For us, the individualities disappear and are noteworthy only as those who realize the will of the popular spirit."[8] The blithely decreed disappearance of individualities—a negative which philosophy presumes to know as positive without any real change having occurred in it—is the equivalent of the continuing break. The power of the world spirit sabotages what a subsequent Hegelian passage extols in the individual: "That he is in line with his substance is due to himself."[9]

And yet the phrasing of the dismissal touches on serious matters. The world spirit is said to be "the spirit of the world as it explicates itself in human consciousness; men relate to it as individuals to the whole, which is their substance."[10] There Hegel is telling off the bourgeois conception of the individual, its vulgar nominalism. The very grimness with which a man clings to himself, as to the immediately sure and substantial, makes him an agent of the universal, and individuality a deceptive notion. On this, Hegel agreed with Schopenhauer; what he had over Schopenhauer was the insight that the abstract negation of individuality is not all there is to the dialectics of individuation and universality. The remaining objection, however—not just against Schopenhauer but against Hegel himself—is that the individual, the necessary phenomenon of the essence, the objective tendency, is right to turn against that tendency, since he confronts it with its externality and fallibility. This is implicit in Hegel's doctrine of the individual's substantiality "by way of himself." Yet instead of developing the doctrine, Hegel sticks to an abstract antithesis of universal and particular, an antithesis that ought to be unbearable to his own method.*[1]

HEGEL SIDING WITH THE UNIVERSAL

Opposed to such a separation of substantiality and individuality, as much as to a narrowly immediate consciousness, is the insight of Hegelian logic into the unity of the particular and the universal, a unity which sometimes strikes him as identity. "Particularity, however, as universality, is such an immanent relation in and for itself, not by way of transition; it is totality in itself and simple definition, essentially a principle. It has no other definition than the one posited by the universal itself and resulting from the universal, as follows. The particular is the universal itself, but it is the universal's difference from or relation to something else, what it seems to be on the outside; but there exists nothing else from which the particular might differ, nothing but the universal itself. When the universal is defined, it is the particular; definition makes the difference; it differs only from itself."[11]

Immediately, then, the particular would be the universal, because it can find no definition of its particularity except by way of the universal only; without the universal, Hegel concludes in an ever-recurring mode, the particular is nothing. The modern history of the human spirit—and not that alone—has been an apologetic labor of Sisyphus: thinking away the negative side of the universal. The Kantian spirit still remembers it, as against necessity: Kant tried to confine necessity to nature. The Hegelian critique of necessity is removed by legerdemain. "The consciousness of the spirit must form in the world; the material, the soil, of this realization is nothing but the universal consciousness, the consciousness of a people. This consciousness contains and directs all of the people's purposes and interests; it makes up the people's rights, customs, religions. It is the substantial part of a people's spirit even if the individuals do not know it, even if it stands as a settled premise. It is like a necessity; the individual is raised in this atmosphere and knows of nothing else. Yet it is not merely education and a consequence of education; rather, this consciousness is developed by the individual himself, not taught to him: the individual has his being in that substance."[12]

The Hegelian phrasing "It is like a necessity" is very adequate to the preponderance of the universal; the "like"—suggesting the merely metaphorical character of such a necessity—fleetingly touches on the semblance character of that which is the most real of things. Doubts whether necessity is good are promptly knocked down with the avowal that, rain or shine, necessity is freedom. The individual, Hegel tells us, "has his being in that substance," in the universality which to him was still coinciding with the popular spirits. But its positivity itself is negative, and the more negative its bearing, the more positive it will be; unity gets worse as its seizure of plurality becomes more thorough. It has its praise bestowed on it by the victor, and even a spiritual victor will not do without his triumphal parade, without the ostentatious pretense that what is incessantly inflicted upon the many is the meaning of the world.

"It is the particular which fights each other to exhaustion, and a part of which is ruined. But it is precisely from struggle, from the fall of the particular, that the universal results. The universal is not disturbed."[13] It has not been disturbed to this day. And yet, according to Hegel, without the particular that defines it, as a thing detached from itself, there would be no universal either. There is only one way for Hegelian logic to succinctly identify a universal and an undefined particular, to equate cognition with the fact that the two poles are mediated; and that is for logic—which Hegel also views as an a priori doctrine of general structures—not to deal with the particular as a particular at all. His logic deals only with particularity, which is already conceptual.[14] Thus established, the logical primacy of the universal provides a fundament for the social and political primacy that Hegel is opting for.

This much should be granted to Hegel: not only particularity but the particular itself is unthinkable without the moment of the universal which differentiates the particular, puts its imprint on it, and in a sense is needed to make a particular of it. But the fact that dialectically one moment needs the other, the moment contradictorily opposed to it—this fact, as Hegel knew well but liked to forget on occasion, reduces neither moment to μὴ ὄν. Stipulated otherwise would be the absolute, ontological validity of the logic of pure noncontradictoriness, which the dialectical demonstration of "moments" had broken through; ultimately stipulated would be the position of an absolute First—the concept—with the fact said to be secondary because according to idealistic tradition it "follows" from the concept. Of a particular, nothing can be predicated without definition and thus without universality, and yet this does not submerge the moment of something particular, something opaque, which that prediction refers to and is based upon. It is maintained within the constellation, else dialectics would end up hypostatizing mediation without preserving the moments of immediacy, as Hegel prudently wished to do everywhere else.

RELAPSE INTO PLATONISM

The immanent critique of dialectics explodes Hegelian idealism. Cognition aims at the particular, not at the universal. It seeks its true object in the possible determination of the difference of that particular—even from the universal, which it criticizes as nonetheless inalienable. But if the mediation of the universal by the particular and of the particular by the universal is reduced to the abstract normal form of mediation as such, the particular has to pay the price, down to its authoritarian dismissal in the material parts of the Hegelian system. "What man must do, what are the duties he has to fulfill to be virtuous, is easily told in a moral community—he has to do nothing other than is prescribed, expressed, and known to him in his circumstances. Probity is the universal that can be demanded of him, partly legally, partly morally. From the moral standpoint, however, it tends to appear as something subordinate, beyond which one ought to ask more of himself and of others; for the urge to be something particular is not contented by that which is in and for itself and universal. It is only in an exception that this urge will find the sense of intrinsicality."[15]

If Hegel had carried the doctrine of the identity of universal and particular farther, to a dialectic in the particular itself, the particular—which according to him is simply the mediated universal—would have been granted the same right as the universal. That he depreciates this right into a mere urge and psychologistically blackens the right of man as narcissism—like a father chiding his son, "Maybe you think you're something special"—this is not an individual lapse on the philosopher's part. Idealistically, there is no carrying out the dialectic of the particular which he envisions. Contrary to the Kantian *chorismos*, philosophy is not supposed to make itself at home in the universal as a doctrine of forms; it is to penetrate the content itself, rather, and this is why, in a grandiosely fatal *petitio principii*, reality is so arranged by philosophy that it will yield to the repressive identification with philosophy.

What is most true in Hegelian thinking, the sense of the particular without whose weight the concept of reality decays into a farce, leads to that which is most false. It removes the particular for which Hegel's philosophy is groping. The more insistently his concept strives for reality, the more benightedly is reality—the *hic et nunc* that should be cracked open as gilded nuts are cracked by children on a holiday—contaminated by him with the concept that covers it. "It is this very attitude of philosophy toward reality which the misconceptions affect, and so I come back to what I said before: that philosophy, because it means to fathom what is rational, means precisely therefore to grasp what is present and real, not to erect a Beyond said to be God knows where—or of which one can in fact say very well where it is, namely, in the error of empty, onesided rationalizing . . . When reflection, feeling, or whatever form the subjective consciousness may take, regards the present as vain, when it goes beyond the present and knows better, it is likewise vain and, being real only in the present, it is nothing but vanity. Conversely, if the idea is taken to be no more than just an idea, a conception held as an opinion, philosophy affords the insight that nothing but the idea is a reality. What matters, then, is that in the semblance of the temporal and transitory we may know the substance which is immanent, and the eternal which is present."[16*[2]]

So Platonic, of necessity, is the dialectician's language. He will not admit that, from the viewpoint of logic as well as of the philosophy of history, the universal contracts into the particular until the latter breaks loose from the abstract universality that has grown extraneous to it—while the universal he vindicates, as a higher objectivity, correlatively declines to a bad subjectivity, to the mean value of particularities. He who was set upon a transition of logic to time is now resigned to timeless logic.

DETEMPORALIZATION OF TIME

The simple dichotomy of temporality and eternity amidst and despite the Hegelian conception of dialectics conforms to the primacy of the universal in *Philosophy of History*. Just as the general concept, the fruit of abstraction, is deemed above time—and just as the loss which the subsumed suffers by the process of abstraction is entered in the profit column, as a draft on eternity—so are history's allegedly supratemporal moments turned into positiva. Hidden in them is the old evil, however. To agree to the perpetuation of the status quo is to discredit the protesting thought as ephemeral. Such an aboutface into timelessness is not extraneous to Hegel's dialectics and philosophy of history. As his version of dialectics extends to time itself, time is ontologized, turned from a subjective form into a structure of being as such, itself eternal.

Based on this are Hegel's speculations which equate the absolute idea of totality with the passing of everything finite. His attempt to deduce time, as it were, and to eternalize it as permitting nothing outside it is as much in line with this conception as with absolute idealism, which can no more resign itself to the separation of time and logic than Kant could to the separation of visuality and intellect. There again, by the way, Hegel, Kant's critic, was Kant's executor. When Kant turns time, as the pure visual form and premise of everything temporal, into an a priori, time on its part is exempted from time.*[3] Subjective and objective idealism concur in this, for the basic stratum of both is the subject as a concept, devoid of its temporal content. Once again, as to Aristotle, the *actus purus* becomes that which does not move. The social partisanship of the idealists goes all the way down to the constituents of their systems. They glorify time as timeless, history as eternal—all for fear that history might begin.

For Hegel, the dialectic of time and temporality logically turns into a dialectic of time in itself.*[4] It offers the positivists their favored point of attack. In fact, it would be bad scholasticism if dialectics were attributed to the formal concept of time, with every temporal content expurgated. In critical reflection, however, time is dialecticized as the internally mediated unity of form and content. Kant's transcendental esthetics would have no answer to the objection that the purely formal character of time as a "form of visuality," its "emptiness," has itself no corresponding visuality whatever. Kantian time defies every possible conception and imagination: to conceive it, we always have to conceive something temporal along with it, something to read it off on, something that permits its passage or its so-called flow to be experienced. The fact is that the conception of pure time does require that very conceptual mediation—the abstraction from all conceptions of time that can be carried out—from which Kant, for the sake of systematics, the disjunction of sensibility and intellect, wished and needed to relieve the forms of visuality.

Absolute time as such, bereft of the last factual substrate that is and passes in it, would no longer be what time, according to Kant, must inalienably be: it would no longer be dynamic. There is no dynamics without that in which it occurs. Conversely, however, a factuality without its place in the time continuum is not conceivable either. Dialectics carries this reciprocity into the most formal realm: of the moments essential to that realm, and opposed to each other, not one is without the other. Yet the reciprocity is not motivated by the pure form in itself that served to reveal it. A relationship of form and content has become the form itself. It is inalienably the form of a content—an extreme sublimation of the form-content dualism in detached and absolutized supjectivity.

An element of truth might even be squeezed out of Hegel's theory of time, provided one will not let logic produce time by itself, as he does; to be perceived in logic, instead, are coagulated time relations, as indicated variously, if cryptically, in *Critique of Pure Reason*, in the chapter on schematism in particular. Preserved likewise in the discursive *Logic*—unmistakeably in its conclusions—are time elements that were detemporalized as subjective thinking objectified them into pure legality; without such detemporalization, on the other hand, time would not have been objectified at all. As cognition of an element, it would be compatible with Hegel to interpret the link between logic and time by going back to something which current positivistic science considers pre-logical in logic. For what Hegel calls synthesis is not simply the downright new quality leaping forth from definite negation; it is the return of what has been negated. Dialectical progress is always a recourse as well, to that which fell victim to the progressing concept; the concept's progressive concretion is its self-correction. The transition of logic to time would like, as far as consciousness is able, to make up to time for the wrongs done to it by logic—by the logic without which, on the other hand, time would not be.

Under this aspect, the Bergsonian duplication of the concept of time is a bit of dialectics unaware of itself. In the concept of *le temps durée*, of lived duration, Bergson tried theoretically to reconstruct the living experience of time, and thus its substantial element that had been sacrificed to the abstractions of philosophy and of causal-mechanical natural science. Even so, he did not convert to the dialectical concept any more than science did. More positivistically than he knew in his polemicizing, he absolutized the dynamic element out of disgust with the rising reification of consciousness; he on his part made of it a form of consciousness, so to speak, a particular and privileged mode of cognition. He reified it, if you will, into a line of business. In isolation, the time of subjective experience along with its content comes to be as accidental and mediated as its subject, and therefore, compared with chronometric time, is always "false" also. Sufficient to elucidate this is the triviality that, measured by clock time, subjective time experiences invite delusion, although there would be no clock time without the subjective time experience which the clock time objectifies.

But the crass dichotomy of Bergson's two times does register the historic dichotomy between living experience and the objectified and repetitive labor process; his brittle doctrine of time is an early precipitation of the objective social crisis in the sense of time. The irreconcilability of *temps durée* and *temps espace* is the wound of that split consciousness whose only unity lies in being split. The naturalistic interpretation of *temps espace* can no more master this than the hypostasis of *temps durée*, in which the subject, flinching from reification, hopes in vain to preserve itself simply by being alive. The fact is that laughter—according to Bergson, the restoration of life from its conventional hardening—has long become the conventions' weapon against uncomprehended life, against the traces of something natural that has not been quite domesticated.

DIALECTICS CUT SHORT BY HEGEL

Hegel's transposition of the particular into particularity follows the practice of a society that tolerates the particular only as a category, a form of the supremacy of the universal. Marx designated this state of facts in a manner which Hegel could not foresee: "The dissolution of all products and activities into exchange values presupposes the dissolution of all fixed personal (historical) dependencies in production as well as the producers' universal dependence on each other. Every individual's production depends as much on the production of all others as the transformation of his product into food for himself has come to depend on the consumption of all others . . . This mutual interdependence is expressed in the constant necessity of exchange, and in the exchange value as universal mediator. The economists put it this way: Everyone pursues his private interest and thus unwillingly and unwittingly serves the private interests of all, the general interests. The joke is not that everyone's pursuit of his private interest will in effect serve the entirety of private interests, that is, the general interest; from this abstract phrase it might as well be inferred that everyone mutually inhibits the pursuit of the others' interest, and that, instead of general affirmation, the result of this *bellum omnium contra omnes* will be general negation. The point is, rather, that the private interest itself is already a socially determined interest, one that can be pursued only on the terms laid down by society and by the means provided by society—hence an interest tied to the reproduction of those terms and means. It is the interest of private persons; but its content as well as the form and means of realization are given by social conditions independent of them all."[17]

Such negative supremacy of the concept makes clear why Hegel, its apologist, and Marx, its critic, concur in the notion that what Hegel calls the world spirit has a preponderance of being-in-itself—that it does not (as would be solely fitting for Hegel) have merely its objective substance in the individuals: "The individuals are subsumed under social production, which exists as a doom outside them; but social production is not subsumed under the individuals who exercise it as their common capacity."[18] The real *chorismos* obliges Hegel, much against his will, to remodel his thesis of the reality of the idea. The theory does not admit this, but there are unmistakable lines about it in *Philosophy of Law*: "For the idea of the state one must not look to particular states or particular institutions; rather, the idea, this real God, must be contemplated by itself. Every state, although a man may call it bad according to the principles he holds, although he may find one or the other flaw in it, always contains the essential moments of its existence, especially if it is one of the developed states of our time. But because finding faults is easier than grasping the affirmative, one will easily fall into the error of letting specific sides make him forget the inner organism of the state itself."[19]

The tenor of the whole work is to dispute away the contradiction between idea and reality; but if the idea "must be contemplated by itself," not in "particular states," and that in principle, with an encompassing structure in mind, this resurrects the contradiction. In keeping with it is the ominous line that finding faults is easier than grasping the affirmative; today this has become the clamor for "constructive criticism," in other words, groveling criticism. Because the identity of idea and reality is denied by reality, ascertaining that identity nonetheless calls, so to speak, for an obsequious special effort on the part of reason; the "affirmative," the proof of positively accomplished reconciliation, is postulated, praised as a superior achievement of consciousness, because Hegel's pure eye witness does not suffice for such affirmation. The pressure which affirmation exerts on a balky reality acts tirelessly to strengthen the real pressure put upon the subject by the universal, its negation. The chasm between the two yawns the more visibly, the more concretely the subject is confronted with the thesis of the objective substantiality of morals.

In Hegel's late conception of education, this is described only as something hostile to the subject: "Absolutely defined, education is thus deliverance and the work on a higher deliverance, namely, the absolute point of transition to the infinitely subjective substantiality of morals, which is no longer immediate and natural but spiritual and likewise raised to the form of universality. —In the subject, this deliverance is the toil of striving against mere subjectivity of conduct, against immediate desire, as well as against the subjective vanity of sensation and the arbitrariness of liking. That it is this toil accounts for part of the disfavor it encounters. But it is by this educational toil that subjective volition gains in itself the objectivity which alone makes it worthy and capable of being the reality of the idea."[20]

Embroidering this is *ὁ μὴ δαρείς*, the Greek school maxim which Goethe—whom it fitted least of all—did not disdain to choose as a Hegelian-minded motto for his autobiography. Yet in trumpeting the truth about the identity it would like first to bring about, the classicist maxim admits its own untruth: literally that of birch rod pedagogy, and metaphorically, that of the unspeakable commandment to submit. Being immanently untrue, the maxim is unfit for the purpose entrusted to it; psychology, belittled by the great philosophy, knows more about that than philosophy knows. Brutality is reproduced by men against whom it is practiced; the abused are not educated but repressed, rebarbarized. An insight of psychoanalysis—that civilization's repressive mechanisms transform the libido into aggression against civilization—cannot be extinguished any more. The man who has been educated by force will channel his aggressions by identifying with force, to pass it on and get rid of it; it is thus that subject and object are really identified according to the educational ideal of Hegel's philosophy of law. If a culture is no culture, it does not even want the people who are caught in its mill to be cultured.

In one of the most famous passages of *Philosophy of Law*, Hegel cites a line attributed to Pythagoras, to the effect that the best way morally to educate a son is to make him a citizen of a state with good laws.[21] This calls for a judgment whether the state itself and its laws are actually good. But to Hegel, order is good a priori; it does not have to answer to those living under it. Ironically, this confirms his subsequent Aristotelian reminiscence that "substantial unity is an absolute and motionless end in itself."[22] Motionless, the end stands in the dialectic that is supposed to produce it. It is thus devalued to an empty avowal that "freedom comes to its supreme right"[23] in the state; Hegel lapses into that insipid edification which he still despised in *Phenomenology*. He reiterates a cogitative cliché of Antiquity, from the stage at which philosophy's victorious Platonic-Aristotelian mainstream proclaimed its solidarity with the institutions, against their bases in the social process; all in all, mankind discovered society much later than the state, which is mediated as such but seems given and immediate to the governed.

Hegel's line "Whatever man is he owes to the state,"[24] that most obvious hyperbole, carries on the antiquated confusion. What induced the thesis is that the "motionlessness" he attributes to the general purpose might indeed be predicated of the institution, once it has hardened, but could not possibly be predicated of society, which is dynamic in essence. The dialectician confirms the state's prerogative to be above dialectics because—a matter he did not delude himself about—dialectics will drive men beyond bourgeois society. He does not put his trust in dialectics, does not look upon it as the force to cure itself, and disavows his own assurance that identity will produce itself in dialectics.

Notes

In this translation, as in the German original, Kant's Works are cited from the German Akademie-Ausgabe (Preussische Akademie der Wissenschaften, Berlin 1900ff.); Hegel's Works, from Jubiläumsausgabe (Glockner, Stuttgart 1927ff.) except for *Reason in History* (from *Die Vernunft in der Geschichte*, 5th ed., Meiner, Hamburg 1955); the writings of Karl Marx and Friedrich Engels, from the new editions published since World War II (Marx, *Grundrisse der politischen Ökonomie*, Berlin 1953).

Footnotes (in original English translation):

*[1] Among the positivists it was in Emile Durkheim's doctrine of collective spirit that Hegel's choice in favor of the universal was maintained and

topped, if possible; in Durkheim's schema there is no more room for a dialectic of universal and particular even in the abstract. In the sociology of primitive religions, Durkheim made the substantial discovery that qualities, the things the particular is boasting of, have been imposed upon it by the universal. He designated to the universal both the delusion of the particular, as a mere mimesis, and the power that makes a particular of it in the first place: "Le deuil (qui s'exprime au cours de certaines cérémonies) n'est pas un mouvement naturel de la sensibilité privée, froissée par une perte cruelle; c'est un devoir imposé par le groupe. On se lamente, non pas simplement parce qu'on est triste, mais parce qu'on est tenu de se lamenter. C'est une attitude rituelle qu'on est obligé d'adopter par respect pour l'usage, mais qui est, dans une large mesure, indépendante de l'état effectif des individus. Cette obligation est, d'ailleurs, sanctionnée par des peines ou mythiques ou sociales." (Emile Durkheim, *Les formes élémentaires de la vie religieuse: Le système totémique en Australie*. Paris, 1912, *Travaux de l'Année sociologique*, p. 568.)

*[2] The cliché "only an idea" had already been criticized by Kant. "The Platonic republic has become proverbial as a supposedly striking instance of imagined perfection, which can be located only in an idle thinker's brain . . . One would do better, however, to pursue this thought some more, and (where the excellent man leaves us without assistance) to illuminate it by new efforts instead of putting it aside as useless, on the very wretched and harmful pretext that it is unfeasible." (Kant, *Kritik der reinen vernunft*, Works III, p. 247.)

*[3] "Time does not pass, but the existence of changeable things passes in it. Since time itself is immutable and enduring, what corresponds to it in phenomenality is the immutable in existence, i.e., substance, and it is by this alone that we can determine the sequence and simultaneity of the phenomena in time." (Kant, ibid., p. 137.)

*[4] "More closely, then, the real I itself belongs to time, with which—if we abstract from the concrete content of consciousness and self-consciousness—it coincides, being nothing but this empty motion of positing myself as something other and voiding this change, i.e., preserving therein myself, the I, and only the I as such. I is in time, and time is the being of the subject." (Hegel, Works 14, p. 151.)

Endnotes (in original English translation):

1. Hegel, *Die Vernunft in der Geschichte*, 5th ed., Hamburg 1955, p. 60.
2. Ibid.
3. Ibid., p. 48.

4. Hegel, Works 7, p. 230.
5. Hegel, *Die Vernunft in der Geschichte*, p. 77.
6. Ibid., p. 78.
7. Ibid., p. 115.
8. Ibid., p. 60.
9. Ibid., p. 95.
10. Ibid., p. 60.
11. Hegel, Works 5, p. 43f.
12. Hegel, *Die Vernunft in der Geschichte*, p. 59f.
13. Ibid., p. 105.
14. Cf. esp. Part One, Being and Existence.
15. Hegel, Works 7, p. 231.
16. Ibid., p. 32ff.
17. Marx, *Grundrisse der Kritik der politischen Ökonomie*, Berlin 1953, p. 73f.
18. Ibid., p. 76.
19. Hegel, Works 7, p. 336.
20. Ibid., p. 268f.
21. Ibid., p. 235.
22. Ibid., p. 329.
23. Ibid.
24. Hegel, *Die Vernunft in der Geschichte*, p. 111.

CHAPTER 12

"Conclusion"

—from *Difference and Repetition* (1968)

Gilles Deleuze

Difference is not and cannot be thought in itself, so long as it is subject to the requirements of representation. The question whether is was 'always' subject to these requirements, and for what reasons, must be closely examined. But it appears that pure *disparates* formed either the celestial beyond of a divine understanding inaccessible to our representative thought, or the infernal and unfathomable for us below of an Ocean of dissemblance. In any case, difference in itself appears to exclude any relation between different and different which would allow it to be thought. It seems that it can become thinkable only when tamed—in other words, when subject to the four iron collars of representation: identity in the concept, opposition in the predicate, analogy in judgement and resemblance in perception. As Foucault has shown, the classical world of representation is defined by these four dimensions which co-ordinate and measure it. These are the four roots of the principle of reason: the identity of the concept which is reflected in a *ratio cognoscendi*; the opposition of the predicate which is developed in a *ratio fiendi*; the analogy of judgement which is distributed in a *ratio essendi*; and the resemblance of perception which determines a *ratio agendi*. Every other difference, every difference which is not rooted in this way, is an unbounded, uncoordinated and inorganic difference: too large or too small, not only to be thought but to exist. Ceasing to be thought, difference is dissipated in non-being. From this, it is concluded that difference in itself remains condemned and must atone or be redeemed under the auspices of a reason which renders it livable and thinkable, and makes it the object of an organic representation.

The greatest effort of philosophy was perhaps directed at rendering representation infinite (orgiastic). It is a question of extending representation as far as the too large and the too small of difference; of adding a hitherto unsuspected perspective of representation—in other words, inventing theological, scientific and aesthetic techniques which allow it to integrate the depth of difference in itself; of allowing representation to conquer the obscure; of allowing it to include the vanishing of difference which is too small and the dismemberment of difference which is too large; of allowing it to capture the power of giddiness, intoxication and cruelty, and even of death. In short, it is a question of causing a little of Dionysus's blood to flow in the organic veins of Apollo. This effort has always permeated the world of representation. The ultimate wish of the organic is to become orgiastic and to conquer the in-itself, but this effort found two culminating moments in Leibniz and Hegel. With the former, representation conquers the infinite because a technique for dealing with the infinitely small captures the smallest difference and its disappearance. With the latter, representation conquers the infinite because a technique for dealing with the infinitely large captures the largest difference and its dismembering. The two are in agreement, since the Hegelian problem is *also* that of disappearance, while the Leibnizian problem is also that of dismembering. Hegel's technique lies in the movement of contradiction (difference must attain that point, it must be extended that far). It consists of inscribing the inessential in the essence, and in conquering the infinite with the weapons of a synthetic finite identity. Leibniz's technique lies in the movement we call vice-diction: it consists in constructing the essence from the inessential, and conquering the finite by means of an infinite analytic identity (difference must be developed to that point). But what is the point of making representation infinite? It retains all its requirements. All that is discovered is a *ground* which relates the excess and default of difference to the identical, the similar, the analogous and the opposed: reason,—that is, sufficient reason—has become the ground which no longer allows anything to escape. Nothing, however, has changed: difference remains subject to malediction, and all that has happened is the discovery of more subtle and more sublime means to make it atone, or to redeem it and subject it to the categories of representation.

Thus, Hegelian contradiction appears to push difference to the limit, but this path is a dead end which brings it back to identity, making identity the sufficient condition for difference to exist and be thought. It is only in relation to the identical, as a function of the identical, that contradiction is the *greatest* difference. The intoxications and giddiness are feigned, the obscure is already clarified from the outset. Nothing shows this more clearly than the insipid monocentricity of the circles in the Hegelian dialectic. Moreover, in another manner perhaps the same should be said of the condition of convergence in the Leibnizian world. Take a notion such as that of Leibnizian incompossibility. Everyone recognizes that incompossibility is not reducible to contradiction, and compossibility is not reducible to the identical. It is indeed in this sense that the compossible and the incompossible testify to specific sufficient reason and to a presence of the infinite—not only in the totality of possible worlds, but in each chosen world. It more difficult to say in what these new notions consist. It seems to us that compossibility consists uniquely in the following: the condition of a maximum continuity for a maximum of difference—in other words, a condition of convergence of established series around the singularities of the continuum. Conversely, the incompossibility of worlds is decided in the vicinity of those singularities which give rise to divergent series between themselves. In short, representation may well become infinite; *it nevertheless does not acquire the power to affirm divergence or decentering*. It requires a convergent and monocentric world: a world in which one is only apparently intoxicated, in which reason acts the drunkard and sings a Dionysian tune while none the less remaining 'pure' reason. The ground or sufficient reason is nothing but a means of allowing the identical to rule over infinity itself, and allowing the continuity of resemblance, the relation of analogy and the opposition of predicates to invade infinity. This is the originality of sufficient reason: better to ensure the subjection of difference to the quadripartite yoke. The damage is done not only by the requirement of finite representation, which consists of fixing a propitious moment for difference, neither too large nor too small, in between excess and default; but also by the apparently contrary requirement of infinite representation, which purports to integrate the infinitely large and the infinitely small of difference, excess and default themselves. *The entire alternative between finite and infinite applies very badly to difference*, because it constitutes only an antinomy of representation. We saw this, moreover, in the case of calculus: modern finitist interpretations betray the nature of the differential no less than the former infinitist interpretations, because both fail to capture the extra-propositional or sub-representational source—in other words, the 'problem' from which the calculus draws its power. In addition, the alternative of the Small and the Large, whether in finite representation which excludes both, or in infinite representation which wants to include both, and each within the other, does not, in general, fit difference. The reason is that this alternative expresses only the oscillations of representation with regard to an always dominant identity, or rather the oscillations of the Identical with regard to an always rebellious matter, the excess and default of which it sometimes rejects and sometimes tries to integrate. Finally, returning to Leibniz and Hegel and their common attempt to extend representation to infinity: we are not sure that Leibniz does not go 'farthest' (nor that, of the two, he is not the least teleological). His conception of the Idea as an ensemble of differential relations and singular points, the manner in which he begins with the inessential and constructs essences in the form of centers of envelopment around singularities, his presentiment of divergences, his procedure of vice-diction, his approximation to an inverse ratio between the distinct and the clear, all show why the ground rumbles with greater power in the case of Leibniz, why the intoxication and giddiness are less feigned in his case, why obscurity is better understood and the Dionysian shores are closer.

CHAPTER 13

"Marx's Relation to Hegel"

—from *Hegel et la Pensée Moderne*
(1970; lecture delivered: 1968)

Louis Althusser

I should like to thank Monsieur Jean Hyppolite for the great honour he has done me in inviting me to his Seminar. I am greatly indebted to M. Hyppolite. Among many other achievements, he will go down in the history of French philosophy as the man who has had the courage to translate Hegel and sponsor the publication of Husserl. He has pulled French philosophy away from the reactionary tradition which has dominated, I say *dominated* (for fortunately there have been other elements beneath this domination), its whole history since the French Revolution, a reactionary tradition reinforced by the academic reigns of Lachelier, Bergson and Brunschvicg. In this tradition French chauvinism took the form of the simplest kind of stupidity: ignorance. M. Hyppolite has had the courage to fight against this ignorance. We owe to him our knowledge of Hegel, and through Hegel, the beginnings of an understanding of, among other things, the distance separating Marx from Hegel. Let us not speak of the fate French philosophy has reserved for Marx. Brunschvicg, who thought Hegel mentally retarded, regarded Marx and Lenin as philosophical nonentities. M. Hyppolite has also had the courage to speak of Marx, and of Freud, those great *damnés de la terre* for academic bourgeois philosophy.

Everyone more or less knows this now. But it is worth saying.

Let me add that I have a debt to M. Hyppolite that he will not suspect. If I have been able to glimpse the revolutionary theoretical scope of Marx's work in philosophy, it is thanks to a very dear friend, Jacques Martin, who died five years ago. Now Jacques Martin was privileged, under the Occupation in Paris, to hear M. Hyppolite, then a *professeur de khâgne* (teacher in Letters in the preparatory class for the École Normale Supérieure), comment on certain passages from the *Phenomenology of Mind*. From what I know of it, these were not, believe me, in that very special period, ordinary commentaries. What M. Hyppolite said then helped several of his students to orientate themselves 'in thought', as Kant put it, i.e. also in politics. M. Hyppolite has certainly forgotten the words he then uttered: but not everyone has forgotten them. I am here to bear witness. Against what common sense, the common sense of financiers and lawyers, tells us, there are many writings that blow away, but a few words that remain. No doubt because they have been inscribed in life and history.

I should like to put forward a few schematic themes about Marx's relation to Hegel.

I renounce rhetoric and maieutics, whether Socratic or phenomenological. In philosophy, the true beginning is the end. I shall begin at the end. I shall lay my cards on the table so everyone can see them. These cards are what they are: they carry the stamp of *Marxism-Leninism*. Exposed in this way, they will naturally have the form of a conclusion without premisses.

Let me start with a fact. The Marx-Hegel relationship is a currently decisive theoretical and political question. A *theoretical* question: it governs the future of the number-one strategic science of Modern Times: the science of history, and the future of the philosophy linked to that science: dialectical materialism. A *political* question: it derives from these premisses. It is inscribed in the class struggle at a certain level, in the past as in the present.

To understand the contemporary importance of this fact of the Marx-Hegel relationship, it must be understood as a symptom, and explained as the symptom of the following realities. In order to situate the symptom, I shall state these realities in the form of *Theses*.

Thesis 1 (a statement of fact). *The union, or fusion of the Workers' Movement and Marxist theory* is the greatest event in the history of class societies, i.e. practically in all human history. Beside it, the celebrated great scientific-technical 'mutation' constantly resounding in our ears (the atomic, electronic, computer era, the space-age, etc.) is, despite its great importance, no more than a scientific and technical fact: these events are not of the same order of magnitude, they only bear in their effects on certain aspects of the productive forces, and not on what is decisive, the *relations of production*.

We are living in the necessary effects of this fusion, of this union. Its first results: the socialist revolutions (USSR, China, etc., revolutionary movements in Asia, Vietnam, Latin America, Communist Parties, etc.).

(a) This union realizes the 'union of theory and practice'.

(b) This union is not an established fact but an endless struggle, with its victories and defeats. A struggle in the union itself. With the 1914 War: the crisis of the Second International. At present: the crisis in the International Communist Movement.

The union brings together: the Workers' Movement and Marxist theory . Here I shall only discuss Marxist theory. What is Marxist theory?

Thesis 2 (a statement of fact). Marxist theory includes a science and a philosophy.

In the great classical tradition of the Workers' Movement, from Marx to Lenin, Stalin and Mao, Marxist theory has been defined as containing two distinct theoretical disciplines: a *science* (designated by its general theory: historical materialism) and a philosophy (designated by the term dialectical materialism). There are very special relations between these two disciplines. I shall not examine them in this paper. I shall suggest the following: of these two disciplines, science and philosophy, it is the science that has the place of determination (in the sense defined in *Reading Capital* and closely specified by Badiou in *Critique*, May 1967).[1] *Everything depends on this science.*

Thesis 3. Marx founded a new science: the *science of the history* of social formations, or the science of history.

The foundation of the science of history by Marx is the most important theoretical event of contemporary history .

Let me use an image.

There are a certain number of sciences. They can be said to occupy a certain site in what can be called a theoretical space. Site, space. Metaphorical notions. But they convey certain facts: the proximity of certain sciences; relations between neighbouring sciences; domination of certain sciences over other sciences; but simultaneously sciences without neighbours, insular sciences (isolated positions in a void: e.g. psychoanalysis, etc.).

From this standpoint it is possible to consider that the history of the sciences reveals the existence, in this problematical theoretical space, of *great scientific continents*.

1. The continent of Mathematics (opened up by the Greeks).
2. The continent of Physics (opened up by Galileo).
3. Marx has opened up the third great continent: the continent of History.

A continent, in the sense of this metaphor, is never empty: it is always already 'occupied' by many and varied more or less ideological disciplines which do not know that they belong to that 'continent'. For example, before Marx, the History continent was occupied by the philosophies of history, by political economy, etc. The opening-up of a continent by a continental science not only disputes the rights and claims of the former occupants, it also completely restructures the old configuration of the 'continent'. A metaphor cannot be spun out indefinitely—otherwise I should here say that the opening-up of a new continent to scientific knowledge presupposes a *change of terrain* or an *epistemological* 'rupture', etc. I leave you the trouble of the temporary needlework required to bring all these metaphors into agreement. But one day we shall have to drop all this sewing and patching for something quite different: to make a theory of the history of the production of knowledges.

Thesis 4. Every great scientific discovery induces a great transformation in philosophy. The scientific discoveries which open up the great scientific continents constitute the major dates in the *periodization* of the history of philosophy:

1st continent (Mathematics): birth of philosophy. Plato.

2nd continent (Physics): profound transformation of philosophy. Descartes.

3rd great continent (History, Marx): revolution in philosophy, announced in the 11th Thesis on Feuerbach. End of classical philosophy, no longer an interpretation of the world, but a '*transformation*' of the world.

'Transformation of the world': an enigmatic word, prophetic but enigmatic. How can philosophy be a transformation of the world? of which world?

Whatever the case, it is possible to say, with Hegel: philosophy always arrives *post festum*. It is always *late*. It is always *postponed* (*différée*).

This thesis is very important to me: in a certain respect (its theoretical elaboration), Marxist philosophy or dialectical materialism *cannot but be behind the science of history*. Time is needed for a philosophy to form and then develop after the great scientific discovery which has silently induced its birth.

All the more so in that, in Marx's case, the scientificity of his discovery has been fiercely denied, fought and condemned by all the self-styled specialists of that continent. The so-called Human Sciences still occupy the old continent. They are now armed with the latest ultra-modern techniques of mathematics, etc., but they are still based theoretically on the same outworn ideological notions as they were in the past, ingeniously rethought and retouched. With a few remarkable exceptions, the prodigious development of the so-called human sciences, above all the development of the social sciences, is no more than the *aggiornamento* of old techniques of social adaptation and social readaptation: of *ideological* techniques. This is the great scandal of the whole of contemporary intellectual history: everyone talks about Marx, almost everyone in the human or social sciences says he is more or less a Marxist. But who has taken the trouble to read Marx closely, to understand his novelty and take the theoretical consequences? Without exception, the specialists of the human sciences one hundred years after Marx work with outdated ideological notions like Aristotelean physicists carrying on with Aristotelean physics fifty years after Galileo. Where are the philosophers who do not take Engels and Lenin for philosophical nonentities? I believe they can be counted on the fingers of one hand. Not all Communist philosophers even, far from it, think well of Engels and Lenin as 'philosophers'. Where are the philosophers who have studied the history of the workers' movement, the history of the 1917 Revolution and the Chinese Revolution? Marx and Lenin have the great honour to share the fate of intellectual pariah with Freud and to be travestied when they are discussed as he is travestied. This scandal is not a scandal: the relations that reign between philosophical ideas are what are called relations of forces, ideological, and therefore political relations of forces. But it is bourgeois philosophical ideas that are in power. The question of power is the number-one question in philosophy, too. Philosophy is indeed in the last instance *political*.

Thesis 5. How is Marx's scientific discovery to be *explained*?

If we take seriously what Marx tells us about the real dialectic of history, it is not 'men' who make history, although its dialectic is realized in them and in their practice, but the masses in the relations of the class struggle. This is true for political history, general history. For the history of the sciences, making due allowances, the same is true. It is not individuals who make the history of the sciences, although its dialectic is realized in them, and in their practice. The empirical individuals known for making such and such a discovery realize in their practice *relations* and a *conjunction* wider than themselves.

This is where we can pose the problem of the relations between Marx and Hegel.

I shall give an extraordinarily schematic figuration. I hope it will be taken only for what it is: the index of a problem, and the indication of the schematic conditions for it to be *posed*.

To pose it thus in outline, I shall start once again from an indication of Engels's, taken up and developed by Lenin and known by the name of the Three Sources of Marxism. *Sources* is an outdated ideological notion, but what matters to us is the fact that Engels and Lenin do not pose the problem in terms of an individual history, but in terms of a *history of theories*. They establish a pattern involving three theoretical 'characters': Classical German Philosophy, English Political Economy and French Socialism. Say: Hegel, Ricardo, and Babeuf-Fourier, Saint-Simon, etc. To simplify and for expositional clarity, I shall partially set aside French Socialism and consider only Ricardo and Hegel, as symbolic representatives of English political economy and German philosophy respectively.

I shall then return to the *extremely* general diagram of 'theoretical practice' which I proposed five years ago in an article on the *Materialist Dialectic*.

Diagram I

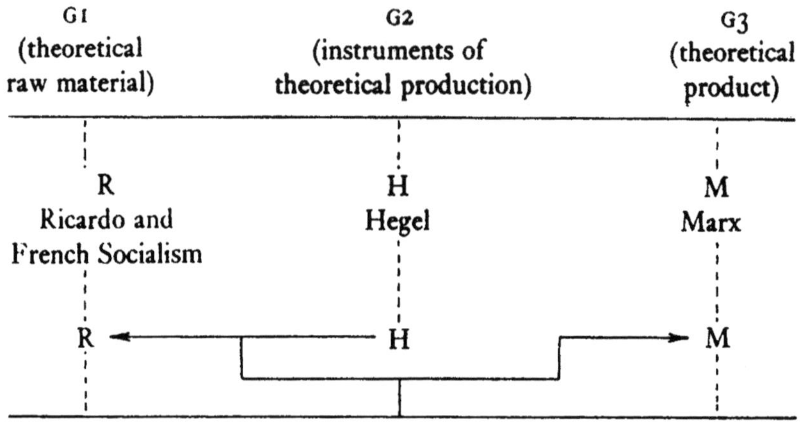

Which means very schematically that Marx (*Capital*) is the product of the work of Hegel (German Philosophy) on English Political Economy + French Socialism, in other words, the *Hegelian dialectic* on: *Labour theory of value* (R) + *the class struggle* (FS).

R + FS = raw material, object of Marx's theoretical practice

H = instruments of theoretical production,

the product of the work of the Hegelian dialectic on Ricardo is then *Capital* = M.

[What we tried to do in *Reading Capital* can be represented, in thoroughly indicative fashion, by the following diagram:

Diagram II

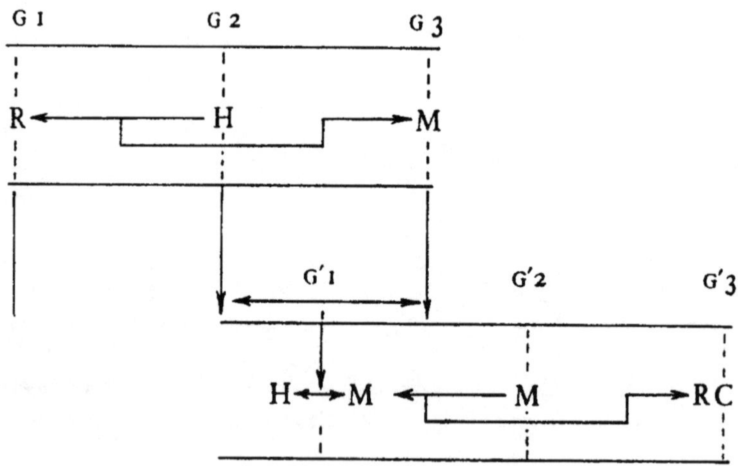

We took as our raw material the *Marx-Hegel* relationship (*G´1*). We set to 'work' on this raw material means of theoretical production *G´2* (Marx himself + certain other categories) to produce a result *G´3*: whatever *Reading Capital* contains that is not aberrant. This labour is provisional—for us above all. The theoretical labour process *must be pursued* in a new cycle in which G 2 might be represented by the (+ or – erroneous) relation between Marx and *Reading Capital*, etc. Experience has very quickly shown that it is impossible to hold to this *internal* circle: the only way to advance is via the experience of the class struggle.]

Let us return to *Diagram I. Capital* is the product of the work of the Hegelian dialectic on Ricardo, etc.

This is a perfectly classical thesis, and one which can, of course, equally well support orthodox-Marxist as anti-Marxist interpretations, since in its schematic formulation, this thesis can give weight to the idea that Marx's relation to Ricardo is reducible to a relation of the *application* of Hegel to Ricardo.

However, this thesis is always stated in the classical tradition along with another equally, if not more, insistent one: the thesis of the *inversion*. It is not Hegel that is applied to Ricardo but Hegel inverted. An enigmatic expression. What does *inversion* mean? The first index of a problem.

A second index. Very many examples can be found in the classics of Marxism. I shall only take one: Lenin's paradoxical and apparently contradictory declarations on the Marx-Hegel relationship.

In *What the 'Friends of the People' are*, Lenin says that Marx has nothing to do with Hegelian triads and that *Capital* is not their application to Ricardo.

But in his *Reading Notes* (known as the *Philosophical Notebooks*), Lenin writes: 'Aphorism: *it is impossible completely to understand Marx's* Capital, *and especially its first chapter*, *without having thoroughly studied and understood the whole of Hegel's* Logic. *Consequently, half a century later none of the Marxists understood Marx*!!'.[2]

However, a page earlier in the same notes, Lenin writes: '*Hegel's analysis of syllogisms . . . recalls Marx's imitation of Hegel in Chapter One*.'[3]

An expression notably recalling a famous and enigmatic expression of Marx, who, in the Afterword to the second German edition of *Capital*, says: 'Just as I was working at the first volume of "Das Kapital", it was the good pleasure of the peevish, arrogant, mediocre *epigonoi* who now talk large in cultured Germany, to treat Hegel in the same way as the brave Moses Mendelssohn in Lessing's time treated *Spinoza*, i.e. as a "dead dog". I therefore openly avowed myself the pupil of that mighty thinker, and even *here and there*, in the chapter on the theory of value, *coquetted* (*kokettieren*) *with the modes of expression peculiar to him*. . . .'

A strange application of Hegel to Ricardo. Let me sum up:

1. Not Hegel: but Hegel *inverted*. Inversion = rational kernel extracted from its mystical shell.

2. Further: 'coquetting' with Hegelian modes of expression (says Marx); an 'imitation' (says Lenin).

3. Leaving aside the imitation and coquettry, there remains the strange inversion. It is the inversion of idealism into materialism: matter in place of the idea. But to say this is to be much too general with respect to what is in question. For Feuerbach had already said and done just this, *in ideology*. Now, our inversion does not only concern the general world outlook but one very precise point: the *dialectic*. Marx 'inverts' it, for his dialectic is the 'direct opposite' of the Hegelian dialectic. What is the opposite of the Hegelian dialectic? A mystery. We must go further: to the *rational kernel*, i.e. to a content with a scientific theoretical value. Then it is no longer a matter of inversion but one of *critical extraction*, of a 'demystification' of the dialectic. What is a demystification? There is no longer any question of an application.

I have brought these indices together and, with considerable difficulty and at the cost of much clumsiness, have advanced the following hypothesis:

1. Marx did not 'apply' Hegel to Ricardo. He made something from Hegel *work* on Ricardo.

2. This something from Hegel is first Hegel *inverted.* The inversion of Hegel only concerns his *world outlook* = the inversion of idealism into materialism. World outlook = *tendency*. Nothing more: the tendency of a World Outlook does not *ipso facto* provide any scientific concepts.

3. This something from Hegel is thus something quite different from the *inversion* of the idealist tendency into the materialist tendency. It is something which concerns the *dialectic*. Here the metaphor of the inversion ceases to serve any useful purpose: it is replaced by a different metaphor. To invert the Hegelian dialectic = to demystify it = to *separate* the rational kernel from the irrational shell. This separation is not a mere sorting out: (take some and leave some). It can only be a transformation. Marx's dialectic can only be the Hegelian dialectic worked-transformed.

4. Thus Marx makes Hegel work on Ricardo: he makes a transformation of the Hegelian dialectic work on Ricardo.

It is indeed necessary to say that the Hegelian dialectic has been *transformed* in the theoretical work it has carried out on Ricardo. The theoretical instrument of labour which transforms the theoretical raw material is itself transformed by its work of transformation.

The result is the dialectic at work in *Capital*: *it is no longer the Hegelian dialectic but a quite different dialectic*.

We took this difference for the raw material of our work, as I have suggested in *Diagram II*.

Hence the results that appear in *For Marx* and *Reading Capital*.

Essentially we found in Marx:
—A non-Hegelian conception of *history*.
—A non-Hegelian conception of the *social structure* (a structured whole in dominance).
—A non-Hegelian conception of the *dialectic*.

Hence, if these theses are well-founded, they have crucial consequences for philosophy: above all, the rejection of the basic system of classical philosophical categories.

This system can be written:
(Origin = ((Subject = Object) = Truth) = End = Foundation)

This system is circular, because the Foundation is the fact that the adequation of subject and object is the teleological origin of all truth. I cannot justify this circular sequence here.

There follows from this rejection a new conception of philosophy—not only a new conception—but a new modality of existence, I shall say a new *practice* of philosophy: a philosophical discourse that speaks *from somewhere else* than classical philosophical discourse did. To make this comprehensible, let me invoke the analogy of psychoanalysis.

1. The point is to carry out a *displacement* = to make something *move over* (*bouger*) in the internal disposition of the philosophical categories.

2. Such that philosophical discourse changes its *modality*—speaks *otherwise* (*autrement*), which creates the difference between interpreting the world and changing it.

3. Without philosophy disappearing nonetheless.

Apparently it is the most conscious discourse there is. *In fact* it is the discourse of an *unconscious*. The point is no more to suppress philosophy than it would be to suppress the unconscious in Freud. What is required is, by working on the phantasms of philosophy (which underly its categories), to make something move over in the disposition of the instances of the philosophical Unconscious, so that the unconscious discourse of philosophy finds its *site*—and speaks at the top of its voice about the very *site* assigned to it by the instances which produce it.

I shall leave these crucial questions here.

One point remains. Everything we have published on Hegel in fact leaves out the positive heritage Marx, by his own confession, owed to Hegel. Marx transformed the Hegelian dialectic, but he owed Hegel a crucial gift: *the idea of the dialectic*. We have not discussed this. I should like to say a little about it.

In the Afterword to the second German edition of *Capital*, Marx discusses the dialectic in the following terms: '. . . The mystification which the dialectic suffers in Hegel's hands, by no means prevents him from being the first to present (*darstellen*) its general form of motion in a comprehensive and conscious manner. With him it is standing on its head. It must be turned right side up again, if you would discover the rational kernel within the mystical shell.

'In its mystified form, the dialectic became the fashion in Germany, because it seemed to transfigure the existing state of things (*das Bestehende*). In its rational shape (*Gestalt*) it is a scandal and abomination to bourgeoisdom and its doctrinaire spokesmen, because it includes in the positive comprehension of the existing state of things at the same time also the comprehension of the negation of that state, of its inevitable breaking up; because it regards every developed form as in fluid movement and thus takes into account its transient nature, lets nothing impose upon it, and is in its essence critical and revolutionary.'[4]

Two notions stand out in this passage:

1. The dialectic is critical and *revolutionary*.

Now, the ambiguity of the dialectic is clear. It can be

(a) either a *transfiguration* of the existing state of things, the '*fait accompli*' *(das Bestehende)*, the existing order. The dialectic: benediction of the existing order (social, scientific).

(b) or *critical and revolutionary*: it implies the *relativity* of every established order, social and theoretical, of societies and of systems, of institutions and of concepts.

The dialectic: a critique of the absolute by historical relativism.

This theme is very clear in Engels: the dialectic sets concepts in motion. A direct adoption of the Hegelian theme: *Reason* as a critique of the *Intellect*. Reason sets the concepts of the Intellect in motion.

The classical opposition in Marxism between

metaphysical materialism
dialectical materialism } = metaphysical/dialectical opposition

is thus no more than the adoption of the Hegelian opposition between *Intellect* and *Reason*.

Stop at this and one has not yet left Hegel. It is still very formal and thus very dangerous. The proof: the spontaneously relativist/historicist interpretation of this conception of the dialectic as a critique of the fixity of the intellect. Counterproof: Lenin's vigorous reaction against relativism and historicism (*Materialism and Empirio-Criticism*), bourgeois ideologies of history and of the dialectic.

2. But there is something else of much greater importance: does the Hegelian *dialectic* contain a *rational kernel*—and if so, what is it?

To see this, a *long detour* is required. It is necessary to go back through Marx's theoretical history. The decisive moment in this history is the rupture with *Feuerbach*. This rupture is announced in the lightning flash of the Theses on Feuerbach. The Theses on Feuerbach were written in haste after a crucial theoretical event: *the introduction of Hegel into Feuerbach* (it took place in the *1844*

Manuscripts). The *Manuscripts* are an *explosive* text. Hegel, reintroduced by force into Feuerbach, induces a prodigious *acting out* of the Young Marx's theoretical contradiction, in which is achieved the rupture with Theoretical Humanism.

To speak of Marx's rupture with Theoretical Humanism is a very precise thesis: if Marx broke with this ideology, that means he had espoused it; if he had espoused it (and it was no unconsummated marriage) that means it existed. The Theoretical Humanism Marx espoused was that of Feuerbach.

Marx 'discovered' Feuerbach, like all the Young Hegelians, in very special conditions, which I have said something about, following Auguste Cornu. For a time Feuerbach 'saved' the young Hegelian radicals theoretically from the insoluble contradictions induced in their liberal-rationalist 'philosophical conscience' by the obstinacy of the damned Prussian State, which, being 'in itself' Reason and Freedom, persisted in misrecognizing its own 'essence', persevering beyond all propriety in the Unreason of Despotism. Feuerbach 'saved' them theoretically by providing them with the reason for the Reason-Unreason contradiction: by a theory of the *alienation of Man*.

Obviously it would be impossible, on whatever basis, even a Marxist one, to think that the matter of Feuerbach can be settled by a confessional note of the kind: a few quotations from him, or from Marx and Engels, who *had* read him. Nor is it settled by that adjective of convenience and ignorance which nonetheless resounds in so many disputes: a *speculative* anthropology. As though it were enough to remove the speculation from the anthropology for the anthropology (assuming one knows what that word designates) to stand up: cut the head off a duck and it won't go far. As though it were also enough to pronounce these magic words to call Feuerbach by his name (philosophers, even if they are not watchdogs, are like you and me: for them to come, they must at least be called *by their names*). Let me therefore try to call Feuerbach by his name, even if need be by an abbreviation of his name.

Of course, I shall only discuss the Feuerbach of the years 1839–45, i.e. the author of *The Essence of Christianity* and the *Principles of the Philosophy of the Future*—and not the post-1848 Feuerbach, who, against his own earlier precepts, put a lot of 'water in his wine' for fear of the (1848) Revolution.

The Feuerbach of *The Essence of Christianity* occupies a quite extraordinary position in the history of philosophy. Indeed, he brings off the *tour de force* of putting an 'end to classical German philosophy', of overthrowing (to be quite precise: of 'inverting') Hegel, the Last of the Philosophers, in whom all its history is summed up, by a philosophy that was *theoretically retrogressive* with respect to the great German idealist philosophy.

Retrogressive must be understood in a precise sense. If Feuerbach's philosophy carried in it traces of German idealism, its theoretical foundations date from *before* German idealism. With Feuerbach we return from 1810 to 1750, from the nineteenth to the eighteenth century. Paradoxically, for reasons that should make a good 'dialectic' derived from Hegel giddy, it was by its *retrogressive* character in theory that Feuerbach's philosophy had fortunate progressive effects in the ideology, and even in the political history, of its partisans. But enough on this.

A philosophy which carries *traces* of German idealism but which settles accounts with German idealism, and its supreme representative, Hegel, by a *theoretically retrogressive* system, what are we to make of that?

The *traces* of German idealism: Feuerbach takes up the philosophical problems posed by German idealism. Above all the problems of Pure Reason and Practical Reason, the problems of Nature and Freedom, the problems of Knowledge (what can I know?), of Morality (what ought I to do?) and of Religion (what can I hope for?). Hence Kant's fundamental problems, but 'returned to' via Hegel's critique and solutions (broadly the critique of Kantian distinctions as abstractions, which for Hegel derive from a misrecognition of Reason reduced to the role of the Intellect). Feuerbach poses the problems of German idealism with the intention of giving them a Hegelian type of solution: indeed, he tries to pose the *unity* of the Kantian *distinctions* or *abstractions* in something resembling the Hegelian Idea. This 'something' resembling the Hegelian Idea, while being its radical *inversion*, is *Man*, or *Nature*, or *Sinnlichkeit* (simultaneously sensuous materiality, receptivity and sensuous intersubjectivity).

To hold all this together, I mean to think as a *single* unit these three notions: Man, Nature and *Sinnlichkeit*, is a dumbfounding theoretical gamble, which makes Feuerbach's 'philosophy' a philosophical velleity, i.e. an actual theoretical inconsistency invested in a 'wish' for an impossible philosophical consistency. A moving 'wish', certainly, even a pathetic one, since it expresses and proclaims in great solemn cries the desperate will to escape from a philosophical ideology against which it remains definitively a rebel, i.e. its prisoner. The fact is that this impossible unity gave rise to a work which has played a part in history and produced disconcerting effects, some immediate (on Marx and his friends), others postponed (on Nietzsche, on Phenomenology, on a certain modern theology, and even on the recent 'hermeneutic' philosophy which derives from it).

It was an impossible unity (Man-Nature-*Sinnlichkeit*) which enabled Feuerbach to 'resolve' the great philosophical problems of German idealism, 'transcending' Kant and 'inverting' Hegel. For example, the Kantian problems of the distinction between Pure Reason and Practical Reason, between Nature and Freedom, etc., find a solution with Feuerbach in a *unique* principle: Man and his attributes. For example, the Kantian problem of scientific objectivity, and the Hegelian problem of religion find a solution with Feuerbach in an extraordinary theory of *mirror* objectivity ('the object of a being is the objectification of its Essence': the object—the objects—of Man are the objectification of the Human Essence). For example, the Kantian problem of the Idea and History, transcended by Hegel in the theory of the Spirit as the ultimate moment of the Idea, finds a solution with Feuerbach in an extraordinary theory of the intersubjectivity constitutive of the human species. As the principal term in all these solutions, we always find Man, his attributes, and his 'essential' objects (mirror 'reflections' of his Essence).

Thus, with Feuerbach, Man is the unique, primordial and fundamental concept, the *factotum*, which stands in for Kant's Transcendental Subject, Noumenal Subject, Empirical Subject and Idea, which also stands in for Hegel's Idea. The 'end of classical German philosophy' is then quite simply a verbal suppression of its solutions which respects its problems. It is a replacement of its solutions by heteroclite philosophical notions gathered from here and there in the philosophy of the eighteenth century (sensualism, empiricism, the materialism of *Sinnlichkeit*, borrowed from the tradition of Condillac; a pseudo-biologism vaguely inspired by Diderot; an idealism of Man and the 'heart' drawn from Rousseau), and unified by a *play on theoretical words* within the concept of Man.

Hence the extraordinary position and the effects Feuerbach could draw from his inconsistency: declaring himself in turn and all at once (and he saw no malice or inconsistency in it himself) a materialist, an idealist, a rationalist, a sensualist, an empiricist, a realist, an atheist and a humanist. Hence his declamations against Hegel's speculation, reduced to *abstraction*. Hence his appeals to the concrete, to the 'thing itself', to the real, to the sensuous, to matter, against all the forms of alienation, whose ultimate essence is for him constituted by *abstraction*. Hence the sense of his 'inversion' of Hegel, which Marx long espoused as the real critique of Hegel, whereas it is still entirely trapped in the empiricism of which Hegel is no more than the sublimated theory: to invert the attribute into the subject, to invert the Idea into the sensuous real, into matter, to invert the Abstract into the Concrete, etc. All that within the category of *Man*, who is the Real, the Sensuous, and the Concrete. An old tune whose worn-out variations are still served up for us today.

There you have the *Theoretical Humanism* which Marx had to deal with. I say *theoretical*, for Man is not just for Feuerbach an Idea in the Kantian sense, but the theoretical foundation for *all* his 'philosophy', as the Cogito was for Descartes, the Transcendental Subject for Kant and the Idea for Hegel. It is this Theoretical Humanism that we find in so many words in the *1844 Manuscripts*.

But before turning to Marx, one more word on the consequences of this paradoxical philosophical position which claims radically to abolish German idealism but which respects its problems and hopes to resolve them by the intervention of a heap of eighteenth century concepts, gathered together within the theoretical injunction of Man, which stands in for their 'philosophical' unity and consistency.

For it is not possible to 'return' with impunity to a position *behind* a philosophy while retaining the problems it has brought to light.

The fundamental consequence of this theoretical retrogression accompanied by a retention of current problems is to induce an enormous *contraction* of the existing philosophical problematic, behind the appearances of its 'inversion', which is no more than the impossible 'wish' to invert it.

Engels and Lenin were perfectly well aware of this 'contraction' with respect to Hegel. 'Feuerbach is small in comparison with Hegel.' Let us go straight to the essential: what Feuerbach unforgiveably sacrificed of Hegel is History and the Dialectic, or rather, since it is one and the same thing for Hegel, History *or* the Dialectic. Here too, Marx, Engels and Lenin made no mistake: Feuerbach is a materialist in the sciences, but . . . he is an idealist in History. Feuerbach speaks of Nature but . . . he does not speak of History—Nature standing in for it. Feuerbach is not dialectical. Etc.

Having obtained this perspective, let us specify these established judgements.

Of course, history certainly is discussed by Feuerbach, who hopes to distinguish between the 'Hindu', the 'Judaic', the 'Roman', etc., 'human natures'. But there is no *theory* of history in his work. And above all there is no trace of the theory of history we owe to Hegel as *a dialectical process of production of forms (figures)*.

Of course, as we can now begin to say, what irremediably disfigures the Hegelian conception of History as a dialectical process is its *teleological* conception of the dialectic, inscribed in the very *structures* of the Hegelian dialectic at an extremely precise point: the *Aufhebung* (transcendence-preserving-the-transcended-as-the-internalized-transcended), directly expressed in the Hegelian category of the *negation of the negation* (or negativity).

To criticize the Hegelian philosophy of History because it is *teleological*, because from its origins it is in pursuit of a goal (the realization of Absolute Knowledge), hence to reject the teleology in the philosophy of history, but to return to the Hegelian dialectic as such at the same time, is to fall into a strange contradiction: for the Hegelian dialectic, too, is teleological in its *structures*, since the key structures of the Hegelian dialectic is the *negation of the negation, which is the teleology itself*, within the dialectic.

That is why the question of the structures of the dialectic is the key question dominating the whole problem of a materialist dialectic. That is why Stalin can be taken for a perceptive Marxist philosopher, at least on this point, since he struck the negation of the negation from the 'laws' of the dialectic. But to the extent, I say to the extent, that it is possible to abstract from the teleology in the Hegelian conception of history and the dialectic, it is still true that we owe Hegel something which Feuerbach, blinded by his obsession with Man and the Concrete, was absolutely incapable of understanding: the conception of History as a *process*. Indisputably, for it passed into his works, and *Capital* is the evidence, Marx owes Hegel this decisive philosophical category, *process*.

He owes him even more, which Feuerbach was again unable even to suspect. He owes him the concept of a process *without a subject*. It is fashionable in philosophical conversations, which are sometimes turned into books, to say that in Hegel, History is the 'History of the alienation of man'. Whatever the intention behind the pronunciation of such a formulation, it *states* a philosophical proposition which has an implacable meaning, one which is locatable in its offspring, if not discernible in their mother. It is to state: History is *a process of alienation which has a subject*, and that subject is man.

Now, as M. Hyppolite has very well noted, nothing is more foreign to Hegel's thought than this *anthropological* conception of History. For Hegel, History is certainly a process of alienation, but this process does not have Man as its subject. First, in the Hegelian History it is not a matter of Man, but of the Spirit, and if one must *at all costs* (which in respect of a 'subject' is false anyway) have a 'subject' in History, it is the 'nations' that should be discussed, or more accurately (and we are approaching the truth) it is the *moments* of the development of the Idea become Spirit. What does this mean? Something very simple, but if it must be 'interpreted', something important from the theoretical point of view: History is not the alienation of Man, but the alienation of the Spirit, i.e. the ultimate moment of the alienation of the Idea. For Hegel, the process of alienation does not 'begin' with (human) *History*, since History is itself no more than the alienation of Nature, itself the alienation of Logic. Alienation, which is the dialectic (in its final principle the negation of the negation or *Aufhebung*), or to speak more precisely, the *process of alienation*, is not, as a whole current of modern philosophy which 'corrects' and 'contracts' Hegel would have it, peculiar to Human History.

From the point of view of Human History the process of alienation has *always already begun*. That means, if these terms are taken seriously, that, in Hegel, History is thought as a *process* of alienation *without a subject*, or a dialectical process *without a subject*. Once one is prepared to consider just for a moment that the whole Hegelian teleology is contained in the expressions I have just stated, in the categories of alienation, or in what constitutes the master structure of the category of the dialectic (the negation of the negation), and once one accepts, if that is possible, to *abstract* from what represents the teleology in these expressions, then there remains the formulation: history is *a process without a subject*. I think I can affirm: this category of *a process without a subject*, which must of course be torn from the grip of the Hegelian teleology, undoubtedly represents the greatest theoretical debt linking Marx to Hegel.

I well know that, finally, there is in Hegel a *subject* for this process of alienation without a subject. But it is a very strange subject, one on which many important comments would have to be made: this subject is the very *teleology* of the *process*, it is the *Idea*, in the process of self-alienation which constitutes it as the Idea.

This is not an esoteric thesis on Hegel: it can be verified at each instant, i.e. at each 'moment' of the Hegelian process. To say that there is no *subject* to the process of alienation whether in History, in Nature or in Logic, is quite simply to say that one cannot at any 'moment' assign as a subject to the process of alienation any 'subject' whatsoever: neither some being (not even man) nor some nation, nor some 'moment' of the process, neither History, nor Nature, nor Logic.

The only *subject* of the process of alienation is *the process itself in its teleology*. The subject of the process is not even the End of the process itself (a mistake is possible here: does not Hegel say that the Spirit is 'Substance becoming Subject'?), it is the process of alienation as in pursuit of its End, and hence the process of alienation itself as teleological.

Nor is teleological a determination which is added to the process of alienation without a subject *from the outside*. The teleology of the process of alienation is inscribed in black and white in its definition: in the concept of *alienation*, which is the teleology itself *in the process*.

Now perhaps it is here that the strange status of *Logic* in Hegel begins to be clearer. For what is Logic? The science of the Idea, i.e. the exposition of its concept, the *concept of the process of alienation without a subject*, in other words, the concept of the process of self-alienation which, considered in its totality, is nothing but the Idea. Thus conceived, Logic, or the concept of the Idea, is the dialectic, the 'path' of the process as a process, the 'absolute method'. If Logic is nothing but the concept of the Idea (of the process of alienation without a subject), it is then the concept of this strange subject we are looking for. But the fact that this subject is only the concept of the *process of alienation itself*, in other words, this subject is the dialectic, i.e. the very movement of the negation of the negation, reveals the extraordinary paradox of Hegel. The process of alienation without a subject (or the dialectic) is the only subject recognized by Hegel. There is no subject to the process: *it is the process itself which is a subject in so far as it does not have a subject*.

If we want to find what, finally, stands in for 'Subject' in Hegel, it is in the teleological nature of this process, in the *teleological* nature of the dialectic, that it must be sought: the End is already there in the Origin. That is also why there is in Hegel no *origin*, nor (which is never anything but its phenomenon) any beginning. The origin, indispensable to the teleological nature of the process (since it is only the reflection of its End), has to be *denied* from the moment it is *affirmed* for the process of alienation to be a process without a subject. It would take too long to justify this proposition, which I propose simply in order to anticipate later developments: this implacable exigency (to affirm and in the same moment to *deny* the origin) was consciously assumed by Hegel in his theory of the *beginning* of Logic: Being is immediately non-Being. The beginning of the Logic is the theory of the non-primordial nature of the origin. Hegel's Logic is the Origin affirmed-denied: the first form of a concept that Derrida has introduced into philosophical reflection, *erasure* (*rature*).

But the Hegelian 'erasure' constituted by the Logic from its first words, is the negation of the negation, dialectical and hence teleological. It is in teleology that there lies the true Hegelian Subject. Take away the teleology, there remains the philosophical category that Marx inherited: the category of a *process without a subject*.

That is Marx's principal *positive* debt to Hegel: the concept of a *process without a subject*.

It underpins *Capital* from beginning to end. Marx was perfectly aware of it. Witness this note added by Marx to the French edition of *Capital*.

Marx: *Le Capital*, tome 1 (a note found only in the French edition!) :

> The word 'procès' (process) which expresses *a development considered in the totality of its real conditions* has long been a part of scientific language throughout Europe. In France it was first introduced slightly shamefacedly in its Latin form—*processus*. Then, stripped of this pedantic disguise, it slipped into books on chemistry, physics, physiology, etc., and into a few works of metaphysics. In the end it will obtain a certificate of complete naturalization. Let us note in passing that in ordinary speech the Germans, like the French use the word *Prozess* (*procès*, process) in the legal sense [i.e., trial].[5]

In passing, let me draw attention to the fact that the concept of a process without a subject also underpins the whole of Freud's work.

But to speak of a process without a subject implies that the notion of a subject is an *ideological notion*.

If the following double thesis is taken seriously:

1. the concept process is scientific,

2. the notion subject is ideological, then two consequences follow:

1. a revolution in the sciences: the science of history becomes formally possible,

2. a revolution in philosophy: for all classical philosophy depends on the categories of subject and object (object = a mirror reflection of *subject*).

But this positive heritage is still *formal*. The question posed then is as follows: What are *the conditions of the process* of history?

Here Marx no longer owes anything to Hegel: on the decisive point he contributes something without any precedent, i.e.:

There is no such thing as a process except in relations (*sous des rapports*): the relations of production (to which *Capital* is restricted) and other (political, ideological) relations.

Our meditations on this scientific discovery and its philosophical consequences are not yet over: we are only beginning to suspect them and assess their extent. It hardly need be said that it is not by dabbling in structuralist ideology that we can obtain the means to explore the immense space of the continent that Marx has opened for us (Marx's *Verbindungen* do not amount to a 'combinatory'!).

The continent was opened up a hundred years ago. The only people who have ventured into it are militants of the revolutionary class struggle. To our shame, intellectuals do not even suspect the existence of this continent, except to annex and exploit it as a common colony.

We must recognize and explore this continent, to liberate it of its occupiers. To reach it it is enough to follow those who went before us a hundred years ago: the revolutionary militants of the class struggle. We must learn with them what they already know. On this condition we too shall be able to make discoveries in it, of the kind announced by Marx in 1845: discoveries which help not to 'interpret' the world, but to change it. To change the world is not to explore the moon. It is to make the revolution and build socialism without regressing back to capitalism.

The rest, including the moon, will be given to us in addition.

23 January 1968

Notes

1. 'Le (Re)-commencement du matérialisme dialectique', *Critique,* no. 240, May 1967.
2. Lenin, *Collected Works*, vol. 38 (London and Moscow, 1961), p. 180.
3. ibid., p. 178.
4. *Capital*, vol. 1 (Moscow, 1961), p. 20.
5. Karl Marx, *Le Capital*, t. 1 (Éditions Sociales, Paris, 1948), p. 181n.

CHAPTER 14

"Hegel's 'Inverted World'"

—from *Hegel's Dialectic: Five Hermeneutical Studies* (1971)

Hans-Georg Gadamer

The function of the "inverted world"[1] within the whole of Hegel's history of the experience of consciousness is much more difficult to ascertain than that of almost any other section. Still, for my part, I would characterize this doctrine of the "inverted world" in the chapter on "Force and Understanding" as one of the most central in the structure of the *Phenomenology of Spirit*. I can tie my argument on this point into what R. Wiehl has shown, namely that the beginning of the *Phenomenology* cannot be comprehended at all without direct reference to Kant's philosophy.[2] If one looks at the main divisions of Hegel's phenomenology of consciousness, one cannot help but see that the task he set for himself was to show how the various modes of knowledge, the interaction of which Kant examines—intuition, understanding, and the unity of apperception or self-consciousness—are actually internally related.

In the final analysis, Hegel's chapter on the phenomenology of consciousness is dominated by the question of how consciousness becomes self-consciousness, i.e., how consciousness becomes conscious of the fact that it is self-consciousness. The thesis that consciousness is self-consciousness has been a central doctrine in modern philosophy since Descartes, and thus, Hegel's idea of phenomenology lies in the Cartesian tradition. This is amply demonstrated by parallels in the work of his contemporaries, in particular the largely unknown book by Sinclair, the friend of Hölderlin and Hegel to whom the "Sphragis" in Hölderlin's *Rhein Hymn* is addressed. The book bears the significant title, *Truth and Certainty*. Obviously, with the same intention as Fichte and at approximately the same time as Hegel, Sinclair attempts to point the way from certainty to truth beginning quite explicitly with the Cartesian concept of *cogito me cogitare*.

Now, when describing the phenomenon of consciousness in his phenomenology of mind or spirit, Hegel assumes from the start that that in which knowing will fulfill itself, that in which alone the concurrence of certainty and truth can be given, cannot merely be consciousness of the objective world which becomes conscious of itself. Rather, it must transcend the ontological status of individual subjectivity. It must be spirit. On the way to this result Hegel's first thesis is: consciousness is self-consciousness. And within Hegel's system the purpose of the first part of the *Phenomenology* is to convincingly justify this thesis. Hegel does this by "demonstrating" the conversion of consciousness into consciousness of itself, i.e., the necessary transition from consciousness to self-consciousness. Thus, Hegel quite consciously makes Kant's conceptual schema—intuition, understanding, and self-consciousness—the basis for his own divisions. It is R. Wiehl's contribution to have shown that in looking back from the chapter on "Force and Understanding," one must view "Sense Certainty" as the point of departure: namely, as consciousness as yet entirely unconscious of its essential self-consciousness.

As a preliminary methodological observation, let me add that we will come to see how Hegel spells out his thesis—and to that end our efforts will be devoted—when we verify in our own experience what Hegel himself requires when he says that everything hinges on the necessity of transitions. We are consciousness looking on. That is the perspective of the *Phenomenology*. And we ourselves must grasp which forms of consciousness appear and in which order they emerge in distinguishing themselves from each other. Hegel's claim that the dialectical transitions are necessary is made good and verified again and again if one reads carefully. Careful reading of him—and not only of him—has the remarkable consequence that precisely that which one extracts in painstaking attempts at interpretation of the section which one is reading, is stated explicitly in the next section. Every reader of Hegel has this experience: the more he explicates the content of a particular train of thought which he has before him, the more certain he can be that that explication will follow in the next section of Hegel's text. That implies that the subject matter of the discussion is always the same and that the same thing is presented on different levels of explication and reveals itself as the proper and single object or content—something of central importance to all philosophy though it is perhaps nowhere as obvious as in Hegel.

At the beginning of the *Phenomenology* this "same thing" takes the form of consciousness as self-consciousness. Thus, from the start, one must understand the task which Hegel proposes for himself in the *Phenomenology*, namely, to treat self-consciousness, Kant's synthesis of apperception, not as something previously given, but as something to be specifically demonstrated as the truth in all consciousness. All consciousness is self-consciousness. If we recognize this as the theme then the position in Hegel's system of the chapter on the "inverted world," which I am about to discuss, becomes clear. It is in the chapter on "Force and Understanding" where the thought-provoking and startling formulation, "the inverted world" is to be found. Hegel is a Schwabian and startling people is his passion, just as it is the passion of all Schwabians. But what he intends here and how he arrives at this turn of speech is particularly difficult to grasp. I shall attempt to show how Hegel's "inverted world" might be understood by means of historical references and in what sense the true world hidden behind the appearances can be called "inverted."

Our concern here is with the text beginning with Ph 110 ff. The decisive phrase, "inverted world," follows on page 121. The true world of which Hegel speaks on page 111 is the world whose inversion, making it the "inverted world," is set forth on page 121. Here, on page 111, it is not yet recognized as the "inverted world," but rather poses as the true world and nothing but the truth.

The train of Hegel's thought has led through the determination of the truth of perception as the concept of force.[3] The perceiving consciousness which the onlooking philosophical consciousness observes learns that the truth intended by the thesis of the "thing with properties" is not the "thing with properties" but rather force and the play of forces. As I see it, that is the step which Hegel demands that the philosophical consciousness grasp. It must realize that the resolution of the thing into many things—i.e., the atomism resulting when one approaches what a thing is or its properties are by means of modern chemical analysis, for example—is not sufficient if one seeks to understand what the reality of the thing and its properties actually is. Perception (*Wahrnehmen*) remains too external. In perceiving, it takes (*nimmt*) properties and things that have properties to be true (*wahr*). But does what is taken in this way to be true, e.g., the chemical structure of things, constitute their entire and true reality? One must see that, in fact, behind these properties there are forces which have their effects in opposition to each other. The formulas of the chemist express the constitution of a substance. But, precisely as the modern development and transformation of chemistry into physics has confirmed, this substance really is a play of forces.

I have now come to the place where a more precise analysis must begin. The dialectic of force is one of those sections of Hegel's work on which he himself has most thoroughly commented, since it not only appears in the *Phenomenology*, but also, in much more lengthy analysis, in the *Logic* and the *Encyclopedia* respectively. It has something so immediately compelling and illuminating about it that Hegel could be said to see what everybody would see if all sophism were dispensed with.

The argument is convincing that a false abstraction is made when one says, "Here is a force which seeks to express itself and which does so when its expression is elicited." To be sure, in this way of putting it the reality of what we have before us would be stated. But, as anyone can see, there is no question that that which elicits an expression of force must in fact be a force itself. What we have before us is thus always a play of forces. In this sense, eliciting and being elicited are the same process. Further, it is equally true—and in this consists the dialectic of force and expression of force—that force is not at all potential force which holds itself back, but rather exists only as its effect. The understanding of this reality as a relationship of self-identical, immutable substances to changing, accidental properties, in fact, proves to be an external one and at that point we become aware of the internal reality of the thing: force. But the assertion that there "exists" a force by itself apart from its expression and isolated from the context of all forces is also a false abstraction. What exists are forces and their interplay. If one examines the forms of consciousness corresponding to these experiences of the object, perception appears to be relating itself to its object externally. It believes it is perceiving the thing which remains the same plus that which changes on its exterior. In comparison to perception, the form of science referred to here as understanding—precisely because it penetrates behind this exterior, strives to get behind it, and searches out the laws governing the forces—has much better comprehension of the real truth.

That is the preparatory step which Hegel takes here (pp. 110 ff). Let me insert ahead of time a general comment about this passage: in analyzing Hegel's *Phenomenology*, one always observes that each new mode of consciousness is presented in two forms. First, in a dialectic or aporetic "for us," Hegel points up the contradiction lying in the presumed object as such and, at the same time, shows how contradictory the consciousness of this object is in the form it presents itself to us. Second, he exhibits the movement in which the consciousness under observation learns of these contradictions itself and is led to abandon its position, i.e., to change its belief about the object; for the object is not at all what it appeared to be. The consequence of this for us observers is that we grasp the necessity of proceeding to a new form of consciousness, and we can expect now that what it believes will actually be the case. It is demonstrated for us that the consciousness, which is given in sense certainty, perception, or understanding, respectively, is not valid. It is not real knowing. Thus we must proceed beyond the consciousness which appears in these forms, for that consciousness involves itself in contradictions which make it impossible for it to stay with the "truth" it had assumed and which make the untruth of its assumptions clear to us. Of course, as whatever particular consciousness it is (e.g., that of the physicist) it persists stubbornly where it finds itself and refuses to move beyond itself. As Hegel puts it, it is forever forgetting what it has learned and thus remains the same form of consciousness. We, the philosophical consciousness, need a better memory and must comprehend that such knowing is not all knowing and the world comprehended by it, not the entire world. Philosophy thus sees the necessity of getting beyond such stubborn consciousness. It is our task here to observe how that transition is accomplished.

What is first developed is the contradiction as it presents itself for us. Properly speaking that is not the dialectic of the phenomenon, for Hegel first treats the contradictions lying in the thought of the object, in its essence. Thus, the dialectic of the essential and inessential, of the thing and its properties, of force and its expression, is a dialectic of the concept and finds its proper place in the *Logic*. The phenomenological insight which Hegel extracts from this subject matter and for the sake of which he develops it, is in respect to knowledge of it: specifically, it is the insight that knowing here must proceed beyond perception if it is to do justice to the task proper to the understanding—finding out what actually is. We are now to look into the inside. At first that is meant quite straightforwardly in comparison to the superficial differentiation of immutable thing and changing properties. If we look in this way into the inside, what do we see? What is the inner essence of the external appearance? One thing is clear: looking into the inside is a matter for the understanding, not sense perception. It is what Plato characterizes as *noein* in contrast to *aisthēsis*. Thus, the object of "pure" thinking (*noein*) is obviously distinguished by the fact that it is not given to the senses.

It is convincing, therefore, when Hegel speaks on page 111 of the "innerly true" as "the *absolute universal*, and thus not merely sense universal, which has developed for the understanding." That is the *noēton eidos*, if I may express myself in Plato's terms for the moment. In it "there now opens up for the first time a supersensible world as the true world above the appearing world." Here is the step which Plato takes.[4] The universal is not the common element in sense appearances which *doxa* has before it. It is the *ontos on*, the *eidos*, the universal of the understanding and not that of the sensuous in its appearing otherness. Hegel's way of building upon this thought has a most singular quality—"above the disappearance of this world, the constant world beyond." Here Plato is made to sound very much like Christianity, and since for Hegel this standpoint is by no means to be the ultimate truth, one can almost hear Nietzsche here and his formulation, "Christianity is Platonism for the masses." Indeed, the structure which Hegel is describing is that of an extreme conceptual abstraction which, as will be demonstrated subsequently, is characteristic not only of the Platonic and Christian position, but also of that of modern science.

The supersensible world is said to be the true world. It is "what remains in disappearance—a way of putting things often found in Hegel. We will encounter precisely this expression again when we set about understanding the "inverted world." For, to give an indication of where we are headed, it will emerge there that what remains is precisely what is real where everything is continually disappearing. The real world exists precisely as continual change, *constant* change. Constancy, then, is no longer merely the opposite of disappearance, rather, it is the truth of disappearance. That is the thesis of the "inverted world."

How does Hegel reach this conclusion? Here, rather than logically reconstructing his course, I would prefer to bring the phenomenon itself so clearly into focus that we can see just what consciousness supposes as the truth in each truth which consciousness believes it has hold of. R. Wiehl has emphasized correctly that belief always remains present in the form of suppositions or contentions which keep the entire process of exhibiting the forms of consciousness moving. Thus Hegel now raises the question of what it is that consciousness supposes here. What is this inner realm into which the understanding peers? What is this consciousness of the beyond? Is an empty beyond meant? Do we have a prefiguration of the "unhappy consciousness" here?

No, Hegel says, that is not true. This beyond is not empty, for "it comes from appearance"—it is the truth of appearance. What kind of a truth? In answer to that Hegel hits upon a brilliant formulation: the beyond, he says, is the appearance *as* appearance. That is, it is appearance which is not the appearance of something else, and which is no longer to be differentiated from something lying beyond it which is "really." On the contrary, it is nothing but appearance, and thus it is not appearance as opposed to reality, but rather appearance as the real itself. Appearance is a whole of showing (*Schein*), as it is put on page 110. Hegel means here that the appearance is not just an expression of force which, when the force weakens, nullifies itself and its effect. Rather, it is the whole of reality. It not only has its ground; it is as the essence showing itself. As opposed to shallow talk of a thing "having" properties, indeed even as opposed to the insight which penetrates behind that to force which either expresses itself or remains potential, there opens up now a view into the inner essence of things as the "absolute reciprocity" of the play of forces. Here the reality is better comprehended than in the superficial view of perception. Insofar as this play of forces proves to be lawful, the "appearances," *ta phainomena*, are redeemed. "The unity in the play of force itself, and the truth of it, is the law of force" (114). Correspondingly, in the *Logic* it is said of the determinations of reflection that their "showing," i.e., the "showing" of the formal determinations, "consummates itself in appearance" (L II, 101). The phrase, "the whole of showing," leads in this way to the concept of law. One can easily see that the law is something simple in comparison to the shifting interplay of forces affecting each other. As the unitary law, it determines the entirety of appearances. The supposed difference between forces which characterizes their effect—eliciting, being elicited, being potential, being expressed—this difference of the universal, is in fact a unity. This way of putting things is peculiarly Hegelian but the truth of it can be seen and verified in the phenomenon: indeed the difference is in no way one between forces separated from each other, which occur by themselves and which one relates *ex post*. Rather it is the appearance of the simple, identical law.

In what follows, accordingly, the law of nature, the one law fully explaining all phenomena and ultimately dominating the realm of mechanics, emerges as the truth of the object under investigation. That is a most important point. Here one might be reminded of those interpreters of Plato who took Plato's idea for the law of nature. Their view was unintentional Hegelianism, for Hegel himself goes so far as to make this identification. However, it will turn out that he does not stay with it, and we shall see why.[5] In any event, he can say for the time being that the universal difference "is expressed in the law as the constant picture of the fluctuating appearance." The law is what remains in disappearance. Reality is viewed as the world of laws, which remains beyond disappearance. "The supersensible world is thus a tranquil realm of laws"—beyond the perceived world, but present in the latter nevertheless as "its immediate, still image." That is on page 114 f., and here Hegel even speaks of this realm as the still image of constant change.

Unquestionably, this phrase not only sounds like Plato but also like Galileo. Galileo is most certainly there in what follows, or more correctly, Newton. For implied here is obviously the completion of Galileo's system of mechanics with implicit reference to gravity as the universal definition of body. Hegel now demonstrates that the step taken here into the supersensible, true world, the step taken by the understanding, is only a first step which must be recognized as falling short of the whole truth. It is impossible to say that the truth of reality is the natural law. (Natorp, for one, has interpreted Plato as saying this.) Hegel shows, namely, that a formulation such as the "realm of laws" always implies that the whole of appearance is not contained therein. Either consciousness necessarily involves itself in the dialectic of the law and its instances or a multiplication of laws results. *In concreto* one might think here of how Galileo's law of falling bodies was contested by the Aristotelians of his time because it did not explain the whole appearance. Indeed, the whole appearance in this case contains the moment of resistance, of friction. Another law must be added here to the law for free falling bodies, which never exist: the law of friction governing the resistance of the medium. That means that in principle no appearance is a "pure" instance of the law.

In the case of our example we thus have two laws if we actually wish to achieve the goal of portraying the real appearance in the still image of laws. The attempt to extend mechanics in this way in order that it might deal successfully with the "impure" instances of the laws, leads at first to a multiplication of the laws. However, the moving appearances are thereby "understood" essentially as a whole, and thus a vision of the unity in lawfulness opens up, a vision which finds its ultimate realization in the integration of terrestrial physics and celestial mechanics. That, according to Hegel, is what is implied in the thesis of "universal attraction," i.e., the thesis that "everything has a constant difference from everything else." This means that the coincidental determinations based on things as they appear to the senses independently of each other are not the basis for differentiating these things. Rather, the proper basis is the essential determination of every body as constituting a force field. That is the new perspective, from which it is seen that force is essentially not one force in distinction from another, but rather distinguished within itself. Thus electricity, for example, is always positive and negative, i.e., exists as the voltage which we call electric power. To be sure, it exists only in the understanding as this difference in designation. If, for instance, the play of forces is taken as the law of positive and negative electricity, the object intended is the voltage, which is actually electric energy and not two different forces. Thus the truth of the play of forces is the unitary lawfulness of reality, the law of appearance (L II 124 ff.).

There is a dialectic on the side of consciousness corresponding to the dialectic of the object which brought out the untruth in talk of different forces. It is the dialectic of explanation, namely, that the law is different from the reality which it determines only in the understanding. The tautologousness of explanation can be demonstrated using the example of phonetic laws. In this instance one speaks of the laws of modification which "explain" the changes in sound within a language. But the laws, naturally, are nothing other than that which they explain. They do not even hint at making any other claim. All grammatical rules have the same tautological character. In these nothing at all is explained. What in truth is the life of the language, is simply stated as a law governing the language.

I spoke just now of the life of the language intentionally, for our explication is headed in the direction of this concept, and that brings me here to Hegel's doctrine of the "inverted world." For what is always lacking when we allow laws to define changes in appearance? Why do these laws fall short of the true reality? Because change as such is missing in this Platonic-Galilean conception of the tranquil realm of laws or unitary lawfulness. Hegel speaks here of the absoluteness of change, i.e., the principle of alteration. Aristotle had a similar criticism of Plato: the ideas, the *eidē*, he argued, are more *aitia akinēsias ē kinēseōs*, more an answer to the question, "What does *not* change in nature?" than an answer to the question, "What is nature?" For nature as a whole, as Aristotle says, is that which has the *archē tēs kinēseōs en eautō*, that which changes of itself.

Here are Hegel's words at the end of this section, in which the "inverted world" is first mentioned by name (p. 121): " For the first supersensible world was only the *immediate* elevation of the perceived world into the element of the universal"—elevation here to be interpreted as the *ascensus* of Plato's allegory of the "cave," i.e., as an ascent to the noetic world of the permanent idea. "The supersensible world necessarily had its corresponding image in the perceived world." The weakness of the world of ideas is, then, that it is only in opposition to the perceived world taken as unreal. Aristotle's objection to Plato's doubling of the world is meant similarly. Why this copy of the perceived world? Why the noetic world? Is not the mathematically figured world lacking in what is most important? Is it not the "true world" only *for* this changing, moving, perceived world, and does it not lack the principle of change and alteration which constitutes the being of the perceived world after all?[6] Accordingly, Hegel concludes,

"The first realm of laws was lacking in this, but as the inverted world it now contains it." A world which contains the *archē kinēseōs*, and as such is the true world, is an inversion of Plato's world in which motion and alteration were supposed to be naught. This world too is supersensible, that is, the alterations here are not merely "different" and hence unreal, but rather are understood *as motions*. This world is not just the tranquil realm of laws which all alteration must obey, rather it is a world in which everything moves because everything contains the origin of change in itself. That appears to be a pure reversal, and modern philosophical research has also struck upon the image of "reversal" for Aristotle's reinterpretation of Plato's doctrine of ideas. The *tode ti*, not the highest *eidos*, is the primary substance (J. Stenzel).

But to what extent does this reversal in ontological emphasis justify calling the true world *verkehrt* in the sense of "perverted"? What form does this second supersensible world take? To achieve complete clarity here I must return to what was under consideration before. As an example of differential in force Hegel uses electricity, which he formalizes as the dialectic of what is of the same and different names. That dialectic appears in electricity as the difference between positive and negative. Hegel's example, however, need not limit us. What Hegel illustrates at any given point with a particular example is often also substantiated in other "spheres." Here the expression "of the same name" shall be our guide. In Greek what is of the same name (homonymous) is called *homōnumon* or in Latin, *univocum*. That of the same name is, if viewed scholastically, the genus. Law and genus are here to be taken as one—they both are characterized by the fact that properly speaking they *exist* only as their various instances. To be clear about this one should say that that of the same name stands in need of, that is, refers to that named differently. The genus of hoofed animals refers to horses, donkeys, mules, camels, etc. The differently named species are what the genus means, its truth. And similarly, each single species refers to the different individuals. If we think that through, we are led to the ultimate conclusion that the difference or what is different, i.e., that which is neither expressed nor contained in that of the same name, is precisely what is real. Again we recognize a theme from antiquity, for this point is basic to Aristotle's criticism of Plato's "idea" and to Aristotle's own teaching. The *eidos* is only an aspect of the *tode ti*: or, as Hegel will put it (p. 124), this "inverted" supersensible world contains the world which it inverts. It contains the *eidos* as *what* constitutes the "this-here" in the *tode ti* and which alone provides the answer to the question which the understanding raises, namely, *ti esti*? (cf. Aristotle's *Categories*). Aristotle too cannot answer this differently from Plato. When I have a this-something before me and am asked, "What is it?" I can only answer with the *eidos*. In this sense the standpoint of the understanding is all-inclusive. But that does not mean that reality is only the *eidos*. Quite the opposite: what is real is the individual which is "of this species" and of which it can be said that it is of this type. But how can Hegel assert that this appearing existent contains its reversal in itself as a perversion? Why is the true reality called the *verkehrte* world?

I would like to pursue a line of thought here which will make the concept of the inverted or perverted world, respectively, comprehensible. What appears in one way or another is never "pure" *eidos*, although the *eidos* is only present in appearance. As Leibniz puts it, no egg is like another. No instance is a pure case of a law. The real world as it exists in opposition to the "truth" of the law is thus perverted. Things do not occur in it in a way that would correspond to the ideas of an abstract mathematician or a moralist. Indeed, the live reality of it consists precisely in its perversion. And that is its function in the *Phenomenology*'s dialectical process of demonstration—the end result will be that being inverted in itself is being turned towards itself or relating itself to itself, and that, precisely, is the structure of Life.

But does Hegel really have a sense of being inverted as being wrong in mind? Does he not always mean the dialectical reversal and does he not want to say here too that the true world is not that supersensible world of tranquil laws, but rather the reverse of this? That of the similar which is dissimilar, the changing, is the truth—in this sense inversion constitutes the essence of one side of the supersensible world (p. 123). But Hegel cautions quite expressly that the matter cannot be imagined in a physical sense, as though it were a case of the inversion (reversal) of something established, i.e., as though there were a supersensible world to begin with and then also a second inverted one. As stated on page 123, the reversal is much more reflection into self and not opposition of one thing to another. The dialectical point of this reversal is obviously that when I take the opposite (the inverted-perverted world) to be true "in and for itself," the truth is necessarily the opposite of itself. For in what it is in and for itself the reality of appearance had, in fact, proven to be more than the pure instances of laws. That implies, however, that that reality is also the law of appearance. It is both: the law and the perversion of the law. It is the opposite of itself. If we take as our example for this Hegel's critique of thought-things which only ought to be, of the hypotheses and all the other "invisible truths of an ever recurring ought" (Ph 190), then, indeed, the reasonable view of reality would reject the vacuous universality of such hypotheses and laws even though reality includes these. What is reasonable and concrete is the reality determined by the principle of change. Abstractions are always confounded because things never turn out as one thought they would.

As is common knowledge, the *Logic* contains the complete development of thought's determinations of being. For this reason it is the natural commentary on the opinions about objective being found in the forms of consciousness developed in the *Phenomenology*. The "inverted world" is also to be found not only in the *Phenomenology* but in the *Logic* too and, specifically, in a form there such that the world in and for itself is the inversion of the world which appears. Obviously reversal is the basic meaning here and nothing here could mislead one into thinking that a perversion of this world in any substantive sense is meant. Still it must not be forgotten that the *Encyclopedia* (also the Heidelberg version) never makes use of the concept of the "inverted world" at all and that the *Logic* develops the dialectic of this concept in a way not entirely consistent with the *Phenomenology*.

It seems as if Hegel might have recognized that the abstract juxtaposition of law and appearance as it is presented in the *Phenomenology*, i.e., as the opposition of the supersensible and sense world, is not at all in keeping with the meaning of law. In the *Phenomenology* he says of the tranquil realm of laws that, though to be sure it is beyond the perceived world, it is also present in the latter as its immediate, still image. However, he says in the same context in the *Logic*, "The law is *not* beyond the appearance, but rather present in it immediately" (L II 127).[7] Corresponding to this, the realm of laws no longer appears in the *Logic* as a *world*, supersensible or otherwise. "The existing world is itself the realm of the laws."

Of course the concept of law goes through the same stages here as in the *Phenomenology*. It is at first the mere basis of appearance and constitutes what stays the same in change—alongside of which the changing content of appearance continues to exist. We have a second step and a changed sense of law when the law itself presupposes the differences which constitute its content. In substance these stages correspond to the first and second supersensible worlds of the *Phenomenology*. But, significantly, only at this point is it said that the law in which the totality of appearance in itself is reflected, has the character of totality, i.e., is a world. In the *Logic*, namely, the tranquil realm of laws is not called the supersensible *world*: "world" first appears in the "world" which is inverted, i.e., totally reflected into itself and existing in and for itself, or what is called in the *Phenomenology* the *second supersensible world*.[8] Only of the latter is it said expressly, "Thus the appearance reflected into itself is now a world, which opens up as existing in and for itself above the appearing world." It is also called the supersensible world (L II 131 f.), and finally proves to be the "inverted world." Many of Hegel's examples of its inversion used here and in the *Phenomenology*, that is, examples for the reversal of the supersensible world, are of no help to us in clarifying the general sense of *verkehrt*. North pole and south pole, positive and negative electricity, illustrate only that these relationships can be turned around and accordingly have a dialectical character (Ph 122; L II 134).

Still the question persists whether the phrase *verkehrte Welt* as much as it might have the dialectical meaning of "turned around" might nevertheless not also connote for Hegel something in line with a double sense of both inverted and perverted. I find a first indication that it does on page 122 of the *Phenomenology*. There one comes across the phrase, ". . . the law of a world which has opposite it a *verkehrte* supersensible world in which that which is scorned in the first is honored in the second and vice versa." The *verkehrte* world is thus a world in which everything is the reverse of the right world. Isn't that a familiar principle of literature, one which we call satire? One might be reminded in this regard of Plato's myths, in particular, of that in the *Statesman*, and of that master of English satire, Swift. Further, as is hinted in the figure of speech, "that's a topsy-turvy world" (*verkehrte Welt*), meaning, for example, when servants play masters and masters, servants, this kind of reversal is illuminating in some way. What is found in the topsy-turvy world is not simply the contrary, the mere abstract opposite of the existent world. Rather this reversal in which everything is the opposite of itself makes visible in a kind of fun house mirror the covert perversion of everything as we know it. If this is so, the topsy-turvy world would be the perversion of perversity. Being the perverted world backwards would amount to displaying the perversion of the latter *e contrario*. And that is certainly the point of all satire.

Such portrayal in a counterfactual possibility illumines for a moment a valid though unreal possibility in the established world as it stands. Indeed, this is precisely the purpose of satirical portrayal. As a form of statement, satirical inversion presupposes that the world will recognize in the reversal of itself its own perversion and thus come to see its true possibilities. Thus, it is the real world itself which splits apart into possibility and counter-possibility. In that the topsy-turvy world displays itself as reversed, it exhibits the wrongness of the established world as it stands. Thus Hegel can justifiably say that this world is "perverted (*verkehrt*) for itself, i.e., the perversion of itself," for it is no mere opposite. The true world, on the contrary, is both the truth projected as an ideal and its own perversion. Now if we keep in mind too that one of the main tasks of satire is to expose moral hypocrisy, i.e., the untruth of the world as it is supposed to be, the real trenchancy of *verkehrt* comes into view. The perversion of the true reality becomes visible behind its false front since in every instance satirical portrayal is the "opposite in itself," whether this takes the form of exaggeration, innocence in contrast to hypocrisy, or whatever.[9]

It is in this sense that the *verkehrte* world is more than a direct opposite of what appears. Hegel states specifically (p. 122) that any view would be superficial in which "the one world is the appearance; the other, the in-itself." That is an opposition which the understanding supposes, but, in truth, it is not a matter here of the opposition of two worlds. Rather, it is the "true, supersensible" world which contains both aspects and which divides itself into this opposition and thereby relates itself to itself.

This interpretation is particularly well documented by a recurring theme in Hegel, one of his favorites, which concerned him from his youth on. It is the problem of punishment and the forgiveness of sins, respectively—a problem which forced the young theologian, Hegel, beyond Kant's and Fichte's moral conception of the world. And, as a matter of fact, to my knowledge the idea of inversion-perversion is first found in Hegel's analysis of the problem of punishment.[10] As the *Phenomenology* expressly states, it would be simplistic if one were to take punishment to be punishment only in appearance here, and, in reality or in another world, to be for the benefit of the criminal (p. 122). Only the abstract thinking of the understanding permits such talk of two worlds and in this account of things there is no speculative reversal. The reversal which punishment implies is also not that of an actual countereffect against which the wrongdoer seeks to defend himself. That would not be the position of justice at all but rather one of vindictiveness. Of course there is such an immediate law of retribution. But punishment has a meaning quite the opposite of this and thus in Hegel it is called the "inversion" of revenge. The individual seeking revenge holds himself to be the essential concern in opposition to the violator and seeks to restore his injured existence through destruction of the wrongdoer. But the concern in punishment is a quite different one, namely, with a violation of law. The countereffect of the penalty is not a mere consequence of the violation, rather it belongs to the very essence of the misdeed. The misdeed as a crime demands punishment, which is to say that it does not have the immediacy of a simple action, but rather exists in the form of universality as crime *per se*. Thus Hegel is able to say that, ". . . the inversion of it (*Verkehrtheit derselben*) is the punishment, i.e., that the crime becomes the opposite of what it was previously." Punishment as inversion (*Verkehrtheit*) plainly implies that punishment has an essential tie to the misdeed. Punishment is reasonable. The wrongdoer, as the reasonable man he wants to be, must turn against himself. In the *System of Ethicality* Hegel describes most impressively how this reversal comes to pass abstractly and ideally in the phenomenon of the bad conscience.[11] The wrongdoer's sensitivity to the division within himself may be anesthetized again and again by the fear of punishment and also by his resistance to its impending reality, but it always returns in the ideal realm of conscience. That means that the wrongness of the deed shows up again and again as long as the punishment is "called for."

But then is it not necessary to take the turning around as it occurs here in relationship to punishment in the double sense which the full meaning of *Verkehrtheit* would imply? That the punishment is required as the necessary inversion of the misdeed means that it is recognized as that inversion. In it, therefore, the reconciliation of the law with the reality of crime opposed to it has occurred. If it is accepted and carried out and thus becomes actual punishment, it cancels itself out and correspondingly the self-destruction of the criminal ends and he is again one with himself. With his acceptance of his fate, the dichotomy prevailing in his existence—on the one hand the fear of punishment, on the other, the pangs of conscience—is eliminated. Here, too, one can say that the *verkehrte* world in which punishment "is not that which damages and annihilates a man, but rather an extension of grace which preserves man's essence," is not simply an inversion of the abstract world where misdeed and punishment are opposed. It also reveals the perversity of that abstract world and elevates it to the "higher sphere"[12] of fate and reconciliation with fate.

The further sequence of the forms of knowledge in the *Phenomenology* also makes it quite clear that "*Verkehrung*" and "*Verkehrtheit*" refer specifically and above all to what is good and evil, and, thus, that the meaning of "*Verkehrt*" is as much substantive as it is formal. In the chapter "Culture and the Realm of Reality" the example used in the *Logic* for the "*Verkehrte Welt*" is made thematic, specifically the fact that "what in phenomenal existence is evil, misfortune, etc., is in and for itself good and fortunate" (L II 134). There it is said that,

> When the upright consciousness, in the only way possible for it here, makes itself the guardian of the good and noble, (i.e., of that which remains constant throughout all expression of itself), in order that the good and noble not be *linked* to the bad or *mixed* with it. . . . this consciousness, though it thinks it is refuting the fact, has only restated in a trivial way, . . . that the noble and good is essentially the inversion-perversion of itself, just as the bad is conversely the most admirable. (Ph 373 f.)

The good *is* the bad. One cannot take Hegel literally enough here. "*Summum ius—summa inuria*" means that abstract justice is perversion of justice, that it not only leads to injustice but is itself ultimate injustice. We are far too accustomed to reading speculative statements as if there were a subject underlying them to which only different characteristics are attributed.[13]

At this point we return from our investigation of the dialectical sense of the "inverted-perverted world" to our consideration of its function in the *Phenomenology*'s train of thought. For my demonstration I have used the example of punishment and acceptance of fate, which came, to be sure, from "another sphere"—one, however, which Hegel himself brings in as an illustration (Ph 122). But though the example is from "another sphere," the structure and inner necessity of the dialectical development which concerns us is confirmed by it. We have no choice but to admit that the unsensed, supersensible world of the universal represents only an aspect of that which really is. The true reality is that of life, which moves itself within itself. Plato conceived of this as the *autokinoun*, Aristotle, as the essence of *physis*. In the progression of the forms of knowing which the *Phenomenology* traverses, an enormous step is made here, where the being of what lives is grasped. What lives is not an instance of law or the composite result of laws bearing on each other, rather it is turned towards itself or it relates itself: it behaves. It is a self. There is an enduring truth here. For however far modern physiology might go in unlocking the secret of organic life, in knowing what lives we will never cease to make a turnabout in our thinking of that which, as the play of forces, lawfully determines organic nature: we will think of it, conversely, as the behavior of the organism and "understand" this organism as living. Though a Newton of the blade of grass may one day appear, in a deeper sense Kant will prove to be right. Our understanding of the world will not cease to judge "teleologically." For us, and not only for Hegel, the transition here is necessary, i.e., the progression to another, higher form of knowing as well as to a higher form of what is known. Indeed, in a decisive sense, that which we look upon as living we must view as a self. A "self," however, means self-identity in all undifferentiatedness and all self-differentiation. The mode of being of what lives corresponds in this to the mode of being of the knowledge which understands what lives. For consciousness of what is as a self has the same structure of differentiation which is no differentiation. Thus the transition to self-consciousness has been essentially completed. We must now grasp that the "inverted world" is in fact the real world—even if in the eyes of the idealist and mathematical physicist it is impure and therefore perverted since the abstract universality of the law and its pure instances are not present in it. That means that there is life in it which maintains itself in infinite change, in the continuing differentiation of itself from itself. And once we have acknowledged this, the mediation which Hegel undertakes in his dialectical exposition of consciousness has been essentially achieved. It has been demonstrated, then, that consciousness is self-consciousness. In its knowing consciousness is actually more sure of this than of all conceptions of what is which have been mediated by the senses and the understanding. This certainty goes beyond all of these conceptions. For if it thinks of what is, as a self, that is, as that which relates itself to itself, what it thinks of is intended as something which has the same certainty of itself which consciousness has. That is the true penetration into the interior of nature, which alone is able to grasp the "natural" in nature, i.e., its life. The living feels the living—it understands it from the inside as it understands itself as a self. The *autokinoun*, abstractly defined, is the act of the living self relating itself to itself. Expressed as knowing, it is the formula of idealism, I = I, self-consciousness.

Thus, the first part of the *Phenomenology* has achieved the goal of pointing out to consciousness that it contains the standpoint of idealism within itself. What leads Hegel beyond the standpoint of idealism, specifically the concept of reason which transcends the subjectivity of the self and which is realized as spirit, has been given a foundation in this first section. Realization of that concept even now exceeds our grasp.

Abbreviations

Ph *Phänomenologie des Geistes*, Meiner, Hamburg, 1952.
L I, II *Wissenschaft der Logik*, Meiner, Leipzig, 1951.

Notes

1. *Verkehrte Welt*. Any single choice in translating *verkehrt* here is unsatisfactory. For Gadamer's analysis turns on the double sense of the word in German—on the one hand, the value free sense of inverted, backwards, upside down, inside out, etc., and on the other, the evaluative sense of perverted, distorted. In this second sense the thing which is "verkehrt" appears as a caricature of itself. (TRANS.)
2. Cf. R. Wiehl, *Hegel-Studien*, supplement 3, 1964, pp. 103 ff.
3. Gadamer is referring here to the development in the first chapters of the *Phenomenology*, which take consciousness from immediate dependency on sense data (sense certainty) through more and more mediated forms of knowledge (perception, understanding). The step referred to here is that from knowing a thing with qualities, e.g., salt with the qualities of white, hard, saline taste, etc., to knowing a universe of objects standing in force relationships to each other. In Hegel's analysis that is the transition from Perception to Understanding. (TRANS.)
4. See Hegel's account of Plato's philosophy in his lectures (XIV 169 ff.).
5. The Marburg school too could not stand pat on this construction of the object through laws. That is demonstrated not only by the later Natorp's concept of *das Urkonkrete* (the originally and ultimately concrete) but also by his understanding of the later Plato, which comes so close to Hegel's. This relationship has been pursued by R. Wiehl in his as yet unpublished studies on Platonic and Hegelian dialectic.
6. This would seem to be the place to point to the ambivalence in Hegel's understanding of Plato. On the one hand, he views him with the eyes of Aristotle: "Plato expresses the essence rather more as the universal and thus the element of reality seems to be missing in him." On the other hand, he recognizes in Plato's dialectic this "negative principle" (i.e., of reality) when he says that principle essentially touches upon reality "if it is the unity of what is opposed" (XIV 322).
7. My italics.
8. My italics.
9. The literary use of the concept of the "inverted world" in the satire of the late middle ages is set forth in *extenso* by Karl Rosenkranz in his *Geschichte der deutschen Poesie im Mittelalter*, Halle, 1830, pp. 586–94. See also Klaus Lazarowicz, *Vekehrte Welt. Vorstudien zu einer Geschichte der deutschen Satire*, Tübingen, 1963, which to be sure does not trace the history of this turn of speech. Somewhat more is to be found in Alfred Liede, *Dichtung als Spiel. Unsinnspoesie an den Grenzen der Sprache*, Berlin, 1963, vol. 2, pp. 40 ff., and some evidence for my thesis from the seventeenth century, in Jean Rousset, *La littérature de l'âge baroque*, Paris, 1963,

pp. 26–28, in particular, p. 27, according to which it would appear that the folk motif of a turnabout into the absurd only gradually assumes the character of a statement of the truth in the sense of satire.

10. Hegel, *Theologische Jugenschriften*, ed. H. Nohl, Tübingen, 1907, p. 280.
11. Hegel, *Schriften zur Politik und Rechtsphilosophie*, ed. George Lasson, Leipzig, 1913, p. 453.
12. Hegel, *Theologische Jugendschriften*, p. 279.
13. See chapter 1 above. In passing it should be mentioned that ordinary German usage quite confidently distinguishes between *falsch* (false) and *verkehrt* (inverted or backwards). Of course an answer which inverts things or gets them twisted is not correct, but the elements of truth are recognizable in it and only need to be put right. A false answer, on the other hand, contains no such possibility of making it right. Thus, for example, the information someone gives you can be called *falsch* if it is deliberately given with the intent of deceiving—but in such a case it could not be called *verkehrt*. For an answer which is *verkehrt* is always one which was meant to be correct and which turned out to be false. In this sense too the *malum* is the *conversio boni*.

CHAPTER 15

Glas

—(1974)

Jacques Derrida

The concept of religion fills itself up, determines itself in opposing itself to itself, then reconciles itself with itself: in three moments that fulfill the absolute spirit. In a first moment, absolute spirit finds its actual existence in religion, but in a religion whose concept yet remains empty and indeterminate. In this moment religion is *immediate* and *natural*. Spirit sees itself outside, apprehends itself as its own proper object in a natural and immediate figure. This is the moment of natural religion (sun, plant, animal, work of the artisan). The spirit loses itself and finds itself again in these external, sensible and natural objects. The last of the three (of the three and not the four, the religion of plants or flowers does not form a settled [*arrêtée*] structure, a true religion), the least natural, the artisan's work secures the mediation toward the following moment: esthetic religion. In the first moment, in natural religion, spirit has not come back to itself, is not yet (it)self (*Selbst*). In denying the natural exterioriry of the sensible thing into which it had lost itself, in consum(mat)ing, interiorizing, relieving that exterioriry, spirit identifies itself, finds itself again, recognizes itself as such (*Selbst*). The second moment of religion then is that of the "figure of *relieved naturalness*, or of the *Selbst*." Moment of esthetic religion: spirit contemplates itself in the object that it has itself produced, in its work. No longer does it have only consciousness of the object (sun, plant, animal, and so on) but consciousness of itself. One has passed from nature to art, as from consciousness to self-consciousness, from the object to subjectivity. This last opposition, like the one-sidedness of these two instances [*instances*], relieves itself in(to) absolute (revealed or manifest) religion. In this ultimate relief, spirit reveals itself in its true figure, but what relieves and reveals itself here (it suffices to think of what withdraws in this veiling movement in order to see announcing itself, in the anagrammatic throw of the d(ie) [*le coup de dé anagrammatique*], the fermentation of truth) yet remains no further than figural representation. "But although in this [in revealed religion], spirit has indeed attained its true *figure* (*zu seiner wahren* Gestalt), yet the *figure* itself and the *representation* (Vorstellung) are still the unvanquished aspect (*unüberwundene Seite*) from which spirit must pass over into the *concept*, in order wholly to resolve therein the form of objectivity, in the concept which equally embraces within itself its own contrary." *Sa* has no figure, is not a figure, while absolute religion is yet (true) figure and representation.

Whence the circle of this syllogistic linking up: natural religion, the first moment of religion (immediate consciousness and sense-certainty) counts three moments whose first (the first moment of the first moment) is also, like *Sa*, at the other end, absence of figure, irrepresentable moment. The figure withdraws at the origin and the end of religion, before and after religion: whose becoming literally describes a consuming destruction of the figure, between two suns. Another jealousy of the Hegelian god who begins and ends by making disappear—in fire—its own proper figural representation. This jealousy, this *zelos* does not boil down to the passion of the Jewish God that never shows himself. Here God shows himself neither at the beginning nor at the end of times, but that is in order to show himself the whole time through his figures and in an absolute light. True, he shows himself better in not showing himself, since the determinate figures dissemble him precisely in their determination. Between the Jewish god and the Hegelian god, the problem, after all, of the remain(s) plays itself out, plays with the remain(s), under the species of an excess of zeal. The jealousy is between them.

In the first moment of natural religion, that of the luminous-essence (*Lichtwesen*), spirit is at first only its own proper concept. But this concept stays in abstract indetermination, has not yet unfolded, manifested, produced itself. It keeps itself back yet in "the night of its essence (*die Nacht seines Wesens*)." In the first split that unveils the secret (*Geheimnis*) of spirit, spirit relates to itself according to a "*simple* relation," without mediation or determination. The Being "filled (*erfüllte*)" by this concept of spirit is indeterminate; it appears, appears itself as such: pure light, simple determinability, pure medium [*milieu*], ethereal transparence of the manifestation in which nothing appears but the appearing, the pure light of the sun. This first figure of natural religion figures the absence of figure, a purely visible, thus invisible sun that allows seeing without showing itself or that shows itself without showing anything, consuming all in its phenomenon: *die Gestalt der Gestaltlosigkeit*. This figure is "the pure, all-embracing and all-filling *luminous essence*," that of the rising [*lever*] or the orient (Lichtwesen *des Aufgangs*). Nothing yet shows itself there; the orient passes here immediately into its pure being-other, absolute dark or occidentality. Analyzed as abstract subjectivity, this figureless figure, first moment of natural religion in the *Phenomenology of Spirit*, corresponds to the third moment of natural religion in the *Lectures on the Philosophy of Religion* ("Historically, the cult of light is the perspective of the religion of the Parsis [founded by Zoroaster]. The cult has its existence in this religion. They do not adore the light under the form of the sun; their adoration is not, in the strict sense, a cult of nature; but the light directly signifies the Good.").

Pure and figureless, this light burns all. It burns itself in the all-burning [*le brûle-tout*] it is, leaves, of itself or anything, no trace, no mark, no sign of passage. Pure consuming destruction, pure effusion of light without shadow, noon without contrary, without resistance, without obstacle, waves, showers, streams ablaze with light: "The movements of its own externalization, its creations in the element without obstacle of its otherness, are effusions of light (*Lichtgüsse*); in their simplicity, they are at the same time (*zugleich*) its becoming-for-(it)self and the return from its being-there, torrents of fire destructive of figuration." By very reason of this indifference—or rather of this absence of opposition—the pure content of this being is without essence. The all-burning is "an essenceless by-play, pure accessory of the substance that *rises* without ever *setting* (*ein wesenloses Beiherspielen an dieser Substanz, die nur* aufgeht, *ohne in sich* niederzugehen), without becoming a subject, and without consolidating through the self (*Selbst*) its differences."

A pure essenceless by-play, a play that plays limitlessly, even though it is already destined to work in the service of essence and sense. But as such, supposing that "as such" can be said of something that is not some thing, this play does not yet work, does not yet have any onto-theo-teleological horizon: fire artist without being. The word itself (*Beiherspielen*) plays the example (*Beispiel*) beside the essence. Here the pure example plays *beside* the essence so much, holds itself so diverted from [*à l'écart de*] the essence, that it has no essence: pure example, without essence, without law. Therefore without example, like God about which Hegel says that an example cannot be made, but because he, God, merges with the pure essence, pure essence is also without example. The all-burning—that has taken place once and nonetheless repeats itself ad infinitum—diverges so well from all essential generality that it resembles the pure difference of an absolute accident. Play and pure difference, those are the secret of an imperceptible all-burning, the torrent of fire that sets itself ablaze. Letting itself get carried away, pure difference is different from itself, therefore indifferent. The pure play of difference is nothing, does not even *relate* to its own blaze [*incendie*]. The light envelops itself in darkness even before becoming subject. In order to become subject, in effect the sun must go down [*décline*]. Subjectivity always produces itself in a movement of occidentalization. Now here the sun does not set—or else it sets immediately, does not know any going down, any route that leads back to self, any season, any season in the sense of cycle, just a pure season, in the sense of the seminal effusion without return. This difference without subject, this play without labor, this example without essence, devoid of self (*Selbst*), is also a sort of signifier without signified, the wasting of an adornment without the body proper, the total absence of property, propriety, truth, sense, a barely manifest unfolding of forms that straightaway destroy themselves; is a One at once infinitely multiple and absolutely different, different from self, a One without self, the other without self that means (to say) nothing, whose language is absolutely empty, void, like an event that never comes about itself.

"Its determinations [those of this pure being or this essenceless play] are only attributes which do not attain to self-subsistence (*Selbständigkeit*), but remain (*bleiben*) merely names of the many-named [empty-named, then: there is not yet any sense, time, circle] One. This One is clothed with the manifold powers of being-there and with the figures of actuality as with an ornament without self (*als mit einem selbstlosen Schmucke*); they are merely messengers, having no will of their own, messengers of its might, visions of its glory, voices in its praise."

How can the self and the for-(it)self appear? How would the sun of the all-burning breach/broach its [*sa*] course and its going down [*déclin*]?

At first approach, that the situation could change and why the void of the concept should fill itself up are not seen.

How, from this consuming destruction without limit, can there remain something that primes the dialectical process and opens history? Conversely, if the process begins, how would it reduce this pure differential consuming, this pure destruction that can proceed only from fire? How would the solar outlay [*dépense*] produce a remain(s)—something that stays or that overdraws itself? How would the purest pure, the worst worst [*le pire du pire*], the panic blaze of the all-burning, put forth some monument, even were it a crematory? Some stable, geometric, solid form, for example, a *pyramis* that guards the trace of death?

Pyramis is also a cake of honey and flour. It was offered as a reward for a sleepless night [*nuit blanche*] to the one who thus remained awake. It was also a cone-shaped cake presented to the dead. The Greeks have given this name to the Egyptian monuments because of the word *pyr*, some think, since the flames end in a point, or because of this cone-shaped flour (wheat, *pyros*) cake.

If the all-burning destroys up to its letter and its body, how can it guard the trace of itself and breach/broach a history where it preserves itself in losing itself?

Here is experienced the implacable force of sense, of mediation, of the hard-working negative. In order to be what it is, purity of play, of difference, of consuming destruction, the all-burning must pass into its contrary: guard itself, guard its own movement of loss, appear as what it is in its very disappearance. As soon as it appears, as soon as the fire shows itself, it remains, it keeps hold of itself, it loses itself as fire. Pure difference, different from (it)self, ceases to be what it is in order to remain what it is. That is the origin of history, the beginning of the going down [*déclin*], the setting of the sun, the passage to occidental subjectivity. Fire becomes for-(it)self and is lost; yet worse [*pire*] since better.

Then in place of burning all, one begins to love flowers. The religion of flowers follows the religion of the sun.

The erection of the pyramid guards life—the dead—in order to give rise to the for-(it)self of adoration. This has the signification of a sacrifice, of an offer by which the all-burning annuls itself, opens the annulus, contracts the annulus into the anniversary of the solar revolution in sacrificing itself as the all-burning, therefore in guarding itself. The sacrifice, the offer, or the gift do not destroy the all-burning that destroys itself in them; they make it reach the for-(it)self, they monumentalize it. The historical placing in orbit of the consuming instant gives the instant the chance of the anniversary movement from orient to occident. The chance of substance, of the *remnance* [restance] determined as subsistence. The last words of "Das Lichtwesen": "But this reeling, unconstrained [tottering, tumultuous, *taumelnde*] life must [*muss*; why must it?] determine itself as being-for-self and give its evanescent figures a stable subsistence (*Bestehen*). The *immediate being* in which this life stands in opposition to its consciousness is itself the *negative* power which dissolves [resolves, *auflöst*] its own differences. This being is thus in truth the *self* (Selbst); and spirit therefore passes on to know itself in the form of self. Pure light disseminates (*wirft . . . auseinander*) its simplicity as an infinity of forms, and offers up itself as a holocaust to the for-(it)self, so that from its substance the individual may take its subsistence."

The difference and the play of the pure light, the panic and pyromaniac dissemination, the all-burning offers itself as a holocaust to the for-(it)self, *gibt sich dem Fürsichsein zum Opfer*. It sacrifices itself, but only to remain, to insure its guarding, to bind itself to itself, strictly, to become itself, for-(it)self, (close)-by-(it)self. In order to sacrifice itself, it burns itself. The burning then burns itself and goes out; the fire appeases itself; the sun begins to go down [*décliner*], to run through the route that will lead it into the occidental interiority (the occidental, one knows this anyway, bears the sun in its heart). This sacrifice belongs, as its negative, to the *logic* of the all-burning, one could say to the double register of its accounting, accountable calculus. If you want to burn all, you must also consume the blaze, avoid keeping [*garder*] it alive as a precious presence. You must therefore extinguish it, keep it in order to lose it (truly), or lose it to keep it (truly). Both processes are inseparable; they can be read in any sense, any direction whatever, from right to left or left to right; the relief of one must value [*faire cas*] the other. A panic, limitless inversion: the word *holocaust* that happens to translate *Opfer* is more appropriate to the text than the word of Hegel himself. In this sacrifice, all (*holos*) is burned (*caustos*), and the fire can go out only stoked.

Here we are at this critical point of the anniversary where we can regard on both sides of the revolution, toward the orient and toward the occident.

What engages itself here? What is the stake at play in this column?

The gage, the engage, the stake at play [*l'enjeu*], that is indeed what is the question here. What puts itself in play in this holocaust of play itself?

This perhaps: the gift, the sacrifice, the putting in play or to fire of all, the holocaust, are under the power of [*en puissance d'*] ontology. They carry and deborder it, but they cannot not give birth to it. Without the holocaust the dialectical movement and the history of Being could not open themselves, engage themselves in the annulus of their anniversary, could not annul themselves in producing the solar course from Orient to Occident. Before, if one could count here with time, before everything, before every determinable being [*étant*], there is, there was, there will have been the irruptive event of the gift [*don*]. An event that no more has any relation with what is currently designated under this word. Thus giving can no longer be thought starting from Being [*être*], but "the contrary," it could be said, if this logical inversion here were pertinent when the question is not yet logic but the origin of logic. In *Zeit und Sein*, the gift of the *es gibt* gives itself to be thought before the *Sein* in the *es gibt Sein* and displaces all that is determined under the name *Ereignis*, a word ofren translated by *event*.

How is the event of an anniversary possible now? What gives itself in an anniversary?

This, perhaps: the process of the gift (before exchange), the process that is not a process but a holocaust, a holocaust of the holocaust, *engages* the history of Being but does not belong to it. The gift *is not*; the holocaust *is not*; if at least *there is some such*. But as soon as it burns (the blaze is not a being), it must, burning itself, burn its action [*opération*] of burning and begin to be. This reflection (in both senses of the word) of the holocaust engages history, the dialectic of sense, ontology, the speculative. The speculative is the reflection (*speculum*) of the holocaust's holocaust, the blaze reflected and cooled by the glass, the ice, of the mirror. The dialectic of religion, the history of philosophy (etc.), produces itself as the reflection-effect of a *coup de don* [the gift's blow, stroke, time, etc.] as/in holocaust.

But if the blazing is not yet philosophy (and the remain(s)), it cannot, nonetheless, not give rise to philosophy, to dialectical speculation, to the annulus of the exchange, to the downward [*déclinante*] course, to the circulating revolution. There is *a fatum* of the gift there, and this necessity was said in the "must" (*muss*, *doit*) we indicated above: the *Taumeln*, the vertigo, the delirium *must* determine itself as for-(it)self and take on a stable subsistence. From the moment this constraint, this constriction of the "must" comes to press the mad energy of a gift, what this constriction provokes is perforce a countergift, an exchange, in the space of the debt. I give you—a pure gift, without exchange, without return—but whether I want this or not, the gift guards itself, keeps itself, and from then on you must-owe, *tu dois*. In order that the gift guard itself, you must-owe. You must at least receive it, already know it, recognize or acknowledge it. The exchange has begun even if the countergift only gives the receiving of the gift. I give you without expecting anything in exchange, but this very renunciation, as soon as it *appears*, forms the most powerful and most interior ligament. This bond of the for-(it)self and the debt, this contracture of sense, is already the ruse of dialectical reason at work as the negative in the holocaust. The gift can be only a sacrifice, that is the axiom of speculative reason. Even if it upsurges "before" philosophy and religion, the gift has for its destination or determination, for its *Bestimmung*, a return to self in philosophy, religion's truth. Always *already*, the gift opens the exchange, chains up, constructs its monuments, calculates on two registers the expenditures and the receipts, the debit [*doit*], the must [*doit*], the goings out, the comings in, to how much it (*ça*) is raised and how much it remains.

So the gift, the giving of the gift, the pure *cadeau*, does not let itself be thought by the dialectics to which it, however, gives rise. The giving of the gift understands itself here before the for-(it)self, before all subjectivity and all objectivity. But when *someone* gives *something* to *someone*, one is already long within calculating dialectics and speculative idealization. I give *me*, I make me the gift [*je me fais cadeau*]. To whom?

If one can speak of the gift in the language [*langue*] of philosophy or the philosophy of religion, one *must say* that the holocaust, the pure gift, the pure *cadeau*, the cake [*gâteau*] of honey or fire hold on to themselves in giving themselves, are never doing anything but exchanging themselves according to the annulus. The gift for (it)self. The prototype of the gift, of the *cadeau*, is then the annulus, the ring or collar or necklace, the chain. The annulus, the chain of the annular anniversary, is not one gift among others; it hands over the gift itself, the very gift of the self (*Selbst*) for (it)self, the present for (it)self. The gift, *cadeau*, names what makes itself present.

Cadeau means *chain*. The word designates, according to Littré, the "Pen strokes [*Traits*] with which the masters of writing embellish their examples," or also, "Large letters placed at the head of acts or chapters in cursively written manuscripts." Or too, "Formerly, feast that one principally gave to women, a pleasure party." The etymology, still according to Littré, would refer to "*Catellus*, small chain, from *catena*, chain . . . because of the chained form of the pen strokes. Household management teaches us that making *cadeaux* is said for making things that appear attractive but are useless, metaphorically compared to those strokes of the hand of the writing masters. From there one passes without trouble to *cadeau* in the sense of diversion, feast, and finally, present." I make me (the) present. In view of whom?

The useless, the specious, the frivolous do not escape the contractual concatenation; on the contrary they engage in it, immediately place in it the debit, the must [*le doit*]. To make themselves [*Se faire*] *cadeau*.

To give means-(to say) to give an annulus, and to give an annulus means-(to say) to guard, to keep: guard the present. (I) give (you) therefore-gift [*donc* as *don*] (I to you) give an annulus therefore-gift (I) guard, keep (you). I lose therefore-gift I win. It is necessary to place the personal pronouns between parentheses. To rethink this movement before the constitution of the *Selbst*. The annular movement re-stricts the general economy (account taken and kept, that is, not taken or kept, of the loss) into a circulating economy. The contraction, the economic restriction forms the annulus of the selfsame, of the self-return, of reappropriation. The economy restricts itself; the sacrifice sacrifices itself. The (con)striction no longer lets itself be circumscribed [*cerner*] as an ontological category, or even, very simply, as a category, even were it a trans-category, a transcendental. The (con)striction—what is useful for thinking the ontological or the transcendental—is then [*donc*] *also* in the position of transcendental trans-category, the transcendental transcendental. All the more because the (con)striction cannot not produce the "philosophical" effect it produces. There is no choosing here: each time a discourse *contra* the transcendental is held, a matrix—the (con)striction itself—constrains the discourse to place the nontranscendental, the outside of the transcendental field, the excluded, in the structuring position. The matrix in question constitutes the excluded as transcendental of the transcendental, as imitation transcendental, transcendental contraband [*contre-bande*]. The contra-band is *not yet* dialectical contradiction. To be sure, the contra-band necessarily becomes that, but its not-yet is not-yet the teleological anticipation, which results in it never becoming dialectical contradiction. The contra-band *remains* something other than what, necessarily, it is to become.

Such would be the (nondialectical) law of the (dialectical) stricture, of the bond, of the ligature, of the garrote, of the *desmos* in general when it comes to clench tightly [*serrer*] in order to make be. Lock [*Serrure*] of the dialectical.

One can follow, if one knows how to read in counter-band [*contre-bande*] (a term borrowed here from the code of blazons), the spiral chaining of the circle of circles. And, the logic of the anniversary, the imposition of the curve on the angle.

How far have we got?

At the limit or the mediation between the first and the second moment of natural religion, between the religion of the pure luminous essence and that of the plant or animal. This is also the passage to the for-(it)self. And, in the history of religion, the passage from sense-certainty to perception.

Why, plant and animal, plant then animal? With the becoming for-(it)self, the opposition interiorizes itself. It no longer scatters itself; it holds itself back, folds itself up, tightly clenched against (it)self, organically unified in the strict unity of the multiplicity. No opposition can form itself without beginning to interiorize itself. This organicity already binds itself again to itself in the plant, but life represents itself therein only by anticipation. The actual war, as opposition internal to the living, is not yet unchained. The plant, as such, lives in peace: substance, to be sure, and there was not yet any substantiality in the light, but peaceful substance, without this inner war that characterizes animality. Already life and self, but not yet the war of desire. Life without desire—the plant is a sort of sister.

Hegel does not say the plant religion, but the "*flower religion*," the "innocence of the *flower religion*." The plant is not the flower, but finds in the flower "*its own* self (ihr eigenes *Selbst*)." The *Encyclopedia* proposes a vast and meticulous deduction of the "vegetable organism," of flowering and fructification (the development of the anther, of the *stilus* (*Griffel*), of the stigma (*Narbe*, scar, cicatrix), and so on), modelled [*réglée*], most often, on *The Metamorphosis of Plants* (Goethe). The subjectivity of the plant is not yet for itself. The criterion for this is classic: the plant does not give itself its own proper place. The "objectivization" by which the vegetal relates itself to itself remains "entirely formal"; it is not "true objectivity." Its differentiation remains external, associative, angular, nearer geometric forms and crystalline regularity. The process of its formation, "the *inner* process of the plant's *relation to itself*" is first a relation to the outside, an exteriorization, an extra-neation, a dispossession (*Entäusserung*); its growth is a hardening, a becoming woody, verily stony (in the case of tabasheer, bamboo salt, for example). The plant is uprooted from itself, toward the outside, by the light. Now the flower sets free an advance in the movement of reappropriation and subjectivization. A moment of relief: the light no longer comes to provoke or uproot from outside; on the contrary, the light engenders itself spontaneously from inside the plant. This passage is analogous to the one that relieves the outer resonance of noise in(to) the voice. Instance of *Klang*. The *color* of the flower manifests this phenomenal auto-determination of the plant. "Consequently, the plant now engenders (*gebiert*) the light from itself, as *its own* self. It does this in the *flower*, in which the neutral color, green, is from the outset determined as a specific color."

A whole theory of colors (here again referred to Goethe and passionately anti-Newtonian) is implied here. And the spontaneous production of the chromatic light, the interiorization of the process, the relation to self, the anthopoetic subjectivity of the plant, all that is also described as the dialectic of a *Hemmung*, of an inhibiting strict-ure. The introjection of the sun, the sublime digestion of the luminous essence, will end in "the heart of the occidental": it begins in the flower.

Flower religion is innocent insofar as the war internal to animality is not yet unchained in it. The relation to self does not yet trigger the war because it does nothing but *represent itself* in the flower. Flower religion (like the flower, as the flower) mimes and anticipates the true self, contains itself in this "self-less representation of the self (*selbstlose Vorstellung des Selbsts*)." The flower plays the "selfsame," does not have the power, or merely has the power to reach there. But as the flower has already begun to subjectivize the luminous essence and the plant, it no longer simply falls (entombed) into dissociative exteriority. The flower is neither an object nor a subject, neither a not-I nor an I, neither a pure alterity without relation to self nor a "*Selbst*." Innocent to be sure, therefore not culpable, not guilty, but its innocence is declared (what would not be done of the sun or the plant) only insofar as the flower is capable of culpability, culpable [*coupable*] of being able to become culpable, cuttable [*coupable*]. Among all these opposites, the essence of the flower appears in its disappearance, vacillates like all the representative mediations, but also excludes itself from the oppositional structure. The flower gives the example of every possible representation, but the circular system of the between-representation permits making the flower the trope of every representative middle or saying that every representation is anthomorphous. The flower at once cuts itself (off) by and from itself and abysses itself.

To adore flowers, to kneel before them, that is possible only on the threshold of culpability. The cult of animals—the totemism to which the *Phenomenology* refers—upsurges, on the contrary, in war, culpability, the struggle to death. Finally relating itself to itself, animal life destroys itself to raise itself to spiritual life, divides itself, opposes itself to itself to erect itself as spirit, in spirit. History, politics begin, in hatred, war, murder, culpability, punishment. One has left the peaceful nomenclature, the taxinomic religion completely occupied with classifying the botanic varieties. This is also the passage from pantheism to polytheism, verily to monotheism. "This pantheism which, to begin with, is the *peaceful* subsistence of these spiritual atoms (*das* ruhige *Bestehen dieser Geisteratome*) develops into a *hostile* movement within itself (feindseligen *Bewegung in sich selbst*)." This movement presupposes a repression of the previous structure: an internal suppression, the effect of a force that is no longer natural, instinctual, and that puts spirit in relation with the universality of the law, whence the origin of culpability. "The innocence of the *flower religion*, which is merely the self-less representation of self (*selbstlose Vorstellung des Selbsts*), passes into the earnestness of warring life, into the culpability of *animal religions*; the tranquility and impotence of contemplative individuality pass into destructive being-for-self. It is of no use to have taken from the things of perception the *death of abstraction*, and to have raised them to the essence of spiritual perception; the animation, the ensoulment (*Beseelung*), of this kingdom of spirits bears this death within it owing to the determinateness and the negativity which encroach upon the innocent indifference of plant life. Through this determinateness and this negativity, the dispersion into multiplicity of peaceful plant forms becomes a hostile movement in which the hatred of their being-for-self consumes them. The *actual* self-consciousness of this dispersed spirit is a host of separate, antagonistic national spirits who hate and fight each other to the death and become conscious of specific forms of animals as their essence; for they are nothing else than animal spirits, animal life that separates itself off from another and conscious of self without universality." In the form and the name of the totemic animal, the spirit calls, names itself, reappropriates itself, but remains yet foreign to itself, does not come back to itself, (close) by itself. The spirit is represented by a determinate, particular, finite species in which its own proper (name) exiles itself. Supplementary classification.

A structural analogy after the other: after the passage from sense-certainty to perception, the dialectic of master and slave. It develops itself in(to) the third moment of natural religion, that of the artisan (*Werkmeister*). Like every moment, that of the artisan announces (itself). Announced and announcing, it represents itself in the previous moment, becomes the representative of the later and higher moment: circle and spiral. But in the moment of the artisan class, one is at the return of the return, the determinate birth of the round form, of the curve, of this particular line that figures however the totality of the process. This befalls the phallic column, according to the very example of Hegel.

So the annulus, the ring, the collar, the necklace, the chain of the gift [*cadeau*], the anniversary circle of the speculative, always turns around a phallic column, whether that column exchanges itself with a finger or an ankle, a waist or a neck [*cou*]. All that finds itself (again) wound round a cylinder, that's the right word, will have placed itself in line with the [à *la taille du*] phallus.

Simultaneously, in the moment of the *Werkmeister* and according to an inner necessity, signification begins to fill itself with voice. Merely begins: in this splendid form, the resonance (*Klang*) that the simple incidence of the light on the stone, the music of the Memnons, produces at dawn.

Let us pick up again. In the totemic war, the for-(it)self is "relieved," destroyed and preserved. It avoids pure and simple death in holding itself back in an object that survives the act of its production, the consuming destruction of its producing self. The spirit then manifests itself as artisan. The artist merely announces and represents himself in the artisan, just as esthetic religion does in the natural religion of the artisan. Spirit appears itself as artisan, and its operation

(*Tun*) makes it yet lose consciousness [*connaissance*]. Spirit produces itself as object, does not retake itself, does not recognize itself entirely. This object is not yet compared to the honey cake but to the *pyramis* whose example does not delay in coming. From the first lines, the operation is nevertheless close, according to a figure that will have become traditional, to the instinctive labor of bees constructing their cells (*ein instinktartiges Arbeiten, wie die Bienen ihre Zellen bauen*). The pyramid erects itself immediately. A lack, however, is remarked there—and thus a representation of what will appear only a little later, the curve, roundness, the curvilinear that can be produced only by the living spirit. Cold, formal, and death-dealing, the understanding proceeds geometrically, cuts [*coupe*] and secures [*arrête*] angular forms. The artisan religion is the history of a rounded angle, the passage from the pyramid to the column, from mathematics or calculus to the incommensurable grace of the spirit. And this passage is a (*re*)(*ful*)*filling*. The round and curvilinear form is more full-of-spirit. "The first form, because it is immediate, is the abstract form of the understanding, and the work (*Werk*) is not yet in its own self filled (*erfüllt*) with spirit. The crystals of pyramids and obelisks, simple combinations of straight lines with plane surfaces and equal proportions of parts, in which the incommensurability of the round is destroyed (*an denen die lnkommensurabilität des Runden vertilgt ist*), these are the works of this artisan of rigid form (*der strengen Form*). On account of the merely abstract intelligibleness (*Verständigkeit*) of the form, this form does not have its signification (*Bedeutung*) within itself, is not the spiritual self. Thus either the works receive spirit into them only as an alien, departed spirit that has forsaken its living interpenetration (*Durchdringung*) with actuality and, being itself dead, takes up its abode in the lifeless crystal; or they have an external relation to spirit as something which is itself there externally and not as spirit—they are related to it as to the dawning light, which casts its significance on them (*als auf das aufgehende Licht, das seine Bedeutung auf sie wirft*)."

One must ceaselessly go back to the philosophy of nature that dictates this interpretation of natural religion. And, in the philosophy of nature, to the relations of space and time, of light and sound in their vast and meticulous deduction. For example, in the course of repeating the "birth of sound" so "difficult to grasp" (*Die Geburt des Klanges ist schwer zu fassen*), the act by which strings, pipes, bars vibrate is described as an "alternating passage from the straight line into the arc." In the process of subjectivizing idealization that the oscillation (*Erzittern*) and the vibration (*Schwingen*) punctuate, the difference between nature and spirit corresponds to the difference between what does not resonate starting from (it)self, the bodies (*Die Körper klingen noch nicht aus sich selbst*), and what resonates with (it)self. The history of *Klang* is what reappropriates itself up to resounding *with* Klang *itself*. "*Klang* properly so called (*eigentliche*)" is in effect pure resonance (*Nachhellen*), "the unhindered inner vibration of the body freely determined by the nature of its coherence." The flux that purely and simply flows [*s'écoule*] does not resonate (*Das bloss Flüssige ist nicht klingend*). The impression freely communicates itself there to the whole, but this communication stems from the total absence of form, to the total lack (*Mangel*) of inner determination. Air and water do not spontaneously resonate, even if their capacity to communicate the *Klang* is recognized. In return, *Klang* presupposes the identity of the determination, is in itself a form. "As compact continuity and equality of matter belong to the pure *Klang*, so the metals (particularly precious metals) and glass (*Glas*) have this clear *Klang* (*diesen klaren Klang*) in themselves. These properties are developed by smelting." If, on the other hand, a bell (*Glocke*) is cracked or scratched (*einen Riss bekommen hat*), no longer is only the pure balancing swinging of the *Klang* heard, but also the noise (*Geräusch*) of the matter that obstructs, that grates, that breaks, that damages the equality of the form. The flat stones, the flagstones (*Steinplatten*) also produce a *Klang*, although they are hard, insensitive, cold, brittle (*spröde*).

In "human song," the external excitation and the vocal timbre are "homogeneous." Only in the voice is "subjectivity or independence of form present." The violin does not *resonate* (*tönt . . . nicht nach*) like the voice; it *sounds* only (*sie tönt nur*) as long as the stretched strings are rubbed.

The process of *Klang* therefore insures the passage from noise to the voice. The description of the *Encyclopedia* takes up again, in its general traits, that of the Jena *Philosophy of Nature*. In the latter, *Klang* was already recognized as that singular repercussion of interiority in exteriority. Sonority in general (*Der Ton*), in the continuity of earthly bodies, has two and only two forms: noise (*Geräusch*) and resonance (*Klang*). Noise expresses merely the immediate, *exterior*, constrained continuity of friction (*Reibung*). *Klang*, on the contrary, its *interior* continuity, by privilege in the case of metal and of glass (*Glas*). But despite this difference (exterior/interior), both, noise and *Klang*, are triggered only by a percussion *come from outside* (*nur ausserlich angeschlagen*). That is what distinguishes them from *sense* (*Sinn*), for example from hearing; is what also distinguishes them from the voice and above all from the reverberating interiority couple that voice and hearing form. Voice is active hearing (*das tätige Gehör*); hearing is the receptive, conceiving voice, as is said of a woman (*die empfangene Stimme*). Through this couple, the sensibility of the individual retakes itself within itself, reassembles itself, gathers itself together, comes to, contracts itself, enters into a contract with itself (*sich in sich zurücknimmt*) and constitutes itself as universal.

Here in this place of the philosophy of nature, in the *Encyclopedia*, heat (the element of fermentation, then of fervor) deduces itself and deduces itself, as strange as that may seem, from *Klang*. For the current representation, sound and heat have nothing to do [*à voir*] with each other, and "it can seem striking (*es kann frappant scheinen*)" to bring them together. *Klang* is the alternation (*Wechsel*) of the reciprocal exteriority of the material parts, of their *Aussereinander*, *and* of its negation, of its being-denied. This negation, as always, produces ideality, but an abstract ideality. The alternation is immediately the negation of the specific exteriority and thus the real identity of cohesion and of specific gravity—what Hegel calls heat. "Sonorous bodies (*klingenden Körper*) will grow hot when they are struck *(geschlagenen)* or rubbed together, and it is in this phenomenon that heat originates with sound in conformity with the concept." There is again a process of *Aufhebung* of materiality there. The setting in motion, swinging, of the body (*Erschütterung*) is not only "relief of matter ideally [*auf ideelle Weise*] presented," it is a "real relief" through heat. Heat is the relief of the body's rigidity (*Aufheben seiner Rigidität*). "There is therefore a direct relation between sound and heat. Heat is the fulfillment (*Vollendung*) of *Klang*. . . . Yet a bell (*Glocke*) will become hot by being struck (*geschlagen*) for example, and this is a heat . . . nor external to it. Not only the musician gets warm, but also the instrument."

From the dead geometric form—rectilinear and plane—the artisan class raises itself to "lifelike roundness." First this is a composite, the mediation of a "blending (*Vermischung*)" announcing the "free architecture" of esthetic religion.

What characterizes this anticipation of the artistic spirit? The hieroglyphic limit of a language insufficiently filled with signification.

This limit also results from a spatialization of language and was already marked in the fact that the sound remains exterior, produced by light, the moment the sun's ray comes to strike the stone. The sun's ray falls on a monument, to be sure, on a stone shaped by the spirit, but which remains stone: white in Egypt, black in Mecca. The limit of language is determined from a certain void in signification. A sensible remain(s) prevents the three-stroke engine from turning over or running smoothly. Yet the remain(s) does nothing but promise a new anniversary.

What the artisan gives a "more lifelike form" to is a habitation (*Behausung*). His art still remains utilitarian; it only anticipates and represents the art of the artist. Nonetheless his art has passed from an unlifelike [*inanimée*] naturalness to a beginning of life and to a prefiguration of the self (*Selbst*).

How did it get there? By making matter vegetate, by bringing matter to a kind of arborescence and efflorescence. Plant-life no longer forms the object of a cult. The flower becomes usable: as an ornament. The *Aesthetics* describes at length the organic figures closest to nature the moment they have just left that nature, when the plant and the tree shoot up into stone structures. Straight up toward the sky, like a "stem," at once supple and rigid (*ein Stamm*, *ein schwanker Stengel*), a slight and strong liana, an erection upheld by a trunk. "The tree trunk already carries, as such, its own corolla, the blade the ear, the stem the flower." The columns derive from the most varied plant-forms (*Pflanzenbildungen*), from lotus plants for example, or onion bulbs. "Then out of this pedestal the slender stem rises up" or climbs by entwining itself (*verschlungen*) as a wreathed column, and the "capital again is a flower-like interlacing of leaves and branches (*blumenartiges Auseinandergehen von Blättern und Zweigen*)." But the imitation of plant nature is not "slavish"; the plant-forms are subject to an architectonic stylization (circle, straight line, regularity of figures): this is the moment of the *arabesque*, the root of "free architecture."

Then the plant is animalized. The artisan resorts to the "*animal form* (Tiergestalt)." The twisted, deformed plant-forms resemble animal bodies. Traversing that rigidity for which the arabesque has been reproached, the for-(it)self constitutes itself.

Recognizing *his* work, the artisan relieves this animal form. The animal form is indeed "*aufgehobene*" the moment it becomes language: first under the form of what is more primitive and subordinated, enslaved in language, to wit a nonphonetic writing: "the animal figure becomes at the same time a relieved figure and the hieroglyph of another signification (*Bedeutung*), of a thought (*Gedankens*)." The animal form makes itself a mute sign or writing the moment the human face [*visage*] appears in the dwelling, the work of the artisan. In Egyptian representations the hieroglyphic blending of animal figures and human figures indicates the specific character of this moment.

The hieroglyph was uprooted from painting, does not show some thing. In expressing a thought the hieroglyph announces language, but its mute writing does not yet reach language. The hieroglyph lacks a self that stands there as such, carrying outside what it is inside, expressing an "inner signification." "It lacks speech," language, tongue (*Sprache*).

What is *Sprache* (*langue* or *langage*, speech or language)? An exteriorization that presents, it gives the there, the *Da-sein*, to the inner signification; but in order to move forward thus into presence, it must first let itself be filled, fulfilled, filled in, accomplished, inflated, curved [*galber*], *rounded* by the sense that penetrates it. It is the "element (*Element*) in which the sense filling itself (*der erfüllende Sinn selbst*) is present (*vorhanden ist*)."

This element is called voice: the spontaneous outside production of an inner sense filling with presence from then on the form of its emission. The spontaneity, the production of self by self gives voice. The sound, resounding ever since the blow [*coup*] struck from the outside, does not utter itself. The sound announces and represents the voice but also holds it back, too much on the outside or too much on the inside.

This moment of the half-voice [*mi-voix*] sculpts its paradigm in the statue of Memnon, son of the dawn, adored by the Ethiopians and the Egyptians. The "colossal sounding statue (*kolossale Klangstatue*)" was ringing under the first rays of the sun. The stroke [*coup*] of light on the block provokes a species of voice, extracts, evokes a voice that is not yet a voice, even when Memnon (*tönend und stimmgebend*) thanks "with its voice" the faithful who come to offer it sacrifices. Even if the work no longer has an animal shape [*figure*], the human face presented there is *tonlose*, noisy but mute: "Therefore the work [of the artisan], even when it is wholly purged of the animal element and wears only the shape of self-consciousness, is still the soundless shape which needs the rays of the rising sun in order to have sound which, generated by light, is even then merely resonance (*Klang*) and not speech (*Sprache*), and shows only an outer, not the inner, self."

The *Klang* of the stony block is *not yet* the voice that it *already* is: neither inside nor outside language, a mediation *or* an excluded middle [*tiers*]. The deciphering of Memnon follows, in the *Aesthetics,* the reading of phallic columns. The Orient, Egypt, Greece used to dedicate a cult to the general vitality (*allgemeine Lebenskraft*) of nature. The cult was directed at the representation of animal "generative organs" that were presented [*mis en scène*] and considered sacred. That above all is the case with the phallus or the *lingam* (a hieratic representation of the phallus for Indians; the word designates the mark and the genre—the class—*and* the phallus). Often cited, Herodotus recalls that on the occasion of the Dionysia, "'instead of phalli they have invented other images, a cubit long, fit with a thread.'" Phallophoric women pull on the thread, and the sex is always raised ('*sich . . . immer hebt*'), nearly as tall as the rest of the body.

In India more than elsewhere the phallic representation is architectural: enormous columns and towers of stone larger at the base than at the top. One begins to worship them for themselves, then sets about making openings (*Öffnungen*), holes, incisions, excavations (*Aushöhlungen*) in which images of gods are inserted. They appear there. This practice is found again in the hermetic columns of Greece. The legendary representation of gods, the images, the idols, the altars come to be inscribed as tattooing on the smooth surface of these rigid columns.

Now the origin of this process [*processus*] of excavation, its *Ausgangspunkt*, is the nonperforated columns (*unausgehöhlten Phallussäulen*). The incisions would have come over columns originally unbreached. Besides, they are rather rare and tend quickly to disappear.

Later the columns are transformed into high and narrow habitations—pagodas—separated into shell and kernel.

Herodotus also mentions male columns that included, by way [*titre*] of ornament or adornment, signs of the feminine organ. He saw them only in Syria, attributes them to Sesostris, and interprets them, according to Hegel, in Greek, in true Greek, in the Greek sense: he transforms their "naturalistic signification" into "one concerned with ethical life (*Sittliche*)." "'In the countries where the people were brave in battle against Sesostris during his wars, he erected columns on which he inscribed (*Inschriften*) his own name and country and how he had reduced these peoples to subjection; where, on the contrary, they submitted without a struggle he added to this inscription on the column a female *pudendum* to indicate that they had been cowardly and unwarlike.'" The properly Greek interpretation, in the Greek sense (*im griechischem Sinne*), deciphers then the ethical in the natural, and this passage from nature to *Sittlichkeit* merges with the phallocentric hierarchization. The Greek interpretation associates the positive ethical values, verily sense itself, with virility.

Then the Memnon statues upsurge. Obelisks had marked the transition. And they have the symbolic value of the sun's rays. Obelisks themselves represent luminous rays, gold ingots, or helioid genitals. Egyptian letters came at times to be engraved in the obelisk's petrified light. Heliogravure, as at Heliopolis where Mithras, god of the Medes and the Persians, let himself be enjoined, through a dream, to build obelisks, "'the sun's rays in stone (*Sonnenstrahlen in Stein*),'" and to engrave thereon letters ('*Buchstaben darauf enizugraben*') "'called Egyptian.'"

At Thebes the large statues of Memnon did not speak, although they had human shape. Some were monolithic (Strabo saw some), others were formed of two colossi seated.

How does language come to the column? By an inner sun. In the meantime, the column must be weaned from the sensible sun. The sensible sun must be denied, and the stone must do without the daylight. Therefore the phallus blinds itself, loses the outside, the light, the form, the *eidos*. The white stone becomes black. The *Behausen*—the casing or abode, *l'habitacle*, as phallus—gains the *Selbst*'s essential interiority only by plunging itself into the night, by elaborating its language in the black and formless stone.

This is the Kaaba, the black stone of Mecca: no remains; all is scraped clean, fished out, inscribed, relieved.

An interiority still negative, covering over the white stone, "cover of the inside": "Over against this outer *Selbst* [Memnon] of the figure stands the other figure which proclaims its possession of an *interior*. Nature, withdrawing into its essence, deposes its living, self-particularizing, self-entangling manifold existence to the level of an unessential casing (*unwesentlichen Gehäuse*), which is the *cover for the interior* (Decke des Inneren); and this interior is, in the first instance, still simple darkness, the unmoved, the black, formless stone."

The artisan finds himself caught in this driving contradiction between the system of the (lost and relieved) white stone and that of the black stone relieving the other only in order yet to lose true interiority by lacking voice. So the two presentations (*Darstellungen*) of the inside and the outside need to be united or reconciled. How is the artisan to elaborate this contradiction?

In an enigmatic way.

Here one has to distinguish between the enigmatic and the oracular. The oracle will be, in esthetic religion, the analog of the enigma, its voiced counterpart.

The artisan resolves the contradiction by producing enigmas composing the two contraries, nature and consciousness, inside and outside, the clear and the obscure. A spirit's word, a witticism [*mot d'esprit*], is in question: difficult to decipher, nocturnal in its form, appealing as well to the unconscious, a profound wisdom unable to give its reasons, a kind of cryptogram the Egyptians themselves, to believe the *Aesthetics* on this, did not understand. The producer of the enigma can be irresponsible, blind to what is written with his own hand. "The artisan therefore unites the two by blending the natural and the self-conscious shape, and these ambiguous essences, enigmas to themselves, the conscious wrestling with the nonconscious, the simple inner with the multiform outer, the darkness of thought mating with the clarity of utterance, these break out in the language of a profound, but scarcely intelligible wisdom."

The first language properly so called is thus "double (*zweideutig*)," enigmatic; it brings into play the contraries between the conscious and the unconscious, on two scenes at once.

The paradigm for this is furnished by the Egyptian religion. The philosophy of religion interprets it as a "religion of enigma," of obscurity, of animal masks, of the walled-in unconscious. The Egyptian spirit lacks that unveiled transparency characterizing the Greek. Its veil *represents by anticipation* the Greek unveiling. So the representation is a veil, the veil a representation. "The most important presentation (*Hauptdarstellung*) by which the essence of this combat [between the conscious and the unconscious, the clear and the obscure, and so on] is made completely accessible to intuition (*anschaulich*) is the image of the goddess at Saïs (Neith) who was presented (*dargestellt*) veiled (*verschleiert*). It is symbolized therein and in the inscription in her temple—'I am what was, is, and shall be; my veil has been lifted by no mortal'—expressly declared that nature *is a being-differentiated in* (*it*)*self*, namely, *an other opposed to its manifestation but which immediately offers itself*, an *enigma*."

The veil does not symbolize the enigma. The enigma is the structure of the veil suspended between the contraries.

Does Hegel then construe [*fait*] a word, does he then play in a vicious way, in the Egyptian manner, on the signifiers? Citing the end of the inscription of Neith's temple in Lower Egypt, he deciphers it in Greek-German in order to read in it the whole course of the sun setting in the West and recalling itself within itself. The history of this *Erinnerung* is a family history. The spiritual sun is at once the son and the father of the sensible sun, the same and the circular inverse of the one that lighted in sum the Republic. Here its purpose is to announce the hermeneutic and teleological resolution of the enigma in the Greek (esthetic) religion, then in the Christian (revealed) religion: "It [nature] has an inner element, something that is hidden (*ein Inneres*, *Verborgenes*). But, it is stated further in this inscription, 'the fruit of my flesh is Helios.' This as yet hidden essence therefore expresses clearness, the sun, the becoming clear to oneself, the spiritual sun (*geistige Sonne*) as the *son* (*den* Sohn) who is born of her. It is this clearness which is attained to in the Greek and Jewish religion, in the former in art and in the beautiful human form, in the latter in objective thought. The *enigma* is solved; the Egyptian *Sphinx*, according to a deeply significant (*bedeutungsvollen*) and admirable myth, was slain by a Greek, and thus the enigma has been solved. This means that the content is *man, free*, *self-knowing spirit*."

The Oedipian resolution of the enigma sounds the end of natural religion in its last moment. Thought attains the clarity of its unveiled there (*Da-sein*); the artisan becomes a "spiritual laborer," conscious of his activity, artist. The instinctive, almost animal, elaboration is now an art.

An essentially Greek history, opened by the death of the Sphinx, the esthetic religion is developed, it too, according to the ternary rhythm of a syllogism: the *abstract* work of art, the *living* work of art, the *spiritual* work of art. This is the same rhythm, with an analogous content, as that of natural religion (indeterminate abstraction of the luminous essence, life of plants and animals, spirituality), each of the three moments dividing itself in its turn in three, according to a syllogistic structure infinitely representative of itself and always abyssal. But is the abyss saturated or hollowed out by a "*mise en abyme*"? Then, to hollow out, is that to run a risk? And in view of what?

The abstract work of art maintains the figure of the gods in the block of the spatial thing. But in this the concept strips off the angular crystal of the understanding, the blending of the inorganic and plant forms, imitation in general. The black stone is drawn out from its animal gangue; the represented figures are no longer the essences of nature but of lucid spirits, the ethical spirits of self-conscious nations. As long as they are singular national figures, Athena for example, they still keep in themselves a certain natural density, a scrap [*relief*] of nature. This naturalness must be relieved. But as long as the work does not belong to the element of the tongue, as long as it extends itself into space, it remains and falls (entombed) outside the operation of the artist. It is opposed to him. The whole of the work is cut off [*coupé*], like a remain(s), from its elaboration.

This caesura takes two contradictory and indissociable forms overlapping each other [*se recoupent*] ceaselessly. On the one hand, this is the effacement, the omission of the artist: he is sufficiently disinterested to declare that his work lives by itself, animates itself without him, removes his signature. But by removing it, the work keeps it, and under this modernic thematic (*thématique modernitaire*], Hegel immediately discloses, on the other hand, the ruse or the dissembled, dissembling reverse, the hypocrisy of the other one-sidedness. In effect the artist verifies that the work, by being able thus to cut itself off and fall (to the tomb) from him, *is not his equal*, that it has not produced an essence equal to its author (kein ihm gleiches *Wesen hervorbrachte*). The animation proper to the work, the admiration of admirers, the offerings, verily the sacrifices it provokes and that bring it to consciousness—the artist therefore knows all that is inferior to his labor, to his elaboration, his production, precisely because that *detaches* itself from him. By his withdrawal [*retrait*] the artist consequently raises himself above his remain(s) and in the same stroke [*du même coup*] detains it as a small part, a morsel of himself. The signature's omission, its nonappearance, simultaneously engages an operation of mastery and the mastery of the operation. All this must be recognized as the *fact* (Tat) of the artist in his untiring strategy. If the admirers "put themselves *below* (darunter *setzen*) it and recognize in it the *essence* which dominates them, he knows himself as the master (*Meister*) of this essence."

Hegel to a lover of autographs: "Had the wish of adding something from my hand as well to a collection of handwriting samples reached me directly, I would have requested some kind of content to be dictated to me. I cannot now make this request in writing, for this very act would render the request superfluous. So allow the superfluity of having submitted the request and thereby at once annihilated it suffice. Berlin, 6 July 1827. H."

In order to cicatrize this cut [*cicatriser cette coupure*] between the elaboration and the work, between the author and his remain(s), in order—then—to think it, the work must *remain present* to the artist, without falling from him like a thing truncated in space, like some wonderful excrement on top of which the master sits enthroned while forgetting himself. The element of art then will no longer be something in space and without consciousness; it will be time and voice. Even if—and insofar as—time is the truth of the space it relieves. The work must find time in order to become consciousness present to itself. The stone must set about speaking: "The work of art therefore demands another element of its *Dasein*, the god another process of coming forth (*Hervorgang*) than this, in which, out of the depths of his creative night, he falls into the opposite [*in das Gegenteil*—its opposing morsel—*herabfällt*], into externality, into the determination of the *thing* unconscious of itself. This higher element is *language* (Sprache)—a *Dasein* that is immediately self-conscious existence (*Existenz*). Just as the *individual* self-consciousness is there (*da ist*) in language, so is it also immediately as a *universal* contagion (*Ansteckung*)." The soul therefore exists "as soul."

The *hymn* is this presence of the universal to the singular, of inside to outside, of the production to the work, of the god to its animated figure. The religious song, the fervent flow of the religious voice gathers the singularities together in one same element of fire and water (*die Andacht, in allen angezündet, ist der geistige Strom*). It flows [*coule*] and consumes all the remains [*tous les restes*].

Yet, contrary to habit, after the hymn a remain(s) is discussed and will form the subject of a longer and more involved development. It is a question of the *oracle*: the oracle relates to the time of speaking [*parole*] as the enigma relates to the space of writing. Simple and universal, oracular propositions come from outside the community (unlike the hymn, the experience of inner communion). They are sublime, but their universality easily turns to triviality, above all in the first time of the oracle, that of natural religion and of the luminous essence. In becoming for-(it)self, the oracle finds again the universal truths in a language *proper* to the community: this is, for example, Antigone's "*sure and unwritten law*," the law of the gods who speak in the citizens' hearts. This relief of the "natural" oracle suspends chance, luck, the throw of the dice in speech [*langue*]. The natural and impulsive oracle is that fortuitous case wherein language [*langage*] falls over/upon universal truth. Whence a kind of dividing in two of the oracle: one's very own [*proper*] language and a foreign language. Socrates, for example, looks within himself for philosophy's voice, but he lets the foreign speaking of his demon inspire, prompt [*souffler*] in him unnecessary counsels, contingent precepts, tell his fortune, talk with him about the opportunity for a journey, and so on. "In the same way the universal consciousness draws knowledge of the contingent from birds, or trees, or the fermenting earth, the vapors from which deprive self-consciousness of its power of reflection. For the contingent is the unreflective and the foreign, and therefore the ethical consciousness lets itself settle such matters too, as by a throw of the dice (*wie durch ein Würfeln*), in an unreflective and foreign manner." The oracle as such, before the inner and unwritten law, is bound to the lot (*Los*). *Das Orakel oder Los*.

The petroglyph remains outside consciousness. Its antithesis, the hymn, immediately disappears, like the voice, the very moment it is produced. Like time, it is no longer *there* straightaway, immediately, as soon as it is *there*, inasmuch as it is *there* (*wie die Zeit, unmittelbar nicht mehr da, indem sie da ist*). The *Da* is posited inasmuch as it withdraws. In its counter-time [*contre-temps*]. Abstract art is made of this double one-sidedness: spatial nonmovement and temporal movement, the double loss of the divine figure, plastic art and lyric art.

This double loss is relieved in(to) the *cult*. From its beyond, the divine essence descends there as far as consciousness. The cult is first of all abstract and is announced in the fervor of the hymn that is limited to its representation: inner, secret, nonactual. This is the moment of inner purification wherein the soul does not know it is the evil. The soul purifies its surface with the waters and re-covers that surface with white linens. But the cult must not be secret; it must give rise to gestures, to actual operations: sacrifice and enjoyment, the ruse of enjoyment in the sacrifice. The act of the cult, its handling (*Handlung*), begins with abandonment (*Hingabe*), the renunciation of possessing and enjoying, without apparent benefit. But the sacrifice recaptures with one hand what it gives with the other, and its account must be kept on a double register. What is sacrificed goes up "in smoke (*in Rauch*)" as the effluvium of a consuming destruction or a decomposition. But it is retained [*gardé*] in the sublimiry of its essence, as a spirit. The sacrificed animal becomes the sign of a god; the consum(mat)ed fruits *are* the living Ceres and Bacchus. The sacrifice reappropriates the enjoyment, but the "ruse" of the enjoyment removes itself; it consumes itself: ". . . the result, in the enjoyment, is itself robbed of its being-there (*das Resultat im* Genusse *sich selbst seines Daseins beraubt*)."

The end of enjoyment is the end of enjoyment: the final point, period. The bone or snag [*L'os*: in German, the lot, *Los*; in Latin, the mouth, *os*] of enjoyment, its chance and its loss, is that enjoyment must sacrifice itself in order to be there, in order to give itself its *there*, in order to touch, and tamper with, its *Dasein*. *Telos* [*tel os*: such *os*] of enjoyment equals death—that would be the end-point (the point-of-no-end-at-all) if there were not, for the untiring desire of speculative dialectics, yet one more turn, annuli yet to be accomplished, and anniversaries to be celebrated.

The antithesis of sacrifice and enjoyment relieves itself in(to) labor, but in(to) the enjoyment of labor, in(to) the enjoyment of the durable products of the elaboration deferring the enjoyment. The dwelling and the ornament of the gods, this whole reliable pomp no longer has the naturalness of statues. And it is elaborated by man reappropriating the enjoyment of this pomp in the feast. The places and the objects of the cult, the altars, the temples, and so on, are like the hard bone [*comme l'os dur*: like the hard mouth, the hard lot] that remains from sacrifices and the consum(mat)ed enjoyment, to be sure, but they occupy the place of labor in the city. With the god the human producer shares in this all the enjoyments of the feast. "At the feast, this people adorns its own dwellings and garments, no less than its ceremonies, with graceful decorations. In this way, they receive in exchange (*Erwiderung*) for their gifts a return from the grateful god (*dankbaren Gotte*) and proofs of his favour, in which through their labor they become bound (*verband*) to him, not as a hope and in a future realization (*späten Wirklichkeit*), but rather, in witnessing to his glory and in bringing (*Darbringung*) him gifts, the nation has the immediate enjoyment of its own wealth and adornment."

This is the feast of labor and the labor of the feast in the Greek city. The sacrifice reappropriates the enjoyment lost through labor in the cult; and the cult is an exchange of labor with the god who restores to the laborers the *immediate* enjoyment of the products they have renounced, without apparent hope of return. The god pays back [*reverse*] to the laborers the sacrifice of the surplus value. Gift contra gift: I give you or sacrifice for you this here that takes on more value in being sacrificed, an object of useless ornament, lost adornment. The recognition of the addressee [*destinataire*] restores the enjoyment; and the feast, this feast at least, far from opening up a pure and impossible disseminal expenditure, organizes, strictly, the circulation of enjoying in the cult. *Telos* of the cult, to speculate the enjoyment of God and to treat oneself to it.

in following the phenomenological gallery ("This becoming presents (*stellt . . . dar*) a slow-moving succession of spirits, a gallery of images (*eine Galerie von Bildern*), . . ."), from station to station, one comes back toward the *IC* and *Sa*, past the "Calvary of absolute Spirit." One finds there again, very close to the "Calvary"—to be inspected on both sides—the "certainty of his throne (*Gewissheit seines Throns*)."
It is enough in sum, only just so, to wait.
All that will have been projected, pulled to pieces, closed, nailed down, fallen (to the tomb), relieved, repeated, round about Easter.
The circle of the phenomenological gallery is reproduced and encircled in the greater *Logic* and the *Encyclopedia*. What is the difference between two editions of the same circle? Hegel, who had just learned of "the rapid sale of the second edition" of the *Encyclopedia*, confides in Winter, in 1827, his worries. He asks Winter to "commit . . . to the prompt payment of the royalty." "For the original eighteen sheets in the first edition we settled upon two-thirds of the 25 florin royalty. For the additional number of sheets we reverted to this original royalty, and for the further eighteen sheets of the second edition we agreed on 22 florins per sheet. In this agreement I reserved for myself the royalties of the first edition for the additional material contained in any new edition. . . . Whether, and by how much, this number of sheets might still be increased in the contemplated new edition I cannot yet say, since the task catches me by surprise, and since I have not yet had a chance to run through the text with this in mind. In general, however, I do not foresee undertaking any significant change or expansion. The printing remains fixed as before at a thousand copies, with eighteen complimentary author's copies, twelve on vellum and six on writing paper. "Since I have been notified so late of the need for a new edition—Mr. Oswald's letter is dated July 13—the manuscript may be sent off later than you probably would wish. Seeing how my work has since piled up, I cannot yet say anything definite on when it will be. I shall do my best, however, to enable the edition to appear by Easter."

We are in the Dionysian circle. The third moment of abstract art, the religion inscribed in that moment, is already the most abstract phase of the subsequent moment, the living work of art. Through its syllogism a process of language still busies itself with the relief of the remain(s).

The first one-sided moment is the bacchic delirium, the *Taumel*, the unbounded intoxication in the course of which the god makes himself present. The ascendant luminous essence unveils itself as what it is. Enjoyment is the mystery of this revelation. For the mystical does not lie in the dissembling of a secre (*Geheimnis*) or an unknown. But what lays itself bare here still belongs to immediate spirit, to spirit-nature. The mystery of bread and wine is *not yet what* it is, *already*, that of flesh and blood. Dionysus then must pass into his contrary, appease himself to exist, not let himself be drunk and consum(mat)ed by the "crowd of frenzied females."

So he does gymnastics.

Apollo is not named, to be sure; but the antithesis, the opposite, the opposing party, the contrary stance into which the Dionysian must pass in order to "appease itself in making itself *object* (*sich zum* Gegenstande *beruhigen*)," stands up as the erect(ed) body in Greek gymnastics, the beautiful "*Körperlichkeit*." The figure of man cultivates itself in place of, on behalf of, the sculptural column of the divinity. The divine lets itself be reappropriated in the human: an exchange still of two erections, two institutions, setting in motion and renewal of life. Surplus value of the contradiction that contracts (itself) with itself, makes itself, after all, the gift of the remain(s) [*se fait du reste cadeau*].

But once more, a balancing movement, everything settles itself in the outer objectivity that was set opposite the Dionysian fiery passion [*embrasement*]. So one has two opposed morsels that contradict one another in their respective one-sidedness. The balance (*Gleichgewicht*] is unceasingly broken. In delirium, the self (*Selbst*) loses consciousness; on the stadium [*sur le stade*, in this stage] spirit is what is outside itself.

Through the spiritual work of art—language right through—reconciliation is announced: the synthesis of esthetic religion (abstraction, life, spirit). The syllogism of spiritual art (*epos*, tragedy, comedy) leads esthetic religion to revealed religion. Through comedy then.

A time to perfect the resemblance between Dionysus and Christ.
Between the two (already) is elaborated in sum the origin of literature.
But it runs to its ruin [*perte*], for it counted without [*sans*]

CHAPTER 16

"The Eternal Irony of the Community"

—from *Speculum of the Other Woman* (1974)

Luce Irigaray

> On the one hand, the uterus in the male is reduced to a mere gland, while on the other, the male testicle in the female remains enclosed within the ovary, fails to emerge into opposition, and does not become an independent and active cerebrality. The clitoris moreover, is inactive feeling in general; in the male on the other hand, it has its counterpart in active sensibility, the swelling vital, the effusion of blood into the corpora cavernosa and the meshes of the spongy tissue of the urethra. The female counterpart of this effusion of blood in the male consists of the menstrual discharges. Thus, the simple retention of the conception in the uterus, is differentiated in the male into productive cerebrality and the external vital. On account of this difference therefore, the male is the active principle; as the female remains in her undeveloped unity, she constitutes the principle of conception.
>
> 'In the case of the eye,' says *Sömmerring,* 'it seems that the arteries are continued in finer branches, which no longer contain red blood. These branches pass initially into a similar vein, but finally into veinlets carrying red blood.'
>
> —Hegel

The purpose that moves blood relatives to action is the care of the *bloodless.* Their inherent duty is to ensure *burial for the dead,* thus changing a natural phenomenon into a spiritual act. One more step (into negation) and we see that it is the task of womankind, guardian of the blood tie, to gather man into his final figuration, beyond the turmoil of contingent life and the scattered moments of his Being-there. Man is thereby raised into the peace of simple universality. In essence, woman has to take it upon herself over and over again, regardless of circumstances, to bury this corpse that man becomes in his pure state. She has to enable man to sublate a universality that smacks too much of the natural, or so it would seem, by affirming—for this is pure truth restored—that death is merely the peace of/and universality of the conscious essence of self. Man is still subject to (natural) death, of course, but what matters is to make a movement of the mind out of this accident that befalls the single individual and, in its raw state, drives consciousness out of its own country, cutting off that return into the self which allows it to become self-consciousness. Just as man must strive to make this negativeness into an ethical action by sacrificing his life for the city—in war for example—so woman must be that external and effective mediation that reconciles the dead man with himself *by taking upon herself the operation of destruction* that the becoming of mind cannot manage without. Thus woman takes this dead being into her own place on his return into the self—a being that is universal, admittedly, but also singularly drained of strength, empty and yielded passively up to others. She must protect him both from all base and irrational individuality and from the forces of abstract matter, which are now more powerful than he. Shielding him from the dishonoring operation of unconscious desires and natural negativeness—*preserving him from her desire, perhaps*?—she places this kinsman back in *the womb of the earth* and thus reunites him with undying, elemental individuality. To do this is also to reassociate him with a—religious—community that controls the violent acts of singular matter and the base urges which, unleashed upon the dead man, might yet destroy him. This supreme duty constitutes the divine law, or *positive* ethical action, as it relates to the individual.

Yet, on the other hand, human law places a negative meaning upon this individualism. In fact each member of the city has a right both to a living and to Being-for-itself, wherein the mind finds its reality and its being-there. But the mind is at the same time the strength of the whole, and hence it gathers *these individual parts* into *one negative entity*. The mind reminds the parts that they are dependent upon this totality and that they owe their *life* to it entirely. Thus any associations—such as families—that one assumes have been founded primarily to serve individual ends, whether the acquisition of personal wealth or the search for sexual pleasures, invite a war that may disrupt their intimate life and violate their independence since these threaten to shatter the whole. All those who persist in following the dictates of individualism must be taught by the government to fear a master: death. They must be prevented from sinking into the neutral Being-there, from regressing into the inner world of the senses, from ecstatically entering a world beyond, lacking all predicates that can be appropriated by the self of consciousness. *The cult of the dead and the cult of death* would thus be the point where divine law and human law join. And also that point where, at least on the higher ethical level, the relationship between man and woman is possible.

This unsullied relationship takes place only *between brother and sister*. They are the same blood, but in them blood is at rest and in balance. Thus they do not desire each other, they have neither given nor received this Being-for-the-self from each other, they are free individualities vis-à-vis each other. What is it, then, that impels them to unite so that finally one passes into the other? What meaning does each have for the other that draws them thus into this exchange? Is it recognition of *blood*? Of their common allegiance to the power of the *same blood*? Could it be their complicity in the permanence, the continuance of blood that a matriarchal type of lineage ensures in its purest and most universal being? In this sense the family of Oedipus would be quite exemplary because the mother of the husband is also his wife, thus re-marking the blood tie between the children of that union—including Polynices and Antigone. Furthermore, the uncle—the mother's brother—will in this family be the representative of an already patriarchal power. Or is it rather that brother and sister share in the *same sperm,* thus giving consanguineity an (other) equilibrium, ridding it of its own magic passion but counterbalancing it with another? In fact, however, the sperm does not join with the blood (though it was long thought to do so) but with the ovum: had this copulation been given its full weight and "effectiveness," it would already have irremediably shattered the unity of mind and ethical substance. Moreover, copulation takes place only in the impure mingling of the marriage of husband and wife. Are we then to seek this pact between sister and brother in a *common name,* in the notion that their co-uterine attraction is matched by their submission—represented by the patronymic—to symbolic rules that might be supposed to carry the potency of blood one step further and already to raise the family community to the types of laws in force in the city?

Thus, for one instant, brother and sister would recognize each other in their single self, each able to affirm a right that is achieved through the power each has when balanced in/by the other; the power of red blood and of its reabsorption, its sublation into a process of denominating—i.e., of semblance. An ideal distribution would hypothetically occur in which the (ethical) substance of matriarchy and of patriarchy would coexist, contributing their own subsistence to each other, in a peace without alloy, a relationship without desire. The war of the sexes would not take place here. But this moment is mythical, of course, and the *Hegelian dream* outlined above is already the effect of a dialectic produced by the discourse of pariarchy. It is a consoling fancy, a truce in the struggle between uneven foes, a denial of the guilt already weighing heavily upon the development of the subject; it is the delusion of a *bisexuality* assured for each in the connection and passage, one into the other, of each sex. Yet both sexes, male and female, have already yielded to a destiny that is different for each. This is so even if rape, murder, breaking and entering, injury, were still, in appearance at least, in general at least, suspended between brother and sister. But in fact such is not the case, as Hegel admits when he affirms that the brother is for the sister that possibility of recognition of which she is deprived as mother and wife, but does not state that the situation is reciprocal. This means that the brother has already been invested with a value for the sister that she cannot offer in return, except by devoting herself to his cult after death.

Certainly, in the work of Sophocles, which marks the historical bridge between matriarchy and patriarchy, things are not yet that clear. No decision has yet been made about what has more value. On the one hand, *blood is no longer pure* in Sophocles: the father, at least for a time, was king; the king thereby affirms his rights as father, as well as the complicity between family (patriarchal) power and that of the State. And tragedy enacts the punishment that is incurred by a taste for blood. On the other hand, *the privilege of the proper name is not yet pure*: the power of the father's name, had its right already been in force, should have prevented Oedipus from committing murder and incest. But this is not what happens. Moreover, the fact that each sister and brother has a double also indicates that this is still a transition in which the extremes—which will later be defined as being more masculine or more feminine: i.e., Eteocles and Ismene—seem almost like caricatures. Now, whereas Ismene is termed a sister because she shares *the same blood* as Antigone, and whereas Polynices is termed a brother because he was born of *the same mother,* Eteocles is brother because he is the son of *the same father and the same mother*.

These things can be stated in other ways. *Ismene* seems indisputably a "woman" in her weakness, her fear, her submissive obedience, her tears, madness, hysteria—all of which in fact are met with condescending scorn on the part of the king. Ismene is subsequently shut up, as a punishment, in the palace, the house, with the other women, who are all thus deprived of their freedom of action for fear they may sap the courage of the most valiant warriors. For *Antigone* things are less simple, and the king himself fears she may usurp his manhood—"Better be beaten, if need be, by a man, than let a woman get the better of us."[1]—if she does not pay for her insolence with death. Antigone does not yield to the law of the city, of its sovereign, of the man of the family: Creon. And she will choose to die a virgin, unwedded to any man, rather than sacrifice the ties of blood, rather than abandon her mother's son to the dogs and vultures, leaving his double to roam in eternal torment. Better to die than to refuse service to the divine law and to the attraction she feels for the gods below. There her jouissance finds easier recognition, no doubt, since her allegiance to them frees her from the inventions of men. She defies them all by/in her relationship to Hades. In her nocturnal passion she acts with a perversity which has nothing in common with the wretched crimes that men stoop to in their love for money, or so the king says. Indeed she boasts of this, stating publicly that she had rather die than give up such practices. And that, moreover, *between her and the king, nothing can be said.* She alone among the Cadmeans, *the literates*, reasons thus. At least out loud. In this way, she becomes the voice, the accomplice of the people, the slaves, those who only whisper their revolt against their masters secretly. Without friends, without husband, without tears, she is led along that *forgotten path* and there is *walled up* alive in *a hole* in the rock, shut off forever from the light of the sun. Alone in her crypt, her cave, her den, her womb, she is given just enough food by those who hold power to ensure that the city is not soiled and shamed by her decay. She is alone in confronting the underground god in order to see—again—if she will survive that solitary ritual.[2] But love, for her, has far too many fatal representations for her desire to recover from such punishments. However guiltless, she feels she bears the burden of her mother's fatal marriage, feels guilty for being born of such terrible embraces. Thus she is damned, and by consenting to a punishment she has not merited and yet cannot escape, at the least she accepts on her own account the death knell of her jouissance—*or is mourning itself her jouissance*?—by killing herself. Does she thus anticipate the decree of death formulated by those in power? Does she duplicate it? Has she given in? Or is she still in revolt? She repeats, in any case, upon herself the murderous, but not bloody, deed of her mother. Whatever her current arguments with the laws of the city may have been, another law is still drawing her along her path: identification with her mother. *But how are mother and wife to be distinguished*? This is the dreadful paradigm of a mother who is both wife and mother to her husband. Thus the sister will strangle herself in order to save at least the mother's son. She will cut off her breath—her voice, her air, blood, life—with the veil of her belt, returning into the shadow (of a) tomb, the night (of) death, so that her brother, *her mother's desire,* may have eternal life. She never becomes a woman. But she is not as masculine as she might seem if seen from an exclusively phallic viewpoint—for it is tenderness and pity that have motivated her. Rather, she is a captive of a desire whose path has reached a dead end, has never been blazed. And did she seek the relationship with the mother in *Polynices* because he was the more feminine of the brothers? The younger? Or at any rate the weaker, the one who is rejected. The more irritable and impulsive one, who in his anger will seek to open the veins of his blood again. He who is armed for/by the love of a woman, married, unlike his siblings, and through that foreign match condemning his sister to die buried alive. At least in his passion for blood he has annulled the right of his brother—*Eteocles*—to command, has destroyed his brother's—his elder's?—relation to power, reason, property, the paternal succession. And has, with the same blow, killed himself.

Yet the government's mode of action remains unchanged. Another man was ready to take up the challenge: *Creon*. He also is alone—like Antigone—but he has the instrument of the law. Desperate he is, no doubt, but he yet claims that all power is his alone. Though he has brought son and wife to utter destruction, he climbs back onto the throne, without love, and the scepter remains in his hands. Death-stricken he is, and/but regulating his practice rigidly. Inflexible in his severity. Implacable in his reasons. His fragile strength, as apt to be broken as to break, demands that he fear pleasure, domination by women, the passion of youth represented by his son, the plots of the people, the slaves' revolt, even the gods (who are still controlled and divided by desires), soothsayers, therefore, and finally the "elders." He defends his privilege of being the sole safeguard of speech, truth, intelligence, reason—the fairest of all possessions—though at the same time he raves a little wildly in his relations with the gods and with women, for example. And in this mass grave of all the members of his family—Ismene is set aside in a golden prison which a change of ruler in fact risks transforming into a simple private home—in this general outflowing of blood, he thus (thereby) remains *one*. But nonetheless, he is *broken* between a self-sureness that is now only misfortune—is he not a superfluous man, weighed down by unbearable destiny, for whom everything and everybody has become equally contingent?—and the rigid sovereignty of a Being-for-the-self empty of content (of the substance of blood), an omnipotence alien to itself. A man who receives his personal power only by exercizing a right that has resolved all (blood) ties between individuals into abstract universality. Soon a God, but a god without any desire but that of submitting everyone to the law of blood congealed in the status of semblance: the Ego.

This is a necessary moment in the development of the mind, but Hegel expresses almost melancholic regret of/in this passage, and the dream of going back to that attraction to the/his sister which is unmingled (by blood). Back to the time when the species and genus had, it seems, not yet come into being, and when that unity, that individuality, *that still living, blood subject* simply took place. And in the nostalgia aroused by this return into the past. Hegel reveals his desire for a relationship that is certainly sexuate but does not need to pass through the realization of sexual desire. Desire intervenes to break the harmony unified in its blood cycle, in which brother and sister are theoretically between the phases—still relatively undifferentiated in their animality—of blood's circulation: inspiration/expiration, fluidity/hardening, apprehension/resorption of an outside. Thus one (male or female) would breathe out while the other would begin to breathe in, he/she would be becoming red blood while the other would return to self in his/her veins, he/she would affirm atomic individuality as cell(s) while the other would remain lymph, he/she would return to the earth in the form of carbon at the very moment when the other is rousing from torpor and taking fire, etc. But perhaps they are already irremediably separated throughout that process called *digestion*. For if the female one can recognize herself in the male one, who has therefore supposedly assimilated her, the reverse is not necessarily true. And if Antigone gives proof of a bravery, a tenderness, and an anger that free her energies and motivate her to resist that *outside* which the city represents for her, this is certainly because she had digested the masculine. At least partially, at least for a moment. But perhaps this will have been possible only at the time when she is mourning for her brother, just long enough to give him back the manhood he had lost in death and to feed his soul therewith. And to die in the act.

Already, then, the balance of blood has been upset, changed, dissolved. And the unadulterated happiness that is to be had from digesting one's own substance, from giving oneself fluidity, from breaking into one's own movement, from giving birth to oneself, is not shared equally between male and female, brother and sister. But, as long as the sister goes on in her living unity she can be the self-representative basis of that substance—the blood—that the brother assimilates in order to return to the self. She can guarantee that the son develops for himself (pour soi), independently of the couple that made him: she is *the living mirror,* the source reflecting the growing autonomy of the self-same. She is the privileged place in which red blood and its semblance harmoniously (con)fuse with each other, though she herself has no right to benefit from this process. And the different recognition that the city pays to their auto-speculation, the one in the other, has always already perverted their union, although sometimes a public remark is needed to make it obvious that the one must eliminate the other.

Thus male and female will be split further and further apart. The wife-mother will henceforward become more and more associated with nourishing and liquefying *lymph*, almost *white* while she loses her blood in cyclic hemorrhages, *neuter and passive* enough in her matter for various members and organs of society to incorporate her and use her for their own subsistence. The man (father) will persevere in developing his individualization by *assimilating* the external other into and for the self, thus re-enforcing his vitality, his irritability, and his activity; a particular triumph is experienced when man absorbs the other into himself in his intestine. The Father-king will repeat the rupture of (living) exchange between man and woman by sublating it into his discourse. Blood is burned to cinders in the writing of the text of law whereby man produces (himself) at the same time (as) the double—differently in him, in his son, and in his wife—and the color of blood fades as more and more semblances are produced, more atoms of individual egos, all bloodless in different ways. In this process some substance is lost: blood in its constitution of a living, autonomous subjectivity.

At the heart of the dialectic is hypochondria, melancholia. It can be linked to a clot of blood, cruor, reminiscent of the bloody calvary that set it on high, or else to the last froth left by an in(de)finite liquid which opens up the cup of its chalice even in Absolute Mind. Such clots and lymph, had they been able to close up wounds without weeping fluids, would have left the mind (only) to stony solitude and innocence. Assuming that the stone referred to serves to close off and mark the space in which femininity dies.

Thus we must go back to the decisive ethical moment which saw the blow struck producing a wound that no discourse has closed simply. The harmonious relationship of brother and sister involved a (so-called) equal recognition and nonviolent co-penetration of two essences, in which femininity and masculinity achieve universality in human and divine law. But this mutual agreement was possible only for as long as *adolescence* lasted and neither was impelled to act. A prolongation of childhood, a kind of Eden shielded from war and blessed by the household gods. But these idyllic and/because *immaculate* loves of childhood could not last. And each will soon realize that his or her equal is also his or her worst enemy, negation, and death. For the rule of law is impossible in a situation of mutual sharing in which one has as much value as the other, is equitably the same. In such circumstances consciousness could not recognize its simplicity or that wholeness which is the pathos of its duty. It must therefore make up its mind to act in accordance with that part of the ethical essence which has become apparent to it—that is, to the part which would correspond to its natural allegiance to one sex. Thus, without realizing it, consciousness finds itself embroiled willy-nilly in the rape of the other, who is henceforward injured by the partial character of such an operation. It is immediately clear, however, that the particular individual is not guilty or at fault. He is but the ineffective shadow acting on behalf of a universal self. And in fact, whatever his lack of personal responsibility, he will pay for his crime by finding that, subsequently, he is cut off from/in himself. In any event, he becomes conscious of that scission whereby the other side is now revealed to him in opposition and enmity. A dark potentiality that has always been on the watch comes suddenly into play when the deed is done: it catches the consciousness of self in the act—the act of also being, or having, that *unconsciousness* which remains alien to it but yet plays a major role in the decision consciousness takes. Thus the public offender who has been killed turns out to be the father, and the queen who has been wedded is the mother. But the purest fault is that committed by the ethical consciousness, which knew in advance what law and power it was disobeying—that is to say, necessarily, the fault committed by femininity. For if the ethical essence in its divine, unconscious, feminine side, remains obscure, its prescriptions on the human, masculine, communal side are exposed to full light. *And nothing here can excuse the crime, or minimize the punishment*. And in its burial, in its decline into ineffectiveness and pure pathos, the feminine must recognize the full measure of its guilt.

What an amazing vicious circle in a single syllogistic system. Whereby the unconscious, while remaining unconscious, is yet supposed to know the laws of a consciousness—which is permitted to remain ignorant of it—and will become even more repressed as a result of failing to respect those laws. But the stratification, on top/underneath, of the two ethical laws, of the two beings-there of sexual difference—which in fact have to disappear as such after the death of brother and sister—comes from Self, of itself. The movement by which the mind ceaselessly sublates necessity, climbing to the top of its pyramid more easily if the other is thrust deeper down into the well. Thus the male one copulates the other so as to draw new strength from her, a new form, whereas the other sinks further and further into a ground that harbors a substance which expends itself without the mark of any individualism. And it is by no means sure that the rape to which she continues to be subjected is visible in broad daylight, for the rape may equally well result in her retreating down into a crypt where she is sealed off. Or else in the resurgence of an "essence" so different, so other, that even to expect it to "work on the outside" reduces it to sameness, to an unconscious that has never been anything but the unconscious of someone conscious of human law alone. Which is as much as to say that the crime can easily occur unnoticed and that the operation may never be translated into a fact. Unless each of these/its terms is doubled so radically that *a single dialectic is no longer sufficient to articulate their copulation*. For if it is asserted that the one character and the other are split into a conscious and an unconscious, with each character itself giving rise to that opposition, there remains the question of how it will be possible to *translate* the laws of the unconscious into those of the conscious, the so-called laws of God into the laws of philosophy, the laws of the female into those of the male. What will be the passage of their *difference* in the subsequent movement of the mind? Or rather, how will that difference be resolved? How does the mind acquire, in a variation of deferred action (après-coup), the right to make laws and official statements about (the) matter, when a certain process of statement has already excluded difference in its desire to return to sameness? This problem can be approached in another way: the masculine will be able to retrace the path of his discursive law, but it is also the role of the masculine to prescribe the law for the female, since she can have no knowledge (of it) for herself. And the fact that, ideally, each is both unconscious and conscious does not in practice prevent the conscious from being identified as masculine, whereas the unconscious remains fixed on the female side, repressed as a result of the impossibility of differentiating the maternal. This implies that masculinity—in man and possibly in woman—will to some extent be able to dialecticize its relationships and identificatory allegiance to the maternal, including a negativization of female singularity, but this would not be true for femininity, which is aware of no difference between itself and the maternal, or even the masculine, except one that is mediated by the abstract immediacy of *the* being (as) or by the rejection of *one* (as) being. The female lacks the operation of affirming its singular and universalizable link to one as self.

Woman has no gaze, no discourse for her specific specularization that would allow her to identify with herself (as same)—to return into the self—or break free of the natural specular process that now holds her—to get out of the self. Hence, woman does not take an active part in the development of history, for she is never anything but the still undifferentiated opaqueness of sensible matter, the store (of) substance for the sublation of self, or being as what is, or what he is (or was), here and now. There is a doubling of a present of utterance in which present is already no more, has already passed into the universal, when woman appears in that *quasi-subjectivity* that is supposedly hers. And that cannot be possessed as consciousness of self. In her case "I" never equals "I," and she is only that individual will that the master takes possession of, that resisting remainder of a corporeality to which his passion for sameness is still sensitive, or again his double, the lining of his coat. Being as she is, she does not achieve the enunciatory process of the discourse of History, but remains its servant, deprived of self (as same), alienated in this system of discourse as in her master and finding some hint of her own self, her own ego, only in another, a You—or a He—who speaks. Her own will is shattered so afraid is she of the master, so aware of her inner nothingness. And her work in the service of another, of that male Other, ensures the ineffectiveness of any desire that is specifically hers.

But, when woman renounces her claim to desire, external things are positively molded, their forms are determined by a self that is not re-marked by any individual pathos or by any contingent arbitrariness, things in which the mind might intuit itself as objectal reality. This would be the final meaning of the obedience demanded of woman. She is merely the passage that serves to transform the inessential whims of a still sensible and material nature into universal will.

Woman is the guardian of the blood. But as both she and it have had to use their substance to nourish the universal consciousness of self, it is in the form of *bloodless shadows*—of unconscious fantasies—that they maintain an underground subsistence. Powerless on earth, she remains the very ground in which manifest mind secretly sets its roots and draws its strength. And self-certainty—in masculinity, in community, in government—owes the truth of its word and of the oath that binds men together to that substance common to all, repressed, unconscious and dumb, washed in the waters of oblivion. This enables us to understand why femininity consists essentially in laying the dead man back in the womb of the earth, and giving him eternal life. For the *bloodless one is the mediation that she knows in her being*, whereby a being-there that has given up being as a self here passes from something living and singular and deeply buried to essence at its most general. Woman can, therefore, by remembering this intermediary moment, preserve at least the soul of man and of community from being lost and forgotten. *She ensures the Erinnerung of the consciousness of self by forgetting herself.*

But at times the forces of the world below become hostile because they have been denied the right to live in daylight. These forces rise up and threaten to lay waste the community. To turn it upside down. Refusing to be that unconscious ground that nourishes nature, womanhood would then demand the right to pleasure, to jouissance, even to effective action, thus betraying her universal destiny. What is more, she would pervert the property/propriety of the State by making fun of the adult male who no longer thinks of anything but the universal, subjecting him to derision and to the scorn of a callow adolescence. In opposition to the adult male, she would set up the strength of youth possessed by the *son*, the *brother*, the *young man*, for in them, much more than in the power of government, she recognizes a *master*, an *equal*, a *lover*. The community can protect itself from such demands only by repressing them as elements of *corruption* that threaten to destroy the State. In fact these *seeds* of revolt, in principle, are quite powerless, are already reduced to nothing by being *separated from the universal goal* pursued by the citizens. Any community has a duty to transform these too immediately natural forces into its own defenders by inciting the young men—in whom the woman's desire takes pleasure—to make war upon each other and slaughter one another in bloody fights. It is through them that the still living substance of nature will sacrifice her last resources to a formal and empty universality, scattering her last drops of *blood* at a multitude of points which it will no longer be possible to gather up in the intimacy of the familiar cave.

And if, in those *points*, the *sperm*, the *name*, the *whole individual* can find a representing basis that allows them to rise up again and recover, blood in its autonomous flow will never re-unite again. But the eye—at least in the absolute—would have no need of blood to see with, anymore perhaps than the Mind to think with.

Notes

(The epigraphs are taken from Hegel's *Philosophy of Nature,* ed. and tr. M. J. Petry [London: Allen & Unwin, 1970], pp. 175 and 123 respectively. Hegel's discussion of Sophocles' *Antigone,* upon which much of this essay is closely based, can most easily be found in English in *Hegel on Tragedy,* ed. Anne and Henry Paolucci [New York: Doubleday, 1962], pp. 260–73.—Tr.)

1. (Sophocles, *The Theban Plays,* "Antigone," tr. E. F. Watling [Penguin Classics, 1947], p. 144.—Tr.)
2. ("I'll have her taken to a desert place / Where no man ever walked, and there walled up / Inside a cave alive, with food enough / To acquit ourselves of the blood guiltiness / That would else lie upon our commonwealth. / There she may pray to Death, the god she loves / And ask release from death or learn at last / What hope there is for those who worship death." Ibid., p. 147.—Tr.)

CHAPTER 17

"Negativity: Rejection"

—from *Revolution in Poetic Language* (1974)

Julia Kristeva

1. The Fourth "Term" of the Dialectic

The notion of *negativity* (*Negativität*), which may be thought of as both the cause and the organizing principle of the *process*, comes from Hegel.[1] The concept of negativity, distinct from that of nothingness (*Nichts*) and negation (*Negation*), figures as the indissoluble relation between an "ineffable" mobility and its "particular determination." Negativity is the mediation, the supersession of the "pure abstractions" of being and nothingness in the concrete where they are both only moments. Although *negativity* is a concept and therefore belongs to a contemplative (theoretical) system, it reformulates the static *terms* of pure abstraction as a process, dissolving and binding them within a mobile law. Thus, while still maintaining their dualism, negativity recasts not only the theses of *being* and *nothingness*, but all categories used in the contemplative system: universal and particular, indeterminate and determinate, quality and quantity, negation and affirmation, etc. Negativity constitutes the logical impetus beneath the thesis of negation and that of the negation of negation, but is identical to neither since it is, instead, the logical functioning of the movement that produces the theses.

Lenin noted Hegel's statement that the "triplicity" of the dialectic is its "external, superficial side."[2] By contrast, negativity is the liquefying and dissolving agent that does not destroy but rather reactivates new organizations and, in that sense, affirms. As transition (*Übergang*), negativity constitutes an *enchaînement* in the choreographical sense, "the necessary connection" and "the immanent emergence of distinctions." Here Lenin writes:

> Very important!! This is what it means, in my opinion:
>
> 1) *Necessary* connection, the objective connection of all the aspects, forces, tendencies, etc., of the given sphere of phenomena;
>
> 2) The "immanent *emergence* of distinctions"—the inner objective logic of evolution and of the struggle of the differences, polarity.

Lenin underscores and accepts the notion of "inherent negativity" as an *objective* principle—the principle of all physical and spiritual life—and not as a simple "subjective craving to shake and break down what is fixed and true."[3] In the final analysis, dialectical materialism will inherit from Hegel's dialectic this and only this founding principle; it will reinstate materialist dualism and see negativity at work in and through two differentiated and heterogeneous orders.

Before returning to this heteronomy, we would like to stress that the Hegelian conception of negativity already prepared the way for the very possibility of thinking a materialist *process*. While remaining an intra-speculative notion, Hegelian negativity bursts, as it were, from within its conceptual unity since it links [*enchaîne*]—unleashes [*déchaîne*]—the "real" and the "conceptual," the objective and the subjective, and, if one wished to find its representation, culminates in the ethical order: although it is *objectivity* itself, negativity is at the same time and for that very reason the "free subject." The *ethics* that develops in the process of negativity's unfolding is not the kind of "ethics" that consists in obedience to laws. It amounts instead to the corruption and absorption of laws by what Hegel calls the aesthetic. The subject of that Hegelian aesthetic—the free subject par excellence—reveals the diremption [*épuisement*] of the ethical subject and effects its *Aufhebung* in order to reintroduce him into a process of transformation of community relations and discursive strata.[4] The logical definition given to this negativity is freedom "for itself": "The highest form of nothingness [takenl for itself is *freedom*, but it is negativity to the extent that it goes as deep into itself as possible, and is itself affirmation."[5]

As the logical expression of the objective process, negativity can only produce a subject in process/on trial. In other words, the subject, constituted by the law of negativity and thus by the law of an objective reality, is necessarily suffused by negativity—opened onto and by objectivity, he is mobile, nonsubjected, free. A subject submerged in negativity is no longer "outside" objective negativity as a transcendent unity or a specifically regulated monad; instead he positions himself as the "*innermost* and *most objective* moment of Life and Spirit." This Hegelian principle is the ferment of dialectical materialism, where it becomes both the concept of *human activity* as revolutionary activity and that of the *social and natural laws* this activity shows to be objective. Hegel writes:

> The negativity which has just been considered is the *turning-point* of the Notion. It is the simple point of negative self-relation, the internal source of all activity, vital and spiritual self-movement, the dialectic

> soul which all truth has in it and through which it alone is truth; for the transcendence of the opposition between the Notion and Reality, and that unity which is the truth, rest upon this subjectivity alone.—The second negative, the negative of the negative, which we have reached, is this transcendence of the contradiction but is no more the *activity* of *an* external reflection than the contradiction is; it is the *innermost* and *most objective* moment of Life and Spirit, by virtue of which a subject, the person, the free, has being.

Lenin notes in the margins of this passage: "the kernel of dialectics," "the criterion of truth (the unity of the concept and reality)."[6]

But the materialist dialectic will retain only one element of the subject's negativation: his subordination, as a unit, to the social and natural process. Inheriting the weak points of dialectical materialist logic, dogmatico-revisionism will either dismiss the very problem of the subject and retain only the process of substance in a Spinozistic sense or the process of modes of production (as in dogmatism); or else it will hypostasize a psychological "subject" that has no process and only an external negativity (as in revisionism).

Let us take a closer look at the vicissitudes and dead ends of Hegelian negativity. If "the truth is, not either Being or Nothing, but that Being—not passes—but *has passed over* into Nothing, and Nothing into Being" (emphasis added), and if "their truth is therefore this *movement*, this immediate disappearance of the one into the other, in a word, *Becoming*; a movement wherein both are distinct, but in virtue of a distinction which has equally immediately dissolved itself,"[7] then we see that this supersession amounts to the erasing of heterogeneity within the Hegelian dialectic. Nothing, posited as such or active as a *relation* in negativity, can only be a *Becoming* or an *abstract negation*: the "absolute void" in Oriental systems. When negativity is considered a logical operation, it becomes reified as a void, as an absolute zero—the zero used in logic and serving at its base—or else as a connective in the logical Becoming. Yet what the dialectic represents as negativity, indeed Nothing, is precisely that which remains outside logic (as the signifier of a subject), what remains heterogeneous to logic even while producing it through a movement of separation or rejection, something that has the necessary objectivity of a law and can be seen as the logic of matter. This notion is possible because of and in spite of Hegel because he maintains, in opposition to Spinoza, the inseparability, the interpenetration, indeed the contradiction of "Being" and "Nothing" even if only within the sphere of the Idea:

> Those who assert the proposition that Nothing is just Nothing, and even grow heated in its defence, do not know that in so doing they are subscribing to the abstract Pantheism of the Eleatics and, in essentials, of Spinoza. That view in philosophy which takes for principle that

> Being is merely Being, and Nothing merely Nothing, deserves the name of system of identity: this abstract identity is the essence of Pantheism.[8]

To those surprised by this thesis of the inseparability of Being and Nothing, Hegel objected that such "wonderment . . . forgets that in this Science [philosophy] there occur determinations quite different from those of ordinary consciousness and so-called common-sense,—which is not exactly sound understanding, but understanding educated up to abstractions and the faith, or rather superstition, of abstractions."[9]

A *negativity* inseparable from the Hegelian notion of *Being* is thus precisely what splits and prevents the closing up of Being within an abstract and superstitious understanding. It points to an outside that Hegel could only think of as something inherent in belief, and which his phenomenological descendants would posit as a negative theology. We nevertheless maintain that Hegelian negativity prevents the immobilization of the thetic, unsettles doxy, and lets in all the semiotic motility that prepares and exceeds it. Hegel, moreover, defines this negativity as the *fourth term* of the true dialectic: triplicity is only an appearance in the realm of the Understanding.[10]

The logic exposed above will become materialist when, with the help of Freud's discovery, one dares think negativity as the *very movement of heterogeneous matter*, inseparable from its differentiation's symbolic function. Although in Kant this material movement of scission, of rejection (to which we shall return), remains a "negative" term for the understanding, it is conceived dialectically, *because it is considered inseparable from Being*, as a fundamental *positivity*: "In this respect therefore mere Unseparateness or Inseparability would be a good substitute for Unity; but these would not express the affirmative nature of the relation of the whole."[11]

Thus, even while maintaining Kantian oppositions, the Hegelian dialectic moves toward a fundamental reorganization of these oppositions—one that will establish an *affirmative negativity*, a *productive dissolution* in place of "Being" and "Nothing." The theology inherent in this reorganization will, however, leave its mark in an implicit teleology: namely, the *Becoming* that subordinates, indeed erases, the moment of rupture.

2. Independent and Subjugated "Force" in Hegel

Already in the *Phenomenology of Spirit* negativity is presented under the rule of the One and the Understanding, even in those moments when it appears most material and independent—closest to what we have called a semiotic *chora* (energy discharges and their functioning)—in other words, when it appears as

Force [*Kraft*]. As an object for the Understanding, Force is always already double in its movement: "One of its moments, *the dispersal of the independent 'matters'* in *their* [*immediate*] *being* [emphasis added], is the *expression* [*extériorisation*] of Force; but Force, taken as that in which they have disappeared, is Force *proper*, Force which has been *driven back into itself* [emphasis added] from its expression."[12] Although, as Notion, Force is driven back into itself, Force as reality is not, and constitutes a freedom from thought. It therefore acts in a space that is *other*, which (Hegelian) speculation, unable to situate it within a concrete signifying practice—in the materiality of the signifying process—ends up superseding not only under the unity of the Understanding, but also under that of reason—but not without first indicating its heterogeneity. This labyrinthian movement recognizes "another subsisting essence" of Force but represses its material negativity, free energy.

> In order, then, that Force may in truth *be*, it must be completely set free from thought, it must be posited as the *substance* [emphasis added] of these differences, i.e., *first* the *substance*, as this whole Force, remaining essentially *in and for itself, and then* its *differences* as possessing *substantial being*, or as moments existing on their own account. Force as such, or as driven back into itself, thus exists on its own account as an *exclusive One*, for while the unfolding of the [different] "matters" is *another* subsisting essence; and thus two distinct independent aspects are set up.[13]

The movement between these two "moments" is that of the Force that will produce a *non-objective inner world*, a return of Forces as a Notion within the Understanding. A play of Forces, the "inner being" will be established as the "beyond of consciousness," a "void": "In order, then, that in this *complete void*, which is even called the *holy of holies*, there may yet be something, we must fill it up with reveries, *appearances*, produced by consciousness itself. It would have to be content with being treated so badly for it would not deserve anything better, since even reveries are better than its own emptiness."[14]

Driving *Force* back under the *Notion* leads Force to an inner world where it is depreciated for precisely that doubling, i.e., its persistence in "expressing" itself and in emptying this inner being, constituted by "Forces," of any possible knowledge. Although posited, the "material" expression of Force, when thought of within the framework of conceptual unity, remains an *opaque* expression and, in ideal totality, this cannot be otherwise. In conceiving radical negativity as an *expression*, the idealist dialectic deprives itself of negativity's powerful moment: the scission that exceeds and precedes the advent of thetic understanding. It closes itself off both to the primacy of the objective laws of material transformation (no longer "exterior" but *heterogeneous* to the zone of the Understanding) and to signifying practices in which material drives striate, displace, and sometimes attain the clarity of the Understanding. Artaud was to give this description: "In it we feel a grinding of sluices, a kind of horrible volcanic shock from which the light of day has been *dissociated*. And from this clash, from the tearing of two principles, all potential images are born in a thrust stronger than a ground swell."[15]

By contrast, for the idealist dialectic, the reality of Force is ultimately the *thought* of it, where Force supersedes itself as Force; conversely, its realization as Force is a loss of reality:

> Force, as *actual*, exists simply and solely in its *expression*, which at the same time is nothing else than a supersession of itself. This *actual* Force, when thought of as free from its expression and as being for itself, is Force driven back into itself; but in fact this determinateness, as we have found, is itself only a moment of Force's expression. Thus the truth of Force remains only the *thought* of it; the moments of its actuality, their substances and their movement, collapse unresistingly into an undifferentiated unity, a unity which is not Force driven back into itself (for this is itself only such a moment), but is its *Notion qua Notion*. Thus the realization of Force is at the same time the loss of reality.[16]

This impeccable logic constitutes signifying unity on the basis of explosions—scissions, impulses, collisions, rejections—yet they remain driven back in the name of and in view of the subjective unity not only of the Understanding but also of reason, which is necessary because it ensures the assertion of reality.

We have seen the way in which Hegel's phenomenological and logical philosophical descendants (Husserl and Frege), in their concern with signifying formation and functioning, tend to bury the negativity that was sketched out albeit already repressed in Hegel. What made its materialist overturning possible, in our view, was the key notion of drives in Freudian theory. [. . .]

7. Freud's Notion of Expulsion: Rejection

Rejection, or expenditure, constitutes the key moment shattering unity, yet it is unthinkable outside unity, for rejection presupposes thetic unity as its precondition and horizon, one to be always superseded and exceeded. Rejection serves to bind only to the extent that it is the *precondition* of the binding that takes place on another scene. To posit rejection as fundamental and inherent in every thesis does not mean that we posit it as origin. Rejection rejects origin since it is always already the repetition of an impulse that is itself a rejection. Its law is one of returning, as opposed to one of becoming; it returns only to separate again immediately and thus appear as an impossible forward movement.

Of the terms "rejection," "scission," and "separation," *rejection* is the one that best designates, archaeologically, the instinctual, repetitive, and trans-signifying aspect of the dynamics of signifiance. It implies a pre-verbal "function," one that is pre-logical and a-logical in the sense that the *logos* signifies a "relation," a "connection." *Scission* and *separation* are more appropriate terms for that rupture when it is considered from the point of view of the subject and already constituted meaning, which is to say, within a perspective that takes into account language and the unity of the subject—a signifying sociality dependent on norms. We shall stress the first term (*rejection*) because it suggests the heterogeneity of signifiance we are attempting to demonstrate, and because, within the text, it opens up an a-signifying, indeed prelinguistic, crucible. But we shall use the other terms (*scission* and *separation*) as well because they emphasize the underlying unity which withdraws and is reconstituted in the return of rejection. They also signal the permanent logical constraint of an insurmountable *consciousness*, which ensures the reactivation of rejection in a process, thus saving it from foundering in inarticulable instinctuality, where signifying production would be impossible. Our conception of rejection will oscillate between the two poles of drives and consciousness, and this ambiguity will reveal the ambiguity of process itself, which is both divided and unitary. But to the extent that these two threads (drives and consciousness) intersect and interweave, the *unity of reason* which consciousness sketches out will always be shattered by the *rhythm* suggested by drives: repetitive rejection seeps in through "prosody," and so forth, preventing the stasis of One meaning, One myth, One logic.

In Freud's article on *Verneinung* [negation], expulsion (*Ausstossung*) is what constitutes the real object as such; it also constitutes it as lost, thus setting up the symbolic function. [. . .]

Now that we have followed the notion of expulsion [*repoussement*] in Freud, let us pick it up again in Hegel who opened the way for the notion of *negativity* outlined at the beginning of this chapter.[17] In Hegel, the term *Repulsion* designates a movement within negativity that comes close to what we have called *rejection* yet does not coincide with it. *Repulsion* is the negative relation of the One with itself, as opposed to *Becoming*, which is "a transition of Being into Nothing."[18] Since it is the fundamental determination of the One and its fragmentation, Repulsion both ensures the preservation of the One and produces the plurality of Ones by the Attraction it presupposes. Thus we see that Hegelian Repulsion is always subordinate to Unicity and that, in beginning to act within it, Repulsion calls Unicity into question only *from the outside*, by adding multiple external meanings. There is no doubt, and Hegel himself stresses, that Repulsion fundamentally interiorizes negativity, in opposition to Kantian analytics where the "two basic forces remain, within matter, opposed to one another, external and independent," and where "Kant determines . . . repulsive force . . . as a *superficial force*, by means of which parts of matter can act upon one another only at the common surface of contact."[19] But in internalizing Repulsion within the One itself, and in making Repulsion what specifies, determines, and, in sum, identifies the One, Hegel subordinates Repulsion to what we have called the "symbolic function"; whereas Freud, on the other hand, joins dialectical logic by making *expulsion* the essential moment in the constitution of the symbolic function. The difference is that, in Freud, what activates expulsion is "another scene" based on the drives. Since he does not have this heteronomy in view, Hegel can only supercede the exteriority of Repulsion that Freud has sketched out.[20] This comes about because separation in Hegel becomes the explanation of what the One is in itself; it gets exported outside this One, which is always already constructed, becomes exteriorized, and, as a result of the dialectic, ends up in an exteriority:

> The self-repulsion of the One is the explication of that which the One is in itself; but infinity, as split-up, is here infinity which has *passed beyond itself*: and this it has done through the immediacy of the infinite entity, the One. It is a simple relation of One to One, and equally, or rather, the absolute unrelatedness of the One; it is the former according to the simple affirmative self-relation of One, and the latter according to the same as negative. In other words, the plurality of the One is its self-positing; the One is its own negative self-relation and nothing else, and this relation (the One itself) is many Ones. But equally, plurality is merely external to the One; for the *One also is the transcending of Otherness. Repulsion is its self-relation and simple self-identity. The plurality of Ones is infinity, as contradiction which unconcernedly produces itself.*[21]

What Hegel does not envisage is the moment the One is *shattered* in a return of Repulsion onto itself, which is to say, a turning against its own potential power for positing and multiplying the One. Nor does Hegelian logic see the heterogeneous parcelling of the symbolic, which underlies the symbolic's very constitution and constantly undermines it even while maintaining it in process; the simultaneous existence of the *boundary* (which is the One) and the a-reasonable, a-relative, a-mediating *crossing* of that boundary; or the possibility of the constitution-unconstitution of One meaning-non-meaning, passing through categorial boundaries ("inside," "one," "multiple," etc.), which is precisely what *rejection* brings about in the "schizoid" process of the text.

The ideational closure of the Hegelian dialectic seems to consist in its inability to posit negativity as anything but a repetition of ideational unity in itself. The exteriority to which it is condemned *in fact* is thus bound up with the ideational enclosure, in which, despite many detours, its trajectory ends.

Repeated rejection, far from purely and simply restoring the series of many Ones, instead opens up in and through Unity—we are tempted to say beyond "signifying unity" and "subjective unity"—*the material process of repeated* (a-signifying and instinctual) *scissions*; these repeated scissions act with the regularity of objective laws and recall, through the rifts or new arrangements they produce, the pulsation of that process through symbolic unification. These are the conclusions we may draw from a materialist interpretation, opened up by the Freudian position on repetition compulsion.

Notes

1. Hegel's terminology poses a problem. Whereas the French translations Kristeva cites are generally consistent in their rendering of key terms, no such "standards" inform the various English translations of either *Phenomenology of Spirit*—even the title is a point of contention—or *Science of Logic*. Both texts, for example, refer to *Nichts*, commonly translated as "*néant*" in French but as "Nothing" in Johnson and Struthers's *Science of Logic* or as "nothingness" in A.V. Miller's *Phenomenology*. The same problem arises with "*le devenir*" ("Becoming" or "process of Becoming"), "*extériorisation*" ("exteriorization" or "expression"), and other such terms. I have not standardized these two different translations. When the discussion of Hegel does not refer to a specific work, I have generally selected French cognates.—Trans.
2. Lenin, "Conspectus of Hegel's Book on *The Science of Logic*," Clemens Dutt, tr. *Collected Works*, Stewart Smith, ed. (Moscow: Foreign Languages Publishing House, 1961), 38: 230.
3. *Ibid.*, p. 97.
4. See "Religion in the Form of Art" in Hegel, *Phenomenology of Spirit*, A.V. Miller, tr. (Oxford: Oxford University Press, 1977), pp. 424–453.
5. Hegel, *Encyclopédie des sciences philosophiques*, vol. 1, *Science de la logique* (1817), B. Bourgeois tr. (Paris: Vrin, 1970), p. 203
6. Lenin, "Conspectus," *Collected Works* 38: 229.
7. *Hegel's Science of Logic*, W. H. Johnston and L. G. Struthers trs. (London: Allen and Unwin, 1929; 1966), 1: 95: emphasis added.
8. *Ibid.*, p. 96.
9. *Ibid.*, p. 97.
10. *Ibid.*, 2: 478–479.
11. *Ibid.*, 1: 104.
12. *Phenomenology of Spirit*, p. 81. "Diese Bewegung ist aber dasjenige, was Kraft gennant wird: das eine Moment derselben, nämlich sie als Ausbreitung der selbstständigen Materien in ihrem Sehn, ist ihre Aeusserung; sie

aber als das Verschwundensehn derselben ist die in sich aus ihrer Aeusserung zurückgedrängte, oder die eigentliche Kraft. Aber erstens die in sich zurückgedrängte Kraft muss sich äussern; und zweitens in der Aeusserung ist sie eben so in sich selbst sehende Kraft, als sie in diesem Insichselbstsehn Aeusserung ist." Hegel, *Sämtliche Werke* (Stuttgart: Fr. Frommans Verlag, 1927), pp. 110–111.

13. Hegel, *Phenomenology of Spirit*, p. 82.
14. *Ibid.*, pp. 88–89.
15. Artaud, "L'Automate personnel," in *Oeuvres completes*, 2 vols. (Paris: Gallimard, 1970), 1: 179.
16. Hegel, *Phenomenology of Spirit*, p. 86.
17. Although the French translators use the term "*repoussement*" for both Freud's *Ausstossung* and Hegel's *Repulsion*, I maintain the standard English translation of these terms, "expulsion," and "Repulsion," respectively—Trans.
18. See *Hegel's Science of Logic* 1: 180–183. Hegel uses the terms "*abstossen*" (to repulse), "*repellieren*" (to repel) and "*Repulsion*" (repulsion). [In French, both verbs are translated as "*repousserî* and the noun as "*repoussement*."—Trans.] See Hegel, *Science de la logique*, Pierre-Jean Labarrière and Gwendoline Jarczyk, trs. (Paris: Aubier-Montaigne, 1972), vol. 1, Book 1 (1812), pp. 138 sq.
19. *Hegel's Science of Logic*, 1: 195; emphasis added.
20. We shall return to this point in part III.
21. *Hegel's Science of Logic*, 1: 182; emphasis added.

CHAPTER 18

"Death and Time"

—from *God, Death, and Time* (1993; lectures delivered: 1976)

Emmanuel Levinas

Hegel's Response: *The Science of Logic*

Friday, February 27, 1976

The nothingness of death is undeniable, but the relationship to death as nothingness is, in any case, a negativity radically other than the negativity thought by Greek philosophy and particularly by Aristotle. In thinking of change all the way to the *metabolē*, one might think that one has isolated the nothingness of being. Actually, in Aristotle, even the *metabolē* preserves the style of alteration, where being subsists in nothingness in such a way that nothingness is not thought as a pure nothing [*néant pur*].

What is knowable and natural to thought is nothingness as *dissolution*; annihilation as *decomposition* in which something subsists even if the forms of things pass away. *Relative* disappearance shows itself without difficulties. Thus, in the two Aristotelian models of the passage from nothingness into being (childbirth and fabrication), *phusis* and material are presupposed. Childbirth is a becoming and not a leap from nothingness to being (the seed was there).

Now, a nothingness like that of death, rigorously thought, *is pregnant with nothing at all*. It is an absolutely indeterminate nothingness that alludes to no being, and it is not a chaos aspiring to form: death is the death of someone, and the having-been of someone is carried not by the one dying but by the survivor.

In Aristotle, being is maintained within nothingness, as potential being. It is always a question of the manner by which one being becomes another. Now, the ontic origin and perishing that a being undergoes are very different from the origin and annihilation *of essance*.[1] Everything unfolds in death as though man were not a simple being that perishes, but one who offered us the very event of finishing or perishing—even if this event occurred in its ambiguity as the unknown.

In the death of another, in his face that is exposition to death, it is not the passage from one quiddity to another that is announced; in death is *the very event of passing* (our language says, moreover, "he has passed" ["*il passe*"]) with its own acuteness that is its scandal (each death is the first death). We should think of all the murder there is in death: every death is a murder, is premature, and there is the responsibility of the survivor.

Aristotle does not think nothingness in this way. For him, that does not "demolish" the world; the world remains.

How is it in Hegel? In order to know this, it is necessary to read the beginning of the *Greater Logic* (book 1, the chapter "With What Must the Science Begin?").[2]

One would say, at first glance, that it is impossible here to think the nothingness of death in all its purity. After having reviewed the different entities (*Seiende*) that philosophy placed at the beginning (water, *noûs*, etc.), Hegel says that the beginning cannot first be thought of as determinate. We must take the beginning in indetermination and in its immediacy. The beginning of philosophy thus becomes a philosophy of the beginning. Thinking will then determine and realize what the determination implies: to determine the various predicates that one might add to this indeterminate beginning.

We must begin, then, with pure being, empty and indeterminate being. What is necessary to the beginning is a nothingness that must become something. "As yet there is nothing and there is to become something. The beginning is not pure nothing, but a nothing from which something is to proceed; therefore being, too, is already contained in the beginning," writes Hegel.[3] Thus, the model of the beginning—though it presents itself as empty and pure—is again the beginning within the world: it is something that begins, a something, and not the beginning of being in general. In the beginning, there is already being. This beginning is the unity of being and nothingness, or a nonbeing that is at once being and nonbeing.

We are thus right away in a situation similar to that which Aristotle contemplated: there is a nothingness, but a nothingness that awaits being, that wants being, that will pass into being. One may therefore wonder whether, in this way, one is not supposing entities as already there. One may wonder whether the beginning is not, thus, the beginning of some thing, the beginning of *that which* begins. This is a beginning that lacks the determinacy of water, as in Thales, but one that has the structure of a something [*du quelque chose*].

The beginning is not yet, but it is going to be. It thus contains that being that grows distant from nonbeing or supersedes it (*aufhebt*) as its opposite.[4] Nothingness and being are here distinguished like that from which the beginning departs and that toward which it aims. The beginning contains both states distinguished from each other; it is their nondifferentiated unity.

But have we not here confused a becoming that is growth with a becoming that is absolute in the sense of an absolute emergence? In these descriptions, is there not a confusion between the relative and the absolute becoming? Would Hegel have been fooled?—as if Hegel could be fooled by something!

Hegel's thought is, in fact, much more radical than this. The absolute beginning is a notion belonging to common sense. When one thinks, one sees that being and nothingness are not separable; one sees that they are identical, and that their unity is becoming.

For Aristotle, the presupposition is that all intelligible meaning must go back to the unmoved mover. It is in this resting of being that all becoming culminates; there is therefore no sense in speaking of absolute nothingness. In Aristotle, we must go back from movement in things to the unmoved mover, whereas Hegel introduces movement *into being itself* and delivers being entirely to movement. "There is not a single proposition in Heraclitus that I have not taken up in my *Logic*," as he will say in this respect.[5]

The difference between absolute emergence and relative emergence is in fact the crude comprehension of being by opinion. Not only does Hegel consciously reject it, he turns it over: what seems to us a relative becoming is precisely the emergence, the origin—which is to say that *becoming is the absolute*, and, consequently, one cannot think before this.

If the beginning must be thought, it is first necessary to bear its emptiness and its indeterminacy. This is a most difficult asceticism, for we are accustomed to beginning where being is strongest and fullest. But what must be uttered about being is, at the beginning, only an empty word, nothing but "being" ["*être*"]. This emptiness is thus the very beginning of philosophy. Being is the first thing that is thought by a thinking that is reasonable.

Yet how must we think it? Therein lies the most important thing to be said.

The philosophical tradition separated being and nonbeing. For Plato and Aristotle, the Eleatic distinction is not valid in the world of becoming: here, there is no pure nothingness. But the distinction is nevertheless maintained: things are "between the two," between being and nothingness. Is it then possible to *think* nothingness? Hegel will set aside every mystical approach to nothingness; nothingness, for him, is going to be *thought*. And to think nothingness is to assert the identity of being and nothingness.

Pure being, indeterminate and without content, is empty; there is nothing to see in it, nothing to intuit. It is therefore "only this pure intuiting itself."[6] There is in pure being, then, nothing to think. Pure being is in fact nothing, neither more nor less than nothing. Pure being is like nothingness. Consequently, being and nothingness have the same structure, they are identical.

But how can the indeterminate be identical to itself? In effect, it is always a content that is identical to itself. In reality, the proposition "pure being is pure nothingness" works on a special level of identity: it is an identity that is speculative, that consists in *becoming* [*consiste à être devenir*]. Being and nothingness are identical in becoming. The coincidence of opposites is not a factual given but is produced as becoming. The simultaneity of opposites is becoming. It is not here a matter of an ordinary becoming; rather, all thinking is in this becoming, and one cannot think outside of it.

> *Pure being and pure nothing are, therefore, the same*. What is the truth is neither being nor nonbeing, but that being does not pass over—but has passed over into nothing, and nothing into being.

Nicht übergeht—sondern übergegangen ist: ALWAYS ALREADY—we have thought being in nothingness, but being is already becoming.[7]

> But it is equally true that they are not undistinguished from each other, that, on the contrary, they are not the same, that they are absolutely distinct, and yet that they are unseparated and inseparable and that each immediately *vanishes in its opposite*. Their truth is, therefore, this movement of the immediate vanishing of the one in the other: *becoming*, a movement in which both are distinguished, but by a difference which has equally immediately resolved itself.[8]

Becoming is thus the difference *and* identity of being and nothingness.

Genesis and corruption return into something that encompasses them. In the absolute, nothing is radically new; nothing subsists that is not handed over to annihilation. The absolute has emptiness not outside itself but in itself. Nothingness runs through being.

One might wonder whether that reaches the level of death, that is, whether what is outside-the-circuit in death—in the death that man knows—finds a place adequate to it in this absolute. The question is in fact posed by Fink.[9]

Reading Hegel's *Science of Logic* (Continued)

Friday, March 5, 1976

The nothingness of death isolated from the process of being, the nothingness of death that is not a moment of this process, the undeniable annihilation of death—

whatever the unknown to which it is attached—appears without common measure with the nothingness about which Aristotle and Hegel, in his *Logic*, are speaking.

"Pure being and pure nothingness are the same," as we read last time. To the degree that they are identical, the truth is not their state of in-differentiation (they are different inasmuch as identical), but the fact that they are not the same, that they are absolutely different; and yet they are just as absolutely un-separated and inseparable, and immediately each one disappears into its contrary. Their truth is therefore that movement of immediate disappearing, the one into the other: their truth is becoming. One cannot think being and nothingness without becoming. "Their truth is, therefore, this movement of the immediate vanishing of the one in the other: *becoming*, a movement in which both are distinguished, but by [the mediation of] a difference[10] which has equally immediately resolved itself." *Becoming is therefore the unity of this difference, which is the greatest possible one, but which has already been the most complete identity.* To think that being comes from nothingness and that there would be an absolute becoming there, or to think that being goes into nothingness as separated and separable nothingness, is a thought insufficiently thought. There is no separable nothingness.

In Hegel's "Remark 1: The Opposition of Being and Nothing in Ordinary Thinking,"[11] he writes: "*Nothing* is usually opposed to *something*; but the being of something is already determinate and is distinguished from another *something*; and so therefore the nothing which is opposed to the something is also the nothing of a particular something, a determinate nothing. *Here, however, nothing is to be taken in its indeterminate simplicity*."[12] If we nevertheless considered it more appropriate to oppose to being not nothingness as the nothingness of something, but *nonbeing*, then the result would still be the same, for "in non-being the relation to *being* is contained."[13] It is both of these two, being and the negation of being. "There is therefore no pure nothing, but nothing such that it is already in becoming."[14]

Hegel will then show the progress toward this speculative thinking on the identity of being and nothingness. When Parmenides inaugurates philosophy, he begins with the absolute distinction between being and nonbeing. For Hegel, this is still an abstract thought: Parmenides saw that the beginning is being, but he did not see that nonbeing in some way is. "Buddhism," in its turn, places nothingness at the beginning. "The deep-thinking Heraclitus brought forward the higher, total concept of *becoming* and said: *being as little is, as nothing is* (*das Sein ist so wenig als das Nichts*), or, everything *flows*, which means, everything is *becoming*."[15]

For Hegel, this unity of being and nothingness is a biblical thought, which for him means a Christian thought. "Later, especially Christian, metaphysics whilst rejecting the proposition that out of nothing comes nothing, asserted a transition from nothing into being; although it understood this proposition synthetically or merely imaginatively, yet even in the most imperfect union there is contained a point in which being and nothing coincide and their distinction vanishes."[16] Thus, creation *ex nihilo* would conform to the speculative proposition, the only reservation being that it is still representative, still abstract.

Now this being/nothingness identity is a speculative proposition, a thought of Reason and not that of the understanding that separates things. We cannot justify this identity by definitions: every definition already presupposes the speculative; every definition is an analysis, a separation, and presupposes the thought of the nonseparable.

We cannot name any difference between being and nothingness; it is impossible to find a difference because, were there one, being would be something other than pure being: there would be a specification here. The difference therefore does not turn on what they are in themselves. The difference appears here as that which embraces them: it is in becoming that the difference exists, and becoming is only possible by reason of this distinction.

But is death equivalent to this nothingness tied to being? Becoming is the phenomenal world, the manifestation of being. Now, death is outside this process: it is a total nothingness, a nothingness that is not necessary to the appearing of being. A nothingness that is obtained not by pure abstraction but as a kind of seizure. In death, one does not make an abstraction of being—it is of us that an abstraction is made.

Death, such is it is appears, concerns and frightens and causes anxiety in the death of an other, is an annihilation that does not find its place in the logic of being and nothingness. It is an annihilation that is a scandal and to which moral notions such as responsibility do not come to be simply added on.

Yet is there not in the *Phenomenology of Spirit* another notion of death? That is what we shall see next time.

From the *Science of Logic to the Phenomenology*

Friday, March 12, 1976

Ours is a questioning about the possibility of responding by way of thought, of being, of world, and of positivity to the undeniable end, the end of being and the annihilation inscribed in the death of another, and imminent in my own time; an annihilation inscribed in death in all the ambiguity of nothingness and the unknown. This is a questioning that is not a simple modality of the theoretical expression of belief, of *doxa*, in which we accede to being, to the world, and to positivity.

In the thinking of being, this nothingness is thought, but it is not the pure nothingness, the annihilation, and the unknown that is death; rather it is a moment of the thinking of being. Do not certain passages in the *Phenomenology of Spirit* treat death in a way that better accounts—not for the constitution of becoming or of the thinking of becoming—but for the *end* of becoming and for the whole scandal that is this end, which is expressed in the affective register (anxiety in Heidegger) and which shall be stated here in moral terms (responsibility for the death of another, the scandal of every new death)? It is that we must search not for a positive thought for death but rather for a responsibility according to the measure or the beyond-measure of death. We must search for a response that is not a response but responsibility, that is not of the same measure as a world but belongs to the beyond-measure of the infinite.

Today we will proceed to a reading of one of the famous pages of the *Phenomenology*, where death is not simply a moment playing its role in the thinking of being. The passage is found in volume 2, on page 14 and the following, in Jean Hyppolite's translation.[17] We should first situate this passage.

It is at the heart of the singular consciousness that Hegel discovers a relation necessary to other singular consciousnesses. The *I think* is only possible if, at the same time as I am in my thought, I am in relation with other thoughts. Each singular consciousness is at the same time for itself and for another. It can be for itself only to the extent to which it is for another. Each one demands recognition by the other to be itself, but it must also recognize the other, because the recognition by the other holds only if the other is himself recognized. Therein resides the surpassing of immediacy (for Hegel, all thinking is a thinking between consciousnesses; it is immediate when it ignores this relationship between consciousnesses; the immediate is the *cogito* all alone).

What Hegel calls Spirit is when this reciprocal recognition of consciousnesses is maintained and transcended (*aufgehoben*) in these relations and conflicts. That is the universal and nonimmediate consciousness. But this universal consciousness is first of all immediate; Spirit is thus like a sort of nature [*comme une nature*] before being opposed to itself. Hegel calls this stage of Spirit's immediacy *substance*. Spirit is substance, and it has before itself a progression whereby it must become a *subject*.[18]

It is substance insofar as it makes its own history, develops itself "insofar as its spiritual content is engendered by itself." It will become a subject, become the Knowledge that Spirit has of itself, that is, absolute thought or the living truth that knows itself. From the Spirit that simply *is*, it will become the Self-Knowledge of that Spirit.

The problem of the relation with death will be posed, for Hegel, at the level of this immediate Spirit, of this Spirit as substance (a people that has not yet put itself in question, that has not yet encountered other peoples). The immediate Spirit is a historical given. The oneself [*soi-même*] adheres immediately to its action. There is no place where the Self [*le Soi*] denies and opposes itself to its being. Concretely, that means that there is an ethical nature (*ἦθος* [*ethos*] means custom).

For Hegel, there is in this substance, in its immediate state, something like a scission between the universality of laws and the singularity of the substance that must itself be understood as a relation between singular consciousnesses. Hegel calls this the scission of this ethical state into human law and divine law.[19]

Human law corresponds to the laws of the city, of the State, and consequently this ethical substance according to human law consists in living the social and political life. What, then, would be the other side of this existence? It is the *family*, which goes back to the obscure origins of all things. Thus the masculine element represents human law and the feminine element the divine law, which is also the law of the home.

The law of the city is public; everyone knows the law, which moreover expresses the will of all. In this human law, man posits himself; he is the very position of self as a self, its style of *self* [*sa manière de soi*]. Man contemplates himself in the public law and opposes himself to the obscurity from which he detached himself. In the law, in broad daylight, he reflects himself.

But there is also the law of the family. These two laws are other than and complementary to each other. The divine law is immediate substance; it is not an operation of thought. It is the being of these men, which has not yet been reflected and which renounces the human law that has detached itself from it.

The State is the dominant order of a people that maintains itself by labor in times of peace and by combat in wartime. Individuals can become aware of their being for self [*leur être pour soi*] within the State, because the awareness the State has of itself is a force from which everyone benefits, since everyone has been recognized by this law. Nonetheless, being recognized in this way, the units inside the State, that is, the families, can in this atmosphere of security separate themselves from the Whole; that is, they can become abstract. It is war that will call back those individuals detached from the Whole. Without war, individuals would return to the state of pure and simple nature, to the immediate, to the absolutely abstract. War, on the contrary, gives them anew the consciousness of their dependency; at the level of the community, war is necessary:

> In order not to let them become rooted and set in this isolation, thereby breaking up the whole and letting the communal spirit evaporate, government has from time to time to shake them to their core, by war. By this means the government upsets their established order, and violates their right to independence [Hyppolite: *l'être-pour-soi*], while the individuals who, absorbed in their own way of life, break loose from the whole and strive after the inviolable independence and security of the person, are made to feel in the task laid on them their lord and master, death.[20]

Here death appears as the absolute Master.

Spirit exists as the individuality of a community, and not in an abstract form. Negation is here present in a double form. On the one hand, the community as a particular people is a determinate people (and every determination is a negation). On the other hand, there is the second negation that is individuality. And war is that negativity that surmounts nature or the possibility for families to fall back into nature. War checks the relapsing of families into the natural being-there far from the ethical being-there.

The State is legislation; it is the action of several in view of a common goal. To the State is opposed the divine law, the family bonded in blood and the relation of the difference of the sexes. The divine law is different from the State because it proceeds from that which is common, whereas the State, by way of the universal law, tends toward what is common. On the basis of this natural unity, from this blood-unity, Hegel expresses this by relating the family to the gods of the Earth (the mysticism of blood and ground in the family!). The State proceeds from Reason conscious of itself and raising itself to the universal. The family, on the other hand, is something natural; it is the substratum of life from which the human law detaches itself. But family is also the immediate nature *of Spirit*, and thus it is not a pure nature; it has an ethical principle. It becomes moral in relation to the *Penates*, to the protective spirits of the household.

What then can the ethical spirit of the family signify? The family's morality is other than that of the State. This morality is in the State and has many of the State's virtues: it raises children, prepares citizens for the State, and in this sense it is for the disappearance of the family. But there exists an ethics proper to the family that, on the basis of its terrestrial morality, relates to the subterranean world and consists in *burying the dead*.

It is here that the relationship with death is inscribed, or more precisely, with the dead *one*.

Hegel first gives a negative definition of the ethical principle proper to the family: "In the first place, because the ethical principle is intrinsically universal, the ethical connection between the members of the family is not that of feeling, or the relationship of love."[21] It is not love, not education, not a contingent service rendered by one family member to another that can furnish the ethical principle proper to the family. It is necessary that there be a relationship with a singularity, and in order for this to be ethical, the content of this relationship must be a universality. "The ethical action can therefore only be related to the *whole* individual, or the singular being *qua* universal."[22]

Hegel thus gives the solution:

> The deed, then, which embraces the entire existence of the blood-relation, does not concern the citizen, for he does not belong to the family, nor the individual who is to become a citizen and *will cease* to count as *this particular individual*; it has as its object and content *this* particular

> individual who belongs to the family, but is taken as a universal essence, freed from his sensuous, i.e. individual, reality. The deed no longer concerns the *living* but the *dead*, the individual who, after a long succession of separate disconnected experiences, concentrates himself into a single completed shape, and has raised himself out of the disquiet of the accidents of life into the peace of simple universality.[23]

One who has a universal essence without being a citizen is the deceased. There is virtue proper to the family in its relationship to the shadows. The duty with regard to the dead is that of burying them, and it is this that makes up the virtue proper to the family. The act of burial is a relationship with the deceased, and not with the cadaver.

Reading Hegel's *Phenomenology* (Continued)

Friday, March 19, 1976

For Hegel, the relationship with death and with the deceased, outside any reference to being and nothingness, is a necessary moment in the logic of the *Phenomenology of Spirit*, that is, of the movement, or the becoming, or the history wherein consciousness attains its full possession of self, wherein its freedom is an absolute thought. This is history not in the empirical sense of the history of the formation of thought, but history coming to pass as history, by way of the articulations necessary to its evolution, in which it becomes Absolute or concrete thought (of what is not separated from anything). At one of these stages, that where we can speak of immediate spirit, this consciousness is produced as an ethical nature, a nature having the content or the *ethos* of the law. This is a stage in which consciousness is not the experience of this Spirit, but immediate Spirit, that is, where Spirit is substance or nature. In this substance, as the immediacy of nature, a scission develops between the universality of laws and the singularity of substance, between the city and the family.

At this stage where the human law is public, what does the divine law or the law of the family consist in as *law*? If the family is an *ethical* substance, if it is not pure nature, in what does its ethic consist? (It is significant that for Hegel, ethics is always universal. The person is always thought of by virtue of the universality of law. On this point Hegel is a Kantian. The person as individual is not Spirit and has no ethic. Here, in our present inquiry, the person is an individual other, and every universal must begin from there. However, in German idealism, the person is the universal.)

The family is the natural community, and yet there is a universality in the family itself. Where is the ethical element peculiar to the family? It will be necessary to invent an exceptional notion in order to speak of the ethics of the family.

There must be a singularity that could also be universal. From this comes Hegel's response, which we saw last time: "This action no longer concerns the living, but the deceased." Death is here understood as a return into self [*recueillemcnt*], as a gathering into oneself. Here is a universality of the person who has fulfilled his destiny: it is an essence. Everything is fulfilled, everything is consummated when one is dead.

The relationship with the deceased and with the universality of death has its decisive trait in burial. There is, in death, something that corresponds to the concept necessary to ethics. The family cannot acknowledge that, with death, he who had been a consciousness is now submitted to matter, that matter has become the master of a being that was formed, that was a self- consciousness. One does not want this conscious being to be given over to matter, for the ultimate being of man, the ultimate fact of man, does not belong to nature. The family accomplishes an act of piety in regard to one who had been active: the appearance of nature's domination over the one who had been conscious must be rendered invisible.

> The blood-relationship supplements, then, the abstract natural process by adding to it the movement of consciousness, interrupting the work of nature and rescuing the blood-relation from destruction; or better, because destruction is necessary, the passage of the blood-relation into mere being, it takes on itself the act of destruction. Through this it comes about that the *dead*, the universal *being*, becomes a being that has returned into itself, a *being-for-self*, or, the powerless, simply isolated individual has been raised to *universal individuality*. The dead individual, by having liberated his *being* from his action or his negative unity, is the empty singular, merely a *passive being-for-another*, at the mercy of every lower irrational individuality and to the forces of abstract material elements, all of which are now more powerful than himself: the former on account of the life they possess, the latter on account of their negative nature. The family keeps away from the dead this dishonoring of him by unconscious appetites and abstract entities, and puts its own action in their place, and weds the blood-relation to the bosom of the earth, to the elemental imperishable individuality. The family thereby makes him a member of a community which prevails over and holds under control the forces of particular material elements and the lower forms of life, which sought to unloose themselves against him and to destroy him.[24]

Thus the blood relatives effect a destruction of death and bring about a sort of return, as though there were a fulfillment, as though beneath terrestrial being there were a subsoil to which one returned and from which one came (cf. in this regard the biblical term for dying, "to sleep with one's ancestors"). In death, there is the idea of a return to a maternal element, to a level situated *beneath* the phenomenological sphere.

The living remove the dishonor of anonymous decomposition by way of the honor of the funeral rites. In this way, they transform the deceased into a living memory. In the act of burial there is an exception relationship of the living with the dead. The burial rite is a deliberate relationship of the living with death, through their relationship with the deceased. Here, death is thought and not simply described. It is a necessary moment in the conceptual progress of thought itself, and in this sense it is thought.

We must wonder whether there is not, in these descriptions, a supplementary element—already stemming from the fact that the region of death is identified with the earth—just as there is also something unfounded in the description, that is, the relationship of death and of blood. As for the enigma of death which the *Logic* reduced to the nothingness that was already thought with being, Hegel comes closer to it here, but he speaks of it on the basis of the behavior of the survivor—although one could not take a less reifying approach to death than Hegel does here, since it is neither a thing nor a person, but a *shadow*.

We can now turn to Hegel's chapter on religion; a religion that, in the development of the *Phenomenology*, represents the penultimate figure of the progress of Spirit, and that is divided into natural religion, aesthetic religion, and revealed religion.

Death is of central importance to religion. In aesthetic religion, tragedy is not simply a literary genre but a certain manner in which consciousness thinks or comprehends itself. Here, Hegel sees in death a subterranean destiny that causes beings to arise that are delivered up to a knowledge that is false, a pure appearing that is but an appearance. And it is the return of destiny that is the tragedy where death plays the role of the subterranean.

In Hegel, the way in which death points to the obscure and veiled ground introduces the world of appearance into thought (Plato's Cave is here one moment of this thought). Again it is burial that remains the symbolic act by which those related through blood freely protect the deceased in returning to him what was in him and was him, even on the eve of his death: ipseity. In the thought expressed in aesthetic religion, death is not only nothingness but a return to the ground. Is it legitimate to interpret death in this way? It can no doubt be *felt* or *sensed* in this way, as the biblical expression cited earlier attests. In the same vein, Eugen Fink quotes the words of a Japanese man condemned to death: "I go to the gallows without pain and without trembling, for I see the smiling face of my mother."[25]

But in this composition of the idea of ground, or final ground, this ground of being and death, there is a certain phenomenal model that seems to remain in Hegel. Likewise in the second aspect of this return: to be taken under the protection of one's blood relatives. There again, a supplementary step is made when the return to the elements is interpreted as a return to the ground of being.

Notes

1. [For a discussion of the word *essance*, see above, note 2 for the lecture "Initial Questions," November 7, 1975; and below in Part II, the lecture "Being and Meaning," November 14, 1975.—Trans.] [The note 2 referred to here reads:]

   "[We are writing] ess*a*nce with an *a* to designate the verbal sense of the word 'to be' or 'being': we mean here the effectuation of being, *Sein* as opposed to the *Seiendes*." Emmanuel Levinas, *De Dieu qui vient à l'idée*, 2d ed. (Paris: Librarie philosophique J. Vrin, 1986), p. 78 n. 1; in English, "From the Carefree Deficiency to the New Meaning," in Emmanuel Levinas, *Of God Who Comes to Mind*, trans. Bettina Bergo (Stanford, Calf.: Stanford University Press, 1998), p. 43 and p. 195 n. 1.

   The preliminary "Note" to *Otherwise than Being* was lexically or orthographically less daring, although the thinking was exactly the same: "The dominant tone, necessary to the understanding of this discourse, and even its title, must be emphasized at the threshold of this book, although it may be frequently repeated at the heart of the work, as well: the term *essence* there expresses being [*l'être*] that is different from beings [*l'étant*], the German *Sein*, distinct from *Seiendes*, the Latin *esse* distinct from the Scholastics' *ens*. We have not dared to write *essance* as the history of the language would require, wherein the suffix *-ance*, coming from *antia* of from *entia*, gave rise to abstract nouns for action." (Emmanuel Levinas, *Autrement qu'être, ou au-delà de l'essence*, 2d ed. [The Hague: Martinus Nijhoff, 1978], "Note préliminaire," p. ix; in English, *Otherwise than Being, or Beyond Essence*, trans. Alphonso Lingis [Dordrecht: Kluwer Academic, 1991], "Note," p. xli.) We note, but simply for curiosity's sake, that in that work one finds the term *essance* written out once (ibid., p. 81; Eng., p. 65). This is a matter of mere curiosity, to be sure, because it is clear that this is a typographical error!
2. [See G. W. F. Hegel, *Hegel's Science of Logic*, trans. A. V. Miller (Atlantic Highlands, N.J.: Humanities Press International, 1969), bk. 1, pp. 67–78.—Trans.]

3. [Ibid., p. 73. Rolland cites from the French translation of the 1812 edition by Pierre-Jean Labarrière and G. Jarczyk, G. W. F. Hegel, *Science de la logique* (Paris: Aubier-Montaigne, 1972), p. 45. The original is on p. 12 of the German text, *Wissenschaft der Logik* (1812; Nuremberg: J. L. Schray, 1816).—Trans.]
4. It is Derrida who, as we know, proposed that we translate the untranslatable Hegelian *Aufhebung* by the term *relève*. The verb *relever* connotes the following: to set something upright or put it in good condition, to gather up, to set something in high relief, to orient it toward a height or give it greater value. [The noun *relève* adds the connotation of replacing something or someone with something, etc. The English "relieve" and "raising up" fail to capture such a wealth of meaning. See Jacques Derrida's essays "Différance" and "The Pit and the Pyramid," in *Margins of Philosophy*, trans. Alan Bass (Chicago: University of Chicago Press, 1982), pp. 19–20 n. 23 and p. 88 n. 16 (the French texts were first published in 1972). Bass leaves *relever* untranslated, arguing that the term "sublation," used in J. B. Baillie's translation of Hegel's *Phenomenology of Mind* (2d ed. {New York: Humanities, 1977}) "is misleading," whereas *relever does* take account {of} the effect of *différance* in its double meaning {of conservation and negation}." Also note Derrida's remarks on *Aufhebung* in his essay on Levinas, "Violence and Metaphysics: Essay on the Thought of Emmanuel Levinas," in Jacques Derrida, *Writing and Difference*, trans. Alan Bass (Chicago: University of Chicago Press, 1978), pp. 113–14.—Trans.]
5. G. W. F. Hegel, *Lessons on the History of Philosophy*, trans. J. Sibree (New York: Dover, 1956).
6. Hegel, *Science of Logic*, p. 82. Levinas translates this passage, combining it with the following line, "only this intuiting itself, pure and empty."
7. [This is Levinas's terse commentary on § C, "Becoming," in Hegel's *Science of Logic*, chap. 1. Levinas capitalizes *d'ores et déjà* ("always and already"), which underscores the difference between, on the one hand, Hegel's nothing and becoming, and, on the other hand, Aristotle's nothingness.—Trans.]
8. [Hegel, *Science of Logic*, pp. 82–83; *Wissenschaft der Logik*, p. 23. I have followed the published English translation here rather than Levinas's French translation. The later introduces no Levinasian idiosyncrasies that would make it deviate significantly from the Miller translation.—Trans.]
9. Eugen Fink, *Metaphysik und Tod* (Stuttgart: W. Kohlhammer, 1969), p. 159.
10. G. W. F. Hegel, *Hegel's Science of Logic*, trans. A. V. Miller (Atlantic Highlands, N.J .: Humanities Press International, 1969), p. 83. [In the French translation, *Science de la logique*, trans. Pierre-Jean Labarrière and G. Jarczyk (Paris: Aubier-Montaigne, 1972), the expression is "Leur vérité est

donc ce mouvement où les deux sont différents, mais *par le truchement d'*une différence qui s'est dissoute." The bracketed words in the passage just quoted in the text, "the mediation of," thus come from the French that Levinas cites, and they concern the question of mediation, which is of great importance to Levinas's thought.— Trans.]

11. [The French title translates as "The Opposition of Being and Nothingness in Representation." Except in citations from Miller's English translation, I translate *néant* as "nothingness."—Trans.]
12. [The French translation adds, at the end of this sentence, a phrase that is not in the German original: "*nothingness purely in and for itself.*" The italics in the quotation in the text are Rolland's.—Trans.]
13. Hegel, *Science of Logic*, p. 83.
14. Ibid., p. 83; in French, Hegel, *Science de la logique*, p. 60; in German, G. W. F. Hegel, *Wissenschaft der Logik* (1812; Nuremberg: J. L. Schray, 1816), p. 24. [The English text here is quite different, so I follow the French.—Trans.]
15. Ibid., p. 83; German, p. 24. [Levinas adds the italics and the German expression.—Trans.]
16. Ibid., p. 84; German, p. 25.
17. [Levinas is citing G.W.F. Hegel, *La phénoménologie de l'esprit*, trans. Jean Hyppolite (Paris: Aubier, 1941), 2: 14ff.; in English, see *Phenomenology of Spirit*, trans. A. V. Miller (Oxford: Clarendon, 1977), pp. 266ff.—Trans.]
18. [See, among Hegel's concluding remarks on Spirit and substance, the following: "This last becoming of Spirit, *Nature*, is its living immediate Becoming; Nature, the externalized Spirit, is in its existence nothing but this eternal externalization of its *continuing existence* and the movement which reinstates the *Subject*." Hegel, *Phenomenology of Spirit*, p. 492.— Trans.]
19. [See ibid., pt. BB, "Spirit," sec. a, "The Ethical World: Human and Divine Law," pp. 267ff.—Trans.]
20. Hegel, *Phénoménologie de l'esprit*, 2: 23; *Phenomenology of Spirit*, pp. 272–73.
21. Ibid., p. 18; Eng., p. 269.
22. Ibid., p. 19; Eng., p. 269 [translation modified for fluency with Levinas's text.—Trans.].
23. Ibid., p. 19; Eng., pp. 269–70 [Levinas's italics; translation modified.—Trans.].
24. G. W. F. Hegel, *La phénoménologie de l'esprit*, trans. Jean Hyppolite (Paris: Aubier, 1941), 2: p. 21; in English, *Phenomenology of Spirit*, trans. A. V. Miller (Oxford: Clarendon, 1977), pp. 271. [Levinas's italicizes "universal identity" and "passive being-for-another."—Trans.]
25. Eugen Fink, *Metaphysik und Tod* (Stuttgart: W. Kohlhammer, 1969), p. 179.

CHAPTER 19

"Hegel's Concept of Presentation: Its Determination in the Preface to the *Phenomenology of Spirit*"

—from *Delimitations: Phenomenology and the End of Metaphysics* (1986; first published: 1977)

John Sallis

For the first issue of the *Critical Journal of Philosophy*, which appeared in January 1802, Hegel wrote a long introduction entitled "On the Nature of Philosophical Criticism in General and Its Relation to the Present Condition of Philosophy in Particular." One of the issues taken up in this Introduction is the peculiarly esoteric character of philosophy. Hegel writes that "philosophy is by its nature something esoteric." He explains: "It is philosophy only by being opposed to the understanding and therefore still more to common sense [*gesunder Menschenverstand*]. . . . In relation to the latter the world of philosophy is in and for itself an inverted world."[1]

Philosophy is esoteric—and yet not in the sense that would entitle it to an indifferent aloofness. It is not such as can remain merely the esoteric possession of a few specially gifted individuals. Hegel is emphatic on this point in the Preface to the *Phenomenology of Spirit*: The elaboration, the form, demanded of philosophy is precisely such as to render it universally intelligible, "capable of being learned and of thus becoming the property of all"—that is, such as to render it "exoteric."[2] Philosophy is esoteric in its way of comporting itself to its *Sache*, its world an inverted world, but it is exoteric in that it offers to all who would undertake it the possibility of undergoing the inversion into philosophy. The formulation in the Introduction of 1802 is succinct: "Philosophy must indeed recognize the possibility of the people elevating themselves to it, but it must not lower itself to the people."[3]

The peculiar esoteric character of philosophy prescribes the rigor demanded of the beginner who would elevate himself to philosophy: The displacement into philosophy requires a radical inversion. And this inversion has as an essential moment a disorientation so radical that only the name "skepticism" is appropriate to it. Yet being in another regard exoteric, philosophy is obliged to hold out to the beginner the possibility of entering into this disorienting inversion, of offering (in the strictest sense) an *introduction* to philosophy. The radically disorienting, inverting movement into philosophy must be *presented*. An initiatory presentation (*Darstellung*) is demanded. The *Phenomenology of Spirit* is intended to satisfy this demand.

Just as philosophy in the form of science cannot begin straightaway as though "shot from a pistol," just as it requires the prior presentation of the movement up to philosophy, so likewise the initiatory presentation has its "prerequisite." The presentation requires a prior determination (appropriately preliminary) of the concept of presentation. Such determining—the introduction to the introduction to philosophy—proves actually to be an anticipatory leap, and as such its necessity for the presentation itself can, at best, be clarified only in and through the determination, not at the outset. My task is to thematize this determination of the concept of initiatory presentation—or, more specifically, to exhibit it up to the point where its necessity for the presentation begins to show itself from out of the determination. I accordingly restrict my attention to the Preface to the *Phenomenology of Spirit*—in fact, to its earlier sections. Rather than proceeding to that second phase, that more specific determination of the concept of presentation which Hegel carries out in the Introduction, in which the considerations, becoming more "procedural," are narrowed down to that point at which the presentation itself can commence—rather than proceeding thus, I shall remain with the Preface and attempt to think through to its end the connection between presentation and presented, as this connection is manifest within that larger sphere opened up by the more dangerous anticipatory leap which Hegel dares in the Preface.

(A) THE FAILURE OF THE PREFACE

Of the nineteen sections into which the Preface is divided,[4] the first is the most starkly reflexive. The theme with which the Preface here begins is *itself*—that is, the idea of a preface as such. More specifically, it begins with a consideration of the questionableness that necessarily infests any preface to a philosophical work, a questionableness rooted in a basic conflict between the character of a preface as such and the demand under which philosophy stands.

Hegel begins: Such explanation as customarily is offered in a preface—an explanation of the aim of the work and of its relation to other treatments of the same subject—"seems in the case of a philosophical writing not only superfluous but in regard to the nature of the thing [*um der Natur der Sache willen*] even unsuitable and inappropriate" (*Phän.* 9). The thing (*Sache*) to which philosophical writing pertains is of such a nature as to render all such prefatory explanations inappropriate. More precisely, such explanations stand in opposition to the way in which philosophy must comport itself to its *Sache*, to its way of having regard for the thing, its way of being for the sake of the thing itself, its letting the thing itself be: "For instead of occupying itself with the thing, such talk is always outside it; instead of abiding in the thing and forgetting itself in it, such knowing always reaches out for something else and really remains involved with itself rather than being involved with the thing and devoting itself to it" (*Phän.* 11).[5] The way of comportment characteristic of prefatory explanations, hence, what is said in such explanations and the manner in which it is said—such "can not hold as the way in which philosophical truth is to be presented" (*Phän.* 9).[6] The Preface determines preliminarily the nature of presentation, but such determining is not itself a presentation. The Preface falls short of those very "standards" which it determines.

From the outset the Preface is thus destined to fail; from its beginning it is already a failure. This character must be directive for the interpretation of the Preface if such interpretation is to avoid duplicating in itself the violence which the Preface does to the *Sache* of philosophical thought. The interpretation is called upon to let the violence ultimately recoil upon and be absorbed by the Preface, to let the things themselves simply stand. There is required, on the side of the interpretation, a certain suspension of judgment regarding those things, a certain "parenthesizing," which is also in a sense a complicity in the violence, or, to the extent that it understands itself, more properly a restraint. This restraint is required most of all in those connections in which the Preface is addressed to such things as the true, knowing, the absolute, God. In *our* time the restraint is more difficult and the demand for it of an entirely different order to the extent that our time is determined by the "death of God"—that is, by the positive lack of a true that could stand correlative to knowing and converge with it in absolute self-consciousness—that is, by the negation of precisely those things which Hegel's presentation would allow to show themselves as the *Sache* of philosophy.

But the Preface cannot allow them genuinely to show themselves. Measured by the demands of the things themselves, it is a failure. This failure of the Preface and its way of determining the further character of the Preface are variously elaborated in the first section. Hegel draws a curious analogy between philosophy and anatomy: Just as no one would suppose that he could learn anatomy merely by acquiring the general idea without mastering the particulars, so in philosophy mere consideration of aims and of other such generalities is inadequate to the thing itself. In fact, the inadequacy is much greater in the case of philosophy, it is even of an entirely different order; for, in the end, anatomy has no right at all to the name of science, and thus the very distinction between the actual elaboration and mere prefatory considerations breaks down, both being equally unscientific. The collapse of this distinction in the case of anatomy and the correlative breakdown of the analogy with philosophy serve, however, to render the distinction still more prominent in the case of philosophy. There is a fundamental opposition between a philosophical work and such general considerations as customarily go to make up a preface. This disparity generates, in turn, a disparity within the Preface itself: "In the case of philosophy, on the other hand, there would arise the disparity that use would be made of such a way [i.e., an unscientific procedure, as an anatomy] and yet, by means of this way itself, it would be exhibited as incapable of grasping the truth" (*Phän*. 10). Such a disparity characterizes the Preface to the *Phenomenology of Spirit*: Its procedure, its way of showing something, is such that the procedure itself gets shown up as inadequate. The Preface is such as to revoke itself. Its exhibition of what is required in order to be equal to the task of grasping the truth recoils upon the Preface itself, which manifestly does not meet the requirement thus exhibited. Nevertheless, in this self-revocation a certain content is preserved, namely, the determination of the nature of presentation; it is preserved inasmuch as it is carried over into *enactment*. The Preface sublates itself; its fundamental movement is an *Aufheben*.[7]

(B) SUBSTANCE AND SUBJECT

The basis for the determination of the concept of initiatory presentation is prepared in sections 5–6 of the Preface. Sections 7–8 explicitly carry through the determinations thus prepared. The subsequent sections of the Preface are then devoted largely to elaborating the determination in various regards and to applying it to certain polemical contexts.

The preparatory sections will require most careful attention and most deliberate restraint. As a guide for thematizing that basis which they prepare for the determination, focus on three principal statements from these sections.

The first of these statements occurs at the beginning of section 5:

> According to my view, which must justify itself [only] through the presentation of the system itself, everything depends on comprehending and expressing the true not as substance but just as much as subject.[8]

Two general observations need to be made before focusing on the principal content of the statement. First, note how the cast of the statement accords with the preliminary, prescientific character which both the determination and the provision of its basis have. The statement incorporates a self-characterization: Hegel is expressing his view (*Einsicht*) to which other views could be opposed, views whose claims to truth could not be effectively countered. Such expression does not belong to the presentation in the proper sense that is to be determined, and consequently what is expressed will eventually need to be genuinely established within the presentation. Second, note Hegel's reference to "comprehending and expressing." This reference poses on the horizon two relevant dualities: the duality of presentation (the comprehending and expressing) and presented (that which is comprehended and expressed); and, within the presentation itself, the duality of comprehension and expression, of thought and language.

The true is to be comprehended and expressed "not as substance"—i.e., not merely as substance, not as though it were substance and nothing more—"but just as much as subject." The true is to be taken as *both* substance and subject, yet in such fashion that the taking of it as subject involves a *negation* of the taking of it as mere substance.

In this context substance is to be understood primarily in the sense determined for it in Spinoza's *Ethics*: "By substance I understand that which is in itself and is conceived through itself."[9] Substance is that which is in itself in the sense of suffering no dependence on anything external to itself, which is absolved from all such dependence and in this sense absolute. Thus, Spinoza poses substance (i.e., the one substance, God) as encompassing both thought and extension as its attributes—hence, as encompassing both subject and object. But, in the end, substance as determined in Spinoza's work proves not to be so encompassing; as Fichte explicitly recognized,[10] substance as so determined remains bound on the side of things. Indeed, as Hegel notes in the present context, Spinoza's own age was outraged by his concept of God as the one substance because of "the instinctive recognition that self-consciousness was only drowned in it and not preserved." To take the true as mere substance is to remain on the side of the object, that is, to establish the identify of subject and object only on the side of the object. In the language of Hegel's *Differenz-Schrift*,[11] Spinoza's substance is, at best, merely an objective subject-object.

What is thus required is that the true be "just as much" subject, that it be not merely substance but *also* subject. In this connection "subject" has, as the primary sense from which Hegel in reforming and further developing its sense will proceed, that sense determined for it in Fichte's *Wissenschaftslehre*: the subject "has no being proper, no subsistence" [*kein eigentliches Seyn*, *kein Bestehen*] but rather is sheer "act" [*Handeln*] and nothing but act, specifically, the act of positing itself.[12] The subject is a movement of self-positing, hence, as both positing and posited, is "a necessary identity of subject and object: subject-object."[13] However, it is an identity of subject and object on the side of the subject, a subjective subject-object.[14] What is thus required is that it unite "with itself the being of the substance" (*Phän.* 19), that is, that the true be both subject and substance. What is required is a synthesis which will yield the identity of subject and substance, that is, the identity of subjective subject-object and objective subject-object, that is, the identity of identity and nonidentity.[15]

But everything depends on how this uniting of subject and substance is carried through, on whether it falls back into "inert simplicity" so as to end up presenting "actuality in a non-actual manner" (*Phän.* 19f.)—that is, on whether this uniting results in an indifference with respect to subject and object in which the negation and opposition between them would be finally eliminated, so that the movement and struggle corresponding to such negation and opposition would be revoked in the end rather than being taken up into the end in that manner which Hegel expresses by restoring to the word "actuality" the fundamental sense which the ancient philosophical tradition gave it. It is not sufficient that the true merely be *also* subject; rather, its way of being subject must be such as to sublate its way of being substance, its being-subject must constitute a sublation of its being-substance. This means that its being-subject must both negate and preserve its being-substance.[16]

Hegel's expression of the relevant negation consists mostly of a recapitulation of the general Fichtean determination of the nature of the subject. He begins: "The living substance is, further, that being which is in truth *subject* or, in other words, which is in truth actual only insofar as it is the movement of self-positing" (*Phän.* 20). It is to be noted how Hegel refers here to *living* substance, which (to say the least) is meant to indicate substance in a sense which, in contrast to that determined in Spinoza's thought, does not remain merely on the side of things. Substance (as living) is in truth subject; that is, substance in respect of its being in the truth, in its character as constituting the truth, *is* subject. Substance, in that sense that would allow one to say "The true is substance," is such as to require that in the end one say instead "The true is subject." Furthermore, "end" is here to be understood as *τέλος*,[17] thus, in correlation with actuality in the sense of *ἐνέογεια*. Substance, as being gathered up into its *τέλος*, as actual, is movement—specifically, the movement of self-positing, the movement which, in the Fichtean determination, does not just belong to the subject but rather *is* the subject.

Hegel continues: "As subject, it is pure, *simple negativity* and thus the bifurcation [*Entzweiung*] of the simple. . . ." This means: As the positing of itself, the subject is both the subject (which posits) *and* the object (which is posited); the subject as posited is object, is what it is not, is pure, simple negativity. As subject, as positing of itself, it is a positing of bifurcation; it posits within itself the bifurcation into subject and object.

Hegel continues, describing the subject, which is the bifurcation of the simple: ". . . or the doubling which opposes [*die entgegensetzende Verdopplung*], which again is the negation of this indifferent diversity and of its opposite." The bifurcation is an opposition *within* the subject; the opposition between subject and object is an opposition within the subject. Thus, it belongs to the movement of the subject (the movement which the subject *is*) to overcome the opposition, to negate the sheer diversity and reestablish its own unity. This overcoming, this reestablishing of its own unity, is not merely something added on, as it were, to the subject's self-positing, to that movement of self-positing which the subject *is*. On the contrary, the movement of self-positing *is* such a reestablishing of unity from out of diversity; it is a self-gathering—neither unity nor diversity but the gathering of diversity into unity. In Hegel's words, "Only this sameness which reconstitutes itself or the reflection into itself in being other—not an *original* unity as such or immediate unity as such—is the true."

The true is subject, that is, the movement of self-gathering into its end: "It is the becoming of itself, the circle which presupposes its end as its aim and has it for its beginning and which is actual only through its execution and end." The true is *not* substance: There can be "alongside" the subject no substance which, as object, would together with the subject constitute the true. There can be no such object, for the very distinction between subject and object is itself posited within the subject. The only being which, in the end, measures up to the Spinozistic criterion of substance is subject, not substance; only subject is "in itself" and "conceived through itself," whereas substance (as object) falls decisively within the sphere of that self-positing which is the subject.

Yet in the issue of subject and substance there is not only the moment of negation but also that of preservation; the opposition between subject and substance is not simply abolished at the level of the true in its actuality but also preserved in a new form. This requirement, that a moment of opposition to the subject be preserved, suddenly bursts forth at the very center of the issue—bursts forth in a language of such sheer strength that it holds together as its content the utmost abstractness and the most stark concreteness. Hegel writes of how matters would stand if such a moment were lacking, if there were merely the moment of negation, if subject were just the negation of substance in the sense of excluding the latter from the true in its actuality: "Thus the life of God and divine knowing may indeed be spoken of as a playing of love with itself; this idea sinks to the level of edification and even insipidity when seriousness, pain, the patience and work of the negative are lacking in it." This playing of love with itself, this play of unification, of self-gathering into unity—what is that seriousness which, if lacking in the idea of such play, reduces what would be the idea of absolute knowing to the level of mere edification?

Hegel continues: "In itself that life is indeed untroubled sameness and unity with itself, which is not serious about otherness and estrangement, nor with the overcoming of this estrangement." Thus, that seriousness which is so crucial is a seriousness regarding otherness; and the insipid idea which fails to include this seriousness is an idea of the divine life merely as *in itself*. What is the character of this seriousness regarding otherness such that it shatters the untroubled unity with self of the divine life in itself? Seriousness about otherness can be thus effective only if it corresponds to an otherness which is in truth serious, a serious other-ness. What, then, is other than life, knowing, subject? And how is it *seriously* other than these? The relevant otherness is simply that of object to subject. It is that otherness constituted by the subject-object bifurcation. What, then, is required in order that this otherness be a *serious* otherness? It is required that the bifurcation be no mere correlate of self-positing, that the otherness of object to subject not be such as to be immediately and totally dissolved into the subject's identity with itself. The bifurcation, the eruption of otherness, must be a rending, a tearing apart, to which belongs the *pain* of dismemberment, a rending which no sheer self-assertion can heal but which requires "the patience and work of the negative." Serious otherness is no mere moment within the identity of the subject; and the overcoming of serious otherness is not to be accomplished by a mere positing of unity correlative to such identity, by a mere positing of a unity that would immediately abolish the diversity of dismemberment. What is required is rather the toilsome gathering of diversity into unity, a gathering which, in overcoming diversity, otherness, lets it nevertheless be preserved in a new form.

Referring still to the divine life regarded in itself, as lacking seriousness about otherness, Hegel continues: "But this in-itself is abstract generality in which is disregarded both the nature of this life *to be for itself* and thus the self-movement of the form." To surpass the level of mere edification, it is thus required that the divine life be regarded in its nature as being-for-itself. For it to be for itself means: to establish the unity of its self-identity (to posit itself) from out of an opposition of such seriousness as to require toil, an opposition of such seriousness that mere negation of it cannot stand, an opposition which, in being overcome, must also be preserved by being granted a new form, an opposition which must be *sublated*. The true is not merely the untroubled self-positing of the divine life, not merely "the pure self-contemplation of the divine"; it is such only *in itself*, not in its *actuality*. The true becomes actual only by troubling itself with the gathering of serious otherness into itself; the true in its actuality is the gathering which *forms* diversity into unity, the gathering movement of informing, "the self-movement of the form."[18]

Hegel concludes: "The true is the whole." He explains: "It should be said of the absolute that it is essentially *result*, that it is only in the end what it is in truth; and precisely in this consists its nature: to be actual, subject, or that which becomes itself." The absolute is the whole of that movement in which self-identity is reconstituted from out of a bifurcation involving serious otherness; it is the whole of the movement in which the otherness of what is seriously other is sublated and that other thus established in its proper identity with the subject; it is the whole of the movement of gathering diversity into unity. And yet, the absolute is *in truth* "only in the end," only as "result." In its way of being the true as such, the absolute is the whole of the movement of gathering *as itself gathered up* into its fulfillment in the end; for what gathers and what is gathered are established in their identity precisely through the gathering, and so the absolute is the self-gatheredness into the τέλος, that is, the absolute is ἐνέογεια.

The true cannot be merely substance in that Spinozistic sense that remains on the side of objects; the true must *also* be subject. Yet, the true cannot be merely both substance and subject; its being-subject must also sublate its being-substance. This means, first, that its being-subject negates its being-substance, i.e., that there can be no mere substance (as object) alongside the subject, since the very distinction between subject and object is posited within the subject; and it means, second, that in its being-subject its being-substance is also preserved, namely, as serious otherness. Yet, now it can be seen, further, that the being-substance which is sublated by being-subject falls as much on the side of the subject as on that of the object: the true in-itself, the divine life as lacking serious otherness, is substance—Hegel calls it "immediate substance"—which the subject, the true in its actuality, negates and preserves in that movement of self-gathering which it is.

(C) KNOWING AS SYSTEM

The present concern is to thematize the basis which Hegel lays in sections 5–6 as preparation for the determination of the concept of presentation. To this end, I have proposed to focus on three principal statements from these sections. The second of these statements occurs at the beginning of the next-to-last paragraph of section 6:

> Among several conclusions which follow from what has been said, one may be singled out: it is only as science or as *system* that knowing is actual and can be presented.[19]

It needs to be asked: From which of the previous considerations does this conclusion follow? And how?

It can be related, first of all, to the consideration of language, specifically, of the proposition, that occurs in the middle of section 6 (*Phän*. 21–23). This consideration falls into two parts, which are separated in the text by a paragraph in which Hegel develops his concept of actuality by bringing it into explicit connection with Aristotle's concept of purposiveness.

The first part of the consideration of language occurs as a response to those who would object to understanding the absolute as result, who would object to doing so on the ground that it introduces mediation into the absolute. Hegel answers this objection by showing how it is based simply on a misunderstanding of the nature of mediation and of the bond between mediation and determination. If the absolute is spoken of *immediately*, if one utters such words as "God," "absolute," "eternal," then the absolute *as* so expressed is merely something general, and such expression is hardly an adequate expression of the absolute. Such single words "do not express what they contain" (*Phän.* 21)—just as the phrase "all animals" does not constitute a zoology. But if to such words anything else is added, if the transition is made to a proposition, then mediation is involved. If, for example, instead of saying merely "God," one says "God is the eternal," then there occurs within the expression the transition from God to something other, the eternal, and then the taking of this other back into God—that is, mediation, which Hegel defines as "nothing else but self-moving self-identity" (*Phän.* 21). Without mediation there could be nothing beyond the mere uttering of names.

The second part of the consideration of language in section 6 is, in effect, an elaboration of Hegel's definition of mediation. In order to express the absolute more adequately than in the previously mentioned single words, one might employ the proposition "God is the eternal." Here one begins with the word "God," which, however, taken by itself, is "a senseless sound, a mere name"; only the predicate gives the name content (*Phän.* 22). And so, one might well ask: Why not just speak of "the eternal"? Why add the senseless sound in the first place? Hegel answers: "But this word signifies that what is posited is not a being or essence or mere generality but rather something reflected into itself, a subject" (*Phän.* 23). The point is that the structure of the proposition anticipates the structure of the absolute as subject: It involves a transition into otherness (bifurcation) and the leading of this other back into the unity of the subject. Nevertheless, the structure of the proposition does *not* duplicate that of the absolute, does not mirror it perfectly; it *only* anticipates it: "The subject is accepted as a fixed point to which the predicates are affixed as to their support, by a movement which belongs to those who know about it and which is not supposed to belong to the fixed point; but only through this [i.e., the recognition that the movement belongs to the subject itself] could the content be presented as subject." The limitation thus lies in the fact that the movement between subject and predicate is taken to belong to the one who knows or asserts the proposition, *not* to the subject itself, which is, rather, posited as a fixed point.

How is this consideration of language linked to that conclusion which Hegel draws: "It is only as science or as *system* that knowing is actual and can be presented"? It is linked, specifically, to that side of the conclusion which pertains to presentation in general; this is indicated at the end of the consideration of language by Hegel's reference to what would be required in order for the structure of the proposition to be more than a mere anticipation of the structure of the absolute, in order that its content be, as Hegel says, "presented as subject." Such presentation would require that the subject (of the proposition) into which the predicate is taken back not be treated as fixed, as unaffected, unchanged, by the synthesis, that the movement not be regarded as belonging on the side of a detached knower who would have the proposition as object of his knowing. Rather, the subject must be treated as moved, as having become a different, more determinate subject by virtue of its taking of the predicate into itself. Yet, this is precisely what a proposition is prevented from accomplishing by its static subject-predicate structure; a proposition can *only anticipate* that movement which the absolute is. The structure of the proposition is such that this movement of becoming determinate cannot be *presented* in a single proposition. This means that the conception of the nature of philosophy in terms of basic propositions (*Grundsätze*) or principles (*Prinzipien*), that conception which dominates almost all modern philosophy up to German Idealism, is decisively transformed in Hegel's development of the issue of presentation. Any such proposition, "if it is true, is also false insofar as it is merely a basic proposition or principle" (*Phän.* 23). How, then, can the movement be presented? Its presentation will (at least) require a *system* of propositions, that is, a chain of propositions systematically connected in such a way that each proposition leads over to another which has as its subject that more determinate subject that results from the determination accomplished through the first proposition.[20] For the sake of presentation, the advance must be made not only from word to proposition but also from proposition to system of propositions. The absolute can be presented "only as science or as system."

Here it is appropriate to recall that peculiar disparity within the Preface of which Hegel spoke at the outset, that disparity which gives to the Preface its self-revoking character: It is to show that the way of showing characteristic of a preface does not measure up to what is required for a *presentation* of philosophical truth. Already this self-revocation is under way: The Preface is not itself such a *system* of propositions as it has shown to be required for the presentation of the truth.[21]

In the statement to which concern is now directed there is a peculiar duality, Hegel referring not only to presentation but also to what is to be presented in the presentation. On the one hand, he says that knowing can be *presented* only as science or as system, the reference being primarily to the requirement that the presentation take the form of a system of propositions, in contrast, for example, to an attempt at presentation through an alleged basic principle. On the other hand, Hegel says also that knowing is itself actual only as science or system. Not only must knowing be presented as science or as system, but also it *is* science or system; and only because it is such does its presentation stand under the requirement that it assume the form of science or system. Knowing, as actual, *is* system, and this is why it must be presented as system. A more fundamental sense of "system" thus begins to emerge: According to this sense, a system is not merely a system of propositions but rather a system of knowing, the system which knowing *is*. But what is this knowing which is actual only as system? It is the knowing *of* the absolute (in the double sense of the genitive). It is the self-knowing of the absolute, in which the absolute reconstitutes its self-identity from out of a serious otherness. Yet, this movement of self-knowing is just the absolute itself; and so in its fundamental sense the system *is* the absolute.

In the first statement that was considered, Hegel calls the absolute "the true"; and, explicitly expressed "not as substance but just as much as subject," it is called "the true in its actuality," "the true as actual." In the second statement, on the other hand, he calls the absolute "knowing," or, more fully, "knowing as actual." The absolute in its actuality is called both "knowing" and "the true." But in so calling it, Hegel has let it become manifest why it may be called by both names: In its actuality, in that self-gatheredness into the τέλος, the absolute finds itself in the other so as to reestablish its own self-identity; such reestablishing, as sublation of the otherness of the object, and, hence, of the otherness of the known, *the true*—such reestablishing is thereby an establishing of the identity of knowing with the true. In its actuality the absolute is both knowing and the true, for in this actuality knowing and the true are identical; the absolute is, most properly, the movement of establishing this identity, the movement in which knowing and the true are gathered into their identity.

(D) SPIRIT

According to the first principal statement, the absolute (the true as actual) is to be comprehended "not as substance but just as much as subject." If the terms are taken in the senses to which the development of this statement leads, that is, if substance is taken as the true in itself, as the "essence" (*Phän.* 20), and subject as the true for itself, as the true in its actuality, then the result of this development may be expressed by saying: Substance is essentially subject. The second statement—that "it is only as science or as *system* that knowing is actual and can be presented"—may be similarly abbreviated if the subordination of presentation to what is presented is taken as granted. It then says: Knowing, i.e., the absolute, i.e., the true as actual, is system; that is, the true is actual only as system. The third of the statements, which stands at the beginning of the final, most crucial paragraph of section 6, brings the results of the other two statements together in the concept of spirit:

> That the true is actual only as system or that substance is essentially subject is expressed in the representation which speaks of the absolute as *spirit*.[22]

It is in the paragraph which this statement introduces that the basis is decisively laid for the determination of the nature of presentation.

The crucial connection is that of spirit to actuality: "The spiritual alone is the actual" (*Phän.* 24). The determinations of spirit are thus to be worked out in terms of the concept of actuality, as the latter has been unfolded throughout sections 5–6. Hegel gives four determinations. First, spirit is "the essence or being-in-itself"—that is, it is immediate substance, the divine life as pure self-contemplation, as involving no serious otherness, as not having undergone the pain of that bifurcation which brings with it radical opposition. In this determination spirit still lacks form and actuality, that is, it is not yet that concrete movement which forms diversity into the unity of the τέλος, into actuality; it is no more than the abstract, still indeterminate assertion of unity, the possibility of self-positing. Second, spirit is "that which relates itself and is determinate" [*das sich Verhaltende und Bestimmte*]—that is, spirit is that which can become determinate, which can concretely posit itself, *only* insofar as it relates itself to an other, only insofar as it undergoes that bifurcation by which radical opposition is brought forth. The third determination is stated together with the second, as though they were one: Spirit is "that which is other and for itself" [*das Anderssein und Fürsichsein*]—that is, the other, which according to the second determination must be brought forth, is brought forth in a rending of spirit itself. It is an other which, however serious its otherness, is ultimately nothing other than spirit itself, an other in which spirit is object for itself. Fourth, spirit is that which "in this determination or being outside itself remains in itself—or it is in and for itself" [*in dieser Bestimmtheit oder seinem Außersichsein in sich selbst Bleibende;—oder es ist an und für sich*]—that is, spirit is the sublation of that bifurcation from which both otherness (being outside itself) and determinateness emerge; it is the gathering of otherness into itself, the positing of the identity of the other with what was subject in itself but is now, through this movement of determination, a reconstituted self-identity. In this fourth determination the others are gathered up: Spirit is being-in-and-for-itself.

Hegel proceeds to develop a curious "doubling" of these determinations:

> This being-in-and-for-itself, however, it is first for us or *in itself*; it is the spiritual *substance*. It must also be this *for itself*, must be the knowing of the spiritual and the knowing of itself as the spirit. (*Phän.* 24)

This doubling indicates a movement. It is a movement of spirit (as being-in-and-for-itself). But, it is characterized in two somewhat different ways. This difference is decisive.

According to the first characterization, the initial term of the movement, i.e., that *from* which there is movement, is: being-in-and-for-itself (only) in-itself. This term Hegel describes as "spiritual substance." At the first level it has, in a sense, no lack: as spirit, as being-in-and-for-itself, it has undergone the pain of bifurcation and the reconstitution of unity out of the diversity. But, at the level of the "doubling" it is only substance, not yet subject; it lacks actuality. Yet, the levels must be brought together, and that requires that this term be regarded as spirit in that condition in which that reunification, without which it would not be spirit, is indeed accomplished *but remains merely implicit*. It is the movement of gathering in that condition in which the moment of being itself gathered up, i.e., the identity of what gathers with what is gathered, is still implicit. In this condition spirit is reunited with itself in the object; it knows itself in the object without, however, knowing that it is itself that it knows. The relevant movement is, then, from spirit in this condition *to* being-in-and-for-itself (also) for-itself—i.e., *to* spirit in that condition in which it knows itself explicitly in its other. Thus, the movement is a movement from spirit in-itself to spirit for-itself, to spirit which is actual in the highest sense. Yet, spirit is itself movement; and so the movement being described is not something which spirit passively undergoes (in the sense, for instance, of a substratum that would remain unchanged through the movement), but rather the movement must belong to that very movement which spirit *is*.

But there is a second, quite distinct characterization given of this movement. According to this second characterization, the relevant movement is a movement from being-in-and-for-itself *for us* to being-in-and-for-itself *for itself*. Taken superficially, this characterization suggests that "we" know something about the absolute which it does not know about itself (namely, that it knows itself in its object). It suggests, in other words, that we know more about the absolute than it knows about itself, so that what would be required is that the absolute raise itself to that level of knowledge which *we* already have. The relevant movement would, then, be a movement by which spirit would come to know as much about its own self-knowing as we knew already before the movement. But clearly this suggested sense of the movement is a *comic sense*; and it collapses as soon as one asks seriously about such knowledge of the absolute as we would presume to have from outside the absolute. What must be the character of a knowing of the absolute in which we—or, more precisely, I—would be the subject of the knowing and the absolute its object? In order for it to be a genuine knowing, it must be true, that is, it must be a knowing of the true. But, the development of the second of the three principal statements has shown that a knowing of the true in its actuality is precisely a movement in which is established the identity of knowing with the true. For genuine knowing there is thus required in the present case a movement through which the mutual externality of the I and the absolute would be retroactively revoked. In other words, the knowing must be such that what the subject knows in knowing the object is just itself and such that the subject comes to recognize this knowing *as* a knowing of itself. Thus, in knowing the absolute, the I would know itself *in* the absolute and would recognize its unity with the absolute. Hence, in the course of knowing the absolute, the I would cease to be a subject situated outside the absolute; its knowing would be, as it were, appropriated to the self-knowing of the absolute.

What, then, is the character of the movement and of its terms? It is a movement *from* a knowing of the absolute which presumes to be outside the absolute and for which spirit would be merely in itself (i.e., its object) *to* a knowing of the absolute which knows itself as not being external but rather as belonging to the absolute's self-knowing. It is a movement of the knowing I *into* the absolute—that is, it is a movement by which the I's knowing is appropriated to the absolute's self-knowing. Considered with respect to its final term, it is a movement in which spirit becomes for-itself by appropriating the self-conscious I, the immediate *cogito*. Contrary to the comic sense at first suggested, the movement is not a movement of the absolute up to the I but of the I up to the absolute; yet, even this conception grants too much externality and so requires qualification, for the I can move up to the absolute only because the absolute is already with it,[23] or, still more strictly, the movement is not something which the I accomplishes alone but is rather a movement of the absolute, i.e., belongs to that movement which the absolute *is*. These qualifications point to a more fundamental perspective on the movement. If the absolute is absolute, then the I cannot have been initially outside it, so as then to undergo movement into the absolute. Rather, the I must already be in the absolute from the beginning, and the movement thus a movement within the absolute. It must be a movement by which the I, which takes itself to be outside the absolute, comes to the awareness that it is always already within the absolute.

Hegel's conclusion to section 6 poses the connection between spirit and science:

> The spirit which, so developed, knows itself as spirit is *science*. Science is the actuality of spirit and the realm that the spirit builds for itself in its own element.

Thus, science is not a theory about spirit, not an account of spirit—just as system is not merely a system of propositions. Rather, science *is* spirit in its actuality. Science *is* the absolute.

The posing of the identity between spirit and science brings to completion the preparation of the basis for the determination of presentation. With this completion two further issues are opened up which point ahead into the complexity of the problem of presentation.

The first concerns the title "System of Science," which Hegel places at the beginning of his work. The title now says: system of spirit in its actuality. Yet, system in its fundamental sense is identical with spirit as actual, the gathering of diversity into the unity of the τέλος. Hence, the title, in this formulation as well as the first, just says the same thing twice—or, it says: system (science) which is spirit in its actuality. "System," "science," "spirit in its actuality"—in their fundamental senses all three say the same thing. And, as long as one adheres solely to this fundamental sense, it makes no sense to speak of *Hegel's system*—or, at best, to speak in this way is only to allude to the problem of withholding from the primary sense of "system" (and "science") a secondary yet in some measure distinct sense; it is to allude to the problem of presentation.

The second issue concerns the becoming of science—specifically, the way in which the sense of such becoming is determined by the posing of the identity of science with spirit in its actuality. Such becoming must belong (in a still to be determined way) to that movement of gathering which is spirit itself. The becoming of science must thus belong to science itself, just as the gathering movement of spirit is itself gathered up into the end. To the extent that the structure of presentation accords with that of what is presented, the presentation of the becoming of science, which Hegel is about to identify as the phenomenology of spirit, constitutes a part of science (as presentation). The presentation of the inverting movement into philosophy falls within philosophy and separates itself decisively from the (self-revoking) prefatory determination of the nature of presentation.

(E) PRESENTATION

In sections 5–6, Hegel has laid the basis for that determination of the concept of presentation that is to be carried out and elaborated in the subsequent sections of the Preface. This basis consists primarily of the determinations of spirit and the peculiar "doubling" then built on these determinations, a "doubling" through which is distinguished, within that whole movement which is spirit as such, the particular movement from spirit in-itself (or for us) to spirit for itself (i.e., spirit in its full actuality). With this basis laid, Hegel proceeds in section 7 to introduce the issue of initiatory presentation and to relate it to that particular movement that has been distinguished.

Hegel introduces into the considerations the peculiar esoteric and exoteric characters of philosophy. These characters in their tension generate the problem of presentation, at least in its most immediate form as that of presenting the inverting movement into philosophy. The esoteric character is expressed first: "Science on its part demands of self-consciousness that it should have elevated itself into this ether to be able to live—and to live—with it and in it" *(Phän.* 25). Science—i.e., in its fundamental sense, spirit as actual and, in its derivative sense, philosophy—brings a demand. It places this demand upon self-consciousness, that is, upon the individual I, the immediate *cogito*, which as such lays claim to knowing. The demand is that the I elevate itself "into this ether," i.e., into the sphere of "pure self-recognition in absolute otherness" (*Phän.* 24)—i.e., up to the level of being-in-and-for-itself for itself, of spirit in its full actuality. That to which elevation is demanded is identical with that which places the demand. And what is demanded, the elevation of self-consciousness into the "ether," is precisely that movement which Hegel distinguished at the end of section 6: the movement of the I into the absolute.

Hegel proceeds to consider the exoteric character of philosophy: "Conversely, the individual has the right to demand that science should at least offer him the ladder to this standpoint and show him this standpoint within himself" (*Phän.* 25). The ladder would lead from the I into the absolute—that is, it would make available to the I the way of that movement into the absolute—that is, it would *present* it. The ladder which the individual can rightly demand is simply the presentation of the movement into the absolute, of the movement up to philosophy. Yet, how does the ladder, the presentation, lead the I to the standpoint of science? It does so, not in the manner of a mere connecting of two otherwise unrelated points, but rather, as Hegel says, by showing the individual "this standpoint within himself." The presentation is to let the standpoint of the I develop itself into what it already implicitly is, the standpoint of science.

However, the movement to be thus presented is not a mere uninterrupted, untroubled unfolding; it is not a movement lacking serious opposition, resistance, tension. In fact, the relevant tension has already come into view in previous considerations as the tension between the I's taking itself to be outside the absolute (such that the absolute would be its *object*) and the I's always already belonging to the absolute. Hegel now extends this into a fundamental tension between science and natural consciousness:

> If the standpoint of consciousness, to know of objective things in opposition to itself and to know of itself in opposition to them, is considered by science as the *other*—that in which it knows itself to be at home with itself, is considered rather as the loss of the spirit—so, on the other hand, the element of science is to it a distant beyond in which it no longer has possession of itself. Each of these two appears to the other to be the inversion of the truth. That the natural consciousness immediately entrusts itself to science is an attempt it makes, attracted by it knows not what, to walk for once also on its head. (*Phän.* 25)

The opposition is fundamental. Science stands at the point of explicit unification of subject and object, of being-in-and-for-itself *for itself*, of "pure self-recognition in absolute otherness"; and at this point the I cannot remain outside as a subject having science (spirit) as its object; the I cannot have "possession of itself" in the sense on which natural consciousness insists. Natural consciousness stands at the point of *merely* implicit unification, and what it asserts is precisely the bifurcation into subject and object; at this point the movement of the I into the absolute is opposed, and the I posited as subject over against object. Therefore, each "standpoint" appears to the other as a perversion, as inverted. The movement into philosophy is a radically disorienting, *inverting* movement.

At the end of section 7, the consideration of the movement into philosophy is explicitly connected with the previous characterizations of this movement (at the end of section 6). Hegel speaks of the demand that the I, "which seems to itself to stand outside science," be appropriated to science, that the belongingness of the I to the absolute be made explicit, that science "show that and how" the I "belongs to it" (*Phän*. 26). At the same time, this movement is precisely the becoming of science, that is, spirit's coming to be for itself:

> As lacking such actuality, it [science] is merely the content as the *in-itself*, the *purpose* which is still only something inward—not yet spirit, only spiritual substance. This *in-itself* has to express itself and to become *for itself*; this means: it has to posit self-consciousness as one with itself. (*Phän*. 26)

It is now possible to formulate the issue of initiatory presentation, that is, to lay out the principal distinctions and questions. The most fundamental distinction is that between the presentation itself and that which is to be presented in the presentation. With respect to the presentation, one can distinguish between two kinds of questions. First, there is the question of the *standpoint* of the presentation, i.e., the question of its stand with respect to what it presents. Second, there is the question of the *form* of the presentation—a question for which Hegel has made preparations in his consideration of the way in which the demand for system is placed upon the presentation by the presented and in his consideration of the structure of the proposition, especially that of the way in which its structure anticipates the movement of the absolute itself.

On the other hand, that which is to be presented in the presentation is that particular movement which Hegel distinguished in his considerations at the end of section 6. It is a movement from being-in-and-for-itself in itself to being-in-and-for-itself for itself; and as such it is identical with the movement from being-in-and-for-itself for us to being-in-and-for-itself for itself. It is the movement of the I into the absolute—that is, the appropriation of immediate self-consciousness to the absolute.

What is especially important at this stage, as the most fundamental development of the issue of presentation is approached, is that the principal items, presentation and presented, be kept sufficiently distinct to allow their intertwining to unfold.

(F) PRESENTATION AND PRESENTED

In sections 5–6 of the Preface, the basis is prepared for the determination of the concept of initiatory presentation. This preparation consists in the distinguishing of the movement that is to be presented in the presentation. In section 7 the demand for initiatory presentation is then introduced, and the movement previously distinguished is identified as that which such presentation is to present. With the presentation and the presented thus identified and distinguished, the task is to determine the precise manner in which they belong together.

Hegel expresses this determination in section 8. I shall attempt to work out the relevant determining methodically, in order then to be able to take up Hegel's expression at its proper level.

At the level of the mere distinction, there is the movement (from being-in-and-for-itself in itself to being-in-and-for-itself for itself), and there is the presentation of this movement. The movement is a movement of spirit, of the absolute. The presentation of the movement would be accomplished by an I, an individual self-consciousness, outside the absolute. Clearly, however, this formulation cannot stand, and the items distinguished cannot remain so totally distinct. For, in this formulation what is manifestly operative is the standpoint of natural consciousness: the formulation is, in effect, an affirmation of sheer bifurcation, of bifurcation between the moving absolute (as object of the presentation) and the presenting I (as subject of the presentation). Such an affirmation cannot stand, because the very movement being presented (the becoming of spirit, of science) is an overcoming of such bifurcation, an inverting of natural consciousness. The character of that which is to be presented must be allowed to recoil upon the determination of its relation to the presentation; the recoil destroys the mere externality that natural consciousness would assert.

Even in the preparatory distinguishing of the movement to be presented, Hegel already points beyond such natural representation by giving a second characterization of the movement, a characterization by which the presenting I is drawn into the movement rather than being simply posed over against it. The movement is a movement from being-in-and-for-itself for us *to* being-in-and-for-itself for itself, and the movement so characterized amounts to a movement of the I into the absolute. Thus, there is the movement of the absolute and the movement of the presenting I into the absolute; that is, the movement of presentation is a movement into the very movement (i.e., the absolute) which it presents.

The connection between these two movements must be determined more precisely. So, the question is: In what way can the presentation be a movement into the very movement presented? What must be the character of this *way* of movement into movement?

The general character of this way is already prescribed by the terms in which the way has become an issue. At a general level it may be said: There can be movement into movement only insofar as the first movement blends into the second. Thus, the presentation can be a movement into the movement presented only if it is of such a character that it comes to coincide with the movement of the presented. The problem is to determine the character of this "coming into coincidence," to exhibit it in terms of the specific character of the two movements involved.

The issue is no simple coincidence, no mere static coinciding, but rather a *coming* to coincidence. That which thus comes to coincidence brings something along to that with which it comes to coincidence, at least a doubling of self. Regarded from the end, the movement of presentation, moving into the movement presented, brings the latter to a completion. The presentation constitutes, in a still to be determined sense, the *completion* of the movement presented; it brings it into its final phase.[24]

Yet, on the other hand, the two movements are the same and not merely coincident in the end. Movement from spirit in itself to spirit for itself and movement of the I into the absolute—these were offered by Hegel as two characterizations of one and the same movement. But, how can the presentation remain in any sense a presentation if it is simply the same as that which it presents? Clearly it cannot remain a presentation if it is *simply* the same as what it presents—that is, the relevant sense of sameness must be other than that of such simple sameness as would exclude all difference. There must be an element of difference which grants to the presentation its distance from the presented, even if the presentation should prove such as to abolish that distance in the end. Such distance is, of course, something utterly different from that distance of subject from object on which natural consciousness would insist.

How, then, can the presentation be the final phase of the movement, that which brings it to completion, and yet be in some determinate sense the same as the movement? Especially if one attends to the peculiar gathering character that belongs to the "ending" of the movement, which would constitute its "final phase," then it can be seen that there is only one way in which this is possible: The presentation must be a retracing of a movement which otherwise is already completed before the inception of the presentation. The presentation as a re-*tracing* is thus identical in content with the presented, but as a *re*-tracing it differs in form and has, thus, its proper distance. The presentation is to retrace the presented in such a way as to gather it into its *τέλος*. The presentation is a *gathering reenactment*.

In section 8, Hegel characterizes the presentation as such a gathering reenactment—that is, as recollection, which is further described as the movement proper to education. It is, more specifically, the recollecting of the past stages of spirit. It is a passage through the contents of the educational stages through which spirit has passed in coming to its present stage, a passage which reenacts, "relives" those stages, not in their original form, but "as shapes already cast off by the spirit": "The content is already actuality reduced to possibility, vanquished immediacy, and the shapes have been reduced to abbreviations, to simple determinations of thought" (*Phän*. 27, 28). What are recollected are the past stages of spirit reduced to simple determinations of thought.

Hegel says that the content thus reduced is something possessed by spirit in its present stage; the reduced content is its property. In other words, the past shapes of spirit are gathered up into spirit in its present condition. Rather than simply leaving its past stages behind in moving to new shapes, spirit reduces these stages in such a way that they can be gathered up into the new stage; with respect to its shape, spirit is a movement of gathering into the τέλος. As so gathered, the content of the past shapes of spirit is "property that has already been acquired by the general spirit which constitutes the substance of the individual" (*Phän.* 27). They belong to spirit as substance, as still in itself to the extent of leaving the gathering of shapes implicit. The gathering has itself still to be gathered into the determination of spirit.

The recollection which the presentation is to accomplish is also a gathering. It is a passage which gathers up that through which it passes, which reenacts in such a way as to gather up that which it reenacts. That which it gathers up are just the stages through which spirit has passed; and it gathers these up in that form in which they now lie in spirit as its property, as thought determinations which are already gathered up. The gathering recollection is a regathering of what is already gathered; it is a regathering which reenacts the self-gathering of the shapes, which lets them show themselves as self-gathering, which thus lets the gathering be itself gathered into the determination of spirit. The presentation brings the gathering which spirit is to its completion by bringing to it the moment of its ending, the gathering of the gathering itself into the end; the presentation, leaving everything on the side of the presented, brings to it the doubling of explicit self-consciousness.

Hegel describes the movement of education, the enactment of initiatory presentation, from the point of view of the individual and from that of the general spirit. With respect to the former, it consists fundamentally in his gaining what is already given over to him, in his appropriating his spiritual substance to himself as self-consciousness. From the point of view of the general spirit as substance, "it is nothing else than that this acquire its self-consciousness [*sich ihr Selbstbewußtsein gibt*], bring forth its becoming and its reflection" (*Phän.* 27). Initiatory presentation has its distance, but only in order that it might properly "rejoin" the movement which is spirit itself and bring the latter to its completion, draw it into the end.[25]

The initiatory presentation, now explicitly identified by Hegel as a "*phenomenology* of spirit," presents the "becoming of science as such" (*Phän.* 26). That is, it presents the movement from spirit in itself (i.e., spiritual substance) to spirit for itself—or, more specifically, the movement from "immediate spirit," which Hegel now identifies as "sensible consciousness," to genuine knowing, i.e., spirit's knowing of itself. Yet, what is distinctive about such presentation is the fact that it is no mere copy set over against an original already complete in itself. It is no mere copy, for it presents the relevant movement, the movement of spirit through its shapes, not in its "original" form, but rather as reduced to thought determinations, to property—that is, *as* already gathered up. Yet, even so regarded, that which is presented is not an "original" already complete in itself, of which the presentation would provide merely a pale reflection easily dispensed with. On the contrary, the presentation brings the reflection by which the presented first comes to its completion, by which spirit becomes for itself, by which the gathering (which spirit is) is itself gathered into the end.

Such is the "standpoint" of the initiatory presentation, that is, its *stand* with respect to what it presents. It is a stand which leaves everything on the side of the *Sache* itself, which lets the *Sache* be, not by turning away and ignoring it but by turning toward it and tending it. The presentation is to free the *Sache* to itself, to let that self-gatheredness (which the matter is) come to fulfillment. The presentation is devoted to that midwifery which assists in the birth of the true; and to that extent it is Socratic.

But what is required in order that thought be able to tend the *Sache* for thought, in order that it be able to free that matter to itself? Must not such thought already have presupposed something in order to occupy the standpoint demanded? Are its presuppositions not then foisted, in turn, upon the *Sache* itself, in such a way that the presentation would end up binding the *Sache* in alien forms rather than freeing it to itself?

Indeed, such thought must already presuppose something in order to attain the required stand with respect to its *Sache*. However, what is of fundamental importance is that its presupposing is not such as to impose upon the *Sache* something alien to that *Sache*, as when, for example, an empirical concept is imposed upon a thing without regard for the nature shown by that thing. The thought which would present the *Sache* has its proper directedness, and without such directedness it could never, for instance, present the transition from one shape of spirit to another, the transition which is unknown to the consciousness within those shapes. But the directedness, rather than imposing the transition onto the *Sache,* only frees the transition that is already in the *Sache* itself, only regathers what is already itself implicitly gathered, or, more precisely, lets it show itself as self-gathering. The presenting thought has undeniably a directedness to unity; more precisely, it has a directedness to gatheredness as such, to unity in the sense of gathering unity. But it does not *impose* this unity upon the diversity that reigns among and within the shapes of spirit. Rather, it *holds out* this unity to the shapes, *lets* them develop into it, that is, lets them show themselves as already self-gathered into such unity.

Indeed, something is required of the thinking that would present the *Sache*. Such thinking does not just observe—as Hegel himself finally grants when he comes to the end of the determination of the concept of initiatory presentation (*Phän*. 74). Yet, all that is required of such thinking is in service to that reticence capable of freeing the *Sache* to itself.

It is to this stand of reticence that the determination of the concept of presentation would provoke one willing to undergo the inverting movement into philosophy. Indeed, the Preface does violence to the *Sache des Denkens*—but precisely in order to contribute to drawing thought to that stand from which it can let the *Sache* be.

Notes

1. *Jenaer Schriften* 1801–1807, vol. 2 of *Werke* (Frankfurt a.M.: Suhrkamp Verlag, 1970), 182.
2. *Phänomenologie des Geistes,* ed. J. Hoffmeister (Hamburg: Felix Meiner Verlag, 1964), 16f. Hereafter *Phän.*
3. *Jenaer Schriften*, 182.
4. Following the division given by Hoffmeister, which is based on that given in the table of contents of the first edition of 1807.
5. Within the Preface, see also the statements in sections 14–15, e.g., "scientific knowing, however, demands rather that one surrender to the life of the object" (*Phän.* 45).
6. Thus, near the end of the Preface Hegel satirizes those who take that "royal road to science" which consists in relying on common sense (i.e., refusing to undergo the inversion into philosophy) and in reading reviews of and *prefaces* to philosophical writings—a "vulgar road [which] can be taken in one's dressing gown" (*Phän.* 56f.), that is, which excuses itself from the "*Anstrengung des Begriffs*."
7. For the purposes of this study, it will suffice to let the usage *of aufheben* and its derivatives be governed by the sense determined in the early stages of the *Phenomenology* and expressed thus in the chapter on Wahrnehmung: "Das Aufheben stellt seine wahrhafte gedoppelte Bedeutung dar, welche wir an dem Negativen gesehen haben: es ist em *Negieren* und ein *Aufbewahren* zugleich" (*Phän.* 90). Hegel's more extended determination is given in *Wissenschaft der Logik*, ed. G. Lasson (Hamburg: Felix Meiner Verlag, 1967), 1: 93–5. No English word suitably translates *aufheben*. However, because of the stylistic difficulty of retaining the German verb with its separable prefix, resort will be had to the frequently used translation *sublate*—which makes it necessary to insist all the more that the sense of the word be taken from Hegel's explicit determinations and not from extraphilosophical preconceptions.
8. "Es kommt nach meiner Einsicht, welche sich [nur] durch die Darstellung des Systems selbst rechtfertigen muß, alles darauf an, das Wahre nicht als *Substanz*, sondern eben so sehr als *Subjekt* aufzufassen und auszudrücken" (*Phän.* 19). *Nur* was added in the revisions for a second edition, which Hegel began to prepare shortly before his death.

9. Part I. Definition 3.
10. Fichte, *Grundlage der gesammten Wissenschaftslehre*, vol. 1 of *Werke* (Berlin: De Gruyter, 1971), 120–22.
11. *Differenz des Fichte'schen und Schelling'schen Systems der Philosophie* (Hamburg: Felix Meiner Verlag, 1962), 75ff.
12. *Erste Einleitung in die Wissenschaftslehre: Werke*, 1: 440; *Zweite Einleitung in die Wissenschaftslehre: Werke*, 498.
13. Note added to the second edition of the *Grundlage* in 1802. *Werke*, 1: 98.
14. Hegel, *Differenz*, 48, 75.
15. In the *Differenz*-Schrift (77) Hegel uses this formulation ("Das Absolute selbst aber ist darum die Identität der Identität und der Nichtidentität") in showing how Schelling's thought goes beyond the limited standpoint (of subjective subject-object) to which Fichte remains attached. The formulation takes on added significance if contrasted with the corresponding formulation given in Schelling's *Darstellung meines Systems der Philosophie*, which was published the same year as Hegel's *Differenz-Schrift*; Schelling's formulation is: "Die absolute Identität *ist* nur unter der Form einer Identität der Identität" (*Sammtliche Werke*. Abt. I/4: 121). In the section of the *Phenomenology* under consideration, Hegel's mention of "intellectual intuition" is presumably to be understood as a reference to Schelling (cf. *Differenz*, 92f).
16. Regarding the governing sense of *sublate*, see note 7 above.
17. Cf. Werner Marx, *Hegels Phänomenologie des Geistes: Die Bestimmung ihrer Idee in "Vorrede" und "Einleitung"* (Frankfurt a.M.: Vittorio Klostermann, 1971), 98.
18. The connection at issue here between self-consciousness and serious otherness can be clarified by reference to Fichte. In Fichte's work there occurs a distinction which, granted certain fundamental differences, corresponds rather closely to Hegel's distinction between the true in itself and the true for itself. In the formulation given in Fichte's *Zweiter Einleitung* (1797), the relevant distinction is that between mere intellectual intuition, i.e., self-reverting activity, which Fichte identifies as constituting the mere *possibility* of self-consciousness, *and* genuine (concrete) self-consciousness, i.e., the positing of the I as determinate (*Werke*, 1: 459). In contrast to the sheer self-positing expressed in the first principle of the *Wissenschaftslehre*, which never occurs unmixed but is arrived at only by abstraction, concrete self-consciousness requires a genuine otherness, an otherness more radical than the always immediately surpassed otherness of abstract self-positing; it requires that a not-I be brought forth. As the matter is expressed in the theoretical part of the *Grundlage*: "An I that posits itself as self-positing, or a *subject*, is impossible without an object brought forth in the manner described (the determination of the I, its reflection upon itself as determi-

nate, is possible only on the condition that it bound itself by an opposite)" (*Werke*, 1: 218). This means: The I's reflection on itself, i.e., determinate self-consciousness, i.e., a determinate I as such, is possible only if a not-I is opposed to the I. The matter is even clearer in the *Zweite Einleitung*: Formulating the task of the *Wissenschaftslehre*, Fichte writes that it will be necessary to show "firstly, how the I is and may be for itself; then, that this being of itself for itself would be impossible, unless there also at once arose for it an existence outside itself" (*Werke*, 1: 458). In other words, opposition (negation) is required for determination; that is, the I can posit itself as determinate only in opposition to the not-I. Thus, for Fichte there is an intrinsic relation between genuine self-consciousness and serious otherness, and this relation has primarily to do with the possibility of determinateness in contrast to the total indeterminateness of the absolutely self-positing I of the first principle. This general connection which Fichte established between self-consciousness and serious otherness, the connecting of them through the concept of determination, remained decisive for Hegel.

On the other hand, the specific context of the connection was transformed when Hegel, following the lead of Schelling, replaced the Fichtean not-I with an object capable of reflection into itself, capable of unfolding into an objective subject-object. Regarding this development, see Marx, *Hegels Phänomenologie des Geistes*, 61ff.

19. "Unter mancherlei Folgerungen, die aus dem Gesagten fließen, kann diese herausgehoben werden, daß das Wissen nur als Wissenschaft oder als *System* wirklich ist und dargestellt werden kann" (*Phän*. 23).
20. Cf. *Phän*. 53, together with Werner Marx, *Reason and World* (The Hague: Martinus Nijhoff, 1971), 36.
21. It must be stressed that these considerations concern presentation *in general*, that is, they take no account of what is peculiar to an *initiatory* presentation or, therefore, of the specific way in which such a presentation would stand under the requirements here prescribed for presentation in general.
22. "Daß das Wahre nur als System wirklich, oder daß die Substanz wesentlich Subjekt ist, ist in den Vorstellung ausgedrückt, welche das Absolute als *Geist* ausspricht . . ." (*Phän*. 24).
23. Cf. Martin Heidegger, *Holzwege* (Frankfurt a.M.: Vittorio Klostermann, 1957), 120.
24. Cf. Marx, *Hegels Phänomenologie des Geistes*, 103f.
25. It is in terms of this "distance" that the problem of the form and, more specifically, of the language required of an initiatory presentation would need to be developed. The basis for such a development is provided by Hegel's determination of the form of speculative presentation, which is carried out in section 17 of the Preface and which is an extension of the considerations of language already given in section 6. The crucial point is that a speculative

presentation is not the same as an initiatory presentation (cf. Marx, *Hegels Phänomenologie des Geistes*, 104); and thus the linguistic requirement under which the former stands cannot simply be carried over to the latter. In other words, it would be necessary to determine in precisely what measure an *initiatory* presentation stands under those requirements. The peculiar "distance" from the presented determines that measure, which may thus be posed (with respect to the single proposition as considered in section 6) as a general structural correspondence: To the extent that presentation is at a distance from the movement presented, so, to that extent the movement within the proposition will be referred to a knower outside the proposition rather than being actually the movement of the subject of the proposition.

CHAPTER 20

"Excursus 7 (after the final day)"[*]

—from *Language and Death: The Place of Negativity* (1982)

Giorgio Agamben

If the Voice indicates the taking place of language as time, if thought is that experience of language that, in every proposition and in every phrase, experiences the very taking place of language (that is to say, it thinks being and time in their co-belonging in the Voice), how is it possible to think the Voice in itself, to think absolute time? In the response to this question it is possible to grasp both the proximity of and the diversity between Hegel's Absolute and Heidegger's *Ereignis*.

At the end of the Jena lessons of 1805–6, Hegel expresses his attitude toward this "thought of time" (*Gedanke der Zeit*). The wisdom of philosophy, absolute wisdom, is a "restored immediateness" (*die wiederhergestellte Unmittelbarkeit*), the spirit that, after having left itself, now returns to its own beginning and knows itself absolutely, overcoming the scission that separated it from itself *at the beginning*:

> Die Philosophie entäussert sich ihrer selbst, kommt bei ihrem Anfange, dem unmittelbaren Bewusstsein an, das eben das Entzweite ist. Sie ist so Mensch überhaupt; und wie der Punkt des Menschen ist, ist die Welt, und wie sie ist, ist er: em Schlag erschafft sie beide. Was ist vor dieser Zeit gewesen? das Andre der Zeit, nicht eine andre Zeit, sondern die Ewigkeit, der Gedanke der Zeit. Darin ist die Frage aufgehoben; denn diese meint eine andre Zeit. Aber so ist die Ewigkeit selbst in der

> Zeit; sie ist ein Vorher der Zeit, also selbst Vergangenheit: es ist gewesen, absolut gewesen: es ist nicht. Die Zeit is der reine Begriff, das angeschaute leere Selbst in seiner Bewegung, wie der Raum in seiner Ruhe. Vorher, eh[e] die erfüllte Zeit ist, ist die Zeit gar nicht. Ihre Erfüllung ist das Wirkliche, aus der leeren Zeit in sich Zurückgekehrte. Sein Anschauen seiner selbst ist die Zeit, das Ungegenständliche. Wenn wir aber sagen: vor der Welt, [meinen wir:] Zeit ohne Erfüllung. Der Gedanke der Zeit [ist] eben das Denkende, das Insich-Reflektierte. Es ist notwendig, hinauszugehen über diese Zeit, jede Periode, aber in den Gedanken der Zeit: jenes [ist die] schlechte Unendlichkeit, die das nie erreicht, wohinaus sie geht.
>
> [Philosophy alienates itself from itself, it arrives at its beginning, at immediate consciousness, which is precisely the scission. This is the case for man in general; and just as the point of man exists, so too the world exists: a blow creates them both. What was there before this time? The other *of time*, not another *time*, but eternity, the thought of time. With that the question is superseded; since this means *another* time. But eternity itself is in time; it is a before time, thus it is itself a past: it was, absolutely was: it is not. *Time* is the pure notion, the empty *itself* intuited in its movement, like space in its rest. Before completed (*erfüllte*) time, time simply does not exist. Its completion is the real, which returns from empty time to itself. Its intuition of itself is time, the Non-objective. If, however, we say: *before* the world, we mean: time without completion. The thought of time is the thinking, the Reflected-in-itself. It is necessary to overcome this time, every period, but in the idea of time; that is the bad infinity, which never reaches its destination.] (Hegel 3, p. 273)

For Hegel, then, the desire to think of eternity as a before all time or as another time is impossible, and any thought of time that desires to cross backward across empty time in order to reach the eternal necessarily leads to a bad infinity. Eternity in this sense is nothing other than the past, and as we know, this does not exist. Only completed time is true and real, that which has returned to itself from empty time. For this reason, Hegel says that the Absolute is not the beginning, what is before time, but only the result that has returned to itself. The Absolute is "only at the end what it truly is." It is "the circle returned on itself which presupposes (*voraussetzt*) its beginning and reaches it only at the end" (Hegel 1, p. 585). If the Absolute can never be itself at the beginning, it cannot, on the other hand, be identified with the infinite empty course of time. It must necessarily complete time, *finish it. Spirit can grasp itself as absolute only at the end of time.*

Hegel affirms this clearly in the final pages of the *Phenomenology*: "Spirit necessarily appears in time and it appears there until it can grasp its pure concept. . . . Until the spirit is completed in itself, as spirit of the world, it cannot reach its completion as self-conscious spirit" (ibid., pp. 584–85).

The beginning, which was presupposed as a past and went to the ground like a foundation, can only be reached at the end, when the history to which it gave a beginning (presupposing itself and going to the ground) is definitely completed.

Hence the essential orientation of the Absolute toward the past, and its presentation in the figure of totality and memory. Contrary to an ancient tradition of thought that considers the present as the privileged dimension of temporality, Hegel's past is completed time, time returned unto itself. It is, however, a past that has abolished its essential relation with the present and with the future. It is a "perfect" past, of which Hegel writes—in the text that most thoroughly explores the *Bewegung* of time—that it is "the dimension of the totality of time" and "the paralyzed restlessness of the absolute concept" (Hegel 4, p. 204). It is this past, this having-been, which thought has to think as absolved in absolute knowledge. (In the terms of our seminar, we might say that we must absolve the Voice from its having-been, from its being presupposed as removed, and thus we must think Voice and the foundation as absolute.)

It is again such a "thought of time" and such a "having-been" that Heidegger begins above all to reclaim as the theme of his thought. In an important passage, he formulates the supreme problem of his own thought in terms of an "advent of the having-been" (*Ankunft des Gewesen*), where "the release of every *it is*" is carried out (*der Abschied von allem "es ist*," Heidegger 1, p. 154). In the "Summary of a Seminar on the Lecture *Zeit und Sein*," Heidegger enunciates the difference between his thought and Hegel's, affirming that "from Hegel's point of view, one could say: *Sein und Zeit* gets caught in Being; it does not develop *Being* to the 'concept'" (Heidegger 2, p. 52; English ed., p. 48). That *Gewesen*, that having-been, which introduces negation and the mediation into immediate consciousness in the beginning of the *Phenomenology*, and which for Hegel is only fully realized *at the end*, still remains problematic for Heidegger. However, even here it is not simply a past, but a *Ge-wesen*; that is, the recollection (*ge-*) of that which lasts and exists (*Wesen*). Even here, the beginning is not something simple, but it hides a beginning (*Anfang*) within itself that only a memorial thought (*Andenken*) can reveal.

Here it is possible to measure the proximity of the Hegelian Absolute to that extreme figure that, in Heidegger, seeks to grasp the advent of the having-been: *Ereignis*. According to Heidegger, *Ereignis* seeks to think the co-belonging (*Zusammengehoren*) of Being and time; that is, it interrogates the *und* of the title *Sein und Zeit* (thus, something that cannot be grasped either as Being or as time; Heidegger 2, p. 46). This reciprocal belonging is not, however, simply conceived as a relation between two preexisting entities, but as that which conveys them in their proper existence, like the *Es* that "gives" in the expressions: *es gibt Sein*, *es gibt Zeit*.

How are we to conceive *Ereignis* in the context of our seminar? The co-belonging and the interweaving of Being and time have been expressed in terms of the taking place of language in time, that is, as Voice. In *Ereignis*, we might then say, Heidegger attempts to think the Voice in itself, no longer simply as a mere logico-differential structure and as a purely negative relation of Being and time, but as that which gives and attunes Being and time. In other words, he attempts to conceive the Voice absolved from negativity, the absolute Voice. In Heideggerian language the word *Ereignis* is semantically related to the word Absolute. In fact, in *Ereignis*, we should understand the *eigen*, the ownmost, as in *Absolute* the self and its own. In this sense, *Ereignis* might have the same meaning as the Latin "ad-*sue*-fectio," habituation, ab*so*lution. The reciprocal appropriation of Being and time that takes place in *Ereignis* is, also, a reciprocal absolution that frees them of all relativity and demonstrates their relation as "absolute relation," the "relation of all relations" (*das Verhältnis aller Verhältnisse*, Heidegger 1, p. 267). For this reason, Heidegger can write that in *Ereignis* he seeks to think "Being without regard for the entity" (Heidegger 2, p. 25)—that is, in terms of our seminar, the taking place of language without regard for that which, in this taking place, is spoken or formulated as a proposition. This does not mean, Heidegger warns, that "the relation with the entity would be inessential to Being or that it would be necessary to exclude this relation" (ibid., p. 35). Rather, it means "to think Being not in the manner of metaphysics," which considers Being exclusively in its function as the foundation for the entity and thus subordinates being to itself. In fact, metaphysics is "the history of the formations of Being (*Seinsprägungen*), that is, viewed from Appropriation (*Ereignis*), of the history of the self-withdrawal of what is sending in favor of the destinies" (ibid., p. 44; English ed., p. 41). In the terms of our seminar, this suggests that, in metaphysics, the taking place of language (the pure fact that language is) is obliterated in favor of that which is said in the instance of discourse; that is, this taking place (the Voice) is thought only as the foundation of the said, in such a way that the Voice itself never truly arrives at thought.

We must now ask if such an absolution and appropriation of the Voice is possible. Is it possible to absolve the Voice from its constitutive negativity and to think the Voice absolutely? Much is determined by the response we give to this question. Yet we can already anticipate that *Ereignis* does not seem to be entirely liberated from negativity or the unspeakable. "We can never represent *Ereignis*" (ibid., p. 24); "*Ereignis* does not exist nor does it present itself"; it is only nameable as a pronoun, as *It* (*Es*) and as *That* (*Jenes*) "which has sent the various forms of epochal Being," but that, in itself, is "ahistorical, or more precisely, without destiny" (*ungeschichtlich*, *besser*: *gesehicklos*; ibid., p. 44; English ed., p. 41).

Even here, as in the Hegelian Absolute, at the point where, in the *Ereignis*, the sender is revealed as the Proper, the history of Being reaches its end (*ist . . . die Seinsgeschichte zu Ende*) and, for thought, there is literally nothing left to say or think other than this "appropriation or habit." But in its essence, this amounts to an expropriation (*Enteignis*) and a hiding (*Verbergung*), which no longer hides itself (*sich nicht verbirgt*) and is no longer veiled in historical figures or words, but is shown as such: as pure sending without destiny, pure forgetting of the beginning (Heidegger 2, p. 44). In *Ereignis*, we might say, Voice shows itself as that which, remaining unsaid and unsignified in every word and in every historical tradition, consigns humanity to history and signification as the unspeakable tradition that forms the foundation for all tradition and human speech. Only in this way can metaphysics think *ethos*, the habitual dwelling place of man.

Here the necessary belonging of self-demonstration to the sphere of the absolute foundation is made clear. In fact, for Hegel the Absolute is not simply the without-relation or the without-movement; rather, it is absolute relation and movement, a complete relation unto itself. Thus, not every significance or every relation to alterity disappears here; but the Absolute is essentially "equal to itself in being-other," "a concept that realizes itself through its being-other and that, through the removal of this reality, is united with itself and reestablishes its absolute reality, its simple self-reference" (Hegel 2, p. 565). That which has returned to itself is not, however, without relation; it is in relation with itself, it shows itself. Signification, which has exhausted its historical figures and no longer signifies *nothingness*, now signifies or *shows itself*. Self-demonstration is the absolute relation that does not show or signify other than itself. *The Absolute is the self-demonstration of the Voice*.

Here, the link between *Ereignis* and the Absolute receives further confirmation. In fact, even in *Ereignis* movement and self-demonstration take place: "the lack of destiny of *Ereignis* does not mean that it has no 'movement' (*Bewegtheit*). Rather, it means that the manner of movement most proper to *Ereignis*, turning toward us in withdrawal, first shows itself as what is to be thought" (Heidegger 1, p. 44). Thus the *Sage*, originary speech, which constitutes "the most authentic mode" of *Ereignis*, is essentially pure self-demonstration, *Zeige* and *sich zeigen* (Heidegger 1, p. 254).

Further examination of the link (and of the differences) between *Ereignis* and the *Absolute* must be deferred until a later date. Such an examination should certainly begin with the problem of completion. If the words Absolute and *Ereignis* have any meaning, this is inseparable from the question of the end of history and tradition. If the Voice is the Insignificant, which goes to the ground so that meaning can be founded, and the beginning, which was presupposed and only came to be replaced in itself at the end, then this Voice can reach meaning only as an end and completion of meaning. The thought of the having-been (of the First) is necessarily a thought of the Last, eschatology.

Does the "conclusion" of the Hegelian figures of the spirit in absolute knowing (*hat also der Geist die Bewegung seiner Gestaltens beschlossen*, Hegel 1, p. 588) truly signify the end of history? Kojève's reading of Hegel, according to which absolute knowing would coincide with a book recapitulating all the historical figures of humanity (and such a book would be identical to the *Science of Logic*), remains hypothetical. But it is probable that, in the Absolute, the labor of human negativity has truly reached completion and that humanity, returned to itself, ceases to have a human figure to present itself as the fulfilled animality of the species *Homo sapiens*, in a dimension where nature and culture are necessarily confused. (Here, Marx's concept of the human condition as post-historical [or truly historical]—that is, after the end of the reign of necessity and the entrance of the "reign of freedom"—is still a contemporary idea.)

In Heidegger, the figure of "appropriated" or post-historical humanity remains ambiguous. On the one hand, the fact that the hiding of Being takes place in *Ereignis*—but no longer veiled in an epochal figure and thus, without any historical destiny—can only signify that Being is now definitively obliterated and that its history, as Heidegger repeatedly suggests, is finished. On the other hand, Heidegger writes that in *Ereignis* some possibilities of unveiling remain that thought cannot exhaust and, thus, there are still some historical destinies (*Schickungen*, Heidegger 2, p. 53). Moreover, man still seems here to maintain the status of the speaking-mortal. Rather, *Ereignis* is precisely the movement that carries language as *Sage* to human speech (Heidegger 1, p. 261). In this sense, "All proper (*eigentlich*) language—as assigned to man through the movement of the *Sage*—is destined (*geschickt*) and thus, destinal (*geschicklick*)" (Heidegger 1, p. 264). Human language, no longer linked to any nature, remains destined and historical.

Since both the Absolute and *Ereignis* are oriented toward a having-been or *Gewesen* of which they represent the consummation, the lineaments of a truly absolved, truly appropriated humanity—one that is wholly without destiny—remain in both cases obscure.

(So if we wished to characterize the perspective of the seminar with respect to the having-been in Hegel and in Heidegger, we could say that thought is oriented here in the direction of a *never-having-been*. This is to say that our seminar sets out from the definitive cancellation of the Voice; or rather, it conceives of the Voice as never having been, and it no longer thinks the Voice, the unspeakable tradition. Its place is the *ethos*, the infantile dwelling—that is to say, without will or Voice—of man in language. This dwelling, which has the figure of a history and of a universal language that have never been and are thus no longer destined to be handed down in a grammar, is that which remains here, to be thought. It is in this context that we should read the poem by Caproni that ended the seminar.)

A final thing remains to be said regarding the Eleusinian mystery. We saw that its simple wisdom, initiating man to negation and to the "mystery of eating bread and drinking wine," was central to the *Phenomenology of Spirit*. How should we understand the solidarity between philosophy and the mysterious wisdom evoked here? And what is meant by this proximity between unspeakable sacrificial wisdom, as the initiation into destruction and violence, and the negative foundation of philosophy? Here the problem of the absolute foundation (of ungroundedness) reveals its full weight. The fact that man, the animal possessing language, is, as such, ungrounded, the fact that he has no foundation except in his own action (in his own "violence"), is such an ancient truth that it constitutes the basis for the oldest religious practice of humanity: sacrifice. However one interprets the sacrificial function, the essential thing is that in every case, the action of the human community is grounded only in another action; or, as etymology shows, that every *facere* is *sacrum facere*. At the center of the sacrifice is simply a determinate *action* that, as such, is separated and marked by exclusion; in this way it becomes *sacer* and is invested with a series of prohibitions and ritual prescriptives. Forbidden action, marked by sacredness, is not, however, simply excluded; rather it is now only accessible for certain people and according to determinate rules. In this way, it furnishes society and its ungrounded legislation with the fiction of a beginning: that which is excluded from the community is, in reality, that on which the entire life of the community is founded, and it is assumed by the society as an immemorial, and yet memorable, past. Every beginning is, in truth, an initiation, every *conditum* is an *abs-conditum*.

Thus the sacred is necessarily an ambiguous and circular concept. (In Latin *sacer* means vile, ignominious, and also august, reserved for the gods; both the law and he who violates it are sacred: *qui legem violavit, sacer esto*.) He who has violated the law, in particular by homicide, is excluded from the community, exiled, and abandoned to himself, so that killing him would not be a crime: *homo sacer is est quem populus iudicavit ob maleficium; neque fas est eum immolari, sed qui occidit paricidi non damnatur*.

The ungroundedness of all human praxis is hidden here in the fact that an action (a *sacrum facere*) is abandoned to itself and thus becomes the foundation for all legal behavior; the action is that which, remaining unspeakable (*arreton*) and intransmissible in every action and in all human language, destines man to community and to tradition.

The fact that, in sacrifice as we know it, this action is generally a murder, and that sacrifice is *violent*, is certainly not casual or insignificant; and yet in itself this violence explains nothing; rather, it requires an explanation (as has been offered recently by Meuli and Burkert [Burkert 1972, English ed. 1983], who place sacrifice in relation to the hunting rites of prehistoric peoples, that is, to the development of hunters from a race of beings that were not biologically destined for hunting). Violence is not something like an originary biological fact that man is forced to assume and regulate in his own praxis through sacrificial institution; rather it is the very ungroundedness of human action (which the sacrificial mythogeme hopes to cure) that constitutes the violent character (that is *contra naturam*, according to the Latin meaning of the word) of sacrifice. All human action, inasmuch as it is not naturally grounded but must construct its own foundation, is, according to the sacrificial mythogeme, violent. And it is this *sacred* violence that sacrifice presupposes in order to repeat it and regulate it within its own structure.

The unnaturalness of human violence—without common measure with respect to natural violence—is a historical product of man, and as such it is implicit in the very conception of the relation between nature and culture, between living being and logos, where man grounds his own humanity. *The foundation of violence is the violence of the foundation*. (In a chapter from *Science of Logic*, titled "The Absolute Relation," Hegel articulates this implication of violence in the very mechanism of every human action as *causative* action; Hegel 2, pp. 233–40.)

Even philosophy, through the mythogeme of the Voice, thinks the ungroundedness of man. Philosophy is precisely the foundation of man as human being (that is, as a living being that has logos) and the attempt to absolve man of his ungroundedness and of the unspeakability of the sacrificial mystery. But precisely in that this absolution is conceived on the basis of a having-been and a negative foundation, the liberation of the sacrificial mythogeme remains necessarily incomplete, and philosophy finds itself obliged to "justify" violence. The *arreton*, the unspeakable tradition, continues to dominate the tradition of philosophy: in Hegel, as that nothingness that we must abandon to the violence of history and of language in order to tear away from it the appearance of a beginning and immediacy; and in Heidegger, as the unnamed that remains unsaid in all speech and in all tradition, and destines man to tradition and language. Certainly, in both cases, the aim of philosophy is to absolve man from the violence of the foundation; but this absolution is possible only *at the end* or in a form that remains, at least partially, excluded from articulation.

A completed foundation of humanity in itself should, however, signify the definitive elimination of the sacrificial mythogeme and of the ideas of nature and culture, of the unspeakable and the speakable, which are grounded in it. In fact, even the sacralization of life derives from sacrifice: from this point of view it simply abandons the naked natural life to its own violence and its own unspeakableness, in order to ground in them every cultural rule and all language. The *ethos*, humanity's own, is not something unspeakable or *sacer* that must remain unsaid in all praxis and human speech. Neither is it nothingness, whose nullity serves as the basis for the arbitrariness and violence of social action. Rather, it is social praxis itself, human speech itself, which have become transparent to themselves.

Note

[*] "Excursus 7 (after the final day)" appears in italics in the original English translation.

Bibliography

Burkert, W.

Homo Necans, The Anthropology of Ancient Greek Sacrificial Ritual and Myth. Berkeley, 1983. Originally published 1972.

Hegel, G. W. F.

1. *Werke*, vol. 3: *Phänomenologie des Geistes*. [English ed.: *Hegel's Phenomenology of Spirit*, trans. A.V. Miller, Oxford, 1977.]
2. *Werke*, vol. 6: *Wissenschaft der Logik*, Part 2.
3. *Jenenser Realphilosophie II, Die Volesungen von 1805–1806*, ed. J. Hoffmeister, Leipzig, 1931 (2nd ed., *Jenaer Realphilosophie*, Hamburg, 1967).
4. *Jenenser Logik Metaphysik und Naturphilosophie*, ed. G. Lasson, Hamburg, 1967 (1st ed., Leipzig, 1923).

Heidegger, M.

1. *Unterwegs zur Sprache*, Pfullingen, 1967. [English ed.: *On the Way to Language*, trans. Peter D. Hertz, New York, 1971.]
2. *Zur Sache des Denkens*, Tübingen, 1969. [English ed.: *On Time and Being*, trans. Joan Stambaugh, New York, 1972.]

CHAPTER 21

"'Not Only as *Substance*, but Also as *Subject*'"

—from *The Sublime Object of Ideology* (1989)

Slavoj Žižek

The Logic of Sublimity

In his essay on 'The Religion of Sublimity' (Yovel, 1982), Yirmiahu Yovel has pointed out a certain inconsistency in Hegel's systematization of religions, an inconsistency which does not result directly from the very principle of Hegel's philosophy but expresses rather a contingent, empirical prejudice of Hegel's as an individual, and can therefore be rectified by consequent use of Hegel's own dialectical procedure. This inconsistency concerns the place occupied respectively by Jewish and by ancient Greek religion: in Hegel's *Lessons on the Philosophy of Religion*, Christianity is immediately preceded by three forms of the 'religion of spiritual individuality': the Jewish religion of Sublimity [*Erhabenheit*], the Greek religion of Beauty, and the Roman religion of Understanding [*Verstand*]. In this succession the first, lowest place is taken by the Jewish religion—that is, Greek religion is conceived as a higher stage in spiritual development than the Jewish religion. According to Yovel, Hegel has here given way to his personal anti-Semitic prejudice, because to be consistent with the logic of the dialectical process it is undoubtedly the Jewish religion which should follow the Greek.

Despite some reservations about the detail of Yovel's arguments, his fundamental point seems to hit the mark: the Greek, Jewish and Christian religions do form a kind of triad which corresponds perfectly to the triad of reflection (positing, external and determinate reflection), to this elementary matrix of the dialectical process. Greek religion embodies the moment of 'positing reflection': in it, the plurality of spiritual individuals (gods) is immediately 'posited' as the given spiritual essence of the world. The Jewish religion introduces the moment of 'external reflection'—all positivity is abolished by reference to the unapproachable, transcendent God, the absolute Master, the One of absolute negativity; while Christianity conceives the individuality of man not as something external to God but as a 'reflective determination' of God himself (in the figure of Christ, God himself 'becomes man').

It is something of a mystery why Yovel does not mention the crucial argument in his favour: the very interconnection of the notions of 'Beauty' and 'Sublimity'. If Greek religion is, according to Hegel, the religion of Beauty and Jewish religion that of Sublimity, it is clear that the very logic of the dialectical process compels us to conclude that Sublimity should *follow* Beauty because it is the point of its breakdown, of its mediation, of its self-referential negativity. In using the couple Beauty/Sublimity Hegel relies, of course, on Kant's *Critique of Judgement*, where Beauty and Sublimity are opposed along the semantic axes quality-quantity, shaped-shapeless, bounded-boundless: Beauty calms and comforts; Sublimity excites and agitates. 'Beauty' is the sentiment provoked when the suprasensible Idea appears in the material, sensuous medium, in its harmonious formation—a sentiment of immediate harmony between Idea and the sensuous material of its expression; while the sentiment of Sublimity is attached to chaotic, terrifying limitless phenomena (rough sea, rocky mountains).

Above all, however, Beauty and Sublimity are opposed along the axis pleasure-displeasure: a view of Beauty offers us pleasure, while 'the object is received as sublime with a pleasure that is only possible through the mediation of displeasure' (Kant, 1964, p. 109). In short, the Sublime is 'beyond the pleasure principle', it is a paradoxical pleasure procured by displeasure itself (the exact definition—one of the Lacanian definitions—of enjoyment [*jouissance*]). This means at the same time that the relation of Beauty to Sublimity coincides with the relation of immediacy to mediation—further proof that the Sublime must *follow* Beauty as a form of mediation of its immediacy. On closer examination, in what does this mediation proper to the Sublime consist? Let us quote the Kantian definition of the Sublime:

> The Sublime may be described in this way: It is an object (of nature) the *representation* [*Vorstellung*] *of which determines the mind to regard the elevation of nature beyond our reach as equivalent to a presentation* [*Darstellung*] *of ideas*. (Kant, 1964, p. 119)

—a definition which, so to speak, anticipates Lacan's determination of the sublime object in his Seminar on *The Ethic of Psychoanalysis*: 'an object raised to the level of the (impossible-real) Thing'. That is to say, with Kant the Sublime designates the relation of an inner-worldly, empirical, sensuous object to *Ding an sich*, to the transcendent, trans-phenomenal, unattainable Thing-in-itself. The paradox of the Sublime is as follows: in principle, the gap separating phenomenal, empirical objects of experience from the Thing-in-itself is insurmountable—that is, no empirical object, no representation [*Vorstellung*] of it can adequately present [*darstellen*] the Thing (the suprasensible Idea); but the Sublime is an object in which we can experience this very impossibility, this permanent failure of the representation to reach after the Thing. Thus, by means of the very failure of representation, we can have a presentiment of the true dimension of the Thing. This is also why an object evoking in us the feeling of Sublimity gives us simultaneous pleasure and displeasure: it gives us displeasure because of its inadequacy to the Thing-Idea, but precisely through this inadequacy it gives us pleasure by indicating the true, incomparable greatness of the Thing, surpassing every possible phenomenal, empirical experience:

> The feeling of the Sublime is, therefore, at once a feeling of displeasure, arising from the inadequacy of imagination in the aesthetic estimation of magnitude to attain to its estimation by reason, and a simultaneously awakened pleasure, arising from this very judgement of the inadequacy of the greatest faculty of sense being in accord with ideas of reason, so far as the effort to attain to these is for us a law. (Kant, 1964, p. 106)

We can now see why it is precisely nature in its most chaotic, boundless, terrifying dimension which is best qualified to awaken in us the feeling of the Sublime: here, where the aesthetic imagination is strained to its utmost, where all finite determinations dissolve themselves, the failure appears at its purest.

The Sublime is therefore the paradox of an object which, in the very field of representation, provides a view, in a negative way, of the dimension of what is unrepresentable. It is a unique point in Kant's system, a point at which the fissure, the gap between phenomenon and Thing-in-itself, is abolished in a negative way, because in it the phenomenon's very inability to represent the Thing adequately *is inscribed in the phenomenon itself*—or, as Kant puts it, 'even if the Ideas of reason can be in no way adequately represented [in the sensuous-phenomenal world], they can be revived and evoked in the mind by means of this very inadequacy which can be presented in a sensuous way.' It is this mediation of the inability—this successful presentation by means of failure, of the inadequacy itself—which distinguishes *enthusiasm* evoked by the Sublime from fanciful *fanaticism* [*Schwärmerei*]: fanaticism is an insane visionary delusion that we can immediately see or grasp what lies beyond all bounds of sensibility, while enthusiasm precludes all positive presentation. Enthusiasm is an example of purely negative presentation—that is, the sublime object evokes pleasure in a purely negative way: the place of the Thing is indicated through the very failure of its representation. Kant himself pointed out the connection between such a notion of Sublimity and the Jewish religion:

> We have no reason to fear that the feeling of the Sublime will suffer from an abstract mode of presentation like this, which is altogether negative as to what is sensuous. For though the imagination, no doubt, finds nothing beyond the sensible world to which it can lay hold, still this thrusting aside of the sensible barriers gives it a feeling of being unbounded; and that removal is thus a presentation of the infinite. As such it can never be anything more than a negative presentation—but still it expands the soul. Perhaps there is no more sublime passage in the Jewish Law than the commandment: Thou shalt not make unto thee any graven image, or any likeness of any thing that is in heaven or on earth, or under the earth, and so forth. This commandment can alone explain the enthusiasm which the Jewish people, in their moral period, felt for their religion when comparing themselves with others. . . . (Kant, 1964, p.127)

In what consists, then, the Hegelian criticism of this Kantian notion of the Sublime? From Kant's point of view, Hegel's dialectics appears, of course, as a repeated fall, as a return to the *Schwärmerei* of traditional metaphysics which fails to take into account the abyss separating phenomena from the Idea and pretends to mediate the Idea with phenomena (as with the Jewish religion, to which Christianity appears as a return to pagan polytheism and the incarnation of God in a multitude of man-like figures).

In Hegel's defence, it is not enough to point out how in his dialectics none of the determinate, particular phenomena represents adequately the suprasensible Idea—that is, how the Idea is the very movement of sublation [*Aufhebung*]—the famous *Flüssigwerden*, 'liquidizing'—of all particular determinations. The Hegelian criticism is much more radical: it does not affirm, in opposition to Kant, the possibility of some kind of 'reconciliation'-mediation between Idea and phenomena, the possibility of surmounting the gap which separates them, of abolishing the radical 'otherness', the radical negative relationship of the Idea-Thing to phenomena. Hegel's reproach of Kant (and at the same time of Jewish religion) is, on the contrary, that *it is Kant himself who still remains a prisoner of the field of representation*. Precisely when we determine the Thing as a transcendent surplus beyond what can be represented, we determine it on the basis of the field of representation, starting from it, within its horizon, as its negative limit: the (Jewish) notion of God as radical Otherness, as unrepresentable, still remains the extreme point of the logic of representation.

But here again, this Hegelian approach can give way to misunderstanding if we read it as an assertion that—in opposition to Kant, who tries to reach the Thing through the very breakdown of the field of phenomena, by driving the logic of representation to its utmost—in dialectical speculation, we must grasp the Thing 'in itself', from itself, as it is in its pure Beyond, without even a negative reference or relationship to the field of representation. This is *not* Hegel's position: the Kantian criticism has here done its job and if this were Hegel's position, Hegelian dialectics would effectively entail a regression into the traditional metaphysics aiming at an immediate approach to the Thing. Hegel's position is in fact 'more Kantian than Kant himself'—it adds nothing to the Kantian notion of the Sublime; it merely takes it more *literally* than Kant himself

Hegel, of course, retains the basic dialectical moment of the Sublime, the notion that the Idea is reached through purely negative presentation—that the very inadequacy of the phenomenality to the Thing is the only appropriate way to present it. The real problem lies elsewhere: Kant still presupposes that the Thing-in-itself exists as something positively given beyond the field of representation, of phenomenality; the breakdown of phenomenality, the experience of phenomena, is for him only an 'external reflection', only a way of indicating, within the domain of phenomenality, this transcendent dimension of the Thing which persists in itself beyond phenomenality.

Hegel's position is, in contrast, that there is *nothing* beyond phenomenality, beyond the field of representation. The experience of radical negativity, of the radical inadequacy of all phenomena to the Idea, the experience of the radical fissure between the two—this experience is already *Idea itself as 'pure', radical negativity*. Where Kant thinks that he is still dealing only with a negative presentation of the Thing, we are already in the midst of the Thing-in-itself—*for this Thing-in-itself is nothing but this radical negativity*. In other words—in a somewhat overused Hegelian speculative twist—the negative experience of the Thing must change into the experience of the Thing-in-itself as radical negativity. The experience of the Sublime thus remains the same: all we have to do is to subtract its transcendent presupposition—the presupposition that this experience indicates, in a negative way, some transcendent Thing-in-itself persisting in its positivity beyond it. In short, we must limit ourselves to what is strictly immanent to this experience, to pure negativity, to the negative self-relationship of the representation.

Homologous to Hegel's determination of the difference between the death of the pagan god and the death of Christ (the first being merely the death of the terrestrial embodiment, of the terrestrial representation, figure, of God, while with the death of Christ it is God of beyond, God as a positive, transcendent, unattainable entity, which dies) we could say that what Kant fails to take into account is the way the experience of the nullity, of the inadequacy of the phenomenal world of representation, which befalls us in the sentiment of the

Sublime, means at the same time the nullity, the nonexistence of the transcendent Thing-in-itself as a positive entity.

That is to say, the limit of the logic of representation is not to 'reduce all contents to representations', to what can be represented, but, on the contrary, in the very presupposition of some positive entity (Thing-in-itself) *beyond phenomenal representation*. We overcome phenomenality not by reaching beyond it, but by the experience of how there is nothing beyond it—how its beyond is precisely this Nothing of absolute negativity, of the utmost inadequacy of the appearance to its notion. The suprasensible essence is the 'appearance *qua* appearance'—that is, it is not enough to say that the appearance is never adequate to its essence, we must also add that *this 'essence' itself is nothing but the inadequacy of the appearance to itself*, to its notion (inadequacy which makes it '[just] an appearance').

Thus the status of the sublime object is displaced almost imperceptibly, but none the less decisively: the Sublime is no longer an (empirical) object indicating through its very inadequacy the dimension of a transcendent Thing-in-itself (Idea) but an object which occupies the place, replaces, fills out the empty place of the Thing as the void, as the pure Nothing of absolute negativity—the Sublime is an object whose positive body is just an embodiment of Nothing. This logic of an object which, by its very inadequacy, 'gives body' to the absolute negativity of the Idea, is articulated in Hegel in the form of the so-called 'infinite judgement', a judgement in which subject and predicate are radically incompatible, incomparable: 'the Spirit is a *bone*', '*Wealth* is the Self', 'the State is *Monarch*', 'God is *Christ*'.

In Kant, the feeling of the Sublime is evoked by some boundless, terrifying imposing phenomenon (raging nature, and so on), while in Hegel we are dealing with a miserable 'little piece of the Real'—the Spirit *is* the inert, dead skull; the subject's Self *is* this small piece of metal that I am holding in my hand; the State as the rational organization of social life *is* the idiotic body of the Monarch; God who created the world *is* Jesus, this miserable individual crucified together with two robbers. . . . Herein lies the 'last secret' of dialectical speculation: not in the dialectical mediation-sublimation of all contingent, empirical reality, not in the deduction of all reality from the mediating movement of absolute negativity, but in the fact that this very negativity, to attain its 'being-for-itself', must embody itself again in some miserable, radically contingent corporeal leftover.

'The Spirit is a Bone'

At the immediate level, that of 'understanding', of 'representation [*Vorstellung*]', this proposition appears, of course, as an extreme variation of vulgar materialism; reducing the spirit, the subject, pure negativity, the most mobile and subtle element, an ever-escaping 'fox', to a rigid, fixed, dead object, to total inertia, to an absolutely non-dialectical presence. Consequently, we react to it like the shocked Soviet bureaucrat in the Rabinovitch joke: we are startled, it is absurd and nonsensical; the proposition 'the Spirit is a bone' provokes in us a sentiment of radical, unbearable contradiction; it offers an image of grotesque discord, of an extremely negative relationship.

However, as in the case of Rabinovitch, it is precisely thus that we produce its speculative truth, because *this negativity, this unbearable discord, coincides with subjectivity itself,* it is the only way to make present and 'palpable' the utmost—that is, self-referential—negativity which characterizes the spiritual subjectivity. We *succeed* in transmitting the dimension of subjectivity *by means of the failure itself,* through the radical insufficiency, through the absolute maladjustment of the predicate in relation to the subject. This is why 'the Spirit is a bone' is a perfect example of what Hegel calls the 'speculative proposition', a proposition whose terms are incompatible, without common measure. As Hegel points out in the Preface to the *Phenomenology of Spirit*, to grasp the true meaning of such a proposition we must go back and read it over again, because this true meaning arises from the very failure of the first, 'immediate' reading.

Does not the proposition 'the Spirit is a bone'—this equation of two absolutely incompatible terms, pure negative movement of the subject and the total inertia of a rigid object—offer us something like a Hegelian version of the Lacanian formula of fantasy: $\$\lozenge a$? To convince ourselves that it does, it is enough to place this proposition in its proper context: the passage from physiognomy to phrenology in the *Phenomenology of Spirit*.

Physiognomy—the language of the body, the expression of the subject's interior in his spontaneous gestures and grimaces—still belongs to the level of language, of signifying representation: a certain corporeal element (a gesture, a grimace) represents, signifies, the non-corporeal interior of the subject. The final result of physiognomy is its utter *failure*: every signifying representation 'betrays' the subject; it perverts, deforms what it is supposed to reveal; there is no 'proper' signifier of the subject. And the passage from physiognomy to phrenology functions as the change of level from *representation* to *presence*: in opposition to gestures and grimaces, the skull is not a sign expressing an interior; it represents nothing; it is—in its very inertia—the immediate presence of the Spirit:

> In physiognomy, Spirit is supposed to be known in its *own* outer aspect, as in a being which is the *utterance* of Spirit—the visible invisibility of its essence. . . . In the determination yet to be considered, however, the outer aspect is lastly a wholly *immobile* reality which is not in its own self a speaking sign but, separated from self-conscious movement, presents itself on its own account and is a mere Thing. (Hegel, 1977, p. 195)

The bone, the skull, is thus an object which, by means of its *presence*, fills out the void, the impossibility of the signifying *representation* of the subject. In Lacanian terms it is the objectification of a certain lack: a Thing occupies the place where the signifier is lacking; the fantasy-object fills out the lack in the Other (the signifier's order). The inert object of phrenology (the skullbone) is nothing but a positive form of certain failure: it embodies, literally 'gives body' to, the ultimate failure of the signifying representation of the subject. It is therefore correlative to the subject in so far as—in Lacanian theory—the subject is *nothing but* the impossibility of its own signifying representation—the empty place opened up in the big Other by the failure of this representation. We can now see how meaningless is the usual reproach according to which Hegelian dialectics 'sublates' all the inert objective leftover, including it in the circle of the dialectical mediation: the very movement of dialectics implies, on the contrary, that there is always a certain remnant, a certain leftover escaping the circle of subjectivation, of subjective appropriation-mediation, and *the subject is precisely correlative to this leftover*: $\$\Diamond a$. The leftover which resists 'subjectivation' embodies the impossibility which 'is' the subject: in other words, the subject is strictly correlative to its own impossibility; its limit is its positive condition.

The Hegelian 'idealist wager' consists, rather, in the conversion of this lack of the signifier into the signifier of the lack; from Lacanian theory we know that the signifier of this conversion, by means of which lack as such is symbolized, is the phallus. And—here we encounter the last surprise in the Hegelian text—at the end of the section on phrenology, Hegel himself evokes the phallic metaphor to designate the relationship between the two level of reading the proposition 'the Spirit is a bone': the usual reading, that of 'representation'/'understanding', and the speculative one:

> The *depth* which Spirit brings forth from within—but only as far as its picture-thinking consciousness where it lets it remain—and the *ignorance* of this consciousness about what it really is saying, are the same conjunction of the high and the low which, in the living being, Nature naïvely expresses when it combines the organ of its highest fulfilment, the organ of generation, with the organ of urination. The infinite judgement, *qua* infinite, would be the fulfilment of life that comprehends itself; the consciousness of the infinite judgement that remains at the level of picture-thinking behaves as urination. (Hegel, 1977, p. 210)

'Wealth is the Self'

When, in the *Phenomenology of Spirit*, we encounter a certain 'figure of consciousness', the question to ask is always: Where does this figure repeat itself—

that is, where do we find a later, richer, more 'concrete' figure which, by repeating the original one, offers us, perhaps, the key to its true meaning? Concerning the passage from physiognomy to phrenology, we do not have to look far: it is resumed in the chapter on the 'Self-alienated Spirit', in the form of a passage from 'language of flattery' to Wealth.

The 'language of flattery' is a middle term in the triad *Noble-minded consciousness—The language of flattery—Wealth.* Noble-minded consciousness occupies the position of extreme alienation: it posits all its contents in the common Good embodied in the State—noble-minded consciousness serves the State with total and sincere devotion, attested by its acts. It does not speak: its language is limited to 'counsels' concerning the common Good. This Good functions here as an entirely substantial entity, whereas with the passage to the next stage of dialectical development it assumes the form of subjectivity: instead of the substantial State, we obtain the Monarch who is able to say 'l'État, c'est moi'. This subjectivation of the State entails a radical change in the mode of serving it: 'The *heroism of silent service* becomes the *heroism of flattery*' (Hegel, 1977, p. 310). The medium of activity of the consciousness is no longer deeds, it is now language, flattery addressed to the person of the Monarch, who embodies the State.

It is not difficult to detect the historical background of this passage: the transformation of medieval feudalism, with its notions of honourable service, and so on, into absolute Monarchy. But here we are far from a simple corruption or degeneration of silent and devoted service into hypocritical flattery. The paradoxical syntagm 'heroism of flattery' is not to be taken as an ironic conjunction of two otherwise opposed notions; here we are concerned with heroism in the full sense of the word. The 'heroism of flattery' is a notion that deserves to be interpreted on the same level as that of 'voluntary servitude'; it announces the same theoretical deadlock: how can 'flattery', usually perceived as a non-ethical activity *par excellence*, as a renunciation of the ethical stance in pursuit of 'pathological' interests of gain and pleasure, obtain a properly ethical status, the status of an obligation whose fulfilment draws us 'beyond the pleasure principle'?

According to Hegel, the key to this enigma is the role played in it by language. Language is, of course, the very medium of the 'journey of consciousness' in *Phenomenology*, to such a point that it would be possible to define every stage of this journey, every 'figure of consciousness', by a specific modality of language; even in its very beginning, in the 'sense-certainty', the dialectical movement is activated by the discord between what the consciousness 'means to say' and what it effectively says. In this series, the 'language of flattery' none the less presents an exception: only here is language not reduced to a medium of the dialectical process but becomes as such, in its very form, what is at stake in the struggle; it 'has for its content the form itself, the form which language itself is, and is authoritative as *language*. It is the power of speech, as that which performs what has to be performed' (Hegel, 1977, p. 308).

This is why 'flattery' is not to be conceived at the psychological level, in the sense of hypocritical and avaricious adulation: what announces itself here is rather the dimension of an *alienation proper to language as such*—it is the very form of language which introduces a radical alienation; noble-minded consciousness betrays the sincerity of its internal conviction *as soon as it starts talking*. That is to say, as soon as we start talking, truth is on the side of the Universal, of what we are 'effectively saying', and the 'sincerity' of our innermost feelings becomes something 'pathological' in the Kantian sense of the word: something of a radically non-ethical nature, something which belongs to the domain of the pleasure principle.

The subject can pretend that his flattery is nothing but a simple feigning, accommodation to an external ritual which has nothing whatsoever to do with his innermost and sincere convictions. The problem is that as soon as he pretends to feign, he is already the victim of his own feigning: his true place is out there, in the empty external ritual, and what he takes for his innermost conviction is nothing but the narcissistic vanity of his null subjectivity—or, in modern parlance, the 'truth' of what we are saying depends on the way our speech constitutes a social bond, on its performative function, not on the psychological 'sincerity' of our intention. The 'heroism of flattery' carries this paradox to its extreme. Its message is: 'Although what I'm saying disavows completely my innermost convictions, I know that this form emptied of all sincerity is truer than my convictions, and in this sense I'm sincere in my eagerness to renounce my convictions'.

This is how 'flattering the Monarch against one's convictions' can become an ethical act: by pronouncing empty phrases which disavow our innermost convictions, we submit ourselves to a compulsive disrupting of our narcissistic homeostasis, we 'externalize' ourselves completely—we heroically renounce what is most precious in us, our 'sense of honour', our moral consistency, our self-respect. The flattery achieves a radical voidance of our 'personality'; what remains is the empty form of the subject—the subject as this empty form.

We encounter a somewhat homologous logic into the passage of the revolutionary Leninist consciousness to the post-revolutionary Stalinist one: here as well, after the revolution, faithful service and devotion to the revolutionary Cause turns necessarily into a 'heroism of flattery' addressed to the Leader, to the subject presumed to embody and personify the revolutionary power. Here too, the properly heroic dimension of this flattery consists in the fact that in the name of our fidelity to the Cause we are ready to sacrifice our elementary sincerity, honesty and human decency—with the supplementary 'turn of the screw' that we are prepared *to confess this very insincerity* and to declare ourselves 'traitors'.

Ernesto Laclau was quite right to remark that *it is language which is, in an unheard-of sense, a 'Stalinist phenomenon'*. The Stalinist ritual, the empty flattery which 'holds together' the community, the neutral voice, totally freed of all 'psychological' remnants, which pronounces the 'confessions' in the staged political processes—they realize, in the purest form to date, a dimension which is probably essential to language as such. There is no need to revert to the pre-Socratic foundation if we want to 'penetrate the origins of language'; the *History of the Communist Party* (*Bolsheviks*) is more than sufficient.

Where can the subject who is thus 'emptied' find his objective correlative? The Hegelian answer is: in Wealth, in money obtained in exchange for flattery. The proposition 'Wealth is the Self' repeats at this level the proposition 'The Spirit is a bone': in both cases we are dealing with a proposition which is at first sight absurd, nonsensical, with an equation the terms of which are incompatible; in both cases we encounter the same logical structure of passage: the subject, totally lost in the medium of language (language of gestures and grimaces; language of flattery), finds his objective counterpart in the inertia of a non-language object (skull, money).

The paradox, the patent nonsense of money—this inert, external, passive object that we can hold in our hands and manipulate—serving as the immediate embodiment of Self, is no more difficult to accept than the proposition that the skull embodies the immediate effectivity of the Spirit. The difference between the two propositions is determined solely by the difference in the starting point of the respective dialectical movement: if we start from language reduced to 'gestures and grimaces of the body', the objective counterpart to the subject is what at this level presents the total inertia—the skullbone; but if we conceive language as the medium of the social relations of domination, its objective counterpart is of course wealth as the embodiment, as the materialization of social power.

Positing. External. Determinate Reflection

This paradox of the 'infinite judgement' is what escapes Kant—why? To put it in Hegelian terms, because Kant's philosophy is one of 'external reflection'—because Kant is not yet able to accomplish the passage from 'external' to 'determinate' reflection. In Kant's view, the whole movement which brings forth the feeling of the Sublime concerns only our subjective reflection external to the Thing, not the Thing-in-itself—that is, it represents only the way we, as finite subjects caught in the limits of our phenomenal experience, can mark in a negative mode the dimension of the trans-phenomenal Thing. In Hegel, however, this movement is an immanent reflexive determination of the Thing-in-itself—that is, the Thing is *nothing but* this reflexive movement.

To exemplify this movement of reflection—namely the triad of positing, external and determinate reflection (Hegel, 1966), let us take the eternal hermeneutical question of how to read a text. 'Positing reflection' corresponds to a naïve reading claiming immediate access to the true meaning of the text: we know, we pretend to grasp immediately what a text says. The problem arises, of course, when there are a number of mutually exclusive readings claiming access to the true meaning: how do we choose between them, how do we judge their claims? 'External reflection' provides a way out of this impasse: it transposes the 'essence', the 'true meaning' of a text into the unattainable beyond, making of it a transcendent 'Thing-in-itself'. All that is accessible to us, finite subjects, are distorted reflections, partial aspects deformed by our subjective perspective; the Truth-in-itself, the true meaning of the text, is lost for ever.

All we have to do to pass from 'external' to 'determinate' reflection is to become aware how *this very externality of the external reflexive determinations of the 'essence'* (the series of distorted, partial reflections of the true meaning of the text) *is already internal to this 'essence' itself*, how the internal 'essence' is already in itself 'decentred', how the 'essence' of this essence itself consists in this series of external determinations.

To make this somewhat speculative formulation clearer, let us take the case of conflicting interpretations of some great classical text—*Antigone,* for example. 'Positing reflection' claims a direct approach to its true meaning: '*Antigone* is in fact a drama about . . .'; 'external reflection' offers us a gamut of historical interpretations conditioned by different social and other contexts: 'We don't know what Sophocles really meant, the immediate truth about *Antigone* is unattainable because of the filter of historical distance, all that is within our grasp is the succession of historical influence of the text: what *Antigone* meant in the Renaissance, to Hölderlin and Goethe, in the nineteenth century, to Heidegger, to Lacan. . . .' And to accomplish the 'determinate reflection', we have only to experience how this problem of the 'true', 'original' meaning of *Antigone*—that is, the status of *Antigone-'in-itself'*, independent of the string of its historical efficacy—is ultimately a pseudo-problem: to resume the fundamental principle of Gadamer's hermeneutics, there is more truth in the later efficacy of a text, in the series of its subsequent readings, than in its supposedly 'original' meaning.

The 'true' meaning of *Antigone* is not to be sought in the obscure origins of what 'Sophocles really wanted to say', it is constituted by this very series of subsequent readings—that is, it is constituted *afterwards*, through a certain structurally necessary *delay*. We achieve the 'determinate reflection' when we become aware of the fact that this delay is immanent, internal to the 'Thing-in-itself': *the Thing-in-itself is found in its Truth through the loss of its immediacy*. In other words, what appears, to 'external reflection', as an *impediment* is in fact a *positive condition* of our access to Truth: the Truth of a thing emerges because the thing is not accessible to us in its immediate self-identity.

Yet what we have just said is insufficient inasmuch as it still leaves room for a certain misunderstanding: if we grasp the plurality of phenomenal determinations which at first sight blocked our approach to the 'essence' as so many self-determinations of this very 'essence'—if we transpose the fissure separating the appearance from essence into the internal fissure of the essence itself—it could still be said that in this way—through 'determinate reflection'—the appearance is ultimately reduced to the self-determination of the essence, 'sublated' in its self-movement, internalized, conceived as a subordinate moment of self-mediation of the essence. We have yet to add the decisive emphasis: it is not only that the appearance, the fissure between appearance and essence, is a fissure internal to the essence itself; the crucial point is that, inversely, *'essence' itself is nothing but the self-rupture, the self-fissure of the appearance*.

In other words, the fissure between appearance and essence is internal to the appearance itself; it must be reflected in the very domain of appearance—*this* is what Hegel calls 'determinate reflection'. The basic feature of Hegelian reflection is thus the structural, conceptual necessity of its *redoubling*: it is not only that the essence must appear, must articulate its inner truth in a multiplicity of determinations (this being one of the commonplaces of Hegelian commentary: 'the essence is only as deep as it is broad'); the point is that it must appear *for the appearance itself*—as essence in its difference to appearance, in the form of a phenomenon which, paradoxically, gives body to the nullity of phenomena as such. This redoubling characterizes the movement of reflection; we run into it at all levels of the Spirit, from the State to religion. The world, the universe, is of course the manifestation of divinity, the reflection of God's infinite creativity; but for God to become effective he must again reveal himself to his creation, embody himself in a particular person (Christ). The State is, of course, a rational totality; but it establishes itself as an effective sublation-mediation of all particular contents only by embodying itself again in the contingent individuality of the Monarch. This redoubling movement is what defines 'determinate reflection', and the element which embodies again, which gives positive form to the very movement of sublation of all positivity, is what Hegel calls 'reflexive determination'.

What we must grasp is the intimate connection, even identity, between this logic of reflection (positing, external, determinate reflection) and the Hegelian notion of the 'absolute' subject—of the subject which is no longer attached to some presupposed substantial contents but posits its own substantial presuppositions. Roughly speaking, our thesis is that what is constitutive for the Hegelian subject is precisely this redoubling of the reflection, the gesture by means of which the subject posits the substantial 'essence' presupposed in the external reflection.

Positing the Presuppositions

To exemplify this logic of 'positing the presuppositions', let us take one of the most famous 'figures of consciousness' from Hegel's *Phenomenology of Spirit*: the 'beautiful soul'. How does Hegel undermine the position of the 'beautiful soul', of this gentle, fragile, sensitive form of subjectivity which, from its safe position as innocent observer, deplores the wicked ways of the world? The falsity of the 'beautiful soul' lies not in its inactivity, in the fact that it only complains of a depravity without doing something to remedy it; it consists, on the contrary, in the very mode of activity implied by this position of inactivity—in the way the 'beautiful soul' structures the 'objective' social world in advance so that it is able to assume, to play in it the role of the fragile, innocent and passive victim. This, then, is Hegel's fundamental lesson: when we are active, when we intervene in the world through a particular act, the real act is not this particular, empirical, factual intervention (or non-intervention); the real act is of a strictly symbolic nature, it consists in the very mode in which we structure the world, our perception of it, in advance, in order to make our intervention possible, in order to open in it the space for our activity (or inactivity). The real act thus *precedes* the (particular-factual) activity; it consists in the previous restructuring of our symbolic universe into which our (factual, particular) act will be inscribed.

To make this clear, let us take the care of the suffering mother as the 'pillar of the family': all other members of the family—her husband, her children—exploit her mercilessly; she does all the domestic work and she is of course continually groaning, complaining of how her life is nothing but mute suffering, sacrifice without reward. The point, however, is that this 'silent sacrifice' is her imaginary identification: it gives consistency to her self-identity—if we take this incessant sacrificing from her, nothing remains; she literally 'loses ground'.

This is a perfect case of Lacanian communication (by which the speaker gets back from the recipient his own message in its inverted—that is, true—meaning). The meaning of the mother's incessant groaning is a demand. 'Keep on exploiting me! My sacrifice is all that gives meaning to my life!', so that by exploiting her mercilessly, other members of the family return to her the true meaning of her own message. In other words, the true meaning of the mother's complaint is: 'I'm ready to give up, to sacrifice everything . . . *everything but the sacrifice itself!*' What the poor mother must do, if she wants to liberate herself effectively from this domestic enslavement, is to *sacrifice the sacrifice itself*—to stop accepting or even actively sustaining the social network (of the family) which confers on her the role of exploited victim.

The mother's fault is therefore not simply in her 'inactivity' in silently enduring the role of exploited victim, but in actively sustaining the social-symbolic network in which she is reduced to playing such a role. Here, we could also refer to the distinction between 'constituting' and 'constituted' identification—between the ideal ego and the ego-ideal. On the level of the ideal-imaginary ego, the 'beautiful soul' sees herself as a fragile, passive victim; she identifies with this role; in it she 'likes herself', she appears to herself likeable; this role gives her a narcissistic pleasure; but her real identification is with the formal structure of the intersubjective field which enables her to assume this role. In other words, this structuring of the intersubjective space (the family network) is the point of her symbolic identification, the point from which she observes herself so that she appears to herself likeable in her imaginary role.

We could also formulate all this in terms of the Hegelian dialectics of form and content, in which the Truth is of course in the form: by means of a purely formal act, the 'beautiful soul' structures its social reality in advance in such a way that it can assume the role of passive victim; blinded by the fascinating content (the beauty of the role of 'suffering victim'), the subject overlooks his or her *formal responsibility* for the given state of things. To explain this notion of form, let us take a historical example: the debate between Sartre and the French Communists immediately after the Second World War (the so-called 'existentialism debate'). The Communists' main reproach to Sartre was as follows: by conceiving the subject as pure negativity, void, emptied of all positive substantial contents, of all determination by some pre-given 'essence', Sartre rejected all bourgeois *content*. What remained, however, was the pure *form* of bourgeois subjectivity, so Sartre had still to accomplish the last and most difficult task: to reject this very form of bourgeois individualistic subjectivity and give himself up to the working class. . . . Despite its simplicity, there is a grain of truth in this argument: is not the blind-spot of so-called 'bourgeois libertarian radicalism' precisely in the way its pathetic sacrificing of all bourgeois content affirms the form of bourgeois subjectivity? In overlooking the fact that the real 'source of evil' is not the positive content but this form itself? This dialectic of form and content is the background for our understanding of the following enigmatic passage from Hegel's *Phenomenology*:

> Action *qua* actualization is thus the pure form of will—the simple conversion of a reality that merely *is* into a reality that results from *action*, the conversion of the bare mode of objective knowledge into that of knowing *reality* as something produced by consciousness. (Hegel, 1977, p. 385)

Before we intervene in reality by means of a *particular* act, we must accomplish the *purely formal* act of converting reality as something which is objectively given into reality as 'effectivity', as something produced, 'posited' by the subject. Here the interest of the 'beautiful soul' is to make us see this gap between the two acts (or two aspects of the same act): on the level of positive content she is an inactive victim, but her inactivity is already located in a field of effectivity, of social reality 'that results from *action*'—in the field constituted by the 'conversion' of the 'objective' reality into effectivity. For the reality to appear to us as the field of our own activity (or inactivity), we must conceive it in advance as 'converted'—*we must conceive ourselves as formally responsible-guilty for it.*

Here we finally encounter the problem of posited presuppositions: in his particular-empirical activity, the subject of course presupposes the 'world', the objectivity on which he performs his activity, as something given in advance, as a positive condition of his activity; but his positive-empirical activity is possible only if he structures his perception of the world in advance in a way that opens the space for his intervention—in other words, only if he retroactively posits the very presuppositions of his activity, of his 'positing'. This 'act before act' by means of which the subject posits the very presuppositions of his activity is of a strictly formal nature; it is a purely formal 'conversion' transforming reality into something perceived, assumed as a result of our activity.

The crucial moment is this previousness of the act of formal conversion in relation to positive-factual interventions, whereby Hegel differs radically from Marxian dialectics: in Marx, the (collective) subject first transforms the given objectivity by means of the effective-material process of production; he first gives it 'human form', and thereupon, reflecting the results of his activity, he formally perceives himself as the 'author of its world', while in Hegel the order is reversed—before the subject 'actually' intervenes in the world, he must formally grasp himself as responsible for it.

In ordinary language, the subject 'doesn't really do anything', he only assumes the guilt-responsibility for the given state of things—that is, he accepts it as 'his own work' by a purely formal act: what was a moment ago perceived as substantial positivity ('reality that merely *is*') is suddenly perceived as resulting from his own activity ('*reality* as something produced by consciousness'). 'In the beginning' is thus not an active intervention but a paradoxical act of 'imitation', of 'pretending': the subject *pretends* that the reality which is given to him in its positivity—which he encounters in its factual substantiality—is his own work. The first 'act' of this kind, the act defining the very emergence of man, is the funeral ritual; Hegel develops this in a formal, explicit way apropos of Polynices' burial in *Antigone*:

> This universality which the individual *as such* attains is *pure being*, *death*; it is a state which has been reached *immediately*, in the *course of Nature*, not the result of an action *consciously done*. The duty of the member of a Family is on that account to add this aspect, in order that the individual's ultimate being, too, shall not belong solely to Nature and remain something irrational, but shall be something *done*, and the right of consciousness be asserted in it. . . . Blood-relationship supplements, then, the abstract natural process by adding to it the movement of consciousness, interrupting the work of Nature and rescuing the blood-relation from destruction; or better, because destruction is necessary, the passage of the blood-relation into mere being, it takes on itself the act of destruction. (Hegel, 1977, pp. 270–71)

The crucial dimension of the funeral rite is indicated in the last phrase quoted: the passage into pure being, death, natural disintegration, is something that happens anyway, with inevitable natural necessity; by means of the funeral rite the subject takes upon himself this process of natural disintegration, he symbolically repeats it, he pretends that this process resulted from his own free decision.

Of course, from a Heideggerian perspective we can here reproach Hegel with bringing subjectivism to its extreme: the subject wants to dispose freely even with death, this limiting condition of human existence; he wants to transform it into his own act. However, the Lacanian approach opens up the possibility of another, opposite reading: the funeral rite presents an act of symbolization *par excellence*; by means of a forced choice, the subject assumes, repeats as his own act, what happened anyway. In the funeral rite, the subject confers the *form* of a free act on an 'irrational', contingent natural process.

Hegel articulates the same line of thought in a more general way in his *Lectures on the Philosophy of Religion*, when he discusses the status of the Fall of man in Christianity—more specifically, the relationship between Evil and human nature. His starting point is of course that human nature is in itself innocent, in a state 'before the Fall'—that guilt and Evil exist only when we have freedom, free choice, the subject. But—and this is the crucial point—it would be quite erroneous to conclude, from this original innocence of human nature, that we can simply distinguish in man the part of nature—which was given to him, for which he is consequently not responsible—from the part of free spirit—a result of his free choice, the product of his activity. Human nature 'in itself'—in its abstraction from culture—is indeed 'innocent', but as soon as the form of spirit begins to reign, as soon as we enter culture, man becomes, so to speak, retroactively responsible for his own nature, for his most 'natural' passions and instincts. 'Culture' consists not only in transforming nature, in conferring on it spiritual form: human nature itself, as soon as it is put in relation to culture, *changes into its own opposite*—what was a moment ago spontaneous innocence becomes retroactively pure Evil. In other words, as soon as the universal form of the Spirit comprises natural contents, the subject is formally *responsible* for it even if it is materially something which he simply *found*: the subject is treated as if, by means of an eternally past, primordial act, he freely chose his own natural-substantial base. It is this formal responsibility, this fissure between the spiritual form and the given content, which drives the subject to incessant activity (Hegel, 1969).

It is thus not difficult to realize the connection between this gesture of 'choosing what is given', this act of formal conversion by means of which the subject assumes—determines as his own work—the given objectivity and the passage from external to determinate reflection accomplished when the positing-producing subject posits the very presuppositions of his activity, of his 'positing': what is 'positing of presuppositions' if not that very gesture of formal conversion by means of which we 'posit' as our own work what is given to us?

It is likewise not difficult to recognize the connection between all this and the fundamental Hegelian thesis that the substance is to be conceived as subject. If we do not want to miss the crucial point of this Hegelian conception of substance as subject, we have to take into account the break that separates the Hegelian 'absolute' subject from the Kantian-Fichtean, still 'finite' subject: the latter is the subject of practical activity, the 'positing' subject, the subject which actively intervenes in the world, transforming-mediating the given objective reality; he is consequently *bound* to this presupposed reality. In other words, the Kantian-Fichtean subject is the subject of the work-process, the subject of the productive relationship to reality. Precisely for this reason he can never entirely 'mediate' the given objectivity, he is always bound to some transcendent presupposition (Thing-in-itself) upon which he performs activity, even if this presupposition is reduced to the mere 'instigation [*Anstoß*]' of our practical activity.

The Hegelian subject is, however, 'absolute': he is no longer a 'finite' subject bound to, limited, conditioned by some given presuppositions; he himself posits these very presuppositions—how? Precisely through the act of 'choosing what is already given'—that is, through the symbolic act, mentioned above, of a purely formal conversion; by pretending that the given reality is already his work; by assuming responsibility for it.

The current notion according to which the Hegelian subject is 'even more active' than the Fichtean subject in so far as he succeeds where the Fichtean subject still fails—that is, in 'devouring'-mediating-internalizing the whole effectivity without any leftover—is entirely wrong: what we must add to the Fichtean 'finite' subject to arrive at the Hegelian 'absolute' subject is just some purely formal, empty gesture—in common parlance: an act of pure feigning by means of which the subject pretends to be liable for what is happening anyway, without taking part in it. *This is the way 'substance becomes subject'*: when, by means of an empty gesture, the subject takes upon himself the leftover which eludes his active intervention. This 'empty gesture' receives from Lacan its proper name: the signifier; in it resides the elementary, constitutive act of symbolization.

In this way, it is also clear how we connect the Hegelian concept of 'substance as subject' with the fundamental feature of the dialectical process: in this process, we can say that in a sense *everything has already happened*; all that is actually going on is a pure change of form through which we take note of the fact that what we arrived at *has always already been*. For example, in the dialectical process the fissure is not 'sublated' by being actively overcome: all we have to do is to state formally that *it never existed*. This happens in the Rabinovitch joke, where the bureaucrat's counter-argument is not actively refuted by Rabinovitch's more accurate arguments; all Rabinovitch has to do is to accomplish a purely formal act of conversion by simply stating that the bureaucrat's very counter-argument is effectively an argument in his favour.

There is no contradiction between this 'fatalistic' aspect of Hegelian dialectics—the idea that we are simply taking note of what has already happened—and his claim to conceive substance as subject. Both really aim at the same conjunction, because the 'subject' is precisely a name for this 'empty gesture' which changes nothing at the level of positive content (at this level, everything has already happened) but must nevertheless be added for the 'content' itself to achieve its full effectively.

This paradox is the same as that of the last grain of sand to be added before we have a heap: we can never be sure which grain is the last one; the only possible definition of the heap is that *even if we take away one grain, it will still be a heap*. So this 'last grain of sand' is by definition superfluous, but none the less necessary—it constitutes a 'heap' by its very superfluity. This paradoxical grain materializes the agency of the signifier—paraphrasing the Lacanian definition of the signifier (that which 'represents the subject for another signifier'), we are even tempted to say that this last, superfluous grain represents the subject for all the other grains in the heap. It is the Hegelian Monarch which embodies this paradoxical function at its purest. The State without the Monarch would still be a *substantial* order—the Monarch represents the point of its subjectivation—but what precisely is his function? Only 'dotting the i's' (Hegel, 1969b, par. 280) in a formal gesture of taking upon himself (by putting his signature on them) the decrees proposed to him by his ministers and councillors—of making them an expression of his personal will, of adding the pure form of subjectivity, of 'It is our will . . .', to the objective content of decrees and laws. The Monarch is thus a subject *par excellence*, but only in so far as he limits himself to the purely formal act of subjective decision: as soon as he aims at something more, as soon as he concerns himself with questions of positive content, he crosses the line separating him from his councillors, and the State regresses to the level of Substantiality.

We can now return to the paradox of the phallic signifier: in so far as, according to Lacan, the phallus is a 'pure signifier', it is precisely a signifier of this act of formal conversion by means of which the subject assumes the given, substantial reality as his own work. This is why we could determine the basic 'phallic experience' as a certain 'everything depends on me, but for all that I can do nothing'. Let us exemplify it by reference to two cases which should be read together: the theory of the phallus found in St Augustine, and a certain well-known vulgar joke.

St Augustine developed his theory of sexuality in one of his minor but none the less crucial texts, *De Nuptiis et Concupiscentia*. His reasoning is extremely interesting because at its very outset it differs from what is commonly regarded as the basic premises of the Christian notion of sexuality: far from being the sin which caused man's Fall, sexuality is on the contrary, the *punishment*, *penitence* for the sin. Original sin lies in man's arrogance and pride; it was committed when Adam ate from the Tree of Knowledge, wanting to elevate himself to the divine heights and to become himself master of all creation. God subsequently punished man—Adam—by implanting in him a certain drive—the sexual drive—which strikes out, which cannot be compared with other drives (hunger, thirst, and so on); a drive which radically exceeds its organic function (reproduction of human species) and which, precisely because of this non-functional character, cannot be mastered, tamed. In other words, if Adam and Eve had stayed in the Garden of Eden they would have had sexual intercourse, but they would have accomplished the sexual act in the same way as they accomplished all other instrumental acts (ploughing, sowing. . .). This excessive, non-functional, constitutively perverse character of human sexuality represents God's punishment for man's pride and his want of power.

How can we detect, where can we locate this uncontrollable character of sexuality? It is at this point that St Augustine proposes his theory of the phallus: if man has a strong will and self-control, he can master the movement of all parts of his body (here Augustine evokes a series of extreme cases: an Indian fakir who is able to stop the beating of his heart for a moment, and so on); all parts of the body are thus in principle submitted to man's will, their uncontrollabilities subsisting only in the *factual* degree of weakness or power of man's will—all parts except *one*: the erection of the phallus escapes *in principle* man's free will. This is therefore according to St Augustine, the 'meaning of the phallus': the part of man's body which escapes his control, the point at which man's own body takes revenge on him for his false pride. Someone with a strong enough will can starve to death in the middle of a room full of delicious food, but if a naked virgin passes his way, the erection of his phallus is in no way dependent on the strength of his will. . . .

This, however, is only one side of the phallus paradox; its reverse is indicated by a well-known riddle/joke: 'What is the lightest object on earth?—The phallus, because it is the only one that can be elevated by mere thought.' And to obtain the true 'meaning of phallus', we have to read both examples together: 'phallus' designates the juncture at which the radical externality of the body as independent of our will, as resisting our will, joins the pure interiority of our thought. 'Phallus' is the signifier of the short circuit whereby the uncontrollable externality of the body passes immediately into something bound to pure interiority of 'thought' and, in contrast, the point at which the innermost 'thought' assumes features of some strange entity, escaping our 'free will'. To use the traditional Hegelian terms, 'phallus' is the point of the 'unity of opposites': not a 'dialectical synthesis' (in the sense of a kind of mutual completion) but the *immediate passage* of one extreme into its opposite, as in Hegel's example where the lowest, most vulgar function of urination passes into the most sublime function of procreation.

It is this very 'contradiction' that constitutes the 'phallus experience': EVERYTHING *depends on me*—the point of the riddle—*but for all that I can do* NOTHING—the point of St Augustine's theory. And from here—from this notion of the phallus as pulsation between 'all' and 'nothing'—we can conceive the 'phallic' dimension of the act of formal conversion of reality *as given* into reality *as posited*. This act is 'phallic' in so far as it marks the point of coincidence between omnipotence ('everything depends on me': the subject posits all reality as his work) and total impotence ('but for all that I can do nothing': the subject can formally assume only what is given to him). It is in this sense that the phallus is a 'transcendental signifier': if, following Adorno, we define as 'transcendental' the inversion by means of which the subject experiences his radical limitation (the fact that he is confined to the limits of his world) as his constitutive power (the a priori network of categories structuring his perception of reality).

Presupposing the Positing

There is, however, one crucial weakness in what we have just articulated: our presentation of the process of reflections was oversimplified at a decisive point which concerns the passage from positing to external reflection. The usual interpretation of this passage, which we have accepted automatically, is as follows: positing reflection is the activity of the essence (pure movement of mediation) which posits the appearance—it is the negative movement sublating every given immediacy and positing it as 'mere appearance';—but this reflexive sublation of the immediate, this positing of it as 'mere appearance', is in itself bound to the world of appearance; it *needs* appearance as something already given, as the basis upon which to perform its negative mediation activity. In short, reflection *presupposes* the positive world of appearance as the starting point of its activity of mediating it, of positing it as 'mere appearance'.

To exemplify this presupposing, let us take the classical procedure of the 'criticism of ideology': this procedure 'unmasks' a certain theoretical, religious, or other edifice by enabling us to 'see through it', by making us see in it 'just an [ideological] appearance', an expression-effect of some concealed mechanisms; this procedure consists thus in a purely negative movement which *presupposes* a 'spontaneous', 'non-reflected' ideological experience in its given-immediate positivity. To accomplish the passage from positing to external reflection, the movement of reflection has only to take note of how it is always bound to some given, external presuppositions which are subsequently mediated-sublated through its negative activity. In short, the activity of positing has to take note of its presuppositions—*external* to the movement of reflection are precisely its *presuppositions*.

In contrast to this current view, Dieter Heinrich, in his excellent study on Hegel's logic of reflection (Heinrich, 1971), demonstrated how *the whole dialectic of positing and presupposing still falls within the category of 'positing reflection'*. Let us refer to Fichte as a philosopher of positing reflection *par excellence*: by means of his productive activity, the subject 'posits', sublates-mediates, transforms the given positivity of objects; he transforms it into a manifestation of his own creativity; but this positing remains for ever bound to its presuppositions—to the positively given objectivity upon which it performs its negative activity. In other words, the dialectic of positing-presupposing implies the subject of the working process, the subject which by means of its negative activity, mediates the presupposed objectivity, transforming it into an objectivation of itself; in short, it implies the 'finite', not the 'absolute' subject.

In this case—if the whole dialectic of positing and presupposing falls within the field of positing reflection—in what consists the passage from positing to external reflection? Now we arrive at the crucial distinction elaborated by Heinrich: it is not enough to determine external reflection by the fact that the essence presupposes the objective world as its basis, as the starting point of its negative movement of mediation, external to this movement; the decisive feature of external reflection is that the essence *presupposes itself as its own other*, *in the form of externality*, *of something objectively given in advance*—that is to say, in the form of immediacy. We find ourselves in external reflection when the essence—the movement of absolute mediation, pure, self-referential negativity—presupposes ITSELF in the form of an Entity existing in itself, excluded from the movement of meditation. To use exact Hegelian terms, we are in external reflection when the essence not only presupposes its other (objective-phenomenal immediacy), but presupposes ITSELF in the form of otherness, in the form of some alien substance.

To exemplify this decisive twist, let us refer to a case which is misleading in so far as it is too 'concrete' in the Hegelian sense; in so far, that is, as it implies that we have already accomplished the passage from pure logical categories to concrete historical spiritual content: the analysis of religious alienation as developed by Feuerbach. This 'alienation', whose formal structure is clearly that of external reflection, does not consist simply in the fact that man—a creative being, externalizing his potentials in the world of objects—'deifies' objectivity, conceiving the objective natural and social forces out of his control as manifestations of some supernatural Being. 'Alienation' means something more precise: it means that man presupposes, perceives *himself*, his own creative power, in the form of an external substantial Entity; it means that he 'projects', transposes his innermost essence into an alien Being ('God'). 'God' is thus man himself; the essence of man, the creative movement of mediation, the transforming power of negativity, but perceived in the form of externality, as belonging to some strange Entity existing in itself, independently of man.

This is the decisive but usually overlooked lesson of Hegel's theory of reflection: we can speak of the difference, the fissure separating the essence from appearance, only in so far as the essence is itself split in the way described above—only, that is, in so far as the essence presupposes itself as something alien, as its own Other. If the essence is not in itself split; if—in the movement of extreme alienation—it does not perceive itself as an alien Entity, then the very duality essence/appearance cannot establish itself. *This self-fissure of the essence means that the essence is 'subject' and not only 'substance'*: to express this in a simplified way, 'substance' is the essence in so far as it reflects itself in the world of appearance, in phenomenal objectivity; it is the movement of mediation-sublation-positing of this objectivity, and the 'subject' is substance in so far as it is itself split and experiences itself as some alien, positively given Entity.

We could say, paradoxically, that the subject is *substance precisely in so far as it experiences itself as substance* (as some alien, given, external, positive Entity, existing in itself): 'subject' is nothing but the name for this inner distance of 'substance' towards itself, the name for this empty place from which the substance can perceive itself as something 'alien'. Without this self-fissure of the essence, there can be no place distinguished from essence in which essence can *appear* as distinct from itself—that is, as 'mere appearance': essence can appear only in so far as it is already external to itself.

What, then, is the nature of the passage from external to *determinate* reflection? If we remain on the level of the common interpretation of the logic of reflection, in which the passage of positing into external reflection coincides with that of positing into presupposing, things are, of course, clear. To accomplish the passage in question, we simply have to take note of the fact that the very presuppositions are already posited—thus we find ourselves already in determinate reflection; in the reflexive movement which retroactively posits its own presuppositions. To refer again to the active-producing subject which mediates-negates-forms the presupposed objectivity: all he has to do is to experience how the ontological status of this presupposed objectivity is *nothing but* the presupposition of his activity, how it exists, how it is here only for him to use, to perform on it his mediating activity: how, then, it is itself retroactively 'posited' through his activity. 'Nature', the presupposed object of activity, is so to speak already 'by its own nature', in itself, the object, the material for the subject's activity; its ontological status is determined by the horizon of the process of production. In short, it is in advance *posited* as such—that is, as a presupposition of subjective positing.

If, however, external reflection cannot be sufficiently defined by the fact that positing is always bound to some presuppositions; if, to reach external reflection, essence must presuppose *itself* as its other, things become a little complicated. At first sight, they are still clear enough; let us refer again to the Feuerbachian analysis of religious alienation. Does not the passage from external to determinate reflection consist simply in the fact that man has to recognize in 'God', in this external, superior, alien Entity, the inverse reflection of his own essence—its own essence in the form of otherness; in other words, the 'reflexive determination' of its own essence? And thus to affirm himself as 'absolute subject'? What is amiss with this conception?

To explain it, we have to return to the very notion of reflection. The key for the proper understanding of the passage from external to determinate reflection is given by the double meaning of the notion of 'reflection' in Hegel—by the fact that in Hegel's logic of reflection, reflection is always on two levels:

(1) in the first place, 'reflection' designates the simple relation between essence and appearance, where the appearance 'reflects' the essence—that is to say, where the essence is the negative movement of mediation which sublates and at the same time posits the world of appearing. Here we are still dwelling within the circle of positing and presupposing; the essence posits the objectivity as 'mere appearance' and at the same time presupposes it as the starting point of its negative movement;

(2) as soon as we pass from positing to external reflection, however, we encounter quite another kind of reflection. Here the term 'reflection' designates the relationship between the essence as self-referential negativity, as the movement of absolute mediation, and the essence in so far as it presupposes itself in the inverse-alienated form of some substantial immediacy, as some transcendent entity *excluded* from the movement of reflection (which is why reflection is here 'external': external reflecting which does not concern the essence itself).

At this level, we pass from external to determinate reflection simply by experiencing the relationship between these two moments—essence as movement of self-mediation, self-referential negativity; essence as substantial-positive entity excluded from the tremor of reflection—*as that of reflection*: by experiencing how this image of the substantial-immediate, positively given essence is *nothing but* the inverse-alienated reflection of the essence as pure movement of self-referential negativity.

Strictly speaking, it is only this second reflection which is 'reflection-into-itself' of the essence, reflection in which the essence redoubles itself and thus reflects itself in itself, not only in appearance. This is why this second reflection is reflection *redoubled*: on the level of 'elementary' reflection, reflection in sense (1), essence is simply opposed to appearance as the power of absolute negativity which, by mediating-sublating-positing every positive immediacy, makes it 'mere appearance'; while on the level of the redoubled reflection, reflection in sense (2), essence reflects *itself* in the form of its own presupposition, of a given-immediate substance. Reflection of the essence into itself is an immediacy which is not 'mere appearance' but an inverse-alienated image of the very essence, essence itself in the form of its otherness, in other words, a presupposition which is not simply posited by the essence: in it, *essence presupposes itself as positing*.

As we have already indicated, the relationship between these two reflections is not that of a simple succession; the first, elementary reflection (1) is not simply followed by the second, redoubled reflection (2). The second reflection is, strictly speaking, the *condition* of the first—it is only the redoubling of the essence, the reflection of the essence into itself, which opens the space for the appearance in which the hidden essence can reflect itself. By taking into consideration this necessity of the redoubled reflection, we can also demonstrate what is amiss with the Feuerbachian model of surpassing the external reflection.

This model, in which the subject overcomes alienation by recognizing, in the alienated substantial Entity, the inverse image of his own essential potential, implies a notion of religion that corresponds to the Enlightenment's portrait of the Jewish religion (almighty God as an inverse image of man's powerlessness, and so on); what escapes such an understanding is the logic behind the fundamental motif of Christianity: God's incarnation. The Feuerbachian gesture of recognizing that God as an alien essence is nothing but the alienated image of man's creative potential does not take into account the necessity for this reflexive relationship between God and man to reflect itself *into God himself*; in other words, it does not suffice to ascertain that 'man is the truth of God', that the subject is the truth of the alienated substantial Entity. It is not enough for the subject to recognize-reflect himself in this Entity as in his inverse image; the crucial point is that this substantial Entity must itself split and 'engender' the subject (that is, 'God himself must become man').

As regards the dialectics of positing and presupposing, this necessity means that it is not enough to affirm that the subject posits its own presuppositions. This positing of presuppositions is already contained in the logic of positing reflection; what defines determinate reflection is, rather, that the subject must *presuppose himself as positing*. More precisely: the subject effectively 'posits his presuppositions' by presupposing, by reflecting himself in them as positing. To exemplify this crucial twist, let us take the two usual examples: the Monarch and Christ. In the immediacy of their lives, subjects as citizens are, of course, opposed to the substantial State which determines the concrete network of their social relations. How do they overcome this alienated character, this irreducible otherness of the State as the substantial presupposition of the subjects' activity-'positing'?

The classical Marxist answer would be, of course, that the State as an alienated force must 'wither away', that its otherness must be dissolved in the transparency of non-alienated social relations. The Hegelian answer is, on the contrary, that in the last resort, subjects can recognize the State as 'their own work' only by reflecting free subjectivity into the very State at the point of the Monarch; that is to say, by presupposing in the State itself—as its 'quilting point', as a point which confers its effectivity—the point of free subjectivity, the point of the Monarch's empty-formal gesture 'This is my will. . .'.

From this dialectic, we can very neatly deduce the necessity behind the double meaning of the word 'subject'—(1) a person subject to political rule; (2) a free agent, instigator of its activity—subjects can realize themselves as free agents only by means of redoubling themselves, only in so far as they 'project', transpose, the pure form of their freedom into the very heart of the substance opposed to them; into the person of the subject-Monarch as 'head of the State'. In other words, subjects are subjects only in so far as they presuppose that the social substance, opposed to them in the form of the State, is already in itself a subject (Monarch) to whom they are subjected.

Here we should rectify—or, more precisely, supplement—our previous analysis: the empty gesture, the act of formal conversion by means of which 'substance becomes subject', is not simply dispersed among the multitude of subjects and as such proper to each of them in the same manner; it is always centred at some point of exception, in the One, the individual who takes upon himself the idiotic mandate of performing the empty gesture of subjectivation—of supplementing the given, substantial content by the form of 'This is my will'. This is homologous with Christ: the subjects overcome the Otherness, the strangeness, of the Jewish God not by immediately proclaiming him their own creature but by presupposing in God himself the point of 'incarnation', the point at which God becomes man. This is the significance of Christ's arrival, of his 'It is fulfilled!': for freedom to take place (as our positing), *it must already have taken place* in God as his incarnation—without it, subjects would remain for ever bound to the alien substance, caught in the web of their presuppositions.

The necessity of this redoubling explains perfectly why the strongest instigation to free activity was procured by Protestantism—by religion putting so much emphasis on predestination, on the fact that 'everything is already decided in advance'. And now, finally, we can also give a precise formulation to the passage from external to determinate reflection: the condition of our subjective freedom, of our 'positing', is that it must be reflected in advance into the substance itself, as its own 'reflexive determination'. For that reason, Greek religion, Jewish religion and Christianity form a triad of reflection: in Greek religion, divinity is simply posited in the multitude of beautiful appearance (which is why, for Hegel, Greek religion was religion of the work of art); in Jewish religion, the subject perceives its own essence in the form of a transcendent, external, unattainable power; while in Christianity, human freedom is finally conceived as a 'reflexive determination' of this strange substance (God) itself.

The significance of these at first sight purely speculative ruminations for the psychoanalytic theory of ideology cannot be overestimated. What is the 'empty gesture' by means of which the brute, senseless reality is *assumed*, accepted as our own work, if not the most elementary ideological operation, the symbolization of the Real, its transformation into a meaningful totality, its inscription into the big Other? We can literally say that this 'empty gesture' *posits the big Other, makes it exist*: the purely formal conversion which constitutes this gesture is simply the conversion of the pre-symbolic Real into the symbolized reality—into the Real caught in the web of the signifier's network. In other words, through this 'empty gesture' the subject *presupposes the existence of the big Other*.

Now, perhaps we are able to locate that radical change which, according to Lacan, defines the final stage of the psychoanalytic process: 'subjective destitution'. What is at stake in this 'destitution' is precisely the fact that *the subject no longer presupposes himself as subject*; by accomplishing this he annuls, so to speak, the effects of the act of formal conversion. In other words, he assumes not the existence but the *nonexistence* of the big Other; he accepts the Real in its utter, meaningless idiocy; he keeps open the gap between the Real and its symbolization. The price to be paid for this is that by the same act he also *annuls himself as subject*, because—and this would be Hegel's last lesson—the subject is subject only in so far as he presupposes himself as absolute through the movement of double reflection.

Bibliography

Hegel, G. W. F. (1966), *Wissenschaft der Logik* I/II, Hamburg.

——— (1969), *Philosophie der Religion* I/II, Frankfurt.

——— (1969b), *Grundlinien der Philosophie des Rechts*, Frankfurt.

——— (1977). *Phenomenology of Spirit,* Oxford.

Heinrich, Dieter (1971), *Hegel im Kontext*, Frankfurt.

Kant, Immanuel (1964), *Critique of Judgement*, Oxford.

Yovel, Yirmiahu (1982), 'La religion de la sublimité,' in *Hegel et la religion*, Paris.

CHAPTER 22

"Stubborn Attachment, Bodily Subjection: Rereading Hegel on the Unhappy Consciousness"

—from *The Psychic Life of Power: Theories in Subjection* (1997; first published: 1995)

Judith Butler

a freedom still enmeshed in servitude
—Hegel, *The Phenomenology of Spirit*

The transition in *The Phenomenology of Spirit* from the section "Lordship and Bondage" to "The Freedom of Self-Consciousness: Stoicism, Skepticism, and the Unhappy Consciousness"[1] is one of the least interrogated of Hegel's philosophical movements. Perhaps because the chapter on lordship and bondage secured a liberationist narrative for various progressive political visions, most readers have neglected to pay attention to the resolution of freedom into self-enslavement at the end of the chapter. Insofar as recent theory has called into question both the assumption of a progressive history and the status of the subject, the dystopic resolution of "Lordship and Bondage" has perhaps regained a timely significance. Foucault suggested that the point of modern politics is no longer to liberate a subject, but rather to interrogate the regulatory mechanisms through which "subjects" are produced and maintained. Although Foucault's vocabulary ought not to be conflated with Hegel's, his concern with the double-edged implications of subjection (*assujetissement*: the simultaneous *forming* and *regulating* of the subject) is in some ways prefigured in Hegel's account of the bondsman's liberation into various forms of ethical self-beratement. In *Discipline and Punish*, Foucault limits the efficacy of prison reform: "the man described for us, whom we are invited to free, is already in himself the effect of a subjection [*assujettissement*] much more profound than himself."[2] The bondsman in Hegel throws off the apparently external "Lord" only to find himself in an ethical world, subjected to various norms and ideals. Or, to put it more precisely, the subject emerges as an unhappy consciousness through the reflexive application of these ethical laws.

The permutations of self-enslavement that Hegel describes appear to take the body as what must be negated, mortified, or subordinated to an ethical demand. The "terror" that seizes the bondsman with his recognition of freedom appears to culminate in the simultaneous fabrication of ethical norms and the beratement of the bodily condition of his own life. In this sense, "The Unhappy Consciousness" establishes a relation between self-enslavement as bodily subjection and the formulation of self-imposed ethical imperatives that prefigures Nietzsche's critique of the same in *On the Genealogy of Morals* and Foucault's appropriation of that critique. In the following citation from Nietzsche's *Genealogy of Morals*, one can discern a temporary convergence between the figures of self-enslavement in Hegel's "Unhappy Consciousness" and the moralized "man" of conscience in Nietzsche: "This *instinct for freedom* forcibly made latent . . . this instinct for freedom pushed back and repressed, incarcerated within and finally able to discharge and vent itself only on itself: that, and that alone, is what the *bad conscience* is in its beginnings."[3]

Underscoring the painful realization that "liberation" from external authorities does not suffice to initiate a subject into freedom, Foucault draws upon Nietzsche and, in particular, upon the self-incarcerating movement that structures modern forms of reflexivity. The limits to liberation are to be understood not merely as self-imposed but, more fundamentally, as the precondition of the subject's very formation. A certain structuring attachment *to* subjection becomes the condition of moral subjectivation. Consider the expanded text of Foucault's remarks on the prisoner's subjection, previously cited, in *Discipline and Punish*: "The man described for us, whom we are invited to free, is already in himself the effect of a subjection [*assujettissement*] much more profound than himself. A "soul" inhabits him and brings him to existence, which is itself a factor in the mastery that power exercises over the body. The soul is the effect and instrument of a political anatomy; the soul is the prison of the body."[4]

How precisely are we to read this "inhabiting" of the body by the soul? Can a return to Hegel help us to read it? What are the points of convergence and divergence in Hegel, Nietzsche, and Foucault on the structure of subjection? Hegel's account in "The Unhappy Consciousness" prefigures a critical discourse on ethical positions that not only seek to institute the denial or sacrifice of bodily life, but that fall into instructive paradoxes when they do. Hegel shows that if the suppression of the body requires an instrumental movement of and by the body, then the body is inadvertently *preserved* in and by the instrument of its suppression. This formulation prefigures the possibility of a convergence with Nietzschean, Foucaultian, and, as we shall see, Freudian perspectives on self-abasement, which Hegel's text, in the transition to Spirit, forecloses. The reading that follows pursues the path that Hegel introduces only to foreclose. Arresting the text prior to its resolution into Spirit, this inquiry seeks to know whether a suppressed link with a Nietzschean and Freudian account of conscience is embedded in Hegel's chapter.

The first section of this essay offers a reading that accounts for how this paradox of bodily subjection is formulated in the transition from "Lordship and Bondage" to "The Unhappy Consciousness" in *The Phenomenology of Spirit*. In the second section, I consider the restatements of that paradoxical formulation in psychoanalytic and Foucaultian terms. Without presuming a direct line of influence, I suggest both that Hegel's insights in "The Unhappy Consciousness" on the ineluctability of the attachment of and to the body in subjection are reiterated in Foucaultian frameworks, and that the Foucaultian account of subjection, despite its significant moves beyond dialectical logic, remains unwittingly tethered to the Hegelian formulation. Furthermore, Hegel tacitly presumes that subjection is understood as a self-negating *attachment* and, in this way, shares an operative assumption with the Freudian notion of libidinal investment.

Hegel and the Production of Self-Enslavement

In Hegel's *Phenomenology*, bodies are almost never to be found as objects of philosophical reflection, much less as sites of experience, for bodies are, in Hegel, always and only referred to indirectly as the encasement, location, or specificity of consciousness. By the time we arrive at the section on the unhappy consciousness, we, the readers, have already encountered the lord and the bondsman, and we have been given to understand these discrepant figures as differentially positioned with respect to bodily life. The bondsman appears as an instrumental body whose labor provides for the material conditions of the lord's existence, and whose material products reflect both the subordination of the bondsman and the domination of the master. In a sense, the lord postures as a disembodied desire for self-reflection, one who not only requires the subordination of the bondsman in the status of an instrumental body, but who requires in effect that the bondsman *be* the lord's body, but be it in such a way that the lord forgets or disavows his own activity in producing the bondsman, a production which we will call a projection.

This forgetting involves a clever trick. It is an action by which an activity is disavowed, yet, as an action, it rhetorically concedes the very activity that it seeks to negate. To disavow one's body, to render it "Other" and then to establish the "Other" as an effect of autonomy, is to produce one's body in such a way that the activity of its production—and its essential relation to the lord—is denied. This trick or ruse involves a double disavowal and an imperative that the "Other" become complicit with this disavowal. In order not to be the body that the lord presumably is, and in order to have the bondsman posture as if the body that he is belongs to himself—and not be the orchestrated projection of the lord—there must be a certain kind of exchange, a bargain or deal, in which ruses are enacted and transacted. In effect, the imperative to the bondsman consists in the following formulation: you be my body for me, but do not let me know that the body you are is my body. An injunction and contract are here performed in such a way that the moves which guarantee the fulfillment of the injunction and the contract are immediately covered over and forgotten.

At the close of the section on lordship and bondage, the bondsman labors away in a repetitive fashion on objects that belong to the lord. In this sense, both his labor and his products are presumed from the start to be other than his own, expropriated. They are given away prior to any possibility of giving them away, since they are, strictly speaking, never the bondsman's to give. And yet, this "contract" in which the bondsman substitutes himself for the lord becomes consequential; the substitution itself becomes formative of and for the bondsman. As the bondsman slaves away and becomes aware of his own signature on the things that he makes, he recognizes in the form of the artifact that he crafts the markings of his own labor, markings that are formative of the object itself. His labor produces a visible and legible set of marks in which the bondsman reads back from the object a confirmation of his own formative activity. This labor, this activity, which belongs from the start to the lord, is nevertheless reflected back to the bondsman as his own labor, a labor that emanates from him, even if it appears to emanate from the lord.

Can, then, the labor reflected back be said finally to be the bondsman's own? Remember that the lord has disavowed his own laboring being, his body as an instrument of labor, and has established the bondsman as the one who will occupy the lord's body for him. In this sense, the lord has contracted the bondsman as a surrogate or substitute. The bondsman thus belongs to the lord, but with a kind of belonging that cannot be avowed, for to avow the belonging would be to avow the substitution and, hence, to expose the lord as being the body which the lord apparently very much does not want to be. Hence, it is as a substitute in the service of disavowal that the bondsman labors; only by miming and covering over the mimetic status of that labor can the bondsman appear to be both active and autonomous. Indeed, the object emerges as the objectification of the bondsman's labor, and thus as an instance of that labor, a congealing and reflection of that labor. But what, then, does the object reflect? Is it the autonomy of the bondsman? Or is it the dissimulated effect of autonomy that results from the contract made between lord and bondsman? In other words, if the bondsman effects autonomy through a miming of the lord's body, a miming which remains hidden from the lord, then the "autonomy" of the slave is the credible effect of this dissimulation. The object of labor thus reflects the autonomy of the bondsman to the extent that the object, too, covers over the dissimulation which is the activity of the bondsman. In his work, then, the bondsman discovers or reads his own signature, but what is it that marks that signature as his own? The bondsman discovers his autonomy, but he does not (yet) see that his autonomy is the dissimulated effect of the lord's. (Nor does he see that the lord's autonomy is itself a dissimulation: the lord effects the autonomy of disembodied reflection and delegates the autonomy of embodiment to the bondsman, thus producing two "autonomies" that appear at the outset radically to exclude one another.)

But here a question emerges: Does the bondsman's activity remain fully constrained by the dissimulation by which it is mobilized? Or does this dissimulation produce effects that exceed the control or dominion of the lord?

If the bondsman is to recognize the marks made on the object as his own, then that recognition must take place through an act of reading or interpretation by which the marks (*Zeichen*) that the bondsman sees are somehow understood to represent the bondsman. It is not that the activity must be witnessed, but that the *signs* produced must be read as an effect of the effectivity that designates the bondsman, must in some way be understood to refer retroactively to the bondsman as signatory. If we are to understand the forming of the object as the inscribing of the bondsman's signature, the formative principle of the object *to be* the formation of his signature, then the bondsman's signature designates a domain of contested ownership. This is *his* mark, which he can read (we shall let the bondsman occupy the site of presumptive masculinity), and so the object appears to belong to him. Yet this object marked by him, which has his mark on it, belongs to the lord, at least nominally. The bondsman signs, as it were, for the lord, as a proxy signatory, as a delegated substitute. Thus the signature does not seal ownership of the object by the bondsman, but becomes the site for the redoubling of ownership and, hence, sets the stage for a scene of contestation.

The mark or sign on the object is not simply the property of the bondsman—this object with his mark on it implies for him that he is a being who marks things, whose activity produces a singular effect, a signature, which is irreducibly his. That signature is erased when the object is given over to the lord, who stamps it with *his* name, owns it, or consumes it in some way. The working of the slave is thus to be understood as a marking which regularly unmarks itself, a signatory act which puts itself under erasure at the moment in which it is circulated, for circulation here is always a matter of expropriation by the lord. The slave, of course, from the start has been working for another, under the name or sign of some other, and so has been marking the object with his own signature under a set of conditions in which that signature is always already erased, written over, expropriated, resignified. If the bondsman writes over the signatory of the lord, temporarily reversing the subordinate position of the proxy to the original, the lord reappropriates the object by writing over the signature of the bondsman. What emerges is less a palimpsestic object—like Kafka's topographies—than a mark of ownership produced through a set of consequential erasures.

Significantly, the bondsman nevertheless derives a sense of self-recognition at the end of the chapter, but not by reading back his signature from the object. After all, that signature has been written over by the signature of the lord. He recognizes himself in the very forfeiture of the signature, in the *threat to* autonomy that such an expropriation produces. Strangely, then, a certain self-recognition is derived from the radically tenuous status of the bondsman; it is achieved through the experience of *absolute fear*.

This fear is a fear *of* a certain loss of control, a certain transience and expropriability produced by the activity of labor. Here the logic of the bondsman's activity appears curiously to converge with that of the lord. Earlier it seemed that the lord occupied the place of pure consumption, appropriating and extinguishing all that the bondsman made. The bondsman, by contrast, achieved the experience of self-reflexivity through working on and creating an object that bore the marks of his being, and thereby understood himself as a being who forms or creates things which outlast him, a producer of permanent things. For the lord, occupying the position of pure consumption, objects were transitory, and he himself was defined as a series of transitory desires. For the lord, then, nothing seemed to last, except perhaps his own consuming activity, his own endless desire.

These two positions, however, are not radically opposed to one another, for each in a different way experiences only and always the loss of the object and, with that loss, the experience of a fearful transience. Work is, for Hegel, a form of desire, a form which ideally suppresses the transitory character of desire; in his words, "work is desire held in check, fleetingness staved off" (118/153). To work on an object is to give it form, and to give it form is to give it an existence that overcomes transitoriness. The consumption of the object is the negation of that effect of permanence; the consumption of the object is its *de*formation. The accumulation of property, however, requires that formed objects be possessed rather than consumed; only as property do objects retain their form and "stave off fleetingness." Only as property do objects fulfill the theological promise with which they are invested.

The bondsman's fear, then, consists in the experience of having what appears to be his property expropriated. In the experience of giving up what he has made, the bondsman understands two issues: first, that what he is is embodied or signified in what he makes, and second, that what he makes is made under the compulsion to give it up. Hence, if the object defines him, reflects back what he is, is the signatory text by which he acquires a sense of who he is, and if those objects are relentlessly sacrificed, then he is a relentlessly self-sacrificing being. He can recognize his own signature only as what is constantly being erased, as a persistent site of vanishing. He has no control over what he puts his name to or over the purposes to which he seeks to fasten his name. His signature is an act of self-erasure: he reads that the signature is his, that his own existence appears to be irreducibly his own, that what is irreducibly his own is his own vanishing, and that this vanishing is effected by another—that is, that this is a socially compelled form of self-erasure. Not only does he labor for another, who takes the yield of his labor, but he gives up his signature for the signature of the other, no longer marking ownership of his own labor in any way.

This expropriation of the object does not negate the bondsman's sense of himself as a laboring being, but it does imply that whatever he makes, he also loses. The determinate thing that the bondsman makes reflects the bondsman himself as a determinate thing. But because the object is given away, he becomes that which can be forfeited. If the object is the congealing or forming of labor, and if the labor is that of the bondsman, then the determinate and transient character of the thing will imply the determinate and transient character of the bondsman. The laboring body which now knows itself to have formed the object also knows that it is *transient*. The bondsman not only negates things (in the sense of transforming them through labor) and is a negating activity, but he is subject to a full and final negation in death. This confrontation of death at the end of the chapter recalls the life-and-death struggle at its beginning. The strategy of domination was meant to replace the life-and-death struggle. But in the earlier version death happened through the violence of the other; domination was a way of forcing the other to die *within* the context of life. The failure of domination as a strategy *re*introduces the fear of death, but locates it as the inevitable fate of any being whose consciousness is determined and embodied, no longer as a threat posed by another. The bondsman verges on this shattering recognition of his own death in the last paragraph of the chapter, but he recoils from recognizing death, attaching himself instead to various attributes of his own, taking up a posture of smugness or stubbornness, clinging to what appears to be firm about himself, firmly clinging to himself, in order not to know that death threatens every aspect of his own firmness: "since the entire contents of its natural consciousness have not been jeopardized, [*Indem nicht alle Erfüllungen seines naturlichen Bewusstseins wankend geworden*] determinate being still *in principle* attaches to it; having a mind of one's own is self-will, a freedom still enmeshed in servitude" (119/155).

The unhappy consciousness emerges here in the movement by which terror is allayed through a resolution of stubbornness or, rather, through the action by which terror of bodily death is displaced by a smugness and stubbornness that, in the next chapter, is revalued as religious self-righteousness. This sanctimonious self is not *without* terror: its reflexivity is self-terrorizing. The body which the bondsmen emblematized as a laboring instrument is recast at the end of the lordship and bondage chapter as a transient object, subject to death. The recognition of the body's death is averted, however, for a mode of living in which the body is ceaselessly dying away: hence, the move from the servitude of the bondsman to that of the unhappy consciousness. The bondsman takes the place of the lord by recognizing his own formative capacity, but once the lord is displaced, the bondsman becomes lord over himself, more specifically, lord over his own body; this form of reflexivity signals the passage from bondage to unhappy consciousness. It involves splitting the psyche into two parts, a lordship and a bondage internal to a single consciousness, whereby the body is again dissimulated as an alterity, but where this alterity is now interior to the psyche itself. No longer subjected as an external instrument of labor, the body is still split off from consciousness. Reconstituted as an interior alien, the body is sustained through its disavowal as what consciousness must continue to disavow.

What is the form that this self-subjection takes in the section on the unhappy consciousness? In the first instance, it is a form of stubbornness (*eigensinnigkeit*). It has a "mind of one's own" or "self-will," but one which is nevertheless still a form of servitude. Consciousness clings or attaches to itself, and this clinging to consciousness is at the same time a disavowal of the body, which appears to signify the terror of death, "the absolute fear." The unhappy consciousness requires and engages this attachment by invoking an imperative. Its fear is allayed by legislating an ethical norm. Hence, the imperative to cling to oneself is motivated by this absolute fear and by the need to refuse that fear. Inasmuch as it is an *ethical* injunction, this imperative is the disarticulated refusal of absolute fear.

The section on the unhappy consciousness explains the genesis of the sphere of the ethical as a defense against the absolute fear by which it is motivated. The fabrication of norms out of (and against) fear, and the reflexive imposition of those norms, subjects the unhappy consciousness in a double sense: the subject is subordinated to norms, and the norms are subjectivating, that is, they give an ethical shape to the reflexivity of this emerging subject. The subjection that takes place under the sign of the ethical is a flight from fear, and so is constituted as a kind of flight and denial, a fearful flight from fear that covers its fear first with stubborness and then with religious self-righteousness. The more absolute the ethical imperative becomes, the more stubborn or *eigensinnig* the enforcement of its law, the more the absoluteness of the motivating fear is at once articulated and refused. Absolute fear is thus displaced by the absolute law which, paradoxically, reconstituted the fear as a fear *of* the law.

Absolute fear would jeopardize all determinate things, including the determinate thingness of the bondsman. The flight from that fear, a fear of death, vacates the thinglike character of the subject. This entails vacating the body and clinging to what appears to be most disembodied: thought. Hegel introduces stoicism as a kind of defensive clinging, one that separates the activity of thinking from any content. For Hegel, stoicism withdraws into a subjective and rational existence that has as its highest aim the absolute withdrawal from existence per se, including its own. This task turns out to be self-refuting, of course, insofar as even self-refutation requires a persistent self to enact the withdrawal from its own and other existences. Because the conceptual act of negation always presupposes a position from which that negation takes place, stoicism ends up underscoring the very positivity of the self that it sought to deny. Skepticism follows upon stoicism for Hegel because skepticism begins by presupposing the insuperability of the thinking subject. For skepticism, the self is a perpetually negating activity, actively refuting the existence of everything as its own constitutive activity.

Skepticism negates the domain of alterity by trying to show that any given determination of logical necessity turns into its opposite and, hence, is not what it is. The skeptic traces and focuses on this constant vanishing of determinate appearance without taking into account the dialectical logic that orchestrates and unifies these various oppositions. Hence, nothing is what it is, and there is no logical or empirical ground accessible to the skeptic on which the domain of alterity might rationally be known. The skeptic's thinking becomes a frantic effort to make every given determination disappear into some other one, so that this constant appearing and vanishing proceeds according to no order or necessity. The skeptic, like some new historicists among us, ends up producing contradiction for its own sake: significantly, Hegel argues that this production of chaos (understood as ceaseless contradiction) is *pleasurable* inasmuch as the skeptic is always able to undermine the position of his philosophical opponent.

This kind of pleasurable and incessant refutation is still a form of stubbornness or *eigensinnigkeit*: "it is in fact like the squabbling of self-willed children [*eigensinniger Jungen*] who by contradicting themselves buy for themselves the pleasure [*die Freude*] of continually contradicting one another" (126/162). The skeptic overrides his own contradictoriness in order to take pleasure in forcing others to witness their contradictions. But this pleasure, a form of sadism, is short-lived, for the stubborn and persistent character of the skeptic's efforts will doubtless be challenged when the skeptic encounters another like himself. If another skeptic exposes the first skeptic's contradictions, then the first skeptic is forced to take account of his own contradictoriness. This understanding of his own contradictoriness will initiate for him a new modality of thought. At this point, the skeptic becomes self-conscious of the constitutive contradiction of his own negating activity and the unhappy consciousness emerges as an explicit form of ethical reflexivity.

In a sense, the childish and stubborn pleasure that the skeptic takes in watching another fall turns into a profound unhappiness when he is, as it were, forced *to watch himself* fall into endless contradictions. Here the distance afforded by watching seems essentially linked to the sadism of the pleasure and to the posture of the skeptic as one who exempts himself through visual distance from the scene that he witnesses. The sadistic pleasure involved in watching another becomes, in the mode of unhappiness, a displeasurable watching of oneself.[5] Witnessing implies a mimetic reduplication of the self, and its "dispassion" is belied by the passion of mimeticism. The self who shored up its identity by encouraging others to fall into contradiction suddenly sees itself as one of those others; this viewing of oneself at a distance not only initiates the unhappy consciousness but also inverts the skeptic's pleasure into pain. The sadism directed toward the other is now turned back on consciousness itself (postponing for the moment whether the pleasure in sadism is also rerouted against consciousness). As a dual structure, the unhappy consciousness takes itself as its own object of scorn.

The philosophical elaboration of this scorn takes the following form: consciousness is now divided into two parts, the "essential" and "unchangeable," on the one hand, and the "inessential" and "changeable," on the other. The watching self, defined as a kind of *witnessing* and *scorning*, differentiates itself from the self witnessed as perpetually falling into contradiction. This watching becomes a way of *re*establishing the visual distance between a subject aloof from the scene and the subject in contradiction. In this case, however, the witnessing and scorning self cannot deny that the contradictory self is its own self; it knows that the contradictory self is *itself*, but in order to shore up an identity over and against it, it renders this contradictory self into an *in*essential part of itself. It thus parts with itself in order to purify itself of contradiction.

As a result, the unhappy consciousness berates itself constantly, setting up one part of itself as a pure judge aloof from contradiction and disparaging its changeable part as inessential, although ineluctably tied to it. Significantly, the activity that in skepticism begins as childish sadism becomes reformulated as ethical self-judgment in the context of the unhappy consciousness: as adult to child, then, the unchangeable consciousness "passes judgment" on the changeable. Implicit in this dual structuring of the subject, however, is the relation between thought and corporeality, for the unchangeable will be a kind of noncontradictory thought, the pure thought sought by the stoics, and the contradictory domain will be that of alternating qualities, the changeable domain of appearance, what pertains to the subject's own phenomenal being. The child who "watches" is transfigured into the judge who "passes judgment," and the aspect of the self on which it passes judgment is steeped in the changeable world of bodily sensation.

Unhappy consciousness seeks to overcome this duality by finding a body which embodies the purity of its unchangeable part; it seeks to come into relation with "the Unchangeable in its incarnate or embodied form." To do this, the subject subordinates its own body in the service of the thought of the unchangeable; this subordinating and purifying effort is that of *devotion* (*Andacht*). Yet, predictably, this effort to deploy the body in the service of thinking the unchangeable proves impossible. Devotion turns out to be pure self-feeling, what Hegel disparagingly refers to as "the chaotic jingling of bells, or a mist of warm incense, a musical thinking" (131/168). As self-feeling, it is the feeling of the body compelled to signify the transcendent and unchangeable, a feeling which nevertheless remains ensconced in the bodily feeling that it seeks to transcend. Indeed, self-feeling refers only and endlessly to itself (a transcendentalized form of *eigensinnigkeit*), and so is unable to furnish knowledge of anything other than itself. Devotion, then, which seeks to instrumentalize the body in the service of the unchangeable, turns out to be an immersion in the body that precludes access to anything else, indeed, an immersion that takes the body to be the unchangeable and so falls into contradiction.

Although devotion appears to be a form of self-immersion, it is also a continuation of self-beratement as self-mortification. This self-feeling, precisely because it does not reach the unchangeable, becomes itself the object of derision and judgment, marking the continuing inadequacy of the self in relation to its transcendent measure. The transcendent is what is always missed, and so haunts this consciousness as a figure of what is permanently inaccessible, forever lost. In the mode of devotion, then, "consciousness . . . can only find as a present reality the grave of its life" (132/169–70). In a transposition of figures, the body survives, and all that is left of the transcendent ideal is a "grave." Whereas devotion, then, begins as an effort to subordinate the body to a transcendent object, it ends by taking the body, that is, self-feeling, as its object of worship, and letting the unchangeable spirit die.

Here we might conclude that a certain form of self-preoccupation, understood as a reformulation of an insurmountable *eigensinnigkeit*, constitutes a narcissism of the subject that defeats the self-sacrificial project of devotion. The subject who would subordinate its body to an ideal, compel its body to embody an ideal, finds itself more fully autonomous from that ideal, outliving it altogether. The collapse of devotion into narcissism, if we can call it that, signifies that there can be no final leave-taking of the body within life. Forced, then, to accept this ineluctability of the body as a presupposition, a new form of the subject emerges, which is distinctly Kantian. If there is a world of appearance for which the body is essential, then surely there is a world of noumena in which the body has no place; the world divides up into beings that are for-itself and in-itself.

In a formulation that will prefigure Kierkegaard's *Philosophical Fragments*, Hegel claims that the unchangeable world surrenders or renounces an embodied form, that it, the in-itself, delivers an embodied version of itself into the changeable world to be sacrificed. This reference to the figure of Christ suggests that the unchangeable world becomes embodied, but does so only to be sacrificed or returned to the unchangeable world from which it came. As a model for the sacred life, Christ is understood as an embodiment which is continually in the mode of giving thanks. In its desire and in its work, this embodied consciousness seeks to give thanks for its own life, capacities, faculties, abilities. These are given to it; its life is experienced as a gift; and it lives out its life in the mode of gratefulness. All of its acts it owes to another; its life becomes understood as a kind of endless debt.

Precisely because, on the one hand, this living being owes its life to another being, it is not the seat or origin of its own actions. Its action is referred to another's action; thus, not being the ground of its own action, it is not responsible for what it does. On the other hand, its own actions are to be construed as a perpetual self-sacrifice by which the self *proves* or demonstrates its own thankfulness. This demonstration of thankfulness thus becomes a kind of self-aggrandizement, what Hegel will call "the extreme of individuality" (134/171).

The renunciation of the self as the origin of its own actions must be performed repeatedly and can never finally be achieved, if only because the *demonstration* of renunciation is itself a self-willed action. This self-willed action thus rhetorically confounds precisely what it is supposed to show. The self becomes an incessant performer of renunciation, whereby the performance, as an action, contradicts the postulation of *in*action that it is meant to signify. Paradoxically, performance becomes the *occasion* for a grand and endless action that effectively augments and individuates the self it seeks to deny.

This consciousness, like the stoic, seeks to know and show itself as a "nothing," yet inevitably becomes a *doing* of nothing. Here the pleasure which earlier appeared to belong to the childish sadism of the skeptic is turned on the self: this "doing of nothing," Hegel argues, finds in "its enjoyment a feeling of wretchedness." This intermingling of pleasure and pain results from a renunciation of the self which can never quite accomplish that renunciation, which, as an incessant accomplishing, carries with it the pleasurable assertion of self. The self-absorption of consciousness does not translate into self-congratulation or simple narcissism. Rather, it appears as negative narcissism, an engaged preoccupation with what is most debased and defiled about it.

Here again the self to be renounced is figured as a bodily self, as "this actual individual in the animal functions." Hegel appears to imply defecation as an object of self-preoccupation: "these [animal functions] are no longer performed naturally and without embarrassment, as matters trifling in themselves which cannot possess any importance or essential significance for Spirit; instead, it is in them that the enemy reveals himself in his characteristic shape, they are rather the object of serious endeavor, and become precisely matters of the utmost importance. This enemy, however, renews himself in his defeat, and consciousness, in fixing its attention on him, far from freeing itself from him, really remains forever in contact with him, and forever sees itself as defiled" (135–36/174). This "enemy," as it were, is described as "the merest particular of the meanest character," one which serves, unfortunately, as an object of identification for this "fallen" consciousness. Here, consciousness in its full abjection has become like shit, lost in a self-referential anality, a circle of its own making. In Hegel's words, "we have here only a personality confined to its own self and its petty actions, a personality brooding over itself, as wretched as it is impoverished" (136/174).

Regarding itself as a nothing, as a doing of nothing, as an excremental function, and hence regarding itself as excrement, this consciousness effectively reduces itself to the changeable features of its bodily functions and products. Yet, since it is an experience *of* wretchedness, there is some consciousness which takes stock of these functions and which is not thoroughly identified with them. Significantly, it is here, in the effort to differentiate itself from its excretory functions, indeed, from its excretory identity, that consciousness relies on a "mediator," what Hegel will call "the priest." In order to reconnect with the pure and the unchangeable, this bodily consciousness offers up its every "doing" to a priest or minister. This mediating agency relieves the abject consciousness of its responsibility for its own actions. Through the institution of counsel and advice, the priest offers the reason for the abject consciousness's actions. Everything that the abject consciousness offers, that is, all of its externalizations, including desire, work, and excrement, are to be construed as *offerings*, as paying penance. The priest institutes bodily self-abnegation as the price of holiness, elevating the renunciatory gesture of excretion to a religious practice whereby the entire body is ritualistically purged. The sanctification of abjection takes place through rituals of fasting and mortification [*fasten und kasteien*]" (137/175). Because the body cannot be fully denied, as the stoic thought, it must be ritualistically renounced.

In its fastings and mortifications, the unhappy consciousness denies itself the pleasures of consumption, figuring perhaps that it will forestall the inevitability of the excremental moment. As self-inflicted bodily acts, fasting and mortification are reflexive actions, turnings of the body against itself. At the limits of this self-mortification and self-sacrifice, the abjected consciousness appears to ground its action in the counsel of the priest, and yet this grounding merely conceals the reflexive origins of its self-punishment.

At this juncture Hegel departs from what has been the pattern of explanation, in which a *self-negating* posture is underscored as a *posture*, a phenomenalization that refutes the negation it seeks to institute. In the place of such an explanation, Hegel asserts that the will of another operates through the self-sacrificial actions of the penitent. In effect, self-sacrifice is not refuted through the claim that self-sacrifice is itself a willful activity; rather, Hegel asserts that in self-sacrifice one enacts another's will. One might expect that the penitent would be shown to be reveling in himself, self-aggrandizing, narcissistic, that his self-punishments would culminate in a pleasurable assertion of self. But Hegel eschews this explanation and thus breaks with the pattern of explanation in the chapter in favor of a religious solution in Spirit.

Indeed, at this juncture one might well imagine a set of closing transitions for "The Unhappy Consciousness" different from the ones Hegel supplies, a set that is, nevertheless, perhaps more properly Hegelian than Hegel himself. The penitent disclaims his act as his own, avowing that another's will, the priest's, operates through his self-sacrifice, and, further, that the priest's will is determined by God's. Installed thus in a great chain of wills, the abject consciousness enters into a community of wills. Although its will is determinate, it is nevertheless bound to the priest's; in this unity, the notion of Spirit is first discerned. The mediator or priest counsels the penitent that his pain will be repaid with everlasting abundance, that his misery will be rewarded with everlasting happiness; misery and pain imply a future transformation into their opposites. In this sense, the minister reformulates the dialectical reversal and establishes the inversion of values as an absolute principle. Whereas in all of the earlier examples of self-negation pleasure was understood to *inhere* in pain (the pleasurable aggrandizement of the stoic, the pleasurable sadism of the skeptic), pleasure is here temporally removed from pain, figured as its future compensation. For Hegel, this eschatological transformation of the pain of this world into the pleasure of the next establishes the transition from self-consciousness to reason. And self-consciousness's recognition of itself as part of a religious community of wills effects the transition from self-consciousness to Spirit.

But what are we to make of this final transition, considering the immanent relation of pleasure and pain in the transitions that precede it? Before the introduction of the "mediator" and the "priest," the chapter on the unhappy consciousness appears to proceed as if it contained a trenchant critique of ethical imperatives and religious ideals, a critique which prefigures the Nietzschean analysis that emerges some sixty years later. Every effort to reduce itself to inaction or to nothing, to subordinate or mortify its own body, culminates inadvertently in the *production* of self-consciousness as a pleasure-seeking and self-aggrandizing agent. Every effort to overcome the body, pleasure, and agency proves to be nothing other than the assertion of precisely those features of the subject.

Post-Hegelian Subjections

The Nietzschean critique of ethical norms, prefigured in "The Unhappy Consciousness" and articulated in Nietzsche's *On the Genealogy of Morals* and *Daybreak*, has received more recent reformulation in Foucault's *Discipline and Punish*. Both Hegel's position and those inspired by Nietzsche might also be usefully compared with Freud's critique of the genesis of moral imperatives in *Civilization and Its Discontents*. Recall that for Hegel ethical imperatives first emerge in a defensive response to absolute fear, and their emergence must be construed as a permutation and refusal of that fear. This absolute fear was the fear of death, hence a fear conditioned by the finite character of the body. The ethical refusal and subordination of the body might then be understood as a magical effort to preempt that existential negation. Moreover, the ideal of radical self-sufficiency is jeopardized by the body's permeability and dependency. In this sense, excretion is not the only "animal function" that would signify "defilement" for this subject. The repeated efforts to sacrifice the body which become repeated assertions of the body are also efforts to defend it against everything that "jeopardizes" it, where to be in "jeopardy" denotes a danger slightly less dire than death, a kind of penetrative paroxysm that implies being moved or shaken sexually "through and through" (*durch und durch angesteckt*). One could then see in the various forms of self-beratement and self-mortification typologized in "The Unhappy Consciousness" a prefiguration of neurosis and perhaps also a specific modality of homosexual panic.[6]

We might then reread the mobilizing fear that is both refused and rerouted by the ethical imperative in terms of the feared "expropriability" of the body. If the bondsman's laboring activity could be expropriated by the lord and the essence of the bondsman's body be held in ownership by that lord, then the body constitutes a site of contested ownership, one which through domination or the threat of death can always be owned by another. The body appears to be nothing other than a threat to the project of safety and self-sufficiency that governs the *Phenomenology*'s trajectory. The anal preoccupation that directly precedes the ascendance into a religious concept of an afterlife suggests that bodily permeability can only be resolved by escape into an afterlife in which no bodies exist at all. This affirmation of the absolute negation of the body contradicts all the earlier efforts to subordinate or master the body *within* life, efforts which culminated in the assertion of the ineluctability of the body. Whereas other religious notions turned out to be surreptitious ways of reasserting the body, this one appears exempt from the dialectical reversal that it resolves.

Psychoanalysis theorizes the failure to maintain the subjection of the body along lines parallel to these earlier dialectical reversals. The repression of the libido is always understood as itself a libidinally invested repression. Hence, the libido is not absolutely negated through repression, but rather becomes the instrument of its own subjection. The repressive law is not external to the libido that it represses, but the repressive law represses to the extent that repression becomes a libidinal activity.[7] Further, moral interdictions, especially those that are turned against the body, are themselves sustained by the bodily activity that they seek to curb:

> An idea . . . which belongs entirely to psychoanalysis and which is foreign to people's ordinary way of thinking . . . it tells us that conscience (or more correctly, the anxiety which later becomes conscience) is indeed the cause of instinctual renunciation to begin with, but that later that relationship is reversed. Every renunciation of instinct now

> becomes a dynamic source of conscience and every fresh renunciation increases the latter's severity and intolerance.[8]

According to Freud, then, the self-imposed imperatives of conscience are pursued and applied precisely because they are now the site of the very satisfaction that they seek to prohibit. In other words, prohibition becomes the displaced site of satisfaction for the "instinct" or desire that is prohibited, an occasion for reliving the instinct under the rubric of the condemning law. This is, of course, the source of the form of comedy in which the bearer of the moral law turns out to be the most serious transgressor of its precepts (Hawthorne's Dimsdale, Tom Stoppard's moral philosopher). Because this displaced satisfaction is experienced through the application of the law, that application is reinvigorated and intensified with the emergence of every prohibited desire. The prohibition does not seek to obliterate prohibited desire; on the contrary, prohibition seeks to reproduce prohibited desire and becomes intensified through the renunciations it effects. The "afterlife" of prohibited desire is in the prohibition itself, where the prohibition not only sustains, but is *sustained by*, the desire that it forces the subject to renounce. In this sense, then, renunciation takes place *through* the very desire that is renounced, which is to say, the desire is *never* renounced, but becomes preserved and reasserted in the very structure of renunciation.

Nietzsche makes a similar argument, deploying a dialectical structure not unlike Hegel's, in his critique of the ascetic ideal in *On the Genealogy of Morals*. The ineluctability of the body in "The Unhappy Consciousness" parallels the ineluctability of "instinct" in Freud and that of the will in Nietzsche. For Nietzsche, the ascetic ideal, understood as a will to nothingness, is a way of interpreting all suffering as guilt. Although guilt works to deny a specific kind of object for human wants, it cannot obliterate the wanting character of humans. According to the dictates of guilt, then, "man had only to *want* something—and to begin with, it mattered not what, whereto, or how he wanted: *the will itself was saved*." The ascetic ideal, very much like Hegel's unhappy consciousness, is to be understood, then, as:

> that hatred against everything human, even more, against everything animal, everything material, this disgust with the senses, with reason itself, this fear of happiness and beauty, this desire to get away from all semblance, change, becoming, death, wish, desire itself—the meaning of all this is a will to nothingness, a will running counter to life, a revolt against the most fundamental presuppositions of life; yet it is and remains a will! . . . rather than want nothing, man even wants nothingness![9]

I do not mean to suggest that Freud's highly problematic notion of instinct, Hegel's inchoate body, and Nietzsche's will are strictly equivalent. Yet I do want to suggest that these three thinkers circumscribe a kind of dialectical reversal which centers on the impossibility of a full or final reflexive suppression of what we might loosely call "the body" within the confines of life. If the suppression of the body is itself an instrumental movement of and by the body, then the body is inadvertently preserved in and by the instrument of its suppression. The self-defeating effort of such suppression, however, not only leads to its opposite—a self-congratulatory or self-aggrandizing assertion of desire, will, the body—in more contemporary formulations it leads to the elaboration of an institution of the subject which exceeds the dialectical frame by which it is spawned.

In Hegel the suppression of bodily life is shown to require the very body that it seeks to suppress; in this sense, the body is preserved in and by the very act of suppression. Freud understood this differently in his analysis of neurosis as a kind of libidinal attachment to a prohibition which nevertheless thwarts libidinal gratification. Where that thwarting constitutes a repression, the splitting off of ideation from affect, neurosis or symptom formation follows. One might read Hegel's references to *eigensinnigkeit* or stubbornness as illustrating the process of splitting and defense in the formation of neurosis. That Hegel refers to this "unhappiness" as a kind of stubborn attachment suggests that, as in neurosis, the ethical regulation of bodily impulse becomes the focus and aim of impulse itself. In both cases, we are given to understand an attachment to subjection which is formative of the reflexive structure of subjection itself. The impulse or bodily experience which would be negated, to return to Hegel, is inadvertently *preserved* by the very activity of negation.

We can see in both Hegel and Freud a certain reliance on a dialectical reversal by which a bodily experience, broadly construed, comes under the censor of the law only to reemerge as the sustaining affect of that law. The Freudian notion of *sublimation* suggests that denial or displacement of pleasure and desire can become formative of culture; his *Civilization and Its Discontents* thus laid the ground for Marcuse's *Eros and Civilization*. The inadvertently productive effects of sublimation in the formation of cultural products appear to exceed the dialectical reversal by which they are generated. Whereas for Marcuse, the drives, or eros and thanatos, precede the regulatory imperatives by which they are rendered culturally livable, for Foucault, the repressive hypothesis, which appears to include within its structure the model of sublimation, fails to work precisely because repression generates the very pleasures and desires it seeks to regulate. For Foucault, repression does not act on a pregiven field of pleasure and desire; it constitutes that field as that which is to be regulated, that which is always potentially or actually under the rubric of regulation. The repressive regime, as Foucault calls it, requires its own self-augmentation and proliferation. As such, this regime requires the field of bodily impulse to expand and proliferate as a moralized domain, such that it will continually have fresh material through which to articulate its own power. Hence, repression produces a field of infinitely moralizable bodily phenomena in order to facilitate and rationalize its own proliferation.

Here we see that Foucault departs from the kind of dialectical reversal we followed in Hegel. In Foucault, the suppression of the body not only requires and produces the very body it seeks to suppress, it goes further by extending the bodily domain to be regulated, proliferating sites of control, discipline, and suppression. In other words, the body *presumed* by the Hegelian explanation is incessantly produced and proliferated in order to extend the domain of juridical power. In this sense, the restrictions placed *on* the body not only *require* and *produce* the body they seek to restrict, but *proliferate* the domain of the bodily beyond the domain targeted by the original restriction. In what many have come to see as a finally utopian gesture in Foucault, this proliferation of the body by juridical regimes beyond the terms of dialectical reversal is also the site of possible resistance. The psychoanalytic discourse that would describe and pathologize repressed desire ends up producing a discursive incitement to desire: impulse is continually fabricated as a site of confession and, hence, potential control, but this fabrication exceeds the regulatory aims by which it is generated. In this sense, criminal codes which seek to catalogue and institutionalize normalcy become the site for a contestation of the concept of the normal; sexologists who would classify and pathologize homosexuality inadvertently provide the conditions for a proliferation and mobilization of homosexual cultures.

Within the Hegelian framework, the subject, which splits itself off from its body, requires that body in order to sustain its splitting activity; the body to be suppressed is thus marshalled in the service of that suppression. For Foucault, the body to be regulated is similarly marshalled in the service of suppression, but the body is not constituted prior to that regulation. On the contrary, the body is produced *as* an object of regulation, and for regulation to augment itself, the body is *proliferated* as an object of regulation. This proliferation both marks off Foucault's theory from Hegel's and constitutes the site of potential resistance to regulation. The possibility of this resistance is derived from what is *unforeseeable* in proliferation. But to understand how a regulatory regime could produce effects which are not only unforeseeable but constitute resistance, it seems that we must return to the question of stubborn attachments and, more precisely, to the place of that attachment in the subversion of the law.

Although Foucault criticizes Freud's hypothesis of repression, he is indebted to this theorization in his own account of the production and proliferation of the regulated body. In particular, the logic of subjection in both Hegel and Freud implies that the instrument of suppression becomes the new structure and aim of desire, at least when subjection proves effective. But if a regulatory regime requires the production of new sites of regulation and, hence, a more thoroughgoing moralization of the body, then what is the place of bodily impulse, desire, and attachment? Does the regulatory regime not only produce desire, but become produced by the cultivation of a certain attachment *to* the rule of subjection? If part of what regulatory regimes do is to constrain the formation and attachments of desire, then it seems that from the start a certain detachability of impulse is presumed, a certain incommensurability between the capacity for a bodily attachment, on the one hand, and the site where it is confined, on the other. Foucault appears to presume precisely this detachability of desire in claiming that incitements and reversals are to some degree *unforeseeable*, that they have the capacity, central to the notion of resistance, to *exceed* the regulatory aims for which they were produced. If a given regime cannot fully control the incitements that it nevertheless produces, is that in part the result of a resistance, at the level of impulse, to a full and final domestication by any regulatory regime?

What Hegel implies in "The Unhappy Consciousness" is not merely that moral wretchedness cannot be coherently sustained, that it invariably concedes the bodily being that it seeks to deny, but that the pursuit of wretchedness, the attachment to wretchedness, is both the condition and the potential undoing of such subjection. If wretchedness, agony, and pain are sites or modes of stubbornness, ways of attaching to oneself, negatively articulated modes of reflexivity, then that is because they are given by regulatory regimes as the sites available for attachment, and a subject will attach to pain rather than not attach at all. For Freud, an infant forms a pleasure-giving attachment to any excitation that comes its way, even the most traumatic, which accounts for the formation of masochism and, for some, the production of abjection, rejection, wretchedness, and so on as the necessary preconditions for love. The gesture of rejection can become masochistically eroticized only because it is a gesture. Although the rejecting gesture's alleged purpose is to thwart an oncoming desire, it nevertheless appears *as a gesture*, thus *making itself present* and lending itself to being read as a kind of offering or, minimally, *presence*. Precisely because the gesture of rejection *is*, it rhetorically denies the threat of withdrawal that it nevertheless purports to signify. For the infant, the presence or determinacy of that object, no matter how persistently rejecting, is nevertheless a site of presence and excitation and, hence, is better than no object at all. This truism is not far from Nietzsche's line that the will would rather will nothingness than not will at all. In both cases, the desire to desire is a willingness to desire precisely that which would foreclose desire, if only for the possibility of continuing to desire.

The question, then, that Hegel and Freud would appear to pose for Foucault is whether this terrain of "stubborn attachment" does not in some way figure in the scenarios of subjection that he describes. To what extent does a regulatory regime exploit this willingness to attach blindly to what seeks to suppress or negate that very attachment? And to what extent does the attachment that a regulatory regime requires prove to be both its constitutive failure and the potential site of resistance? If desire has as its final aim the continuation of itself—and here one might link Hegel, Freud, and Foucault all back to Spinoza's *conatus*—then the capacity of desire to be withdrawn and to reattach will constitute something like the vulnerability of every strategy of subjection.

Notes

1. In the following text I refer to this chapter in abbreviated form as "The Unhappy Consciousness." English citations are from *The Phenomenology of Spirit*, trans. A. V. Miller (Oxford: Oxford University Press, 1977); German citations are from G. W. F. Hegel, *Werke in zwanzig Bänden*, vol. 3 (Frankfurt am Main: Suhrkamp, 1980). Page numbers for later citations will appear in the text.
2. Michel Foucault, *Discipline and Punish: The Birth of the Prison* (New York: Pantheon, 1977), p. 30; *Surveiller et punir: Naissance de la prison* (Paris: Gallimard, 1975), p. 30.
3. Friedrich Nietzsche, *On the Genealogy of Morals*, trans. Walter Kaufmann (New York: Random House, 1967), p. 87; *Zur Genealogie der Moral*, in Nietzsche, *Sämtliche Werke: Kritische Studienausgabe in 15 Einzelbänden*, ed. Giorgio Colli and Mazzino Montinari, vol. 5 (Berlin: de Gruyter, 1988), p. 325.
4. Foucault, *Discipline and Punish*, p. 30/34.
5. The relevance of the psychoanalytic understanding of the "phantasmatic" and, in particular, the view of Laplanche and Pontalis that the subject is *dissimulated* in the scene of phantasy. We might consider the various stages of progress in the *Phenomenology* as successive forms of the phantasmatic, that is, successive ways in which the subject becomes dissimulated in and as the scene of its action.
6. See Sigmund Freud, "On Narcissism: An Introduction," *The Standard Edition of the Complete Psycholological Works of Sigmund Freud*, ed. and trans. James Strachey, 24 vols. (London: Hogarth, 1953–74), 14: 73–104, for a discussion of the origins of conscience in the repression of homosexuality.
7. Here one can see that Foucault's critique of Freud in *The History of Sexuality, Volume I* is partially wrong. Foucault's view that psychoanalysis fails to understand how law produces desire is itself a failure to understand the way in which prohibition is productive. Foucault reserves the term "power" for a productive operation that is understood not to apply to "law." Yet we see that an insurmountable equivocation between the two terms is produced once law is understood as productive.
8. Sigmund Freud, *Civilization and Its Discontents*, trans. James Strachey (New York: Norton, 1977), p. 84.
9. Nietzsche, *Zur Genealogie der Moral*, 411–12; my translation. Kaufman's equivalent is on pp. 162–63.

CHAPTER 23

"Freedom" and "We"

—from *Hegel: The Restlessness of the Negative* (1997)

Jean-Luc Nancy

Freedom

Equality, not as the abstract equation of a subject = X in every subject, but as the effective equality of concrete singularities (absolute equality of the absolute): such is the element of sense, and desire is its liberation. The concept must enter into existence,[1] and effective existence can only be effective singularity, in which "the absolute return of the concept into itself, and at the same time the posited loss of itself," comes to pass.[2] Conception or grasp is not the subsumption of the particular under a generality; it is precisely the movement that negates the general as well as the particular (movement that therefore also negates abstract relation), in order to affirm what alone affirms itself in itself and for itself: the concrete singular, here and now, the existent as such, in the concrete relation of separation. Grasp is thus the grasping of the singular in its singularity, that is, in what is unique and unexchangeable about it, and therefore at the point where this unicity is the unicity of a desire and a recognition in the other, in all the others. The ones and the others—the ones who are all others for each other—are among themselves equals in desire.

Desire is thus the freedom of the singular insofar as the latter is grasped according to the "absolute separation of the concept," in other words, as detached from a mere "return in itself," from the simple return into self of the identical.

In the concept, everything is grasped as necessity: it is necessary that the self return to itself even as it separates itself from itself. In this respect, "self" is the name of necessity itself, and its movement is pure logic. One is therefore tempted to conclude hastily that Hegel's thought is a "panlogism," or the system of an inhuman mechanics of the absolute. But this is to forget that necessity must itself have a necessity, a sufficient reason: which, since its beginnings, is what philosophy has signified with *logos*. And this necessity of necessity is freedom.

In fact, freedom is the name for the necessity to be in itself and for itself detached from all fixity, all determination, from every given, and every property. But even more, it is the necessity to be detached, not as an independence fixed in itself, but as the movement of detachment right at the surface of every determinacy. In exposing this necessity as such, one gives it the form of a constraining logic. But one also exposes that its veritable content is "freedom and independence."[3]

The necessity of the concept and of thought in general—the necessity of the *logos*—is the form that the absolute of freedom takes in order to expose itself as such and as absolute constraint. The absolute of freedom is not, however, dissimulated beneath this form, as a secret that would be merely to come, or only located in a divine realm. Freedom consists in the necessity that form again dissolve itself of itself, and that the "content" be its own "form": the concrete, singular manifestation of self-liberation.

Freedom is therefore not given as a property or as a right. Freedom is nothing given: it is the negation of the given, including this given that would be a "free subject" defined only by determined rights and liberties. Being itself the appropriation of the subject, freedom is nothing that a subject might appropriate. If Hegel refers to Spinoza on the subject of freedom,[4] it is because he recognizes in Spinoza the thought of the only true freedom in the absolute, as distinct from the illusory freedom of men who believe themselves masters of their acts because they are unaware of the real determinations of these acts. Free will is only a moment and a figure of freedom: for in it there subsists, and even prevails, the given fixity of the subject as master of its choices. In affirming myself as free, I adhere to this position of an ego that is "master of its domain": this adherence has already deprived me of freedom.

Freedom is indeed independence, but independence from the "despotic ego" as much as from any political or domestic despot whatsoever. It is indeed autonomy, but the law it gives itself is precisely itself: it therefore gives itself the law to have no law, if it is itself, for itself, the law.

Generally speaking, the law is a "relation of universal determinations":[5] it posits, each time, that this is (in the law of physics) or should be (in the moral law) universally according to a universal condition. Thus "the law is something differentiated within itself." It is not a particularity differing from a generality; rather, the law states that *this* is a *universal* (for example, a body is heavy). Being for itself, the law is thus nothing other than being *self*: interior difference, or "the difference which is not one." This is not, however, the pure and simple absence of difference, the consistent unity of an "itself," but rather "difference in itself," and the step out of self that is the entirety of self-manifestation.

Freedom is the law or the necessity that posits the self outside of itself. It is thus the law of what first posits itself without law, whose law lies, precisely, in that positing. But this law—manifestation or mediation—cannot be represented as a law, for a (physical or moral) law is always "the stable image . . . unaware of the restlessness of negativity."[6] Freedom is the position of negativity as such.

Because such a "position" is just the contrary of a being-posited, deposited as given, and because it is eminently "position" in the active sense,[7] freedom is the position . . . of nothing, and the liberation . . . of everything. Necessity and anarchy of the absolute.

Once again, the apparent dialectical ease should not mislead. It will have always been premature to impute sleight of hand. The Hegelian thought of freedom is the most difficult because it gathers and knots together all the aporias that intersect at the term "freedom"—and because it expends much effort showing the way to freedom from these same aporias. Freedom is par excellence the concept that consciousness or the understanding expects to be a given—whereas it must be the concept of nothing given, the very concept of the nongiven and the ungiveable. Here, thought forcefully states: you ask to have a freedom, whereas you have to become it.

This is also why the freedom of the absolute, or the absolute in and as freedom, is anything but the "absolute freedom" that Hegel deciphers in the Terror. This is the freedom that posits itself as absolute: it therefore posits its pure equality with itself as being immediately universal will, or as containing this equality with itself as pure and annulled difference of the law. It is thus foreign to the singularity and the diversity of effective existence. Under its juridical, economic, political, and moral forms, the pure "self-certainty"[8] of freedom is precisely only its ineffectivity; and, consequently, when it aspires to effectuate itself, its concrete inequality with itself is equal to the inequality of concrete subjects.

The experience of deliverance from tutelages and tyrannies that was the experience of Hegel's time immediately opens onto this other experience: that the erection of a free subject, of an absolute worth as such and in itself, is the alienation of the very movement of emancipation. Whether this subject be represented as individual or as collective, as law of the global market or of a universal morality, it simultaneously freezes both the concrete becoming of singular freedoms and their movement of becoming through each other into this abstract given. Freedom can lay down the law (in the sense of the law that has been specified), and can effectuate itself as the *sublation* of every law, only through the concrete equality of all: not as a legal equality, but as the real equality of an appropriation (each time, concretely singular) of my being-free. A being-free that cannot be concretely separated from yours, nor from ours, from a being-free-with-each-other.

Freedom is freedom-with or it is nothing, because it is neither independence, nor autonomy, nor the free will of a subject—no more than it is the independences of many juxtaposed subjects, even to imagine them without oppositions. It is rather the liberation of the subject: its taking leave of the density of being. One cannot say that the self is free, for such a *being* is in itself the negation of freedom. Freedom, to the contrary, is the negation of this negation, or negativity for itself. "The pure idea . . . is an absolute *liberation*."[9] If it is liberation, and not given freedom, it is because it liberates itself in and through its other: the movement of recognition is also the movement of liberation.

Freedom and negativity thus mutually expose one another. On the one hand, the negation of the given or of being-in-itself, in other words, its entry into becoming, into manifestation and desire, goes toward nothing other than freedom—more precisely, to *its* freedom, and still more precisely, to its *liberation*. Negation is first of all this movement of a self-liberation-from-immediate-being: negativity is from the very first nothing other than the hollowing out of being by its own liberation. And, on the other hand, liberation is nothing other than negativity for itself, for it is the negation of this simple negation that is the being held-back-in-itself of being.

The Hegelian privilege of negativity and the decisive character of the formula "negation of the negation" is thereby justified: the first negation is the position of the given, the fixity of which holds back, freezes, and annuls the movement of sense. To posit that being is in itself nothing is not to open an abyss in which speculative ideality would plunge the entirety of the real; to the contrary, it is to posit the thoroughgoing insufficiency of the self considered in itself—and even, in truth, the impossibility of considering the *self* for itself, of identifying it as a substance or subsistence, as an assurance or a certitude. The first negation is already freedom, but still only negatively indicated. If I penetrate this first truth, that neither the stone nor the ego has the value of simple being-there or of an identity (for example, my name, but also my self-image), this penetration is already liberation. And it is liberation of the grasping of this: that the *self* is not *there*, that it does not assume the form of being-given-there.

The second negation denies that the first is valid on its own: it negates pure nothingness, the abyss or lack. It is the positive liberation of becoming, of manifestation, and of desire. It is therefore self-affirmation. But as this liberating affirmation is not a return to the point of departure—to the stone or to me, which in turn was already only a derived given, a provisional deposit along the way and the fleeting instant of a presentation—it is also not a new, simple position. It is infinite negativity in and as act. I cannot say that the stone has become free just because it has moved from its position beside the path any more than I can say that I have become free just because I have recognized myself as different from my nominal or imaginary identity. Neither one nor the other has *become* free (as if freedom could be a result). But the stone in my slingshot, in the wall that I have built, or in the statue that a sculptor exhibits to us, indefinitely liberates itself from its exteriority, enters into a history and into multiple senses, and brings us along with it. The result is again a liberation—and that is what negativity means.

This result, however, is not indefiniteness as such—the "bad infinity" of an abstract circulation from one sense to another, from one usage to another, from one identification to another, which would always be in search of a final, sovereign, and total freedom (nature and history reconciled, postulated kingdom of ends). It is the infinite in and as act: liberation in the present of presence itself, and therefore the manifestation of singularity as such. There is indeed return to being: we have said that the *self* is return to self. It is indeed a matter of this stone and indeed a matter of me, of us. It is matter of nothing other than this world.

Now, "absolute liberation" signifies that return is a return to nothing given, but return to the given as that which gives *itself*—or to the "self" insofar as self is nothing other than a self-giving. Not, then, if one likes, a return to the world, but to the creation of the world. Not, then, to conclude, a "return," but the liberation once again of what infinitely liberates itself, starting from nothing. The ultimate signification of negativity as freedom—or of "negativity for itself"—is therefore still a negation: it is not a matter of hailing, celebrating, consecrating, or accepting the course of the world such as it is. And because it is also not a matter of measuring the world, with the edifying powerlessness of the "beautiful soul,"[10] against what it should be, it is once again a matter of liberating it. Thus, we will also not say that such and such a juridical, social, or political regime makes us free and equal. Freedom and equality are always in opposition to the exteriority of the law.

Which means liberation can be for no freedom that would one day become its given result, that would present itself as its law and would incarnate itself in a figure. Liberation for nothing, in this sense, but therefore liberation for a death that would not be a "death without signification."

Such a death is at least, and first of all, death that does not come from the outside as another given, in order to reduce my presence to being only a given. It cannot be inflicted death, but only the death that individuality, as simply natural and immediate, *gives itself* [*se donne*].[11] This is not a suicide; that is, this individuality does not treat itself as if from outside, submitting to a foreign and abstract subject. Rather, it dies in and to the immediacy that is all it was as something given. This does not suppress the uncanniness [*étrangeté inquiétante*] of death: on the contrary, it is what makes it absolutely unsettling, and what provokes the fulgurant contradiction, the absolute pain of having to sojourn in this thought, of having to become in this penetration.

What is to be thought, then, is not that death has its signification beyond itself, like a subsistence beyond the end of subsistence, or as a surviving relic. Such a signification would be precisely only a signification, and, appropriately enough, a signification attached to another subsistence-in-itself, which would do nothing more than replay the entire drama or process. It is to think—and this is thought itself—that the death which is not "death without signification" is still death without signification, but in such a fashion that the nothingness of signification is also the appropriating movement of the proper "self," the grasping-and-penetration of the truth of sense.

This movement cannot be represented to the self—it is its own becoming, its manifestation, and its desire—and, moreover, it is in this way that the subject is not a subject of representation in general, but the subject of an infinite appropriation, and the subject of this appropriation in the other. This movement is not represented, but posited, in the other: in the most immediate manner, in mourning and in burial, the others bear witness to appropriation insofar as it is not that of self-consciousness in itself, but is a singular appropriation that falls outside of all immediate particularity.[12] In this way, death is an event: the appropriating event of the proper that is the outside-of-self; passage into the other, and absolute giving over to the other, to every other and to all the others, of that which can only be given over as passage itself. The other is the one who recognizes that my death is mine and is thus the "sojourn of spirit." Infinite recognition of this: an absolute singular desire has passed through here.

The event is therefore nothing other than the penetration into "completely free manifestation."[13] As such it is not different from the event of birth, from the creation of the world or the upsurge of the existent in general—that is, as singular. As long as we grasp it only on its formal side and presented as a truth, it is this event that is at stake as thought. But this event is therefore at stake as effective liberation each time that a simple given is refused, each time that a given death or a murder [*mort donnée*] is refused, each time that the "despotic ego's" law of nothingness is refused.

The return of freedom in itself—if one can still speak of return and of the in-itself—will therefore be nothing other than the return to the decision with which, each time, thought will have begun. Because the I is absolutely undetermined, it will have had to decide *itself*. Not in order to choose between possibilities given to the free will of its subjectivity: for this subjectivity is not, or is no more than, a one-sided abstraction, to which nothing is therefore given. But the I will have had to know itself precisely as "the infinity of subjectivity,"[14] to which nothing is given or prescribed in advance, and for which, consequently, there is no "good" or "duty" laid out beforehand. It "knows itself then as what chooses and decides," which is also to know itself infinite in and as act, and to become.

I do not therefore decide in favor of things proposed as possible, because I exist as "me" only in my decision. But the truth and the sense of free decision is this: I decide *myself*, I decide on myself; more precisely, I take leave of my universal indetermination and realize my infinity as singularity. It is not "starting out from myself" that I decide, as if I *was* free; in liberating myself, it is on myself, from out of myself, that I decide. Deciding oneself, liberating oneself, and giving oneself are one and the same: the self outside itself in the blossoming, the supreme manifestation of manifestation in general.

I will not have known "beforehand" what I was choosing, because there was no beforehand. But, in deciding, each time, I decide on my singularity itself that knows itself to be decisive. Either this self-knowing posits itself as "pure identity with immediate self" and thereby as subjective "interest"—which is what the word *evil* designates—or this self-knowing posits itself as this very deciding identity that does not retain itself in itself, that is thus not pure identity, but decision of self as other—this is what the word *good* designates. But this "good" cannot be designated as given, present, and qualified. The decisive subject, who is only a subject in the act of deciding, decides, as undetermined, either for the pure determinacy of "I = I," or for the infinite determination of the "I = becoming-other."

The freedom of decision is the very thing that thought, in order to begin or end, has to penetrate. But since it cannot merely penetrate it "in thought," it is not enough to have decided to philosophize in order to have penetrated the truth of decision, which is only its concrete act. So too the decision to philosophize leads only to exposing what is at stake in the form of the act—and also to exposing that this form itself is nothing yet without its effectuation as content. One could say, summarily, that everything that can be formally exposed reduces itself to this: the decision is made between the self and the other. But only on the condition of adding: this means, between the given immediate and the non-given infinite. On the one hand, consequently, the self grasps itself, knows itself, and affirms itself as the whole content of its decision. On the other hand, it decides itself for the infinite recognition of and in the other. But it does not know this, for this is not a knowledge in its possession, and it cannot, nor should it, know itself as "good"—unless it relapses into a given identity, and into a moral imaginary.

Decision is the act of concrete singularity, and the becoming of liberation. Its knowing is only absolute knowing: absolutely concrete knowing, of everyone and no one, that absolutely negates the independence and consistency of all self-certainty. Knowing of restlessness, knowing without rest—but thus, and not otherwise, *knowing*.

We

This knowing is not a knowing that would remain that of the absolute in itself and for itself. It is not the knowing of the subject, as if the subject were the absolute other, the Self contemplating itself in itself in its pure logic, its pure becoming, and its pure decision, forever returning to itself from all exteriorization and from all alienation.

Hegel has often been read as if he exhibited the autodevelopment of an anonymous Subject or Reason, foreign to us, the big Other of an autistic Self that, moreover, would only be the fantasmatic correlate of the subject of a proprietary and securitary individualism: two subjects each the mirror for the other, each one as stupid and wretched as the other.

But the *truth* of a self-knowing that must be the knowing of manifestation, of the desire of the other, and of decision cannot be a truth that simply returns to itself. Truth must itself be the manifestation, the desire, and the becoming of truth—or its sense. And in this way, truth comes back to us. It finds or happens upon itself *as us*, and it is *to us* that it is entrusted.

"We" means two things:

1. The knowing that is "for us" is knowing that is not merely "for consciousness."[15] Consciousness is indeed only the knowledge of objects, and as self-consciousness, it still has the self as an object, as its other that remains its correlate. The knowing of the truth of this other as the truth of the passage-out-of-self is the knowing *for us* of what consciousness, as consciousness, is unaware of in its own experience. *For us* there is sense and truth of what remains for consciousness representation and isolated signification.

But who is *we*? It seems first of all that this is us, right here, with Hegel, in the exercise of the work of thought. "We," then, seems to designate the philosopher, or those who have understood the lesson of philosophy, a more refined consciousness and knowledge that would grasp what escapes common consciousness. This appearance must be dispelled if thought is not to remain pure thought.

Without a doubt, it is correct to say that consciousness, in the movement of its experience, does not present to itself the knowing of this movement as a separate and distinct knowledge. It is, however, no less correct to say that what absolute knowing knows is nothing other than the "movement of birth and passing away."[16] It is knowing of passage, not as passage of an object, but as that of the subject itself: it is this passage itself, and knowing "for us" is essentially *the same* as that of common consciousness. And this latter, in its turn, is nothing other than the manifestation and becoming of the former.

Consequently, "we" designates neither a corporation of philosophers nor the point of view of a more elevated knowledge—and this, quite precisely, because this "we" *is us*, us all. If the moment of philosophy—of the knowing, the work, and the patience that are proper to it—must initially posit itself as a separate knowledge, as an abstract discipline of thought and as a book difficult to read, a book one will have to reread or whose reading will have to be effaced in order to penetrate the sense[17] (but whose rereading, as a separate act, is never not indispensable to the experience of truth)—if this separation is therefore necessary, it is only so as to expose this: that it is indeed a matter of *us*, and that the truth or sense staged before us as "philosophy" only has sense and truth for us.

Not that philosophy is enlisted to give them to us: for, under these conditions, truth and sense would only be something given to us, with which we have nothing to do. But they are for us, for us all—that is, they have sense and truth only in us, in our concrete existences, and only to the extent that these existences are not separate individuals, but the sharing of singularities in movement, becoming, desire, and decision.

2. "We" is defined by this: "the absolute . . . from the beginning, is and wants to be in itself and for itself near to us."[18] The total movement of the "self" in-right-at-near-to-for-itself [*en-à-même-auprès-de-pour-soi*] would have no sense if this movement was not that of this proximity with us. "Near" (or *chez*) signifies that among us it is not simply in-and-for-itself that this comes to pass: neither in the in-and-for-itself of the individual, nor in that of an all-encompassing Power of the world. Neither nature nor history, neither capital nor technology is capable of being such a power; nor can the gods be other powers that would save us from the first. Rather, all of these figures expose us, through their determinateness, to the unbinding or dislocation of every "Self," of all self-certainty. It is *we* who are exposed, and it is therefore *to us* that we are exposed.

To us: to the upsurge of our existences, together, as the surging up of sense. To the upsurge of this, that the world is precisely what does not remain an inert weight, but what manifests itself as a restlessness. This restlessness is not only ours, it is itself "us"— that is, it is the singularity of singularities as such.

"We" is not something—neither object nor self—that the absolute would be near, as if the absolute were itself another thing or another self. On the contrary: that the absolute be or wants to be near us means that it is our "near us," our just-between-us [*entre-nous*], the just-between-us of our manifestation, our becoming, and our desire.

The absolute is between us. It is there in itself and for itself, and, one might say, the self itself is between us. But "the self itself is unrest":[19] between us, nothing can be at rest, nothing is assured of presence or of being—and we pass each after the others as much as each into the others. Each with the others, each near the others: the *near* of the absolute is nothing other than our *near* each other.

We never stop losing the "fixity of self-positing."[20] And this unrest that *we are* and that we desire (even as consciousness believes it only wants its self and its objects) is where the proximity of the absolute finds, or happens upon, itself: neither possession, nor incorporation, but proximity as such, imminence and coincidence, like the beat of a rhythm.[21] So beats the passage of sense: as the interval of time, between us, in the fleeting and rhythmic awakening of a discrete recognition of existence.

Abbreviations

Citations of works by Hegel are given with the following abbreviations. When indicated, the translations have been modified in compliance with Nancy's use of the French translations.

PM *Hegel's Philosophy of Mind: Part III of the Encyclopedia of Philosophical Sciences (1830)*. Translated by William Wallace. London: Oxford University Press, 1971.

PN *Hegel's Philosophy of Nature: Part II of the Encyclopedia of Philosophical Sciences (1830)*. Translated by A. V. Miller. London: Oxford University Press, 1970.

PS *Hegel's Phenomenology of Spirit*. Translated by A. V. Miller. London: Oxford University Press, 1977.

SL *Hegel's Science of Logic*. Translated by A. V. Miller. New York: Humanities Press, 1989.

Notes

1. *PN*, §359, p. 385.
2. *SL*, III, chap. 1, B, p. 612; translation modified.
3. Ibid., Preface to the Second Edition, p. 40.
4. G. W. F. Hegel, *Encyclopedia of the Philosophical Sciences*, Preface to the Second Edition (1827), *LL*, pp. 8–10.
5. *PM*, §423, p. 164; translation modified.
6. *SL*, II, §2, chap. 2, II, A, pp. 503–4. [The citation given is a piecing together of two different passages.—*Trans*.]
7. The sense that Hegel gives to "position" by the "concept": the latter grasps and posits. But what it posits is its own activity.
8. *PS*, BB, "Spirit," C, pp. 364ff.
9. *SL*, III, §3, chap. 3, "The Absolute Idea," p. 843.
10. *PS*, BB, "Spirit," C, pp. 383ff.
11. *PN*, §375. War, which Hegel certainly does not perceive in the same fashion we do, would have to be given particular treatment on its own. [The expression "donner la mort" means to murder or kill; "se donner la mort" would therefore mean to murder oneself. Hence the reference to suicide in the next sentence.—*Trans*.]
12. Cf. *PS*, BB, "Spirit," A, a, pp. 267–78.
13. *SL*, III, §1, chap. 1, A, p. 603. [The citation given here is a compression of two paragraphs, in other words, an "allusion."—*Trans*.]
14. *PM*, §427, then §§428–30, pp. 168–71.
15. *PS*, Introduction.

16. Ibid.
17. Ibid. Cf. the opening pages of the Preface.
18. Ibid., Introduction, p. 47; translation modified.
19. Ibid., Preface, p. 12; translation modified.
20. Ibid., p. 20.
21. Ibid., pp. 36, 38.

Bibliography

Adorno, Theodor W. "World Spirit and Natural History: An Excursion to Hegel." In *Negative Dialectics*. Translated by E. B. Ashton, 300–360. New York: Continuum, 1973.

———. *Hegel: Three Studies*. Translated by Shierry Weber Nicholsen. Cambridge, Massachusetts: MIT Press, 1993.

Agamben, Giorgio. "Excursus 7 (after the final day)." In *Language and Death: The Place of Negativity*. Translated by Karen E. Pinkus and Michael Hardt, 99–106. Minneapolis: University of Minnesota Press, 1991.

Althusser, Louis. "Marx's Relation to Hegel." In *Politics and History: Montesquieu, Rousseau, Hegel and Marx*. Translated by Ben Brewster, 161–186. London: Verso, 1972.

———. *The Spectre of Hegel: Early Writings*. Translated by G. M. Goshgarian. Edited by François Matheron. London: Verso, 1997.

Bataille, Georges. "Hegel, Death and Sacrifice." In *Yale French Studies* 78 (1990): 9–28. Translated by Jonathan Strauss.

Blanchot, Maurice. "Literature and the Right to Death." In *The Gaze of Orpheus, and Other Literary Essays*. Translated by Lydia Davis. Edited by P. Adams Sitney, 21–62. Barrytown, New York: Station Hill Press, 1981, reprinted in *The Work of Fire*, 300–344. Stanford: Stanford University Press, 1995.

———. *The Step Not Beyond*. Translated by Lycette Nelson. Albany: State University of New York Press, 1992.

Butler, Judith. *Subjects of Desire: Hegelian Reflections in Twentieth-Century France*. New York: Columbia University Press, 1987.

———. "Commentary on Joseph Flay's 'Hegel, Derrida, and Bataille's Laughter.'" In *Hegel and His Critics: Philosophy in the Aftermath of Hegel*. Edited by William Desmond, 174–178. Albany: State University of New York Press, 1989).

———. "Stubborn Attachment, Bodily Subjection: Hegel on the Unhappy Consciousness." In *Intersections: Nineteenth-Century Philosophy and Contemporary Theory*. Edited by Tilottama Rajan and David L. Clarke, 173–196. Albany: State University of New York Press, 1995, reprinted in *The Psychic Life of Power: Theories in Subjection*, 31–62. Stanford: Stanford University Press, 1997.

———. *Antigone's Claim: Kinship Between Life and Death*. New York: Columbia University Press, 2000.

Deleuze, Gilles. *Difference and Repetition*. Translated by Paul Patton. New York: Columbia University Press, 1994.

———. *Nietzsche and Philosophy*. Translated by Hugh Tomlinson. New York: Columbia University Press, 1983.

Derrida, Jacques. "From Restricted to General Economy: A Hegelianism without Reserve." In *Writing and Difference*. Translated by Alan Bass, 251–277. Chicago: University of Chicago Press, 1978.

———. "Outwork, prefacing." In *Dissemination*. Translated by Barbara Johnson, 1–59. Chicago: University of Chicago Press, 1981.

———. "The Pit and the Pyramid: Introduction to Hegel's Semiology." In *Margins of Philosophy*. Translated by Alan Bass, 69–108. Chicago: University of Chicago Press, 1982.

———. "The Age of Hegel." In *Demarcating the Disciplines: Philosophy, Literature, Art*. Translated by Susan Winnett. Edited by Samuel Weber, 3–35. Minneapolis: University of Minnesota Press, 1986.

———. *Glas*. Translated by John P. Leavey, Jr. and Richard Rand. Lincoln: University of Nebraska Press, 1986.

Fanon, Frantz. "The Negro and Hegel." In *Black Skin, White Masks*. Translated by Charles Lam Markmann, 216–222. New York: Grove Press, 1967.

Gadamer, Hans-Georg. "Hegel's 'Inverted World.'" In *Hegel's Dialectic: Five Hermeneutical Studies*. Translated by P. Christopher Smith, 35–53. New Haven: Yale University Press, 1976.

Hyppolite, Jean. *Studies in Marx and Hegel*. Translated by John O'Neill. New York: Basic Books, 1969.

———. *Genesis and Structure of Hegel's* Phenomenology of Spirit. Translated by Samuel Cherniak and John Heckman. Evanston: Northwestern University Press, 1974.

———. *Introduction to Hegel's Philosophy of History*. Translated by Bond Harris and Jacqueline Bouchard Spurlock. Gainesville: University Press of Florida, 1996.

———. "Logic and Existence." In *Logic and Existence*. Translated by Leonard Lawlor and Amit Sen, 177–189. Albany: State University of New York Press, 1997.

Irigaray, Luce. "The Eternal Irony of the Community." In *Speculum of the Other Woman*. Translated by Gillian C. Gill, 214–226. Ithaca, New York: Cornell University Press, 1985.

———. "The Universal as Mediation." In *Sexes and Genealogies*. Translated by Gillian C. Gill, 125–149. New York: Columbia University Press, 1993.

Kojève, Alexandre. *Introduction to the Reading of Hegel: Lectures on the* Phenomenology of Spirit. Translated by James H. Nichols, Jr. Edited by Allan Bloom. Ithaca, New York: Cornell University Press, 1969.

———. "Hegel, Marx, and Christianity." In *Interpretation: A Journal of Political Philosophy* 1 (1970): 21–42. Translated by Hilail Gildin.

———. "The Idea of Death in the Philosophy of Hegel." In *Interpretation: A Journal of Political Philosophy* 3, no. 2, 3 (1973): 114–156. Translated by Joseph J. Carpino.

Kristeva, Julia. "Negativity: Rejection." In *Revolution in Poetic Language*. Translated by Margaret Waller, 107–164. New York: Columbia University Press, 1984.

Lacan, Jacques. "The Subversion of the Subject and the Dialectic of Desire in the Freudian Unconscious." In *Écrits: A Selection*. Translated by Alan Sheridan, 292–325. New York: W.W. Norton & Company, 1977.

Levinas, Emmanuel. "Death and Time." In *God, Death, and Time*. Translated by Bettina Bergo, 5–117. Stanford: Stanford University Press, 2000.

Lukács, Georg. "'*Entäusserung*' ('Externalization') as the Central Philosophical Concept of *The Phenomenology of Mind*." In *The Young Hegel: Studies in the Relations between Dialectics and Economics*. Translated by Rodney Livingstone, 537–568. Cambridge, Massachusetts: MIT Press, 1976.

Merleau-Ponty, Maurice. "Hegel's Existentialism." In *Sense and Non-Sense*. Translated by Hubert L. Dreyfus and Patricia Allen Dreyfus, 63–70. Evanston: Northwestern University Press, 1964.

Nancy, Jean-Luc. "The Jurisdiction of the Hegelian Monarch." In *The Birth to Presence*. Translated by Mary Ann and Peter Caws, 110–142. Stanford: Stanford University Press, 1993.

———. *The Speculative Remark: One of Hegel's Bons Mots*. Translated by Céline Surprenant. Stanford: Stanford University Press, 2001.

———. "Freedom" and "We." In *Hegel: The Restlessness of the Negative*. Translated by Jason Smith and Steven Miller, 66–79. Minneapolis: University of Minnesota Press, 2002.

Sallis, John. "Hegel's Concept of Presentation: Its Determination in the Preface to the *Phenomenology of Spirit*." In *Hegel-Studien* 12 (1977): 129–156, reprinted in *Delimitations: Phenomenology and the End of Metaphysics*, 40–62. Bloomington: Indiana University Press, 1986, and in *The*

Phenomenology of Spirit *Reader: Critical and Interpretive Essays.* Edited by Jon Stewart, 25–51. Albany: State University of New York Press, 1998.

———. "Imagination and Presentation in Hegel's Philosophy of Spirit." In *Hegel's Philosophy of Spirit.* Edited by Peter Stillman, 66–88. Albany: State University of New York Press, 1987.

———. "Ending(s): Imagination, Presentation, Spirit." In *Spacings—of Reason and Imagination in Texts of Kant, Fichte, Hegel*, 132–157. Chicago: University of Chicago Press, 1987.

———. "From Tower to Cathedral." In *Stone*, 32–79. Bloomington: Indiana University Press, 1994.

———. "Mimesis and the End of Art." In *Double Truth*, 171–189. Albany: State University of New York Press, 1995.

Sartre, Jean-Paul. "Husserl, Hegel, Heidegger." In *Being and Nothingness: A Phenomenological Essay on Ontology.* Translated by Hazel E. Barnes, 315–339. New York: Washington Square Press, 1956.

Wahl, Jean. "Mediation, Negativity, and Separation." In *Le Malheur de la conscience dans la philosophie de Hegel.* Translated by Christopher Fox and Leonard Lawlor, 81–118. Presses Universitaires de France, 1951, deuxieme edition.

Žižek, Slavoj. "'Not Only as *Substance*, but Also as *Subject*.'" In *The Sublime Object of Ideology*, 201–231. London: Verso, 1989.

———. *For They Know Not What They Do: Enjoyment as a Political Factor.* London: Verso, 1991.

———. *Tarrying With the Negative: Kant, Hegel, and the Critique of Ideology.* Durham: Duke University Press, 1993.

———. *The Indivisible Remainder: An Essay on Schelling and Related Matters.* London: Verso, 1996.

Index

Achille, 172n3
Adam, 151, 408
Adonis, 11
Adorno, 409
Agathon, 232
Alcibiades, 232
alienation, 56, 91, 96, 97, 106–19, 175–86, 223, 265, 267, 269, 270, 397, 398, 410, 411, 413, 439, 444
anthropology, 28, 68, 69, 72n2, 176, 181, 185, 189, 221, 265
Antigone, 311, 317, 318, 320, 321
Antigone, 400, 404
anxiety, 17, 129, 132, 133, 181, 222, 225, 231, 342, 343, 431
Apollo, 252, 314
Aquinas, 210
Aristotle, 40, 41, 243, 280, 281, 286, 288n6, 337, 338, 339, 341, 361
Artaud, 332, 336n15
Athena, 309
Augustine, 407–9

Baader, 18
Babeuf-Fourier, 259
Bacchus, 312
Badiou, 257
Bauer, 105, 116, 117
Beauvoir, 133n7
Bergson, 21n3, 244, 255
Blake, 8, 15
Boehme, 8, 12, 24n11, 24n20, 25n22
Bosanquet, 3
Bruno, 6, 123
Brunschvicg, 255
Büchner, 238
burial, 315, 323, 346, 347, 348, 404, 442
Burkert, 385, 387

capitalism, 96, 98, 106, 107, 108, 115, 118, 120, 123, 125, 179, 272
Caproni, 384
castration complex, 228, 229
Catholic, 203n10
Catholicism, 203n10
Ceres, 312
Christ, 1, 2, 10, 15, 20n1, 23n7, 25n25, 35, 227, 314, 390, 393, 394, 401, 413, 414, 427
Claudel, 233
Communism, 179
community, 8, 58, 59, 61, 68, 69, 241, 311, 315–25, 328, 344, 345, 346, 347, 385, 398, 430
Condillac, 267
Copernicus, 208
Cornu, 265
creation, 6, 8, 23n9, 24n19, 32, 42, 46, 54, 61, 71, 103, 118, 142, 146, 151, 170, 178, 185, 201n1, 208, 293, 401, 408, 441, 442
    See also self-creation

creation *ex nihilo*, 342
Creon, 318, 320
crime, 21n3, 51, 56, 285, 319, 322, 323, 385

Damascius, 24n11
Damourette, 219, 224
Darwin, 103, 208
David of Dinant, 10
death, 10, 11, 20, 21n3, 25n27, 27–71, 73n6, 74n9, 79, 83, 88, 89, 130–33, 148–66, 167n9, 170, 171, 172n3, 177, 181, 187–201, 202n6, 203n10, 211, 212, 214, 219, 220, 235n11, 252, 294, 300, 301, 309, 312, 316, 317, 318, 319, 321, 322, 323, 326n2, 337–49, 404, 405, 408, 423, 424, 431, 432, 441, 442
  being-unto-, 88, 89
  -dealing, 302
  of Christ, 20n1, 393
  of God, 1, 14, 19, 190, 355, 393
  -stricken, 320
death instinct, 213
Derrida, 270, 350n4
Descartes, 28, 41, 72n2, 80, 92, 93, 258, 267, 273
Deshaies, 172n3
Diderot, 267
Dilthey, 25n26, 25n27
Dionysus, 252, 313, 314
Durkheim, 173n3, 247n1

Eckhart, 12, 15, 24n17, 25n23
Ehrenberg, 3, 4, 22n5
Empedocles, 19, 20, 24n11
empiricism, 180, 207, 267
Engels, 100, 106, 115, 117, 119, 120, 121, 123, 125n5, 247, 259, 264, 268
enjoyment, 58, 60, 64, 162, 311–12, 313, 390, 428
  See also jouissance
Eteocles, 318, 319
Eve, 408
evil, 2, 24n19, 107, 122, 154, 164, 242, 286, 311, 403, 405, 443
externalization, 95–125, 293, 429

Fall, the, 23n9, 24n19, 107, 405, 407
fetishism, 98, 99
Feuerbach, 105, 106, 110, 114, 115, 117, 118, 119, 120, 175–80, 258, 262, 264–68, 410
Fichte, 1, 4, 5, 6, 7, 8, 9, 10, 11, 14, 17, 22n3, 23n8, 23n10, 28, 72n2, 97, 98, 102, 123, 172, 273, 284, 357, 376n10, 376n15, 376n18, 410
Fink, 340, 349, 351n25
Flaubert, 158
forgiveness, 2, 16, 284
Foucault, 251, 417–18, 430, 433–35, 436n2, 436n4, 436n7
Frazer, 200
freedom, 5, 10, 14, 22n3, 33, 34, 35, 38, 43, 44, 48, 51–54, 55, 57, 58, 59, 61, 68, 73n6, 79, 87, 89, 95, 97, 98, 102, 131, 132, 133, 140, 143, 145, 146, 147, 148–50, 153, 156, 165, 170, 171, 172, 179, 181, 182–85, 219, 220, 238, 240, 247, 265, 266, 318, 328, 331, 346, 384, 405, 414, 417, 418, 423, 437–43
Frege, 332
Freud, 205–34, 234n1, 235n14, 255, 259, 263, 271, 330, 333, 334, 336n17, 430–35, 436n6, 436n7, 436n8
funeral rite, 348, 405

Gadamer, 400
Galileo, 257, 259, 279
games theory, 216
gift, 2, 295–98, 301, 312, 314, 428
Gnosticism, 24n19
Gnostics, 24n11
Goethe, 5, 6, 19, 25n23, 25n27, 101, 102, 124, 125, 246, 299, 400
Groos, 24n19
guilt, 132, 230, 317, 323, 404, 405, 432
Günderode, 20
Gurvitch, 7

Hadlich, 24n18
Hawthorne, 432
Haym, 20n1
Hebbel, 20

Heidegger, 73n4, 73n6, 74n9, 86–91, 132, 133n6, 194, 201n1, 203n6, 238, 343, 377n23, 379–86, 387, 400
Heimann, 9, 24n13
Heine, 115, 116
Heinrich, 410, 415
Heraclitus, 339, 341
Herder, 25n23
Herodotus, 306
Hodgskin, 98, 99
Hoffmeister, 130
Hölderlin, 7, 8, 11, 17, 18, 20, 151, 153, 273, 400
holocaust, 295–97
homosexuality, 434, 436n6
hope, 20, 95, 142, 152–54, 160–66, 209, 266, 312, 326n2
Husserl, 75–78, 80, 86, 87, 255, 332
Hyppolite, 127–33, 133n1, 166n1, 255, 256, 269, 343, 344

incarnation, 42, 185, 392, 413, 414
Ismene, 318, 320

Jacobi, 5
Jaensch, 172n3
Jakobson, 210
Jolas, 204n12
jouissance, 220, 227–33, 318, 319, 325, 390
    See also enjoyment
Joyce, 198
Judaism, 17, 130

Kadmon, 24n19
Kafka, 138, 161, 163, 164, 422
Kant, 2, 5, 14, 24n17, 28, 72n2, 76, 77, 98, 101, 124, 129, 133n4, 240, 243, 247, 248n2, 248n3, 256, 266, 267, 273, 274, 284, 287, 330, 334, 390–94, 399, 415
Kierkegaard, 81, 128, 171, 427
Kojève, 167n5, 167n7, 187–201, 201n1, 201n2, 201n3, 202n6, 203n10, 384
Kraus, 237
Kroner, 1, 2

Lacan, 390, 400, 406, 407, 415
Lachelier, 255
Laclau, 398
Lafargue, 102, 121
Lalande, 92
Laplanche, 436n5
Lautréamont, 160
Lazarowicz, 288n9
Lazarus, 154
Leibniz, 72n2, 252, 253, 282
Lenin, 121, 122, 123, 126n37, 255, 257, 259, 261, 262, 264, 268, 272n2, 327, 328, 329, 335n2, 335n6
Léon, 6
Lessing, 8, 10, 15, 261
Levinas, 161, 167n8
Lévi-Strauss, 229
liberation, 61, 171, 173, 179, 238, 386, 417, 418, 437–43
Liede, 288n9
literature, 135–66, 195, 284, 314
Littré, 297
Loustalot, 116
love, 2, 9, 15, 18, 19, 20, 48, 132, 144, 172, 176, 222, 232, 295, 319, 322, 326n2, 345, 359, 435
Luther, 13

MacCulloch, 99
MacTaggart, 21n3
madness, 150, 158, 213, 318
Malebranche, 91
Mallarmé, 151, 158, 212
Mao, 257
Marcuse, 433
Martin, 255, 256
Marx (Karl), 74n9, 79, 95–125, 126n27, 127, 128, 144, 175–81, 186, 245, 247, 249n17, 255–72, 272n5, 384, 404
Marx (Werner), 376n17, 377n18, 377n20, 377n24, 378n25
Marxism, 121, 122, 234, 259, 261, 264
materialism, 99, 100, 105, 106, 114, 117, 119, 121, 124, 179, 180, 256, 257, 258, 262, 264, 267, 328, 394
Mauss, 229, 230

Mehring, 121
Memnon, 301, 305, 306, 307
Menades, 14
Mendelssohn, 261
Meuli, 385
Milrx, 102
Mithras, 307
Montanists, 15
Moses, 227
Mosheim, 15
Mounier, 172, 173n7
murder, 68, 153, 167n7, 219, 300, 318, 338, 385, 442, 446n11
Myers, 234n1
mysticism, 18, 25n23, 102, 203n6, 345

Napoleon, 59
Natorp, 279, 288n5
Neith, 308
Newton, 279, 287
Nicolas of Cusa, 123
Nietzsche, 20, 127, 172, 183, 266, 277, 418, 430, 432, 435, 436n3, 436n9
nihilism, 152
nihilist, 147
Novalis, 2, 14, 20

Oedipus, 317, 318
Oedipus complex, 221, 227, 228

pain, 4, 11–20, 21n3, 349, 359, 360, 365, 426, 428, 430, 435, 441
Parmenides, 28, 29, 35, 41, 341
Pascal, 12, 13, 219
patience, 4, 359, 360, 444
Paulhan, 160
Pavlov, 225
Penates, 345
phantasy, 222–233, 436n5
Phoenix, 17
Pichon, 219, 224
Plato, 207, 232, 258, 277, 279, 280, 281, 284, 286, 288n4, 288n5, 288n6, 339, 348
Plekhanov, 121
Plotinus, 21n3
Polynices, 317, 318, 319, 404
Ponge, 159
Pontalis, 436n5
psychoanalysis, 127, 206, 208, 209, 214, 220, 221, 227, 228, 230, 232, 246, 257, 263, 431, 436n7
punishment, 21n3, 284, 285, 286, 300, 318, 319, 323, 407, 408
    See also self-punishment
Pushkin, 124
Pythagoras, 247

reconciliation, 9, 15, 16, 18, 20, 21n3, 128, 175, 176, 246, 285, 286, 314
redemption, 9, 11, 24n19
Reinhold, 6
renunciation, 182, 297, 311, 397, 428, 431, 432
resurrection, 11, 23n7, 69, 178
revelation, 17, 18, 28, 30, 36, 45, 47, 88, 104, 152, 155, 156, 175, 176, 181, 185, 194, 199, 200, 201, 313
Revolution
    Chinese, 259
    1848, 120, 265
    French, 95, 122, 124, 148, 255
    Industrial, 124
    1917, 259
revolution, 53, 54, 55, 59, 74n9, 115, 120, 148–50, 208, 213, 258, 259, 271, 272, 295–97, 398
Ricardo, 99, 259, 260, 261, 262
ritual, 199, 319, 398, 404, 429
Robespierre, 149
Rodin, 3
Rosenkranz, 12, 25n21, 125n9, 288n9
Rousseau, 8, 267
Rousset, 288n9
Royce, 22n5

sacrifice, 1, 4, 6, 14, 56, 64, 140, 182, 193–201, 203n8, 203n10, 229, 233, 295–98, 309, 311–12, 318, 325, 385–86, 398, 402, 418, 431
    See also self-sacrifice
Sade, 150, 160

sadism, 131, 425, 426, 428, 430
Saint-Just, 149
Saint-Simon, 259
Sartre, 131, 132, 221, 234n1, 403
Saussure, 210
Schad, 7
Schelling, 1, 4, 5, 6, 7, 8, 12, 16, 17, 22n6, 23n8, 23n10, 27, 35, 41, 96, 97, 98, 102, 113, 123, 124, 376n15, 377n18
Schiller, 6, 8, 14, 15, 19, 126n13, 238
Schilling, 8
Schlegel, 3, 7
Schönberg, 238
Schopenhauer, 16, 239
self-creation, 30, 31, 66, 68, 125
self-punishment, 429
self-sacrifice, 428, 429, 430
Sesostris, 306
sin, 6, 9, 11, 23n9, 24n19, 33, 197, 228, 407, 408
Sinclair, 273
Sisyphus, 240
skeptic, 193, 425, 426, 428, 430
skepticism, 17, 147, 183, 354, 417, 425, 426
Smith, 99
socialism, 116, 259, 260, 272
Socrates, 232, 311
Sophocles, 318, 325, 400
Sphinx, 309
Spinoza, 33, 35, 41, 261, 329, 357, 358, 435, 438
Stalin, 122, 123, 257, 268
Stenzel, 281
Stirling, 24n12, 24n20
Stirner, 105
stoic, 15, 147, 426, 428, 429, 430
stoicism, 17, 147, 417, 424, 425
Stoppard, 432
Strabo, 307
Sublime, 389–94, 399
Sublimity, 212, 389–94
suffering, 8, 16, 19, 178, 357, 402, 432
suicide, 66, 68, 172n3, 441, 446n11
Swift, 284

Terror, the, 53, 54, 74, 148–50, 439
Thales, 28, 338
Thomas, 235n11

unhappy consciousness, 1–20, 118, 147, 210, 278, 417–35

Valéry, 138, 140, 186n1
Vico, 103
violence, 129, 130, 131, 142, 156, 189, 192, 219, 355, 375, 385, 386, 423

Wagner, 20
Wahl, 205
war, 55–59, 149, 171, 203n10, 299, 300, 301, 316, 317, 322, 325, 344, 345, 446n11
Wiehl, 273, 274, 278, 288n2, 288n5
woman, 150–51, 197, 230, 303, 315–25, 332
Wright, 172n3

Yovel, 389, 390, 415

Zagreus, 24n11
Zeus, 7, 8